D0039448

Myanmar
(Burma)

RETIRÉ DE LA COLLECTION UNIVERSELLE
Bibliothèque et Archives nationales du Québec

Robert Reid

Joe Bindloss, Stuart Butler

LEGEND

Primary Road
Secondary Road
Tertiary Road
Unsealed Road

0 — 200 km
0 — 120 miles

ELEVATION

3000ft
1500ft
0

RIVERBOAT TO MANDALAY (p307)
Myitkyina: starting point for a long, lazy ride with locals down the Ayeyarwady

HSIPAW (p300)
Low-key Shan State village, with great treks to waterfalls

KENGTUNG (p247)
Thai-style pagodas, hot springs and exotic hill-tribe treks

INLE LAKE (p232)
Canoe trips to Intha villages, floating gardens and tribal markets – plus pizza for dinner

KALAW (p224)
Myanmar's top trekking hub, with overnight trips to hill-tribe villages led by guides versed in hill legends

MANDALAY (p255)
Burma's last royal capital, home to traditional theatre and moustached jokesters, and near ancient cities

AMARAPURA (p277)
World's longest teak bridge, commuting monks and sublime sunset views

BAGAN (p177 & p203)
Vast plain dotted with 800-year-old temples on the curve of the Ayeyarwady

MRAUK U (p327)
Goat shepherds and ancient temples mingle in this sleepy, timeless backwater

CHINA (TIBET)

CHINA

INDIA

BANGLADESH

VIETNAM

LAOS

THIMPHU
BHUTAN

DHAKA

Chittagong

Imphal

Hkakabo Razi (19,321ft)

Putao

Sumprabum

Pangsaw Pass

Ledo

Khamti

Pakhan

Homlin

Tamu

Tiddim

Hakha

Mawlaik

Kalaymyo

Ye-U

Shwebo

Monywa

Pakokku

Nyaung U

Bagan

Salay

Kyaukpadaung

Magwe

Minbu

Maungdaw

Paletwa

Mrauk U

Minbya

Sittwe

Kyaukpyu

Yinbye

Kyun

Teknaf

Mt Victoria (10,016ft)

CHIN STATE

RAKHAING STATE

Rakhaing

MAGWE DIVISION

SAGAING DIVISION

KACHIN STATE

Myitkyina

Bhamo

Katha

Namhkan

Ruili

Muse

Luxi

Mogok

Namsan

Hipaw

Kyaukme

Lashio

Kunlong

Mong Ping

Kengtung

Mong La

Loi-Awe

Tachileik

Mae Sai

Chiang Rai

Mae Hong Son

SHAN STATE

Shan Plateau

Thanlwin River

Mekong River

Loilem

Namsang

Nyaungshwe

Taunggyi

Pindaya

Kalaw

Heho

Thazi

Meiktila

Kyaukse

Amarapura

MANDALAY

Sagaing

Myingyan

KAYAH STATE

Loikaw

Lawpita

Taungdwingyi

Pyinmana

NAY PYI TAW

Bago

MANDALAY DIVISION

Mt Popo

Ayeyarwady

Chindwin

Indawgyi Lake

Irrawaddy

Brahmaputra

Ganges

20° N

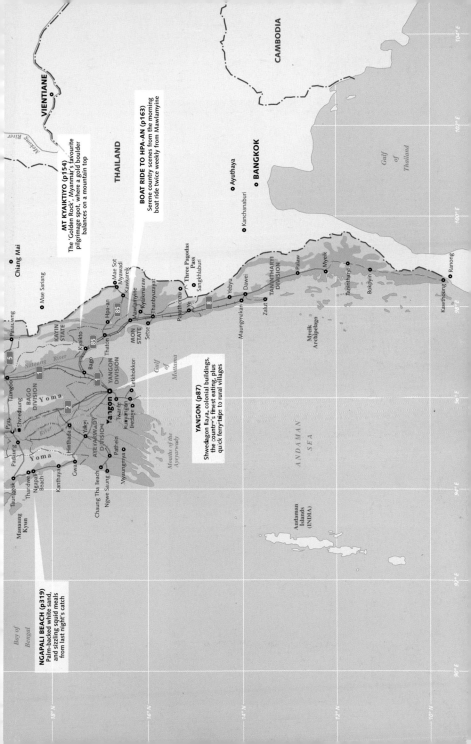

NGAPALI BEACH (p319)
Palm-backed white sand, and sizzling squid meals from last night's catch

MT KYAIKTIYO (p154)
The 'Golden Rock', Myanmar's favourite pilgrimage spot, where a gold boulder balances on a mountain top

BOAT RIDE TO HPA-AN (p163)
Serene country scenes from the morning boat ride twice weekly from Mawlamyine

YANGON (p87)
Shwedagon Paya, colonial buildings, the country's finest eating, plus quick ferry trips to rural villages

Bay of Bengal

THAILAND

CAMBODIA

VIENTIANE

Mekong River

Chiang Mai

Mae Sariang

Pasawng

KAYIN STATE

Kyaikto

Hpa-an

Mae Sot

Myawadi

Kawkareik

Kyaikmaraw

Mawlamyine

Thanbyuzayat

Setse

Three Pagodas Pass

Sangkhlaburi

Payathonzu

Kanchanaburi

Ayuthaya

BANGKOK

Gulf of Thailand

Ranong

Kawthaung

Bokpyin

Taninthayi

TANINTHARYI DIVISION

Myeik

Myeik Archipelago

Palaw

Zalut

Maungmakan

Dawei

Yebyu

Ye

MON STATE

Thaton

Thanbyuzayat

Bago

Letkhokkon

YANGON DIVISION

Yangon

Twante

Taungdaung

Shwedaung

Pyay

Prome

Yoma

BAGO DIVISION

Sittoung River

Taungoo

Taunggok

Thardwe

Ngapali Beach

Kanthaya

Gwa

Chaung Tha Beach

Ngwe Saung

Myaungmya

Pathein

Hinthada

AYEYARWADY DIVISION

Ayeyarwady River

Mouths of the Ayeyarwady

Gulf of Mottama

ANDAMAN SEA

Andaman Islands (INDIA)

Manaung Kyun

On the Road

ROBERT REID
Coordinating Author
At a Rakhaing wrestling match I found myself surrounded by locals happily willing to explain the throw-down sport in which winners and losers leave the ring arm in arm. 'Villagers practise harder', one local told me. 'Us Sittwe guys always get beat.' I caught the eye of a 70-year-old 'legend', who waddled over to yell out: 'Very good. We have a new wrestler!'

JOE BINDLOSS Cycling over the fields between two small pagodas in Bagan, I stumbled across a small headless buddha statue sticking out of the mud. It seemed only appropriate to return it to its proper place, so I climbed to the upper terrace of the nearest stupa and placed the statue in a niche looking over the plain of temples. That's the wonder of Bagan – history literally coming out of the ground.

STUART BUTLER Taking my 'see and experience everything' brief a little too much to heart I somehow ended up in the ring with a famous kickboxer, practising my right hook. It may look like I'm losing this fight, but actually I'm just humouring him before turning into a British Chihuahua and giving my opponent a bit of good old-fashioned what for.

For full author biographies see p390.

Myanmar Highlights

1 SHWEDAGON PAYA

Sunset at the incredible Shwedagon Paya (p92), one of the world's most spectacular religious monuments, is not to be missed. The golden dome of the Shwedagon Paya rises 322ft above its base, can be seen for miles and is covered with 60 tons of pure gold. There are always many Myanmar people praying and making offerings at the Shwedagon and it is a fascinating place to spend time watching the world go by.

Nikom Annan, Traveller, Thailand and USA

2 INLE LAKE

Life revolves around this rich, abundant lake (p232). Hire a boat and marvel at the fishers with their one-legged rowing style, visit homes on stilts above the water and watch farmers tend their floating fruit and vegetable gardens.

gotchagirl, Traveller

MT KYAIKTIYO (GOLDEN ROCK)

During holidays there are thousands of pilgrims and at the top Mt Kyaiktiyo (p154) will be bristling with energy. From the pathway are sweeping views of nothing but untouched jungle. The small stops on the way up have resting platforms where pilgrims can take a break or even spend the night (especially the elderly who take so long to make the journey). The place is breathtaking at sunset.

Plasterer, Traveller

3

BAGAN

Countless temples spread across a vast plain (p203). It's impossible to do them all justice in only one or two days. Rent a bike to explore the closer sites, or hire a horse-drawn cart as it will let you see much more in your time, as well as further temples. If you're flush with money, a sunset/sunrise balloon ride is an unforgettable experience.

santamonica811, Traveller

4

5

MRAUK U

Mrauk U (p327) was one of the most special places I've ever been in my life: completely deserted; ruins falling into ruins; sandstone buddha heads falling off walls into the sand; some mysterious temples with secret passages and chambers; and goats, snakes and farmers escaping the summer heat by sleeping through noon beside an altar. You can also take upriver trips to minority villages.

Sanny Albers, Traveller, USA

PYIN U LWIN

Escape the heat of Mandalay in the mountains of this former British hill station (p294). Cooler temperatures, the charming town, good food and pony carts make this a pleasant stop. Spend Sunday afternoon at the botanic garden speaking English with local students.

gotchagirl, Traveller

6

BERNARD NAPTHINE

HSIPAW

Hsipaw (p300) is an untouched town with wonderful family-run teashops, beautiful mountain scenery, a traditional popcorn factory, ageing ruins tucked away in the jungle, and an old wooden movie theatre that shows cheesy action movies. It's really fantastic.

Murray Newham, Traveller, Australia

7

EITAN SIMANOR / ALAMY

BURMAPHOTOS / ALAMY

8

NGAPALI BEACH

The Naples of the East, as it is known, is situated on the Rakhaing coast. Ngapali (p319) is one of the most beautiful beaches in Myanmar. It stretches about 2 miles, with blue sea, white sand and swaying palm trees. For those who love the five Ss – sea, sand, sun, swimming and snorkelling – a visit to Ngapali is a must.

mosegrisen, Traveller, Australia

KEVIN LANG / ALAM

9 KALAW

Discover Myanmar with your own two feet – and explore 22 miles of trails that wind through mountains, pine forests, plantations and villages inhabited by hill tribes. On the western edge of the Shan Plateau, the old colonial hill station of Kalaw (p224) is a base for trekking.

Cheryn Flanagan, Traveller, USA

CHRISTIAN KOBER / ALAM

10 CHAUNG THA BEACH

Christmas holidays at Chaung Tha Beach (p140) are packed with thousands of local tourists. You can walk or rent a bike to ride just a quarter of a mile to a stretch of beach that is full of white sand and lined with millions of coconut palms. The beach is untouched by development of any kind. Rocky points every once in a while are each topped with a golden stupa, and bamboo fishing villages are hidden back in the palms. There were no other tourists; it was beautiful!

Mark Maxwell, Traveller, USA

Contents

Regional Map Contents

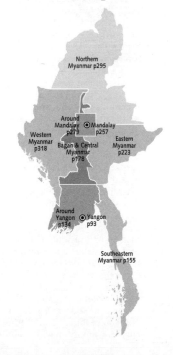

Northern Myanmar p295

Around Mandalay p279

Mandalay p257

Western Myanmar p318

Bagan & Central Myanmar p178

Eastern Myanmar p223

Around Yangon p134

Yangon p93

Southeastern Myanmar p155

Destination Myanmar (Burma)

The temples are 2000 years old and covered in gold. Locals reach street markets or river ferries by trishaw and ox cart. Yangon businessmen wear skirtlike *longyi* and women decorate their faces with dollops and stripes of tree-bark paste. Some travellers leave saying: 'It's like Asia 75 years ago', but it's much more than that. As Rudyard Kipling wrote a century ago, Myanmar is 'quite unlike any land you know about'.

Locals cherish an outsider's ear, and yours is likely to be filled with your trip's most memorable moments. Much of it is good-natured, delivered with a sweet dose of 'Burmeseness' – the gentle trait that favours subtlety to making waves. This happens when, say, that 70-year-old grandfather stops you to talk for a few minutes about the nation's three great passions: family, football or Buddha. Then thanks you for listening. Despite limited access to the internet or (for many) proper education, you'll find a public that is remarkably well informed of outside events, thanks to Burmese-language radio shows from the BBC or Voice of America, which the government bans and calls 'killers of the airwaves'. Such government decrees are frequently taken with a shrug or an ironic smirk. A Rakhaing woman footballer described the generals to us as 'Christmas trees with all their medals', and a farmer near Sagaing drily likened the intelligence of passing cows to that of the leaders.

There's also a local saying that 'bad news only lasts seven days' – wait it out and it'll be forgotten. But it's probably going to take a lot longer for anyone to forget a couple of recent events that stunned locals and outsiders watching a drip-drop of news relayed by smuggled video and on-scene reports. First, in September 2007, after monks peacefully protested rising gas prices, military forces cracked down on unarmed protestors and raided monasteries. Then, in May 2008, Cyclone Nargis blew across the Ayeyarwady (Irrawaddy) Delta, leaving tens of thousands dead and many more homeless.

During this book's research period we witnessed many whispered conversations at homes and in teashops from Mandalay to Sittwe, Taunggyi to Mawlamyine – all of which hovered on the immediate future and the promise of 'multiparty elections' by 2010. Most locals remain frustrated that change for a country without regular electricity is 'beyond hope'. Many found solace in Sylvester Stallone, who took on the military in *Rambo IV;* the banned film appeared on the Yangon black market in 2008. It sounds tense but after the disturbing events the bulk of day-to-day life soon returned to discussing Champions League scores, eating curry, drinking tea and going to temple.

Visitors can ease into this day-to-day with little difficulty around most areas, though most first-timers are content with seeing the main destinations – Yangon (Rangoon), Mandalay, Bagan and Inle Lake – in 10 to 14 days. Traffic is lighter than in some of Southeast Asia, but miles on bumpy roads tend to pass slowly. So does time spent waiting for answers. Many locals don't get why you'd use '10 words when a thousand would do' (author Peter Olszewski)…and never really get around to answering the question. Basic enquiries can often yield long, thrilling replies, which tap into things like local nicknames for ghosts that drowned nearby a couple of centuries before. In Myanmar, more so than most places, this is where the real trip lies. If you're in a hurry here…well, try not to be.

If you're thinking of visiting Myanmar, please read our Should You Go? chapter (opposite), which outlines the pros and cons of a visit.

FAST FACTS

Population: 47.4 million (officially)

Population growth rate: 0.8% (2008 estimate)

Area: 421,600 sq miles

GDP: $13.7 billion

GDP per capita: $1900

Cost of a mobile phone SIM card: $1000

Favourite ring tone in Yangon: 50 Cent or Beyoncé songs

Number of refugees or displaced persons: at least 500,000 before Cyclone Nargis; the current number is unknown

Internet users: 0.1% of the population

Government's self-proclaimed slogan: 'Everybody's friend but nobody's ally'

Should You Go?

No-one argues Myanmar (Burma) isn't one of the world's most exciting destinations, but a complex question mark has hovered over the country since the birth of a tourism boycott in 1995. Does your money, no matter how carefully spent, sustain a military dictatorship that has imprisoned political dissidents, used forced labour, cracked down on peaceful demonstrations (as was seen in September 2007) and seized foreign aid (most notably following Cyclone Nargis in May 2008)? Or does isolating one of the world's poorest countries not only deprive a burgeoning private sector of income, but also push the government into the arms of neighbours with bigger bankrolls and their own serious human rights issues?

'We don't care if we have a military government, a socialist government or a democratic government. We just want one who will care about the people,' a retired doctor told us in 2008.

Essentially, no outsiders are happy with the situation, but not all agree on what to do about it. Some activists, quoting prodemocracy leader Aung San Suu Kyi, liken a visit to 'condoning the regime'; others suggest boycotts have only snoozed possible change for over a decade – that, with more engagement (including tourism), Myanmar could have opened and risen like Vietnam has.

So, should you go? Lonely Planet believes all prospective visitors must ask, and answer, this question for themselves. This section outlines all sides of the argument, as well as showing how, if you go, to keep the bulk of your money in private hands.

THE BOYCOTT

After decades of self-imposed isolation, and a crumbling economy that necessitated the former 'rice bowl' importing food for survival, in the 1990s Myanmar began opening itself up. The world's longest running military dictatorship invited foreign investment, bumped up the tourist visa from a week to 28 days, and readied itself for a massive 'Visit Myanmar Year' in 1996, with hopes for half a million visitors. Some hoped that the government that had ignored the results of the 1990 election (see p47) was changing. But then word leaked out about what was happening. Numerous sources, including Burma Campaign UK and the *New York Times*, reported that hundreds of thousands of forced labourers were being used to build airport runways and roads, and ready tourist sites like Mandalay's palace moat. In other places, such as Old Bagan, whole villages were forcibly relocated to make way for high-end hotels.

The boycott worked, at least by its original goal: Myanmar received fewer than 200,000 visitors during its Visit Myanmar Year (1996), well below the government's initial target of 500,000.

The responding tourism boycott had an immediate effect. The government cut back its target to 200,000 arrivals – and eventually even that number wasn't met.

Governments – even the US and those in the EU, who have signed on sanctions against Myanmar generals, banks and exports – have been shy to endorse an all-out tourism ban, but other outsiders haven't. Some activist groups continue to encourage foreign businesses and tourists to stay away, and many tour operators, travellers and celebrities have backed the boycott.

Groups like Amnesty International and Human Rights Watch claim forced labour has decreased this decade but still continues, particularly in remote, mountainous regions. Allegedly none is connected with tourism.

Other activists, including many exiled Myanmar citizens who ran from government bullets during the 1988 prodemocracy demonstrations, believe the boycott has outlived its purpose, pushing the generals into far more lucrative deals with fellow Asean countries and neighbours like India and China. Author of *The River of Lost Footsteps* and one-time supporter of sanctions, Thant Nyint U, called further isolation of a self-sustained government 'counterproductive and dangerous'.

Occasionally overlooked in the debate are the locals themselves, many of whom privately declare unconditional support for the 'lady' (as Aung San Suu Kyi is known) but disagree with her on the boycott, believing that isolation only strengthens the generals' position. Many locals point out that over the past decade and a half the tourism sector has become increasingly privatised – visitors can now choose from several hundred private hotels and keep up to 80% of expenses in private hands. Those locals that have qualms about tourism stress that they don't want visitors 'just to come and admire the scenery' (to quote Suu Kyi), they want them to be thoughtful and informed and engage with locals.

One '1988 generation' protestor told us after the 2007 protests: 'I love Aung San Suu Kyi. We all do. I used to agree with her on the boycott, but things have changed. It doesn't work.'

DIVIDED VOICES

Other than the generals themselves, essentially everyone speaking out on the boycott hopes for the same thing: a democratic Myanmar, the release of political prisoners (including Aung San Suu Kyi), and an improved economy and public services. The difference is in how this can be achieved.

Aung San Suu Kyi

'The bulk of the money from tourism goes straight into the pockets of the generals.'

Aung San Suu Kyi, 1995

For many would-be travellers the most compelling reason to support a total boycott is that Nobel Laureate for Peace Aung San Suu Kyi apparently says to. Or does she? Considering she's been under house arrest for much of the time since the boycott's birth, there are many divergent interpretations on what exactly her policy is regarding tourism.

Governments tend to shy away from all-out endorsements of the tourism boycott (unlike the USA's clearer restrictions for Cuba), though the UK's Foreign & Commonwealth Office urges visitors 'to consider carefully whether by their actions they are helping to support the regime'.

In 1995 Suu Kyi asked travellers to 'visit us later', insisting that visiting at that time was 'tantamount to condoning the regime'. However, in her conversations with Alan Clements in 1995 and 1996 (included in the 1997 collection *The Voice of Hope*) she said, in response to his question about whether she was advocating would-be travellers to stay away: 'No, we are not doing anything like that. What we are asking for is a boycott of Visit Myanmar Year 1996.' At the time she suggested an 'alternative guide' to the country needed to be made. In 2002 she told the BBC that the National League for Democracy (NLD; the opposition party, which she leads) stand on tourism 'has not changed'.

She's expressed many opinions about the effect tourism may or may not have. She said in 1995: 'Visitors to the country can be useful, depending on what they do, or how they go about it,' and that 'tourists can open up the world to the people of Burma just as the people of Burma can open up the eyes of tourists to the situation in their own country if they're interested in looking.' But she also expressed concern that tourists who 'go around in air-conditioned taxis' don't see anything that's going on in the country.

After Aung San Suu Kyi's 1995 suggestion for an 'alternate guide' to Myanmar, the proboycott group Burma Campaign UK published *Burma: The Alternative Guide*, which was actually more of a detailed manifesto against tourism.

In 2002 she said, 'the people of Burma, in general, do not depend on…foreign visitors to bring them information' but obtain knowledge of the international world via – 'limited', she admitted – radio broadcasts such as BBC, Radio Free Asia and Democratic Voice of Burma. Suu Kyi has remained an influential figure for worldwide political agendas. Her captivity often tops the list of outside rebukes of Myanmar. In 2007 an *Economist* article confessed that when she burst onto the scene, many journalists were 'a little in love with her'. Even as supporters begin to criticise some of her decisions, locals' reverence to the 'lady' is not in doubt. When she was allowed to make her first brief public appearance since 2003, just as the 2007 protests started to swell on the Yangon (Rangoon) streets, one monk told Human Rights Watch, 'we got strength from [seeing] her'.

TO GO OR NOT TO GO?

Reasons Not to Go

▪ Aung San Suu Kyi has asked tourists not to come.

▪ The government used forced labour to develop tourist-related sights and services.

▪ Thousands of families have been forcefully relocated to make room for some tourism facilities, such as in Old Bagan.

▪ International tourists can be seen as a symbolic stamp of approval for the Myanmar government.

▪ It's impossible to visit without some money going to the military junta (eg $20 for a visa, $10 departure fee, entry fees at Bagan or Inle Lake, up to 12% tax on many services).

▪ Activists claim that tourism dollars help directly fuel government repression.

▪ The government forbids travel to many areas (p359 and p133), particularly those inhabited by minority groups, due to unrest.

Reasons to Go

▪ The vast majority of locals you meet – including many veterans of the 1988 prodemocracy protests – want you to come.

▪ The majority (possibly 80%) of a careful independent traveller's expenses goes to the private sector, a higher percentage than the government allocates for the public.

▪ Many observers point out that a four-decade (and going) trade boycott against Cuba never changed its leadership, and Myanmar gets more outside investment than Cuba.

▪ Through 'direct aid' efforts (p25), visitors can help a local community facing a humanitarian crisis.

▪ The government's biggest source of income from foreign visitors – requiring they change $200 for government FEC notes (Foreign Exchange Certificates; see p347) upon arrival – ended in 2003.

▪ As outside communication is regulated, tourism provides an open two-way exchange between many locals and the outside world: locals see that they're not forgotten and visitors take away images and stories to share outside Myanmar. Bear in mind, though, the sensitivity around political issues (see p24).

▪ Human-rights violations are less likely to occur in areas where international visitors are present.

Proboycott Activists

'Nowhere else in the world have human rights abuses and tourism been so closely linked.'

www.burmacampaign.org.uk

Many proboycott activists, who are fighting for the military government to hand over power to the NLD, interpret all visitors as a financial and symbolic endorsement of the military junta, whether they be $5-a-night backpackers, package tourists, meditation tourists or businesspeople. Often the argument refers to the government's abusive use of forced labour to build tourist infrastructure and services in the past, as well as the forced relocation of thousands of families from their homes (evident in Yangon, Mandalay and Old Bagan). But, ultimately, it's Aung San Suu Kyi who makes up the backbone of most proboycott stances. In a 2007 report, the pro-Burma group Tourism Concern stated they'd support the boycott 'unless we hear otherwise' from her.

Burma Campaign UK estimates that only a third of the country has access to outside radio programs by the BBC, Radio Free Asia or Voice of America.

ACTIVIST WEBSITES

Many groups have websites that outline Myanmar's prodemocracy movement, as well as providing details on human-rights abuses sustained since 1988. See also p29 for a list of other useful websites.

■ **Amnesty International** (www.amnesty.org) Regular updates on the status of 1150 political prisoners behind bars before the September 2007 protests, and the 700 arrested afterwards.

■ **Burma Campaign UK** (www.burmacampaign.org.uk) One of the more outspoken proboycott groups, which has written numerous articles and keeps a tab of celebrities enlisted in their 'I'm Not Going' campaign.

■ **Burma Project** (www.burmaproject.org) This organisation is focused on human-rights abuses and suggests travellers 'think twice' before going.

■ **Free Burma Coalition** (www.freeburmacoalition.org) Run by Myanmar-exile figure Zarni, who reversed his proboycott stance in 2003. The site includes links to Myanmar-related news.

■ **Voices for Burma** (www.voicesforburma.org) This group, founded in the UK in 2003, supports 'alternative tourism', and provides lengthy tips on how to best visit the country.

One of the most active groups, Burma Campaign UK (BCUK; formerly Burma Action Group), calls the ongoing boycott a 'short-term strategy to ensure long-term prosperity' and one that requires cutting off the country from investment, including tourism. They doubt tourism provides a positive effect economically. 'Almost all of the money goes to the regime's pocket in one way or another,' says their website. And the organisation dismisses reports that most locals support tourism, saying it comes from those 'almost exclusively…working in the tourism industry', Mark Farmaner, acting director of BCUK, told the *Times* in 2007 that the 'real Burma' is only witnessed once you see the forced labour, political prisoners and palatial homes of the generals.

The Burma Campaign UK maintains that 'it is impossible to know whether services sold to private individuals haven't in fact been sold to the regime's own families.'

> 'Increased numbers of tourists to Burma would have some economic trickle down to local people but when compared to the millions in revenue it would earn the government…we believe it is not a fair trade.' – Tourism Concern

Protourism Voices

'At the heat of passion in 1995 and 1996, I supported the tourism boycott. It was a major mistake. The whole boycott and sanctions campaign, in which I played a lead role, was a major strategic mistake.'
Zarni, Free Burma Coalition

Many activists now championing engagement and tourism with Myanmar once argued against it. Zarni, founder of Free Burma Coalition, reversed his take on the boycott in 2003. He told us that proboycott activists these days are 'more keen to prove their strategy right than the considerations of the public welfare'. He joins some locals who now rebuke the NLD and Aung San Suu Kyi for inexperienced leadership (as well, former British ambassador to Myanmar Derek Tonkin calls Aung San Suu Kyi 'an idealist unable to compromise with the rough reality of Southeast Asian politics'). Many believe she and the NLD missed an opportunity by not communicating with more open (and now removed) factions of the military (including the now-ousted former prime minister Khin Nyunt).

The tourist industry is now far more privatised than during its first toddler steps two decades ago, when the government controlled everything. Many argue that, while billions of dollars in foreign trade come annually (often with little distinction between private and government sectors), as much as

> A grandmother veteran of the 1988 demonstrations in central Myanmar told us, 'I love Aung San Suu Kyi. We all do. She's a very good person, but too straightforward. That may work in the West, but this is Asia and you have to be more cunning.'

80% of an independent tourist's budget stays in local hands (see boxed text, p19). The tourism sector employs 300,000, not including grassroots businesses (eg trishaw driver, curry makers, handicrafts makers).

Some activists plug the benefits of 'alternative travel' – borrowing the term from an Aung San Suu Kyi quote. One is the UK-based Voices for Burma, formed in 2003, which draws a clear line between potentially negative and positive trips. They promote staying at private guesthouses, travelling to off-the-beaten-track locales and ensuring that for every dollar that goes to the government two more are spent in the private sector. Their website explains: 'By accepting the standard boycott view…we may miss an important opportunity to help the Burmese people.'

Tourism isn't only about bringing in money, in these viewpoints, but opening a two-way exchange. Zarni, once a tourist guide in the 1980s and now working on political transitions at Oxford University, told us: 'Tourism is a rare window for any Burmese to really learn about the outside world – in a way no electronic medium would allow. Tourists that sit and talk with locals can bring ideas, and ideas are oxygen.' This is something Vietnam knows a little about, some observers and locals like to point out. While the West argued about Myanmar, they embraced Vietnam – overlooking its record of thuggish leadership and intolerance of political dissidence – and the country has emerged as a new tiger with a growing middle class.

Author Thant Nyint U sees tourism as playing a notable factor in creating new freedoms and growth. He writes of the best-case scenario in *The River of Lost Footsteps*: 'If Burma were less isolated, if there were more trade, more engagement – more tourism in particular…then perhaps the conditions for political change would emerge over the next decade or two.'

A point occasionally still heard from some proboycott groups is outdated. The National Coalition of the Union of Burma (www.ncgub.net), for example, still ranks the requirement of changing '$300' with government changers as the top negative impact of tourism; this requirement (for $200 actually) ceased in 2003.

An NLD official told Al Jazeera in November 2006 that he had 'no objection' to 'real tourists…who are really interested in the social, economic and cultural conditions. I think these people can always come to us, no problem.'

'Tourism is the thin end of the wedge to opening up Burma to international influences, but it is bound to be a long, slow process. The sanctions of the last 10 years have simply set the clock back.' Derek Tonkin, former British ambassador to Myanmar and chairperson of Network Myanmar

THE ECONOMY

Part of the question of whether it's ethical to visit Myanmar is whether the money is what keeps the junta in power. While the government once hoped tourism would provide a huge source of hard currency, it's clear that, as time's passed, they've depended little on it. They now receive the lion's share of their income from trade of gems, timber, textiles and, most notably, oil and gas.

TOURISM'S EFFECTS

'Tourism is peanuts for the generals.'
          Ma Thanegi, former aide to Aung San Suu Kyi

There are two ways of tracking tourists' expenses: the $240 of a careful visitor's $300 budget that stays in the private sector (eg family guesthouses, curry restaurants, trishaws and private buses); and the $60 that joins the government's estimated $13.7 billion GDP. Does either outweigh the other in importance?

Despite an official annual earnings of $1900, many locals make much less – about $440 according to the Burma Campaign UK's findings of £0.60 per day. The UN Development Program claims the people of Myanmar have the 13th-lowest income in the world. So a little goes a long way in helping. But, as proboycott advocates point out, tourism reaches only a

Moustache Brother Lu Maw (p270), a political comedian in Mandalay, told us in 2008: 'I need the tourists to pass on the news. We are always skating on thin ice here… Tomorrow? I'm not sure what'll happen.'

small percentage of the population. In an August 2008 report, the World Travel and Tourism Council estimated that tourism provides about 5.8% of Myanmar's jobs (about 1.3 million) and that tourism was likely to rise another 4% that year, despite the negative impact of international coverage of the protests and the government's slow reaction to Cyclone Nargis. It's a figure many are reluctant to agree on. Meanwhile, local businessman and author Paul Strachan argued, in one protourism presentation, that there's a 10:1 'trickle-down' effect, as one local receiving money from tourism can end up helping nine others.

Obviously not all tourists come on the same type of trip nor for the same time periods. Of the 660,000 visitors in 2006, nearly 60% were Asian. About 65% of all tourists come on 'border trips', meaning a day across the border from Thailand or China – sometimes just for casinos (or brothels). The rest arrive in Myanmar through Yangon (the only practical way to reach its main destinations). About half are 'FITs' (foreign independent tourists); a quarter of these come on package trips.

No matter how tourists come, the government does receive money from a few direct expenses during a trip: the $20 visa fee, the $10 departure tax, at least a portion of entry fees at many sites (see the boxed text, p19), and something like 12% of tax on hotel accommodation.

Its fellow Asean countries see many more tourists but Myanmar's tourism has risen in recent years, from 62,000 in 1994 to 650,000 in 2006. Peak season arrivals dipped to 250,000 after the September 2007 protests, according to Asean statistics.

Adding it up, Myanmar certainly depends far less on tourism than its neighbour Thailand does (where 6% of GDP, or about $14 billion annually, comes from tourism). Myanmar receives, at most, 0.7% of its GDP through tourism (calculated with CIA statistics and proboycott activists' estimates of the government receiving $100 million per year).

THE WORLD & MYANMAR

'China is the key.'

Human Rights Watch

Treatment of Myanmar by other nations seems to be governed by how far from the border they are: the closer, the less offensive the regime; the further, the less countries want to interact.

Asian Partners

A pivotal moment in the past two decades came following the brutal crackdown on protests in the 1988 election. As the generals carted away thousands of prisoners and chased others to the hills, what would the world do? There was a moment when a financially ruined government stood alone. But then a long-time rival, Thailand, signed on to huge timber deals – just enough to ensure the regime's survival. And the generals haven't looked back since.

Soon after, additional support came through tourism – there has been $1.1 billion in foreign investment in hotels and tourism services since 1988. But this focus faded a bit as bigger pies came into view. General Than Shwe has courted Myanmar's neighbours, discussing trade, oil and timber deals with India to the west, China to the north and its new Asean cousins to the south and east.

The Shwe gas reserves off the coast are valued at up to $17 billion over the next 20 years. And in 2006 Thailand bought $2.16 billion in natural gas. Despite Western sanctions against timber and jade, much of these materials

Former aide to Aung San Suu Kyi, Ma Thanegi, spent three years in Yangon's Insein prison, and told us many NLD members have always been against the boycott: 'Many people around Aung San Suu Kyi tried to dissuade her on the boycott. In '96, '97, '98, '99. I gave up trying around then.'

A member of pro-democracy local rap band Myanmar for Future Generations told us that 'boycott methods don't work any more and they don't affect the dictators much directly. If the country becomes isolated, can any exiled politician promise that we'll be free?'

Bribery is essentially part of *all* behind-the-scenes business in Myanmar. One private guesthouse owner told us they have to bribe their tax official. 'We pay the tax man 25% of the taxes we would have paid. He's a very rich man.'

HOW DEEP ARE THE GOVERNMENT'S POCKETS?

It's impossible to say exactly how much the government makes in a year, in tourism or other sectors. Several activist groups, including the Burma Campaign UK, have suggested that tourism brings the government $100 million per year (or about $167 per visitor, if calculated with 600,000 visitors annually). The estimates of *Xinhua News* in China (referring to Myanmar's official figures) suggested tourism brings in $200 million (to private and government sectors), before operating costs are deducted.

Considering the visa fee of about $20, departure tax of $10 and the 12% tax on purchases, a traveller staying away from government hotels and using privately run transport spends as much as 80% of their budget in the private sector – a bit less for shoestring travellers (see boxed text, p23).

Here are a few known figures to consider:

- **$114** average daily expense per tourist to Myanmar (*Xinhua News* estimates)
- **$900** spent per person per visit to Vietnam on average; thought to be comparable to Myanmar (source: Vietnam National Administration of Tourism)
- **$1900** Myanmar's annual per-capita income; many locals earn $200 annually (source: CIA)
- **$50 million** estimated value of wedding gifts at General Than Shwe's daughter's wedding in 2006 (source: *Guardian*)
- **$122–244 million** one estimate of the cost of building the new capital at Nay Pyi Taw (source: International Monetary Fund)
- **$241 million** UK investment in Myanmar's oil businesses in 2007 (source: *Myanmar Times*)
- **$300 million** value of showcased items at Myanmar Gems, Jade & Pearl Emporium in Yangon, held shortly after the EU's 2007 sanctions against gems (source: *Myanmar Times*)
- **$470 million** foreign investment in oil/gas in 2006–07 fiscal year (source: *Myanmar Times*)
- **$1.1 billion** amount of foreign investment in hotels and tourism since 1988 (source: *Xinhua News*)
- **$2 billion** foreign exchange reserves (source: International Monetary Fund)
- **$2.16 billion** estimated natural gas sales with Thailand (2006; government sources and Human Rights Watch)
- **$4.3 billion** approximate value of exports in 2006, up 48% from 2005 (source: Asian Development Bank)
- **$12–17 billion** estimated profits in Shwe gas deposits in next 20 years (source: government sources and Human Rights Watch)
- **$13.7 billion** Myanmar's GDP (2007; source: CIA)

are reportedly exported to China, Thailand and Singapore, then used to make furniture or jewellery for export.

The flow of foreign investment isn't likely to slow soon. The next round of multimillion dollar investments focus on trade connections with Myanmar's neighbours. In early 2008, India signed on to spend about $100 million developing a port in Sittwe to access more oil reserves in the Bay of Bengal, supposedly worth billions. Around the same time, Thailand won a bid to develop a new seaport at Dawei, while China will pay most of the costs of a massive highway from Kunming to a new Rakhaing seaport it will build at Kyauk Phyu, giving western China increased access to international trade routes.

Some observers had hoped that Asean could levy its influence for, at least, Aung San Suu Kyi's release. On occasion Asean officials have frowned over the generals' goings-on – even expressing 'revulsion' over the violent response

One Yangon local told us: 'Asean treats the generals like spoiled kids. They need discipline!'

GOVERNMENT FEES

Entry Fees

This box lists many of the government fees visitors to Myanmar will face, including those to visit some popular attractions such as Shwedagon Paya in Yangon or the Bagan Archaeological Zone. Many can be avoided if you alter your destination or the way you travel, while a few other fees (including sales tax and tax on accommodation) cannot be avoided if you visit.

- **Alaungpaya Palace**, Shwebo (K50; see p290)
- **Bagan Archaeological Zone** Even if you don't visit temples ($10; p177)
- **Bago sites** ($10; p147)
- **Chin State** Requires permit and taking either government or private guide (p334)
- **Elephant camps** Near Taungoo (p194) and Ngwe Saung (p145)
- **Hpo Win Daung Caves**, near Monywa ($2; p289)
- **Inle Lake Zone** ($3; p232)
- **Inwa** (see Mandalay Archaeological Zone)
- **Kachin State Cultural Museum**, Myitkyina ($2; p308)
- **Khamti** Must take tour with government's Myanmar Travels & Tours (from $1200 per person; p286)
- **Kyaiktiyo** (Golden Rock; $6; p154)
- **Mandalay Archaeological Zone** Includes entry to Inwa ($10; p261)
- **Mawlamyine's Mon Cultural Museum** ($2; p159)
- **Mingun** Includes Sagaing Hill ($3; p284)
- **Mrauk U** ($5; the museum is $5 extra; p328)
- **Putao** Must pay government fee to visit (p313)
- **Sagaing Hill** (see Mingun)
- **Shwedagon Paya**, Yangon ($5; p92)
- **Sittwe Museums** Rakhaing State Cultural Museum ($2; p325) and Buddhistic Museum ($5)
- **Thanboddhay Paya**, near Monywa ($3; p288)
- **Thayekhittaya ruins**, near Pyay ($5; p200)
- **Yangon museums** ($3 to $5; p104)
- **Youqson Kyaung**, Salay ($3; p190)

Other Services

- **Beer** Myanmar Beer is a joint-venture operation
- **City buses** From K50 a ride
- **Gas** Official ration is two gallons per week per vehicle, beyond that requires black market
- **Golf** Many courses are government controlled
- **Inland Water Transport (IWT)** Government ferries
- **Internet** As with electricity, post and telephone, the dial-up service is government controlled
- **Licences** As with all business, guesthouse owners and private guides must get licences from government; also restaurants with alcohol licences pay an extra fee for the right to sell beer etc
- **Myanma Airways** Government's domestic airline
- **Myanma Railways** Government's train service, with foreigner fares marked up over 500% of local fares (p368)
- **Myanmar Travels & Tours (MTT)** Government-run tourist information service
- **Newspapers** *Myanmar Times* and *New Light of Myanmar*
- **Post and telephone** All calls and faxes run by Ministry of Post & Telecommunications; international calls of $5 or $6 per minute

---

WHO IS TAY ZA?

Some 'private' companies in Myanmar are run by government members on the sly, or by their family members or cronies. Most of this business is linked with high-income sectors like gems and timber, but some is in tourism services.

The most infamously linked with tourism is Tay Za, founder of Htoo Trading Company. The 40-something businessperson initially made his money in the '90s from timber, having procured access to virgin forests. Though married, he is rumoured to be connected with one of the daughters of head honcho Than Shwe.

Earlier this decade (in 2004), he founded Air Bagan and set up two luxury hotel chains: Aureum Palace (in Ngwe Saung, Ngapali, Bagan, Nay Pyi Taw and Pyin U Lwin) and Myanmar Treasure Resort (in Yangon, Pathein, Ngwe Saung, Mawlamyine, Bagan and Inle Lake).

EU and US sanctions in October 2007 directly targeted Tay Za. By November 2007, Air Bagan, which apparently loses $1 million monthly, had to suspend international service to Singapore.

On the Air Bagan website, Tay Za maintains his independence from the junta and calls the sanctions 'misguided and unfair'. Despite a 2008 report in independent news organisation *Irrawaddy*, which quoted an unnamed Yangon-based businessperson saying that Tay Za's relationship with the government 'is not in fact as close as the press reported', most locals and observers remain doubtful.

---

to the September 2007 protests – but it's not been followed with action. One-time adviser to Asia for George W Bush, Michael J Green, likened Myanmar to a 'crazy drunk' on a block of Asean homes – it would take their unified confrontation to get the bottle away.

Western Sanctions

The West, meanwhile, has given a totally different response, by imposing economic sanctions against individuals and industries, and blocking involvement by the World Bank and IMF. Following Aung San Suu Kyi's arrest in 2003, the US targeted the textile industry, which led to the reported loss of 40,000 to 60,000 jobs.

More ambitious 'targeted sanctions' followed the September 2007 protests. The Australian government enacted the toughest, prohibiting the transfer of funds to a list of 418 government members or government cronies, including Tay Za (see boxed text, above). Many of these individuals are on the EU and US lists too, and both these entities have also banned the import of Myanmar timber and gems. Derek Tonkin, former British ambassador to Myanmar, said these targets 'represent only about 1% of Burmese exports to the EU' and has accused some targeted sanctions of simply lifting company names from a Myanmar Yellow Pages listings, thus affecting many 'prodemocracy supporters'.

What are missing from these lists, of course, are oil and gas, Myanmar's top draw and a field that 13 countries invest in currently – including $241 million annually from UK companies. Bo Kyaw Nyein, an author for Myanmar news site Mizzima (www.mizzima.com), predicts 'the Burmese generals will laugh all the way to the bank' unless sanctions are expanded to include this gap.

The other part of the picture is the UN. Over six months after the 2007 protests, the UN visited the generals three times and had the chance to meet with Aung San Suu Kyi. The visits appeared to accomplish little. At research time there was a question about whether the Security Council would call for any weapons embargos or sanctions against military officials.

Myanmar makes no weapons or military equipment. Much of it comes through sales from Russia, China, India and North Korea.

Myanmar locals aren't free to publicly discuss many things including politics. Throughout this book we've quoted many locals we met on this trip but, for their protection, haven't identified them by name.

If You Go

'Don't come in with your camera and take only pictures. We don't need that kind of tourist. Talk to those who want to talk. Let them know of the conditions of your life.'

Yangon resident

This guidebook is geared for independent travellers, not those on group tours. Not only can you get more out of a trip travelling independently and meeting locals, but you can be more responsible for where your money goes.

A great thing about the tourism boycott to Myanmar is how thoroughly it reminds us all to re-evaluate the effect of travel on the places we visit. If you do go to Myanmar, there are myriad opportunities to make some little differences that can mean a lot to a growing number of locals. Some of it is keeping in mind where your money goes, and spreading it further than the normal tourist trails; another is (and it may sound goofy) talk and talk and talk, and make new friends. Many locals cherish outside contact – they have so little – and the two-way exchange that comes from it is reassurance for them that Myanmar isn't forgotten. If you're spending all your time with one guide, or on your own, you're not really seeing Myanmar right. The temples and mountains and markets are lovely, but ultimately a trip to Myanmar is mostly about the people. After we spent a few hours with a *nat* expert in Bagan while researching this book, for instance, the grey-haired local, offering a second cup of tea in his home, said, 'I'll remember you till the end of eternity.'

We recommend against treating a trip as a means for political change. Foreigners who've handed out leaflets have been jailed (p341) and locals can be implicated by your gestures (eg taking a taxi to photograph Aung San Suu Kyi's house).

DIY OR PACKAGE TOUR?

'If you want to go, go. I just try to discourage people from taking package tours. Nothing goes to the people. I encourage people to go individually.'

Pascal Khoo Thwe, author of From the Land of Green Ghosts

GIVING GIFTS & DONATIONS

Travellers handing out candies, pens or money to kids on hiking trails or outside attractions have had a negative impact (as you'll certainly see when begging kids follow you around a pagoda). It's not the best way to contribute to those in need, and many locals will advise you not to give to children anyway. If you want to hand out useful items keep this in mind:

- Try to give to schools or village leaders, not kids. Although a rewarding way to spend a day is going to a village school, asking a teacher what supplies are lacking, buying them and handing them out to each of the students.

- If you want to help a begging family, ask what they need. Often you can accompany them to the market and pick up food (a bag of rice, some vegetables, some fish) and be invited to see their home.

- Foreign-made gifts (eg pens) are generally cherished items, and more likely to find a place in a bookcase than actually being used. If you want to give useful items, buy locally. It not only puts money into the local economy, but locals are more likely to use the gift!

- Some items from outside the country are greatly appreciated though. It's a good idea to carry books and magazines and discreetly give them to people you meet (for instance, leaving one behind in a guesthouse), particularly if there are any potential political overtones (eg copies of the *Economist*).

WHERE THE MONEY GOES

Travel costs (and other economic transactions) in Myanmar come in many forms. Some estimates suggest foreign travellers spend an average of $114 per day per person, but it is much lower for those sticking with budget accommodation and getting about by private buses. This table gives *estimated* average breakdowns of how much the government may get from different types of travellers. The figures include government taxes such as a visa, fees and a 12% tax on all purchases.

In some places, there are ways around the imposed fees, such as in Mandalay (p261). Also see p33 for an itinerary that skips all sites and destinations that require government fees.

Travel budget	Amount the government receives	Type of trip
$0	$0	People who stay at home and read about Myanmar
$300	$85	A two-week trip skipping all government fees (eg Bagan, Inle Lake) and services, and sticking with family guesthouses and public buses
$300	$105	Another shoestring trip, but one that includes government fees at Shwedagon Paya, Bagan and Inle Lake
$850	$150	A two-week trip that includes three flights, a boat ride to Bagan and accommodation at midrange hotels
$1100	$175	A 10-day trip with a private car for a week and accommodation at midrange hotels
$1750+	$250+	A one-week trip staying at higher-priced hotels, taking several guided day trips, eating at hotels and taking four domestic flights
$5000	$575	The minimum amount that goes to the government for a deluxe cabin on a seven-night luxury cruise
$1200	$1200	The part going to the government from an Myanmar Travels & Tours (MTT) guided, three-day trip to Khamti (Nagaland)

Many locals who support tourism favour individual travellers over package tourists, who often pay their money outside the country and have far less local interaction while in Myanmar. Another criticism of such tours is that the government, in some cases, takes 7% of remittances to local agents who arrange things, and 'encourages' certain services to be used. We can't say it's a rule, but we've seen a high-end European agent almost exclusively use Tay Za's Air Bagan and Aureum Palace hotels (see p21).

If you're used to having a car at the airport waiting for you, and guides showing you where to go, that can be done *and* arranged privately. Just because some roads are rough doesn't mean you have to sacrifice all comforts. Either contact a Yangon-based agent (p92) before a trip, or give yourself a couple of days to do so once you arrive, and they can help set up private guides, transport and hotels. Ask to pay as you go to ensure your money is spread out. And consider talking with more than one agent, telling them what you want, to gauge offers.

Better agents sometimes have some charity services in place: one private Yangon (Rangoon) agent started a small-loans program so that trishaw or boat drivers or weavers can purchase their means and slowly pay the loan back. Ask about contributing directly to a clinic or school as part of a trip (always do this in person).

Note that some high-end hotels import their furnishings, supplies and even food. Ask about it. Staying at hotels that use local products can keep more of your money in the country.

PICKING HOTELS

The days when uninformed travellers checked into government-run hotels are now almost entirely past. The dwindling number of government hotels – usually named for the city they're in (eg Sittwe Hotel in Sittwe) and haphazardly run – are frequently vacant these days. We recommend choosing from the 600 private accommodation choices, which we focus on in this book. That said, some money from your accommodation expenses – an estimated 12% tax – goes to the government no matter where you stay.

Visitors who want to be sure the least amount of their money goes to the government can stick with budget family-run guesthouses and minihotels. Those who want their stay to reach the most people sometimes choose to stay in midrange and top-end hotels, which can employ staff of 100 or more and often fund community projects.

We point out government hotels to avoid in this book, and flag some known government-crony hotels that we suggest passing on as well. See p336 for more on the types of hotels and where your accommodation spending goes.

SPREAD YOUR MONEY

Critics of independent travel argue that travellers' spending usually bottlenecks at select places, even if those spots are privately run. Familiarity can be reassuring – such as your trishaw-driver buddy, or the plate of noodles that didn't get you sick – but try to mix it up a bit. A few things to consider:

- Don't buy all of your needs (bed, taxi, guide, rice) from one source.
- Be conscious that behind-the-scenes commissions are being paid on most things you pay for when in the company of a driver or guide. If all travellers follow the same lead, the benefits only go to a select few.
- Plan en-route stops, or take in at least one off-the-beaten-track destination, where locals are less used to seeing foreigners.
- Mix up locations where you catch taxis and trishaws – and try to take ones from guys not lingering outside tourist areas.
- Try to eat at different family restaurants and if you're staying at a hotel, eat out often; eg in Ngapali Beach, local restaurants are just across the road from the beach and hotels.
- Either buy handicrafts directly from the artisans, or, if not, don't get all your souvenirs from one private shop.

DON'T COMPROMISE LOCALS

In a country that imprisons its people for disagreeing with the government's line, travellers need to ensure that they don't behave in a way that will lead to locals being compromised in the eyes of the junta.

- Don't raise political questions and issues in inappropriate situations; let a local direct the conversation. For example, don't come out with something like: 'Did you march with the monks in 2007?' or any-

---

All trains and most ferries are government run. Many visitors choose to go by private car with driver, private buses or air – but note that some runways were built with forced labour and there are government contacts in some airline companies (p361).

Unless otherwise specified, all sights and organisations reviewed in this book are believed to be locally owned and run businesses.

See p55 for a list of some dos and don'ts to remember on your trip.

SPIES LIKE THEM

At some point on your trip, you may be followed by local authorities, though few visitors ever realise it. (Our efforts to create a map of Taungoo – failed, sorry – certainly got their attention.) One way to get the eyes of military intelligence off your back is do what Emma Larkin does in her book *Finding George Orwell in Burma*: duck into a church. She writes: 'Since the Burmese assume that most Westerners are Christians, going to a church is a fairly innocent thing to be doing.'

AID & DIRECT-AID VOLUNTEERS

Sometimes it takes more than tourism and a trickle of money to reverse a situation. Even before Cyclone Nargis claimed up to 140,000 lives in May 2008, groups like Refugees International and Human Rights Watch were frantically waving a warning flag that Myanmar was facing a humanitarian crisis. And considering the block the military government made towards outside groups, including the UN, after the cyclone hit, there's little reason to believe much help will come from within.

Of the 50 poorest nations, Myanmar is last in per-capita aid – receiving about $2.88 per person compared with an average of $58. For years, sanctions (and the government's restrictions) have curbed many NGO efforts, but that may soon be changing. In 2008, for example, the UK doubled its total aid (to $35 million), and Australian and European donors are giving $104 million through to 2013 to fight disease like AIDS and malaria.

Tourism isn't going to fix this problem on its own, of course, but there are some small things you can do to help during your visit. Ask guesthouse owners, agents, teachers and monks about donations you'd like to make for medical or school supplies. Or stop in a village school and ask what materials they lack. Often about $75 can get a book, notepad and pen for everyone needing them. Also consider taking some simple, locally bought medicines. When routes into the Ayeyarwady Delta reopen, see if there are things locals might need in areas damaged by Cyclone Nargis.

One remote Chin village we visited in Rakhaing State sees occasional tourists, and donations to the village leader had resulted in something they quickly pointed out: a corrugated metal roof on a stilt-house. 'Tourists paid for the roof of our school,' the leader told us.

Outside of small donations, some NGOs prefer tourists to stick with their trips and leave bigger projects for them. Joel Charny at Refugees International, who supports tourism in the private sector, told us, 'I am not a fan of tourists trying to turn into development workers. Let tourists be tourists.'

During research for this guide, however, we met several retired travellers who were new 'direct-aid volunteers'. They felt there wasn't time to wait for aid to reach locals so they come twice yearly to fund projects on their own. One, who has built and overseen many new school projects, told us: 'When I finish one, I only have to drive 10 minutes to the next village to find another in need.'

Another is a retired 'millionaire' from Switzerland, who has dug water wells, built homes for the elderly and set up schools for years. He advised: 'Never give money. Go in a shop and buy a kilo of rice for someone. Ask what they need and get it, not money.'

thing about Aung San Suu Kyi or the NLD where there are others that may be listening in – even if you are riding on a trishaw.

- Show equal caution regarding what you ask or say on the phone or via email.

- Asking a taxi driver to take you past Aung San Suu Kyi's house or to a NLD office could implicate them.

- Exercise care in handing over anything to a local that could carry political overtones (such as a copy of the *Economist* or Myanmar-related books).

- Outside of politics, be wary of places that treat minority groups as 'attractions'. The 'long-necked' Paduang women in Shan State (p239) have led to a zoolike tourist event. This is particularly problematic from visitors on the Thai side of the border, where Thai agencies offer $8 tours of women who aren't allowed to leave. The Office of the UN High Commissioner for Refugees told the BBC in 2008 that 'one solution is for tourists to stop going'.

For safe hiking guidelines see p340, or p228 for suggestions on how trekking trips can bring helpful gifts to remote communities. For tips on responsible snorkelling and diving, see p339.

BACK AT HOME

Your trip to Myanmar doesn't end once you're back home. Alert us and fellow travellers via the Thorn Tree discussion board (www.lonelyplanet .com/thorntree) if you've stumbled onto a new or changed government-operated service or have a suggestion on how to minimise money going to the government. Consider posting photos and perceptions of your trip on a blog. Write to your local Myanmar embassy to express your views about the human-rights situation there. And be sure to keep in contact with new friends made on the road.

Getting Started

WHEN TO GO

The best time to visit Myanmar is between November and February. During these months it rains least (if at all in places) and it is not so hot. March to May brings intense heat. At this time, the daily temperatures in Yangon (Rangoon) often reach 40°C, while areas around Bagan and Mandalay go a few digits higher. The cool hill towns of Shan State offer relief from the heat, though.

The southwest monsoon starts between mid-May and mid-June, bringing frequent rains that dunk the country through till October, peaking from July to September. The dry zone (between Mandalay and Pyay) gets the least rain, though roads anywhere (and particularly in the delta region) can become impassable. Rakhaing State bears the full force of the rains – often exceeding 195in of rain annually.

COSTS & MONEY

Even though fuel prices jumped by 500% in 2007 and the government keeps a 'foreigner price' system (affecting all transport, accommodation and entrance fees), Myanmar can still be very cheap to visit.

On a 10-day trip to the 'big four' (Yangon, Mandalay, Inle Lake and Bagan), staying in budget family-run guesthouses (about $7.50 to $10 for a single, $12 to $15 for a double), eating your free breakfast and other meals at local rice-type eateries ($1.50 or $2 a meal, perhaps a $1 beer) and using buses to get around, you could comfortably get by with $400 per person.

Doing the same 10-day trip with a bit more comfort – staying at midrange hotels (from $15/25 for a single/double), adding a nicer meal each day (about $5 to $10 per person), hiring a local guide a couple of times (maybe $7 to $10 per day), buying a puppet and adding a couple of internal flights – will be more like $600 or $700 per person.

Add more if you're planning to get a private driver and car (around $80 or $100 per day for a good one). And more if you're going for the top-end hotels (up to $400 per night!).

Only US dollars and euro can be exchanged in Myanmar. Baht can be exchanged only at the border with Thailand. Official rates at the airport were K450 for $1. Also see p346 regarding money in Myanmar.

TRAVEL LITERATURE

Few countries warrant more pretrip reading than Myanmar.

Thant Myint U's engaging *River of Lost Footsteps* (2006) has recently emerged as the new must-read historical overview. The grandson of former UN Secretary-General U Thant, Thant Myint recounts kings' blunders and successes, while adding occasional family anecdotes of Burma's early days of independence. He ends with a passionate case against isolation.

HOW MUCH?

Ride on a Yangon city bus K100

Burmese all-you-can-eat buffet lunch K1500

Overnight bus from Yangon to Mandalay K10,000

Hired car with driver per day $40-100

Local phone call: about K200

'The number one concern visitors have is coming without cash!' – the British Consulate in Yangon

Check p340 for climate charts for Yangon and Mandalay.

GET YOUR CASH READY

Considering Myanmar has essentially no places that accept a credit card, travellers cheques or ATM cards, you need to plan how much money you're going to spend – and get the *right kind* of bills (clean, crisp, new US dollar bills) well before your plane lands in Yangon (Rangoon). Many, many visitors forget to do this, and end up heading back to Thailand to get some. See p347 for more on moneychangers.

TOP PICKS
Bangladesh · India · MYANMAR (BURMA) · Vietnam · Laos

KEY FIRST QUESTIONS

1 Burma or Myanmar? Britain renamed 'Myanma' as Burma (after the majority Bamar, or Burmese, people); the junta restored the original name of Myanmar in 1989; 'Burmese' in this book refers to the food, the Bamar people and the language.

2 Where to change money? Not at the airport. You get better rates from your hotel or in town.

3 Should I lie about my profession? If you're a writer or journalist, put down your dream job instead.

4 Men in skirts? Most Myanmar men wear *longyi* (saronglike wraparound 'skirts').

5 Mud on face? No, that's *thanakha* (powdered bark) used as a make-up and sunblock.

6 Is that blood? No, those puddles of red on the ground are from spit betel nuts – known to revive if you're tired.

7 Is the water OK? Go with bottled water. Many guesthouses give a free bottle.

8 How to shake hands? It's local custom to shake hands or hand money with your right hand, with your left hand 'holding up' your right arm.

9 Will I be followed? At some point, most likely, though very few visitors ever realise it.

FESTIVALS & EVENTS

1 Independence Day, 4 January (p30)

2 Kachin State Day (Myitkyina), 10 January (p308)

3 Shwedagon Festival (Yangon), February/March (p116)

4 Buddha's birthday, full moon, April/May (p30)

5 Water Festival (Thingyan) & Burmese New Year, mid-April (p67)

6 Dawei Thingyan, April (p171) – giant bamboo effigies and drums

7 Nat Festival (Mt Popa), Nayon full moon, May/June (p189)

8 Start of Buddhist Rains Retreat, full moon June/July (p30)

9 Nat Festival (near Amarapura), after Wagaung full moon, August (p280)

10 Taunggyi's balloon festival, October/November (p245)

SOUVENIRS

1 *Longyi* (sarong-style lower garment) – found wherever a breeze might blow.

2 Marionettes from Yangon's Bogyoke Aung San Market (p128) or in Mandalay (p272).

3 Pathein's paper parasols (p139).

4 Myanmar's best lacquerware at Myinkaba (p186).

5 Glazed pottery from workshops in Kyaukka (p290).

6 Moustache Brothers T-shirt from Mandalay (p270).

7 Tatmadaw army hat. Public markets sell the (infamous) floppy green hats that many locals wear.

8 Mini sheets of gold leaf. Locals put it on buddhas, and occasionally on bananas (p271).

9 Kachin jewellery or ceremonial swords (p307).

10 Water buffalo in Kengtung (p248), or maybe just browse for one.

DON'T LEAVE HOME WITHOUT...

- Reading up on the political situation as well as the question of 'Should You Go?' (p13)
- Having enough US dollars in cash for your full trip (see p27)
- Getting your visa (p352)
- Packing a sweater or fleece jacket for chilly overnight bus rides or the mountains
- Passport photocopies, which can be useful for permits in some, far-flung places
- Flip-flops or sandals
- Bug spray

You can find things like batteries, video tape and tampons in bigger destinations like Yangon and Mandalay.

From the Land of Green Ghosts: A Burmese Odyssey (2002), by Pascal Khoo Thwe, is a self-told tale of a reluctant rebel of the government from a hill tribe in Shan State who escaped – unlike many of his friends – out of Myanmar.

In Andrew Marshall's excellent *The Trouser People: A Story of Burma in the Shadow of the Empire* (2002), the British author retraces the steps of a gutsy Scot named Sir George Scott who traversed unmapped corners of British Burma ('where people are small and ghosts are big') in the late 1800s.

Emma Larkin's *Finding George Orwell in Burma* (2004) ploughs a more delicate path, following Orwell's footsteps of his days here. It could do with fewer forced comparisons of *1984* and the military junta, but it's worth it for the inside looks of backwaters like Mawlamyine (Moulmein) and the delta.

Peter Olszewski may not be the sort of guy you want to share a tea with, but his *Land of a Thousand Eyes* (2005) is a refreshing look at day-to-day life in modern Myanmar (without fixating much on politics). The ageing Australian journalist came for long enough to train journalists at the *Myanmar Times* (and find a wife), but it's not quite as sleazy as it sounds.

April may be Myanmar's new year, but to TS Eliot April in Myanmar is 'the cruellest month'.

INTERNET RESOURCES

Here are some useful sites to refer to when planning your trip:
Burma Today (www.burmatoday.com) Posts recent Myanmar articles.
Irrawaddy (www.irrawaddy.org) Bangkok-based publication focuses on political issues, but covers many cultural news topics.
Lonely Planet's Thorn Tree (www.lonelyplanet.com/thorntree) Best resource to mix and mingle with fellow travellers.
Mizzima (www.mizzima.com) A nonprofit news service organised by Myanmar journalists in exile.
Myanmar Home Page (www.myanmar.com) Provides a funny government dictum, and two local English-language papers.
Online Burma/Myanmar Library (www.burmalibrary.org) Comprehensive database of books and past articles on Myanmar.

Events Calendar

Festivals usually take place or culminate on full-moon days, but the build-up can last for a while. Many follow the 12-month lunar calendar (p353). Also, nearly every active paya or *kyaung* (Buddhist monastery) community hosts occasional celebrations of its own, often called *paya pwe* or 'pagoda festivals'. Many occur on full-moon days and nights from January to March, following the main rice harvest.

JANUARY

INDEPENDENCE DAY   4 Jan
This major public holiday is marked by a seven-day fair at Kandawgyi Lake (p104) in Yangon (Rangoon), and nationwide fairs.

KACHIN STATE DAY   10 Jan
Rice beer and buffalo sacrifices in Myitkyina (see p308).

FEBRUARY–MARCH

UNION DAY   12 Feb
This two-week festival celebrates Bogyoke Aung San's (short-lived) achievement of unifying Myanmar's disparate ethnic groups.

SHWEDAGON FESTIVAL
The lunar month of Tabaung brings the annual Shwedagon Festival (p116), the largest *paya pwe* in Myanmar.

PEASANTS' DAY   2 Mar
Dedicated to the nation's farmers.

**ARMED FORCES
(OR RESISTANCE) DAY**   27 Mar
Myanmar's army stages parades to celebrate its resistance against Japanese occupation during WWII.

APRIL–MAY

BUDDHA'S BIRTHDAY
The full-moon day of Kason is celebrated as Buddha's birthday, the day of his enlightenment and the day he entered *nibbana* (nirvana).

WATER FESTIVAL (OR THINGYAN)
This is the celebration of the Myanmar New Year. See p67 for more details.

JUNE–JULY

START OF THE BUDDHIST RAINS RETREAT
The full moon of Waso is the beginning of the three-month Buddhist Rains Retreat (aka 'Buddhist Lent'), when young men enter monasteries and no marriages take place.

MARTYRS' DAY   19 Jul
This date commemorates the assassination of Bogyoke Aung San and his comrades on this day in 1947.

JULY–AUGUST

WAGAUNG FESTIVAL
During Wagaung, many offer alms to monks; a highlight event is at Taungbyone, near Mandalay (see p266).

SEPTEMBER–OCTOBER

BOAT RACES
In the rainy season, boat races fill rivers, lakes and ponds nationwide. The best is in Inle Lake (see p234).

THADINGYUT
During Thadingyut, the Buddhist Rains Retreat ends, a popular time for weddings and monk pilgrimages to Mt Popa or Kyaiktiyo.

OCTOBER–NOVEMBER

TAZAUNGMON
The full-moon night of Tazaungmon, known as Tazaungdaing, is the biggest 'festival of lights', particularly famous for the fire-balloon competitions in Taunggyi (see p245).

KAHTEIN
Tazaungmon also brings Kahtein, a one-month period during which new monastic robes and requisites are offered to the monastic community.

NOVEMBER–DECEMBER

NATIONAL DAY
Myanmar's national day falls in late November or early December.

NADAW
During Nadaw, many *nat pwe* (spirit festivals) are held; Nadaw is spelt with the characters for *nat* and *taw* (a respectful honorific).

CHRISTMAS
A surprisingly popular public holiday in deference to the many Christian Kayin, Kachin and Chin.

DECEMBER–JANUARY

KAYIN NEW YEAR
On the first waxing moon of Pyatho, the Kayin New Year is considered a national holiday, with Kayin communities (Insein in Yangon, Hpa-An) wearing traditional dress.

ANANDA FESTIVAL
Enormous religious festival in Bagan (p210).

Itineraries
CLASSIC ROUTES

THE BIG FOUR   11 Days / Yangon to Inle Lake

Starting in **Yangon** (Rangoon, p87), visit the **Shwedagon Paya** (p92) at night, when its golden *zedi* (stupa) glows under floodlights. The next day, wander around **downtown** (p114) and shop for handicrafts at **Bogyoke Aung San Market** (p128). Overnight on a bus to **Mandalay** (p255), climb **Mandalay Hill** (p258), see the famed **Mahamuni Paya** (p263) and **Moustache Brothers** (p270). The next day take a morning boat trip to **Mingun** (p284) to see an earthquake-cracked stupa, then take a sunset boat ride past U Bein's Bridge at **Amarapura** (p278). Bus to the often-missed **Monywa** (p288), home to a colourful buddha-rama (Thanboddhay Paya). Catch the next morning bus to **Pakokku** (p191) for a private boat ride to **Bagan** (p183) and take a horse cart or cycle around Bagan's 800-year-old temples. Catch the 4am bus towards **Inle Lake** (p232) then, after a day on the lake, where dugout canoes take you to floating markets under the flight path of egrets, consider a day trip to **Pindaya Caves** (p229) to see 8000 buddha images. Take an overnight bus back to Yangon.

Most first-time visitors with a week-and-a-half stick with Myanmar's four most-popular attractions. Flying saves a couple of travel days, but we've planned it with two overnight buses and the off-the-beaten-track 'Monywa loop' from Mandalay to Bagan instead.

NO FEES PLEASE!   17 to 18 Days / Yangon to Hsipaw & Chaung Tha

Start with two nights in **Yangon** (p87). Skip the $5 Shwedagon Paya fee and visit the 2000-year-old **Sule Paya** (p114) while on a downtown walking tour. The next day, ferry to nearby rural villages **Thanlyin** and **Kyauktan** (p133), then return for an overnight bus to **Mandalay** (p255). The government $10 fee is easily skipped (p261) with alternative sights, such as **Yankin Paya** (p264) and a day trip to **Amarapura** (p277). Bus or taxi into the Shan Hills at **Hsipaw** (p300) and take a privately guided trek to Palaung villages. After two nights, taxi downhill to **Pyin U Lwin** (p294) for a night in the old British hill station. Get back to Mandalay in time for the night bus to Yangon, but stop in the wee hours at **Bago** (p147; don't stay, it's $10 to visit). Catch an 8am bus to Kipling and Orwell's old stomping grounds at far-flung **Mawlamyine** (Moulmein, p159) in Mon State. You'll want two nights, enough to make a day trip to the 'Burma Railroad' **cemetery** (p165) two hours south. Try timing your trip for the lovely boat ride to Kayin State's **Hpa-an** (p167), which goes Monday or Friday. Stay a couple of nights and climb nearby Mt Zwegabin for a free breakfast with monkeys (not of monkeys!). Afterwards bus back to Yangon.

If there's time, bus the next day to low-key **Pathein** (Bassein, p136) to pick up a sun parasol from private workshops, then finish with a couple of days at the locals' favourite sun spot at **Chaung Tha Beach** (p140). At the time of writing, travel restrictions in the delta area (p133) prevent foreigners travelling to Pathein and Chaung Tha Beach so check for updates before you travel.

Some destinations (eg Bagan, Inle Lake, Golden Rock and Bago) can't be seen unless you pay a fee that goes to the government. This itinerary skips them all – and gets more out of Myanmar by going local.

ROADS LESS TRAVELLED

AYEYARWADY HO!   24 to 28 Days / Myitkyina to Yangon

Fly to **Myitkyina** (p307), where you can wait for the next ferry south by taking in Kachin culture; every 10 January animal sacrifices are made to satisfy the *nat*. Begin the river ride on a small local boat for a full-day drift, changing in Sinbo, to reach **Bhamo** (p309), a leafy town with 5th-century Shan ruins. A fast boat or ferry (thrice weekly) heads south for an eight-hour trip to **Katha** (p312), where George Orwell based his *Burmese Days* and where you can visit an elephant camp. The ferry out of Katha goes overnight so consider a cabin. Get out in the morning at **Kyaukmyaung** (p292) for a quick look at riverside pottery factories, then catch a pick-up ride an hour west to the former Burmese capital **Shwebo** (p290) for the night. Detour from the river via a 3½-hour bus ride to pleasant **Monywa** (p286), near a **buddha-shaped mountain** (p289) with budda-filled caves (and monkeys).

Take a bus to **Mandalay** (p255) and spend three or four days visiting the **ancient cities** (p277) and maybe one of the local **festivals** (p277); then get back on the Ayeyarwady (Irrawaddy) to **Bagan** (p177), to witness the 3000 temples. If you're worn out by boats, take the morning bus south to Magwe (four hours) and peek at a gurgling mound of sludge at Nga Ka Pwe Taung at **Minbu** (p202); then hop on an afternoon bus to **Pyay** (Prome, p198) and stay a couple of nights. On one day you can go by ox around the ruins and see a nearby spectacled buddha at **Shwemyetman Paya** (p201). Frequent buses reach **Yangon** (p87), six hours south.

This may be Myanmar's ultimate journey – from top to bottom, mostly following the Ayeyarwady, hitting the far-flung backwaters *and* still making it to Mandalay and Bagan. It's not all on the water so savour those ferry trips – they're best for meeting locals.

TAILORED TRIPS

THE ACTIVE LIFE

Many activities take place under the hot Myanmar sun and more travellers are planning their own loops on treks in Shan State. The best, and certainly most popular, are the overnight treks from **Kalaw** to **Inle Lake** (p226), while day treks around **Kengtung** (p250) see more traditional garb, and those from **Hsipaw** (p302) take in waterfalls. With a government permit, you can hike **Mt Victoria** (p334), which is popular with birders. The journeys to some religious sites are hikes in themselves, famously up **Mt Kyaiktiyo** (the Golden Rock; p154), up Mandalay Hill (p258) or past monkeys at **Mt Popa** (p188), the spiritual centre of the 37 *nat*.

Bicycles are regular transport around towns. Long-distance cyclists, often on tours, enjoy the ride from **Mandalay** to **Bagan** (p338) via Myingyan – or take to the hills along the road from **Pyin U Lwin** (p338) to **Lashio** (p304).

You can take kickboxing classes at the YMCA in **Yangon** (p115) or if you have less angst in your system opt for t'ai chi in the city's central **Mahabandoola Garden** (p104).

Ngapali Beach (p319) has low-key island snorkelling tours; **Chaung Tha Beach** (p140) has plenty of snorkelling options too, though travel restrictions (put in place after Cyclone Nargis in 2008, p133) may prevent foreigners reaching it. The best diving by far is off the islands near **Kawthoung** (p173), currently reached with diving operators from Phuket. And in the far north, at the foothills of the Himalaya, you can go white-water rafting on the **Maykha River** (p314).

MYANMARVELS & THE OUTRIGHT ODD

Certain aspects of Myanmar are a little 'unusual' – and memorable. In **Myingyan** (p192) the remains of a famous monk have been on view since 1951. Snakes are another thing: three pythons in **Paleik** (p282) are lovingly fed at 11am daily; in **Minbu** (p202) the Nga Ka Pwe Taung (p202) is guarded by a snake or two, and you can dip your toe into a 'volcano' of bubbling butane gas.

Buffalo-browse at the water-buffalo market in **Kengtung** (p248) or see monk-trained cats jump through rings at Nga Hpe Chaung at **Inle Lake** (p240). No tricks are needed – just nerve – to eat live wriggling larva, served at many **street markets** (p78).

The wonder of Myanmar is the Golden Rock at **Kyaiktiyo** (p154), a gravity-defying boulder atop a mountain. The lesser-seen **Nwa-la-bo** (p164), near Mawlamyine, features three sausage-shaped boulders topped by a stupa. The unique spectacled buddha of Shwemyetman Paya sits in a temple at **Shwedaung** (p201). Across the river from Yangon, **Thanlyin** (p134) hosts a hot coal–walking, skin-piercing festival in January. If that's too much to stomach, sip a German-made wine from a **Shan State winery** (p245) near Inle Lake. Now, that's odd.

History

Six decades since independence from Britain, Myanmar remains a rocky work in progress. In fact, it's never enjoyed stability for long.

Squabbling kingdoms plagued the area for hundreds of years, till the British took it in three waves in the 19th century. Britain managed the mountainous border regions separately from the fertile plains and delta of central and lower Myanmar, building on a cultural rift between the lowland Bamar and highland ethnic groups that lingers today. Civil war erupted between minority groups after independence in 1948, and continues still.

General Ne Win wrested control from a failing government in 1962 and began the world's longest-running military dictatorship, which quickly pursued xenophobic policies and led the country to full isolation. Ruined by a rapidly deteriorating economy and a major currency devaluation in the 1970s and '80s, many thousands of locals flooded the streets – peacefully – on 8 August 1988. The prodemocracy marches saw Aung San Suu Kyi emerge as a leader, who was recognised worldwide. After a violent reaction by the military, the administration, to everyone's surprise, called a national election. It thought it couldn't lose. But it did. At the 1990 election, Aung San Suu Kyi's National League for Democracy (NLD) won 82% of the assembly seats, but the military refused to transfer power.

In the years since, Myanmar's neighbours (particularly China) and its membership in Asean (since 1997) have ensured that the government has been able to withstand increased scorn from the USA and EU. But in 2007, after gas prices jumped by 500%, nationwide protests erupted for the first time since '88. The world watched as the generals' army clamped down, leaving a number of fatalities in the streets. Then, on 3 May 2008, Cyclone Nargis tore through the Ayeyarwady (Irrawaddy) Delta, claiming nearly 140,000 lives. The government blocked any foreign help for weeks, as some local groups and monks strove to get food and supplies to victims.

Many outsiders hoping for democracy, like author U Than Nyint and activist Dr Maung Zarni, feel that the past two decades have been a waste of time and are beginning to wonder if it'll take more than peaceful marches to ignite any meaningful communication.

The Rakhaing claim the Buddha visited their kingdom in the 6th century BC.

Per local tradition, Buddha gave eight of his hairs to a couple of visiting Burmese merchants 3000 years ago. They took them back to be enshrined in what is now Yangon's Shwedagon Paya.

THE BIRTH OF KINGS

When the British arrived on the scene in the 1800s, jockeying for more colonial turf in their ongoing competition with France, they found an unorganised, sparsely populated empire of five million, already in decline.

TIMELINE

483 BC	3rd century BC	1st century BC
Age 30, Buddha pronounces that 'all creations are impermanent, work diligently for your liberation', shortly before going into meditation and – through his death – passing into nirvana	The Mon, who migrated into the Ayeyarwady Delta from present-day Thailand (and from China before that), establish their capital Thaton, and have first contact with Buddhism	Possible founding of Beikthano (named after the local word for Vishnu), a Pyu town east of current-day Magwe; it's believed to have flourished for about 400 years

The notion that the area had been settled for long was dismissed by many early British reports, but they were wrong. Myanmar's region has a long, complex history

At least 2500 years ago, the area was a key land link between traders from India and the Middle East and China – a link that's being renewed now, as China plots a pipeline across Myanmar. The first archaeological evidence of life here goes further back – perhaps as far as 2500 BC. Local farmers domesticated chickens and had made bronze by 1500 BC. Ancient Greeks knew of the country too.

The Myanmar government, however, contends that this is modern history compared to the area's real roots. Apparently in the 1990s, a 45-million-year-old fossil (an anklebone of a primate) was found in central Myanmar. The Myanmar government is fond of its belief that this broad fertile flatland, rimmed by a horseshoe of mountains and carved by long navigable rivers, may be the birthplace of *all* the world's humans.

History of Burma (1925), by GE Harvey, gives a chronological rundown of Myanmar's kingdoms (from the Pyu era until 1824). Harvey almost audibly sighs at the kings' blunders, and faithfully recounts many fanciful legends.

EARLY KINGDOMS

Four major precolonial ethnic groups peppered the flatlands with kingdoms for centuries, while smaller ethnic groups lived – mostly untouched – in the remote hills beyond.

Mon The Mon (Tailing), who may have originated from eastern India or mainland Southeast Asia, settled fertile lowlands on the Ayeyarwady River delta across Thailand to Cambodia. They developed the area as Suvannabhumi (Golden Land), the capital either being near present-day Thaton in Myanmar, or in Thailand's Nakhon Pathom.

Pyu Arriving from the Tibeto-Burman plateau or from India around the 1st century BC, the Pyu established the first major kingdom of sorts, with city-states in central Myanmar including Beikthano, Hanlin (p292) and Sri Ksetra (Thayekhittaya; p200). In the 10th century, Yunnanese invaders from China enslaved or scared off most Pyu (though some Pyu art remains, showing a blend of Hinduism and Theravada and Mahayana Buddhism).

Bamar The Bamar people, or Burmans, arrived from somewhere in the eastern Himalaya in the 8th or 9th century, supplanting the vanquished Pyu in central Myanmar and establishing the cultural heartland of Myanmar as it's still known. It's believed the first Bamar here arrived with royal prince Abhiraja, escaping political troubles with his army. They first converged at Tagaung, north of Mandalay, before founding Bagan (Pagan) in 849. Centuries of conflict with the Mon erupted after their arrival. Although the Bamar came out on top, the result was really a merger of the two cultures.

Rakhaing Sometimes linked with present-day Bangladesh, the Rakhaing (Arakanese) claim their kingdom was well under way by the 6th century BC. Certainly it was in full force by the 15th century, when their Buddhist kingdom was based in Mrauk U (p327) and their navy controlled much of the Bay of Bengal.

What is currently considered traditional 'Burmese culture' is really a fusion of Mon and Bamar cultures that came about at the height of the Bagan era.

THE 'FIRST BURMA'

Bagan was nearly 200 years old when its 'golden period' kicked off – when energetic, can-do (and can-kill) King Anawrahta took the throne in 1044.

AD 754	849	1044
Nanzhao soldiers of Yunnan, China, conquer the hill tribes in the upper reaches of the Ayeyarwady River and come into contact with the Pyu	Bagan is founded on the site of a once-thriving Pyu city; its first name may have been Pyugan, something recorded 200 years later by the Annamese of present-day Vietnam	Anawrahta takes the throne in Bagan and the 'golden period' of the First Burmese Empire emerges, including such military achievements as sacking the ancient Mon city of Thaton 13 years later; Anawrahta would rule until 1077

Converted to Buddhism by a Mon monk, Anawrahta quickly became a fanatic. When he demanded the Mon king Manuha of Thaton hand over their Tripitaka (the holy canon of Theravada Buddhism), and Manuha refused, Anawrahta marched south and conquered Thaton in 1057, bringing back both the scriptures and the king. The resultant injection of Mon culture into Bagan inspired a creative energy. It quickly became a city of glorious temples and the capital of the First Burmese Empire. For more on the history of Bagan see p203.

In 1077 the kingdom took a steady slip downward when a lowly buffalo killed mighty Anawrahta. None of his successors (Kyanzittha, Alaungsithu and Htilominlo) had his vision, and the kingdom's power slowly declined. In 1273 King Narathihapate made the diplomatic mistake of offending the growing power of Kublai Khan and his Tartars (assassinating diplomats will do that). The Mongols invaded in 1287, but didn't stay long. Shan tribes (closely related with the Siamese) from the hills to the east took the opportunity and grabbed a piece of the low country, while the Mon in the south broke free of Bamar control and established their own kingdom. An empire ended in chaos.

> The first record of European contact with present-day Myanmar came when Venetian trader Nicolo di Conti travelled along the coast in the 1420s, but it's often claimed that Marco Polo dropped by in the late 13th century.

THE 'SECOND BURMA'

The 200 years following the collapse of Bagan were chaotic, with pieces of the puzzle ruled by various factions. In the 13th century the Mon re-established Hanthawady as a fairly stable kingdom at Bago (Pegu) near Yangon (Rangoon). In 1472, Dhammazedi, the greatest of Bago's kings, came to the throne. He prompted a Buddhist revival, set up diplomatic contact with Europe and set the first stones for the great Shwedagon Paya in Yangon.

Meanwhile the Shan had taken over northern Myanmar and founded the Kingdom of Inwa (mistakenly called 'Ava' by the British) near present-day Mandalay in 1364, and the Rakhaing people flourished in western Myanmar, building fields of temples to rival Bagan (see p317 for more on the Rakhaing).

Amidst all the flowing testosterone, the tiny settlement of Bamar refugees in central Taungoo (surviving between the Mon and Shan by playing the larger forces off against each other) managed eventually to egg on the so-called 'Second Burmese Empire'. In the 16th century, a series of Taungoo kings extended their power north, nearly to the Shan's capital at Inwa, then south, taking the Mon kingdom and shifting their own capital to Bago. In 1550 Bayinnaung came to the throne, reunified all of Myanmar and defeated the neighbouring Siamese so convincingly that it was many years before the long-running friction between the two nations resurfaced.

> Some of the first British encounters with Burmese kings were in the early 18th century, when Bodawpaya dressed up in so much gold (to impress) that he needed assistants to help move him to his throne.

As had happened with Anawrahta, the union slipped into decline following Bayinnaung's death in 1581. The capital was shifted north to Inwa in 1636. Its isolation from the sea – effectively cutting off communication around the kingdom – ultimately contributed to Myanmar's defeat by the British.

1273	**1290s**	**1364**
In a curious gesture of diplomacy against far-superior forces to the north, the Burmese in Bagan slay Tartar ambassadors, prompting a peeved Kublai Khan to invade 14 years later	Marco Polo becomes possibly the first Westerner to travel in Myanmar (then known to foreigners as Mien), and publishes an account of his travels in 1298	After the collapse of Bagan, Burmese leaders settled Inwa, southwest of present-day Mandalay, which was eventually conquered by the Shan 163 years later (in 1527)

BURMA'S LAST KINGS

With all the subtlety of a kick to the groin, King Alaungpaya launched the third and final Burmese dynasty by contesting the Mon when the latter took over Inwa in 1752. Some say Alaungpaya's sense of invincibility deluded the Burmese into thinking they could resist the British later on. After Alaungpaya's short and bloody reign (see below), his son Hsinbyushin charged into Thailand and levelled the capital of Ayuthaya, forcing the Siamese to relocate their capital to what would eventually become Bangkok. His successor, Bodawpaya (another son of Alaungpaya), looked for glory too, and brought the Rakhaing under Burmese control. This eventually led to tension with the British (who had economic interests in Rakhaing territory) that the dynasty would not outlive.

With eyes on Indochina, Britain wrested all of the increasingly isolationist Burma from the kings in three decisive swipes. In the First, Second and Third Anglo-Burmese Wars they picked up Tanintharyi (Tenasserim) and Rakhaing in 1824, Yangon and southern Burma in 1853, and Mandalay and northern Burma in 1885. The first war started when Burmese troops, ordered by King Bagyidaw, crossed into British-controlled Assam (in India) from Rakhaing to pursue refugees. General Maha Bandula managed some minor victories using guerrilla tactics, but eventually was killed by cannon fire in 1824. Burmese troops then surrendered. The Treaty of Yandabo, helped by the translator of missionary Adoniram Judson (whose name is on many Baptist churches in Myanmar still), gave Rakhaing and Tenasserim to the British.

Irrawaddy Flotilla, by Alister McRae, highlights the British-bred fleet of steamers that continue to ply Myanmar's many waterways, while *The Longest War 1941–45*, by Louis Allen, gives an excellent account of the WWII campaign in Burma.

PAIR OF KINGS

Myanmar's royal history is an account of endless streams of kings – some quiet poets reluctantly in power, others bloody killers who trampled rival family members by elephants. A couple stand out as the favourites:

■ **Bayinnaung** Aided by Portuguese mercenaries, this 16th-century king of Taungoo is steeped in nationalism today. Bayinnaung is famed for unifying Burma for its 'second empire' and conquering Ayuthaya, the capital of Siam (Thailand), in 1569. Since 1996, his likeness has ominously looked over Thailand from near the border at Tachilek. It is sometimes the target of home-made bombs, but is still standing.

■ **Alaungpaya** With no royal roots, this hometown hero of Mokesebo (Shwebo) kick-started Burma's final dynasty. After the Mon (Tailing) army of Bago conquered a passive Burmese capital at Ava (Inwa) in 1752, he went on the warpath. He recruited soldiers, picked up weapons from slain soldiers (including the French who aided the Mon) and took Inwa in 1753, Pyay (Prome) in 1755, Dagon in 1755 (he'd rename it 'Yangon', or 'end of strife') and Bago in 1757. He played up a macho image, apparently mocking English dignitaries on occasion ('like women with soft skin and no tattoos!'). His reign lasted only eight years, ending when he died at 46 – some say from poisoning – on retreat from Siam, after being turned back by rains.

---

early 15th century	1472	1527
Italian merchant and traveller Nicolo di Conti travels to Bago, arriving overland from India and continuing to Java	The great Mon King Dhammazedi takes the throne, unifies the Mon, moves the capital from Inwa to Bago, and sets up diplomatic contact with Europe	The Shan, who had exercised increasing control over the area following the fall of Bagan, defeats the kingdom at Ava (Inwa) and rules Upper Burma for 28 years

Two Burmese kings later, Bagan Min started his reign in the same manner that many did: with mass executions to rid the capital of his potential rivals. An 1852 incident involving the possible kidnapping of two British sea captains – some argue it never happened – gave the British a welcome excuse for igniting another conflict, and an opportunity for more land. The British quickly seized all of southern Burma, conquering Yangon and Pathein (Bassein). They then marched north to Pyay (Prome), facing little opposition.

The unpopular Bagan Min was ousted in favour of the more-revered Mindon Min, who moved the capital to Mandalay in 1857. Mindon Min built Mandalay, but unhappily didn't adequately provide for his successor. After he died in 1878, the new (rather reluctant) king, Thibaw Min, was propelled to power by his ruthless wife and scheming mother-in-law. The following massive 'massacre of kinsmen' (79 of his rivals) made many British papers. Alas, previous kings hadn't had to face the consequences of world media attention, and this act did little to generate much public backlash against a Britain seeking full control.

For a very readable fictionalised, but accurate, retelling of Burma's days from the fall of King Thibaw to the modern era, read Amitav Ghosh's *The Glass Palace*.

FINDING INDEPENDENCE

ENTER BRITAIN

Burma's last king, King Thibaw, was totally ineffective and ruthless. Under his rule gangs of thugs replaced relative order in northern Burma. In 1885 it took Britain two weeks to conquer Mandalay, the final piece in the Burmese acquisition puzzle. Some locals today shake their heads, stating that Ayeyarwady forts weren't used adequately to repel the British ships.

The conflict is sometimes called 'the war over wood', as Britain's victory allowed it to secure rights to the growing teak industry. Focused on controlling the rice, gem, petroleum and teak exports, England found that, to control Burma, they needed to apply direct rule only where the Bamar were the majority (ie in the central plains). The 'hill states' of the Chin, Kachin, Shan, Kayin and Kayah were allowed to remain largely autonomous. This division would contribute to a rocky start when Myanmar became independent in 1948, due to ill-feeling between the groups.

As British warships overtook Mandalay in 1885, ending the Burmese kingdom, one of the biggest meteor showers in modern history filled the sky. Locals saw it less as a scientific phenomenon than as an omen. Their kingdom was conquered.

Division among the indigenous population was brought about in other ways too. As part of 'British India' after 1885, Myanmar saw a flood of Indians (whom the Burmese traditionally looked down on) come into the country and became the 'second colonisers', by building businesses and taking rare low-level government jobs. The less commercially experienced Burmese were unable to compete. Chinese were also encouraged to immigrate and set up businesses to stimulate the economy. Cheap British imports poured in, fuelled by rice profits. At this time many old

1550	1634–80	1753–55
Bayinnaung ascends to the throne and reunifies all of Myanmar as the Second Burmese Empire; he goes on a rampage, taking the Siam capital of Ayuthaya in 1569	The Dutch East India company sets up trading posts in Syriam (Thanlyin), Ava (Inwa) and Pegu (Bago), and a factory in Prome (Pyay); a combination of factors sees the company withdraw in 1680	Burmese king Alaungpaya – who once mocked English dignitaries as 'like women with soft skin and no tattoos' – conquers Inwa, then Dagon, which he renames 'Yangon'

CAPITAL HOPSCOTCH

Myanmar's generals surprised many by moving the capital from Yangon (Rangoon) to Nay Pyi Taw in 2005. Some say astrologers advised them, others say they feared an Iraqlike invasion, but they may have just been following a long tradition.

Kingdom	Location of capital	Era
Pyu	Beikthano	1st century BC–5th century AD
	Hanlin	3rd–9th century
	Thayekhittaya	3rd–10th century
Rakhaing	Dhanyawady	?–6th century AD
	Wethali	4th–9th century
	Mrauk U	13th–18th century
Mon	Thaton (Dvaravati)	?–10th century
	Hanthawady (Bago)	6th–16th century; 1740–57
Bamar	Bagan (Pagan)	10th–14th century
	Sagaing	1315–64
	Inwa (Ava)	1364–1555; 1636–1752; 1765–83; 1823–37
	Taungoo	1486–1573
	Shwebo (Mokesebo)	1758–65
	Konbaung	1783–1823; 1837–57
	Mandalay (Yadanapon)	1857–85
British	Sittwe & Mawlamyine (Moulmein)	1826–52
	Mandalay	1852–86
	Yangon	1886–1947
Myanmar	Yangon	1947–2005
	Nay Pyi Taw	2005–present

names got new British ones: Rangoon for Yangon, Prome for Pyay, Burma for Myanmar.

Contrary to the romantic tone of modern English-language accounts of 'Burma under the Raj', much of Myanmar was considered a hardship posting by British colonial officials, who found the Burmese difficult to govern (to be fair, many of the British officials were insensitive and incompetent). The country had the highest crime rate in the British Empire. Along with railroads and schools, the British built prisons, including the infamous Insein prison, the Empire's largest (and still in use by the current government).

1760	**1784**	**1812**
Alaungpaya conquers Tenasserim and marches on Ayuthaya but falls ill before the invasion is complete; he withdraws and dies on the return journey	Burmese king Bodawpaya sends soldiers to capture the Mahamuni Buddha image in present-day Rakhaing State; the image, now in Mandalay, was supposedly cast during Buddha's legendary visit to the area in 554 BC	Adoniram Judson, a Baptist missionary from Massachusetts, arrives to convert souls and translate the Bible; he finds many willing converts among the Karen, who remain heavily Christian still

RISE OF NATIONALISM

In *The River of Lost Footsteps,* Thant Nyint U writes, 'for many Indian families, Burma was the first America'. After Britain colonised the nation, hundreds of thousands of Indians poured in; in 1927 a majority of Yangon's population was Indian.

Of course, many Burmese were not happy with the British presence, and nationalism burgeoned in the early days of the 20th century – often led by Buddhist monks. In 1919, at Mandalay's Eindawya Paya (p265), monks evicted Europeans who refused to take off their shoes; one monk, U Kettaya, was given a life sentence. U Ottama, a Burmese monk who had studied in India and returned to Myanmar in 1921, promoted religious liberation as a way to bring the independence movement to the attention of the average local Buddhist. After numerous arrests, U Ottama died in prison in 1939. Another monk, U Wizaya, died in prison after a 163-day hunger strike, which began as a protest against a rule that forbade imprisoned monks from wearing robes.

University students in Yangon went on strike on National Day in 1920, protesting elitist entrance requirements at British-built universities. The students referred to each other as *thakin* (master), as they claimed to be the rightful masters of Burma (present leader General Than Shwe was among them). One *thakin* – a young man called Aung San – was expelled from university in 1936 for refusing to reveal who wrote a politically charged article.

'Democracy is the only ideology which is consistent with freedom… It is therefore the only ideology we should aim for.'

– AUNG SAN

The British were eventually forced to make a number of concessions towards self-government. In 1937 Myanmar was separated administratively from India, but internally the country was still torn by a struggle between opposing political parties and sporadic outbursts of anti-Indian and anti-Chinese violence.

Aung San & WWII

The British built Yangon's Insein Prison to hold 2500 prisoners. Today, some estimates suggest there are 10,000 or more there.

More famous in the West as Aung San Suu Kyi's father, Bogyoke Aung San is still revered as national hero number one by most Myanmar people, from prodemocracy activists to the military regime. His likeness is seen throughout Myanmar. Aung San Suu Kyi, who was only two when he died, called him 'a simple man with a simple aim: to fight for independence'.

WWII SITES IN MYANMAR

- **Lashio** (p304) Where the infamous Burma Road began
- **Taukkyan War Cemetery** (p146) Final resting place of over 33,000 allied soldiers
- **'Death Railway' terminus** (p166) Western end of Japanese-designed Burma–Siam Railway (of *Bridge over the River Kwai* fame), built by Allied POWs and Asian coolies, which claimed over 100,000 lives
- **Meiktila** (p197) Japanese memorial, plus British colonial diplomat house used as Japanese interrogation centre (now a so-so hotel)

1826	**1852**	**1857**
Launched as England eyed French expansion in the region, the three-year First Anglo-Burmese War concludes with England annexing Rakhaing and Tenasserim from Burma	England gets uppity over minor offences, which kick-starts the Second Anglo-Burmese War; Mindon Min wrestles control from his brother in Amarapura	On the 2400th anniversary of Buddha's purported prophecy that a great city would be built at the site of Mandalay 2400 years later, Mindon Min moves the capital from Amarapura to newly built Mandalay

---

LOVING THE TATMADAW

Outsiders hearing reports of human rights abuses, village relocation, rape and murder have a hard time understanding how divided many locals feel about the army. Founded by Aung San – Aung San Suu Kyi's father and 'something like a god' to locals – the Tatmadaw is universally credited with earning Myanmar its independence from the British after WWII. Aung San's aggressive negotiating won the country immediate freedom, instead of a 10-year transition. Current leader, Than Shwe, calls the Tatmadaw 'born of the people and one with the people'. For decades since, and still today, for poor families, having a son join the army is something that can be celebrated for the financial security. And when the coup took over the government in 1962, many locals believed, at least initially, it was a step in the right direction.

Born in 1915, Aung San was an active student at Rangoon University. He edited the newspaper and led the All Burma Students' Union. At 26 years old, he and the group called the 'Thirty Comrades' looked abroad for support for their independence movement. After initially planning to seek it in China, they negotiated for military training in Japan, and returned as the first troops of the Burmese National Army (BNA) with the invading Japanese troops in 1941. By mid-1942 the Japanese had driven retreating British-Indian forces, along with the Chinese Kuomintang (KMT), out of most of Myanmar. But the harsh and arrogant conduct of the Japanese soon alienated the Myanmar people. Aung San complained at Japan's 15th Army headquarters in Maymyo (now Pyin U Lwin): 'I went to Japan to save my people who were struggling like bullocks under the British. But now we are treated like dogs.'

Despite a British-held ban against visiting Buddhist sites (because of the tradition of being asked to remove their shoes), aviator Amelia Earhart visited them anyway (and took off her shoes).

Aung San and the BNA switched allegiance to the Allied side. The British, helped by the imaginative 'Chindit' anti-Japanese operation, ultimately prevailed. The Allies suffered about 27,000 casualties, while nearly 200,000 Japanese perished during the campaign.

Footsteps to Independence

In January 1947, Aung San visited London as the colony's deputy chairperson of the Governor's Executive Council, and signed a pact (the Aung San-Attlee agreement) allowing self-rule within a year. Plans included an April election of a constituent assembly, made up of nationals of Burma only; also Burma would receive an interest-free loan of £8 million from Britain.

Many soldiers during WWII fought for the Japanese, then against them. Armed Forces Day (March 27) commemorates when Burmese soldiers left to confront British troops then, instead, attacked the Japanese, whose thuggish rule was seen as worse.

A month later, Aung San met with Shan, Chin and Kachin leaders in Panglong, in Shan State. They signed the famous Panglong Agreement in February 1947, guaranteeing ethnic minorities the freedom to choose their political destiny if dissatisfied with the situation after 10 years. The agreement also broadly covered absent representatives of the Kayin, Kayah, Mon and Rakhaing.

1866	1885	1886
Mindon's sons conspire against the heir apparent – beheading him in the palace – prompting Mindon to pick Thibaw, who showed no interest in the throne, as his successor	The final conflict between Britain and Burma, the Third Anglo-Burmese War, results in the end of the era of Burmese kings, as Britain conquers Mandalay and sends Thibaw into exile in India	Britain makes Myanmar a province of India, with the capital at Yangon; it takes several years for the British to successfully suppress local resistance

In the elections for the assembly, Aung San's Anti-Fascist People's Freedom League (AFPFL) won an overwhelming 172 seats out of 225. The Burmese Communist Party took seven, while the Bamar opposition (led by U Saw) took three. The remaining 69 seats were split between ethnic minorities (including four seats for the Anglo-Burman community).

Britain hoped to maintain influence and wanted a gradual transition. Aung San wanted immediate independence with a democratic, civilian government.

He wouldn't live to see it. On 19 July 1947, the 32-year-old Aung San and six aides were gunned down in a plot ascribed to U Saw. (Some speculate that the military was involved, due to Aung San's plans to demilitarise the government.) Apparently U Saw thought he'd walk into the prime minister's role with Aung San gone; instead he took the noose, when the British had him hanged for the murders in 1948.

U NU & EARLY WOES

While Myanmar mourned the death of a hero, Prime Minister Attlee and Aung San's protégé, U Nu, signed an agreement for the transfer of power in October 1947. On 4 January 1948, at an auspicious middle-of-the-night hour, Burma became independent and left the British Commonwealth. As Aung San had promised, the national presidency was given to a representative from an ethnic minority group: Sao Shwe Thaike, a Shan leader, became the first president of the Union of Burma.

Almost immediately, the new government had to contend with the complete disintegration of the country, involving rebels, communists, gangs and US-supported anticommunist Chinese KMT forces.

The hill-tribe people, who had supported the British and fought against the Japanese throughout the war, were distrustful of the Bamar majority and went into armed opposition. The communists withdrew from the government and attacked it. Muslims from the Rakhaing area also opposed the new government. The Mon, long thought to be totally integrated with the Burmese, revolted. Assorted factions, private armies, WWII resistance groups and plain mutineers further confused the picture.

In early 1949 almost the entire country was in the hands of a number of rebel groups, and there was even fighting in Yangon's suburbs. At one stage the government was on the point of surrendering to the communist forces, but gradually fought back. Through 1950 and 1951 it regained control of much of the country.

Also, with the collapse of Chiang Kai-Shek's KMT forces to those of Mao Zedong, the tattered remnants of the KMT withdrew into northern Burma and mounted raids from there into Yunnan, China. Being no match for the Chinese communists, the KMT decided to carve their own little fiefdom out of Burmese territory.

'How long do national heroes last? Not long in this country.'

– AUNG SAN, SHORTLY BEFORE HIS ASSASSINATION IN 1947

U Nu led Myanmar's brief democratic experiment, ruling twice between independence and the 1962 takeover. Generally considered a charming goofball, his intense passion for Buddhism helped unravel his popularity when he tried to enforce it as a national religion.

Ne Win ran things from 1958 to 1960, when a fresh election could be held to heal a fractured government. Those two years were, according to Thant Myint U, 'the most effective and efficient in modern Burmese history'.

1927	**1934**	**1937**
Yangon overtakes New York City as the world's top immigrant port, as 480,000 come (mostly from India) for work in the British-held capital	Fussy publishers ask George Orwell to fudge some details of his first novel Burmese Days – changing the town name from Katha to Kyauktada for example – to obscure some of the characters' real-life inspirations	Hundreds of thousands of labourers (mostly Chinese) begin building the first leg of the 'Burma Road', which expands during WWII and is used to ship weapons to the Kuomintang army to fight the Japanese

NE WIN & THE ROAD TO SOCIALISM

By the mid-1950s, the government had strengthened its hold on the country, but the economy slipped from bad to worse. A number of grandiose development projects succeeded only in making foreign 'advisers' rather wealthy. In 1953 Myanmar bravely announced that aid or assistance from the USA was no longer welcome, as long as US-supplied Chinese KMT forces were at large within the country. U Nu managed to remain in power until 1958, when he voluntarily handed the reins over to a military government under General Ne Win.

Considering the pride most of the country had in the Burmese army, which had helped bring independence, this was seen as a welcome change. Freed from the 'democratic' responsibilities inherent in a civilian government, Ne Win was able to make some excellent progress during the 15 months his military government operated. A degree of law and order was restored, rebel activity was reduced and Yangon was given a massive and much-needed cleanup.

In early 1960, elections were held and U Nu regained power with a much-improved majority. However, once again political turmoil developed. His party threatened to break into opposing groups and in early 1962 Ne Win assumed power again and abolished the parliament. He established his own 17-member Revolutionary Council, announcing that the country would 'march towards socialism in our own Burmese way'. This time U Nu did not hand over power voluntarily. Along with his main ministers he was thrown into prison, where he remained until he was forced into exile in 1966.

'The Burmese Road to Socialism' was a steady downhill path. A rice-growing wonder went into economic free fall. Nationalisation policies were extended right down to the retail-shop level in 1966, when it was announced that a long list of items would only be available from 'People's Shops'. The net result was frightening: many everyday commodities immediately became available only on the black market, and vast numbers of people were thrown out of work by the closure of retail outlets.

A disingenuous 'sock the rich' measure demonetised the largest banknotes (K50 and K100). Anybody so unfortunate as to have these notes found them to be worthless. Many of the traders who became unemployed following the nationalisation of retail trade were Indians and Chinese – vestiges of the colonial era in Bamar eyes – and they were hustled out of the country with Draconian thoroughness. No compensation was paid for their expropriated businesses, and each adult was allowed to depart with only K75 plus K250 in gold. As many as 250,000 people of Indian and Chinese descent left Burma during the 1960s. Anti-Chinese riots in Yangon in 1967, spurred by fears that the Chinese were about to 'import' China's Cultural Revolution, resulted in hundreds of Chinese deaths.

Following Ne Win's military coup in 1962, the country started closing off the outside world, limiting foreigners' visits to just 24-hour visas.

The 1988 demonstrations followed a students' fight at the Rangoon Institute of Technology (that's right, RIOT). Some locals like to say Slorc changed many names around the country simply to avoid the continuation of this one unfortunate acronym.

1939	1941	1947
Still under British watch, the leader of Burma's government, U Saw, holds office until his arrest by the British in January 1942 for communicating with the Japanese	After training with the Japanese during WWII, Aung San – the father of Aung San Suu Kyi – founds the Burmese Army, which switches sides and fights the Japanese a year later	Aung San seeks agreement for independence from Britain and rallies ethnic groups to a 10-year deal where they can secede from Burma by 1958 – Aung San is assassinated by rivals

---

WRITINGS OF AUNG SAN SUU KYI

Aung San Suu Kyi's interviews in 1995 and 1996 with journalist Alan Clements, described in *Voices of Hope* (1997), often intermingle politics and Buddhism. *Freedom from Fear* (1991) is a collection of her writings on topics ranging from her father to winning the Nobel Peace Prize. *Letters from Burma* (1997) features a collection of letters Suu Kyi wrote on Burmese culture for a Japanese publication.

In late 1974 there were serious student disturbances over the burial of former UN secretary-general and long-time Ne Win political foe U Thant (grandfather of author Thant Myint U). Yet, overall, the government appeared firmly in control and determined to continue its strange progress towards a Burmese Utopia. In late 1981 Ne Win retired as president of the republic (retaining his position as chair of the Burmese Socialist Programme Party, the country's only legal political party at the time) but his successor, San Yu, and the government remained guided very much by Ne Win's political will.

THE '88 GENERATION

Aung San Suu Kyi returned to Burma from Britain in 1988 to tend to her dying mother. At the time disquiet with the government was at a peak.

With the standard of living on a continual downward spiral, something happened that no-one foresaw. In 1987 and 1988 the people of Myanmar decided they had had enough of their incompetent and arrogant government and packed the streets in huge demonstrations, insisting that Ne Win go.

Ne Win voluntarily retired as chairperson of the party in July 1988, but it was too late to halt the agitation of the people. The massive pro-democracy demonstrations, spurred by the further demonetisation of large notes and a prophecy that Burma would become a 'free country' on the auspicious date of 8 August 1988 (8-8-88), were brutally crushed by the government, with at least 3000 deaths recorded over a six-week period.

Ne Win's National Unity Party (NUP; formerly the Burmese Socialist Programme Party) was far from ready to give up control, and the public protests continued as two Ne Win stooges succeeded him. The third Ne Win successor came to power after a military coup in September 1988, which, it is generally believed, was organised by Ne Win.

A newly formed State Law & Order Restoration Council (Slorc) established martial law under the leadership of General Saw Maung, commander in chief of the armed forces, and promised to hold democratic National Assembly elections in May 1989.

The opposition quickly formed a coalition party called the National League for Democracy (NLD) and campaigned for all it was worth. The Myanmar

1948	1950	1958
Myanmar achieves independence from the British on 4 January; the first year of independence is marked by various ethnic and political conflicts	Chiang Kai-shek's armies from China invade border regions, prompting the need for a bigger military – a move the chaotic democratic Burma would later second-guess	The country's economic situation improves but a split in the Anti-Fascist People's Freedom League heralds further political problems; the parliament becomes unstable and U Nu barely survives a no-confidence vote

population rallied around charismatic NLD spokesperson Aung San Suu Kyi, daughter of hero Aung San. Suu Kyi, conversant in Burmese, Japanese, French and English, and married to an Oxford University professor, brought a hitherto-unseen sophistication to Myanmar politics.

Nervous, Slorc tried to appease the masses with new roads and by adding a coat of paint to many buildings in Yangon. Then it attempted to interfere in the electoral process by shifting villages from one part of the country to another and by postponing the election. Perhaps the biggest surprise came with the announcement that the government was abandoning socialism in favour of a capitalist economy in all but a few industries.

In July 1989 Aung San Suu Kyi was placed under house arrest.

A VOTE FOR THE NLD

Convinced it had effectively dealt with the opposition, the government allowed an election in May 1990 (the first in 30 years). In spite of all its preventive measures, the NUP lost the election to the NLD, which took 392 of the 485 contested seats (or about 60% of the vote). Slorc barred the elected members of parliament from assuming power, decreeing that a state-approved constitution had to be passed by national referendum first. In October 1990 the military raided NLD offices and arrested key leaders. Since that time over 100 elected parliamentarians, according to Human Rights Watch, have been disqualified, imprisoned, exiled or killed. Some observers wonder if the election was a ruse to get members of the opposition out in the open, where they could be more easily crushed.

Before her arrest in 1989, Suu Kyi had been appointed secretary-general of the NLD. The main NLD candidates in line for potential premiership, had the 1990 election results been recognised by the current regime, were U Aung Shwe, U Tin Oo and U Kyi Maung, all ex-officers. It was widely acknowledged, even back in 1990, that Slorc would never allow a person of Aung San Suu Kyi's background (an ex-resident of the country, and married to a Briton) to run for office. It was equally acknowledged that the candidates who stood the best chance of acceptance by the military dictatorship were those with a military background. It turned out that even this was not enough to make the ruling junta relinquish control.

After the events of 1988–89, the world press at first gave little coverage to politics in the country that had been renamed Myanmar. In January 1991, Suu Kyi was awarded the Sakharov Prize for freedom of thought by the European Parliament, and in October of the same year she was honoured with the Nobel Peace Prize. Another international honour came her way in June 1992 when Unesco awarded Suu Kyi the Simón Bolívar Prize. In May 1995, Suu Kyi was honoured with a fourth international award when India presented the leader, in absentia, with the Jawaharlal Nehru Award for International Understanding. As the world media began to follow

In the decade following the 1988 demonstrations, the Myanmar military more than doubled in size – to over 400,000, about the same size as the USA's. Some reports have the government spending at least 40% of the budget on the military, compared with 4% in the USA.

Slorc hired a Washington, DC public-relations firm to improve its image, which suggested changing its name to the State Peace & Development Council (SPDC). The change was made in November 1997.

1961	March 1962	July 1962
U Thant is elected secretary-general of the United Nations, the first non-Westerner to lead the international organisation; his grandson U Than Nyint discusses his grandfather's role with the UN in the book *The River of Lost Footsteps*	Four years after General Ne Win headed a brief, quite popular 'caretaker' government during a period of chaos, he takes power from U Nu after a coup, setting up a military government that is still in control today	A peaceful student protest at Rangoon University is suppressed by the military – over 100 students are killed and the Student Union building is dynamited; hundreds are arrested in Yangon and elsewhere

events in Myanmar, prodemocracy elements, both within the country and abroad, proved themselves to be much more media savvy than the military junta. The democratisation of 'Burma', as most prodemocracy groups still call the country, soon became a cause célèbre for sundry activists and Hollywood celebrities.

Much to the joy of the people of Myanmar and her supporters abroad, the government released Suu Kyi from house arrest after nearly six years, in July 1995. Suu Kyi's detention was the most potent symbol of government repression and the biggest magnet for international attention, but many other high-level dissidents, including the NLD's Tin U and Kyi Maung, were also released (from prison) at this time. For several months Suu Kyi was allowed to address crowds of supporters from her residence. In May and September 1996, Suu Kyi held a congress of NLD members in a bold political gambit to demonstrate that the NLD was still an active political force. The junta responded by detaining hundreds who attended the congress and the street leading to Suu Kyi's residence was blockaded, prohibiting her from making speeches at her residence.

In 1998 18 foreign activists were arrested in Yangon for distributing anti-government leaflets. In the same year Suu Kyi attempted to leave Yangon to meet with supporters outside the city but was blocked by the military and forcibly returned to Yangon. In 1999 Suu Kyi's husband, Oxford professor Michael Aris, died of cancer shortly after Yangon denied him a visa to see Suu Kyi in Myanmar. Although they hadn't seen each other since January 1996, Suu Kyi felt she had no choice but to stay in Myanmar, fearing that if she left the country to visit her husband's deathbed in England, she would be refused re-entry and forced into exile.

Suu Kyi made a second attempt to leave Yangon to meet with supporters in September 2000, but was stopped at a military roadblock. After spending six days in her car by the roadside, Suu Kyi was once again placed under house arrest.

In October 2000, secret talks began between Suu Kyi and the junta – the most significant step towards reconciliation since the elections. Brokered by Rizali Ismail, a former Malaysian diplomat and special envoy to UN Secretary-General Kofi Annan, the talks resulted in the release of hundreds of political prisoners. A very noticeable result of the talks was the cessation of crude attacks against Suu Kyi in the Myanmar media. The NLD in return stopped its direct criticism of the Myanmar government.

In May 2002 Suu Kyi was released from house arrest and immediately announced that her demands for political reform had not changed as a result of the talks with the junta. Her unconditional release promised the opposition leader freedom of movement for the first time in over 12 years. In the weeks following her release she visited NLD offices in townships in the Yangon area, and in late June made a triumphant visit to Mandalay. It was Suu Kyi's

---

Aung San Suu Kyi has been under house arrest three times: from July 1989 to July 1995; from September 2000 to May 2002; and from May 2003 to the present.

Although Ne Win had retired from all official positions by 1988, he was widely believed to call the shots for many years thereafter – possibly up till his death in December 2002.

1964	1974	1975
All opposition political parties are banned, commerce and industry are nationalised and Ne Win begins the process of isolating Myanmar from the rest of the world	Massive anti-government demonstrations break out when U Thant, considered to be a symbol of opposition to the military regime, does not get the state funeral many believe he deserves	A powerful earthquake registering 6.5 on the Richter scale rocks Bagan, toppling many temples; reconstruction begins almost immediately, using many traditional techniques, and later falls, for a spell, under Unesco's direction

first trip to Myanmar's second-largest city since 1989 (her September 2000 attempt to visit Mandalay was thwarted by the military).

In May 2003, while touring Sagaing District outside Budalin (north of Monywa), Suu Kyi and a party of 250 NLD members were attacked. It's believed as many as 100 people were killed. Many others were held in detention. Suu Kyi spent several months in jail and underwent a hunger strike. She was eventually transferred to her house. She is still there.

THE WORLD & MYANMAR

Initially after 1988, the West established embargoes on arms sales and most foreign aid to Myanmar. But some companies – such as UK's Premier Oil, France's Total and USA's Unocal – helped develop offshore gas fields. Stronger international sanctions were taken in 1997 by the USA, usually the regime's harshest critic, when it banned new investment by American companies in Myanmar. Strong lobbying by activists and threats of consumer boycotts forced some major companies (including PepsiCo, Heineken, Carlsberg and Levi Strauss) to either pull out or decide against investing in the country.

In November 1999, the UN International Labour Organization took the unprecedented step of recommending sanctions against Myanmar, for its use of civilians for forced labour and treacherous tasks of porterage for the military (including serving as 'human landmine detectors'). Its 174 member nations were advised to review their links with Myanmar and ensure they did not support forced labour there. In June 2001, UN agencies in Myanmar warned, in a joint letter to their headquarters, that Myanmar was facing a humanitarian crisis and that it was a 'moral and ethical necessity' for the international community to extend more aid. The letter stated that a quarter of Myanmar babies were born underweight and, as of the end of 1999, an estimated 530,000 people were HIV-positive. The letter also stated that Myanmar only receives annual foreign aid equivalent to about $2.88 per capita, compared with $35 for Cambodia and $68 for Laos.

In a controversial move, in 2001 Japan broke ranks in the embargo on nonhumanitarian aid to Myanmar when it offered $28 million in technical assistance to repair the Baluchaung hydroelectric power plant in Kayah State as an incentive for the regime to press ahead with reconciliation talks with Suu Kyi. And even before Cyclone Nargis hit Myanmar in May 2008, many nations were upping aid due to what some outsiders called a humanitarian 'crisis' (see p25). Any question of a 'crisis' became a certainty in the aftermath of the cyclone, when as many as 1.5 million locals were in need of food, medicine and shelter. The government kept out many offers of assistance, frustrating the UN, NGOs and foreign governments trying to provide aid.

The sanctions got stronger following Aung San Suu Kyi's third arrest in 2003. US President George W Bush authorised full economic sanctions,

1976	1979	1987–88
A group of officers conspire to assassinate Ne Win and San Yu but are found out; the ringleader is tried and hanged	Television is introduced to Burma, and the public feeds off such regretful imports as the *Love Boat*, *Dynasty* and, a bit more impressively, James Bond flicks	Rising debt and an economic crisis lead the government to introduce economic reforms that relax several of the socialist controls and encourage foreign investment

which resulted in foreign banks in Myanmar packing up and leaving. The wording of the EU's sanctions, however, allowed France's Total gas company to continue operating there. Critics of the use of sanctions argue that these measures hurt the local workforce. After the strengthening of the US sanctions, many garment factories, virtually all of which are privately owned, closed down, reportedly leading to the loss of 40,000 to 60,000 jobs. For more on the sanctions debate, see p13.

'When fuel prices went up...suddenly people who make K2000 a day had to pay K500 for the bus to work. It's just not enough for even one person to live, much less a family.'
– MANDALAY PROTESTOR

Despite the Myanmar government's human-rights record, a number of foreign investors – most of them Asian (particularly Chinese, but also Singaporean, Japanese, Indian and Thai) – continue to invest huge amounts of foreign currency into private development projects, especially in the Yangon to Mandalay corridor. The land border between Myanmar and China stands wide open for legal and illegal trade, and acts as the main supply line for millions of dollars worth of Chinese weaponry destined for Myanmar's military, and India and Myanmar have signed a deal for India to develop Sittwe as a port to access untapped offshore oil reserves. See p17 for more on foreign investment.

LOOKING AHEAD

REPOSITIONED JUNTA

After years of isolation, the government actively tried to open itself up in the '90s. But a disappointing turnout for the official 'Visit Myanmar Year 1996' and increased sanctions from the West led the government to other outlets: namely trade with China, India and Thailand, and joining Asean in 1997. The organisation has done little to control its wildcard member other than murmur discontent over Aung San Suu Kyi's continued captivity and 'repulsion' over the bloody response to monk-led protests in 2007. Despite Asean's policy of non-interference, many observers believe the association could have done more to discourage Myanmar from acting as a 'spoiled child', misbehaving without response.

'The soldiers that moved in were half Rakhaing, half Burmese. We heard the Rakhaing soldiers tell the Burmese soldiers: "Hey asshole, if you shoot you'll get my peanut [bullet]." No shots were fired.'
– PROTESTOR IN SITTWE

Former Prime Minister Khin Nyunt, a disciple of Ne Win, sought to re-create his role (and that of the government) after Ne Win's death in 2002 with a seven-step 'Roadway to Democracy'. In 2004, however, the government split when hard-liner Secretary-General Than Shwe ousted Khin Nyunt and his league CIA-style intelligence officers in 2004 (many were imprisoned). Than Shwe initially promised to continue the transition to democracy but spent more time negotiating deals with China, India and Thailand, and importing weapons from Russia.

He stunned many (inside and outside of the largely impoverished nation) by moving the capital from Yangon to an arid field near Pyinmana in 2005. The move was so expensive and wasteful (an International Monetary Fund es-

July 1988	August 1988	1990
General Ne Win steps down, prompted by massive popular demonstrations against his rule; however, the military remains in power and civilian unrest grows as the standard of living continues to fall	On 8/8/88 (8 August), huge nonviolent prodemocracy marches across Yangon (and other points around the country) end with the military killing over 3000; these events lead to a democratic election	In May the National League for Democracy, led by Aung San Suu Kyi, wins 82% of the assembly seats in the first nationwide election in three decades, but the military never hands over power

timate suggests nearly $250 million) that even the usually aloof Chinese shook their heads. The junta named the city-in-the-making Nay Pyi Taw (Royal Capital), leaving little doubt that Than Shwe's strategies and inspirations are aligned less with the modern world than with Burmese kings of centuries past. A year later, video of his daughter's lavish wedding – with wedding gifts alone supposedly worth over $50 million – appeared on YouTube.

SEPTEMBER 2007

Though Myanmar has the largest oil and gas reserves in Southeast Asia, natural gas prices rose in mid-2007 by 500% (and petrol by 200%). The reason is unclear though there was speculation that the government was short on money after sinking untold millions into construction of the new capital. This led to price hikes for everything from local bus transport to rice. In late August a group of '1988 generation' protestors were arrested for making a first march against the inflation. It wasn't until 5 September, when monks – long a behind-the-scenes player in politics – denounced the price hikes in a demonstration in Pakokku, that the protests escalated. The military responded with gunfire and allegedly beat one monk to death. In response, the All Burma Monks Alliance (ABMA) was formed, denouncing the ruling government as an 'evil military dictatorship' and refusing to give alms to military officials (a practice called *pattam mikkujana kamma*), a move that stunned the government. 'If generals were going to visit their monastery, the monks would disappear,' one local in Mandalay told us a couple of months afterward.

By 17 September daily marches began, swelling in numbers across Myanmar – particularly in a couple of dozen cities including Yangon, Mandalay, Meiktila and Sittwe. Unexpectedly, monk-led crowds were allowed to pray with Aung San Suu Kyi from outside her house gates. By 24 September, 150,000 were protesting in Yangon, including up to 50,000 monks. International media covered the events, and smuggled-out video images of the marches hit YouTube. All the while the government watched, photographing participants. The next day the government announced a curfew and moved troops into Yangon and other cities. On 26 September shots were fired, a monk was beaten to death, monasteries were raided and 100 monks were arrested. The following day a soldier was caught on video shooting dead Japanese photographer Kenji Nagai at the southwest corner of Sule Paya Rd and Anawrahta Rd in central Yangon (he may have been mistaken for a local, as he was wearing a *longyi*). Two days later, the protests were stopped, the national internet access cut off (only the second time a nation has done so; the first was in Nepal in 1995) and an unsettled quiet hung over Myanmar's cities.

According to UN estimates, nearly 3000 were arrested and 31 were killed. A few celebrities were among the arrestees, including comedians Zagana

---

Moustache Brother Par Par Lay told us about his 35 days in jail in 2007: 'Every night we had no sleep. They'd wake us and ask who organised the monks. They couldn't believe they could organise on their own.'

'This is only the second time in our history that our leaders killed monks,' one furious Yangon resident told us. 'And the first time was from a non-Buddhist 500 years ago. They just don't care.'

One 2007 protestor told us that many locals still have hope for change. 'We don't see the coast yet, so we must keep paddling.'

1991

Aung San Suu Kyi wins the Nobel Peace Prize for her struggle for democracy and human rights; the government expects her to pay tax on her winnings, despite being held under house arrest in Yangon

1995

The government uses forced labour to ready some sites for the official 'Visit Myanmar Year' and a tourism boycott is established by Aung San Suu Kyi, the NLD and many outside activist groups

1997

Myanmar's government hires a US PR firm to help improve its image and changes the name of the State Law & Order Restoration Council (Slorc) to the State Peace & Development Council – but gets a bigger boost that year by joining Asean and Par Par Lay. The latter is the head comedian of Mandalay's Moustache Brothers (p270); he spent 35 days in jail.

CYCLONE NARGIS

In the aftermath of the 2007 demonstrations, Than Shwe made a couple of promises to fend off outside criticism, drafting a new constitution and holding another free election. The government announced a national referendum for a new constitution for May 2008 but, a few days beforehand, the second-deadliest cyclone in recorded history tore across an unaware Ayeyarwady Delta. On 3 May 2008, Cyclone Nargis' 121mph winds and the tidal surge that followed swept away bamboo hut villages, leaving in all over two million survivors without shelter, food or drinking water, and with damages totalling an estimated $10 billion. Yangon saw diminished winds, but still strong enough at 80mph to overturn power lines and trees, leaving the city without power for a couple of weeks.

The aftermath was brutal. Outside aid groups were held up by a lack of visas and the Myanmar military's refusal to allow foreign planes to deliver aid while, according to the UN, one million waited. All the while, the government kept the referendum on schedule, outraging many locals and outside observers.

Nargis' final death count may never be known. Several months afterward, a group organised by Asean and the UN documented 84,537 deaths and 53,836 missing people – 138,373 in all, 61% of whom were female. Other estimates are even higher, suggesting 300,000 were lost. Children, unable to withstand the inflow of water, were most vulnerable to drowning.

The military government's reaction led to international scandal. Fearful of opening the doors to British, French and American planes and ships, the junta simply refused entry to all for the first full week, letting victims, more or less, fend for themselves.

This reality gap became chillingly clear nine days later when, on 12 May 2008, the world saw how China swiftly reacted to the Sichuan earthquake. Within 90 minutes China's leaders had sent an expert to oversee relief efforts, and the nation welcomed international relief groups like the Red Cross who donated $20 million in assistance.

Meanwhile, local relief efforts in Myanmar – run by monasteries, private businesses and NGOs – were immediate and effective. One Yangon businessman told us that he and a few colleagues 'formed a small team to help the poor areas in town, then gradually reached more remote areas as far as Bogole' (a town that lost 10,000 lives). Such efforts continued regularly, essentially, he said, 'sneaking' supplies into the delta such as 'clean water, biscuits, T-shirts, blankets, plastic sheets'.

Eventually programs like the UN's World Food Programme (WFP) were allowed entry; the WFP brought 4000 tonnes of supplies from late May to

2000	2003	2004
The EU intensifies its economic sanctions against Myanmar, following a similar move by the US in 1997; concerns over human rights abuses are at the core of the decisions	A group of National League for Democracy members are attacked by the militia in northern Myanmar; up to 100 are killed and Aung San Suu Kyi, released the year before, is again placed under house arrest	Myanmar opens the world's largest tiger reserve in the 2500-sq-mile Hukaung Valley in the far north and ousts Prime Minister Khin Nyunt, the moderate voice in the military who outlined a seven-point 'roadmap' for democracy

late August. Some reports, including by Unicef, have suggested government efforts eventually did a good job at reaching all victims, while independent Myanmar news organisation *Irrawaddy* (www.irrawaddy.org) had a different take. In one report several months after the cyclone, the news outlet noted a stream of refugees leaving the delta with hopes of work in bigger towns and Yangon. One told an *Irrawaddy* reporter: 'We do not have food in our villages.'

THE FUTURE

Those locals who believe in omens – like King Thibaw's dying white elephant shortly before the British took Mandalay – had much to say about the timing of the storm and the first Myanmar vote in nearly two decades. Even before the storm, activist groups and NLD members had urged the public to vote 'no' at the referendum to change the constitution. They feared that it would enshrine the power of the generals. Others worried that not voting would only deepen the military hold on the government and leave no wiggle room for other political parties to contribute. The voting took place in two rounds during May 2008, while a reported 2.5 million people still required food, shelter and medical assistance. The junta reported that a majority of voters approved the military-backed constitution. A purported 'multiparty' election will follow in 2010, the first such election since 1990.

2005	2007	2008
In an unexplained move that some credit to astrology or fear of an Iraqlike invasion, General Than Shwe and the government move the capital from Yangon to unsettled Nay Pyi Taw in central Myanmar	Following fuel price hikes, monk-led protests hit Myanmar's streets – the first such demonstrations since 1988; the government cracks down in force, killing at least 31 and briefly cutting off all outside access	A few days before Myanmar has its first election in nearly two decades, Cyclone Nargis tears across the delta, killing tens of thousands and leaving many more without homes – the election takes place on schedule

The Culture

NATIONAL PSYCHE

Ever proud of their country's centuries-old culture, the Myanmar people live, often, with a shrug over their day-to-day conditions of poverty, isolation and corruption. That electricity comes and goes (more often goes) is part of life. And talk about such problems, as well as more positive things like a local *pwe* (festival), family, football or *mohinga* (noodle soup with fish or eel), comes with a healthy dosage of *bamahsan chin* (Burmeseness) – that Buddhism-influenced personality trait that favours gentleness and subtlety over directness or confrontation.

Another common trait is *ah har de,* a sense of not wanting to 'make waves' or pass on unpleasant news. Even small-scale open dialogue is not an everyday aspect of life. One exiled Myanmar man explained: 'The most important thing I got out of being in England was watching political TV shows, where people were arguing, explaining different viewpoints. That never happens at home.'

On occasion that tendency wavers and talk *can* be quite 'direct', particularly in private places likes homes and some teashops. Such an occasion came in the aftermath of the September 2007 protests. That 31 died (per UN reports) was less offensive for many than the fact that monks were killed. One Yangon (Rangoon) resident bitterly explained, 'I never thought they could kill monks.' A retired doctor in central Myanmar said: 'It's depressing. I've been working 40 years under this government and they just don't care.' Another, a Buddhist grandmother and veteran of the 1988 marches, wondered, 'perhaps we need Molotov cocktails now.'

Locals are also fond of poetic images, reading between the lines and messages in code of various sorts. On Valentine's Day 2008, a Yangon poet was arrested when it was revealed the first letters of each word of a poem spelled 'power crazy Senior General Than Shwe'. Many locals considered the children's film *The Lion King* to be about Aung San Suu Kyi – the offspring of the slain lion, Aung San. Meanwhile, there's a saying that '1000 words beats 10 words', and sometimes simple yes/no questions – 'how long have you been a trishaw driver?' – yield lively, long-winded answers with no resolution.

LIFESTYLE

Exiled writer Pascal Khoo Thwe writes that, growing up in Myanmar's hills, traditional family life meant that 'earth is round at school and flat at home', meaning some aspects of modern life are left, along with your shoes, outside the door at home.

Families in Myanmar are big, and the birth of a boy or girl is a big occasion. While boys are coddled more, girls are equally welcomed, as they're expected to look after parents later in life. You might find three or four generations of a family living in a two- or three-room house. Some thatched huts in the countryside have generators pumping life into the TV a couple of hours a night. Running water outside the cities and bigger towns is rare. Many families put coconut symbols of the house guardian *nat* (spirit) inside their homes (see p65).

About three-quarters of the people farm, so much of local life revolves around villages and the countryside. Here, Yangon's politics or dreams of wealth can pale in importance to the season, the crop and the level of the river (where they bathe, clean and get their drinking water). Everywhere, people are known for helping each other when in need and call each other 'brother' and 'sister' affectionately. In *Finding George Orwell in Burma,*

Khin Myo Chit's English-language *Colourful Myanmar* highlights many customs and traditions of Myanmar life. It's available in many Yangon bookshops.

Superstitions run deep in Myanmar. Many people consult astrologers to find mates, plan events or even schedule a haircut! Eight is considered an unlucky number. One trishaw driver quoted us a K800 ride as 'double four'.

DOS & DON'TS

Many locals are too kind to mention to a traveller when they're being insensitive. So, let it be your role to (politely) tell fellow travellers when they're acting inappropriately. Also see p22 for tips on giving gifts.

Here are the basics:

- When visiting a Buddhist sight, don't wear shoes, shorts, short skirts or have exposed shoulders.
- Don't thrust a camera into a monk's (or anyone's) face for a photo.
- Don't pose with or sit on buddha images.
- Take your shoes off (not necessarily socks) when entering private homes.
- Don't touch somebody on the head (including patting a child's head).
- Don't point your feet at anybody or anything – apologise if you accidentally brush someone with your foot.
- When shaking hands or handing over something, do so with your right hand, while touching your right elbow with your left hand.
- Don't step over somebody who is sitting or lying on the floor (such as on a boat deck).

Emma Larkin recounts how a Mandalay cemetery worker saved some dirt from a moved gravesite, just in case the family ever returned, so they could have 'some soil from around the grave'.

Death, of course, is a big deal, though mourned for less time than in much of the West. To miss a funeral is an unimaginable faux pas. If a heated argument goes too far, the ultimate capper is to yell: 'Oh yeah? Don't come to my funeral when I die.'

> 'Ghosts? It's nothing unusual, it's part of our life,' one Taungoo local said, describing a few local ones. 'Most are drowning victims.'

EDUCATION

Literacy rates are high in Myanmar – about 93% to 98%. This is largely due to the fact that primary education (roughly ages five to 10 or 11) is mandatory. Conditions, though, can be limited to makeshift spaces with a single blackboard shared by students of all ages. A common donation made by some travellers is school supplies – including pens, notebooks and textbooks – at village and town schools. According to Unesco, enrolment dips to below half the country's population at secondary school level.

After the military dictatorship took control of Myanmar in 1962, all universities were privatised and quality took a nose dive. After the 1988 democratic demonstrations, all universities were closed and changes have been made, some argue, to make it more difficult for students to gather. In some towns, you'll see some of the nation's 101 universities split into branches, often far apart and far outside town centres. In other instances students have 'home study' programs – not living/staying at a campus.

The brain drain – of eligible students leaving the country to study abroad – is growing in recent years. Many choose not to return, largely because they can't afford to pay school bills on local salaries.

> Many locals believe you need to be extra careful – about everything! – during the months of December, January and February, when 'you're not permitted to go into the dragon's mouth!' – so play it safe if you go then.

ECONOMY

Rich in jade, teak and offshore oil, Myanmar doesn't suffer for resources, yet its people remain one of the poorest in Asia. The government exports $2 billion of natural gas annually to Thailand alone, yet the average per-capita income is about $1900 annually (about 70% of the country works on farms); a third of the nation is below the poverty line, striving to make just $1 a day, if that. There are rumours that the government may use the Chinese *yuan* in

---

HOW MANY DID YOU SAY?

The Myanmar people may seem, to outsiders, to have an imaginative understanding of maths. We had a resident of Mrauk U tell us, in all earnestness, the local area had six million temples, and a Sittwe resident insisted the largest minority group in the city of 150,000 were the '800,000 Muslims'. Locals count 4000 islands in the Mergui (Myeik) Archipelago, while detailed British surveyors found only 804. A trishaw driver in Mandalay suggested that to start a guesthouse you'd need – after spending several minutes tabbing it up by pen and paper – about $400 million. Minimum. Historical accounts include hundreds of thousands of soldiers marching to battle; numbers often contradicting later British accounts. The age of the 'antique' you're holding is often wildly, um, optimistic too.

Nothing to fuss over, though. Locals are more accustomed to counting with the *lakh* (equal to 100,000) than in millions, so it's possible a zero or two gets added there. Also, Myanmar's largest bill is just K1000 (about $0.85), and many people are happy to earn K2000 a day. For nearly everyone, $40,000 is about as likely to fall into their laps as $400 million.

---

international transactions to bypass sanctions against trade and investment by the US and EU, which were expanded after the September 2007 military crackdown. For more on the economy, see p17.

POPULATION

About 11% of Myanmar's 47 million people live in the former capital Yangon. Unlike many developing-world countries, there isn't a massive flocking to the big cities: jobs are scarce in the capital with inflation soaring at 40% and international banks fleeing in 2003 due to economic sanctions imposed by the international community.

Historically, the diverse ethnic make-up of the country has been separated by its topography. The broad central plain, with the Ayeyarwady (Irrawaddy) River and Myanmar's most fertile soil, has been run by whichever group was strongest (usually the Bamar, or Burmese, in the past few hundred years). Most ethnic groups continue to live in some sort of troubled isolation in the mountains lining much of Myanmar's international borders, notably the Shan, Kayah and Kayin (Karen) in the east; the Kachin to the north; and the Chin and Rakhaing to the west (see p58). The Bamar make up 68% of the population.

Myanmar is not densely populated. There are roughly 70 people per square kilometre (compared to 1124 per square kilometre in neighbouring Bangladesh) and outside Yangon or Mandalay there's Laos-like elbow room.

> Everyone who can afford a car – 20-year-old Toyotas go for $40,000 – ends up buying most gas from the black market. Per-gallon prices rose from about K2000 in 2004 to K6000 in 2008.

SPORT

Football (soccer) is the most popular sport to watch. Sometimes local TV even broadcasts European games. Sporting events peak in December because of the cool temperatures.

Martial Arts

Myanmar has a tradition of kickboxing that's said to date back to the Bagan era, although the oldest written references are found in chronicles of warfare between Burma and Thailand during the 15th and 16th centuries. *Myanma let-hwei* (Myanmar kickboxing) is very similar in style to *muay thai* (Thai kickboxing), although not nearly as well developed as a national sport.

The most common and traditional kickboxing venues are temporary rings set up in a dirt circle (usually at *paya pwe* rather than sports arenas). All fighters are bare-fisted. All surfaces of the body are considered fair targets

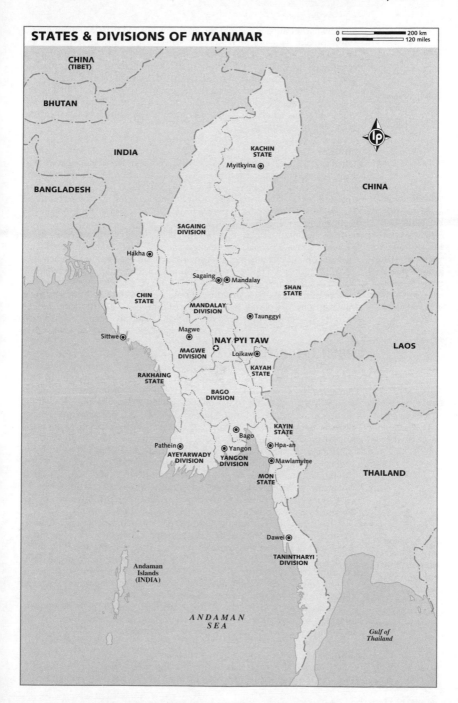

and any part of the body except the head may be used to strike an opponent. Common blows include high kicks to the neck, elbow thrusts to the face and head, knee hooks to the ribs and low crescent kicks to the calf. Punching is considered the weakest of all blows and kicking merely a way to 'soften up' one's opponent; knee and elbow strikes are decisive in most matches.

Before the match begins, each boxer performs a dancelike ritual in the ring to pay homage to Buddha and to Khun Cho and Khun Tha, the *nat* whose domain includes Myanmar kickboxing. The winner repeats the ritual at the end of the match.

Chinlon

Often called 'cane ball' in Burmese English, *chinlon* refers to games in which a woven rattan ball about 5in in diameter is kicked around. It also refers to the ball itself, which resembles the *takraw* of Thailand and Malaysia. Informally, any number of players can form a circle and keep the *chinlon* airborne by kicking it soccer-style from player to player; a lack of scoring makes it a favourite pastime with locals of all ages.

In formal play six players stand in a circle of 22ft circumference. Each player must keep the ball aloft using a succession of 30 techniques and six surfaces on the foot and leg, allotting five minutes for each part. Each successful kick scores a point, while points are subtracted for using the wrong body part or dropping the ball.

A popular variation – and the one used in intramural or international competitions – is played with a volleyball net, using all the same rules as in volleyball except that only the feet and head are permitted to touch the ball.

MULTICULTURALISM

One of the more exciting aspects of travel in Myanmar is getting the opportunity to experience a corner of Asia that in many ways has changed little since British colonial times. Due to its isolation – self-imposed and otherwise – Myanmar has yet to be completely overwhelmed by outside clothing influences. Nowhere else in Southeast Asia will you see so many sarongs, turbans and other exotic apparel. Of course, differences in dress are just a hint of the distinctions between Myanmar's diverse ethnic populations.

Officially Myanmar's 47 or so million residents (not including Chinese, Indian, Nepalese and other groups) are divided into eight nationalities – the Bamar, Shan, Mon, Kayin, Kayah, Chin, Kachin and Rakhaing. The Myanmar government further subdivides these eight groups into 67 subgroups. In the following pages we discuss the 10 groups visitors to Myanmar are most likely to encounter or read about.

As in many other ethnically (and religiously) diverse countries, feelings of pride and prejudice cause friction between Myanmar's ethnic groups – some sort of tension lingers over any area that is home to ethnic minorities. Ask a Bamar (or a Shan or a Kayin) their opinion about their countryfolk of different ethnic or religious backgrounds and you'll get an idea of what kinds of challenges governments in Myanmar have faced in their efforts to keep the peace and preserve the borders.

In recent years there's been a massive influx of Chinese people into northern Burma, evident in Mandalay and certainly in border towns such as Mong La, where the *yuan* is the local currency.

Bamar

The Bamar – also known as Burman or Burmese – make up the majority (68%) of the population and, not surprisingly, rule the country. Thought to

National population statistics range from 47 million to 54 million.

The number of people who died during May 2008's Cyclone Nargis may never be known, but one report claimed it could be nearly 140,000 – with 84,537 known casualties and 53,836 people still missing many months after the storm.

Ethnologists have suggested there are 135 distinct ethnic groups living in Myanmar.

Living Silence: Burma under Military Rule (2001), by Christina Fink, sums up Myanmar's military years and how the military affects various aspects of life. It's peppered with fascinating quotes from a wide cross-section of Myanmar people.

have originally migrated from the Himalaya, the Bamar ruled much of what is now Myanmar from Bagan (Pagan) by the 11th century. When the British conquered Myanmar in the 19th century, it was the Bamar who had to relinquish the most. Many ancient court customs and arts were lost as the Bamar monarchy was abolished.

Devout Theravada Buddhists, the Bamar – from the top generals to trishaw drivers – believe that being Buddhist is a key aspect of being Bamar, and the Myanmar media reports daily on the merit-making of top officials at the country's principal Buddhist places of worship. Government nation-building efforts have included establishing the Bamar language (Burmese) as the language of instruction in schools throughout Myanmar. So most non-Bamar speak Burmese as a second language.

Chin

The Chin inhabit the mountainous region (mostly corresponding with Chin State) that borders India and Bangladesh to the west. In the past, the Chin, as with most highland dwellers, led labour-intensive lives and their relatively simple traditional dress reflected this. Men wore loincloths in the warmer months and draped blankets over themselves when the weather turned cool. The women wore poncho-like garments woven with intricate geometric patterns. These garments and Chin blankets are highly sought after by textile collectors today.

The most extraordinary (and now dying out) Chin fashion was the custom of tattooing women's faces. Chin facial tattoos cover the whole face – starting at just above the bridge of the nose and radiating out in a pattern of dark lines that resemble a spider's web. Even the eyelids were tattooed. The tattooing was traditionally done to girls once they reached the age of 12 or 13. Legend has it that this practice was initiated to keep young Chin maidens from being coveted by Rakhaing princes whose kingdom bordered the southern Chin Hills. The practice died out after WWII, but in many Chin villages (particularly in the more traditional southern areas) you can see a few tattooed grannies.

Many Chin, particularly in the north, are Christian, following the efforts of American missionaries during the British colonial period. Chin State is restricted to travellers, but can be visited with government permission (p334).

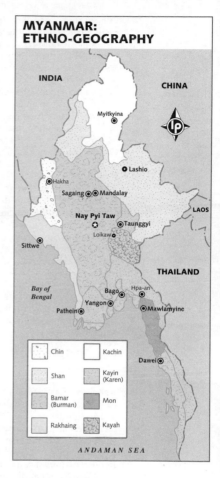

MYANMAR: ETHNO-GEOGRAPHY

Kachin

The Kachin (who call themselves Jingpaw) were heavily targeted by Christian missionaries during British colonial times (about 36% of the population are Christian, mostly Baptists and Catholics). As much of Kachin State lies above the tropic of Cancer, the climate is more extreme – stifling hot in the summer months and downright cold in the winter – and the Kachin seem

The so-called 'Monk from Brooklyn' (www.speak adventure.com) has a video project of the Shan State Army shot from behind the scenes.

to have abandoned their traditional dress for Western clothes that can be easily changed to suit the seasons.

About the only vestige of Kachin dress that foreign visitors are likely to encounter are men's *longyi* (saronglike lower garment) of indigo, green and deep-purple plaid. During festive occasions, Kachin women sport finely woven wool skirts decorated with zigzag or diamond patterns, and dark blouses festooned with hammered silver medallions and tassels.

Following independence from Britain, Kachin relations with the Burmese-run government strained. After U Nu dictated in 1961 that Buddhism would be the state religion, the Kachin formed an army. A ceasefire agreement was made only in 1994, though organisations like the Kachin National Organisation (www.kachinland.org) still strive for independence.

> Travellers can visit the Kachin in Myitkyina, home to the Kachin State Cultural Museum (p308), Bhamo (p309) and – with a permit – Putao (p313).

Kayah

Also known as the Karenni or Red Karen, the Kayah are settled in the mountainous isolation of Kayah State – an area completely closed to travellers.

As with many of Myanmar's ethnic groups that traditionally practised animism, the Kayah were targeted for conversion to Christianity by Baptist and Catholic missionaries during the colonial period. The name 'Red Karen' refers to the favoured colour of the Kayah traditional dress and the fact that their apparel resembles that of some Kayin (Karen) tribes – a resemblance that caused the Kayah to be classified by colonisers and missionaries as 'Karen'.

Today the Kayah make up a very small percentage of the population of Myanmar – perhaps less than 1% – and the vast majority lead agrarian lives. A significant number of Kayah also live in Thailand's Mae Hong Son Province.

> In recounting his efforts to form the world's biggest tiger reserve in Kachin State, American Alan Rabinowitz shows much of the local life in the Kachin hills in his fascinating *Life in the Valley of the Death*.

Kayin (Karen)

The Kayin (also known as Karen) are a large and diverse group, divided into numerous subgroups. They were originally animists, but some Kayin villages were heavily targeted by Christian missionaries in the 19th and early 20th centuries, while other villages converted to Buddhism.

The only major ethnic group to never sign peace agreements with the military government, the Kayin are an independent-minded people. However, the sheer diversity of the many Kayin subgroups has made it impossible for them to achieve any real cohesion. To this day Buddhist Kayin often side with the Buddhist Bamar against their Christian Kayin kin. Meanwhile, the head of the Karen National Union (a group devoted to Karen independence), Pado Mahn Sha, was shot and killed near the Thai border in February 2008.

The typical dress of both the Kayin men and women is a *longyi* with horizontal stripes (a pattern that is reserved exclusively for women in other ethnic groups). The Kayin are thought to make up about 7% of the total population of Myanmar.

> Presently the only place in Kayin State that travellers can visit is Hpa-an (p167).

Mon

The Mon (also called the Tailing by Western historians) were one of the earliest inhabitants of Myanmar and their rule stretched into what is now Thailand. As happened with the Cham in Vietnam and the Phuan in Laos, the Mon were gradually conquered by neighbouring kingdoms and their influence waned until they were practically unknown outside present-day Myanmar. As in Thailand, which also has a Mon minority, the Mon have almost completely assimilated with the Bamar and in most ways seem indistinguishable from them. In the precolonial era, Mon Buddhist sites including Yangon's Shwedagon Paya were appropriated by the Bamar (though the

---

HTOO TWINS

For a few years in the Kayin hills, twin kids Johnny and Luther Htoo – Christian Kayin – led a 'God's Army' in attacks against the Myanmar military. They famously held a Thai hospital hostage in 2000. Their quest began in 1997, when the Htoo's village was attacked. The 12-year-old twins supposedly rallied some men and sent Myanmar troops into retreat. As many as 150 armed followers praised their magic, believing they couldn't be harmed. In 2001 the Htoos – innocent-looking Johnny with long hair and the tougher cigarette-smoking Luther – surrendered to Thai authorities, who placed them in a refugee camp. In 2006 Johnny escaped to Myanmar and surrendered, with a few followers, to Myanmar authorities.

Golden Rock is still in Mon State), and Mon tastes in art and architecture were borrowed as well.

Today the Mon make up just over 2% of the population of Myanmar, but Mon art and culture have influenced that of the Bamar quite thoroughly, as a trip to the Mon Cultural Museum (p159) in Mawlamyine will attest.

A few Mon groups still fight for independence, though peace talks with the government are frequently in progress.

Apparently a Karen told George Orwell (reported in Emma Larkin's *Finding George Orwell in Burma*) that they hoped the British would stay for 200 years because 'we do not wish to be ruled by the Burmese'.

Naga

The Naga are mainly settled in a mountainous region of eastern India known as Nagaland, but significant numbers live in the western Sagaing Division between the Indian border and the Chindwin River.

When the British arrived in the mid-19th century, the Naga were a fragmented but fearsome collection of tribes. Headhunting was a tradition among them and for many decades they resisted British rule, though a lack of cooperation between the tribes hindered their efforts to remain independent. After nearly 17,000 Naga fought in WWI in Europe, a feeling of unity grew, which led to an organised Naga independence movement.

The Naga sport one of the world's most exotic traditional costumes. Naga men at festival time wear striking ceremonial headdresses made up of feathers, tufts of hair and cowry shells, and carry wicked spears.

Rakhaing

The Rakhaing (formerly called Arakanese), who make up about 4% of the population of Myanmar, are principally adherents of Buddhism. Their last ancient capital was centred at Mrauk U in Rakhaing State, which borders Bangladesh. Their language is akin to Bamar but, due to their geographical location, they have absorbed a fair amount of culture from the Indian subcontinent. In the eyes of most Bamar, the Rakhaing are a Creole race – a mixture of Bamar and Indian – a perception that Buddhist Rakhaing strongly resent. The Rakhaing are skilled weavers and are known in Myanmar for their eye-catching and intricately patterned *longyi*. Also see p317.

Rakhaing State also has a minority population of Muslim Rakhaing, some of whom are known as the Rohingya (see p317).

The only way to visit the Naga is with a very expensive government trip during the Naga new year in January. It's easier, and more rewarding, to visit on the Indian side of the border, where the majority of Naga live.

Shan

Making up 9% of the Myanmar population, the Shan are the biggest ethnic group in Myanmar other than the Bamar. The Shan, most of whom are Buddhists, call themselves Tai ('Shan' is actually a Bamar word derived from the word 'Siam'). This name is significant, as the Shan are related ethnically, culturally and linguistically to Tai peoples in neighbouring Thailand, Laos and China's Yunnan Province. In fact, if you've spent some time in northern Thailand or Laos and learned some of the respective languages, you'll find

---

ONGOING SUBJUGATION

With the complete takeover of Myanmar by the British in 1886, new borders were drawn. As with so many of the boundaries superimposed on maps during the European colonisation of the world, these borders had little to do with ethnic groupings, and there were many old rivals and enemies within the borders of British Burma. The colonisers managed to keep animosity between ethnic groups under control by utilising the carrot of semi-autonomy or the stick of arrest and imprisonment. Over a century later, despite a different bunch of rulers, little has changed.

Acts of insurgency between Bamar-majority government troops and minority ethnic groups that smouldered for four decades after independence have been largely quelled. Groups that signed ceasefire agreements with the government (the Kachin, Kayah etc) have been granted limited economic autonomy.

Not all have stopped fighting. Those who haven't (including some Shan and the Kayin) have been dealt with severely. In rebel-controlled areas, government troops have been accused of using rape as a weapon and adopting a scorched-earth policy that regularly sends groups of refugees fleeing across the borders into Thailand and Bangladesh. In 2003 the US State Department investigated, and found credible, reports of systematic military rapes of Shan and other ethnic groups. Some observers of politics in Myanmar predict that, given a choice, many of Myanmar's ethnic groups would opt for independence and break away from Bamar-controlled Myanmar. It's a problem that loomed over Burma's quest for independence after WWII – and would certainly be revived if any new leadership ever assumes power in the future.

---

you can have a basic conversation with the Shan. Many Shan groups have fought the Bamar for control of Myanmar, and a few groups continue a guerrilla-style conflict in the mountains near Thailand.

Traditionally, the Shan wore baggy trousers and floppy, wide-brimmed sun hats, and the men were known for their faith in talismanic tattoos. Nowadays Shan town-dwellers commonly dress in the Bamar *longyi*, except on festival occasions, when they proudly sport their ethnic costumes.

In former times the Shan were ruled by local lords or chieftains called *sao pha* (sky lords), a word that was corrupted by the Bamar to *sawbwa*.

Besides the ruins at Mrauk U (p328), the most visible vestige of the Rakhaing's illustrious past is the Mahamuni Buddha image (p263), now in Mandalay. Sittwe is home to a Rakhaing State Culture Museum (p325).

Wa

During British colonial times the Wa (who come from the still-remote north-eastern hills of Shan State) were hated and feared. The British distinguished two groups of Wa according to how receptive they were to the coloniser's attempts to control them. The 'Wild Wa' were headhunters, and decorated their villages with the severed heads of vanquished enemies to propitiate the spirits that guarded their opium fields. (Apparently they only stopped the practice in the 1970s!) The so-called 'Tame Wa' allowed the colonisers to pass through their territory unimpeded, yet the area inhabited by the Wa – east of the upper Thanlwin (Salween) River in northern Shan State – was never completely pacified by the British. For years the 20,000-strong United Wa State Army gathered power and money through the production of opium and methamphetamine. Allegedly the Wa are now drug free.

Pascal Khoo Thwe's *From the Land of Green Ghosts: A Burmese Odyssey* shares many insights from local Shan life, including a recipe for smoked pigeon with marijuana sauce.

MEDIA

The government tries to keep a tight grip on all information leaving and entering the country. Foreign journalists are denied visas (Lonely Planet researchers must fib their profession) and all printed materials in Myanmar must be cleared by the military's censorship boards. Other than sports and a few surprises here and there (eg the English-language *Myanmar Times* put stories on the UN's calls to meet with Aung San Suu Kyi on the front cover; a new Myanmar-language paper is provocatively named *Action Times*), very little breaks from the generals' typical dicta. The best way to get a sense of the propaganda locals must wade through is by thumbing through the English version of the generals' own mouthpiece, the *New Light of Myanmar,* which features generals' visits of plants and monasteries on the front page. Many locals skip the nightly 'news' read by a beehive-haired woman in front of a power-plant pictorial at 9.15pm, but movie-goers are subjected to dry newsreels before films at theatres. One of the best sources of information on Myanmar is *Irrawaddy* (www.irrawaddy.org), a Bangkok-based news magazine run by Myanmar exiles.

See the boxed text on p302 for more on the subjugation of the Shan.

Locals get hard news from satellite broadcasts of foreign news (in English), banned radio programmes translated into Burmese, such as the BBC, VOA (Voice of America) and RFA (Radio Free Asia), or via internet cafés that allow access to sites such as BBC or Myanmar-related blogs. But, following the September 2007 protests, the government made several moves to fight the inflow of outside news. First the government cut off all internet access for several days, in the aftermath arrested several journalists, and threatened to increase the yearly satellite licence fee from a few dollars to one million kyat (about $850).

Internet continues to be a sore spot for the generals – as many as 1000 internet cafés operate without a licence. The government slowed the (already slow) dial-up connection to 256 Kbps to limit the number of users. As this book was going to press, the government was updating a list of internet cafés and requiring that they all get new 'Public Access Centre' permits. One internet café owner told *Irrawaddy* that they usually pay bribes to operate, but the new permits would make it difficult to keep working.

United Wa State Army leader Bao You-Xiang promised his head if poppy production was found in the Wa area after a June 2005 deadline. The area is now drug free. But one NGO official claims three-quarters of the local population now don't have enough rice to eat.

See p29 for a list of online resources.

RELIGION

About 89% of the people of Myanmar are Buddhist, and the monks – numbering 500,000 – are seen as the nation's only real civil institution. Locals are proud of their religion and keen to discuss it. Knowing a little about it is a prerequisite for outsiders wishing to better understand the Myanmar mind. During the U Nu period, Buddhism functioned as a state religion of sorts – as embodied in such catch phrases as 'the Socialist Way to Nibbana'. Nowadays there is complete freedom of religion, though within the government Buddhists tend to attain higher rank more easily than non-Buddhists.

Many locals like calling the generals' mouthpiece paper *The New Light of Myanmar* 'the dim light of Myanmar'. It includes anti-West poems but, then again, what country's newspaper doesn't?

Buddhism in Myanmar
EARLY HISTORY
The Mon were the first people in Myanmar to practise Theravada Buddhism. King Asoka, the great Indian emperor, is known to have sent missions here (known then as the 'Golden Land') during the 3rd century BC. A second wave is thought to have arrived via Sinhalese missionaries between the 6th and 10th centuries.

By the 9th century the Pyu of northern Myanmar were combining Theravada with elements of Mahayana and Tantric Buddhism brought from their homelands in the Tibetan Plateau. During the early Bagan era (11th century), Bamar king Anawrahta decided that the Buddhism practised in his realm should be 'purified' from all non-Theravada elements. It never completely shed Tantric, Hindu and animist elements, but remains predominately Theravada.

American shows like *Love Boat* and *The Bold and the Beautiful* delighted TV watchers in the past, but now the local imagination leans to Korean soap operas. 'Sometimes I give my grandkids a little money to play elsewhere so I can watch TV,' one Mandalay woman explained.

THERAVADA & MAHAYANA
Theravada Buddhism (also followed in Cambodia, Laos, Sri Lanka and Thailand) differs from Hinduism, Judaism, Islam or Christianity in that it is

News finds its way into Myanmar's most remote pockets – a local in a western Myanmar village without roads or electricity told us: 'We listen to the BBC and VOA every couple of days. We were very worried about the monks during the protests.'

not centred around a god or gods, but rather a psycho-philosophical system. Today it covers a wide range of interpretations of the basic beliefs, which all start from the enlightenment of Siddhartha Gautama, a prince-turned-ascetic and referred to as the Buddha, in northern India around 2500 years ago.

In the Theravada (Doctrine of the Elders) school, it's believed that the individual strives to achieve *nibbana* (nirvana), rather than waiting for all humankind being ready for salvation as in Mahayana (Large Vehicle) school.

The Mahayana school does not reject the other school, but claims it has extended it. The Theravadins see Mahayana as a misinterpretation of the Buddha's original teachings. Of the two, the Theravada is more austere and ascetic and, some might say, harder to practise.

TENETS

Buddha taught that the world is primarily characterised by *dukkha* (unsatisfactoriness), *anicca* (impermanence) and *anatta* (insubstantiality), and that even our happiest moments in life are only temporary, empty and unsatisfactory.

The ultrapragmatic Buddhist perception of cause and effect – *kamma* in Pali, *karma* in Sanskrit, *kan* in Burmese – holds that birth inevitably leads to sickness, old age and death, hence every life is insecure and subject to *dukkha*. Through rebirth, the cycle of *thanthaya* (*samsara* in Pali) repeats itself endlessly as long as ignorance and craving remain.

After a monk was reportedly beaten to death in Pakokku in September 2007, the All Burma Monks Alliance (ABMA) was formed – a surprisingly direct confrontation with the government, and one credited for kick-starting nationwide protests.

Only by reaching a state of complete wisdom and nondesire can one attain true happiness. To achieve wisdom and eliminate craving one must turn inward and master one's own mind through meditation, most commonly known in Myanmar as *bhavana* or *kammahtan*.

The Buddha taught four noble truths:

1 Life is *dukkha*.
2 *Dukkha* comes from *tanha* (selfish desire).
3 When one forsakes selfish desire, suffering will be extinguished.
4 The 'eightfold path' is the way to eliminate selfish desire.

The eightfold path consists of:

1 Right thought
2 Right understanding
3 Right speech
4 Right action
5 Right livelihood
6 Right exertion
7 Right attentiveness
8 Right concentration

Regarding the monk-led protests in 2007, Sein Win of *Mizzima* wrote: 'The monks have done what they had to do…they have opened the flood gates.'

Devout Buddhists in Myanmar adhere to five lay precepts, or moral rules (*thila* in Burmese, *sila* in Pali), which require abstinence from killing, stealing, unchastity (usually interpreted among laypeople as adultery), lying and intoxicating substances.

In spite of Buddhism's profound truths, the most common Myanmar approach is to try for a better future life by feeding monks, donating to temples and performing regular worship at the local paya (Buddhist monument). For the average person everything revolves around the *kutho* (merit), from the Pali *kusala* (wholesome), one is able to accumulate through such deeds.

Many visitors come to Myanmar to meditate; see p341 for more on this.

MONKS & NUNS

Socially, every Myanmar male is expected to take up temporary monastic residence twice in his life: once as a *samanera* (novice monk) between the ages of 10 and 20, and again as a *hpongyi* (fully ordained monk) sometime after the age of 20. Almost all men or boys aged under 20 'take robe and bowl' in the *shinpyu* (novitiation ceremony).

All things possessed by a monk must be offered by the lay community. Upon ordination a new monk is typically offered a set of three robes (lower, inner and outer). Bright red robes are usually reserved for novices under 15, darker colours for older, fully ordained monks. Other possessions a monk is permitted include a razor, a cup, a filter (for keeping insects out of drinking water), an umbrella and an alms bowl.

In Myanmar, women who live the monastic life as *dasasila* ('10-precept' nuns) are often called *thilashin* (possessor of morality) in Burmese. Myanmar nuns shave their heads, wear pink robes and take vows in an ordination procedure similar to monks. Generally, nunhood isn't considered as 'prestigious' as monkhood, as nuns generally don't perform ceremonies on behalf of laypeople, and keep only 10 precepts – the same number observed by male novices.

> 'Auspicious', or 'favourable' or 'prosperous', is a word used daily in Myanmar.

MONASTERIES

Monastic communities are called *kyaungtaik, hpongyi-kyaung,* or simply *kyaung* for short. There are over 50,000 in Myanmar. The most important structure on the monastery grounds is the *thein* (a consecrated hall where monastic ordinations are held). *Kyaung* may also be associated with one or more *zedi* (stupa) or *pahto* (temple). An open-sided resthouse or *zayat* may be available for gatherings of laypeople during festivals or pilgrimages.

The 37 *Nat*

One of the most fascinating things about Myanmar is the ongoing worship of the *nat* (spirit) – a link to the pre-Buddhism era when animism (associated with hills, trees and lakes) held undisputed dominion over the land. Though some Buddhist leaders downgrade the *nat,* the *nat* are very much alive in the lives of the people of Myanmar.

> In mornings, you'll see rows of monks carrying bowls to get offerings of rice and food. It's not begging. It's a way of letting locals have the chance of doing the deed of *dhana,* thus acquiring merit.

HISTORY

The powerful *nat* of Myanmar has evolved into a spirit that may hold dominion over a place (natural or human-made), person or field of experience. Orthographically, the written Burmese word *nat* is likely derived from the Pali-Sanskrit *natha* (lord or guardian).

Separate, larger shrines were built for a higher class of *nat,* descended from actual historic personages (including previous Thai and Bamar kings) who had died violent, unjust deaths. These suprahuman *nat,* when correctly propitiated, could aid worshippers in accomplishing important tasks, vanquishing enemies and so on.

In Bagan, King Anawrahta stopped animal sacrifices (part of *nat* worship at Mt Popa) and destroyed *nat* temples. Realising he may lose the case for making Theravada Buddhism the national faith, Anawrahta wisely conceded the *nat's* coexistence with Buddha. There were 36 recognised *nat* at the time (in fact, there are many more). Anawrahta sagely added a 37th, Thagyamin, a Hindu deity based on Indra, whom he crowned 'king of the *nat'*. Since, in traditional Buddhist mythology, Indra paid homage to Buddha, this insertion effectively made all *nat* subordinate to Buddhism. Anawrahta's scheme worked, and today the commonly believed cosmology places Buddha's teachings at the top.

> For more on Buddhism, check websites like www .buddhanet.org, www .dharmanet.org or www .accesstoinsight.org.

WORSHIP & BELIEFS

In many homes you may see the most popular *nat* in the form of an unhusked coconut dressed in a red *gaung baung* (turban), which represents the dual-*nat*

Eindwin-Min Mahagiri (Lord of the Great Mountain Who Is in the House). Another widespread form of *nat* worship is exhibited through the red-and-white cloths tied to a rear-view mirror or hood ornament; these colours are the traditional *nat* colours of protection.

'I worship Buddha, but I make friends with the *nat*.'

– PAKOKKU LOCAL

Some of the more animistic guardian *nat* remain outside home and paya. A tree-spirit shrine, for example, may be erected beneath a particularly venerated old tree, thought to wield power over the immediate vicinity. These are especially common beneath larger banyan trees *(Ficus religiosa)*, as this tree is revered as a symbol of Buddha's enlightenment. A village may well have a *nat* shrine in a wooded corner for the propitiation of the village guardian spirit. Such tree and village shrines are simple, dollhouselike structures of wood or bamboo; their proper placement is divined by a local *saya* (teacher or shaman), trained in spirit lore. Such knowledge of the complex *nat* world is fading fast among the younger generations.

See p330 for an interview with a Rakhaing State local who calls himself the 'Only Guardian of Buddha Wisdom', among other things.

Those with a general fear of *nat* will avoid eating pork, which is thought to be offensive to the spirit world. The main fear is not simply that spirits will wreak havoc on your daily affairs, but rather that one may enter your mind and body and force you to perform unconscionable acts in public – acts that would cause others to shun you. Spirit possession – whether psychologically induced or metaphysical – is a phenomenon that is real in the eyes of the people of Myanmar.

NAT FESTIVALS

On certain occasions the *nat* cult goes beyond simple propitiation of the spirits (via offerings) and steps into the realm of spirit invocation. Most commonly, this is accomplished through *nat pwe* (spirit festivals), special musical performances designed to attract *nat* to the performance venue. Nearly all indigenous Burmese music is designed for this purpose.

To lure a *nat* to a loud *pwe* (festival) takes the work of a spirit medium, or *nat-gadaw* (*nat* wife), who is either a woman or a male transvestite who sings and dances to invite specific *nat* to possess them.

The *nat* like loud and colourful music, so musicians at a *nat pwe* bang away at full volume on their gongs, drums and xylophones, producing what sounds like some ancient form of rock and roll.

Every *nat pwe* is accompanied by a risk that the invited spirit may choose to enter, not the body of the medium, but one of the spectators. One of the most commonly summoned spirits at *nat pwe* is Ko Gyi Kyaw (Big Brother Kyaw), a drunkard *nat* who responds to offerings of liquor imbibed by the *nat-gadaw*. When he enters someone's body, he's given to lascivious dancing, so a chance possession by Ko Gyi Kyaw is especially embarrassing.

Once possessed by a *nat*, the only way one can be sure the spirit won't return again and again is to employ the services of an older Buddhist monk skilled at exorcism – a process that can take days, if not weeks. Without undergoing such a procedure, anyone who has been spirit possessed may

---

NUMBER NINE (SAY IT NINE TIMES!)

Myanmar astrology, based on the Indian system of naming the zodiacal planets for Hindu deities, continues to be an important factor in deciding proper dates for weddings, funerals, ordinations and other events. Burma became independent at 4.20am on 4 January 1948, per U Nu's counsel with an astrologer. Numerology plays a similar role in Myanmar.

Nearly everyone in Myanmar reveres the number nine, which is thought to have an inherent mystic significance. The Burmese word *ko* (nine) also means 'to seek protection from the gods'. General Ne Win, too, was fascinated with numerology, especially that relating to the cabalistic ritual Paya-kozu (Nine Gods). He replaced common currency with 45-kyat and 90-kyat notes, because their digits' sum equalled nine. It is considered no accident that the prodemocracy marches were staged on 8 August 1988 (8-8-88); for many, eight is considered an 'unlucky' number.

THE WATER FESTIVAL

Around the middle of April, the three-day Thingyan (Water Festival) starts the Myanmar New Year. This event occurs at the height of the dry and hot season and, as in Thailand's Songkran, is celebrated in a most raucous manner – by throwing buckets of cold water at anyone who dares to venture into the streets. Foreigners are not exempt!

In cities, temporary stages called *pandal* (from the Tamil *pendel*) are erected along main thoroughfares, with water barrels ready to douse all passersby.

On a spiritual level, Myanmar people believe that during this three-day period the king of the *nat* (spirit beings), Thagyamin, visits the human world to tally his annual record of the good deeds and misdeeds humans have performed. Villagers place flowers and sacred leaves in front of their homes to welcome the *nat*. Thagyamin's departure on the morning of the third day marks the beginning of the new year, when properly brought-up young people wash the hair of their elder kin, buddha images are ceremonially washed, and *hpongyi* (monks) are offered particularly appetising alms food.

Although the true meaning of the festival is still kept alive by ceremonies such as these, nowadays it's mainly a festival of fun. In between getting soaked, there will be dancing, singing and theatre. And drinking. In theatre, the emphasis is on satire – particularly making fun of the government, the latest female fashions and any other items of everyday interest. Cultural taboos against women acting in a boisterous manner are temporarily lifted, so women can 'kidnap' young men, blacken the men's faces with soot or oil, bind their hands and dunk their heads in buckets of water until they surrender and perform a hilarious monkey dance for the women.

---

carry the *nat* stigma for the rest of their lives. Girls who have been so entered are considered unmarriageable unless satisfactorily exorcised.

Other Religions

Among the non-Buddhist people of Myanmar, 1% are animist, 4% Christian, 4% Muslim and 1.5% Hindu. Most Muslims and Hindus, as well as many Christians, are of Indian descent and live in the larger towns and cities.

Most other Christians in Myanmar are found among the tribal minorities, though the majority of the tribal people remain animist. Baptist, Catholic and Anglican missionaries have been active in Myanmar for over 150 years. Ethnic groups that traditionally practised animism were more receptive to conversion, especially the Kayin, Kachin and Chin.

Myanmar had 2500 Jews before the wake of nationalism encouraged most to leave; today Myanmar has only about 25 Jews. The best Jewish site to visit is Yangon's 19th-century Moseah Yeshua Synagogue (p103).

There is sometimes friction between religious groups. In October 2001, riots between Buddhists and Muslims caused the government to impose temporary curfews in Taungoo and Pyay. Many Muslims endure restrictions on their ability to travel, and often can stay only at family homes, not hotels.

The country's biggest *nat pwe* is held in August at Taungbyone, about 12 miles north of Mandalay (p266). Irinaku Festival (p280) follows thereafter at Yadanagu, south of Amarapura, where there's a ritual bathing of *nat* images in the Ayeyarwady River.

WOMEN IN MYANMAR

In most respects Myanmar women (who make up 48.5% of the population) enjoy legal rights equal to those of Myanmar men; for example, they own property and aren't barred from any profession. Unlike in the West, females do not traditionally change any portion of their names upon marriage; in the event of divorce, they are legally entitled to half of all property accumulated during the marriage. Inheritance rights are also equally shared. Aung San Suu Kyi wrote that a baby girl is as equally celebrated as a baby boy, as they're believed to be 'more dutiful and loving than sons'. Girls are educated alongside boys and, by university age, women

Plumpness is a sign of health for local women. To say *'wa-laiq-ta!'* (how fat you're looking!) is quite a compliment.

outnumber men in university and college enrolment. Most white-collar professions grant women paid maternity leave of six weeks before birth and one or two months afterwards.

Religion is one arena in which women perpetually take a back seat. Any man, regardless of desire, is seen as possessing the potential of becoming a buddha; women cannot. A small number of Buddhist shrines, for example Mandalay's Mahamuni Paya, have small areas around the main holy image that are off limits to women.

Many people in Myanmar – women as well as men – believe the birth of a female indicates less religious merit than the birth of a male, and that it is easier for males to attain *nibbana*. Just as boys between the ages of five and 15 usually undergo a prepuberty initiation as temporary novice monks, girls around the same age participate in an initiatory ear-piercing ceremony (often called 'ear-boring' in Burmese English). Some also become temporary nuns at this age.

Saw Myat Yin, the insightful author of *Culture Shock! Burma*, expresses a viewpoint common among the majority of Myanmar women, who see their role as equal but 'supportive and complementary…rather than in competition' and that 'if they accept a role a step behind their menfolk they do so freely and willingly'.

One Mandalay grandmother told us things are changing somewhat: 'There used to be that belief that women aren't clean – because they have periods. We used to have to sleep on the floor, or apart from our husbands at least, when we had periods. That's changed. Some things still need to change!'

ARTS
Dance & Theatre

Myanmar's truly indigenous dance forms are those that pay homage to the *nat*. Most classical dance styles, meanwhile, arrived from Thailand. Today the dances most obviously taken from Thailand are known as *yodaya zat* (Ayuthaya theatre), as taught to the people of Myanmar by Thai theatrical artists taken captive in the 18th century.

The most Myanmar of dances feature solo performances by female dancers who wear strikingly colourful dresses with long white trains, which they kick into the air with their heels – quite a feat, given the restrictive length of the train.

An all-night *zat pwe* involves a re-creation of an ancient legend or Buddhist Jataka (life story of the Buddha) while the Yamazat picks a tale from the Indian epic Ramayana.

Classical dance-drama is performed nightly at Mandalay's Mintha Theater (p271) and occasionally performed at the National Theatre in Yangon (p126). In Mandalay, Yamazat performers even have their own shrine. Since Myanmar classical dancing emphasises pose rather than movement, and solo rather than ensemble performances, it can soon become a little boring for TV-hyped Western tastes. By contrast the less common, but livelier, *yein pwe* features singing and dancing performed by a chorus or ensemble.

Most popular of all is the *a-nyeint pwe*, a traditional *pwe* somewhat akin to early American vaudeville (see the boxed text on p270 for a description).

Marionette Theatre

Youq-the pwe (Myanmar marionette theatre) presents colourful puppets up to 3.5ft high in a spectacle that many aesthetes consider the most expressive of all the Myanmar arts. Developed during the Konbaung period, it was so influential that it became the forerunner to *zat pwe* as later performed by

---

Myanmar women keep their beauty by staying away from alcohol and cigarettes, washing with cold water, and lathering up their whole bodies in *thanakha* paste at night.

Some Buddhist women look to the story of Visakha, an early disciple of Buddha, whose rather traditional virtues (looking after house, family, relatives, husband) act as a 'guide to women', in the words of local author Khin Myo Chit.

Myanmar dance scholars have catalogued around 2000 dance movements, including 13 head movements, 28 eye movements, nine neck movements, 24 ways of moving only one hand and 23 of both, 38 leg movements, eight body postures and 10 walking movements.

actors rather than marionettes. As with dance-drama, the genre's 'golden age' began with the Mandalay kingdoms of the late 18th century and ran through to the advent of cinema in the 1930s.

The people of Myanmar have great respect for an expert puppeteer. Some marionettes may be manipulated by a dozen or more strings; certain *nat* may sport up to 60 strings, including one for each eyebrow. The marionette master's standard repertoire requires a troupe of 28 puppets including Thagyamin (king of the gods); a Myanmar king, queen, prince and princess; a regent; two court pages; an old man and an old woman; a villain; a hermit; four ministers; two clowns; one good and one evil *nat*; a Brahmin astrologer; two ogres; a *zawgyi* (alchemist); a horse; a monkey; a *makara* (mythical sea serpent); and an elephant.

These days it's rare to see marionette theatre outside tourist venues in Yangon, Mandalay or Bagan.

Music

Much of classical Myanmar music, played loud the way the *nat* like it, features strongly in any *pwe*. Its repetitive, even harsh, harmonies can be hard on Western ears at first, as Myanmar scales are not 'tempered', as Western scales have been since Bach. Traditional Myanmar music is primarily two dimensional, in the sense that rhythm and melody provide much of the musical structure, while repetition is a key element. Subtle shifts in rhythm and tonality provide the modulation usually supplied by the harmonic dimension in Western music.

CLASSICAL MUSIC

Classical music traditions were largely borrowed from Siam musicians in the late 1800s, who borrowed the traditions from Cambodian conquests centuries earlier. Myanmar classical music as played today was codified by Po Sein, a colonial-era musician, composer and drummer who also designed the *hsaing waing* (the circle of tuned drums, also known as *paq waing*) and formalised classical dancing styles. Such music is meant to be played as an accompaniment to classical dance-dramas that enact scenes from the Jataka or from the Ramayana.

Musical instruments are predominantly percussive, but even the *hsaing waing* may carry the melody. These drums are tuned by placing a wad of *paq-sa* (drum food) – made from a kneaded paste of rice and wood ash – onto the centre of the drum head, then adding or subtracting a pinch at a time till the desired drum tone is attained.

In addition to the *hsaing waing*, the traditional *hsaing* (Myanmar ensemble) of seven to 10 musicians will usually play: the *kye waing* (a circle of tuned brass gongs); the *saung gauq* (a boat-shaped harp with 13 strings); the *pattala* (a sort of xylophone); the *hneh* (an oboe-type instrument related to the Indian *shanai*); the *pa-lwe* (a bamboo flute); the *mi-gyaung* (crocodile lute); the *paq-ma* (a bass drum); and the *yagwin* (small cymbals) and *wa leq-hkouq* (bamboo clappers), which are purely rhythmic and are often played by Myanmar vocalists.

FOLK

Older than Myanmar classical music is an enchanting vocal folk-music tradition still heard in rural areas where locals may sing without instrumental accompaniment while working. Such folk songs set the work cadence and provide a distraction from the physical strain and monotony of pounding rice, clearing fields, weaving and so on. You'll hear this type of music most readily in the Ayeyarwady Delta (p133) between Twante and Pathein.

Enjoying *zat pwe*, according to writer Khin Myo Chit, 'you must be prepared to stay the whole night'. In the morning you'll be 'relaxed and happy' and can sleep until you 'wake up, a giant refreshed, equal to face life for quite a while to come.'

Famously, the 1988 protests began when two student groups argued over what kind of music to play at a teashop. The police moved in, a student was killed, and the students banded in protest. An apology never came, and soon the nation stormed the streets.

TRADITIONAL BURMESE MUSIC CDS

These music CDs can generally be found outside Myanmar:
Mahagitá *Harp & Vocal Music from Burma* (2003; Smithsonian Folkways)
Music of Nat Pwe: Folk & Pop Music of Myanmar (2007; Sublime Frequencies)
Pat Waing *The Magic Drum Circle of Burma* (1998; Shanachie)
U Ko Ko *Performs on the Burmese Piano* (1995; Ummus)
White Elephants & Golden Ducks *Musical Treasures from Burma* (1997; Shanachie)

ROCK & RAP

Modern music has taken off in Myanmar, with a host of rap and rock bands influenced by the introduction of MTV Asia. Western music's influence first came in the 1970s, when singers such as Min Min Latt and Takatho Tun Naung sang shocking things such as Beatles cover versions or 'Tie a Yellow Ribbon 'round the Old Oak Tree'. This led to long-haired, distorted-guitar rock bands such as Empire and Iron Cross in the 1980s. Even today, no-one's bigger than Iron Cross – try to see them live (you're sure to see them on videotape at teashops or on all-night buses). Another big band is Lazy Club.

Bands such as these (all of whom usually sing in Burmese, even if they have English names) have a stable of several singers who split stage time with the same backing band. Iron Cross, for example, features one of Myanmar's 'wilder' singers, Lay Phyu, whose *Butterfly* album has him done up like the insect. Iron Cross also tones it down as a backing band for the poppier stuff of other singers. One local aficionado explained: 'There's no competition between a band's many singers. They help each other. Our rock singers don't throw TVs out the windows. On stage they jump around and all, but offstage they're very good-natured.'

Female singers like Sone Thin Par and actor Htu Eindra Bo win fans for their melodies – and looks – but the most interesting is Phyu Phyu Kyaw Thein, a sort of 'Sporty Spice', who has fronted both Iron Cross *and* Lazy Club. In a 2007 show we attended, she came out in a grim reaper costume, then tore it off to reveal a sparkling gold outfit. 'Many people like her voice,' one Yangon resident said. 'But her performance? So confident, so strong; some say it's too much.'

Rap is the latest trend, with Min Min Latt's son, Anega, now busting beats with other big-name rappers Barbu, Myo Kyawt Myaung and heart-throb Sai Sai. Songs often deal with gossip, or troubles between parents and kids. One rap band, 9mm, was briefly detained in 2004 for performing political songs written by an anonymous prodemocracy group of exiled and local rappers called Myanmar Future Generations (MFG); download their songs for free at www.mm-fg.net.

A famed exiled singer Mun Awng (a Kachin singer) has recorded political songs, including his *Battle for Peace* album, which is available through the underground only.

Yangon is the best place to catch a show; look out for advertisements.

When government censors wouldn't go for a literal translation of Eminem's lyric ('shake that ass') in Sai Sai's cover version in 2007, Sai Sai sang 'shake that water pot' *(o lay, hloke pa ohn!)*.

All lyrics must pass the government's censor board. In 1998 blues singer Nyi Pu had to rename his debut *Everything's Going to Be Good* to *Everything's Good;* a few years later, Iron Cross' Myo Gyi changed his *Very Wild Wind* album to a tamer *Breeze.*

Architecture

It is in architecture that one sees the strongest evidence of Myanmar artistic skill and accomplishment. Myanmar is a country of *zedi,* often called 'pagodas' in English. Wherever you are – boating down the river, driving through the hills, even flying above the plains – there always seems to be a hilltop *zedi* in view. It is in Bagan (p203) that you see the most dramatic results of this national enthusiasm for religious monuments.

PAYA, *ZEDI* OR *PAHTO*?

Paya (pa-*yah*), the most common Myanmar equivalent to the often-misleading English term pagoda, literally means 'holy one' and can refer to people, deities and places associated with religion. Often it's a generic term covering a stupa, temple or shrine. There are basically two kinds of paya: the solid, bell-shaped *zedi* and the hollow square or rectangular *pahto*. A *zedi* or stupa is usually thought to contain 'relics' – either objects taken from the Buddha himself (especially pieces of bone, teeth or hair) or certain holy materials. Both *zedi* and *pahto* are often associated with *kyaung* (Buddhist monasteries).

The term *pahto* is sometimes translated as temple, though shrine would perhaps be more accurate as priests or monks are not necessarily in attendance. The so-called Mon-style *pahto* is a large cube with small windows and ground-level passageways; this type is also known as a *gu* or *ku* (from the Pali-Sanskrit *guha,* meaning 'cave'). The overall Bamar concept is similar to that of the Mayan and Aztec pyramids of Mesoamerica: worshippers climb a symbolic mountain lined with religious reliefs and frescoes.

If all this seems too confusing, just remember that the generic Myanmar term for all these structures is paya. The famous Mon *zedi* in Yangon is called Shwedagon Paya (p92), and Bagan's greatest *pahto* is often called Ananda Paya (p210).

DJ & Thar Soe's unusual 2007 hit 'I Like Drums' merged *nat* music with trance. The video featured a transvestite *nat-gadaw* and an old guy overwhelmed by the music who dies then comes back to life yelling: 'I like drums!' Who doesn't, brother?

ZEDI STYLES

Early *zedi* were usually hemispherical (the Kaunghmudaw at Sagaing near Mandalay) or bulbous (the Bupaya in Bagan), while the more modern style is much more graceful – a curvaceous lower bell merging into a soaring spire, such as the Shwedagon Paya in Yangon. Style is not always a good indicator of the original age of a *zedi,* as Myanmar is earthquake-prone and many (including the Shwedagon) have been rebuilt again and again.

OTHER BUILDINGS

Traditionally, only the *zedi, gu* and *pahto* have been made of permanent materials. Until quite recently all secular buildings – and most monasteries – were constructed of wood, so there are few old ones to be seen. Even the great palaces were made of wood and, since the destruction of Mandalay Palace during WWII, there is no remaining wooden Myanmar palace. A few surviving examples of wooden buildings are in Mandalay (p261), Inwa (Ava; p281), Salay (p190) and near Pakokku (p191).

BUDDHA'S HAND SIGNS

While visiting some of Myanmar's thousands and thousands of buddha images, look out for the following hand signs, which have different meanings:

- **Abhaya** Both hands have palms out, symbolising protection from fear.
- **Bhumispara** The right hand touches the ground, symbolising when Buddha sat beneath a banyan tree until he gained enlightenment.
- **Dana** One or both hands with palms up, symbolising the offering of *dhamma* (Buddhist teachings) to the world.
- **Dhyana** Both hands rest palm-up on the buddha's lap, signifying meditation.
- **Vitarka or Dhammachakka** Thumb and forefinger of one hand forms a circle with other fingers (somewhat like an 'OK' gesture), symbolising the first public discourse on Buddhist doctrine.

Although so little remains of the old wooden architectural skills, there are still many excellent wooden buildings to be seen. The people of Myanmar continue to use teak with great skill, and a fine country home can be a very pleasing structure indeed.

Buildings erected during the British colonial period feature a variety of styles and materials, from the rustic wood-and-plaster Tudor villas of Pyin U Lwin to the thick-walled, brick-and-plaster, colonnaded mansions and shop houses of Yangon, Mawlamyine and Myeik (Mergui). An interesting example of a fusion of Myanmar and European styles is the City Hall building in Yangon (p114). Until recently scant attention was paid to preserving colonial architecture – for political as well as economic reasons. Nowadays some are being restored, but many have been demolished and replaced by new structures in recent years.

Sculpture & Painting

Early Myanmar art was always a part of the religious architecture – paints were for the walls of temples, sculpture to be placed inside them. Remarkably little research has been carried out on Myanmar religious sculpture other than that from the Bagan and Mandalay eras. Many pieces, formerly in paya or *kyaung*, have been sold or stolen. Mandalay's Mahamuni Buddha image, a Rakhaing sculpture, is the country's most famous image of any age. Unfortunately, you'll easily find more Myanmar religious sculpture for sale or on display in Bangkok, Chiang Mai, San Francisco and London than in Myanmar.

In the immediate aftermath of the 1988 demonstrations, the government forbade 'selfish' or 'mad art' that didn't have clear pro-government themes. One artist, Sitt Nyein Aye, spent two months in custody for sketching the ruins of the former student union, which Ne Win had blown up in 1962. Things seem to have relaxed a little, evident in national galleries, though most works are rather predictable tourist-oriented works. The government's social posters – anti-AIDS, antidrugs, pro–traffic safety, or just pro-government! – are often just simple messages, but occasionally are interesting pieces of propaganda artwork found on many main streets.

Literature

Religious texts inscribed onto Myanmar's famous *kammawa* (lacquered scriptures) and *parabaik* (folding manuscripts) were the first pieces of literature as such, and began appearing in the 12th century. Until the 1800s, the only other works of 'literature' available were royal genealogies, classical poetry and law texts. A Burmese version of the Indian epic 'Ramayana' was first written in 1775 by poet U Aung Pyo. The first printed books in the country were produced by missionaries; the American Baptist Mission was responsible for virtually all publishing until the late 19th century, when the first press owned by a Myanmar local began printing a Burmese-language newspaper.

Today the people of Myanmar are great readers, as you'll realise from the piles of books in the street at every night market.

When royal palaces ceased to be built, woodcarving skills rapidly declined. There has been a small renaissance in recent years, mostly seen in hotels.

Food & Drink

STAPLES & SPECIALITIES

Myanmar's food may never overtake regional cuisines such as Thai or Vietnamese on the worldwide dining map, and possibly for a reason. While Burmese food shows great variety, and can be quite tasty at times, very few visitors come away from a visit boasting more about the food than the people or sights seen. This section gives an overview to help you persevere and get the most out of your meals.

Burmese Cuisine

Mainstream Burmese cuisine represents a blend of Bamar, Mon, Indian and Chinese influences. *T'ămin* (rice), also written as *htamin,* is the core of any Burmese (or Bamar) meal, to be eaten with a choice of *hìn* (curry dishes), most commonly fish, chicken, prawns or mutton. Very little beef or pork is eaten by people in Myanmar – beef because it's considered offensive to most Hindus and Burmese Buddhists, and pork because the *nat* (spirits) disapprove (see p66). Many Burmese Buddhists abstain from eating the flesh of any four-legged animal and, during the Buddhist rain retreat around the Waso full moon, may take up a 'fire-free' diet that includes only uncooked vegetables and fruit. Nearly all butchers in Myanmar are either Muslim or Chinese.

> Foods in Myanmar are believed to have 'hot' or 'cool' qualities. Chicken, chocolate and mango are 'hot', pork and dairy products are 'cool'.

Unlike many Chinese dishes, Burmese food takes a long time to prepare. It is often best eaten in homes or at lunch in restaurants (when it tends to be freshest). Burmese curries are the mildest in Asia in terms of chilli power – in fact most cooks don't use chillies at all in their recipes, just a simple *masala* of turmeric, ginger, garlic, salt and onions, plus plenty of peanut oil and shrimp paste. Heat can be added in the form of *balachaung,* a table condiment made from chillies, tamarind and dried shrimp pounded together, or from the very pungent, very hot *ngapi jaw* (salty shrimp paste fried in peanut oil with chilli, garlic and onions; it can be an acquired taste). A thin sauce of pressed fish or shrimp called *ngan-pya-ye* may also be used to salt Bamar dishes.

> One of the seminal works on Myanmar cuisine is *Cook and Entertain the Burmese Way,* by Mi Mi Khaing, available in many Yangon bookshops.

Curries are generally cooked until the oil separates from all other ingredients and floats on top. Some restaurants will add oil to maintain the correct top layer, as the oil preserves the underlying food from contamination by insects and airborne bacteria while the curries sit in open, unheated pots for hours at a time.

One of the culinary highlights of Burmese food is undoubtedly *dhouq or thouq* (also *lethouq*) – light, spicy salads made with raw vegetables or fruit tossed with lime juice, onions, peanuts, chillies and other spices. Among the most exquisite are *maji-yweq dhouq,* made with tender young tamarind leaves, and *shauk-thi dhouq* mixed with pomelo, a large citrus fruit similar in appearance to grapefruit, but sweeter. *T'ămin let-dhouq* are savoury salads made with cooked rice.

A popular finish to Burmese meals is *la-hpeq dhouq* (a saladlike concoction of pressed, moistened green tea leaves mixed with a combination of sesame seeds, fried peas, dried shrimp, fried garlic, peanuts, toasted coconut and ginger, and other crunchy flavourings). The 'slimy-looking' mass of leaves puts some foreigners off, but it's actually quite tasty once you get beyond the dish's exotic appearance.

> Food is so enjoyed in Myanmar that standard greetings to friends and foreigners include: *sar pyi bi lar?* ('have you eaten your lunch yet?') and *bar hìn ne sar le?* ('what curry did you have for lunch?').

A common side dish is Indian-influenced *peh-hìn-ye* (lentil soup, or dhal); the classier restaurants may serve dhal fortified with chunks of boiled turnips, potatoes and okra. A *hìn-jo* (mild soup) of green squash may also be available. Once you've ordered one or more curries at an authentic *t'ămin zain* (rice shop), rice, dhal, soup, side dishes and Chinese tea come automatically for no charge.

Noodle dishes are most often eaten for breakfast or as light meals between the main meals of the day. By far the most popular is *mohinga* (rice noodles with fish, eel or chicken), which is eaten with a spoon and *tu* (chopsticks). Another popular noodle dish, especially at festivals, is *oun-no hkauq-sweh,* Chinese-style rice noodles with pieces of chicken in a spicy sauce made with coconut milk.

REGIONAL CUISINE

Local cuisine can be broadly broken down into dishes found in 'lower Myanmar' (roughly Yangon – Rangoon – and the delta), with more fish pastes and sour foods; and 'upper Myanmar' (centred at Mandalay), with more sesame, nuts and beans used in dishes.

In Mandalay and around Inle Lake, it is also fairly easy to find Shan cuisine, which is very similar to northern Thai cuisine. Popular dishes are *k'auk sen* (Shan-style wide rice noodles with curry) and various fish and meat salads. Large *maung jeut* (rice crackers) are common throughout Shan State.

Shàn k'auk swèh (Shan-style noodle soup), thin wheat noodles in a light broth with chunks of chilli-marinated chicken, is a favourite all over Myanmar but is most common in Mandalay and Shan State. A variation popular in Mandalay, called *myi shay,* is made with rice noodles and is often served with pork. Another Shan dish worth seeking out is *t'ămin chin* (sour rice; a turmeric-coloured rice salad).

Mon cuisine, most readily available in towns stretching from Bago to Mawlamyine (Moulmein), is very similar to Burmese food, with a greater emphasis on curry selections. While a Burmese restaurant might offer a choice of four or five curries, a Mon restaurant will have as many as a dozen, all lined up in curry pots to be examined. Mon curries are also more likely to contain chillies than those of other cuisines.

Rakhaing (Arakan) food most resembles dishes found in Bangladesh and India's Bengal state, featuring lots of bean and pulse dishes, very spicy curries and flatbreads.

Chinese & Indian Cuisines

In towns large and small throughout Myanmar you'll find plenty of Chinese restaurants, many of which offer regional specialities that are a world (well, half of China anyway) away from the Chinese food found in Western countries. For example, there are Muslim-Chinese restaurants that serve Yúnnánese specialities.

Indian restaurants are also common, although much more so in Yangon than elsewhere. Most are run by Muslim-Indians, a few by Hindus. Excellent chicken *dan bauk* (biryani), as well as all-you-can-eat vegetarian *thali* served on a banana leaf, is easy to find in the capital. The Myanmar people call Indian restaurants that serve all-you-can-eat *thali* 'Chitty' or 'Chetty' restaurants. Many Indian places outside of Yangon can be very basic.

DRINKS
Nonalcoholic Drinks

Only drink water in Myanmar when you know it has been purified – which in most restaurants it should be. You should be suspicious of ice although we've had lots of ice drinks in Myanmar without suffering any ill effects. Many brands of drinking water are sold in bottles and are quite safe. A 1L bottle, usually kept cool by ice or refrigerator, costs about K150 or K200.

Myanmar's fruit offerings vary by region and season. Don't miss Pyin U Lwin's strawberries and Bago's pineapples. Mango is best March through July; jackfruit June to October.

If you're not bonding with Myanmar's curry-based meals, go for noodles. *Mohinga* (fish noodle soup) is a tasty breakfast, while *myi shay* is a Shan-influenced noodle soup with pickled tofu and pork (most famous in Mandalay).

Pregnant women, stay away from bananas! Per local beliefs, your baby will be born overweight if you indulge while pregnant.

Burmese tea, brewed in the Indian style with lots of milk and sugar, is cheap. If this is not to your liking, ask for Chinese tea, which is weak and comes without milk. Many restaurants, the Chinese ones in particular, will provide as much weak Chinese tea as you can handle – for free if you order some food. It's a good, safe thirst quencher and some people prefer it to regular Burmese tea. You can always buy a little snack if you'd like some tea but not a meal. Teashops (p77) are a good place to drink safely boiled tea and munch on inexpensive snacks such as *nam-bya, palata* (kinds of flat breads) or Chinese pastries.

Soft drinks are more costly but reasonable by Asian standards. Since the privatisation of industry there has been a boom in new made-in-Myanmar soft-drink brands, including Fantasy, Max, Star, Fruito and Crusher. They taste pretty much the same as Coke and are not frequently found outside Yangon or touristy areas.

Coffee drinkers will find themselves growing disturbingly attached to the 'three-in-one' packets of instant coffee (the 'three' being coffee, milk and sugar), which you can have in teashops for about K200.

Alcoholic Drinks

In the past the people of Myanmar were not big drinkers. This was partially due to the general lack of disposable income but also because alcohol drinking is looked down upon by the many Burmese Buddhists who interpret the fifth lay precept against intoxication very strictly. However, with the advent of 'beer stations' – places that serve cheap draught beer – the number of urban locals who can afford a few glasses of beer after work is on the rise.

Any place selling beer or alcohol must pay (sometimes relatively expensive) 'alcohol licence fees' to the government. See p77 for information on drinking venues.

BEER

Apart from international brands such as Tiger, ABC Stout, Singha, San Miguel, Beck's, and other beers brewed in Thailand, Singapore and Indonesia (typically costing K1700 for a 375mL can or bottle), there are a couple of Myanmar brews. These include long-established, joint-venture Myanmar Beer, which is very similar to Indian or Sri Lankan beer and equal to Tiger (to the palate of at least a couple of researchers). A more watery beer is Mandalay Beer. If you order it, some waiting staff may double-check to see if you meant 'Myanmar' beer. Some bottles contain a layer of sediment on the bottom resulting from inadequate filtration. Founded in 1886, Mandalay Brewery, in Yangon, also produces the New Mandalay Export label, which is the best-tasting local beer. Some fine, newer brands brewed in Myanmar include Dagon and Skol.

Among the locals, Myanmar draught is the favourite; a glass of it will only set you back K400 or so.

LIQUORS & WINES

Very popular in Shan State is an orange brandy called *shwe leinmaw*. Much of it is distilled in the mountains between Kalaw and Taunggyi. It's a pleasant-tasting liqueur and packs quite a punch. Near Taunggyi, there's a German-run winery (p245) and in Pyin U Lwin there are several sweet strawberry-based wines.

There is also a variety of stronger liquors, including *ayeq hpyu* (white liquor), which varies in strength from brandylike to almost pure ethyl; and *taw ayeq* (jungle liquor), a cruder form of *ayeq hpyu*. Mandalay is

A monastery near Yankin Paya (p264), east of Mandalay, is famed for the 'purest' water ever found. It certainly seemed the smoothest, tastiest we've tried. For more tips on drinking water, see p376.

Fountain of youth in a bottle! (And with models on the label no less.) Spirulina Beer, made from a lake algae near Monywa, is revered for its 'anti-ageing' qualities (less so for the slightly sweet aftertaste).

TODDY

Throughout central Myanmar and the delta, *t'àn ye* (or *htan ye;* palm juice) or toddy is the farmer's choice of alcoholic beverage. *T'àn ye* is tapped from the top of a toddy palm, the same tree – and the same sap – that produces jaggery, or palm sugar. The juice is sweet and nonalcoholic in the morning, but by midafternoon ferments naturally to a weak, beerlike strength. By the next day it will have turned. The milky, viscous liquid has a nutty aroma and a slightly sour flavour that fades quickly.

Villages in some areas have their own thatched-roof toddy bars, where the locals meet and drink pots of fermented toddy. The toddy is sold in the same roughly engraved terracotta pots the juice is collected in, and drunk from coconut half-shells set on small bamboo pedestals. Some toddy bars also sell *t'àn-ayeq* (toddy liquor, also called jaggery liquor), a much stronger, distilled form of toddy sap.

---

well known for its rums and there is also, of course, the fermented palm juice known as toddy (above).

CELEBRATIONS

A part of life in Myanmar are huge feasts *(soon kway)* of giant family-style portions of food, drink and dessert. These often mean huge expenses for the family, leading many into debt, but are popular ways of celebrating special occasions such as birthdays, when a child 'takes the robe' and joins a monastery, and certainly funerals (or anniversaries of deaths). These meals are huge family-and-friends affairs, with monks invited to bless the family.

WHERE TO EAT & DRINK

Myanmar has essentially three dining/drinking scenarios: what's in Yangon (including many expat-oriented, high-end choices); what's in other oft-visited places, including Mandalay, Bagan (Pagan), Inle Lake and Ngapali Beach (many traveller-oriented menus, with Thai and pizza); and everywhere else. Food can be quite cheap (from K1200 or K1500 for a full stomach) if you stick to the roadside restaurants with their curry-filled pots or pick-and-point rice dishes. In some mid-sized towns, there are basic stands and maybe a Chinese restaurant or two – and that's it.

Because almost all accommodation options include a free breakfast of eggs – or, on occasion, *mohinga* – many travellers don't venture out in the morning.

Quick Eats

By far the bulk of eateries throughout Myanmar are basic, with concrete floors, a wide-open front for ventilation and often a menu in English. Burmese eateries are busiest (and many say freshest) at lunch. No menus are necessary at most; just go to the line of curries and point to what you want. A meal comes with a tableful of condiments, all of which are automatically refilled once you finish them. An all-you-can-eat meal is about K1500.

Another abundant option is the (usually) hole-in-the-wall Indian curry shop, which generally serves veggie dishes only and no beer.

Like most Southeast Asians, the people of Myanmar are great grab-and-go snackers. Stands at night markets, selling a host of sweets and barbecued meals and noodles, get going around 5pm to 8pm or later. Generally you can get some fried noodles, a few pieces of pork, or sticky rice wrapped in banana leaf for a few hundred kyat.

Half of Ba Than's fun little book *Myanmar's Attractions & Delights* (2003) features snippets on the backgrounds of various dishes and food-related customs. The book is available in some Yangon bookshops.

When you're served a bowl of *hìn* (curry), you're not expected to consume all the oil; just spoon out the ingredients from underneath the layer.

Restaurants

Most restaurants keep long hours daily, usually from 7am to 9pm or until the last diner wants to stumble out, their belly full of curry or beer.

Chinese restaurants are found in most towns and can be quite appealing after a week or so of Burmese food. Most have similar sprawling menus, with as many as 50 rice or noodle and chicken, pork, lamb, fish, beef or vegetable dishes. Veggie dishes start at around K800 or K1000; meat dishes about K1200 or K1500.

SWISHY EATS

More upmarket restaurants – some serving a mix of Asian foods, others specialising (the ever-present pizza, Thai etc) – can be found in Bagan, Mandalay, Inle Lake and (especially) Yangon. Also, most top-end hotels offer plusher eating places, sometimes set around the pool (but not always that much better). Such comfort is rarer to come by off the beaten track.

Drinking Venues

Outside Yangon, drinking gets done at restaurants or open-air barbecue restaurants, sometimes cutely called 'beer stations' in Burmese-English. Opening hours are therefore the same as for restaurants. All but Indian restaurants keep cold bottles of Tiger and Myanmar Beer handy (charging from K1700 in basic restaurants, upwards to K3000 or so in swankier ones). It's perfectly fine to linger for hours and down a few beers.

Men and women don't often intermingle at restaurants, so in many places you may see red-faced men lingering over a slowly amassing number of empty bottles, with full ones always kept nearby by waiting staff.

More upmarket restaurants will serve foreign wines and mixed cocktails. For information on Yangon's lively drinking scene, see p125.

Teashops

Teashops are an important social institution in Myanmar, a key meeting place for family, business associates or conspirators speaking of potentially freer times. You'll do well to hang out in a few during your trip to soak up some local atmosphere. Any time is fine. Locals like to sit and chat while sipping tea – sometimes for hours. At many, noodles, fried snacks or pastries are served. 'Morning teashops' typically open from 5am to 5pm, while evening ones open from 4pm or 5pm and stay open till 11pm or later.

The quality of tea can vary dramatically from one teashop to the next. The best use only fresh, top-quality Indian-style tea for every brewing cycle, while the worst recycle tea leaves until the flavour and colour are gone.

Getting tea with milk at a teashop can be one of the country's great challenges. Some servers know the English word 'tea' but you may end up with Chinese-style tea (and no milk) unless you're willing to point and nod at fellow sippers' tables, or learn a couple of phrases.

- *lăp'eq·ye* – tea water; it will come with a dollop of condensed milk
- *cho bawq* – less sweet version of *lăp'eq·ye*
- *kyauk padaung* – very sweet; the phrase comes from a famous sugar palm–growing region near Bagan
- *cho kya'* – strongest tea, also served with condensed milk

VEGETARIANS & VEGANS

Vegetarians will be able to find fare at most restaurants in Myanmar. Even meaty barbecues have a few skewered vegetables that can be grilled up. The easiest way to convey your needs is saying 'I can't eat meat' *(ăthà măsà-nain-bù)*. Some Indian or Nepali restaurants are vegan. In western Myanmar,

---

Streetside stands hawk barbecue and various pig parts in most towns. Some can be appetising, but be wary of cleanliness – particularly if slabs of meat have been left out all day.

Servers in teashops around Myanmar are 'tea boys', poor kids from the countryside who bring snacks and drinks to tables. They work daily in exchange for room, board and several dollars a month. One told us: 'Some day I hope to be a tea maker or a teashop manager.'

Myanmar's teashops are often excellent places to go for breakfast.

'Burmese tea' (or 'Indian tea') is tea with milk, and costs about K300 per cup. 'Chinese tea' (or green tea) is served in pots and is free at nearly all teashops and restaurants.

STREET SNACKS: WE DARE YOU

Myanmar *thǎye-za* (literally 'mouth-watering snacks') come in an eye-popping, cheap, bite-sized array that line 'night markets' all around the country. Most of the stuff isn't threatening – multicoloured sticky-rice sweets, poppy-seed cakes, dried salt fish split open and deboned, and banana or potato puddings. A bag of the sweet offerings can be taken to a restaurant for a cheap BYO dessert.

Other options are a little more of a challenge to Western stomachs. Some locals boast that 'anything that walks on the ground can be eaten'. The following list is testimony to that saying:

- items at a *wek thaa douk htoe* (barbecue stand) – these stands are a few tiny plastic stools around a boiling pot and a circular grill filled with various sliced-up pig organs (liver, intestine, lung, pancreas, heart, head, lip, ears, nose, tongue). Grab and grill and dip in the spicy sauce for about K50 or K100 per piece.

- *pa-yit kyaw* (fried cricket) – like the ol' adage goes, there's nothing like a 10-pack of fried crickets for a few hundred kyat to kick off an evening; sometimes they are sold on a skewer. One local explained how to eat them: 'take off the head, peel off the wings and gulp it.'

- *bi-laar* (beetle) – prepared like crickets, except diners 'suck the stomach out, then chew the head part'.

- *thin baun poe* (larva) – these thick, cocoonlike insect larvae, freshly taken from bamboo poles, are lightly grilled and served still wriggling. A vendor explained: 'It's best to eat raw because it's good for your stomach'. Apparently there's a big demand in China for these, so eat them while you can.

Rakhaing State's (p323) specialised dishes include many excellent local vegetable dishes, such as cauliflower.

Throughout the regional chapters, we highlight some particularly good vegetarian options or restaurants.

HABITS & CUSTOMS

At home, most families take their meals sitting on reed mats around a low, round table about 1ft in height. In restaurants, chairs and tables are more common. The entire meal is served at once, rather than in courses. In basic Burmese restaurants, each individual diner in a group typically orders a small plate of curry for himself or herself, while side dishes are shared among the whole party. This contrasts with China and Thailand, for example, where every dish is usually shared.

Traditionally, Burmese food is eaten with the fingers, much like in India, usually with the right hand (but using the left doesn't seem to be taboo as it is in India). Nowadays, it's also common for urban Myanmar people to eat with a *k'ǎyìn* (or *hkayin*; fork) and *zùn* (tablespoon). These are always available at Burmese restaurants and almost always given to foreign diners.

If you eat at a private home, it's not unusual for the hostess and children to not join you at the table.

EAT YOUR WORDS

For some general Burmese phrases and pronunciation guidelines see p380.

Useful Phrases

FINDING FOOD

Is there a ... near here?	... di·nà·hma shí·dhǎlà?	... ဒီနားမှာရှိသလား။
Chinese restaurant	tǎyouq·s'ain	တရုတ်ဆိုင်
food stall	sà·thauq·s'ain	စားသောက်ဆိုင်
restaurant	sà·daw·s'eq	စားတော်ဆက်
Shan noodle stall	shàn·k'auk·swèh·zain	ရှမ်းခေါက်ဆဲအာ\ˆဆိုင်

ORDERING

I can't eat meat.
> *ăthà măsà·nain·bù.*   အသား မစားနိုင်ဘူး။

Do you have any drinking water?
> *thauq·ye shí·dhălà?*   သောက်ရေရှိသလား။

What's the best dish to eat today?
> *di·né ba·hìn ăkaùn·zoùn·lèh?*   ဒီနေ့ ဘာဟင်းအကောင်းဆုံးလဲ။

I didn't order this.
> *da măhma·bù*   ဒါ မမှာဘူး။

Please bring (a) …
> *… yu·pè·ba*   … ယူပေးပါ။

chopsticks	*tu*	တူ
fork	*k'ăyìn*	ခက်ရင်း
spoon	*zùn*	ဇွန်း
knife	*dà*	ဓါး
glass	*p'an·gweq*	ဖန်ခွက်
plate	*băgan·byà*	ပန်းကန်ပြား
bowl	*băgan·loùn*	ပန်းကန်လုံး
cup	*k'weq*	ခွက်

Food Glossary

MEALS

breakfast	*măneq·sa*	မနက်စာ
lunch	*né·leh·za*	နေ့လည်စာ
dinner	*nyá·za*	ညစာ
snack/small meal	*móun/thăye·za*	မုန့်/သရေစာ

TYPICAL BURMESE DISHES

ămèh·hnaq	အမဲနှပ်	beef in gravy
ceq·thà·ăc'o·jeq	အ၊းကြက်သားအချို၊ချက်	sweet chicken
ceq·thà·gin	အ၊းကြက်သားကင်	grilled chicken (satay)
ceq·thà·jaw	အ၊းကြက်သားအေ၊းက်	fried chicken
hìn	ဟင်း	curry
ămèh·dhà·hìn	အမဲသားဟင်း	beef curry
ceq·thà·hìn	အ၊းကြက်သားဟင်း	chicken curry
hìn·dhì·hìn·yweq·hìn/	ဟင်းသီးဟင်းရွာ၊က်ဟင်းအ၊ယ	vegetable curry
thì·zoun·hìn	သီးစုံဟင်း	
hìn·jo	ဟင်းချို၊	soup (clear or mild)
s'an·hlaw·hìn·jo	ဆန်လှော်ဟင်းချို၊	sizzling rice soup
s'eh·hnămyò·hìn·jo	ဆယ့်၊နှစ်မျို၊းဟင်းချို၊	'12-taste' soup
móun·di	မုန့်၊တီ	*mount-ti* (Mandalay noodles and chicken/fish)
móun·hìn·gà	မုန့်၊ဟင်းခါး	*mohinga* (noodles and chicken/fish)
móun·s'i·jaw	မုန့်၊ဆီအေ၊းက်	sweet fried-rice pancakes
móun·zàn	မုန့်၊ဆန်း	sticky rice cake with jaggery (palm sugar)

DOS & DON'TS

- A fork is held in the left hand and used as a probe to push food onto the spoon; you eat from the spoon.
- Locals tend to focus on the flavours, not table talk, during meals.
- If you're asked to join someone at a restaurant, they will expect to pay for the meal.

myi shay	မြီးရှည်	Shan-style noodle soup
ngà·dhouq	ငါးသုတ်	fish salad
ngà·baùn·(douq)	ငါးပေါင်း(ထုပ်)	steamed fish (in banana leaves)
t'ămin	ထမင်း	rice
kauk·hnyìn·baùn	ကောက်ှင်းပေါင်း	steamed sticky rice
oùn·t'ămin	အုန်းထမင်း	coconut rice
t' ămìn·gyaw	ထမင်းအေါ\:ကk	fried rice
t'àn·thì·móun	ထန်သိးမုန်ဒ\ç	toddy-palm sugar cake
weq·thà·ni	ဝက်သားနီ	red pork

MEAT & SEAFOOD

ămèh·dhà	အမဲသား	beef
ceq·thà	အ\:ကက်သား	chicken
k'ăyú	ခရ	shellfish
ngà	ငါး	fish
ngăk'u	ငါးခူ	catfish
ngăshín	ငါးရှဉ်ဒ\ç	eel
pin·leh·za/ye·thaq·tăwa	ပင်လယ်စာအ\:ယရေသတ\:ဝါ	seafood
pyi·ji·ngà	ပြိ-အ\:ကီးငါး	squid
thălauq·paùn	သလောက်ပေါင်း	carp
weq·thà	ဝက်သား	pork

VEGETABLES

bù·dhì	ဘူးသီး	zucchini/gourd
ceq·thun·ni	အ\:ကက်သအ\^န်နီ	onion
gaw·bi·douq	ဂေါသ\ယဖီထုပ်	cabbage
hìn·dhì·hìn·yweq	ဟင်းသိးဟင်းရအ\^က	vegetables
hmo	မှ\ç	mushrooms
hngăpyàw·bù	ငှက်ပျောဖူး	banana flower
kălăbèh	ကုလားပဲ	chick peas
k'ăyàn·dhì	ခရမ်းသီး	eggplant/aubergine
k'ăyàn·jin·dhì	ခရမ်းချဉ်သီး	tomato
moun·la·ú·wa	မုန်လာဥဝါ	carrot
pàn·gaw·p'i	ပန်းဂေါသ\ယဖီ	cauliflower
p'ăyoun·dhì	ဖရုံသီး	pumpkin
pèh·dhì	ပဲသ\း	beans
pyaùn·bù	ပြောင်းဖူး	corn (cob)

FRUIT

àw·za·thì	အ\:သဇာသီး	custard apple ('influence fruit')
ceq·mauq·thì	အ\:ကက်မောက်သီး	rambutan ('cocksomb fruit')
cwèh·gàw·dhì	ကအ\ှ]ကောသီး	pomelo
dù·yìn·dhì	ဒူးရင်းသီး	durian
lain·c'i·dhì	လိုင်ချီးသီး	lychee
lein·maw·dhì	လိမ္မော်သီး	orange
meq·màn·dhì	မက်မန်းသီး	plum (damson)
măji·dhì	မန်ကျ\း-သီး	tamarind
na·naq·thì	နာနတ်သီး	pineapple
ngăpyàw·dhì	ငှက်ပျောသီး	banana
oùn·dhì	အုန်းသီး	coconut
pàn·dhì	ပန်းသီး	apple ('flower fruit')
shauq·thì	ရှောက်သီး	lemon
t'àw·baq·thì	ထောပတ်သီး	avocado ('butter fruit')
than·bằya·dhì	သံပရာသီး	lime
thiq·thì/a·thì	သစ်သီးအ\:ယအသီး	fruit

thăyeq·dhì	သရက်သီး	mango
thìn·bàw·dhì	သဘော?\?ာသီး	papaya ('boat-shaped fruit')

SPICES & CONDIMENTS

ceq·thun·byu	အ\:ကက်သအ\^နဖြူ	garlic
gyìn	ဂျင်း	ginger
hnàn	နှမ်း	sesame
hnìn·ye	နှင်းရည်	rose syrup
kalà t'àw·baq	ကုလားထောပတ်	ghee
kùn·ya	ကအ\^မ်းယာ	betel quid
meiq·thălin	မိတ်သလင်	galangal (white gingerlike root)
mye·bèh·(jaw)	မြေပဲ(အေ\:ကာ်)	peanuts (fried)
nan·nan·bin	နံနံပင်	coriander
ngan·pya·ye	ငံပြာရည်	fish sauce
ngăyouq·thì	ငရုတ်သီး	chilli
ngăyouq·ye	ငရုတ်ရည်	chilli sauce
oùn·nó	အုန်းနို၃\၄	coconut cream
p'a·la·zé	ဖါလာစေ၃\၄	cardamom
paun·móun·dhì	ပေါင်မုန်၃\၄	bread
pèh·ngan·pya·ye	ပဲငံပြာရည်	soy sauce
t'àw·baq	ထောပတ်	butter
tha·gu	သာဂူ	sago/tapioca
t'oùn	ထုံး	lime (for betel)
s'à	ဆား	salt
s'ănwìn	ဆနအ\^င်း	turmeric
sha·lăka·ye	ရှာလကာရည်	vinegar
thăjà	သအ\:ကား	sugar
tó·hù/tó·p'ù	တိုဟူး/တိုဖူး	tofu (beancurd)

COLD DRINKS

ăyeq	အရက်	alcohol
bí·laq·ye/p'yaw·ye	ဘိလပ်ရည်-အ\ယဖျော်ရည်	soft drink
bi·ya/tăbălìn	ဘီယာ	beer
can·ye	အ\:ကံရည်	sugarcane juice
lein·maw·ye	လိမ္မော်ရည်	orange juice
nwà·nó	နအ\^ားနို၃\၄	milk
oùn·ye	အုန်းရည်	coconut juice
s'o·da	ဆိုဒါ	soda water
t'àn·ye	ထန်းရည်	toddy
than·băya·ye	သံပရာရည်	lime juice
ye	ရေ	water
thán·ye	ရေသန်၃\၄	bottled water ('clean water')
ye·è	ရေအေး	cold water
ye·jeq·è	ရေချက်အေး	boiled cold water
ye·nwè	ရေနအ\^း	hot water

HOT DRINKS

kaw·fi	ကော်ဖီ	coffee
dhăjà·néh	သအ\:ကားနဲ၃\၄	with sugar
nó·s'ì·néh	နို၃\၄ဆီနဲ၃\၄	with condensed milk
nwà·nó·néh	နအ\^ားနို၃\၄နဲ၃\၄	with milk
lăp'eq·ye·jàn/ ye·nwè·jàn	လက်ဖက်ရည်-အ\:ကမ်း-အ\ယ ရေနအ\^း-အ\:ကမ်း	green tea (plain)
leq·p'eq·ye	လက်ဖက်ရည်	tea (Indian)

Environment

THE LAND

Extraordinary in its diversity, Myanmar contains a slice of almost every habitat but desert. From frozen alpine country to steamy jungles, blushing coral reefs to open grasslands, you name it, Myanmar's got it. A bit bigger than France and slightly smaller than Texas, Myanmar covers 421,600 sq miles. It borders (clockwise from west) Bangladesh, India, Tibet, China, Laos and Thailand, with 1199 miles of coastline facing the Bay of Bengal and Andaman Sea.

Geographically, Myanmar's south is similar to Malaysia and its north to northern India or China. The centre is an overlap of the two, producing unique 'zones' manifest in the scenery and creatures that hop around in. In the central broad flat heartland, much of the country's history was played out and lots of rice is currently grown. This area is surrounded by protective mountain and hill ranges. Most notable are: the rugged Kachin Hills, which serve as the first steps into the Himalaya to the north; Hkakabo Razi, on the Tibetan border, is Southeast Asia's highest mountain at 19,321ft; and Mt Victoria, west of Bagan (Pagan) in Chin State, rises to 10,016ft. The area southwest of Yangon (Rangoon) is a vast delta region.

Three major rivers – fed by monsoon downpours and melted Himalayan snows from Nepal and India – cut north to south through the country. The 1240-mile-long Ayeyarwady (Irrawaddy) River, one of Asia's most navigable big rivers, feeds much of the country's rice fields. It connects lower Myanmar (based around Yangon) with upper Myanmar (around Mandalay). North of Mandalay, the Chindwin River connects the hills to the north; while the Thanlwin River leads from China to the Gulf of Mottama through Myanmar's east. Also, the Mekong River passes by on the short border with Laos.

Politically, the land is divided into seven *tain* (divisions) and seven *pyi* (states) as shown on the map on p57.

WILDLIFE

Myanmar's wildlife is as rich and diverse as its habitats and the country, which sits on a transition zone between the plants and creatures of the Indian subcontinent, Southeast Asia and the Himalayan highlands, is known as a biodiversity hotspot.

Animals

When Marco Polo wrote about Myanmar in the 13th century, he described '...vast jungles teeming with elephants, unicorns and other wild beasts'. Though Myanmar's natural biodiversity has no doubt altered considerably since that time, it's difficult to say by just how much. It's estimated that

From the local perspective, the 1860-mile-long Himalaya mountain chain begins in Myanmar. This is true enough, as one end of the chain, formed when the Indian and Eurasian tectonic plates collided 140 million years ago, extends to Myanmar's northern Kachin State.

Possession of a sacred 'white (albino) elephant' supposedly ensured Burmese kings a prosperous reign. In 1885 Burma's last royal white elephant died during the reign of King Thibaw. Shortly thereafter British colonial forces took over the country.

WHERE THERE BE WERE-TIGERS

The forests of Myanmar are said to provide a home to more than just elephants and birds. In some regions locals will warn you to steer clear of the jungles at dusk for that is when the Were-Tiger emerges. As yet unconfirmed by science, the Were-Tiger, a half-tiger, half-human creature, is bad news indeed. At night the creature takes on its big cat form and hunts for human prey. As the sun rises, it reverts to human form and continues with village life. It's also said that the Were-Tiger can change its form, and stories abound of the creature appearing to hunters as a pretty woman who seduces and then eats the hunter.

OF BUMBLEBEES AND PITTAS

The closed forests of Myanmar have long intrigued scientists who believed that many critically endangered species, or even species that were new to science, might be living here. As remote parts of the country have opened up, the scientists' hopes have been proven correct. One of the more unusual creatures recently described in Myanmar for the first time is the bumblebee bat, or Kitti's Hog-nosed Bat, which, at a length of 1.25in to 1.5in and weighing in at just 0.07oz, is not just the world's smallest bat but potentially the world's smallest mammal (it vies with the Etruscan pygmy shrew for this honour). Long thought to live only in a tiny part of western Thailand, it has recently been discovered in Myanmar. This tiny mammal, with a skull less than 0.5in long, is considered to be one of the rarest creatures on Earth.

Few birds come more stunningly bright than the Gurney's pitta. Unfortunately, like so many creatures, this small bird underwent a dramatic decline during the 20th century, until only a single population in Thailand was known. However, it too has recently been discovered in Myanmar, giving hope that it may also be able to survive.

Myanmar is presently home to 300 mammals, 687 birds, 262 reptiles and 80 amphibians. Of these species, 94 are endangered, including the tiger, two species of rhinoceros and the red panda (see p84).

The most comprehensive wildlife survey available was undertaken by the Bombay Natural History Society between 1912 and 1921 and published as the *Mammal Survey of India, Burma and Ceylon*. In Myanmar *The Wild Animals of Burma*, published in 1967, is the most 'recent' work available and even this volume simply contains extracts from various surveys carried out by the British between 1912 and 1941, with a few observations dating to 1961. The US-based Wildlife Conservation Society has engaged in a number of localised surveys, primarily in the far north, over the past few years, but currently nobody is attempting a full nationwide stocktake of plants and animals.

As with Myanmar's flora, the variation in Myanmar's wildlife is closely associated with the country's geographic and climatic differences. Hence the indigenous fauna of the country's northern half is mostly of Indo-Chinese origin, while that of the south is generally Sundaic (ie typical of Malaysia, Sumatra, Borneo and Java). In the Himalayan region north of the Tropic of Cancer (just north of Lashio), the fauna is similar to that found in northeastern India. In the area extending from around Myitkyina in the north to the Bago Mountains in the central region there is overlap between geographical and vegetative zones – which means that much of Myanmar is a potential habitat for plants and animals from all three zones.

Distinctive mammals found in dwindling numbers within the more heavily forested areas of Myanmar include leopards, fishing cats, civets, Indian mongooses, crab-eating mongooses, Himalayan bears, Asiatic black bears, Malayan sun bears, gaur (Indian bison), banteng (wild cattle), serow (an Asiatic mountain goat), wild boars, sambar, barking deer, mouse deer, tapirs, pangolin, gibbons and macaques. Sea mammals include dolphins and dugongs.

Some 8000 Asiatic elephants – roughly a third of all those on the planet – are distributed throughout Myanmar. Among these, roughly 4000 are working elephants, most of which are used in logging and agriculture. The number of wild elephants is steadily dropping, primarily due to logging, which leads to habitat destruction. Ironically, domesticated elephants (which are frequently taken from wild stocks) are widely used by the logging industry to knock down the forests on which their wild cousins depend. As the logging industry continues to expand in Myanmar at a dizzying rate, the number of wild elephants is only likely to fall still further.

An excellent resource on feathered friends in Myanmar is provided by www.birdlifeindochina .org.

In 2008 the Korea International Cooperation Agency (KOICA) announced that it would be donating $1.5 million for a reforestation project in Myanmar's dry central zone. The project aims to turn some 495 acres in Mandalay Division back into forest.

INTRODUCING...THE LEAF DEER

In the 1990s the 'leaf deer', a 2ft-tall deer, amazed scientists in northern Myanmar just by existing. Locals called it 'leaf deer' because it's so small they could wrap it in a leaf. Genetically ancient, and considered the most primitive deer species, it offers insight into evolution. The New York–based Wildlife Conservation Society (WCS) was the first to bring the leaf deer to the attention of the world. The WCS also broke ground by becoming, in 1993, the first international NGO in three decades to work with the junta to set up wildlife reserves in Myanmar.

Reptiles and amphibians include four sea turtle species, along with numerous snake varieties, of which an astounding 52 are venomous, including the common cobra, king cobra (hamadryad), banded krait, Malayan pit viper, green viper and Russell's viper. This makes Myanmar home to more venomous snakes than any other country in the world.

Myanmar is rich in birdlife, with an estimated 687 resident and migrating species. Coastal and inland waterways of the delta and southern peninsula are especially important habitats for Southeast Asian waterfowl. Two of the best birding spots are Mt Victoria, which requires taking an expensive government guide (see p334), and the Moeyungyi wetlands (p152), not far from Bago and easily slotted into a trip to that town.

Alan Rabinowitz's Beyond the Last Village: A Journey of Discovery in Asia's Forbidden Wilderness *(2001) describes the rolled-up-sleeve efforts by Rabinowitz and the Wildlife Conservation Society to set up reserves and parks in Myanmar's northern areas.*

ENDANGERED SPECIES

Of some 8233 known breeding species (of which 7000 are plants) in Myanmar, 132 of these (animals, birds and plants) are endangered, including the flying squirrel, tiger and three-striped box turtle. The main threats to the country's wildlife are deforestation and poaching.

As recently as the mid-1990s, an estimated 2000 tigers (about 40% of Southeast Asia's total, some suggest) were thought to inhabit the primary forests. Recent surveys by the Wildlife Conservation Society suggest that there are now closer to just 200 of these beautiful cats, half of which are to be found in the newly created Hukuang Valley Tiger Reserve (p314).

Both the one-horned (Javan) rhinoceros and the Asiatic two-horned (Sumatran) rhinoceros are believed to survive in very small numbers near the Thai border in Kayin State. The rare red panda (or cat bear) was last sighted in northern Myanmar in the early 1960s but is thought to still live in Kachin State forests above 6500ft.

Plants

As in the rest of tropical Asia, most indigenous vegetation in Myanmar is associated with two basic types of tropical forest: monsoon forest (with a distinctive dry season of three months or more) and rainforest (where rain falls more than nine months per year). It's said there are over 1000 plant species endemic to the country.

Myanmar may contain more species of bamboo than any country outside China. One pure stand of bamboo forest in Rakhaing State extends over 4828 sq miles.

Monsoon forests are marked by deciduous tree varieties, which shed their leaves during the dry season. Rainforests, by contrast, are typically evergreen. The area stretching from Yangon to Myitkyina contains mainly monsoon forests, while peninsular Myanmar to the south of Mawlamyine (Moulmein) is predominantly a rainforest zone. There is much overlapping of the two – some forest zones support a mix of monsoon forest and rainforest vegetation.

In the mountainous Himalayan region, Myanmar's flora is characterised by subtropical broadleaf evergreen forest up to 6500ft; temperate semi-deciduous broadleaf rainforest from 6500ft to 9800ft; and, above this, evergreen coniferous, subalpine snow forest and alpine scrub.

Along the Rakhaing (Arakan) and Tanintharyi coasts, tidal forests occur in river estuaries, lagoons, tidal creeks and along low islands. Such woodlands are characterised by mangroves and other coastal trees that grow in mud and are resistant to seawater. Beach and dune forests, which grow along these same coasts above the high-tide line, consist of palms, hibiscus, casuarinas and other tree varieties that can withstand high winds and occasional storm-sent waves.

The country's most famous flora includes an incredible array of fruit trees, over 25,000 flowering species, a variety of tropical hardwoods, and bamboo. Cane and rattan are also plentiful.

Myanmar holds 75% of the world's reserves of *Tectona grandis,* better known as teak (*kyun* in Burmese). This dense, long-wearing, highly prized hardwood is one of Myanmar's most important exports, for which the biggest consumers are China, Singapore and India.

NATIONAL PARKS

By an optimistic account, about 4.5% of Myanmar's land area is made up of national parks and national forests, wildlife sanctuaries and parks, and other protected areas. However, only around 2.1% has what could be described as anything approaching adequate protection (and this tally takes in zoos and the like). The government has pledged to increase the area, much to the credit of the efforts of the New York–based Wildlife Conservation Society. The government recently expanded the Hukuang Valley Tiger Reserve (p314) in Kachin State to 8452 sq miles, making it easily the largest tiger reserve in the world. When set up in 2001, a mere 100 tigers roamed the area; hunting (for the Chinese market) has been a major cause of the decline. There has recently been talk of creating a cross-border, 4660-mile-long 'genetic corridor' for tigers stretching from Bhutan to Malaysia, with a large part of the corridor passing through Myanmar. The idea has already been presented to the UN and been endorsed by the King of Bhutan.

Most of the 'ecotourist' sights touted by the government are in remote areas and require special permission to visit. The most visited national park is Mt Popa (p188), which receives 150,000 visitors annually. The Moeyungyi Wetlands (p152), close to Bago, are a protected haven for waterfowl; they are very simple to visit yet, strangely, receive few visitors.

Myanmar supposedly contains more standing forest, with fewer inhabitants, than any other country in Indochina. That said, it's also disappearing faster than almost anywhere else in Asia, and Myanmar's forests remain the most unprotected in the region. A few years ago the government planned to expand protection to 5%, then 10%, of the country. Though these plans haven't been officially dropped, concerns are being expressed that the future of even famous reserves such as the Hukuang Valley might be in doubt, due

Environment watchdog Global Witness says 1.5 million cu yards of Burmese timber (worth $350 million) was exported to China in 2005, most of it illegally. Myanmar has one of the worst deforestation rates in the world.

Myanmar is the world's second-leading producer of heroin. Its share of the world market fell from 63% to 6% between 1998 and 2006 but, reports the UN, in 2007 poppy cultivation suddenly rose by 29%.

DAMN THE TAMANTHI DAM

The biggest construction project currently under way in Myanmar is the Tamanthi Dam, which is being built on the Chindwin River in northwestern Myanmar. When finished, the dam will be the biggest in the country and will produce in the region of 1200 megawatts of power. The problem is that the dam and its future reservoir sit very close to the Hukuang Valley Tiger Reserve and virtually on top of the Tamanthi Wildlife Sanctuary, also an area of exceptional biodiversity. To make matters even worse the residents of 35 Kuki tribal villages are to be forcibly relocated to make way for the dam waters. And what will happen to all the electricity generated? The government itself says that some surplus power will be sold to India, but the Anti-Tamanthi Dam Campaign Committee believes that India will actually receive around 80% of the power produced.

LOME

One of the first grassroots environmental organisations in Myanmar is **Lovers of Myanmar Environment** (LOME; ☎ 01-374 714). Established in 2007 by seven young friends in Yangon, the organisation has been gathering national publicity in its bid to rid the nation of the scourge of plastic bags. The group started life by purchasing cotton bags, which they then sold to retail shops, which in turn sold them to customers as an alternative to plastic bags. The money the group raised from this was then used to make small bags out of recycled newspapers and magazines, which were distributed free to shops on the condition that they stopped using plastic bags. The project, though very much in an early stage, has met with some success and at least one supermarket chain in Yangon, Orange, has taken the hint from their lead and swapped to fully recyclable bags.

LOME has also printed a number of pamphlets explaining the benefits of recycling to the people of Yangon, including that picking up rubbish in the street is actually an act of religious merit.

---

to the government selling off forests to neighbouring countries who may not have regard for environmental sustainability. Much of the land the Hukuang Valley reserve occupies is the home of various minority tribal groups and is a stomping ground of the Kachin Independence Army. Control of these lands is now with the government.

In 2007 the US-based Wildlife Conservation Society and Panthera Foundation announced that they are helping Myanmar establish the country's first postgraduate-level diploma course on wildlife management.

ENVIRONMENTAL ISSUES

Though most locals recycle non-biodegradable material as a matter of course (disposability is still only a luxury for the rich here), and despite government's plans to expand 'protected' areas, there is little in the way of an 'environmental movement' in the country as such. Essentially no environmental legislation was passed from the time of independence until after 1988, and most of the government's acts, such as recent efforts to 'green the Dry Zone' and protect wildlife, have been ineffective.

About 70% of the population are farmers, and much of Myanmar's forests have fallen to the axe – for fuel sources, or legal and illicit timber exports. One of the most troubled areas is the so-called 'Dry Zone', made up of heavily populated Mandalay, lower Sagaing and Magwe divisions. Little of the original vegetation remains in this pocket (which is about 10% of Myanmar's land, but home to one-third of the population), due to growth in the area's population and deforestation. The problem isn't new. Much of Britain's 19th-century industrialisation, as well as the train tracks made here in Myanmar, were built from Burmese timber. Following the 1988 putting down of the prodemocracy protests, the government relaxed timber and fishing laws for short-term gains, causing more long-term problems.

See www.nationalgeographic.com/adventure (search for 'Rabinowitz') for an in-depth interview with Alan Rabinowitz, the man who has done more for conservation in Myanmar than anyone else.

Deforestation by the timber industry poses the greatest threat to wildlife habitats. In areas where habitat loss isn't a problem, hunting threatens to wipe out the rarer animal species. Wildlife laws are seldom enforced and poaching remains a huge problem in Myanmar, where tigers, elephants, pythons, turtles and eagles are frequently sold in Mandalay (usually en route to China). Almost all of the protected wildlife sanctuaries (13 of 16) are smaller than 135 sq miles – not big enough to make much of a difference.

Marine life is threatened by a lack of long-range conservation goals. Myanmar's move to industrialise means that the release of pollutants into rivers and the sea is steadily increasing, and overfishing, especially in the delta regions, is also a growing problem. The country must also deal with illegal encroachment on national fisheries by Bangladeshi, Thai and Malaysian fishing boats.

Yangon

ရန်ကုန်

Once upon a time in the land of Suvannabhumi, a great king was presented with a gift of eight strands of hair. The bearers of these gifts, two merchant brothers who had journeyed from faraway lands after looking for an enlightened one, told King Okkalapa that he should guard these strands well for they were no ordinary hairs.

The king set to his task with zeal and on the summit of a 10,000-year-old sacred hill he enshrined the hairs in a temple of gold, which was enclosed in a temple of silver, then one of tin, then copper, then lead, then marble and, finally, one of plain iron-brick.

Two and a half thousand years after the death of good King Okkalapa, the small town that had sprung up around the shrine on the hill has grown into a city.

A half-finished work in progress, a picture of dishevelment, the city of Yangon, recently dethroned capital of Myanmar, might have lost its good kings of old, but it has matured into the most fascinating city in the country. From the fading yesterdays visible in the crumbling colonial architecture of downtown, to the glass office blocks pointing to a wealthier tomorrow, this is an endlessly exciting city of startling contradictions. No visitor can hope to understand anything of modern Myanmar without first knowing something of Yangon – the city King Okkalapa conceived when he enshrined a gift from faraway lands in that star-studded pinnacle of gold that dominates Yangon and Myanmar to this day. This is Yangon. This is the city of the Shwedagon Paya.

HIGHLIGHTS

- Offer a slack-jawed prayer of wonder at the **Shwedagon Paya** (p92), the pyramid of gold that is the Burma of old
- Overload your bags in the **Bogyoke Aung San Market** (p128), a bargain-shopper's paradise
- Massage the person-sized toes of the jewel-bedecked enlightened one at the **Chaukhtatgyi Paya** (p101)
- Have your palm read on the watercolour streets and search for a glittering paya and Chinese dragons on a walking tour through **downtown Yangon** (p114)
- Eavesdrop on the gossip at a street-side teashop and chow down on flavours from around the world in Yangon's excellent **restaurants** and **teashops** (p120)

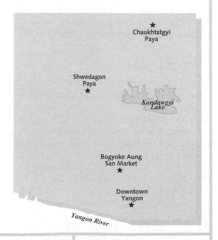

★ Chaukhtatgyi Paya

★ Shwedagon Paya

Kandawgyi Lake

★ Bogyoke Aung San Market

★ Downtown Yangon

Yangon River

■ TELEPHONE CODE: 01	■ POPULATION: 6 MILLION	■ ELEVATION: 46FT

HISTORY

Myanmar's biggest city, Yangon is comparatively young. It only became the capital in 1885 when the British completed their conquest of northern Myanmar, and Mandalay's brief period as the centre of the last Burmese kingdom ended.

Despite its short history as the seat of national government, Yangon has been in existence for a long time – although as a small town for much of that time, in comparison to places such as Bago (Pegu), Pyay (Prome) or Thaton. In 1755 King Alaungpaya conquered central Myanmar and built a new city on the site of Yangon, which at that time was known as Dagon. Yangon means 'end of strife': the king rather vainly hoped that with the conquest of central Myanmar, his struggles would be over. In 1756, with the destruction of Thanlyin (Syriam) across the river, Yangon also became an important seaport.

In 1841 the city was virtually destroyed by fire; the rebuilt town again suffered extensive damage during the Second Anglo-Burmese War in 1852. The British, the new masters, rebuilt the capital to its present plan and corrupted the city's name to Rangoon.

Yangon's early history as Dagon is tied very closely to its grand Buddhist stupa, the Shwedagon Paya. It doesn't stand in the city centre (rather about 2 miles to the north) yet it totally dominates the Yangon skyline.

In 1988 around 15% of Yangon's city centre population – all squatters – were forced to move to seven *myo thit* (new towns) northeast of the city centre. Many of the old colonial buildings once occupied by the squatters have now been refurbished for use as offices, businesses and apartments.

The city has changed dramatically following the 1989 banishment of socialism. Starting in the early 1990s, the government began sprucing up the city's appearance by cleaning the streets and painting many public buildings. Since 1992, when the procapitalist General Than Shwe took power, new cars and trucks have taken to city roads, mobile phones are commonly seen in the city centre and satellite dishes dot the horizon. To try and keep blood-red spittle off the streets, the selling of betel nuts was banned in 1995. As with many such decrees, the results have been negligible.

From the early '90s until 2006 Yangon pottered along nicely. In November 2005, quite unexpectedly, the government announced that the newly constructed city of Nay Pyi Taw in central Myanmar was to be the nation's capital. Despite the government upping sticks for the new capital, Yangon remains the commercial and diplomatic capital and by far the largest city. However, many Yangon residents say that basic public services, which had long been poor, have got even worse since the move to the new capital.

In late 2007 Yangon was the centre of huge nationwide fuel protests, which were led by the monks. The protests quickly escalated into antigovernment demonstrations, which resulted in the deaths of many protestors, and worldwide condemnation.

ORIENTATION

The city is bordered to the south and west by the Yangon River (also known as the Hlaing

---

CYCLONE NARGIS

In May 2008 the worst natural disaster in Myanmar's recent history hit the south of the country (see p52 for more). Yangon was declared a disaster area by Myanmar's government. Many of the city's pagodas and temples, shops and hotels had minor to serious damage from falling trees, lampposts and fences. However, when reconstruction work began, it was found that most of the city had escaped major structural damage. By mid-June 2008 electricity and telecommunications were back to normal, and shops and restaurants had reopened with brand-new corrugated tin roofs. Yangon returned to business as usual – aside from a lack of customers.

Bus and taxi fares rose for a few weeks after the storm but soon returned to normal. Highway buses were not affected, except those running to the Ayeyarwady (Irrawaddy) Delta (p133), where roads were badly damaged.

Recovery in Yangon happened quickly, particularly when compared with rescue efforts in the delta area, but the effects of Nargis can be seen in the lack of shady trees. For many years these beauties played a significant role in the identity of Yangon, which in the 1960s was known as 'the garden city of the East'.

River) and to the east by Pazundaung Chaung (Pazundaung Canal), which flows into the Yangon River. The city is divided into townships, and street addresses are often suffixed with these names (eg 126 52nd St, Botataung Township – or Botataung t/s). North of the centre the city opens up like the top of a funnel and spreads along a network of long, curving avenues.

At the northern end, most businesses and hotels are found along Pyay Rd, Kaba Aye Pagoda Rd or Insein Rd – long thoroughfares running south from the airport area to the city centre. Addresses in this northern area often quote the number of miles from Sule Paya – the landmark paya (stupa or pagoda) in the city's centre. For example, 'Pyay Rd, Mile 8' means the place is 8 miles north of Sule Paya on Pyay Rd.

Two of the most important townships outside the central area are Dagon – where you'll find Shwedagon Paya, People's Park and several embassies – and Bahan, site of many of the city's midrange and top-end hotels and inns. Kandawgyi Lake interrupts the flow of traffic from north to south; roads extend from it like spokes in a wheel, and it is a convenient landmark with which to orient yourself.

Central Yangon (Map p102) is a relatively simple area to find your way around, and pleasant enough to explore on foot. The main central streets are laid out in a grid pattern, with the minor north–south streets numbered in the North American fashion. Many of the major roads were renamed after independence.

INFORMATION
Bookshops
It's worth checking out the many bookstalls around Bogyoke Aung San Market or along 37th St (Map p102), which is also regarded as something of a university library for the people. Several stalls have small selections of novels and nonfiction books in English, French and German. Good-quality books are hard to come by in Myanmar and many of those on sale are patiently made photocopies, which are stitched and bound ready for your reading pleasure.

Bagan Bookshop (Map p102; ☎ 377 227; 100 37th St; ☺ 9am-5.30pm) The most complete selection of English-language books on Myanmar and Southeast Asia. The front gate pulled across the entrance doesn't necessarily mean the place is closed unless the door inside the gate is closed too.

Inwa Bookshop (Map p102; Sule Paya Rd) This bookshop next to the Nay Pyi Daw Cinema sells old issues of foreign magazines such as *Newsweek* and *Der Spiegel* as well English-language airport paperbacks and romance novels.

Cultural Centres & Libraries
At Shwedagon Paya (p92), you can visit the Library & Archives of Buddhism, located in the western arch. There is no public library system in the country.

Alliance Française (Map p93; ☎ 536 900; Pyay Rd; ☺ Tue & Fri) French culture, reading material and various French-language evening courses.

American Center (Map p98; ☎ 223 140; 14 Taw Win St; ☺ 9am-4pm Mon-Fri) Behind the Ministry of Foreign Affairs. It also has a collection of books and magazines, which can be perused.

British Council Library (Map p102; ☎ 254 658; Strand Rd; ☺ 9am-6pm Mon-Sat, 9am-1pm Sun) A very modern and plush facility connected to the British embassy. It has a small library of English-language magazines, books and videos and one of the most complete collections of English-language history books on Myanmar.

Emergency
Your home embassy (see p344) may be able to assist with advice during emergencies or serious problems. It's a good idea to register with your embassy upon arrival or, if possible, register online before you arrive, so that the embassy staff will know where to reach you in case of an emergency at home.

There isn't always an English-speaking operator on the following numbers; you may have to enlist the aid of a Burmese speaker to make these calls.

Ambulance (☎ 192)
Fire department (☎ 191)
Police (☎ 199)
Red Cross (☎ 383 680)

Internet Access
Most top-end hotels and many midrange ones offer internet access, as do a steadily growing number of small hotels and ready-made cyber cafés. Rates are by the hour – usually pro rata if under an hour – and most of the central cyber cafés (as well as many hotels) know how to outwit the censors, meaning that you can normally log onto pretty much any website. Server speeds have improved over the last couple of years but still tend to be frustratingly slow in comparison to almost any other country.

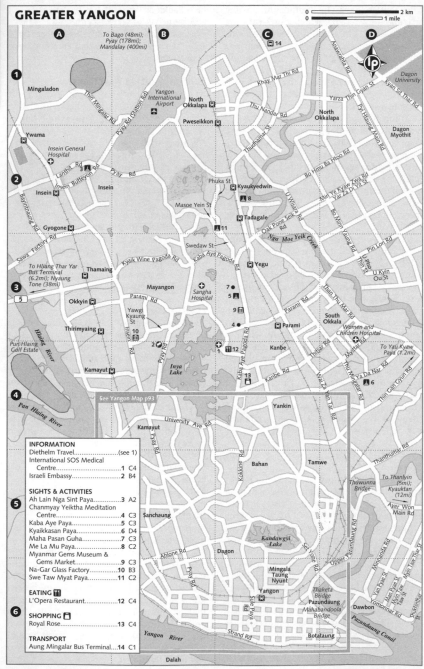

GREATER YANGON

Castle Internet & Café (Map p102; 140 Sule Paya Rd; per hr K400; ☺ 8am-11pm) Modern and plush with café attached.

Cyber World (Map p98; 4th fl, La Pyat Wun Plaza, 37 Ah Lan Paya Pagoda Rd; per hr K800; ☺ 9am-9pm) Faster than most.

Cyber World I (Map p102; ground fl, Nay Pyi Daw Cinema, 246-248 Sule Paya Rd; per hr K400; ☺ 9am-9pm) Busy and frequented by foreigners because of its central location, but with slow connections.

Net Station 1 (Map p98; 121 51st St; per hr K1000; ☺ 9am-10pm) Close to several midrange hotels and with very good connections.

SMG Skyline Internet (Map p102; Bo Aung Kyaw St; per hr K400; ☺ 10am-11pm) Large central cyber café. Some claim it has the fastest connections in the city.

Laundry

Almost all of Yangon's budget and midrange guesthouses and hotels offer inexpensive laundry services including ironing (about K1000 per load). Rates at the top-end hotels are not cheap. Another option is **Ava Laundry** (Map p98; ☎ 392 416; 305 Mahabandoola Rd, btwn 41st & 42nd Sts; ☺ 8am-8pm) though it's no quicker than the guesthouses and is expensive.

Medical Services

There are several private and public hospitals in Yangon but the fees, service and quality may vary. There are also some useful pharmacies in town.

AA Pharmacy (Map p102; ☎ 253 231; 142-146 Sule Paya Rd; ☺ 24hr) Just north of Sule Paya.

City Mart Supermarket (Map p98; cnr Anawrahta Rd & 47th St) Well-stocked place (tampons available), which includes a pharmacy.

Global Network Co (Map p102; 155-161 Sule Paya Rd; ☺ 24hr) Pharmacy just north of Sule Paya and opposite the AA Pharmacy.

International SOS Clinic (Map p90; 24hr alarm centre ☎ 667 879; 37 Kaba Aye Pagoda Rd; ☺ 24hr) On the ground floor of the Renaissance Inya Lake Hotel, this is your best bet in Yangon if you want medical attention.

Pacific Medical Centre & Dental Surgery (Map p93; ☎ 548 022; 81 Kaba Aye Pagoda Rd)

Money

You can pay for your taxi from the airport to the city in US dollars and there's no reason to buy kyat in the terminal. Most hotels and guesthouses sell kyat for rates slightly lower than the usual street rate. One hotel in particular known to offer competitive rates is the **Central Hotel** (Map p102; 335-357 Bogyoke Aung San Rd)

YANGON STREET NAMES

The English terms 'street' and 'road' are often used interchangeably in Yangon for the single Burmese word *làn*. Hence, some local maps may read Shwegondine Rd, while others will say Shwe Gone Daing Rd or Shwe Gone Daing St; in Burmese, it's simply Shwe Gone Daing Làn. This chapter uses the most common English version that travellers encounter.

Just to make matters a little more confusing, different maps present the actual names of streets differently; eg Shwegondine Rd is Shwegondaing Rd on some local maps. Similarly, U Wi Za Ra Rd may appear as U Wizara Rd, Dhama Zedi Rd as Dhammazedi Rd, and Sule Paya Rd as Sule Pagoda Rd, and there are many other differences.

---

near Bogyoke Aung San Market. The market itself has a fair number of moneychangers who generally offer the highest rates; odds are you'll be approached if you wander down the centre aisle. Before you go, ask around to establish the going rate. You should not pay any commission or tip for their services.

A few of the top-end hotels including the **Sedona Hotel** (Map p93; 1 Kaba Aye Pagoda Rd) accept credit cards (Visa is the favourite) and a few will give guests cash advances on their cards. Any transaction with plastic involves commissions from 3% to 12%. Travellers cheques are even less likely to be recognised as legal tender (see p347). Again, only a few hotels accept them, and they charge a hefty commission.

Post

DHL (Map p98; ☎ 664 434; Park Royal Hotel, 33 Ah Lan Paya Pagoda Rd; ☺ 8am-6pm Mon-Fri)

Main post office (Map p102; Strand Rd; ☺ 7.30am-6pm Mon-Fri) A short stroll east of the Strand Hotel. Stamps are for sale on the ground floor but go to the 2nd floor to send mail.

Tourist Information

Myanmar Travels & Tours (MTT; Map p102; ☎ 382 243; Sule Paya Rd; ☺ 8.30am-5pm) is a government-run travel agency on the corner of Mahabandoola Rd and across the street from Sule Paya. It seems modern when compared with MTT's other offices, but is so unhelpful it's not worth the effort of visiting – use a private travel agency instead.

Travel Agencies

Most visitors to Myanmar only use private domestic travel agencies to book a tour, hire a car or book a domestic flight (air-ticket prices are usually cheaper through a private travel agency). However, of the more than 100 enterprises in Yangon calling themselves travel agencies, only a handful can be considered full-service, experienced tour agencies. Yangon is the best place in the country in which to book tours to difficult and remote regions.

Among the more reliable agencies:

Columbus Travels & Tours (Map p98; ☎ 229 245; www.travelmyanmar.com; 586 Strand Rd) It's on the corner of Strand Rd and 7th St. There's also a branch office on the 3rd floor of the Sakura Tower, next to Exotissimo Travel.

Diethelm Travel (Map p90; ☎ 662 898; leisure@ diethelm.com.mm; 37 Kaba Aye Pagoda Rd)

Exotissimo Travel (Map p102; ☎ 255 266; www.exoti ssimo.com; 3rd fl, Sakura Tower, 339 Bogyoke Aung San Rd)

Good News Travel (Map p102; ☎ 09-5137 5050; www.myanmargoodnewstravel.com; 4th fl, FMI Centre, 380 Bogyoke Aung San Rd) The owner, William Myat-wunna, is extremely personable and knowledgeable. Highly recommended.

Gulliver Tours & Travel (Map p93; ☎ 526 100; gulliver @mptmail.net.mm; 51A Inya Myaing Rd)

Myanmar Himalaya Trekking (Map p93; ☎ 227 978; www.myanmar-explore.com; Room 215, Summit Parkview hotel, 350 Ahlone Rd)

New Horizons Travels & Tours (Map p93; ☎ 540 902; tun@mptmail.net.mm; 64 B2R Shwe Gon Plaza)

Woodland Travels (Map p98; ☎ 202 101; www.wood landtravels.com; 7 FJV Commercial Centre, 422-426 Strand Rd)

DANGERS & ANNOYANCES

Yangon is an incredibly safe city: you are far less likely to get robbed here than almost any other big city in Southeast Asia. Having said that, rich foreigners and badly lit side streets at night don't mix and you should show some caution at such times. A far bigger danger is stumbling on the uneven paving slabs in central Yangon or even disappearing completely into a sewage-filled pot hole. Keep your eyes peeled for such obstacles and carry a torch at night.

SIGHTS
Shwedagon Paya
ရွှေတိဂုံဘုရား

Heart stopping at any time, the **Shwedagon Paya** (Map p93 & p95; admission $5; 5am-10pm) glitters bright gold in the heat of the day. Then, as the sun casts its last rays it turns a crimson gold and orange, magic floats in the heat and the mighty diamond surmounting the summit casts a beam of light that reflects sheet white, bloody red and jealous green to the far corners of the temple platform. It can be quiet and contemplative or colourful and raucous, and for the people of

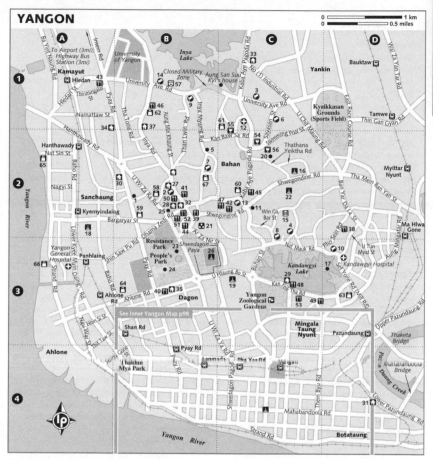

Myanmar it is the most sacred of all Buddhist sites, one that all Myanmar Buddhists hope to visit at least once in their lifetime.

Visible from almost anywhere in the city, Shwedagon is located to the north of central Yangon, between People's Park and Kandawgyi.

The admission fee, which goes to the government, includes a lift ride to the raised platform of the stupa. Of course, like most local visitors, you may walk up one of the long graceful entrances, by far the more exciting method of entry. There's also a $5 camera fee, not always enforced. The north gate is especially photogenic at night.

For more on the history of the paya, see p105.

DESIGN

There are four covered walkways up Singuttara Hill to the platform on which Shwedagon stands. The southern entrance, from Shwedagon Pagoda Rd, is the one that can most properly be called the main entrance. Here, and at the northern entrance, there are lifts available, should you not feel fit enough for the stroll up the stairs. The western entrance features a series of escalators in place of stairs, and is the only entrance without vendors. The eastern stairway has the most traditional ambience, passing adjacent *kyaung* (monasteries) and vendors selling monastic requisites.

Two 30ft-high *chinthe* (legendary half-lion, half-dragon guardian figures) loom over the

YANGON

YANGON IN...

Two Days

Start the morning with a traditional Myanmar breakfast of fish soup and tea. No matter how early you begin the city will already be up and buzzing. Before the sun gets too high in the sky and the heat becomes oppressive take a walk around the city centre using the suggested **walking tour** (p114). Allow yourself plenty of time to play in the markets, dawdle in the temples and fawn over the rickety architecture. The **Sule Paya** (p100), the geographic heart of the city, will be the highlight of the morning. Lunch in one of the Indian eateries nearby before doing some cruising around temples north of the city centre, including the **Chaukhtatgyi Paya** (p101) and nearby **Ngahtatgyi Paya** (p101). Then, if time allows, take a stroll around **Kandawgyi Lake** (p104), and maybe stop in for a drink at one of the lakeside restaurants or hotels.

The second day can begin much like the first at a street-side teashop. Morning is the best time for a **ferry** (p131) back and forth to Dalah, on the other side of the Yangon River, to provide a little taste of delta life. Back on dry ground, the **Botataung Paya** (p100) near the jetty is the next logical stop. Take a walk along Strand Rd for the British colonial-era architecture or head directly to lunch at one of the restaurants around **Bogyoke Aung San Market** (p128). Then move on to the main event: the **Shwedagon Paya** (opposite). The highlight of any tour in Yangon, the paya deserves time, attention and the perfect light of a Yangon sunset. Dine at one of the excellent restaurants – Bamar, Thai, Korean, Japanese, French or Italian – in the immediate vicinity.

Four Days

The sensible should try to give themselves more time to devote to the city and if you're one of the lucky blighters able to do this then Yangon has some treats in store! Spend the first two days following the Yangon in Two Days suggestions and then, after another teashop breakfast on day three, head to the **National Museum** (p104) to swoon over treasures that would make Aladdin jealous. If that's not enough culture then follow up with the dazzling **Myanmar Gems Museum** (p113), but don't purchase any of the stones on sale on the lower floors – bad karma. In the afternoon hit up Chinatown and the incense-clouded temple **Kheng Hock Keong** (p103), and finish with a slap-up dinner in one of the many cheap Chinese restaurants in this quarter (p122). By day four you'll probably feel the need to stretch your wings a little so choose from one of three easy day trips out of the city. The first involves floating temples and off-beat adventure around **Thanlyin** and **Kyauktan** (p133). The second involves more water with a slow ferry ride and temple tour of **Twante** (p135). The third is for those for whom one buddha is never enough: temple-packed **Bago** (Pegu; p147) is where you're off to today.

---

southern entrance. You must remove your shoes and socks as soon as you mount the first step. Like the other entrances, the southern steps are lined with a series of shops, where devotees buy flowers – both real and beautifully made paper ones – for offerings. Buddha images, ceremonial paper umbrellas, books, golden thrones, incense sticks, ivory combs and antiques are also on sale. However hot it may be outside, you'll find the walkway cool, shady and calm. It's this quiet, subdued atmosphere on the entrance steps that makes the impact so great as you arrive at the platform.

You emerge from semi-gloom into a deafening explosion of technicoloured glitter – for Shwedagon is not just one huge, glowing *zedi* (stupa). Around the mighty stupa cluster an incredible assortment of smaller *zedi*, stat-

ues, temples, shrines, images and *tazaung* (small pavilions). Somehow, the bright gold of the main stupa makes everything else seem brighter and larger than life.

Stupas – indeed, all Buddhist structures – should be walked around clockwise, so turn left at the top of the steps and, like the crowds of locals, start strolling. During the heat of the day you'll probably have to confine yourself to the mat pathway laid around the platform – unless your bare feet can take the heat of the uncovered marble paving.

THE STUPA & ITS TREASURES

The hill on which the stupa stands is 190ft above sea level and the platform covers over 12 acres. Prior to the British takeover of southern Myanmar there had been defensive

SHWEDAGON PAYA PLAN

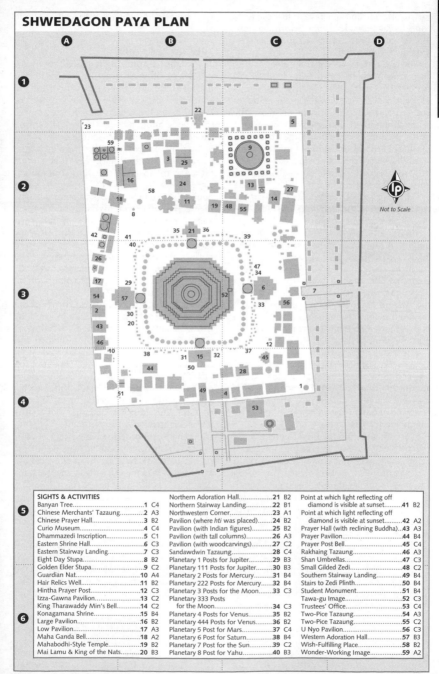

Not to Scale

YANGON

earthworks around the paya, but these were considerably extended by the British. The emplacements for their cannons can still be seen outside the outer wall.

The main stupa, which is completely solid, rises from its platform in a fairly standard pattern. First there is the plinth, which stands 21ft above the clutter of the main platform and immediately sets Shwedagon above the lesser structures. Smaller stupas sit on this raised platform level – four large ones mark the four cardinal directions, four medium-sized ones mark the four corners of the basically square platform and 60 small ones run around the perimeter.

From this base, the *zedi* rises first in three terraces, then in the 'octagonal' terraces and then in five circular bands – together these elements add another 98ft to the stupa's height. A standard architectural problem associated with stupas is how to change from the square base to the circular upper elements. Here, as in many other *zedi* in Myanmar, that transition is achieved with the help of the octagonal sections, which make a transition from the horizontal design of these lower elements to the smooth vertical flow of the bell.

The shoulder of the bell is decorated with 16 'flowers'. The bell is topped by the 'inverted bowl', another traditional element of stupa architecture, and above this stand the mouldings and then the 'lotus petals'. These consist of a band of down-turned petals, followed by a band of up-turned petals.

The banana bud is the final element of the *zedi* before the *hti* tops it. Like the lotus petals below, the banana bud is actually covered with no fewer than 13,153 plates of gold, measuring 1 sq ft each – unlike the lower elements, which are merely covered with gold leaf. The seven-tiered *hti* is made of iron and again plated with gold. Even without the various hanging bells, it weighs well over a ton.

The *hti* tiers descend in size from bottom to top, and from the uppermost tier projects the shaft, which is hung with gold bells, silver bells and various items of jewellery. The top-most vane, with its flag, turns with the wind. It is gold- and silver-plated and studded with 1100 diamonds totalling 278 carats – not to mention 1383 other stones. Finally, at the very top of the vane rests the diamond orb – a hollow golden sphere studded with 4351 diamonds, weighing 1800 carats in total. The very top of the orb is tipped with a single 76-carat diamond.

AROUND THE STUPA

The mighty central *zedi,* regilded every year, is only one of many structures on the hilltop platform. Reaching the platform from the southern stairway (**49**), you encounter the first shrine (**15**), which is to Konagamana, the second buddha. Almost beside the shrine stand the planetary posts for Mercury (**31** and **32**). If you were born on a Wednesday morning (as was the Buddha), then this is your post, and the tusked elephant is your animal sign. Continuing around the plinth, you pass a double-bodied lion with a man's face, a laughing necromancer with his hands on his head, and an earth goddess. At the southwestern corner of the plinth, you reach the planetary post for Saturn (**38**). Come here if you were born on a Saturday; your animal sign is the *naga* (serpent being). The pavilion (**44**) directly opposite has 28 images to represent the 28 previous buddhas.

Back towards the southwest corner of the platform is a monument (**51**) with inscriptions in four languages, recounting a 1920 student revolt against British rule. Continuing around the platform, you come to a glass case with two figures of *nat* (**10**; spirits) – one is of the guardian *nat* of Shwedagon Paya. Close to these figures is a prayer hall (**46**), quite bare inside but with fine woodcarving on the terraced roof. It is known as the Rakhaing Tazaung, as it was donated by brokers from the Rakhaing (Arakan) coast bordering Bangladesh. A 26ft-long reclining buddha can be seen in the next prayer hall (**43**). Next to this is the Chinese Merchants' Tazaung (**2**), with a variety of buddha figures in different poses.

On the plinth opposite this prayer hall are figures of Mai Lamu and the king of the *nat* (**20**), the parents of King Okkalapa who, according to the legend, originally enshrined the Buddha hairs here. The figures stand on top of each other. The western adoration hall (**57**) was built in 1841 but was destroyed in the fire that swept the *zedi* platform in 1931. The planetary posts for the Thursday-born (**29** and **30**) stand to the right and left of this pavilion: your planet is Jupiter and your animal sign is the rat. A figure of King Okkalapa can be seen further to the left, on the *zedi* plinth.

Directly opposite the west adoration hall is the Two Pice Tazaung (**54**) located at the head of the western stairway. The low pavilion (**17**) next to the entrance was built by manufacturers of monastery requirements – in contrast to the rather Chinese-looking roof. Next along is a pavilion (**26**), with tall columns and the *pyatthat* (wooden, multiroofed pavilion) rising from the upper roof. Almost opposite this *tazaung,* at the northwestern corner of the main *zedi,* is the planetary post (**40**) for those born on Wednesday afternoon, whose animal symbol is the tuskless elephant, and whose planet is Yahu (Rahu, a mythical planet in Hindu astrology that allegedly causes eclipses).

As the sun goes down you can see red, green and yellow light reflecting off a diamond halfway up the paya from two exact spots (**11** and **12**) on the western edge of the complex. Look for a couple of small markers on the ground, though you'll probably need someone to point them out to you.

A small stupa with a golden spire (**8**) has eight niches around its base, each with a buddha image. Between the niches are figures of animals and birds – they represent the eight directions of the compass and the associated sign, planet and day of the week. To get over the small complication of having an Eight Day Stupa and a seven day week, Wednesday is divided into Wednesday morning and Wednesday afternoon (see p353).

Wishes & Floating Bells

Close to this small Eight Day Stupa stands the bell pavilion (**18**) housing the 23-ton Maha Ganda Bell. Cast between 1775 and 1779, it was carted off by the British after the First Anglo-Burmese War in 1825. The British dropped it into the Yangon River while trying to get it to the port for shipping to England. After repeatedly trying to raise it from the river bottom, they gave up and told the people of Myanmar they could have the bell back if they could get it out of the river. The locals placed logs and bamboo beneath the bell until it eventually floated to the surface.

Venturing back into the open area of the platform, you come to the star-shaped 'wish-fulfilling place' (**58**), where there will often be devotees, kneeling down and looking towards the great stupa, praying that their wishes come true.

The large pavilion (**16**) across from the bell pavilion houses a 30ft-high buddha image

and is often used for public meetings. Behind this pavilion stands a small shrine (**59**) with a highly revered 'wonder-working' buddha image covered in gold leaf. From the northwestern corner of the platform (**23**) you can look out over some of the British fortifications and the country to the north of the hill. There are also two banyan trees growing here, one of them grown from a cutting from the actual tree at Bodhgaya in India, under which the Buddha sat and was enlightened.

Among the cluster of buildings on this side of the platform is the Chinese prayer hall (**3**), with good woodcarvings and Chinese dragon figures on the sides of the *zedi* in front of it. The adjacent pavilion (**25**) has life-size figures of Indians guarding the side and front entrance doors. No one quite understands their relevance or that of the very British lions that guard the next pavilion.

In 1824 a force of Myanmar 'Invulnerables' fought their way up the northern stairs to the entrance (**22**) of the platform before being repulsed by the better-armed British forces occupying the paya. The crocodile-like stair banister dates from 1460. The Martyrs' Mausoleum of Bogyoke Aung San and his compatriots stands on the western side of the hill reached from this stairway.

Walking back towards the stupa, you pass the pavilion (**24**) built on the site where the great *zedi's hti,* provided by King Mindon Min, was placed before being raised to the *zedi* summit. The Hair Relics Well (**11**) was located at the position of the Sandawdwin Tazaung (**28**; on the opposite side of the paya) and is said to reach right down to the level of the Ayeyarwady (Irrawaddy) River and to be fed from it; the Buddha hairs were washed in this well before being enshrined in the *zedi.* In the northern adoration hall (**21**), the main image is of Gautama, the historical Buddha. On either side of the hall stand planetary posts for Friday (**35** and **36**), domain of the planet Venus, and the guinea pig or mole.

Modelled after the Mahabodhi temple in Bodhgaya, India, the temple (**19**) a few steps away is distinctly different from the general style of buildings on the platform. A small gilded *zedi* (**48**) stands next to this temple, and next again is another 'two-pice' *tazaung* (**55**) enshrining a 200-year-old buddha image. An opening behind this image is, according to legend, the entrance to a passage that leads to the chamber housing the Buddha

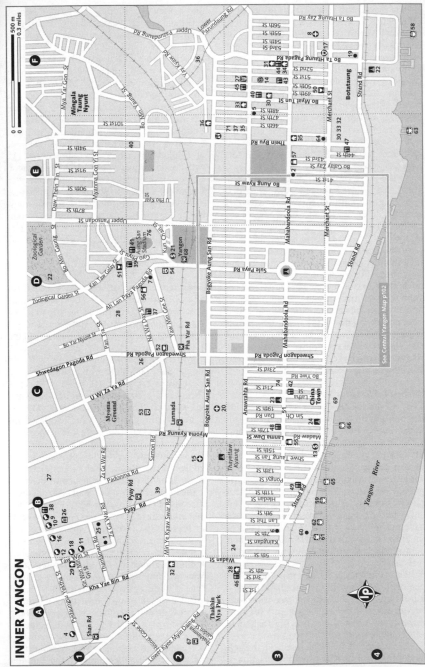

hair relics. Although seen from the 'two-pice' *tazaung,* the buddha image is actually in the adjacent stupa.

All-Seeing Goats

Izza-Gawna (which means 'goat-bullock') was a legendary monk whose powers enabled him to replace his lost eyes with one from a goat and one from a bullock. In his pavilion (**13**), the figure off to the left of the main buddha image has eyes of unequal size as a reminder of this unique feat. The golden Elder Stupa (**9**; also known as the Naungdawgyi Stupa) is built on the spot where the hair relics were first placed before being enshrined in the great *zedi.* A straight line drawn from the centre of this stupa to the centre of Shwedagon would pass through the small stupa reputed to be the entrance to the passage that leads to the relic chamber. Women are not allowed to ascend to the platform around the Elder Stupa.

Back in the corner of the platform is the Dhammazedi inscription (**5**), which dates from 1485 and was originally installed on the eastern stairway. It tells in three languages – Pali, Mon and Burmese – the story of Shwedagon.

Cast in 1841, King Tharawaddy Min's bell is housed in an elegant pavilion (**14**). The Maha Titthadaganda (three-toned bell) weighs 42 tons. Note the ceiling made of lacquer inlaid with glass. If you look closely, you can also discern red-billed green parrots nearly hidden in the scrolling among the *devas* (celestial beings). The adjacent small pavilion (**27**) has some good panels of woodcarvings. Back on the main platform the planetary post (**39**) for those born on Sunday (the sun) stands at the northeastern corner of the stupa platform. The bird-like creature beneath the post is the Garuda of Hindu-Buddhist mythology, called *galoun* in Burmese. Further around you will see golden Shan umbrellas (**47**) among the plinth shrines; there is also one over the Friday planetary post near the northern pavilion.

Facing the eastern stairway, the eastern shrine hall (**6**) is said to be the most beautiful on the platform. It was renovated in 1869, but destroyed by the 1931 fire and subsequently rebuilt. The main image is that of Kakusandha, the first buddha. The eastern stairway (**7**) is the longest and is lined with shops selling everyday articles as well as religious goods and antiques. On either side of the hall, the people who were born on Monday worship at the planetary posts (**33** and **34**) ruled over by the moon and the tiger.

The graceful U Nyo pavilion (**56**), beside the eastern entrance, has a series of interesting woodcarved panels illustrating events in

YANGON

the life of Gautama Buddha. The prayer post (**12**) close to the southeastern corner of the *zedi* is topped by a mythological *hintha* bird. An interesting bell (**45**) hangs near this prayer post. Opposite these on the *zedi* plinth is the planetary post for Tuesday (**37**), presided over by the lion and the planet Mars.

In the corner of the platform stands another sacred banyan tree (**1**), also said to be grown from a branch of the original tree under which Gautama Buddha gained enlightenment in India. There is a good view from this corner of the platform over Yangon and across the Yangon River towards Thanlyin. On a clear day, you can see the Kyaik-khauk Paya, just beyond Thanlyin. The paya trustees have their office (**53**) on this side of the platform, and there's also a small curio museum (**4**). In front of the museum is a pavilion (**28**) with very fine woodcarvings. There is also a revolving *hti* and a telescope, possibly for looking at the real *hti* on top of the *zedi*.

Beside the southern shrine (**15**), the first stop on this circular tour, stairs (**50**) lead up onto the *zedi* plinth. With permission from the paya trustees, men only are allowed to climb up to the plinth terrace. Men come up here to meditate; the terrace is about 20ft wide – a circular walkway between the great *zedi* and its 68 surrounding *zedi*. Behind the eastern shrine is a buddha image (**52**) known as the Tawa-gu, which is reputed to work miracles.

Sule Paya

ဆူးလေဘုရား

It's not every city whose primary traffic circle is occupied by a 2000-year-old golden temple. Surrounded by government buildings and commercial shops, the tall *zedi* at **Sule Paya** (Map p102; cnr Sule Paya & Mahabandoola Rds; admission $2) is another example of the strange incongruity of the Yangon cityscape. Yet, it's this mix of modern Asian business life melding with ancient Bamar tradition that is the highlight of the Sule Paya. Early evening, just after the sun has gone down, is the most atmospheric time to both visit the temple and make a turn of the streets surrounding it when all the workers rush off home for the night. Many take the time to pause by the Sule Paya to pray and meditate on the day's events.

The central stupa's name, Kyaik Athok, translates in the Mon language as 'the stupa where a Sacred Hair Relic is enshrined'. As with many other ancient Myanmar shrines, it

has been rebuilt and repaired many times over the centuries, so no-one really knows exactly when it was built.

The golden *zedi* is unusual in that its octagonal shape continues right up to the bell and inverted bowl. It stands 151ft high and is surrounded by small shops and all the familiar nonreligious activities that seem to be a part of every *zedi* in Myanmar. Besides its significance as a landmark and meeting place, maybe its most mundane function is as a milestone from which all addresses to the north are measured.

Botataung Paya

ဗိုလ်တထောင်ဘုရား

One of Yangon's 'big three' payas, and said to contain hair relics of the Buddha, the **Botataung Paya** (Map p98; Strand Rd; admission $2) was named after the 1000 military leaders who escorted relics of the Buddha from India to Myanmar over 2000 years ago (*Bo* means leader, usually in a military sense, and *tataung* means 1000). For one six-month period this paya is said to have harboured all eight strands of the Buddha's hair before they were distributed elsewhere. It's not as breathtaking as the Shwedagon, or as striking for being so out-of-place like Sule Paya, but Botataung's spacious riverfront location and lack of crowds give it a more down-to-earth spiritual feeling than the other two.

Its proximity to fresh air and the Yangon wharves were less fortuitous when a bomb from an Allied air raid in November 1943 scored a direct hit on the unfortunate paya. After the war the Botataung was rebuilt in a very similar style to its predecessor, but with one important and unusual difference: unlike most *zedi*, which are solid, the Botataung is hollow, and you can walk through it. There's a sort of mirrored maze inside the stupa, with glass showcases containing many of the ancient relics and artefacts, including small silver-and-gold buddha images, which were sealed inside the earlier stupa. Reconstruction also revealed a small gold cylinder holding two small body relics and a strand of hair, said to be that of the Buddha's, which is reputedly still in the stupa. Above this interesting interior, the golden stupa spire rises to 131ft.

To the western side of the stupa is a hall containing a large gilded bronze buddha, cast during the reign of King Mindon Min. At the time of the British annexation, it was kept in King Thibaw Min's glass palace, but after King Thibaw was exiled to India, the British shipped the image to London. In 1951 the image was returned to Myanmar and placed in the Botataung Paya. Also on the grounds is a *nat* pavilion containing images of Thurathadi (the Hindu deity Saraswati, goddess of learning and music) and Thagyamin (Indra, king of the *nat*) flanking the thoroughly Myanmar *nat* Bobogyi.

There's also a large pond full of hundreds of terrapins. Most are fairly small but every now and again a truly monstrous one sticks its head out of the water.

A short walk from Botataung Paya at Botataung jetty, you can watch ferryboats and oared water taxis cross the Yangon River.

Chaukhtatgyi Paya
ခြောက်ထပ်ကြီးဘုရား

Fifty years ago there was a giant standing buddha poking his head above the temples and monasteries here, but one day he got tired and collapsed into a heap on the floor, whereupon he was replaced with the monster-sized lazy reclining buddha you see today. One of Myanmar's more beautiful reclining buddhas, the placid face of the **Chaukhtatgyi Buddha** (Map p93; Shwegondine Rd; admission free; 24hr) is topped by a crown encrusted in diamonds and other precious stones. Housed in a large metal-roofed shed, only a short distance northeast of the Shwedagon Paya, this huge figure is surprisingly little known and hardly publicised at all. Close to the buddha's feet is the small shrine to Ma Thay, a holy man who has the power to stop rain and grant sailors a safe journey. Fortune-tellers on the surrounding platform offer astrological and palm readings.

Attached to the temple complex is the Shweminwon Sasana Yeiktha Meditation Centre, where large numbers of locals gather to meditate. It's not hard to find someone to show you around the adjoining monasteries, which until the protests of September 2007 housed 500 monks but now provide a home for only 300 – many of them returned to a civilian life where it's easier to hide from the authorities.

Kaba Aye Paya
ကမ္ဘာအေးဘုရား

When the designers were asked to come up with a suitable blueprint for the 'world peace'

zedi, which was built for the 1954–56 Sixth Buddhist Synod, they obviously decided that Mickey Mouse and friends were the epitome of world peace, because this paya has an uncouth, Disneyesque feel and look to it. The 112ft-high **paya** (Map p90; Kaba Aye Pagoda Rd; admission free; 24hr) also measures 112ft around its base. It stands about 5 miles north of the city centre, a little beyond the Renaissance Inya Lake Hotel. The interior of the monument is hollow and contains some nice Buddhist sculptures, including a *lei-myet-hna* (four-sided Buddha sculpture).

Maha Pasana Guha
မဟာပါသာဏလိုဏ်ဂူ

The 'great cave' (Map p90) is a totally artificial one, built close to the Kaba Aye Paya. It was here that the Sixth Buddhist Synod was held in 1954–56 to coincide with the 2500th anniversary of the Buddha's enlightenment. It looks even tackier than the next-door Kaba Aye Paya. This enormous cave (measuring 456ft by 371ft; it can accommodate up to 10,000 people) took only 14 months to build. It helped that they had 63,000 labourers. The cave is still used to hold grand religious ceremonies.

Maha Wizaya (Vijaya) Paya
မဟာဝိဇယ

Linked by a pedestrian bridge to the Shwedagon complex's southern gate, the **Maha Wizaya** (Map p93; U Htaung Bo St; admission K200; 24hr) is unavoidably dull in comparison. It's a rather plain but well-proportioned *zedi* built in 1980 to commemorate the unification of Theravada Buddhism in Myanmar. The king of Nepal contributed sacred relics for the *zedi's* relic chamber and Myanmar military strongman Ne Win had it topped with an 11-level *hti* – two more levels than the *hti* at Shwedagon.

Foreign media and some locals often refer to the monument as 'Ne Win's paya', due to Ne Win's involvement in the project (a common practice among top military figures). However, many Myanmar citizens resent this phrase, pointing out that, as the *zedi* was built by donations from the people, it should rightfully be called the 'people's paya'.

Other Paya, Temples & Shrines
South of the Chaukhtatgyi Paya is a gorgeous seated buddha image at the **Ngahtatgyi Paya** (Map p93; Shwegondine Rd; admission $2; 24hr).

YANGON

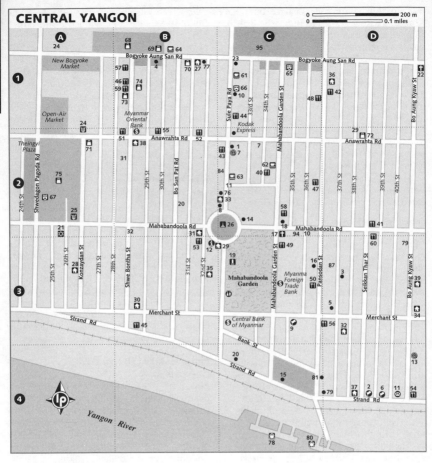

CENTRAL YANGON

0 — 200 m
0 — 0.1 miles

Sitting in calm gold and white repose with a healthy splash of precious stones to boot, it's one of the most impressive sitting buddhas in southern Myanmar. In fact it's worth going to see for its carved wooden backdrop alone. In Kyemyindaing (also called Kyimyindine and Kemmedine), in the west of the city, there's another huge seated buddha over in the **Kohtatgyi Paya** (Map p93; Bargaryar St); it stands (or sits) 66ft high. There are many monasteries in the vicinity. Kyemyindaing also has a busy night market.

Near the airport, the **Me La Mu Paya** (Map p90; Wai Za Yan Tar Rd; admission free; ☯ 24hr) has a series of images of the Buddha in his previous incarnations, and a reclining buddha image. The paya is named after the mother of King

Okkalapa, the founder of the city of Dagon. In Insein, west of the airport, you'll find the five-storey **Ah Lain Nga Sint Paya** (Map p90; cnr Lanthit & Insein Butteyon Rds; admission free; ☯ 24hr).

Near the International Buddhist University, between Kaba Aye Pagoda Rd and Thudhamar St, is wedding-cake shaped **Swe Taw Myat Paya** (Buddha Tooth Relic Pagoda; Map p90; Swedaw St; admission free; ☯ 24hr). Not that you'd ever know it, nor should it affect your appreciation of the paya architecturally, but it contains not just another tooth relic from the Buddha, but a replica of a relic brought from China in 1997 by pilgrims.

The **Yau Kyaw Paya** (off Map p90) is a 30-minute drive northeast of the city centre, past the Kyaikkasan Paya (Map p90). It's an interesting complex of buildings with tableaux depicting Buddhist legends, pet monkeys, deer and peacocks, and an interesting museum crammed full of Myanmar antiques. The paya is beside the Pazundaung Chaung in a rural setting.

At the time of writing, construction was almost complete on a **replica of the Thatbyinnyu Paya**, in the North Okkalapa section of Yangon; the Thatbyinnyu is the tallest structure in Bagan. It was due to open in 2009 – maybe.

For a change of scenery check out the dragons and incense of the **Kheng Hock Keong** (Map p98; Strand Rd; admission free; 24hr), the largest Chinese temple in Yangon. Supported by a Hokkien association, the 100-year-old temple is most lively from around 6am to 9am when it's thronged with worshippers offering candles, flowers and incense to the Buddhist and Taoist altars within. Old men play Chinese checkers in the temple compound throughout the day. There is another, smaller, but equally interesting Chinese temple on nearby Mahabandoola Rd.

The crumbling **Moseah Yeshua Synagogue** (Map p102; 85 26th St), near Mahabandoola Rd, was founded over 100 years ago by Sephardic Jews. In the classic Sephardic style, it contains a *bimah* (platform holding the reading table) in the centre of the main sanctuary and a women's balcony upstairs. The wooden ceiling features the original blue-and-white Star of David motif.

Myanmar had around 2500 Jews – a combination of B'nai Israel, Cochin (Indian) and Iraqi heritages – until nationalisation in the 1960s and '70s, when many began leaving the country. Today there are no more than 25 or so Jews left in the country.

Several colourful Hindu temples can be found in the centre of the city, including **Sri Kali** (Map p102; Anawrahta Rd; 5-11am & 3-9pm), between 26th and 27th Sts, **Sri Siva** (Map p102; Mahabandoola Rd) and the **Sri Devi** (Map p98; cnr Anawrahta Rd & 51st St; 6.30-11.30am & 4.30-8.30pm), all of which are sickeningly sweet temples following the classic South Indian style of god-lined towers. These are the centres for the city's annual Murugu Festival, famous for colourful street processions featuring acts of ritual self-mutilation.

Christians get in on the act in Yangon as well with **St Mary's Cathedral** (Map p102; cnr Bo Aung Kyaw St & Bogyoke Aung San Rd), built in a bizarre red brick (and equally bizarre red, green and white interior), which will excite colonial buffs. Here in Myanmar, where religion in all its forms is the core of life, the clergy have enough churchgoers to hold services in English twice daily (Monday to Saturday 6am and 5pm, Sunday 6am and 8am) and in Burmese on Sundays (5pm). This is exactly the sort of religious building that developers in Europe would have turned into a crazy paved nightclub.

National Museum
အမျိုးသားပြတိုက်

Try to ignore the fact that the priceless collection at the **National Museum** (Map p98; ☎ 371 540; Pyay Rd; admission $5; ☉ 10am-4pm) is appallingly labelled and lit, and just focus on the treasures that lie within this cavernous building.

Highlights of the collection include the 26ft-high Sihasana (Lion Throne), which belonged to King Thibaw Min, the last king of Myanmar. It's actually more of an entrance doorway than a throne but let's not pick at straws, because it's certainly a damn sight more impressive than your front door! Further signs that the kings of old didn't understand the meaning of the word subtlety are the jewel-encrusted beds, silver and gold rugs, flashy palanquins (one of which is palatial in its size and splendour), kitchen chairs made of ivory, some breathtaking ceremonial dresses and a large collection of betel-nut holders and spittoons, which alone could make the British Crown Jewels look like cheap tack picked up at an 'everything for a dollar' shop.

The upper floors are less impressive and take you on an amble through natural history, prehistory and a very poorly lit art gallery.

Bogyoke Aung San Museum
ဗိုလ်ချုပ်အောင်ဆန်းပြတိုက်

The little-visited **Bogyoke Aung San Museum** (Map p93; ☎ 541 359; Bogyoke Aung San Museum St; admission $3; ☉ 10am-3pm, closed Mon & public holidays) is the former home of General Aung San and his wife Daw Kin Kyi, and contains remnants of another era. The government, perhaps fearing its revolutionary overtones, have closed it to

TIP

Ride the lift to the top of the **Sakura Tower** (Map p102; Bogyoke Aung San Rd), an office building across from Traders Hotel, for the best 360-degree views of the city.

locals, but foreign tourists hanging around the gates will normally be allowed in. Inside the 1920s house you will find several old family photos, which of course include daughter Suu Kyi as a little girl. A glass-encased English-language library reveals the general's broad interests: titles range from *Cavalry Training*, *Armoured Cars*, *A History of the US*, *Left-ing Democracy in the English Civil War* and Adam Smith's *The Wealth of Nations*.

Martyrs' Mausoleum
အာဇာနည်ဗိမာန်

Close to Shwedagon, on a hill offering a good view over the city, stands this **memorial** (Map p93; Ar Za Nir St) to Bogyoke Aung San and his fellow cabinet officers who were assassinated with him. It was also here that a bomb set off by North Koreans killed a number of South Korea's top government officials in late 1983. The mausoleum itself is only open one day a year – 19 July.

Mahabandoola Garden
မဟာဗန္ဓုလပန်းခြံ

Just southeast of the Sule Paya, this square urban **park** (Map p102; admission K500) offers pleasant strolling in the city centre's heart, especially in the early morning when the Chinese come to practise t'ai chi, and the air hasn't yet filled with traffic fumes. Occupying the centre of the northern half of the park is the **Independence Monument**, an obelisk surrounded by two concentric circles of *chinthe*.

For a year or two following the 1988–90 prodemocracy uprisings, the park was occupied by soldiers; many of the more violent events of the time took place nearby.

Kandawgyi Lake
ကန်တော်ကြီး

Occupying prime Yangon real estate, this natural lake (Map p93) close to the city centre is a good place for a stroll. Don't expect untamed nature or meditative quiet here, as

(Continued on page 113)

Shwedagon Paya

Young monk at the Shwedagon Paya

FELIX HUG

The dome of the most sacred Buddhist site in Myanmar

CAROL WI

When the mythmakers of the ancient world spoke of mountains made of gold it must surely have been the Shwedagon Paya that they had in mind. It's said that there is more gold plastered onto the sides of the Shwedagon than in all the vaults of the Bank of England. To this you can also add all of the diamonds, all of the rubies and all of the emeralds.

But to many the Shwedagon is so much more than just the jewel-box pinnacle of human creation. Kipling famously wrote of it, in his book *Letters from the East:* 'A golden mystery upheaved itself on the horizon – a beautiful winking wonder that blazed in the sun, of a shape that was neither Muslim dome nor Hindu temple spire… "There's the old Shway

Dagon," said my companion…the golden dome said: "This is Burma, and it will be quite unlike any land you know about".'

For in truth this two-and-a-half-thousand-year-old testament to religious faith, this gold-draped symbol of exotica, is the very heart and soul of this country. It is the reason for all the smiles in Myanmar and it has witnessed all of the tears. Once seen it can never be forgotten and once experienced it will hold you spellbound forever.

HISTORY

The great golden dome rises 322ft above its base. According to legend this stupa – of the solid *zedi* (conelike) type – is 2500 years old, but archaeologists suggest that the original stupa was built by the Mon people sometime between the 6th and 10th

Buddha image inside a golden shrine
JANE SWEENEY

Girls in traditional costume preparing for an ear-piercing ceremony
MICHAEL GEBICKI

centuries. In common with many other ancient *zedi* in earthquake-prone Myanmar, it has been rebuilt many times and its current form dates back only to 1769.

During the Bagan period of Myanmar's history (10th to 14th centuries), the story of the stupa (see p111) emerged from the mists of legend to become hard fact. Near the top of the eastern stairway you can see an inscription recording the history of the stupa to 1485.

In the 15th century, the tradition of gilding the stupa began. Queen Shinsawbu, who was responsible for many improvements to the stupa, provided her own weight (88lb) in gold, which was beaten into gold leaf and used to cover the structure. Her son-in-law, Dhammazedi, went several better, offering four times his own weight and that of his wife in gold. He also provided the 1485 historical inscription on the eastern stairway.

The *zedi* suffered from a series of earthquakes during this time, which caused great damage. In 1612 Portuguese renegade adventurer Philip De Brito raided the stupa from his base

A shimmering detail of the Shwedagon Paya

DOUBLE IMAGE STUDIO / ALA

The grounds of the Shwedagon Paya

JANE SWEENEY

Flowers and wheels made from money, for sale on the streets below the Shwedagon Paya

CAROL WIR

in Thanlyin and carried away Dhammazedi's great bell, with the intention of melting it for cannons. As the British were to do later with another bell, he dropped it into the river. During the 17th century, the monument suffered earthquake damage on eight occasions. Worse was to follow in 1768, when a quake brought down the whole top of the *zedi*. King Hsinbyushin had it rebuilt to virtually its present height, and its current configuration dates from that renovation.

British troops occupied the compound for two years immediately after the First Anglo-Burmese War in 1824. In 1852, during the Second Anglo-Burmese War, the British again took the paya, the soldiers pillaged it once more and it remained under military control for 77 years, until 1929. In 1871 a new *hti* (the umbrella-like decorative top of a stupa), provided by King Mindon Min from Mandalay, caused considerable head-scratching for the British, who were not at all keen for such an association to be made with the still-independent part of Myanmar.

During the 20th century, the Shwedagon Paya was the scene for much political activity during the Myanmar independence movement. The huge earthquake of 1930, which totally destroyed the Shwemawdaw in Bago, caused only minor damage to Shwedagon. Less luck was had the following year when the paya suffered from a serious fire. After another minor earthquake in 1970, the *zedi* was clad in bamboo scaffolding, which extended beyond King Mindon's 100-year-old *hti,* and was refurbished.

THE LEGEND OF THE SHWEDAGON PAYA

The legend goes that for 10,000 years Singuttara Hill, in lower Myanmar, had been a holy place, containing as it did the relics of three past buddhas. But it was also said that a new buddha was due to arrive on Earth at any moment and when that day came Singuttara Hill would lose its special powers – unless it contained something of this new buddha. This knowledge caused King Okkalapa, ruler of this area of Myanmar, a bit of a headache and so, in order to try and prevent this catastrophe, he spent days and days praying on top of the hill.

Unbeknownst to him, at that time a certain royal gentleman by the name of Gautama was within a buddha's eyelash of achieving enlightenment under the Bodhi tree in Bodhgaya, India. The king was also unaware that, at that very moment, two merchant brothers called Bhallika and Tapussa, who hailed from his kingdom, were leaving gifts of honey-coated cakes for Gautama. Having just spent 49 days meditating, Gautama was getting peckish. To show his gratitude for these gifts he presented the two brothers with eight strands of his hair to take to their king.

Despite a rough journey, in which they were robbed of two hairs by the king of a neighbouring land and lost another two to the salty clutches of the king of the *naga* (dragon serpents), who rose from the seabed to attack their ship as they crossed the Bay of Bengal, the brothers finally made it home. When they presented the casket containing their gift to King Okkalapa, he opened it to discover that, miraculously, there were now eight hairs again. Then some quite amazing events took place:

There was a tumult among men and spirits…rays emitted by the Hairs penetrated up to the heavens above and down to hell…the blind beheld objects…the deaf heard sounds…the dumb spoke distinctly…the earth quaked…the winds of the ocean blew…Mount Meru shook…lightning flashed…gems rained down until they were knee deep…all trees of the Himalaya, though not in season, bore blossoms and fruit.

Disappointingly, perhaps, hairs of the Buddha are not unveiled every day.

Once the relics were safely enshrined in a temple on Singuttara Hill, a golden slab was laid on the chamber and a golden stupa built over it. Over this, a silver stupa was built, then a tin stupa, a copper stupa, a lead stupa, a marble stupa and finally, an iron-brick stupa. Later, the legend continues, the stupa fell into disuse. It is said that the great Indian Buddhist emperor Ashoka came to Myanmar and, after finding the site only with great difficulty, had the encroaching jungle cleared and the stupa repaired.

Young Buddhist monks at the Shwedagon Paya

YADID LEVY / ALAMY

Golden buddha statue, Shwedagon Paya

JANE SWEENEY

(Continued from page 104)

the footpath surrounding the circumference of Kandawgyi also runs alongside a busy road. Also known by its literal translation, Royal Lake (Dawgyi Kan), the lake seems at its most attractive at sunset, when the glittering Shwedagon is reflected in its calm waters. You'll find the best sunset view from the lake's eastern edge.

Several of the city's embassies, clinics and smaller hotels are in the lake's vicinity, the majority north of the lake. Just east of the Kandawgyi Palace Hotel, on the southern side of the lake, floats a **Shin Upagot shrine** (Map p93). Upagot is a Bodhisattva or Buddhist saint who is said to protect human beings in moments of mortal danger.

The eastern side of the lake is dominated by a very expensive government-financed project including a small park and playground for children, as well as the fanciful or monstrous (depending on your taste) **Karaweik** (Map p93), a reinforced concrete reproduction of a royal barge. Apart from being something of a local attraction in its own right, the Karaweik (Sanskrit for Garuda, the legendary bird-mount of the Hindu god Vishnu) is also the name of a government-owned restaurant nearby. Traditional dance performances are held here in the evenings.

Inya Lake
အင်းယားကန်

Inya Lake itself is hidden from street level view – a shame as a drive around the perimeter reveals only that something is probably on the other side of the earthen berms. The **lake** (Map p90) is roughly five times larger than Kandawgyi but to see actual water you must explore on foot and brave the powerful sun. There aren't many opportunities for shade, only scattered umbrellas, which are popular with young couples sneaking a little alone time.

Inya is north of the city, stretching between Pyay Rd to the west and Kaba Aye Pagoda Rd to the east. Certain areas along the lakeshore – occupied by state guesthouses and ministerial mansions – are off limits to the general public.

Before reclusive dictator Ne Win died in December 2002, he lived on University Ave Rd at one end of the lake while Aung San Suu Kyi, who at the time of research was still under house arrest at number 54, was at the other end. For years these two important figures in contemporary Myanmar history resided like powerful *nat* locked in a battle of wills.

Myanmar Gems Museum & Gems Market
မြန်မာ့ကျောက်မျက်ပြတိုက်နှင့် အရောင်းပြခန်း

Just north of Parami Rd, this government-owned **museum** (Map p90; ☎ 665 365; 66 Kaba Aye Pagoda Rd; admission $3; ☼ 9am-5pm Tue-Sun) is meant to impress – starting with the world's largest sapphire, which comes from Mogok (to the northeast of Mandalay). The sapphire measures 6.7in in height, and is nearly 26lb in weight – this somehow translates to 63,000 carats. The museum also boasts the world's largest jade boulder, rough ruby, and star sapphire. Other not-so-impressive claims include the only mineral with 'imperial' in its name.

The Gems Market, essentially a government shop, is spread over the three lower floors, while the museum takes up the top floor. In a currently poor country famous for valuable resources, the museum offers an unintended lesson in beauty, politics and money.

Na-Gar Glass Factory
နဂါး:ပန်ရေမြမုန်ရေမြစက်ရုံ

The **glass factory** (Map p90; ☎ 526 053; 152 Yawgi Kyaung St, Hlaing Township; admission free; ☼ 9.30-11am & 12.30-3.30pm) is an interesting place to explore, with lots of hand-blown glass on display in a surprisingly pleasant indoor-outdoor setting. It was this place that provided the huge, mesmerising eyes of the reclining Buddha at Chaukhtatgyi Paya (p101). Unusual wine glasses, small vases and the like are also for sale.

The factory isn't signposted and is well hidden down a jungly driveway. Most taxi drivers in the downtown area aren't familiar with the factory, and it definitely helps if you tell them it's located in Hlaing (pronounced lie-eng) Township. At the time of research it was closed because of a lack of gas for the kiln. However we were assured it would reopen shortly. Best call ahead to make sure.

Other Attractions
Opposite the Shwedagon Paya to the west, the **People's Park** (Map p93; admission $3; ☼ 7am-7pm) is a huge expanse of grass and trees, which is bisected by **People's Square**, a wide,

YANGON

socialist-style pedestrian promenade that is kept firmly out of bounds to the public. Near a set of fountains, just to the south of People's Square, is a children's playground area, and in the southeastern corner of the park there are a couple of armoured tanks on display. The entrance to the park is on the eastern side, by the Shwedagon Paya's western gate.

ACTIVITIES
Traditional Myanmar Massage
After a long day slogging around the city what could be better than a massage? A professional centre with no dodgy side is **Seri Beauty and Health** (Map p93; ☎ 534 493; 103 Dhama Zedi Rd).

Train Ride
More in the category of sightseeing rather than transportation, the **Yangon Circle Line** (☎ 274 027; tickets $2) is a slow-moving, not particularly comfortable two-hour trip around Yangon and the neighbouring countryside. However, it's a great way to experience commuter life in the big city. You can always hop off at any station and take a taxi back to the city centre. The first train leaves around 6am from platform 6/7 at the **Yangon Train Station** (Central Train Station; Map p98; Bogyoke Aung San Rd) and the last trip of the day departs around 5pm (though the lack of electricity means it gets very dark inside the carriages of the later trains). Trains depart approximately every 30 minutes though not all do the full circuit. The train is least crowded on weekends.

To buy tickets look for the ticket window next to an oval track map at the eastern end of the station.

WALKING TOUR – DOWNTOWN YANGON
This tour takes in the best of colonial Yangon, flirts with Indian flamboyance, gets serene in Buddhist temples, lightens your wallet in the markets and throws in some pickled serpents and crystal-ball gazing for good measure. Depending on how long you shop, it should take around two or three hours. Start your tour of downtown Yangon at the 2200-year-old **Sule Paya (1;** see p100), the geographic and commercial heart of the city, and where the British-designed grid street pattern was centred. After a complete rotation or two and inside visit, cross the busy traffic circle to the east and you'll find the twice rebuilt **City Hall (2)**, a yellow colonial building with ori-

ental overtones. On the next corner further east on Mahabandoola Rd is the **Immigration Office (3)**, once one of the largest department stores in all of Asia. Across the street is the **Immanuel Baptist Church (4)** originally built in 1830, though the present structure dates from 1885. Continuing east on Mahabandoola Rd you'll pass a couple of alleyways crammed with **food stalls** and **markets**. Take the next major right onto Pansodan St with its many stalls selling second-hand and photocopied books. About halfway down this block you'll see the **High Court Building (5)** on your right: in name at least, the highest legal authority in the land. Further down, on your left, are the grand **Inland Water Transport** offices and even grander **Myanma Port Authority** building. Continue south to Strand Rd, the last east–west thoroughfare before the Yangon River.

Two blocks to your left is the **Strand Hotel (6;** p118), whose restored façade evokes another era and whose air-conditioned lobby, café and bar make a good rest-stop along the way. When you're ready to brave the heat and uneven sidewalks again, walk west along Strand Rd for a block past Pansodan St where you'll see the **Customs House (7)**, built in 1915, on one corner and the **Law Court (8)**, an impressive-looking colonnaded building on the other (police will prevent you approaching this last building). Turn north, just past the Customs House, and then left onto boisterous Bank St and up onto Sule Paya Rd, where you can discover how the remainder of your walking tour will pan out by consulting one of the many **fortune-tellers** who hang out under the trees. Bordering this street is a 55yd obelisk, a monument to the country's independence, standing in the middle of the heat-stained **Mahabandoola Garden (9;** p104).

This brings you back to the Sule Paya, from where you can continue west down Mahabandoola Rd through the chaotic **Indian** and **Chinese quarters (10)** of the city. Every block along the way is crammed with shops and street vendors selling everything under the

---

WALK FACTS

- **Start** Sule Paya
- **Finish** Bogyoke Aung San Market
- **Distance** Approx 1.4 miles
- **Duration** Two to three hours

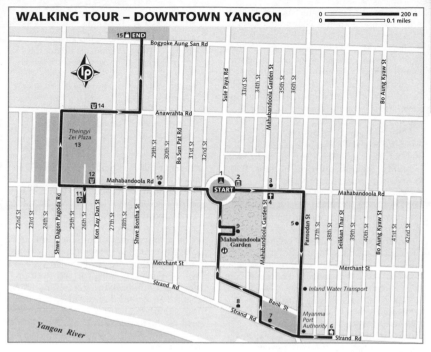

WALKING TOUR – DOWNTOWN YANGON

sun. Detour south onto 26th St in order to pay a visit to the **Moseah Yeshua Synagogue** (**11**; p103). Return to Mahabandoola Rd and pause at the **Sri Siva temple** (**12**; p103) with its bizarre clock tower. Carry on westwards a little further until you reach the bursting **Theingyi Zei** market (**13**; p128), where you can engage in a little pickled-snake hunting. Exit onto Anawrahta Rd and head east until you crash into the **Sri Kali temple** (**14**; p103). From here it's only a short hike north to the sprawling mess of the **Bogyoke Aung San Market** (**15**; p128), where you can begin a new sort of tour, a slightly more difficult one that combines walking *and* shopping.

COURSES
Meditation

Several monasteries in Yangon welcome foreigners to meditation courses. The most famous centre in Yangon is the **Mahasi Meditation Centre** (Map p93; ☎ 541 971; 16 Thathana Yeiktha Rd, Bahan Township), founded in 1947 by the late Mahasi Sayadaw, perhaps Myanmar's greatest meditation teacher. The Mahasi Sayadaw technique strives for intensive, moment-to-moment awareness of every physical movement, every mental and physical sensation and, ultimately, every thought. The centre only accepts foreigners who can stay for at least one week.

Two of the Mahasi centre's chief meditation teachers, Sayadaw U Pandita and Sayadaw U Janaka, have established their own highly regarded centres in Yangon: **Panditarama Meditation Centre** (☎ 535 448; http://web.ukonline.co.uk/buddhism/pandita.htm; 80-A Than Lwin Rd, Bahan Township) and **Chanmyay Yeiktha Meditation Centre** (Map p90; ☎ 661 479; www.chanmyay.org; 55-A Kaba Aye Pagoda Rd). Both have second branches with private quarters, especially geared for foreigners. **Panditarama's forest meditation centre** (☎ 247 211) is 2 miles northeast off the highway to Bago. Chanmyay's **branch** (☎ 620 321), set among gardens in Hmawbi, is a 50-minute drive north of Yangon; one-month stays are preferred. Each of these centres represents a slight difference from the Mahasi Sayadaw technique.

T'ai Chi & Martial Arts

T'ai chi is practised daily at dawn at Mahabandoola Garden, near the Sule Paya. It's an informal gathering of the Chinese community.

Myanmar kickboxing instruction for beginners is offered on the ground floor of the **YMCA** (Map p98; ☎ 294 128, 296 435; Mahabandoola Rd, near Thein Byu Rd; ☷ 4-6pm Mon, Wed & Fri). There's usually someone around who can translate the essentials, though you should mostly expect to learn by example, which we imagine would be quite painful. Techniques taught here incorporate some moves borrowed from Thai and international boxing.

Upon becoming members, visitors are welcome to participate in boxing ($6); it's then a further K5000 for unlimited lessons. Enquire at the main office on the upper floor for more information.

FESTIVALS & EVENTS

Crowds of pilgrims descend on the Shwedagon for a *paya pwe* (pagoda festival), one of the more important Myanmar holidays. This takes place over the March full moon day, the last full moon before the Myanmar New Year. In the Western calendar it normally falls in late February/early March.

Other major festivals in Yangon:

Independence Day (4 January) Includes a seven-day fair at Kandawgyi; see p30.

Water Festival/Thingyan (April) The Myanmar New Year is celebrated in wet pandemonium; see p30 for more details.

Buddha's birthday (April/May) Celebrate Buddha's enlightenment; see p30.

Martyrs' Day (19 July) Commemorating the assassination of Bogyoke Aung San and his comrades; see p30.

Murugu Festival (March or April depending on lunar calendar) Held at Yangon's Hindu temples (see p104), it involves colourful processions.

SLEEPING

Judging by the number of large top-end business-style hotels cropping up all over the city, the hospitality industry in Yangon seems alive and well. Low occupancy rates, though, belie the wisdom of the hotel building boom and heavy rebates are to be had by the savvy traveller. The prices quoted here are published walk-in rates, but almost all midrange and top-end hotels offer discounts of up to 50%. In general the hotels with the most character are either budget or top-end establishments; midrange hotels tend to be very dull Chinese-built high-rise blocks with only slightly more character than a wet rag.

Many of the midrange and top-end hotels provide airport pick-ups, internet access and

> **ALL IS NOT AS IT SEEMS**
>
> Many of the top-end hotels are joint ventures with the government, although the exact percentage of ownership – whether the government is a majority or minority shareholder and exactly what this means – is difficult to ferret out (see p336). As far as we are aware those listed here have a fairly minimal government ownership share – if any.

full-service business centres. Only a few of the top-end hotels accept credit cards and some also add on an additional 10% service charge and 10% government tax. Almost all hotels, even the mostly lowly budget place, will store luggage while you're away upcountry.

The obvious appeal of the hotels just north of the city centre, in the Kandawgyi area, are the breathtaking views of the Shwedagon Paya, especially at night. The lake itself provides a peaceful backdrop for several hotels clustered around its shores. The city becomes more suburban and spread out the further north you go towards Inya Lake.

City Centre
BUDGET

Prices quoted generally include a rudimentary eggs-and-toast breakfast. Payment is accepted in US dollars, and sometimes kyat. Street noise, especially in the early morning, is a nuisance at many of the options.

Golden Smiles Inn (Map p102; ☎ 373 589; myathiri@ mptmail.net.mm; 644 Merchant St; s & d $8-12, without bathroom $5-8; ☷) The cheaper rooms, without bathrooms, are noticeably cleaner than those with bathrooms and, strangely, are the better deal. It's one of the better bare-bones hotels and has a nice breakfast/hang-out balcony.

ᴏᴜʀ ᴘɪᴄᴋ Motherland Inn 2 (Map p93; ☎ 291 343; www.myanmarmotherlandinn.com; 433 Lower Pazundaung Rd; s & d from $7-10; ☷ ☐) Take a pinch of backpacker bohemia, a dollop of professional service, a massive portion of cleanliness, mix well with a generous helping of travel advice and services and leave to marinate with enviously attired and proportioned rooms and, voila, it's the Motherland Inn 2 (the original Motherland has long since closed), the king of Yangon backpacker hotels. There are of course downsides, namely that it's a long walk or a short taxi ride from the centre.

Otherwise this is a budget traveller's dream and the rooms give those of some of the mid-range hotels a real hard time. The internet access here might well be Yangon's best, the breakfast outstanding for this category and the restaurant a great place to hook into the traveller's grapevine. Pricier rooms have private bathrooms.

Tokyo Guest House (Map p102; ☎ 386 828; 200 Bo Aung Kyaw St; s/d $7/12; ❷) Squeeze through the doorway between the knick-knack stall and up the betel-stained stairs and you'll come to this little and welcoming guesthouse. Highlights are the sunny terrace with views and the room cleanliness. Lowlights are the fact that said rooms are windowless and very cramped. And the communal bathrooms and toilets are located right inside the open-plan kitchen – nice!

May Fair Inn (Map p102; ☎ 253 454; mayfair.inn@mpt mail.net.mm; 57 38th St; s/d $7.50/15; ❷) This family run inn has freshly painted rooms that are a little spartan but ever reliable. It's more equipped to deal with the traveller looking for tranquillity rather than a party and it has a loyal clientele of returnees for a good reason. The complimentary breakfast is served in the small communal area.

Ocean Pearl Inn (Map p98; ☎ 297 007; www.ocean pearlinn.com; 215 Bo Ta Taung Pagoda Rd; s/d $7.50/15; ❷ 🖳) In the same neighbourhood as the Haven and Three Seasons, the Ocean Pearl is another high-value option. While the rooms don't have as much charm as the other two, the snap-to-attention staff and rooms that are washed and polished by a team of cleaning addicts make this a sure-fire bet. There is satellite TV and plenty of solid travel advice.

YMCA (Map p98; ☎ 294 128; 263 Mahabandoola Rd; s/d $10/19, without bathroom $8/15; ❷) As the sign says: 'Staying at the YMCA helps the needy.' This is a very valid reason for giving them your money but if comfort and value for money are more important to you than saving the planet then you'd better look elsewhere because the rooms are overpriced and tatty.

The following are bare-bones and only last resorts:

Mahabandoola Guest House (Map p102; ☎ 248 104; 93 32nd St; s/d $4/6) It's cheap. The end.

Daddy's Home (Map p102; ☎ 252 169; 107 Kon Zay Dan St; s/d $9/18, without bathroom $5/8) A drab tower-block hotel with the largest bathrooms in the budget category. The cleaners could do with purchasing a broom, but otherwise it's friendly and adequate.

Garden Guest House (Map p102; ☎ 253 779; 441-445 Mahabandoola Rd; s/d from $6/12) The sign on the stairway reads: 'Effort exerted bears fruit of success.' It's not a proverb the hotel staff have taken to heart. It does have stunning, but noisy, views of the Sule Paya.

MIDRANGE

ourpick Haven Inn (Map p98; ☎ 296 449; phyuaung@ mptmail.net.mm; 216 Bo Myat Tun St; s/d $10/15; ❷) There's no more homy and inviting place to retire to after a busy day of sightseeing in Yangon than this matchbox-sized gem, which was built back in the days when houses came with class. The Haven Inn, announced only by a small neon sign, is located on a relatively quiet street east of the city centre and has just five rooms. The old-fashioned wood panelled interior is a real blast from the past and makes you feel like a hibernating squirrel tucked up inside a hole in a tree. Each room has an array of wooden furniture and bathrooms with hot water. Dr Htun, the friendly owner, is an excellent source of information. Staying in his guesthouse is a good way of experiencing Myanmar family life, while also allowing you to meet fellow travellers.

Three Seasons Hotel (Map p98; ☎ 293 304; phyu aung@mptmail.net.mm; 83-85 52nd St; s/d $12/18; ❷ 🖳) Run by the stars who created the Haven Inn, this, the sister hotel, is equally endearing. Though not as cosy it's just as full of wood-created charm. The outdoor terrace, with tree shade, is a nice place to sit and watch the world cruise on by, whilst the cool and dark interior invites a siesta. Once again the nine rooms are large and well-endowed with everything that would make your granny smile. It's very friendly and helpful and comes with a superb part-Western, part-Burmese breakfast. This is an especially quiet block at night so you should be able to sleep undisturbed.

Okinawa Guest House (Map p102; ☎ 385 728; 64 32nd St; dm/s/d $5/13/17; ❷) Halfway up a mucky street of alternate high rises and tumbledowns is the red pitched roof of this charming bougainvillea-fronted guesthouse. The interior is a bizarre hotchpotch of decorations and building styles that mix wood, bamboo and red brick perfectly. The handful of rooms are small but very clean, but it's the bathrooms that are the real prize – neat, tidy and with a toilet separated behind a wall from the shower and sink. There's also a cosy dorm upstairs for penny-pinchers and a number of communal areas with old wooden chairs and tables. The

Sule Paya is just 109yd away. Breakfast and friendly vibes included in the price.

Yoma Hotel (Map p98; ☎ 299 243; www.yoma hotelone.com; 146 Bogyoke Aung San Rd; s/d $15/18; 🅧 🖵) Not as nice as its Yoma 2 counterpart (p120), the Yoma gets by on its central location. Run by a friendly bunch who give you all the time you need, the low-ceilinged rooms are decent enough but, like many such poor man's business hotels, they lack any real sparkle. There are five floors and no lift, so if you're on the top floor you can eat that extra cake without guilt. Monthly rates are available on request.

Sunflower Hotel (Map p102; ☎ 252 197; www .myanmarsunflower-hotel.com; 259/263 Anawrahta Rd; s/d $15/20; 🅧) Located in the heart of the busy Indian quarter and appropriately colourful. The rooms are bright and adequate but could do with a wash more often. Ask for room 401 – it'll make you feel like a prostitute! Not used to foreigners.

Mayshan Guest House (Map p102; ☎ 252 986; www .mayshan.com; 115-117 Sule Paya Rd; s/d $15/20; 🅧 🖵) It's hard to top the Mayshan's location, half a block north of Sule Paya. The vibe is less family and intimate than others; nevertheless the small, tiled modern rooms are well kept and have satellite TV. To be honest you pay for the location and, like most of the hotels around the Sule Paya, it's not very good value. Even so it remains the pick of the bunch around the exotic pagoda. Quite a few hustlers congregate outside.

Queen's Park Hotel (Map p98; ☎ 296 447; www .myanmarqueensparkhotel.com; 132 Anawrahta Rd; s/d from $15/20, ste $35; 🅧 🖵) Unusually for a hotel in this category, the rooms are more appealing than the dowdy reception area – though only by a little. The staff are sweet, and slow days means easy discounts. The superior double offers the best value by far. There's a generator to cover frequent power outages and free airport transfer for groups of six or more.

Friendship Hotel (Map p98; ☎ 228 841; 97 4th St; s/d $15/20; 🅧) It's out on a bit of a limb and you'll be one of the first Western guests but that's no bad thing. The freshly painted rooms have very little character but the manager, who is as friendly as the hotel name indicates, soon makes up for that. It's down a little side alley so should ensure a quiet night's kip and is very handy for the excitement of Chinatown.

New Aye Yar Hotel (Map p102; ☎ 256 941; www .newayeyarhotel.com; 170-176 Bo Aung Kyaw St; s/d $17/20; 🅧) This good-value high-rise has avoided the tropical rot that has struck down so many of its cousins and has vast rooms with starched sheets and equally vast city views. The cheapest rooms are carpeted and more musty than the enjoyable wooden-floored rooms (single/ double $20/25). You might need binoculars in order to make out the river from the famous 'river view' rooms.

Panorama Hotel (Map p102; ☎ 253 077; panorama@ mptmail.net.mm; 294-300 Pansodan St; s/d $25/30; 🅧 🖵) Within walking distance of the train station and the Bogyoke Market, the aptly named 10-storey Panorama offers some of the best value in this price range. Its wide marble atrium lobby seems slightly dated but the rooms themselves serve their purpose well and provide excellent levels of comfort and cleanliness at a memorable price. Some have vague views over the distant Shwedagon Paya. Professional and attentive service.

Central Hotel (Map p102; ☎ 241 001; www.central hotelyangon.com; 335-357 Bogyoke Aung San Rd; s/d $30/35; 🅧 🖵) 'Bond, James Bond.' With its whispered conversations and surreptitious glances there is no place you are more likely to hear these words uttered than in the lobby of this long-standing, good-value midrange hotel. Day and night locals and tourists alike dash in and out for secret rendezvous, and intrigue hangs in the air. Away from 007 fantasies the plain and sterile upstairs rooms contain no surprises – though some may find the old-fashioned décor a little kitsch – don't worry it'll grow on you! The enduring popularity of this hotel means that there is money to spare for repairs and cleanliness. The lifts feature government-sponsored posters, which ask tourists to respect human rights. The hotel has a good Chinese restaurant and why not stop by the very popular bar/café, the Diamond White Bar, which is a good place to change money and have a martini – shaken, not stirred.

TOP END

Strand Hotel (Map p102; ☎ 243 377; www.ghmhotels.com; 92 Strand Rd; superior ste $550, Strand ste $1100; 🅧 🖵) Royalty (the Hollywood kind and the traditional) make the Strand their home away from home. Mick Jagger, Oliver Stone, the King of Tonga and George Orwell all slept here. Like the most stylish of creations this Grande Dame wears her dress in the most subtle of manners and the mode is 100% colonial. In reward for her class she was voted one of Asia's top hotels by *Travel + Leisure*

HOTEL MANAGER, YANGON

I'm 33 years old and was born in Yangon. I wanted to work in the tourist industry in order to meet foreigners and learn about other people and their country. I have been working in the tourist industry for eight years.

What is your favourite thing to do in Yangon? I'm religious so I like all of the pagodas but every morning I go to the one near my home. I go and pray at 4am and stay until 6am. I meditate whilst I am there and give rice and other donations.

What do you like to do on your day off? I have a daughter and like to take her and my husband to the zoo on my day off or I like to go shopping.

What is your favourite place in Myanmar? I have only been to Bago and Kyaiktiyo. I liked Kyaiktiyo best. One day I would like to go to Mandalay to visit the temples.

And if you could go anywhere in the world where would you go? I would like to visit Bangkok for the shopping and Singapore for the work. I think the management system in Singapore is good and that it would be a good place to work.

Yes, but if you could go anywhere in the world, just for a holiday, where would that be? Just for a holiday? I don't know. I have never thought about that because we cannot go abroad.

magazine in 2007. Though well beyond the accommodation budget of many visitors, the Strand is well worth a visit for a drink in the bar, high tea in the lobby lounge or a splurge lunch at the café.

Shwedagon & Kandawgyi Area

This area of the city is generally quieter than central Yangon. It's also convenient for walking to Shwedagon Paya and Kandawgyi Lake. It's not a place to seek out budget accommodation.

MIDRANGE

Comfort Inn (Map p93; ☎ 525 781; Inya Rd; s/d $15/25; ✷) A quiet family-run guesthouse on a side street close to the Bangladeshi embassy and within walking distance of the Shwedagon Paya. The wood-panelled rooms are decent enough, but do little to set the imagination alight. On the positive side the bathrooms are a solid plus and for this area it's cheap as chips. The gardens have a mini Niagara Falls and a crazy aquarium/pond.

Winner Inn (Map p93; ☎ 535 205; www.winnerinnmyanmar.com; 42 Than Lwin Rd; r from $20; ✷ ▯) Something of a 'posh backpackers', the Winner is a real find. This low-slung building is in a quiet, leafy suburb and has spotless rooms with desks, and pictures on the walls. The communal areas have plenty of well-positioned chairs waiting for you to collapse into with a book. The service is excellent and it has a good restaurant but remember if you use the internet service 'not to look at political sites', as the sign requests.

Summer Palace Hotel (Map p93; ☎ 527 211; sph@myanmar.com.mm; 437 Pyay Rd; s/d $20/30; ✷ ▯ ▣) There's nothing wrong with this small, business hotel, but nothing ever so right about it either. The biggest selling point, if you're that way inclined, is the popular karaoke bar, where already terrible love songs get a regular beating. The large rooms are at least clean and the staff friendly, if a little confused about what to do with a Western tourist.

Guest Care Hotel (Map p93; ☎ 511 118; www.guestcarehotel.com; 107 Dhama Zedi Rd; s/d $24/34; ✷ ▯) All guests at the Guest Care have access to the top-floor viewing area with spectacular unobstructed views of the nearby Shwedagon Paya. There are several classes of room (with little noticeable difference between them) and it's worth taking a look at a few before committing, as some are in much better nick than others. For character you'll find a few bits of beautifully carved wooden furniture tossed about the place.

Panda Hotel (Map p98; ☎ 212 850; www.myanmarpandahotel.com; 205 Wadan St; s/d $30/40; ✷ ▯) One of the more appealing hotels in this price range is this 13-storey high-rise west of the city centre. It has bright and enticing rooms with excellent bathrooms. It's in a peaceful residential area but is close enough to downtown to be worthwhile. Popular with tour groups.

TOP END

Summit Parkview (Map p93; ☎ 211 888; www.summityangon.com; 350 Ahlone Rd; s/d $50/55; ✷ ▯ ▣) Normally there would be little to capture the imagination in a business-class hotel like this, but this one, owned by the Singapore government, is different. How many hotels do you know of with breathtaking views over one of the wonders of the universe? If a bargain-rated, orderly and civilised room overlooking the jewel-encrusted Shwedagon Paya isn't for you then feel free to take the same type of room overlooking the pool (open to non-guests for $5 per day). For the price you'd have to rate this as one of the best deals in town. Has a plethora of gyms, travel agencies, shops and restaurants, which, though pricey, do make passable Basque starters.

Savoy Hotel (Map p93; ☎ 526 289; www.savoy -myanmar.com; 129 Dhama Zedi Rd; s/d $140/150; ⚙ 💻 🏊) Everything inside the Savoy is done so perfectly that it's easy to forgive the fact that it's situated right on a busy street corner with heavy traffic. Hallways, rooms and even the lavish bathrooms are stocked with photographs, antiques, handicrafts and sculptures and it takes little imagination to feel as if you are some Raj-like king. Basically what you get at this Myanmar-German joint venture is Strand Hotel standards without the price tag.

Kandawgyi Palace Hotel (Map p93; ☎ 249 255; www .kandawgyipalacehotel.com; Kan Yeik Tha Rd; s/d $140/160; ⚙ 💻 🏊) Almost monstrous in its over-the-top design, yet somehow the dragon- and shrine-filled gardens, courtyards and communal areas work to produce one of Yangon's more memorable places to stay. The smart rooms are simple and classy and some have little private wooden balconies jutting out towards the lily-coated lake. There's a beautiful multilevel swimming pool, which merges into jungle gardens where even the odd dinosaur can be found lurking! There are also a handful of insanely decadent bungalows which have private pools, Jacuzzis and a personal butler service. Huge discounts off the above rack rates are normal if you book through a travel agency in Yangon. The Thai-owned hotel has several fine restaurants including the oh-so-chic La Maison du Lac.

our pick **Governor's Residence** (Map p98; ☎ 229 860; www.governorsresidence.com; 35 Taw Win St; r from $195 plus 20% tax & service charge; ⚙ 💻 🏊) If you'd like to live like a sovereign, this UK-owned teak mansion of period elegance and modern luxury in the leafy embassy district is for you. In the '20s the Governor's Residence was a guesthouse for important nationals of the Kayah ethnic group but now, after a masterful restoration, it's a tourist's ideal of colonial

luxury. A waiter with a crystal cocktail is always on hand and the pool merges gently into the lawns and sparkles in reflected beauty. The glorious rooms have ever-so-lightly perfumed air, teak floors, cloudy soft beds and stone baths with rose-petal water. This really is the Shwedagon of hotels. The excellent restaurant, Mandalay, serves expensive but superb French and Asian cuisine in a pond-side setting and a stylish bar. The pool is open to nonguests if they eat at the restaurant.

North Yangon & Inya Lake Area

The remainder of the hotels are well north of the city centre.

MIDRANGE

Yoma Hotel 2 (Map p93; ☎ 502 506; yoma_two@mail4u .com.mm; 24A Inya Rd; s/d from $15/20; ⚙ 💻) A sharp customer-service oriented hotel tucked up a lane of flowering trees. The cathedral-sized deluxe rooms are a good deal but the cheaper rooms' showers have windows that let all the world see you in your birthday suit.

Liberty Hotel (Map p93; ☎ 501 793; liberty@mpt mail.net.mm; 343 Pyay Rd; s/d $18/20; ⚙) The staff will get in a right tizz-wiz when they see a foreigner approaching but after the initial shock they'll cope admirably, which is good because the clean, high-ceilinged rooms on offer in this colonial-era mansion offer great value for money. The manager is a huge goldfish fan and has some of the biggest you'll ever see, in the reception-area aquarium. There's a nice garden out the back.

TOP END

Sedona Hotel (Map p93; ☎ 666 900; www.sedona myanmar.com; 1 Kaba Aye Pagoda Rd; r $100; ⚙ 💻 🏊) You know exactly what you'll be getting at the Singapore-owned Sedona: peace, quiet and very professional service. What you won't be getting is any kind of indication that you are in Myanmar but, as you sink into one of the comfortable beds, you probably won't be that bothered. The Atlantic-sized swimming pool (nonguests $5) is a real plus as is the downstairs Mediterranean-tasting Orzo restaurant (though you'd better like pasta).

EATING

Yangon is the culinary capital of the country. From street food, to cheap Bamar and Indian eateries, to high-end restaurants with creative chefs serving European, Thai and Japanese cuisine, eating is an unexpected highlight of a visit to the city. Eat early – by 10pm all but a couple of places and a few large hotel restaurants will be closed. Unless otherwise specified all the places listed are open for lunch and dinner (noon to 3pm and 6pm to 9pm). Teashops and cafés serving breakfast are also open from at least 8am (and often much earlier).

Travellers keen to avoid government-owned places should bypass the Karaweik Palace Restaurant, which is a remarkable-looking structure on Kandawgyi.

Bamar

Eating options outside Yangon are limited to mostly Bamar cuisine so many travellers take advantage of the relative diversity until they leave the capital. While this is an understandable strategy to keep the taste buds guessing, it would be unfortunate, as there are several excellent Bamar restaurants that are more interesting than those upcountry.

The more humble-looking the restaurant appears, the more locals probably frequent it. Figure on spending no more than K1500 per person at a cheap joint for a full spread, not including beverages.

Aung Thuka (Map p93; 17A 1st St; venison curry K1000; 10am-7pm) Hidden on a side street of teashops and mechanics, this is an ever busy, and very cheap, local chop house. Some people swear by this place, some swear about it – certainly the food can be a little oily (maybe from the mechanics?!). It's best to eat here only at lunchtime when the food is fresh. It's not far from the northern entrance to the Shwedagon Paya.

Taw Win Myanmar Food Centre (Royal Myanmar Food Centre; Map p102; ☎ 387 618; Merchant St; mains K1000-2000) It's for good reason that this cheap eat gets top marks from staff and guests at the nearby May Fair Inn – its curries really are excellent.

Hla Myanma Htamin Zain (Beautiful Myanmar Rice Shop; Map p93; 27 5th St; curries K1500; 10am-7pm) This place is sometimes called Shwe Ba because a famous actor of that name once had his house nearby. Like its neighbour Aung Thuka it's a very simple, plain restaurant, where the food is served from rows of curry pots. There are also some Chinese and Indian dishes.

Happy Café & Noodles (Map p93; ☎ 525 112; 62 Inya Rd; mains K2000) Do we like noodles? Yes we do! Then Happy Noodles, which, needless to say,

has noodles in all their magnificent forms, will make you happy indeed. This new setup for the fashion fiends of Yangon has outdoor roadside seating (perfect for seeing and being seen), tables in the garden or a more discreet air-con indoor section for those who feel they've committed a fashion faux pas. If you don't dig noodles then there are a few rice dishes too.

our pick **Monsoon** (Map p98; ☎ 295 224; 85-87 Thein Byu Rd; mains from K2500) Inside this classic colonial town house is quite possibly the best Southeast Asian restaurant in Yangon. It's a fully multicultural affair both in terms of the cuisine, which smoothly mixes the highlights of Burmese cooking with dishes from Thailand, Vietnam, Cambodia and Laos, and the staff, who are a Myanmar-Anglo mix. Often in these jack-of-all-trades restaurants the food isn't that hot, but you needn't worry about that here. Everything that emerges from the kitchen is exceptional, and the atmosphere relaxed and cosmopolitan without letting standards of service slip. Many locals consider it a lunchtime-only restaurant but the dinner service is just as good. Upstairs is an equally good handicraft shop, which, like the restaurant, offers the best-quality products for prices that cannot be faulted.

Feel Myanmar Food (Map p98; ☎ 725 736; 124 Pyidaungsu Yeiktha St; meals K3000) This sophisticated jungle-shack restaurant is reminiscent of a north Myanmar house. It's a superb place to get your fingers dirty experimenting with the excellent range of Bamar dishes, which are laid out in little trays that you can just point to. It's very popular at lunchtime with local businesspeople and foreign embassy staff.

Sandy's Myanmar Cuisine (Map p93; ☎ 382 918; Kan Yeik Tha Rd; entrées K1500, mains from K3000) There's no better place to try Bamar cooking than at Sandy's, overlooking serene Kandawgyi. The colonnaded colonial building and outdoor patio seating heighten the surprisingly affordable dining experience. The *mohinga* (rice noodles with chicken or fish) breakfast here, compared with the same meal served in the average teashop, is like the difference between haute couture and sweat pants.

Green Elephant Restaurant (Map p93; ☎ 535 231; www.greenelephant-restaurants.com; 519A Thirimingalar St; dishes K5000) Tour groups make this restaurant, which is tarted up like a Chinese temple, part of their Yangon itinerary. If you don't mind rubbing elbows with other foreigners, the upmarket and slightly Westernised Bamar curries, salads, meat and seafood dishes are fair game – just try talking about the beef with yoghurt and grapes without feeling hungry! Service is very good and the restaurant includes an upmarket craft shop.

Shan

999 Shan Noodle Shop (Map p102; 130B 34th St; most noodle dishes K400; 6am-7pm) Four or five tables are crammed into this tiny, brightly coloured eatery behind City Hall and a short walk from Sule Paya. The menu, printed in English and Burmese, includes filling *Shàn k'auq swèh* (thin rice noodles in a slightly spicy chicken broth) and *myi shay* (Mandalay-style noodle soup). Noodle dishes are served with fried tofu triangles and jars of pickled cabbage. The kitchen may sell out of some items by early evening.

Lashio Lay Shan Restaurant (Map p98; 295 015; 71 51st St; mains under K1000) A simple little, sub-road-level place near the corner of Mahabandoola Rd and 51st St, serving the sort of Shan delicacies the less-exciting may prefer not to subject their tummies to. Dried eels is a favourite snack.

Aung Mingalar Shan Noodle Restaurant (Map p98; Bo Yar Nyunt St; dishes K1000) Aung Mingalar is an excellent place to indulge simultaneously in people watching and the sweet sound of noodle sipping. There are always plenty of students hanging around and conversations come easy – though if they don't you can stick your nose in one of the magazines or newspapers lying around. It's a simple and fun restaurant with trendy city café overtones.

Maw Shwe Li Restaurant (Map p98; 221 103; 316 Anawrahta Rd, Lanmadaw Township; curries K1200) This small, friendly, out-of-the-way place is usually crowded with locals, and the curries are excellent and cheap. Shan specialities include *pei pot kyaw* (sour bean condiment) and *hmo chawk kyaw* (fried mushrooms). It doubles as a bar and can be a little dark but the food gets plenty of local support.

Thai

Black Canyon Coffee (Map p93; 395 052; Ahlone Rd; dishes from K2000;) Located next door to the Summit Parkview hotel, this is a swish little Thai restaurant, which also delves into fusion foods, eg spicy pasta. The noodles are decent as are the Wellington boot–shaped coffees. Lots of locals stop by here.

Yinn Dee Thai Restaurant (Map p93; 526 526; 126 Dhama Zedi Rd; mains K2500-3000;) Many people will tell you that this informal Thai restaurant, set back from the street, is the best place on the block to eat at and we won't disagree. You could come here every day for a year and still not work your way through everything on the mammoth menu.

Sabai Sabai Thai Restaurant (Map p93; 544 724; 232 Dhama Zedi Rd; dishes K3000;) You can tuck in alfresco at this, one of the best-regarded Thai restaurants in the city, or hide yourself away in the formal indoor dining room. The range of salads is particularly impressive for someone craving a light lunch in the heat of the day. It's very much an expat hang-out.

Padonmar Restaurant (Map p93; 536 485; 78 Inya Rd; mains K3000-4500;) Dine on the mighty fine Thai and Bamar food in the wood-stained interior or take it easy in the bamboo garden room. After eating knock back a few drinks in the stylish bar and then knock down a few balls at the pool table. It's set in a lovely old house and the trek out here is well worthwhile.

Chinese

You can sample the whole range of Chinese cuisine in Yangon – from the familiar Cantonese to the less well known Shanghai, Sichuan, Beijing or Hokkien dishes.

For noodles, fried rice and other quick Chinese meals, try the **night market** (Map p98; Madaw Rd) in Chinatown, around the corner from the Cantonese temple.

Palei Kywe Restaurant (Map p102; 380 288; 44 Bo Aung Kyaw St; dishes K1200; 9am-9pm) This restaurant is a two-part affair: one part formal and one part chilled. The menu and prices are the same no matter which room you feel more suited to. Chinese duck is the house speciality and the staff speak English and can advise on dishes.

Okinawa Restaurant (Map p102; 385 7283; 32nd St; meals K1500) Owned by the same family as the Okinawa Guest House down the road, this funkily decorated eatery has a long list of Chinese delights and fresh fruit juices. It's also a neat place for a beer in front of a satellite TV that plays a never-ending stream of films. The Singapore-style fried rice is decent.

Nan Yu (Map p102; 252 702; 81 Pansodan St; mains K1500-5000;) The small and attentive Nan Yu is one of the more popular Chinese restaurants in the city centre and has all the usual Cantonese specialities.

Golden Duck Restaurant (Map p102; ☎ 231 234; 222-224 Strand Rd; duck mains K2000; ☺ 10am-10pm) The Golden Duck is a real-deal Chinese restaurant with all manner of 'exotic' ingredients in its dishes – if you know what we mean! Fortunately it also has some more user-friendly meals that have taste.

Mandarin Restaurant (Map p102; ☎ 252 986; 126 Mahabandoola Garden St; mains K2500) Soak up views of the Sule Paya while you eat in this tranquil English-speaking Chinese, run by the same family that owns the Mayshan Guest House. The Mandarin offers the usual assortment of northern Chinese dishes, vegetarian fare and fresh fish in a clean and fan-cooled setting.

Singapore's Kitchen (Map p98; ☎ 226 297; 524 Strand Rd; dishes K3000; ☺ 6pm-3am; ✖) This is one of the best Chinese restaurants in town and its waterfront location ensures that the fish is as fresh as can be. The food is excellent and the service good, and it has tables that spill onto the footpath during fair weather. At night it's a bright and busy place, and even better is the late closing time. Besides seafood, it does a good job of crispy-fried duck, as well as lots of veggie and noodle dishes.

Yin Fong Seafood Restaurant (Map p93; ☎ 546 149; Kan Yeik Tha Rd; dishes K4500-8000; ✖) The setting, beside a busy main road, isn't ideal but the seafood sure is. This pricey restaurant has carved a well-founded reputation as one of the top Chinese restaurants in Yangon.

Indian

Along Anawrahta Rd, west of Sule Paya Rd towards the Sri Kali temple, are a number of shops serving Indian biryani (*kyettha dan bauk* in Burmese), and at night the *roti* and *dosa* (a thin crepe filled with potato; spelt *toeshay* on menus) makers set up along the pavement on the side streets. Indian food is probably the cheapest way of eating in Yangon, particularly at places that serve *thali* (all-you-can-eat meals of rice and vegetable curries piled on a fresh banana leaf or stainless-steel plate), which often cost only K300. Biryani costs a bit more, around K500. Most places shut around 7pm or 8pm.

New Delhi Restaurant (Map p102; Anawrahta Rd; meals from K600) The tiny, and therefore rather hard to find (look carefully for the small opening hidden amongst the shops), New Delhi is a superb place for genuine South Indian dishes. The selection includes *puris* (puffy breads), *idli* (rice ball in broth), breathtaking

masala dosa and banana-leaf *thalis* as well as a wide variety of curries. Overhead fans keep the swarms of bugs attracted by the ceiling lights from dive bombing your food. The *chai* ain't bad either. The restaurant opens onto the street between 29th and Shwe Bontha Sts.

Shwe Htoo Restaurant (Map p102; cnr Anawrahta Rd & 30th St; meals from K700; ☺ 6-9.30pm) This excellent Indian joint is perfect for either a full meal or just a quick snack (the samosas are superb). It's open later than most, though you're not encouraged to linger, and its *palata* (fried flatbread) and biryani plate is worthy of mention.

our pick Nila Biryani Shop (Map p102; Anawrahta Rd; meals from K800) Giant cauldrons full of spices, broths and rice bubble away at the front of this bright and brash Indian joint. It's never less than packed, and for good reason: the biryanis are probably among the best that your lips will ever embrace. The chicken has been cooked so slowly and for so long that the meat just drips off, the rice itself is out of this world and the banana lassi (spelt *laci*) is divine. Nothing on the menu costs more than K1700 and most is a fraction of that. It's far and away the best of several similar nearby places.

Bharat Restaurant (Map p102; ☎ 281 519; 356 Mahabandoola Rd; mains from K1000) One of the most reliable Indian restaurants in the city centre, this place has a strong focus on the coconut flavours of the southern half of the subcontinent. Bharat's marble-topped tables make a nice change from the long cafeteria-style tables at the Indian places on Anawrahta Rd.

Golden City Chetty Restaurant (Map p102; Sule Paya Rd; mains K1500; ☺ 6-9.30pm) There are two branches of this restaurant, very close to each other a little to the north of the Sule Paya. Packed day and night, these two white-tiled Indian extravaganzas offer some of central Yangon's finest spice and rice meals. The speedy turnover of food ensures that everything is fresh and hygienic, as well as very tasty. It's one of the few city-centre Indian places open after 7pm.

Ashoka Indian Restaurant (Map p93; ☎ 555 539; 28B Pho Sein Rd; mains from $2; ☺ 6-10pm; ✖) The creamy curries of north India are the main event here and they are an event worth getting seriously worked up about. The portions are small but that justifies ordering several courses including piping hot breads and filling samosas. The colonial villa the restaurant is housed in is as gorgeous as the food. The service is formal and attentive.

Japanese

Yakiniku Japanese Barbeque (Map p102; ☎ 274 738; 357 Shwe Bontha St; BBQ dishes K1500; ⏱ 9am-10pm; ☒) A fun Japanese restaurant where the tables open up to reveal that favourite of men the world over – a barbecue! Yes, the chefs have it easy here because you cook your own meat and so, if you're a woman and want to eat something vaguely edible then it's best to go without a man! The menu is full of pictures of what your dinner should, but probably won't, end up looking like.

Furusato Japanese Restaurant (Map p93; ☎ 556 265; 137 West Shwegondine Rd; mains K2500) Furusato, a traditional Japanese restaurant (no shoes, floor seating), enjoys a stellar reputation because of its high-quality sushi and sashimi. The hotpot and barbecue dishes are also excellent and the wood-panelled building itself is lovely.

Japan Japan (Map p102; ☎ 09-513 0016; 239 Pansodan St; mains K2500-3000) A kitschy-decorated, but strangely cool, new Japanese restaurant with Japanese staff who like to make a fuss over you. The food is cheap, filling and mouth-watering with some superb sushi. We've had a number of raving reports from travellers over this place.

Ichiban-Kan (Map p98; ☎ 803 1583; 17-18 Aung San Stadium; noodle dishes $5-7; ☒) An intimate and tasteful restaurant, which seems to have been lifted straight from the backstreets of the Tokyo of yesteryear. It's a perfect spot for couples wishing to indulge in a little romantic smooching over dinner. The food is as well presented and created as the décor, and the small menu focuses on soup and noodle dishes.

Korean

Lavender Food and Drink (Map p98; 179-181 Bo Ta Htaung Pagoda Rd; mains K2000; ⏱ 10am-10pm) Slick and modern restaurant with a relaxed atmosphere and a tasty range of Korean and Japanese dishes. If you don't want a meal then the inexhaustible range of milk shakes and yoghurt drinks (K1400) might tempt.

World Cup (Map p93; ☎ 525 728; Dhama Zedi Rd; mains K4000-5000) This rare Korean restaurant is a little hard to find (it's diagonally opposite the Savoy Hotel), and is located inside a family home. You eat in the front room, which gives it a laid-back family vibe, but bring a friend

or you'll feel a bit lonely and it's best to call ahead just to check it's open.

French

Le Planteur (Map p93; ☎ 541 997; 22 Kaba Aye Pagoda Rd; mains $15-25; ☒) Widely considered the best restaurant in Yangon and with meal prices to match its exalted reputation. A list of just a few of the delicacies that will whet the appetite of foodies: chowder of Japanese scallops with black truffles and Myanmar white beans, and locally caught filet of parrot fish. Book ahead and dress sharp.

Italian

our pick **Café Dibar** (Map p93; ☎ 500 6143; 14/20 Than Lwin Rd; mains K4000; ☒) An unassuming and romantic restaurant heavy with Mediterranean senses. The food, which is Italian through and through, is well priced and comes with all the olives attached in just the right places. The beef lasagne (K4500) is superb and the staff normally chuck in a free antipasto as well. It has a comprehensive wine list (Italian and local) and is popular at lunch and dinner with well-to-do locals. If you've been on the road a while this is exactly what you're looking for.

Cia Pizzeria Italiana (Map p102; ☎ 249 992; 262 Pansodan St; mains K5000) Small and simple Italian restaurant without any unnecessary fuss, and with passable imitations of Rome's finest, including spaghetti with seafood and a decent selection of pizzas. The Myanmar chef has been trained by an Italian.

L'Opera Restaurant (Map p90; ☎ 665 516; 62D U Tun Nyein St; mains from $10; ☒) One of the better and more elegant restaurants in Yangon, L'Opera boasts well-trained and smartly dressed waiters, but more important is the Italian owner and chef's meticulous preparation. The outdoor garden seating is a bonus in good weather. Lunch is cheaper than the dinner service, but on Fridays there is a $15 all-you-can-eat-and-drink special.

Teashops

Yangon's numerous teashops are not just places to have cups of milk tea and coffee or tiny pots of Chinese tea. They are great places for cheap Burmese, Chinese and Indian snacks. For breakfast, in fact, you're often better off spending a few kyat in a teashop, rather than eating the boring toast, egg and instant-coffee breakfasts provided by many hotels and guesthouses. As well as serving food and drink, teashops are a social institution where gossip is passed around, deals made and, if you believe the rumours, government spies are rampant. There are so many teashops in the city that in parts (such as central Yangon) they virtually merge with one another to create a single, huge multi-coloured teashop. Just park your bottom on any spare doll's-house-sized plastic chair and get into the spirit of things.

Sei Taing Kya Teashop (Map p93; 53 Za Ga War St; ☺ 7am-5pm) This is the most famous tea-tippling spot in Yangon. It has six branches but this one is the most happening. It serves top-quality tea, samosas, *palata, mohinga* (rice noodles with chicken or fish and eggs) and *ei-kya-kwe* (deep-fried pastries). A branch east of the city centre is at 103 Anawrahta Rd, on the corner of 51st St. There's another just south of the Theinbyu Playground and by Kandawgyi, on Thein Byu Rd.

Yatha Teashop (Map p102; ☎ 349 341; 353 Mahabandoola Rd; ☺ 7am-5pm) Mahabandoola Rd has a couple of more modest establishments that typify the general division between Chinese- and Indian-influenced teashops. This place, between Seikkan Thar and 39th Sts, represents the latter, providing fresh samosas and *palata*.

The **Golden Dragon Teashop** (Map p98; cnr Anawrahta Rd & 19th St) and **Lucky Seven Teashop** (Map p98; Anawrahta Rd) are lively teashops serving good snacks and are in the vicinity of several mid-range guesthouses east of the city centre.

Street Food

Lit up like Times Square, little makeshift grills and small plastic tables line 19th St between Mahabandoola and Anawrahta Rds in Chinatown. To order, point to what you want – a selection of meat and fish skewers (K300) or artichokes and bean curd. It's a bit of a men's club, though there's no reason to think women aren't welcome. Another good Indian stall (Map p98), selling good barbe-cued fish, is nearby on Latha St, just south of Mahabandoola Rd, next to Vilas Beauty Salon. Snack places for dessert are around the corner on Mahabandoola Rd.

The noodle stalls on 32nd St, near the Sule Paya, are very cheap and very good. Food stalls serving curries and rice – for experienced stomachs only – can be found along the eastern side of Bo Galay Zay St (east of Sule Paya).

Quick Eats

If you're seeking more of a café-style atmosphere, see p126.

Sharkey's (Map p93; Inya Rd) More of a shop than a restaurant, but whatever it is there's no denying its popularity with the expat community. It sells locally made cheese, yoghurt, pizzas (part cooked – you need your own oven to finish them off), pesto, olives and sundried tomatoes, as well as home-grown rocket and other vegetables and fresh herbs.

Ginza Pan Food Center (Map p98; ☎ 379 234; 29 Gyo Phyu Rd; mains K1500; 🔀) The Ginza Pan, across from Aung San Stadium, is a pop place for well-to-do local teenagers who can't decide if they are feeling Italian, Japanese or Chinese today. As it happens it does all of the above adequately.

Tokyo Fried Chicken (Map p102; 156 Mahabandoola Garden St; mains K1500; 🔀 8am-9pm; 🔀) There are several outlets of TFC, Yangon's very own version of KFC. One is just north of Mahabandoola Rd and the other is across the street from Bogyoke Aung San Market.

J' Donuts (Map p102; Shwe Bontha St; snacks from K1000; ☺ 8am-9pm) is just south of Bogyoke Aung San Rd and there is another branch on Pansodan St (Map p102; open 8am to 9pm) between Mahabandoola and Anawrahta Rds.

DRINKING

Apart from the following listed bars and cafés, Yangon abounds in teashops, where milk tea or coffee, endless tiny pots of Chinese tea and cheap snacks are available. As these places are a good choice for breakfast, we have included them opposite.

Bars

Most of the city goes dark around 9pm. A lively expat scene rotates around the city during the week: Wednesday nights are for the Savoy (Captain's Bar), and Friday nights the Strand.

Strand Bar (Map p102; ☎ 243 377; 92 Strand Rd; ☺ 11am-11pm) Primarily an expat scene, this classic bar inside the Strand Hotel has any foreign liquors you may be craving behind its polished wooden bar. Occasionally there's someone around to play the baby grand. Friday afternoon and early evening is a two-for-one happy hour (there's a standard happy hour all other days from 5pm to 7pm). The bar is pleasantly relaxed and comfortable despite the price of the rooms above.

Mr Guitar Café (Map p93; ☎ 700 446; 22 Sayasan St; ⏰ 6pm-midnight) Founded by famous Myanmar vocalist Nay Myo Say, this dark café-bar features live folk music from about 7pm to midnight nightly. Well-known local musicians drop by frequently to sit in with the regular house group. The clientele is a mix of locals and expats.

Frenz Bar & Grill (Map p93; ☎ 547 324; Kaba Aye Pagoda Rd; ⏰ noon-late) A sleek place, especially for Yangon, Frenz keeps the décor minimalist and, like trendy bars everywhere, risks style over substance. Live music, mostly covers, is on offer most nights.

50th Street Bar & Grill (Map p98; ☎ 298 287; 9-13 50th St, ⏰ 11am-10.30pm) Popular with locals and expats on Wednesday nights, when it has $5 pizzas to soften the drinking. Many people go straight from here to the Savoy.

British Club Bar (Map p98; off Gyo Byu St; ⏰ 1st Fri evening of month until midnight) Think ambassadors sit around at night discussing world peace? Think again! Once a month the ever-so-prim British Club throws open its doors and discussion moves from world peace to beer consumption. Expats (of all nationalities) rate this as the social event of the month. Bring your passport.

Captain's Bar (Map p93; ☎ 526 289; Savoy Hotel, 129 Dhama Zedi Rd; ⏰ until midnight) This bar at the Savoy is popular with locals and expats, especially on Wednesday and Friday nights, when there's live jazz.

Ginki Kids (Map p93; Kan Baw Sa Rd; ⏰ until midnight) This new, small and cosy bar is fast gaining a reputation on the expat circle as the coolest in Yangon.

Cafés

Zawgyi's House (Map p102; ☎ 256 355; 372 Bogyoke Aung San Rd) The city's hippest coffee shop is a bold display of what could be if the city was ever allowed out of its doldrums. It's a café/gift shop ensemble with a cool interior and shady terrace perfect for people watching. It's very much a hang-out for expats and passing businesspeople, all of whom appreciate the expensive shakes, juices, ice creams and sandwiches.

Ritz Café (Map p98; ☎ 253 680; 296 Shwedagon Pagoda Rd; meals K2000-3000; ⏰ 10.30am-10.30pm Mon-Sat, 4-10.30pm Sun; 🔾) Much more informal than the name implies, this trendy café is for the young or young at heart. It has a wide range of Asian favourites, a dozen or

more coffees and juices and you can download some Western treats including – wait for it – a full English breakfast (K1800)! It has a cool decoration theme including beach-flavoured tables.

Café Aroma (Map p102; Sule Paya Rd; ⏰ 8am-9.30pm; 🔾) The Starbucks of Yangon, this café has several outlets around the city. The Sule Paya Rd branch, next to the cinema, is the most central, and offers fine, freshly brewed coffee and fruit smoothies (from about K500) in a stylish setting. Pasta and pizza dishes are also available for K800 to K1400. Other Café Aroma outlets are at the Yuzana Plaza, just east of Kandawgyi, and at the La Pyat Wun Shopping Centre (opposite).

Parisian Cake & Café (Map p102; Sule Paya Rd; ⏰ 8am-7pm; 🔾) It certainly ain't as chic as a café in its namesake city, but it's cool, relaxing and has an arm-length list of teas and coffees, as well as cold juices and shakes, a variety of cakes and light pasta lunches. There is another branch in the heart of Chinatown at 778 Mahabandoola St (Map p98).

Mr Brown Café (Map p102; Mahabandoola Garden St; 🔾) Another place to get a break from the heat, sip a cold drink and chow down on a cake.

ENTERTAINMENT

Nightlife and Yangon aren't usually used in the same sentence. The main form of local recreation is hanging out in teashops or 'cold drink' shops. While Bangkok makes an evening in Yangon seem quaint and provincial, entertainment can be found for those who are keen.

On festival days (some are listed on p116), local bands occasionally organise live outdoor concerts. During the water festival in April, sizable rock-music shows are set up along Inya Rd and University Ave Rd, and feature local underground rockers.

National Theatre

The Yangon government revived the performance of Myanmar classical dance-drama at the **National Theatre** (Map p98; Myoma Kyaung Rd; tickets K1000-4000), a government-sponsored facility, northwest of Bogyoke Aung San Market.

Dinner Shows

There are a couple of large, banquet-style restaurants with floorshows in Yangon. Heavily used by the visiting business community, these dining spots are typically Chinese-owned and feature extensive Chinese menus plus a few Burmese dishes. Entertainment is provided by bands that perform a mixture of local, Western and Chinese pop songs. Some places also feature Myanmar classical dance and/or marionette theatre.

LakeView Theatre Restaurant (Map p93; ☎ 249 255; kphotel@mptmail.net.mm; Kan Yeik Tha Rd; dinner & show $6) Attached to the Kandawgyi Palace Hotel, the entertaining show includes 10 traditional Burmese dances; one involves a woman balancing on one foot on a chair while juggling a cane ball. It all kicks off at 7pm.

Clubs

Yagon's own interpretation of club culture involves competitive fashion shows and mostly listless groups of men sipping bottles of beer. Most clubs have a nominal cover charge that includes the first drink.

There are several rooftop clubs in Theingyi Zei Plaza, on Shwedagon Pagoda Rd in Chinatown. They tend to be open from early evening until late.

You might find yourself straining to hear the gentle lap of ocean waves at **Zero Zone Rock Restaurant** (Map p102; ☎ 373 384; 4th fl, 2 Theingyi Zei market), whose bamboo shelters seem more appropriate for a beach club than a Yangon rooftop. It's a very male kind of place and there are some even more male-only dives nearby (think Bangkok...). **BME Entertainment** (Map p93; ☎ 512 670; 881A University Ave Rd) is a seedy dive club close to the US embassy.

Cinemas

There's no better city for Myanmar cinephiles than Yangon. By a conservative estimate there are over 50 theatres, a half-dozen or so found along Bogyoke Aung San Rd, east of the Sule Paya. Tickets are K800 or less per seat. Critically acclaimed films are in short supply; rather there is a succession of syrupy Myanmar dramas, Bollywood musicals, kung-fu smash-ups, plus a few Hollywood blockbusters.

Nay Pyi Daw Cinema (Map p102; ☎ 252 115; Sule Paya Rd; 🏱) This cinema across from Traders Hotel and next to Café Aroma has showings throughout the day. It's one of the busiest cinemas in the city.

Thamada Cinema (Map p98; ☎ 246 962; 5 Ah Lan Paya Pagoda Rd; 🏱) Easily the best cinema for foreigners, it is comfortable and shows fairly recent international (including American) films.

American Center (Map p98; 14 Taw Win St) This American-sponsored centre shows free American movies at noon every Monday.

SHOPPING

It's unfortunate that shipping goods from Myanmar is either prohibitively expensive or simply not possible because of political reasons; travellers are therefore limited to whatever can fit in their carry-on baggage. While it isn't quite the shoppers' mecca that Bangkok is, Yangon does offer a more manageable alternative as there are fewer and smaller outlets, and prices tend to be cheaper all around.

Arts & Handicrafts

A small but thriving local gallery scene exists in Yangon; the majority are spread around the relatively posh Golden Valley neighbourhood. Several painters have achieved recognition abroad and prices in general are not cheap.

Nandawun (Map p93; ☎ 221 271; cnr Baho & Ahlone Rds) It deals in rare books on Myanmar, ethnic minority costumes, lacquerware and gems.

Traditions Gallery (Map p93; ☎ 513 709; 24 Inya Myaing Rd) Quality reproductions of traditional Myanmar handicrafts are sold here. The director is Claudia Saw Lwin.

Ivy Gallery (Map p102; ☎ 500 0677; 152 Konzaydan St) Features a fine collection of modern Myanmar art.

Both **Golden Valley Art Centre** (Map p93; ☎ 513 621; 54(D) Shwe Taung Gyar St) and **Inya Gallery of Art** (Map p93; ☎ 534 327; 50(B) Inya Rd) feature exhibits by contemporary Myanmar painters.

Malls

There are a number of modern Western-style shopping malls selling everything from hipster jeans to flat-screen TVs. The largest and most convenient:

Blazon Centre (Map p93; 72 U Wi Za Ra Rd)
Dagon Centre (Map p93; 262-264 Pyay Rd)
Excel Treasure (Map p93; Kaba Aye Pagoda Rd)
FMI Centre (Map p102; 380 Bogyoke Aung San Rd) Just east of Bogyoke Aung San Market.
La Pyat Wun Plaza (Map p98; 37 Ah Lan Paya Pagoda Rd) Not far north of the train station.

Markets

Shopping at the *zei* (markets, often spelt *zay*) in central Yangon can be fun, educational and a chance to interact with the locals.

The long southern stairway at Shwedagon Paya is lined with small shops catering to pilgrims and tourists alike. Popular items include sandalwood bracelets, small drums and papier-mâché animals. Bargaining is expected here.

Bogyoke Aung San Market (Map p102; Bogyoke Aung San Rd; ☷ 8.30am-5pm Tue-Sun) A half-day could easily be spent wandering around this 70-year-old sprawling market (sometimes called by its old British name, Scott Market). Besides the fact that it has over 2000 shops and the largest selection of Myanmar handicrafts you'll find under several roofs, the market is a fantastic opportunity to smile, laugh and haggle alongside local shoppers. You'll find a whole variety of interesting souvenirs, from lacquerware and Shan shoulder bags to T-shirts and puppets. Pick up some nice slippers here, convenient for all the on-and-off demanded by paya protocol. Gems and jewellery are also on hand. If you need somewhere to store all this booty, several shops in the market across Bogyoke Aung San Rd (and in the New Bogyoke Market, which caters more to household needs) sell an extensive variety of backpacks of all sizes and brands, some more authentic than others. All in all, though, this market isn't as exotic as some travel brochures like to make out.

Theingyi Zei (Map p102; Shwedagon Pagoda Rd) The biggest market in Yangon, this is especially good for locals, who find Bogyoke Aung San Market a little too pricey. Most of the merchandise is ordinary housewares and textiles, but the market is renowned for its large selection of traditional herbs and medicines, which can be found on the ground floor of the most easterly building. Traditional herbal shampoo, made by boiling the bark of the Tayaw shrub with big black *kin pun* (acacia pods), is sold in small plastic bags; this is the secret of Myanmar women's smooth, glossy hair. There used to be a sizable snake section, which featured the fresh blood and organs of various snakes as well as live ones being disembowelled on the spot for medicinal consumption. This trade has died off (or gone fully underground) and what remains of it can be found on the 4th floor. In all truth, though, there is little to see in this dark and lonely corner of the market, save possibly a solitary jar of pickled serpents, and the atmosphere is a little weird. A new mall-like section on Shwedagon Pagoda Rd, Theingyi Zei Plaza, contains some less-interesting modern shops.

Thirimingala Zei (Map p93; Yangon River bank, Ahlone Township) Off the northern end of Strand Rd (almost a mile west of People's Park) is a labyrinth of vendors selling fresh foodstuffs, vegetables, fruits and meat. It's worth a stroll for the amazing sights and smells, not all of them especially pleasant. Of all the markets in Yangon this one is probably the most exotic and interesting for those just watching rather than shopping.

San Pya Fish Market (Map p93; Nat Sin St) Catch even more of an aroma further north along the riverfront.

Mingala Zei (Map p93; cnr Ban Yar Da La St & Set Yone Rd) A little southeast of Kandawgyi, this market proffers textiles, clothes, electrical appliances, plasticware, preserved and tinned foodstuffs, modern medicines, and even cosmetics from China, Thailand and Singapore.

Iron bazaar (Map p98; cnr Mahabandoola & Madaw Rds) Located in Yangon's Chinatown. You can find all the items that are used in Chinese cooking here.

Itinerant vendors set up along Anawrahta Rd east and west of Sule Paya Rd from about 6pm to 10pm nightly, selling everything from Chinese toothbrushes to fresh fruit and shish kebabs. Chinatown itself extends east–west between Madaw and Shwedagon Pagoda Rds, and north–south between Mahabandoola and Strand Rds.

Speciality Shops

J's Irrawaddy Dream (Map p102; ☎ 243 377; Strand Hotel, 92 Strand Rd; ☷ 9am-8pm) This shop features high-quality Myanmar textiles, clothes, lacquer and other handicrafts. It's an especially good place to find stylish women's dresses.

Royal Rose (Map p90; ☎ 662 576; www.kyolone.com; Inya Yeiktha St) East of Inya Lake, Royal Rose sells handbags and beautifully crafted women's slippers, better than the kind sold in Bogyoke Aung San Market.

Monsoon (Map p98; ☎ 295 224; 85-87 Thein Byu Rd; ☷ 10am-10pm) Above the excellent restaurant is an equally excellent craft shop selling high-quality products for prices that don't send waves of shock through your body.

If your prescription spectacles should go missing, optometry shops line both sides of Shwe Bontha St between Bogyoke Aung San and Anawrahta Rds (Map p102).

The inappropriately named **Morning Market** (Map p102; cnr 38th St & Anawrahta Rd) is a much more raw and gritty version of the Bogyoke Aung San Market. To temper the perfume of all the fresh flowers sold here it's also the city centre's smelly, fresh fish pick-up point.

Yangon is a surprisingly good place to find DVDs of American, British, French and Hong Kong films. Be aware that almost all DVD shops, many of which are in Chinatown, deal in pirated copies.

Tailors

Yangon isn't a place you'd usually think of for tailor-made clothes, but prices are among the lowest in Southeast Asia. The selection of fabrics at tailor shops, however, is mostly restricted to synthetics. Cotton in prints, plaids, solids and batiks can easily be found in the larger markets, so you may do better to buy cloth at a market and bring it to a tailor for cutting and sewing.

J's Clothes (Map p102; 243 377; Strand Hotel, 92 Strand Rd; 9am-8pm) Part of J's Irrawaddy Dream, this place works with high-quality Myanmar and imported fabrics.

Globe Tailoring (Map p102; 273 416; 367 Bogyoke Aung San Rd) Well regarded by local expats for women's and men's tailoring.

Tip-Top Tailors (Map p98; 245 428; cnr Mahabandoola Rd & 43rd St) A friendly tailors, which is open 'everyday, except some of the days when we are shut'. Some of the days when it is most likely to be shut are Fridays and Sundays.

GETTING THERE & AWAY
Air

See p355 for information on international air travel, and p359 for details on domestic air travel to and from Yangon.

Boat

Along the Yangon River waterfront, which wraps around the south of Yangon, are a number of jetties that are home to long-distance ferry services. The four main passenger jetties (Pongyi St, Lan Thit St, Kaingdan St and Hledan St; Map p98) service long-distance ferries headed up-delta towards Pathein or north along the Ayeyarwady River to Pyay (Prome), Bagan and Mandalay. Named after the respective streets that extend north from each jetty, all four are clustered in an area just south of Lanmadaw township and southwest of Chinatown. When you purchase a ferry ticket from the government's **Inland Water Transport** (IWT; Map p98; 381 912, 380 764) deputy division manager's office, at the back of Lan Thit jetty, be sure to ask which jetty your boat will be departing from.

Myanma Five Star Line (MFSL; Map p98; 295 756; cnr Merchant St & Thein Byu Rd) used to have passenger-carrying ships that sailed between Yangon and Dawei, Myeik (Mergui) and Kawthoung. They now only carry cargo, but if you're planning on heading that way it can't hurt to ask about paying passengers. Boats leave from the **MFSL jetty** (Map p102; Chanmayeiseikan jetty).

There are several privately owned companies that operate luxury cruises from Yangon to Bagan and Mandalay (see p364).

PATHEIN

IWT boats depart from the Lan Thit jetty in Yangon for Pathein at 5pm daily (arriving 11am the next day). The cost is $7 for deck class (an easy chair if you're early enough) or $42 per person for a cabin with private bathroom. From Pathein to Yangon, boats also leave at 5pm and arrive at 11am the next day.

TWANTE

The alternative to getting to Twante by the Dalah ferry/bus combo is to take the two-hour scenic trip along the Yangon River and Twante Canal (see p135 for details).

Bus

There are two major bus terminals in Yangon: Aung Mingalar Bus Terminal (p130) and Hlaing Thar Yar Bus Terminal (p130).

A third station, smaller and less important than the previous two (known as Tha-khin Mya Pan-gyan Gate, Map p98), is near the Western Park Chinese Restaurant. Buses from here, which are generally older and lack air-con, service Bago, Mawbi and Taikgyi. Companies based in Aung Mingalar also travel to Bago so the only real reason to leave from Tha-khin Mya Park is because the station is within walking distance of the city centre.

Most signs at the bus terminals are in Burmese; however, English-speaking touts anxious to steer you in the right direction are in abundance. To avoid the hassle and attention make sure your taxi driver (both of the major terminals are around 45 minutes from the city centre) knows where you want to go and, even better, the name of the specific bus company. Showing the driver your ticket will do; if you don't have a ticket, ask a Burmese speaker to write the information on a slip of paper.

You can buy tickets at the bus terminals or at several central locations, mostly opposite the central Yangon train station), alongside

Aung San Stadium. Many hotels can book tickets for you.

Bus companies with offices at the Aung San Stadium:

Mann Shwe PYI Express (☎ 88267, 73882)
MAW Travelling (☎ 393 066)
New Mandalar Htum (☎ 701 772)
PTT Express (☎ 705 833)
Shwe Buses (☎ 249 672)
Teht Lann Express (☎ 254 485)

AUNG MINGALAR BUS TERMINAL (HIGHWAY BUS STATION)

Located to the northeast of the airport, Aung Mingalar (Map p90) is the only official bus terminal for all 150 bus lines leaving for the northern part of Myanmar, as well as for Kyaiktiyo (Golden Rock), Mawlamyine (Moulmein) and destinations to the south.

To Thandwe & Ngapali Beach

There are about seven or eight bus lines operating on this route (Yangon to Thandwe K12,000, 18 hours). Almost all leave around 3pm and 4pm.

To the North

Some destinations served by Aung Mingalar follow. Journey times depend on road conditions and the health of your bus.

Bagan (K20,000, 16 hours) To go there via Pyay requires bus changes in Pyay and Magwe – this seems to be a route only used by those on package bus tours, or with a private car.
Kalaw (K15,000, 15 to 17 hours) Buses depart in the late afternoon and go over the mountains.
Mandalay (K10,000, 12 to 15 hours) Buses leave from around 4.30pm to 6pm.
Pyay (K4000-6000, six hours)
Taunggyi for Inle Lake (K15,000, 17 hours) Get off in Shwenyaung and then grab a pick-up or taxi to Nyaung-shwe on Inle Lake.

To Bago, Kyaiktiyo, Hpa-An & Mawlamyine

Bago (K6000, two hours) Buses leave every 30 minutes from the early morning to early afternoon.
Kyaiktiyo and Kinpun (K8000, 4½ hours) Buses leave between 7am and 1pm. There are also several companies with ticket booths along Pansodan St in Yangon with trips to Kinpun on similar large, air-con buses. However, these leave around 9pm and aren't very desirable unless you prefer to arrive in the middle of the night.
Hpa-An (K8000, eight hours) Buses from 6.30pm to 8pm.
Mawlamyine (K13,000, 8 hours) A handful of buses which leave either early in the morning or later in the evening. Try to avoid the evening bus as you will arrive at the massive bridge leading into Mawlamyine at around 3am, but for security reasons will not be allowed across it until daybreak.

HLAING THAR YAR BUS TERMINAL

This is the bus terminal for travel to the delta region (called Ayeyarwady Division) to the west of Yangon, including destinations such as Pathein (K7000, 3½ hours), Chaung Tha Beach (K8000, six to seven hours) and Ngwe Saung Beach (K8000, five hours).

It's 45 minutes to an hour away by taxi (K7000) west of the city centre on the other side of the Yangon River on Hwy 5 (Yangon–Pathein Rd). More than 20 bus lines operate out of here.

Car

Many people choose to forgo both public transport and package tours by hiring a guide and car, and maybe an additional driver for doing DIY tours. For some this combines the best of both worlds – relative comfort and safety, and flexibility and personalised itineraries. This can be arranged through a travel agent (p92) or hotel front desk. See p366 for information on car rental.

Train

The most frequented train from Yangon is the 14-hour trip north to Mandalay. Prices vary depending on the train: an ordinary-class seat costs $11 to $15, an upper-class seat $30 to $35, and a sleeper $33 to $40. Departure times from Yangon are 4.30am, 5am, 5.30am and 12.45pm. Tickets can normally only be bought up to five days in advance but two days is more usual. Theoretically foreigners are not allowed to buy tickets for any berths below upper-class but ordinary-class tickets are sometimes offered. It's possible to get off anywhere, the most relevant stops being Bago, Taungoo and Thazi. Another line heads north to Pyay and another to Kyaiktiyo and Mawlamyine in the south.

For general train enquiries call **Yangon train station** (Map p98; ☎ 202 178; ☆ 6am-4pm). See p368 for information on rail travel within Myanmar using the government's Myanma Railways.

GETTING AROUND
To/From the Airport

Taxi drivers will approach you before you exit the airport terminal. The standard fare for a ride from the airport to anywhere in the city is $8. It's best to have a few single bills so that you don't have to change money in the airport. From the city centre to the airport it can cost slightly less (K6000 or about $5).

Boat

Cross-river ferries to Dalah ($1), on the southern bank of the Yangon River, leave about every 20 minutes from Pansodan St jetty (Map p102), at the foot of Pansodan St, from the early morning to the evening.

You can hire privately owned sampans (flat-bottomed skiffs) from the Pansodan or Botataung jetties for K1500 per hour if you just want to have a look at the river life.

Bus

Over 40 city bus routes connect the townships within Yangon. Many buses are wonderfully old-fashioned 1940s buses. Plans to phase out these beauties have been in the making for a few years but, so far, nothing has come of them. Often, the buses are impossibly crowded – a Myanmar bus is not full until every available handhold for those hanging off the sides and back has been taken. Other routes use newer air-conditioned Japanese and Korean buses that aren't too bad; some routes also use pickup trucks with benches in the back.

If you can find a space on a bus you can go anywhere in central Yangon for K100. Prices often double at night, but they're still cheap and still crowded. Prior to the summer of 2007 most local bus fares used to be K5 but overnight, due to government fuel price hikes, prices rose by 2000% to K100. The majority of Yangon workers, who earn just K9000 a month, suddenly found themselves forking out K6000 for transport to and from work. It was anger over these price increases that eventually led to the huge September protests (see p51).

The *Yangon Bus Directory* (K13,000) is a spiral-bound colour map book with 336 pages. It has all bus stops in English and Burmese.

Some useful bus routes:

Bogyoke Aung San Market to Mingala Zei (southeast of Kandawgyi) Japanese pick-up number 1
Chaukhtatgyi Paya Buses 42 and 47
Insein to Thein Byu Rd Near the YMCA, Three Seasons Hotel and Cozy Guest House – green pick-up 48
Kaba Aye Paya to Mae La Mu Paya Bus 43
Shwedagon Paya Buses 37, 43 and 46
Sule Paya to the airport Via Hledan junction, Pyay Rd, University of Yangon, western side of Inya Lake and Yangon City Hotel – blue buses 51 and 53, and air-con 51

Sule Paya to Aung Mingalar Bus Station Buses 43, 45 and 51
Sule Paya to Thamaing Junction (8 Mile Junction) Along Insein Rd – buses 44, 45 and 53
Sule Paya to Hlaing Thar Yar Bus Station Buses 54, 59 and 96

Taxi

All licensed taxis have a visible taxi sign on the roof. The less expensive licensed taxis are the usually older, midsized Japanese cars, many missing their door handles and other 'extras'.

Fares are highly negotiable: most trips around the central area shouldn't cost more than K1000 one way, and K1000 to K1500 for longer trips. You can also hire a taxi for about K4000 an hour. For the entire day, you should pay from $20 to $35 depending on the quality of the vehicle and your negotiating skills. Be sure to work out all details before you agree to a price and itinerary.

From downtown to the highway bus terminal, drivers ask for K7000 and the trip takes from 45 minutes to an hour. To the Hlaing Thar Yar Bus Terminal taxis charge around K7000.

For all types of taxis the asking fares usually leap by 30% or so after sunset and on weekends, when rationed petrol isn't available. Late-night taxis – after 11pm or so – often cost double the day rate, mainly because the supply of taxis is considerably lower than in the day, so the drivers are able to charge more.

Many drivers speak enough English to understand directions to your destination but it's advisable to have someone write them out for you in Burmese as insurance.

Train

A circular train route loops out north from Yangon to Insein, Mingaladon and North Okkalapa townships and then back into the city. For more info see p114.

Trishaw

Every Asian country seems to have its own interpretation of the bicycle trishaw. In Myanmar, trishaw passengers ride with the driver, but back-to-back (one facing forward, one backward). These contraptions are called *saiq-ka* (as in side-car) and to ride one across the city centre costs roughly K300 to K500.

Nowadays trishaws are not permitted on the main streets between midnight and 10am. They're most useful for side streets and areas of town where traffic is light.

Around Yangon

Let the adventure begin! As the last of the Yangon (Rangoon) suburbs disappear into the rear view mirror you enter an older world where time is measured less by the tick-tocking of a clock and more by the passing of the seasons.

Immediately south of the big city are the vast, squelchy swamps and river channels of the delta region. Travel here might be tough, but the rewards include starry nights on chugging river ferries and pagodas that float on rivers full of fish that jump in anticipation of your arrival. West, across more rivers and past paddy field after gorgeous green paddy field, is sticky Pathein, home of golden monuments to love and a Buddha who sailed on a raft from far away Sri Lanka. Beyond that charming city is carefree Chaung Tha Beach and the refined sands of Ngwe Saung, either of which are exquisite enough to send you to cloud nine.

Heading east out of Yangon it's only a short hop to Bago (Pegu), the former capital born of a chivalrous bird. Today Bago might look a little down at heel, but it has treasures to make any monarch jealous. Some, built by nasty kings who tried to block the path of true love, are obvious enough, but others, such as saintly snakes that speak to those who care to listen, are a little more off-beat. And off-beat sums this region up well – little visited and full of the weird and wonderful, this fascinating corner of the country promises adventures and escapades you'll remember forever.

HIGHLIGHTS

- Scan the horizon for giant purple swamp hens and relax to a chorus of frog croaks in the fresh air of the **Moeyungyi Wetlands** (p152)
- Search for monks disguised as giant pythons and *nat* (spirit beings) disguised as masculine women in **Bago** (p147)

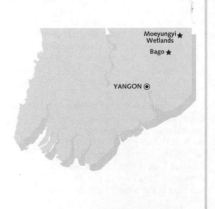

GETTING THERE & AROUND

To the west, Pathein is the transport hub with buses and boats to/from Yangon and minibuses to Chaung Tha and Ngwe Saung.

Bago, easily reached from Yangon by bus or train, is a natural stop before heading north or south to Kyaiktiyo (Golden Rock; p154) and beyond.

Getting to most other places mentioned in this chapter will require some patience, particularly if you take public transport. The southwest part of the region affords travellers the chance to ride the same river ferries that the locals use. For information on travel restrictions and getting around in the delta region, see below.

DELTA REGION

A vast, wobbly mat of greenery floating on a thousand rivers, lakes and tributaries, like a squishy waterbed, the delta region south of Yangon is one of the most fertile and dazzlingly green regions of Myanmar. A trip through this waterlogged land is nothing short of genuine adventure full of gentle rewards for the discerning traveller.

This riverine network irrigates millions of hectares of farmland, making the delta essentially one of the 'rice bowls' of Myanmar. In addition, the estuarine environments along the coast provide much of the country's saltwater and freshwater fish harvest.

THANLYIN & KYAUKTAN

သန်လျင် / ကျောက်တန်

☎ 056

One of the easiest escapes from the glamour and noise of Yangon is to the small, rural towns of Thanlyin and Kyauktan, just across the river from Yangon. The official goals of the trip are a couple of interesting religious sites, but the true goal is just getting into the groove of rural Myanmar.

During the late 16th and early 17th centuries, Thanlyin was the base for the notorious Portuguese adventurer Philip de Brito. Officially a trade representative for the Rakhaing (Arakan), he actually ran his own little kingdom from Thanlyin, siding with the Mon (when it suited him) in their struggle against the Bamar. In 1599 his private army sacked Bago, but in 1613 the Bamar besieged Thanlyin and de Brito received the punishment reserved for those who defiled Buddhist shrines – death by impalement. It took him two days to die, due, it is said, to his failure to take the recommended posture where the stake would have penetrated vital organs.

Thanlyin continued as a major port and trading centre until it was destroyed by Bamar King Alaungpaya in 1756, after which Yangon took over this role. Today Thanlyin is a low-key industrial town as well as the home of a large Hindu community.

Cyclone Nargis caused significant damage to this area; for more see p134.

Sights

Thanlyin is a relaxing place, with shaded streets and a busy market to stroll through, but there is little of the ancient city to be seen.

A short bus ride out of town will take you to the **Kyaik-khauk Paya**, a scaled down Shwedagon with stupendous views from its hilltop location. It's said to contain two Buddha hairs delivered to the site by the great sage himself. Most likely the first stupa on this hillock was erected by the Mon 600 to 800 years ago. You can hire a horse cart to the paya for about K500 each way.

Thanlyin was also the first place in Myanmar to receive Christian missionaries and the first place to have its own church. You can visit the remains of the Portuguese-built **church**, which was constructed in 1750.

Yele Paya (Midriver Paya; admission $1) at Kyauktan, 7.5 miles southeast of Thanlyin, is a sparkling floating temple adrift on a chocolate river.

TRAVEL RESTRICTIONS

Foreign tourists are not able to access many areas of the delta due to post–Cyclone Nargis travel restrictions. Even undamaged areas like Pathein, Chaung Tha Beach and Ngwe Saung Beach could not be reached at the time of writing because travellers must go through the delta to get to them. These restrictions are likely to be lifted as roads are mended – an undertaking that had not begun at the time of writing, as conditions in the wet season make road repair difficult. Check with local travel bureaus for up-to-date information.

For more on Cyclone Nargis, see p52.

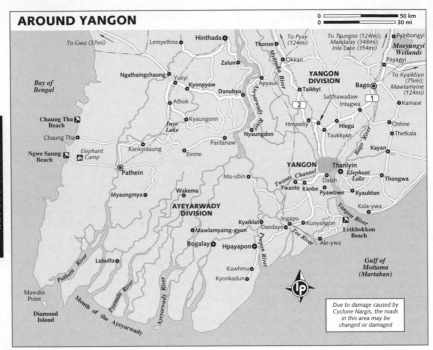

AROUND YANGON

Due to damage caused by Cyclone Nargis, the roads in this area may be changed or damaged

You can re-enact *Jaws* by feeding the massive catfish splashing about at the temple complex's edge. To reach the islet, catch one of the launch ferries reserved for foreigners from the riverbank (K4000 return). Also in the town is a small pagoda perched on the top of a hill beside the river and a hectic, flyblown and rather fishy market, which reaches its climax in the morning.

In between both towns are numerous pagodas, churches and Hindu temples. With your own set of wheels you could have great fun ferreting through this religious mosaic. The inappropriately named **Elephant Lake** makes a good picnic and bird-watching halt.

In the third week of January Thanlyin's Hindu community celebrates (or endures depending on your opinion) **Thaipusam**, the ritual of penitence in which devotees repent for bad deeds by impaling themselves with hooks and nails and walking over hot coals.

Sleeping & Eating

There is no licence for foreigner accommodation in either town, but the **White House Restaurant & Guest House** (☎ 21827; dishes about K700),

about 100yd off the main road in Thanlyin, can conjure up some decent Chinese fare.

Near the ferry landing in Kyauktan are several food vendors.

Getting There & Away

The most convenient way to visit both Thanlyin and Kyauktan on the other side of

---

CYCLONE NARGIS

Thanlyin and Kyauktan are in one of the areas hardest hit by Nargis. Because almost all buildings except the pagodas and temples were made of wood, around 90% of both towns were damaged, including most of the residential areas. Although some of the shops and restaurants have reopened, sourcing clean water remains a problem.

At the time of writing, recovery was still underway. Buses, trains and taxis are running to normal timetables and these areas can be visited by tourists but the roads were severely damaged and are still very bad in parts.

the river is to hire a taxi in Yangon ($15 for a half-day). By taxi, it takes about 30 minutes to get to Thanlyin.

However, if you're passionate about Myanmar's uncomfortable local transport or are counting kyat, very slow minibuses to Thanlyin (K200, one hour, 16 miles) leave frequently throughout the day from a spot at the corner of Bogyoke Aung San and Lower Pazundaung Rds. It costs an extra K100 if you continue by minibus from Thanlyin to Kyauktan and the Yele Paya.

In Thanlyin, horse carts are a good way to get around.

TWANTE

တွံတေရှ

☎ 045

The small town of Twante was noted for its pottery, cotton-weaving and an old Mon paya complex. Sadly, much of the town was destroyed by Cyclone Nargis in May 2008.

Reports at the time of writing indicated that resettlement and reconstruction are occurring very slowly. The exception is the renovation of temples and pagodas, which progressed very quickly thanks to donations from Buddhists around the world.

At the time of writing, foreigners were unable to visit Twante because of travel restrictions in the Ayeyarwady Delta.

When travel is again allowed, the journey to Twante, by rickety ferry, is the best reason of all for coming to the town. You'll glide past fishers in little wooden boats hauling in nets, larger cargo boats steaming towards Yangon and, on land, small villages where kids spill out from thatched huts to play.

Sights

SHWESANDAW PAYA

ရွှေဆံတော်ဘုရား

Standing 250ft tall, the **Shwesandaw Paya** (camera fee K200) is a Mon-built *zedi* (stupa), just a few years younger than Yangon's Shwedagon Paya, making it over 1000 years old. One corner of the compound commemorates King Bayinnaung's (also spelt Bayint Nyaung) defeat of a local rebellion.

Near the southern entrance is a 100-year-old sitting bronze buddha in Mandalay style. Instead of focusing on the floor, the buddha's eyes stare straight ahead. Along the western side of the *zedi* stand some old bronze buddhas.

Fortune tellers, such as readers of palms, tarot cards and *kywe-zi-be-din* (cards and shells used to predict the future) are found around the edges of the paya platform. You can also purchase small songbirds to release for good karma and a long life, and by the main entrance is an amazing set of mechanical toys – drop a coin into the slot and watch them crank into life.

Technically, from the ferry dock to Shwesandaw Paya a horse cart shouldn't cost more than K500, but in reality you'll pay K1500 return with waiting time.

OTHER SIGHTS

There is a stocky **reclining buddha** lying on a pillow of sparkling mirrors a couple of miles east of town. Next to that is an upright version.

Pottery is a major cottage industry in Twante, which supplies much of the delta region with well-designed, utilitarian containers of varying shapes and sizes. The pots were made in huge thatched-roof sheds in the **Oh-Bo Pottery Sheds** (အိုးဗိုအိုးလုပ်ငန်း) in the Oh-Bo district south of the canal, about 15 minutes' walk from the dock.

This area was severely damaged by Cyclone Nargis and, at the time of writing, had not been repaired. It may be ready for visitors (travel restrictions permitting) but check with a travel agent before you come.

Getting There & Around

The easiest way to hit up Twante from Yangon, when the area is again opened to foreign travellers, is via a short cross-river ferry and public jeep or pick-up ride. Pedestrian ferries from Pansodan St jetty (near the foot of Pansodan St and opposite the Strand Hotel) take passengers across the Yangon River to Dalah ($1, five minutes). To return to Yangon take a taxi or bus from the main street.

In Dalah, taxis, jeeps, minibuses and pick-ups leave for Twante every half-hour or so throughout the day. All leave only when completely full. The ride takes around 45 minutes in a taxi and the fare is K1500 for a back seat or K2000 for the front seat. A jeep or pick-up takes just over an hour and costs K200.

By far the most enjoyable way of getting to Twante is to take the slow ferry from Yangon ($1; departing Yangon at 7am Saturday, Monday and Wednesday). It's a colourful and action-packed two-hour journey and for those without the strength to cope with some of Myanmar's longer ferry rides this is without a doubt the best way to get your water wings without turning into an old seadog.

The ferry itself is a chaotic floating market in the early morning, cool at the start of the journey but gradually, as the journey heats up, things calm to a sleepy stupor. The boat is very cramped and you should bring a piece of matting to sit on or get there early to bag one of the few deck chairs for hire (K400).

Strangely, ferries only travel from Yangon to Twante and not the other way around. Presumably after leaving Twante they sail off the end of the world…

PATHEIN

ပုသိမ်

☎ 042 / pop 300,000

The noisiest vehicle in the river town of Pathein is a trishaw and greenery very much has the upper hand over concrete. It's the kind of place where the roll of the seasons rules over the click of a clock, yet despite these impressions it's actually Myanmar's fourth city and the most important delta port outside Yangon.

It's in the heart of a major rice-growing area that produces the finest in Myanmar, including *pawsanmwe t'ămin* (fragrant rice). The growth of the delta trade, particularly rice exports, has contributed to a general air of prosperity in the city. It receives few visitors so you're likely to draw lots of smiles and curious stares. Most travellers only stop off on their way to the beaches, but the workshops that produce colourful, hand-painted parasols, along with the shady, tree-lined village lanes to the northeast of the market, are worth a little more than this token glance.

A boat trip between Pathein and Yangon along the river, where large boats are laid up on the mud flats like dinosaurs taking their last gasp of air, is a rare window on the pattern and pace of the everyday lives of locals in the delta region.

Cyclone Nargis bypassed Pathein but, at the time of writing, the roads in the Ayeyarwady Delta between Yangon and Pathein were still badly damaged and tourists were not permitted to visit this area. Check with local tourist bureaus for updates before you travel.

History

The town was the scene of major clashes during the struggle for supremacy between the Mon and the Bamar. Later it became an important trade relay point for goods moving between India and Southeast Asia. The city's name may derive from the Burmese word for Muslim – *Pathi* – due to the heavy presence of Arab and Indian Muslim traders here centuries ago. The colonial Brits – or more likely their imported Indian civil servants – corrupted the name to Bassein.

Today, Pathein's population includes large contingents of Kayin (Karen) and Rakhaing. Although once part of a Mon kingdom, Pathein is now home to only a few Mon. During the 1970s and '80s, the Kayin villages surrounding Pathein generated insurgent activity that has since generally calmed.

Information

Despite the city being one of Myanmar's largest, there are no banks here offering foreign exchange and there are no internet services.

Sights & Activities

If you want to check out Pathein's parasol workshops, see p139.

The following sights don't charge an admission fee.

SHWEMOKHTAW PAYA

ရွှေမုဋ္ဌောဘုရား

Looming with grace over central Pathein is the golden bell of the Shwemokhtaw Paya. This large complex is unusually well-layered in legend. One states that it was originally built by India's Buddhist King Ashoka in 305 BC. Standing just 7.5ft tall, this original stupa supposedly enshrined Buddha relics and a 6in gold bar.

Another legend says a Muslim princess named Onmadandi requested each of her three Buddhist lovers build a stupa in her honour. One of the lovers erected Shwemokhtaw, the others the less distinguished Tazaung and Thayaunggyaung paya.

Whichever story you choose to believe, Bagan's King Alaungsithu is thought to have erected an 46ft stupa called Htupayon over this site in AD 1115. Then, in 1263, King Samodagossa took power, raised the stupa to 132ft and changed the name to Shwemokhtaw Paya, which means Stupa of the Half-Foot Gold Bar.

The *hti* (umbrella-like pinnacle) consists of a topmost layer made from 14lb of solid gold, a middle tier of pure silver and a bot-

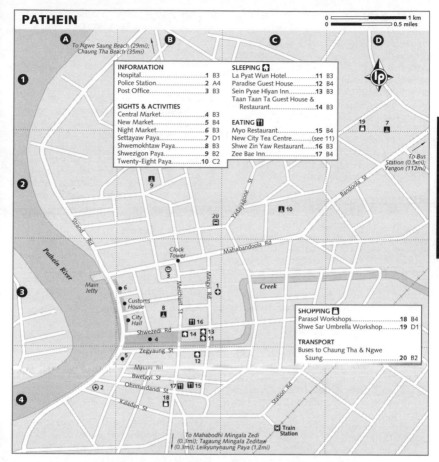

PATHEIN

INFORMATION	
Hospital.....................................**1** B3	
Police Station.........................**2** A4	
Post Office..............................**3** B3	

SIGHTS & ACTIVITIES	
Central Market.......................**4** B3	
New Market............................**5** B4	
Night Market..........................**6** B3	
Settayaw Paya........................**7** D1	
Shwemokhtaw Paya................**8** B3	
Shwezigon Paya......................**9** B2	
Twenty-Eight Paya................**10** C2	

SLEEPING	
La Pyat Wun Hotel................**11** B3	
Paradise Guest House............**12** B4	
Sein Pyae Hlyan Inn...............**13** B3	
Taan Taan Ta Guest House &	
Restaurant.......................**14** B3	

EATING	
Myo Restaurant......................**15** B4	
New City Tea Centre...........(see **11**)	
Shwe Zin Yaw Restaurant......**16** B3	
Zee Bae Inn............................**17** B4	

SHOPPING	
Parasol Workshops..................**18** B4	
Shwe Sar Umbrella Workshop.........**19** D1	

TRANSPORT	
Buses to Chaung Tha & Ngwe	
Saung.................................**20** B2	

To Ngwe Saung Beach (29mi);
Chaung Tha Beach (35mi)

To Bus
Station (0.5mi);
Yangon (112mi)

Pathein River

Strand Rd

Merchant St

Mingyi Rd

Yadayatone St

Mahabandoola Rd

Bandoola St

Clock
Tower

Main
Jetty

Customs
House

City
Hall

Shwezedi Rd

Zegyaung St

Myoma Rd

Bwetgyi St

Ohnmardandi St

Kaladan St

Creek

Station Rd

Train
Station

To Mahabodhi Mingala Zedi
(0.3mi); Tagaung Mingala Zeditaw
(0.3mi); Leikyunyhaung Paya (1.2mi)

AROUND YANGON

tom tier of bronze; all three tiers are gilded and reportedly embedded with a total of 829 diamond fragments, 843 rubies and 1588 semiprecious stones.

The southern shrine of the compound houses the **Thiho-shin Phondaw-pyi** sitting buddha image, which, the story goes, floated to the delta coast on a raft sent from Sri Lanka during ancient times. According to the legend, an unknown Sinhalese sculptor fashioned four different buddha images using pieces from the original Bodhi tree mixed with cement composite. He then placed the images on four wooden rafts and set the rafts adrift on the ocean. One landed in Dawei (Tavoy), another at Kyaikkami (Amherst), another at Kyaiktiyo (this one is now at

Kyaikpawlaw); and the fourth landed near Phondawpyi, a fishing village about 60 miles south of Pathein, from where it was transferred to Pathein.

A **marble standing buddha** positioned in a niche in the fence running along the western side of the stupa marks a spot where Mon warriors once prayed before going off to battle. In the northwestern corner of the compound is a **shrine** dedicated to Shin Upagot, the Bodhisattva who floats on the ocean and appears to those in trouble. Turtles swim in the water surrounding the small pavilion.

Also in this northwest corner is an unusual golden **Ganesh shrine**, the elephant-headed god worshipped by Hindus as the god of wisdom and wealth.

SETTAYAW PAYA

စက်တော်ရာဘုရားရှု

Of the several lesser-known shrines in Pathein, perhaps the most charming is the **Settayaw Paya**, dedicated to a mythical Buddha footprint left by the Enlightened One during his legendary perambulations through Southeast Asia.

The paya compound in the northeast of town wraps over a couple of green hillocks that are dotted with well-constructed *tazaung* (shrine buildings) – altogether a nice setting and a change from the flat paya compounds near the river. The footprint symbol itself is an oblong, 3ft-long impression.

OTHER RELIGIOUS MONUMENTS

The **Twenty-Eight Paya** is a rectangular shrine containing 28 sitting and 28 standing buddha images. None of them are particularly distinguished except that the latter appear in the open-robe style rather than the closed-robe pose that is typical of Mandalay standing images.

At one end of the hall stands a group of crude sculptures depicting a scene from the Buddha's life in which he teaches a disciple the relativity of physical beauty by comparing a monkey, the disciple's wife and a *deva* (celestial being). You may have to ask the caretaker to unlock the building.

More interesting from an artistic perspective is **Tagaung Mingala Zeditaw** (Tagaung Paya), south of town, which is centred on a graceful stupa that sweeps inward from a wide, whitewashed base to a gleaming silver superstructure.

Look for the small squirrel sculpture extending from the western side of the upper stupa, representing a previous life of the Buddha as a squirrel. One of the pavilions at the base of the stupa contains a very large sitting buddha image.

West of Tagaung Mingala Zeditaw, a little way towards the river, stands **Mahabodhi Mingala Zedi**, patterned after the Mahabodhi stupa in Bodhgaya, India. **Leikyunynaung Paya**, about a mile directly south of Mahabodhi, was renovated by the State Law & Order Restoration Council (Slorc), now the State Peace and Development Council (SPDC), in the early 1990s to create a facsimile of Ananda Paya in Bagan. Few people outside the government worship here now, reportedly because forced labour was used in the renovation.

Half a mile or so northeast of Leikyunynaung Paya is **Leimyetna Paya**, which features a large, but particularly ugly, sitting buddha. Even worse, aesthetically, is the gaudily painted sitting buddha at **Shwezigon Paya**, at the northern end of town.

MARKETS

At the **night market** (Strand Rd) that is set up each evening in front of Customs House, teenagers cruise, flirt and hang out while vendors purvey food, clothing and tools and just about every other requisite for daily life at low prices. Just south of Shwemokhtaw Paya is the **central market** (🕑 Mon-Sat), and just south of that is a newer **market** (🕑 Mon-Sat), with all manner of goods.

Festivals & Events

The people of Pathein celebrate **Vesakha** (a celebration of the Buddha's birth, enlightenment and passing away) with a huge *paya pwe* (pagoda festival) during the full moon of Kason (April/May). The festival is held at the Shwemokhtaw Paya (p136).

Sleeping

The sleeping options in this city are a sorry lot, no doubt because most people race right on through to the beaches. The hotels' electricity supplies are at the mercy of the city-wide rationing schedule, which means power generally is available from early evening to early morning.

Those hoping to avoid government-owned properties should steer clear of the Pathein Hotel, a two-storey building on spacious grounds near the bus station.

Sein Pyae Hlyan Inn (☎ 21654; 32 Shwezedi Rd; s/d without bathroom $3/8; r with bathroom $15; 🔀) Certainly the cheapest hotel in town, and it shows. The rooms with communal baths are the best value, though still dirty and very hot. Trade up to the 'deluxe' rooms and you get just as much dirt but also air-con, though it rarely works. The showers are of the cold-bucket-of-water type.

Paradise Guest House (☎ 25055; off Zegyaung St; r $5; 🔀) For the price this actually isn't far off paradise (well a cut-price version anyway). Tucked down a side street away from road noise, it has cramped but clean rooms, a large communal balcony, a karaoke bar and an obscene amount of very aggressive mosquitoes. All that for five bucks – you could hardly ask for more. But there is more! – a free breakfast and a half-decent restaurant.

Taan Taan Ta Guest House & Restaurant (☎ 22290; 7 Merchant St; s $5-6, d $10-12; ✗) This, the best and most popular budget guesthouse with locals and foreigners alike, has spacious and colourful rooms and friendly staff, but the secret's out and it fills up quickly.

La Pyat Wun Hotel (☎ 24669; 30 Mingyi Rd; s/d $10/20; ✗) The town's most prestigious address offers white-tiled rooms that are as polished as the staff. The huge bathrooms, rather bizarrely, only have cold showers. Breakfast isn't included and loving couples will be delighted to hear that it's twin rooms only – so we'll have none of that hanky-panky please!

Eating

New City Tea Centre (Mingyi Rd; snacks from K100; ✗ 7am-8pm) Next to the La Pyat Wun Hotel and perfect for replacing the breakfasts that hotel doesn't provide. This shady teashop provides plates of greasy, sugar coated doughnuts and other snacks and a morning caffeine kick.

Myo Restaurant (☎ 21367; 5 Aung Yadana St; mains around K1000) A bustling, retro bar and restaurant that extends a loving welcome to all-comers. The meals, which focus on all your favourite Bamar staples, are done with more style than most places and, to keep you entertained while you wait for your supper, there is a TV playing all the premiership matches and there's good draught beer to boot.

Zee Bae Inn (Merchant St; dishes K1000; ✗ to 10pm; ✗) Zee Bae is among the more well known and longest running Chinese places and has been producing large bowls of noodles since the 1950s. It has a grubby backstreet Shanghai look and feel to it and a suitably feisty woman boss.

Shwe Zin Yaw Restaurant (24/25 Shwezedi Rd; mains K1400) Oh you lucky, lucky taste buds, finally you're going to get something different, including goat curry and sardine salad! A handy place for lunch before hopping on a bus out of here.

Shopping

Most of the 'umbrellas' made in Pathein are actually parasols; ie they aren't waterproof, but are used to counter the hot delta sun. There are a few workshops scattered throughout the northern part of the city, particularly in the vicinity of Twenty-Eight Paya, off Mahabandoola Rd.

The parasols come in a variety of bright and bold primary colours. One type that can be used in the rain is the saffron-coloured monks' umbrella, which is waterproofed by applying various coats of tree resin; a single umbrella may take five days to complete, including the drying process. Parasols and umbrellas can be ordered in any size directly from the workshops, and are cheap.

Workshops welcome visitors who want to observe this craft, which is a lot more interesting than it might sound!

Shwe Sar Umbrella Workshop (☎ 25127; moemoe@carefreight.com.mm; 653 Tawya Kyaung Rd; ✗ 8am-5pm) This family-run affair with high-quality work is just around the corner from the Settayaw Paya. If you decide to purchase these beautiful handiworks in bulk – you won't find the same quality elsewhere, even in Yangon – they can be securely and conveniently packaged, though getting them posted to your home country is another matter altogether.

Getting There & Away

At the time of writing, foreigners were not permitted to travel to Pathein because of damage to the roads caused by Cyclone Nargis, but these restrictions are likely to be lifted when the roads are repaired.

BOAT

Inland Water Transport (IWT; Map p98; ☎ in Yangon 381 912, 380 764; Lan Thit jetty, Yangon) is a government operation that runs Chinese triple-decker ferries between Yangon and Pathein. Ordinary class costs $7 and puts you on the open deck (with an easy chair if you get in early). For $42 you can get an air-conditioned cabin with private bathroom. These 'express' boats leave Yangon's Lan Thit jetty daily at 5pm, arriving the next morning in Pathein at 10am and run at the same times going the other way. Foreigners must buy tickets from the deputy division manager's office next to Building 63 on Lan Thit jetty.

BUS

Buses to Pathein are available from Yangon's Hlaing Thar Yar bus station; there are several departures from 5am to 3pm (K7000, four hours, 112 miles). The same applies when heading from Pathein to Yangon. You should try to buy tickets a day in advance.

Insanely uncomfortable minibuses ply the route from Pathein to Chaung Tha Beach

AROUND YANGON

(K4000, 2½ hours, 36 miles); departures are at 7am, 9am, 11am, 1pm and 3pm from Pathein's **bus station** (Yadayagone St).

It's best to book a couple of hours in advance. Around these parts it seems that rice is more valuable than people because the sacks of rice get all the seats and you get to sit on top of them, knees crunched up to your chin and head banging off the roof. If you're tall you may seriously want to consider forking out some greenbacks for a private taxi ride.

The other option is to ask your guesthouse if it's possible to book a seat on the more comfortable Yangon–Chaung Tha buses (see p143). You'll be asked to pay the full fare but it's worth it.

Buses take around 1½ hours to travel the 29 miles from Pathein to Ngwe Saung (K3000); departures are at 7am, 8am, 9am, 11am and 3pm from the bus station on Yadayagone St as well.

TAXI
Share taxis for up to four people can be arranged from your hotel in Pathein for Chaung Tha (K50,000), Ngwe Saung (K40,000) and also Yangon (K70,000).

AROUND PATHEIN
Horseshoe-shaped **Inye Lake**, 44 miles northeast of the city near the village of Kyonpyaw, is a favourite weekend picnic spot.

If you follow the Pathein River south till it empties into the Andaman Sea you'll reach **Mawdin Point** (Mawdinsoun), site of the massive **Mawdin Point festival** during the lunar month of Tabodwe (February/March). On the sea side of the cape, at its point, is a sandy beach and the revered stupa of **Mawdin Paya**.

During the festival there are special boats running from Pathein daily. Other times, boats go only once a week or so, leaving the main Pathein jetty around 6am and arriving at 2pm. Be aware that there's no lodging licences for foreigners at Mawdin, so this is strictly a trip for risk-takers. During the festival more guesthouses are open, which makes it the best time of year to attempt a trip.

CHAUNG THA BEACH
ချောင်းသာကမ်းခြေ

☎ 042

Chaung Tha Beach, 25 miles west of Pathein, is a place of holiday excess for the Myanmar middle class. There's paddling in the water, floating about on rubber rings, plodding up and down on ponies, wasting money on tacky souvenirs, boisterous beach football games and happy family picnics.

It might not sound the most promising of places for a Western tourist wanting nothing more complicated than a hammock and some peace. But prepare to be surprised, because there's more to Chaung Tha than candy floss holiday crowds. You can exchange the noisy main beach for heaven by walking 20 minutes or so north of the village to some utterly gorgeous, immaculately clean and totally empty white-sand beaches that rival any in the country.

Then, after a blissful day of dozing in the sun, take advantage of the wide range of restaurants serving seafood to make you drool and some superb value hotels. And if that's not enough enticement then there's always the pony rides and rubber rings!

Cyclone Nargis skipped Chaung Tha Beach but, as with all delta-area sites, travel was restricted in this area at the time of writing.

Sights & Activities
The village **market** is most active from 6am to 9am. East of the main village area is a mangrove wetland and a **canal beach** with a wooden jetty. It isn't hard to convince a fisherperson to take you up the river and around the mangroves for a few thousand kyat.

BOATING TRIPS
A modest coral reef lies a short way offshore with decent **snorkelling** possible both here and around the headland at the beach's northern end. During the rainy season the water clarity is terrible.

The best snorkelling though is about a two-hour boat ride away. Boats, which should be arranged through your hotel, cost K30,000 per hour for six people. If you haven't got your own gear some of the hotels might conjure up a tatty snorkel and mask for your use – ask at the Shwe Hin Tha Hotel.

The appropriately named **Whitesand Island** which is visible a short way offshore can be explored in a day trip from Chaung Tha Beach. Boats (K3000 one way, 30 minutes) leave from the jetty in the village every hour or so from 8am (last one back leaves at 5pm). There's good **swimming** and **snorkelling** around the island, but very little shade. Bring plenty of water and, finally, don't attempt to swim over – it's a very long way and around the halfway point the *Jaws* theme tune gets lodged in your head! For more information, ask at any of the hotels.

OTHER ACTIVITIES

You can rent **canoes** for about K1000 a half-day, or **bicycles** for about K500 per hour or K1000 a day, at hotels and guesthouses.

Sleeping

Of all the beach destinations in Myanmar, Chaung Tha offers the most affordable accommodation. All but a few hotels close down from 15 May to 15 September; those that remain open discount room rates

Most of the big beachfront hotels are owned by businesspeople in Yangon or even outside the country and it's likely that many are joint ventures. In Chaung Tha more than most places in the country, it's worth staying in smaller and cheaper, locally run establishments so as to ensure your money stays in the community.

With the exception of Woody Guesthouse, all hotels are located along Main Rd.

BUDGET

Win Guesthouse (☎ 42186; s/d $3/6) A red colonial villa surrounded by a gaggle of cheap restaurants with very basic rooms. However, it's cheap, family-run and the deaf owner will appreciate your custom.

Woody Guesthouse (☎ 42372; s/d $5/6) Hidden away from all the beach hullabaloo this charming and simple guesthouse run by U Tin Htut Aung and family is a real gem. On the edge of the village and surrounded by squawking chickens, his six Swiss Alpine–style huts are neat and tidy and contain no unnecessary fuss. Breakfast isn't part of the deal but invites into the family home are a certainty.

Shwe Chaung Tha Hotel (☎ 42249; s/d $4/8) Unusually, the rooms here are actually inside a traditional wooden house rather than the standard 10-a-penny beach bungalows. The all-wood rooms have some old-fashioned charm and there's a monster-sized balcony. Look at several rooms before committing as some are better than others.

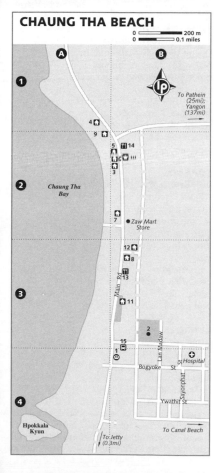

CHAUNG THA BEACH

0 —————— 200 m
0 —————— 0.1 miles

To Pathein (25mi); Yangon (137mi)

Chaung Tha Bay

Zaw Mart Store

Main Rd

Lan Madaw

Bogyoke St

Hospital

Sayonphat St

Ywathit St

Hpokkala Kyun

To Jetty (0.3mi)

To Canal Beach

OUR PICK **Top Chaung Tha 2 Guesthouse & Restaurant** (☎ 42127; s/d $5/10; ✖) Let's start with the bad news, and this won't take long. It's on the opposite side of the road from the beach. Now that's out of the way we'll hastily move onto the good news, which will take a little longer. Small individual cottages sit behind an excellent terracotta restaurant (right), and each one is scrubbed clean, neatly tiled and comes with desk, soft bed (bring your own mosquito net) and a bathroom with highly original wash basins. The clothes dryer for wet beach things and outside taps to wash sandy feet are well-considered extras, but the best asset is the local family who run this establishment; they simply cannot do enough for you and nothing will wipe the smiles off their faces. All up it's one of the best bargains in southern Myanmar.

Shwe Hin Tha Hotel (☎ 42118; s $10-12, d $12-15; ✖) The only beachfront hotel with budget prices, this is the most popular backpacker choice. It's at the quiet northern end of the beach and the English-speaking staff are eager for your custom. Perhaps a little too eager. When the bus from Pathein stops opposite the hotel, touts rush over, unload your gear and cart it into the hotel without you having a chance to breathe. If such presumptuous behaviour weren't bad enough, we have also received a number of complaints regarding both the state of the rooms and some of the tours the hotel organises. Having said all that, when we visited, the rooms, especially the more expensive ones, seemed very clean and good value and the reception staff couldn't have been more helpful. However, they did attempt the unloading-our-bags-from-the-bus trick…

MIDRANGE

Coe Coe Beach Resort (☎ 42345; s $7-15, d $10-20; ✖) Formally known as Ambo's, this is one of the cheapest beachside hotels and the rooms without air-con are actually better value than those with. All in all the large and airy bungalows have seen better times, but they are just a sandy step from the tranquil northern part of the beach. If you do take an air-con room, you not only get a free breakfast but also a TV, in case all that sun and sand gets boring.

Diamond Hotel (☎ 13109; s $10-20, d $15-30; ✖) Another in the flurry of large and impersonal complexes on the beach. This one has had a recent makeover so is slicker than most, and has some of the best bathrooms this side of

the Indian Ocean. The bright and colourful bungalows are the same no matter what price you pay, but if you opt for the Mr Mean price then you won't be allowed to use the air-con (it's OK, Chaung Tha's erratic electricity supply means it never works anyway!) and hot water will come in a bucket rather than from the tap (well, that's logical).

Golden Beach Hotel (☎ 200 565; r $28-35; ✖ ⚏) These big, bright beachside bungalows come with individual back and front porches, comfortable, modern bathrooms and a couple of small double beds per bungalow. Try to look at a couple of rooms as some are starting to look a bit tired. There is a well-used pool table and a little-used pool. Like many of the more expensive hotels it's a bit large and impersonal for the beach. The stretch of sand out the front is especially popular with middle-class Myanmar tourists.

Chaungtha Oo Beach Hotel (☎ 42353; r $30-35; ✖) If you're English the quaint and colourful beachside huts at this hotel, situated at the quiet northern end of the beach, will remind you of a row of multicoloured Torquay beach huts. They are kept very clean, though unfortunately are about as tiny as a Torquay beach hut. This hotel marks the point at which the coconut trees begin to replace the concrete hotels.

TOP END

Belle Resort (☎ 42320; www.belleresort.com; s/d $60/75; ✖ ⚏) Chaung Tha's plushest hotel is so new that you can almost smell the paint drying and for the price it offers superb value for money. The rooms are understated sophistication with stone walls, sprawling beds, massive windows with equally massive ocean views and satellite TV. Enter the bathrooms, made of stylish black stone, and things get even better. There is an enticing swimming pool and equally enticing service.

Eating

Most hotels and guesthouses have small restaurants, but there's generally better quality food in the small locally run restaurants outside the hotels.

Top Chaung Tha 2 (☎ 42127; mains K1500-2000) This Mediterranean-coloured restaurant, which is part of the guesthouse of the same name, feels just right for the beach with intimate alfresco dining on stunning seafood, pancakes that are literally cakes and, in case you're getting nostalgic, all the favourites of inland Myanmar.

Rhythm Food House (☎ 09-501 6902; mains K2000, fish K3000; 🕙 9am-10pm) Eating in this informal roadside restaurant is a guaranteed musical experience. The palm leaves rustle like backing singers, the wind chimes twinkle and the musician owners stage regular jam nights (there are some spare guitars so passing musicians can jump right in). The atmosphere might be informal but the food is more sophisticated than you would expect with the highlights being the grilled fish stuffed with herbs with a side portion of homemade chips.

Aung Myin Restaurant (dishes K2000-7000) A pleasant wooden shack set back from the beach with decent seafood including lobster (K7000), crab stuffed with ginger and lemongrass (K3000) and sardines soaked in a spicy tomato sauce.

Getting There & Around

At the time of writing, foreigners were not permitted to travel to Chaung Tha because travel in the delta was restricted but this is likely to change as reconstruction continues.

BUS

The rough 22-mile road between Chaung Tha and Pathein can be traversed in two hours by private car, buses, minibuses and pick-ups usually take about 2½ hours. The route to/ from Pathein passes through jungle hills – well, OK, ex-jungle – it's a depressing example of the effects of deforestation. Over half the villages passed along the way are Kayin.

Uncomfortable minibuses leave from Chaung Tha Beach for Pathein (K4000, 2½ hours) at 7am, 9am, 11am, 1pm and 3pm from the bus station in the village.

A direct Yangon-bound bus departs at 6.30am (K7000) or at 10.30am you can hop onto a more comfortable air-conditioned bus (K10,000). It's a six- to seven-hour trip.

It's theoretically possible to travel north via the town of Gwa all the way to Ngapali without first having to go through Yangon and Pyay. It's an exciting, beautiful but very demanding two-day journey on very local minibuses.

MOTORBIKE & BOAT

Motorbike taxis can be hired to take you directly to Ngwe Saung Beach, which saves having to waste a day backtracking to Pathein. In fact, the trip between these two beaches is a real highlight of a beach holiday. The route, which takes about two hours, is through wild and glorious country and involves three river crossings on small wooden country boats that have just enough room for the motorbike and a couple of passengers. You will pass serene beaches, several untouched villages, heavy forests and whiz over tracks and trails between shocking-green rice paddies. With just a backpack the journey is a breeze, but it's just about possible to do it with more baggage (the author managed it while carrying a backpack, a large surfboard bag and an insanely oversized camera/computer bag – nothing like travelling light!). It costs K18,000 per person. Ask your hotel a few hours in advance to organise it.

If it's calm you can also hire a boat (seats six; K40,000) to and from Ngwe Saung. This is handy if you're in a group but be prepared to wade ashore with your bags and ask to be dropped as close to your hotel as possible. Bring plenty of water and sunblock. The journey takes around 1½ hours. Again organise this through your hotel a few hours in advance.

TAXI

Share taxis for up to four people to Pathein (K50,000) and Yangon (K120,000) can be arranged with your hotel's assistance.

NGWE SAUNG BEACH

ငွေဆောင်

☎ 042

On the steamy shores of the Bay of Bengal is a special kind of place where salty, seaborne breezes, drenched in the scent of jasmine, play among the twitching coconut palms of a beach that looks and feels like the stunning daughter of African, Indian and Caribbean lovers. It's a place of sinking sunsets and tomorrows that never come. Its name is Ngwe Saung. It will transport you to seventh heaven.

Although Ngwe Saung was not hit by Cyclone Nargis, at the time of writing travellers were not permitted to travel through the delta to reach it. Check with local tourist bureaus for updates before you travel.

Sights & Activities

Above all else Ngwe Saung is an indulgent, lie-back-and-do-absolutely-nothing sort of beach and most visitors are happy to comply. However, if sitting around doing nothing more strenuous than wiggling your toes in the

AROUND YANGON

AROUND YANGON

sand sounds boring then there are a few calorie-burning activities you can partake in.

A boat trip out to **Bird Island**, just visible way out on the horizon, for a day of snorkelling and, dare we say it, bird-watching, is the most popular water-based excursion. Boats can be arranged through many hotels for a cost of $70.

A cheaper place to **snorkel** among dancing clouds of tropical fish is just behind the island perched off the southern tip of the beach. Masks and snorkels can be hired from some hotels (Shwe Hin Tha Hotel is the most reliable) for K2500 per day.

Traditional Myanmar puppet shows blast into life at the **Shwe Yoe Gardens** (Myoma St; admission K6000), whenever a foreigner rocks up (evenings only).

A less organised, but very rewarding activity, and one that's a million miles from the luxury resort life, is to follow one of the tracks on the other side of the road into the countryside where you'll discover delightful hamlets and farmsteads where children still leap into the air in excitement at the sight of you.

Several of the resorts can arrange day trips to an elephant camp halfway between Ngwe Saung and Pathein (see opposite).

Sleeping

In the last couple of years Ngwe Saung has developed enormously and hotels now proudly back the whole beach. Fortunately the authorities have, for once, shown some care and restraint and the result is that the fringing layer

---

BETTER ON A BUDGET

Until recently there was no budget accommodation at Ngwe Saung, but things have changed for the better and there are now a couple of places right at the southern end of the beach. Getting between these hotels and the village is a pain, but enough trishaws drift on past to allow some means of escape.

Most of the remainder of the hotels are aimed more at the upper price range and many of the top-end hotels (not reviewed here) are thought to have strong government ties – best go cheap. The number one problem with Ngwe Saung is the feeling of living in a resort-inspired bubble utterly removed from Myanmar life.

---

of palm trees remains relatively intact. With all the beachfront space taken it also looks hopeful that it may well remain as such.

BUDGET

Royal Treasure Resort (☎ 581 101, in Yangon 01-543 689; r $15; 😷) Ignore the run-down reception area, because the stumpy pink bungalows here are cheaper than anywhere else and have large, clean rooms that catch lots of light. The family who run this hotel, right at the southern end of the beach, speak very little English but try their hardest and are friendly. You can safely skip the restaurant – we were served a completely raw egg on toast!

Golden Sea Resort (s/d $15/20) One of the cheaper places to stay in Ngwe Saung at the moment. The Golden Sea is simplicity in itself and much more in keeping with beach life than many of its flashy competitors. The rustic rooms come in concrete or, more enticing, bamboo flavours and the women running it speak good English. It's the only hotel that has hammocks strung between the palms.

Shwe Hin Tha Hotel (☎ 40340; r $15-30) Set at the blissful southern end of the beach, this place is almost within paddling distance of the jungle-covered island. It has a magnetic pull for backpackers who agonise over whether to opt for cheap-and-simple bamboo huts or one of the more solid and luxurious bungalows. Either way they can be sure that it will be clean and well maintained and that hot water will appear on request. There's a book exchange, various travel services and plenty of like-minded clientele to waste away the days with. It's the sister hotel of the one in Chaung Tha but comes with much higher recommendations.

MIDRANGE & TOP END

Chaungtha Oo Beach Resort (☎ 40324, in Yangon 01-254 708; htoo.maw@mptmail.net.mm; r $35; 😷) About as far down the beach from the village as you can get, this secluded resort is a bargain hunter's fantasy, featuring delightful beachside bungalows with finesse and character. There's plenty of space, lots of light and hardly a soul around to disturb the peace of your own slab of palm-be-decked perfection. Price reductions are available for those who agree to cut their electricity requirements.

Yamonnar Oo Resort (☎ 40338, in Yangon 01-538 080; kbzinfo@bzbank.com.mm; r $50) Down at the southern end of the beach this modern hotel offers good value for money. The red-and-white bunga-lows are stylish yet informal with lots of clean lines, well-placed pot plants and pleasant ter-races overlooking the sea. The landscaped gardens are another highlight. Sadly the staff don't speak much English.

our pick **Emerald Sea Resort** (☎ 40247, in Yangon 01-5200 890; r from $55; ☒) Service really counts in this small hotel, privately owned by Myanmar businesspeople. It's the kind of place where you'll emerge in the morning for breakfast to discover that a table has been set up for you right by the water's edge and that fresh jasmine flowers have been left outside your door. Yes, it's true that groups of blokes trav-elling together might feel a bit silly staying at such a romantic hotel, but newlyweds will be in matrimonial bliss, unwed couples might be inspired and, you never know, even cynical old timers might feel something! The resort, which consists of half-a-dozen thatch-roofed bungalows (it's worth paying the extra $15 for a sea-view room) has been designed by a respected Yangon architect and it really shows. The rooms themselves are beautifully created with minimal décor making the virgin-white, and very comfortable, interiors all the more classy. There's a decent restaurant (advance notice often required) and a beautiful stretch of beach out front, but let's give credit where it's due – it's the staff that really make this place as good as it is.

Eating
You should try your hardest to break out of your hotel restaurant at least once in order to eat in the village where there are a good range of cheap restaurants. is little to distinguish one from the other – all sell excellent fish for K3000 or lobster for K18,000 to K20,000 (order a day in advance).

Ngwe Hline Si Restaurant (☎ 40292; mains K3500) Maybe the pick of the bunch in the village, the Ngwe Hline Si has all the usual seafood and mixes it up with pastas and a variety of tasty starters.

U San Min Restaurant (mains K2000) If you're staying at the southern end of the beach, fill-ing your belly, which always used to involve a major migration, is now a little easier thanks to a couple of cheap and simple shacks op-posite the Yuzana Resort. One of these, the U San Min Restaurant, must be run by a family with a crystal ball because for the last couple of years they have been proudly advertis-ing themselves as 'recommended by Lonely Planet' – long before any of our authors had the chance to check them out! Fortunately, they really are deserving of our recommen-dation and certainly have the edge over their two neighbours.

Getting There & Around
At the time of writing, foreigners were not permitted to travel to Ngwe Saung but check with local tourist bureaus for an update as this is likely to change.

A bus leaves for Yangon at 6.30am (K8000, six hours) from the crossroads between the village and the beach resorts.

Minibuses from Pathein (K3000, two hours) stop first at the intersection between the beginning of the village and the Treasure Beach Resort. If staying further south the bus should be able to drop you at your resort; conversely, you should be able to catch the bus leaving Ngwe Saung (7am, 8am, 9am, 11am and 3pm) by waiting by the side of the road.

Taxis can be arranged for Pathein (K40,000) and Yangon (K110,000).

For information on motorbike taxis and boats between Ngwe Saung and Chaung Tha Beach see p143. There are a few trishaws avail-able to carry you between the resorts and the village (K500), and motorbikes can be hired from most hotels for an average of K5000 per hour and K15,000 per day.

AROUND NGWE SAUNG
Elephant Camps
If you go down to the woods today you're sure to find – a herd of elephants! Crashing through what little is left of the forests between Ngwe Saung and Pathein are several groups of working elephants (as well as a handful of their wild brothers and sisters). Myanmar actually has the world's largest population of working elephants who are used, primarily, by the local logging industry.

Around half an hour from Ngwe Saung is an **elephant camp** (admission $5, elephant ride $5; ☯ 8am-noon). Though the dozen elephants here are working elephants, the camp itself is purely for tourists and no logging actually takes place. It's possible to go for a half-hour elephant ride through the forest – the romance of which wears off in about 30 seconds. If you thought horses attracted a lot of large biting insects just wait until you get on the back of an elephant!

THE JUNGLE BOOK

While most 13-year-old boys dream of being a racing car driver when they are older, Mogley has his eyes set firmly on being the driver of a much slower, but much greener, form of transport. When we met up with him in the forests of southern Myanmar he was well on his way to achieving this dream.

Leaning his head against that of Khin Tazin Kyu and tickling the edge of his friend's ear, Mogley told us that both Khin Tazin Kyu and himself were 13 years old and that he would work as Khin Tazin Kyu's *oozie* until either of them dies.

An *oozie* isn't Sylvester Stallone's favourite machine gun or even a drunk Aussie, but rather an elephant handler, and Khin Tazin Kyu is a beautiful half-tonne Asian elephant. Currently Mogley isn't a fully-fledged *oozie*, but rather a *pejeik*, or trainee elephant handler. He only went to school for three years, but his brother and father work as *oozies* and he grew up with elephants and always wanted to work with them. He told us he started riding elephants at eight years old and it took him three months to learn how to ride one properly.

Anyone who spent most of their childhood wishing they had an elephant would be intrigued to know where one gets one from. Khin Tazin Kyu was caught in the wild. Mogley told us how difficult it is to catch and train an elephant. The latter is done over two months – by tying the elephant up, not feeding it and scaring it with fire. Now Mogley will stay with this elephant forever because it knows him, but Khin Tazin Kyu belongs to the forestry department – when it's older it will be used for logging. The forestry department and the elephant camp pay Mogley's wages – between them he gets K18,000 a month. When Mogley is not with the elephants he spends time with his family or hunting in the forest with a bow and arrow for monkeys, which he either takes home to eat or sells in the market.

At night Khin Tazin Kyu goes with the other elephants into the jungle. They have bells around their necks so they can be found the next morning, but sometimes the elephants fill the bells with mud and cannot be heard. Mogley has never seen elephant poachers in these parts but, when looking for the elephants, Mogley sometimes finds wild elephants, which can be dangerous.

With childhood fantasies of owning an elephant resurfacing, we asked Mogley what it's like to actually have his own elephant. He told us Khin Tazin Kyu is very clever and is like family – actually he's better than Mogley's big sister. And with that comment, which will resonate with every 13-year-old boy with a big sister, even those without their own elephant, he turned and rode back into the forest.

The camp used to be government run but is now a joint venture tied to the Treasure Resort in Ngwe Saung, which in turn is owned by Tay Za (p21).

NORTH OF YANGON

TAUKKYAN

ထောက်ကြံ့

☎ 01

On the road to Bago, beyond Yangon's airport at Mingaladon, you reach Taukkyan, where you will find the huge **Taukkyan War Cemetery**, maintained by the Commonwealth War Graves Commission.

It contains the graves of 6374 Allied soldiers who died in the Burma and Assam campaigns of WWII. There is also a memorial bearing the names of the almost 27,000 soldiers who died with no known grave. Slowly, as you walk around reading the names of those who died and the epitaphs commemorating them, the heat of the sun seems to fade and the noise of the road recedes, leaving you alone in the silence of your own thoughts in this immensely sad place.

Some of the more personal messages of remembrance bring a tear to the eye: 'Only one to all the world, but all the world to me. Always in my thoughts. Mum.', for SE Sanders who died age 24; 'It is not goodbye darling, only goodnight. Loving wife Madge and sons', for AE Foulds who died age 28. Or the one that best sums up the waste of war, 'We had a son.', for RAW Barr who died age 24.

You can get to Taukkyan on bus 9 from Yangon or aboard any Bago-bound bus from either the Aung Mingalar Bus (highway) terminal (p130) or the Tha-khin Mya Pan-gyan Gate terminal (p129; K650 to K1000).

Taukkyan was not hit by Cyclone Nargis and there are no travel restrictions affecting foreigner movement in this area.

BAGO (PEGU)

ပဲခူးမြို့

☎ 052 / pop 48,000

Bago, a former capital, is a Disney-flavoured theme park of gaudy religious sites. It would be fair to say that this small and scrappy town probably contains a greater density of blissed-out buddhas and treasure-filled temples than any other similar-sized town in southern Myanmar. All this makes Bago a superb and simple day trip from Yangon, or the ideal first stop when you leave the city behind.

Bago was out of the direct path of Cyclone Nargis but was still affected by strong winds. By mid-2008 reconstruction was well underway. Shops, restaurants and hotels had reopened and transport services were back to normal.

History

Bago was reputedly founded in AD 573 by two Mon princes from Thaton, who saw a female *hamsa* (mythological bird) standing on the back of a male *hamsa* on an island in a huge lake. Taking this to be an auspicious omen, they founded a royal capital called Hanthawady (from the Pali-Sanskrit 'Hamsavati', meaning the 'kingdom of the *hamsa*') at the edge of the lake. During the later Mon dynastic periods (1287–1539), Hanthawady became the centre of the Mon kingdom of Ramanadesa, which consisted of all southern Myanmar.

The Bamar took over in 1539 when King Tabinshwehti annexed Bago to his Taungoo kingdom. The city was frequently mentioned by early European visitors – who knew it as Pegu – as an important seaport. In 1740 the Mon, after a period of submission to Taungoo, re-established Bago as their capital, but in 1757 King Alaungpaya sacked and utterly destroyed the city. King Bodawpaya, who ruled from 1782 to 1819, rebuilt it to some extent, but when the river changed its course the city was cut off from the sea and lost its importance as a seaport. It never again reached its previous grandeur.

Information

Sitthugyi Email Centre Very basic email service east of the river.

Sights & Activities

Though foreigners can visit the town for free, officially they must buy an entrance ticket valid for all the town's sights for $10. This can only be purchased from the Shwethalyaung Buddha and the Shwemawdaw Paya. We are not recommending this, but the town's guides may offer to get you into the sights for free as long as you pay them the $10 instead (they then don't charge you for transport between the sights). If you choose to do this you won't be alone and we've never heard of any problems when doing so (though you will still have to pay the nominal camera fee that many places charge). For information on guides and transport between the sights see p151. All the sights are open from just before sunrise until well after dark.

SHWETHALYAUNG BUDDHA

ရွှေသာလျောင်းဘုရားလျ

Once upon a time a nasty king, who went by the name of Mgadeikpa, ruled the lands around what is today Bago. His reign was marked by corruption and violence, but one day his son was out hunting in the forests when he came upon the village of Suvannabhumi, where his eye fell upon a Mon girl who caused his heart to flutter. Even though she was a Buddhist and he, like everyone in his father's kingdom, worshipped pagan idols, the two became lovers and married after he promised her that she could continue to practise Buddhism.

Back at the court the king was furious when he discovered this and ordered both the girl and his son executed. Yet, when the new bride prayed in front of the pagan idol it cracked

---

THE HAMSA

In deference to legend, the symbol for Bago is a female *hamsa* (*hintha* or *hantha* in Burmese; a mythological bird) standing on the back of a male *hamsa*. At a deeper level, the symbol honours the compassion of the male *hamsa* in providing a place for the female to stand in the middle of a lake with only one island. Hence, the men of Bago are said to be more chivalrous than men from other Burmese areas. In popular Burmese culture, however, men joke that they dare not marry a woman from Bago for fear of being henpecked!

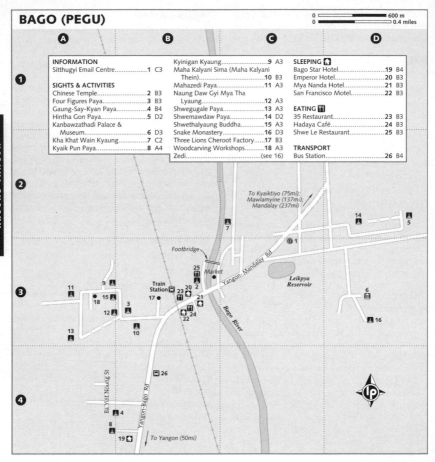

BAGO (PEGU)

and broke. The king was seized with fear and, realising the error of his ways, he ordered a statue of the Buddha to be built and the population to convert to Buddhism.

The gorgeous reclining buddha that you see here today is said to be the result of this doomed love. Measuring 180ft long and 53ft high, the Shwethalyaung is certainly the kind of overwhelming object you would expect to be constructed by an absolute monarch with a guilt complex – the little finger alone extends 10ft.

Since its original construction the statue underwent several restorations before the destruction of Bago in 1757. The town was so completely ravaged that the huge buddha was totally lost and overgrown by jungle. It was not rediscovered until 1880 and restoration began in 1881. The 1930s saw another flurry of renovation activity, as a mosaic was added to the great pillow on which the buddha's head rests.

Near the huge head of the image stands a **statue of Lokanat** (Lokanatha or Avalokitesvara), a Mahayana Buddhist deity borrowed by Burmese Buddhism.

A Japanese war cemetery, **Kyinigan Kyaung**, can be seen on the grounds of a monastery just north of Shwethalyaung.

SHWEMAWDAW PAYA

ရွှေမောတော်ဘုရားလျှ

A pyramid of washed-out gold in the midday haze, and glittering perfection in the evening gloss, the 376ft-high Shwemawdaw

Paya stands tall and proud over the town. According to murky legend the original stupa was a small, ramshackle object, built by two brothers, Kullasala and Mahasala, to enshrine two hairs given to them by Gautama Buddha. In AD 982 a sacred tooth was added to the collection; in 1385 another tooth was added and the stupa was rebuilt to a towering 277ft. In 1492 strong winds blew over the *hti* and a new one was raised.

The stupa has collapsed and been rebuilt many times over the last 600 years, each time it has grown a little taller and the treasures mounted in it grown a little thicker. The last time it was destroyed was in 1930 when a huge earthquake completely levelled it and for the next 20 years only the huge earth mound of the base remained.

Today the gaudy golden top of the stupa reaches 46ft higher than the Shwedagon in Yangon. At the northeastern corner of the stupa, a huge section of the *hti* toppled by the 1917 earthquake has been mounted into the structure of the stupa.

KANBAWZATHADI PALACE
ကမ္ဘောဇသတိ နန်းတော်

Recently, the original site of Hanthawady (see p147), which surrounded Kanbawzathadi Palace, a former Mon palace, was excavated just south of the huge Shwemawdaw Paya. Walled in the Mon style, the square city measured a mile along each side and had 20 gates.

When we visited, the site was closed for renovations (ie they're building a new one). It's due to re-open in 2010 – maybe!

HINTHA GON PAYA
ဟင်္သာကုန်ဘုရား

Located behind the Shwemawdaw, this shrine was once the one point in this whole vast area that rose above sea level and so was the natural place for the *hamsa* to land.

A statue of the bird, looking rather like the figures on opium weights, tops the hill. The stupa was built by U Khanti, the hermit monk who was the architect of Mandalay Hill. Walk to it by taking the steps down the other side of the Shwemawdaw from the main entrance. This paya is also a big spot for *nat* (spirit beings) worship and festivals and with a bit of luck you'll catch the swirling, veiled forms of masculine-looking *nat* dancers accompanied by the clanging and crashing of a traditional orchestra.

KYAIK PUN PAYA
ကျိုက်ပွန်ဘုရား

The Gautama Buddha and his three predecessors can all be found hanging out together about a mile south of Bago just off the Yangon road.

Built in 1476 by King Dhammazedi, the Kyaik Pun Paya consists of four 100ft-high sitting buddhas placed back-to-back around a huge, square pillar. According to legend, four Mon sisters were connected with the construction of the buddhas; it was said that if any of them should marry, one of the buddhas would collapse. One of the four buddhas disintegrated in the 1930 earthquake, leaving only a brick outline (since restored) and a very old bride.

En route to the Kyaik Pun Paya, you can detour to the picturesque **Gaung-Say-Kyan Paya**, reached by crossing a wooden bridge over a small lake.

MAHA KALYANI SIMA
(MAHA KALYANI THEIN)
မဟာကလျာဏိသိမ်

This 'Sacred Hall of Ordination' was originally constructed in 1476 by Dhammazedi, the famous alchemist king and son of Queen Shinsawpu. Like almost everything in Bago it has suffered a tumbledown history and has been destroyed and rebuilt many a time.

Next to the hall are 10 large tablets with inscriptions in Pali and Mon describing the history of Buddhism in Myanmar.

If you can't get enough of buddha statues then across the road from the Maha Kalyani Sima is the **Four Figures Paya**, with four buddha figures standing back to back. An adjacent open hallway has a small reclining buddha image, thronged by followers, and some macabre paintings of wrongdoers being tortured in the afterlife.

Relaxing in the sun next to these two monuments is the **Naung Daw Gyi Mya Tha Lyaung**, a reclining buddha sprawled out over 250ft, which is almost as long as its name. It was built in 2002 with donations from the people and, though locals adore it, you probably won't find it all that interesting.

MAHAZEDI PAYA
မဟာစေတီဘုရား

The design of the Mahazedi Paya (Great Stupa), with its white-washed stairways leading almost to the stupa's summit, is unusual for southern Myanmar and certainly one of the more attractive religious buildings in Bago.

Originally constructed in 1560 by King Bayinnaung, it was destroyed during the 1757 sacking of Bago. An attempt to rebuild it in 1860 was unsuccessful and the great earthquake of 1930 comprehensively levelled it, after which it remained a ruin. This current reconstruction was only completed in 1982.

The Mahazedi originally contained a Buddha tooth, at one time thought to be the most sacred of all Buddha relics, the tooth of Kandy, Sri Lanka. After Bago was conquered in 1539, the tooth was moved to Taungoo and then to Sagaing near Mandalay. Together with a begging bowl supposed to have been used by the Buddha, it remains in the Kaunghmudaw Paya (p283), near Sagaing, to this day.

The shady corners of the paya contain various sad-looking chained monkeys.

SHWEGUGALE PAYA
ေရႊ ဂူ က ေလး ဘု ရား

A little beyond the Mahazedi, this *zedi* has a dark *gu* (tunnel) around the circumference of the cylindrical superstructure. The monument dates to 1494 and the reign of King Byinnya Yan. Inside are 64 seated buddha figures. In the evening many locals venture out here.

OTHER ATTRACTIONS
The **Kha Khat Wain Kyaung** is one of the three largest monasteries in the country and watching the long line of monks and novices file out in the early morning for their daily round of alms is quite a sight.

Busloads of tourists visit the monks at lunchtime (10.30am). You're free to wander around the eating hall, and most of the monks think it's hilarious that tourists come and watch them eat, but the atmosphere is a bit like a zoo. Prior to the protests of 2007 there were supposedly 1500 monks in residence here but afterward that figure fell to just 400.

A short distance from the Kanbawzathadi Palace and Museum is the **Snake Monastery**, where you'll find a former head of a monastery in Hsipaw reincarnated in the form of an enormous 118-year-old Burmese python.

Apparently the snake told its owner up north the exact address he needed to go to in Bago in order to complete the construction of a stupa begun in a previous life. Streams

of pilgrims come to pay fearful homage to the snake.

Even if the snake isn't actually a monk it is amazing simply because of its sheer size. Burmese pythons are regarded as one of the world's largest snakes but this one, which chows down 11lb of chickens every 10 days, has to be at least 17ft long and a foot wide, making it probably one of the largest in the world. Don't worry though, it's harmless.

There's a **zedi** nearby on a small hilltop that's great for watching sunsets, and close to the Shwe Le restaurant is a small and colourful **Chinese temple**.

Many Bago women work in local cheroot factories. The **Three Lions cheroot factory**, a little north of the road to Shwethalyaung, claims to welcome visitors but they weren't exactly waiting with open arms when we rocked up. Further west, towards Mahazedi Paya, you can visit a **woodcarving workshop**.

Festivals & Events
On the full moon of the Burmese lunar month of Tagu (March/April) the **Shwemawdaw Paya Festival** attracts huge crowds of worshippers and merrymakers.

Sleeping
The quality of accommodation reflects the fact that many travellers visit Bago only for the day. Most options are on the busy, and make no mistake about this, noisy main road, so rooms towards the back of these hotels are the choice pickings. Electricity is generally available only from the evening to early morning.

Travellers keen to avoid government-owned hotels should bypass the Shwewatun Hotel, out towards the Shwemawdaw Paya.

San Francisco Motel (☎ 22265; Main Rd; s/d from $4/8; ❄) The rooms are rough and ready but fear not, for this is an excellent budget hang-out in the true sense of the word. The guys who run it organise excellent motorbike tours of Bago's sights and are so knowledgeable that by all rights they should actually be a tourist office. Another huge tick in this hotel's favour are the hot showers, which as your, by now, slightly whiffy armpits will know only too well, are a real rarity in this price range.

Emperor Hotel (☎ 21349; Main Rd; s/d $6-11; ❄) From the exterior the Emperor looks like a right fancy-pants hotel, but get on the inside of those pants and you'll find they're horribly stained! On the plus side at least it's friendly and its size allows some escape from road noise.

Mya Nanda Hotel (☎ 19799; 10 Main Rd; s/d from $8-10; 🔀) This place has clean tiled rooms that are the cleanest and most inviting of the Bago budget rooms, but it lacks the atmosphere of the San Francisco Motel. Fight tooth and nail to get a room at the back of the hotel otherwise the crazy road noise will be making sleep a wishful dream. The staff here can also arrange motorbike taxis and guides in order to check out the sights.

Bago Star Hotel (☎ 23766; bagostar@myanmar.com .mm; 11-13 Kyaikpon Pagoda Rd; s/d $24/30; 🔀 🔊) The Star, the nicest and most expensive hotel in Bago, is located just off the highway and only a short walk to the ever-watching eyes of the Kyaik Pun Paya. This smart complex, built entirely of dark stained wood, is a little like kipping in a child's tree-house, though fortunately with a little more comfort. The showers are hot, the swimming pool murky and the restaurant echoing and formal. Bikes can be rented for K1000 a day. Generators keep the air-con humming.

Eating

35 Restaurant (dishes K1200; 🔀) A friendly but shabby place a few doors west of the Emperor Hotel. The menu is a combination of Bamar, Chinese, Indian and European, the food is cheap and good, and the menu includes 'goat fighting balls' (goat testicles), prepared in a number of ways.

Shwe Le Restaurant (☎ 22213; mains K1300) This cheap restaurant has real character. Located on the bottom floor of the owner's house, and looking as much like his front room as a restaurant, it has a slight time-warp atmosphere. Most locals regard it as the best restaurant in town and certainly the Chinese staples are superb and the drinks very cold.

Opposite the Emperor Hotel, the Hadaya Café is a popular teashop with a nice selection of pastries, and good quality tea and coffee.

Getting There & Away
BUS
The bus station is on the Yangon–Bago road, about halfway between the centre and the Bago Star Hotel. Many buses passing though Bago can also be waved down from outside your hotel, though unless you have booked a ticket in advance there is less likelihood of a seat.

Buses to Yangon (K2500) operate approximately hourly from 5am and the journey takes a couple of hours.

Buses to Kyaiktiyo leave every hour or so, and the 3½-hour ride costs K4000. To Mawlamyine departures are at 8am (K10,000) and 9pm (K12,000).

Heading north to Mandalay will set you back K8000 to K12,000 depending on the class of bus. Most of these buses originate in Yangon and getting a ticket can be a little problematic – try to book ahead and ask your hotel to help.

For Taungoo and Inle Lake there are 10 departures a day and you're looking at between K12,000 and K14,000 for a seat. The journey time is 12 hours but it will feel longer, much longer. Again most of these buses originate in Yangon.

TAXI
A more expensive but more convenient alternative is to hire a taxi for a day trip from Yangon. With bargaining this should cost about $35, but it does give you the additional advantage of having transport between sites once you get to Bago and saves traipsing all the way out to the bus station in Yangon. One-way taxis back from Bago straight to your hotel in Yangon can be had for as low as K10,000, well worth it when you consider that if you take the bus to Yangon you'll need to pay K7000 for a taxi from the bus station in Yangon to the city centre. Ask at any hotel about organising this but give at least half a day's notice.

A guide and driver to Kyaiktiyo (Golden Rock, p154) can be hired through any of the central Bago hotels for around $40 return.

TRAIN
Trains from Yangon come through Bago for Mandalay at 6.50am, 7.20am, 10.39am and 1.50pm (ordinary/upper class $11/29, 14 hours).

Trains to Mawlamyine pass by at 9.15am and 11.45am (ordinary/upper class $13/5, two hours).

To Yangon, there are about six trains a day from around 6am to 8pm (ordinary/upper class in express train $2/5).

Getting Around
Trishaw is the main form of local transport in Bago. A one-way trip in the central area

should cost no more than K500. If you're going further afield – say from Shwethalyaung Buddha, at one end of town, to Shwemawdaw Paya, at the other – you might as well hire a trishaw for the day (about K2500 to K3000). Horse carts are another option (K4000 to K5000 for a day). Most people choose to take a motorbike tour and, though less civilised than travelling by trishaw or horse and cart, it's probably the easiest way to go.

A day tour to all of Bago's sites costs K5000 and can be arranged through any hotel, though the best guides are to be found at the Mya Nanda Hotel and San Francisco Motel.

AROUND BAGO
Moeyungyi Wetlands

ရိုးယွန်းကြီး

Myanmar isn't known for its environmental awareness and the nation's few national parks and protected areas are largely inaccessible to foreigners. Moeyungyi Wetlands, about an hour northeast of Bago and close to the village of Pyinbongyi, is the one real exception to this rule.

The wetlands originally started life as an artificial water storage reservoir in the 19th century, but over time the reservoir naturally morphed into a 15-sq-mile lake and marsh. Sitting on a migration route of birds fleeing the icy Siberian winter and attracting thousands of local waders, the wetlands will bring a big grin to any birder's face. The last census

revealed some 125 different species including great flocks of egrets, cormorants, white stalks and large numbers of the beautiful swamp hen (purple gallinule) as well as sarus cranes with their brilliant red heads.

Even if you are not a bird-watcher you will enjoy the experience of escaping the crushing cities and remembering what fresh air and peace and quiet feel like. The wetlands are at their most beautiful around sunset when thousands of egrets return to the trees surrounding the marsh to roost and the light is gorgeous.

A small 'resort' offers excellent boat tours (up to six people) out onto the lake for $10 for half an hour (though in reality you get an hour out on the water). As well as the boat driver, you will be accompanied by a guide – normally the very knowledgeable and informative Mr Aung Ko Oo. The boat will take you whizzing over the lake to the marshy reed beds in the centre where the birds congregate in vast numbers.

Should you want to stay, the resort offers **accommodation** (☎ 01-526 633; per person $55) in floating houseboats. The price includes three meals and a boat ride and it's essential that you book in advance. The rooms, though novel, are insanely overpriced and even serious birders may prefer to make a half-day tour from Bago.

The resort is privately owned by Myanmar businesspeople though the wetlands themselves belong to the government.

Southeastern Myanmar

Slithering like a serpent away from the heartland, southeastern Myanmar is a slippery ride into an extraordinary world of half-true legends and impossible-to-believe facts. This finger of land, extending along the border of Thailand, lapping the lapis lazuli shores of the Andaman Sea and pointing south to Malaysia, contains maybe more variety and vitality than almost any other corner of this country.

In the north columns of saffron, robed monks trudge to a giant sized boulder of gold at Kyaiktiyo that floated to its precarious mountain summit on a ship of stone. Not far away wooden decked ferries voyage upriver from the literary greatness of the stupas of Mawlamyine (Moulmein) to the bat-filled caves of hell near Hpa-an. South still further and hell presents itself in a more poignant manner aboard the death railway heading to the forgotten WWII cemeteries of Thanbyuzayat. Ever further south, close to the serpent's head, you enter a brighter land of singing palm trees, Robinson Crusoe beaches and, strung like sparkling beads across the sultry waters of the Andaman Sea, an archipelago of glittering islands that are a watery home to the romantic sea gypsies.

However, this beautiful region is not without its problems, and while the northern half of the serpent, including Kyaiktiyo, decrepit Mawlamyine and gentle Hpa-an make an easy and trouble-free loop from Yangon (Rangoon), the same cannot be said of the far south. Down here access is only by very unreliable air services and, once in the towns of Dawei, Myeik (Mergui) or Kawthoung, your movements will be highly restricted, which essentially makes the most gorgeous coastline in Southeast Asia out of bounds for all but the most determined.

SOUTHEASTERN MYANMAR

HIGHLIGHTS

- Reach for enlightenment at the home of the *nat* (spirit beings), the golden, gravity-defying **Kyaiktiyo** (Golden Rock; p154)

- Compose prose to rival Kipling's 'By the old Moulmein Pagoda, lookin' lazy at the sea' in go-slow **Mawlamyine** (p159)

- Grapple with reality in Myanmar's parallel world of ghosts, monsters and sausage-shaped rocks of gold at the extraordinary **Nwa-La-Bo Pagoda** (p164)

- Tremble with fear in the dark bowels of hell and fawn over a hidden gallery in the caves close to charming **Hpa-an** (p167)

★ Kyaiktiyo (Golden Rock)

Nwa-La-Bo Pagoda ★ ★ Hpa-an
Mawlamyine ★

| ■ POPULATION: 5.16 MILLION | ■ HIGHEST POINT: MT WEIK-ZAR (3681FT) |

DANGERS & ANNOYANCES

Foreigners are generally restricted from travelling by road south of Thanbyuzayat. The government attributes road attacks in this area to Mon or Kayin (Karen) insurgents, but the motive always seems to be robbery and it's very unclear whether these assaults are politically motivated or whether the robbers are simple bandits. The government tends to lump both kinds of attacks together as 'insurgent activity'. Both sides have laid antipersonnel mines, often near villages, along the lengthy and mountainous border with Thailand.

GETTING THERE & AWAY

From a foreign traveller's perspective there are really two parts to southeastern Myanmar: the first is the northern part that includes Kyaiktiyo, Hpa-an, Mawlamyine and a few places a little further south. All of these destinations are accessible by a combination of boat, bus, car and train with no more than the usual number of hassles of travelling in Myanmar.

The second part to the region – covering Dawei, Myeik, Kawthoung and the archipelago of islands off the coast – is a different story. Foreigners cannot use overland transport. Therefore, to reach any of these places from within Myanmar you will have to fly and, at the time of research, schedules were highly erratic to completely nonexistent. In addition, the border to Thailand at Kawthoung is closed for overland entry and exit.

Of course, the situation, especially in regards to flights, can and will change very fast and it's worth checking to see if flight schedules have normalised.

Until things change, we don't recommend visiting the area – and some Yangon agents will hesitate to even book you a ticket! Check with Yangon travel agents when you arrive to see if the situation has changed.

MON STATE

မွန်ပြည်နယ်

Magnificent Mon State is so full of wonders that it's a wonder that the whole world isn't wondering about holidaying here. There are two dominant colours: the gold of a zillion breathtaking temples and the green of a million, zillion flouncy palm trees. Travelling in this region is generally easy (at least for Myanmar) and distances short, yet strangely few visitors seem to make it down here.

Once native to a broad region stretching from southern Myanmar to Cambodia, the Mon have been absorbed – sometimes willingly, sometimes unwillingly – by the more powerful Bamar and Thai cultures in Myanmar and Thailand over the last 1000 years.

Though no-one knows for sure, the Mon may be descended from a group of Indian immigrants from Kalinga, an ancient kingdom overlapping the boundaries of the modern Indian states of Orissa and Andhra Pradesh. They are responsible for much of the early maintenance and transmission of Theravada Buddhism in mainland Southeast Asia.

Since 1949 the eastern hills of the state (as well as mountains further south in Tanintharyi Division) have been a refuge for the New Mon State Party (NMSP) and its tactical arm, the Mon National Liberation Front (MNLF), whose objective has been self-rule for Mon State.

In 1995, after years of bickering and fighting, the NMSP signed a ceasefire with the Myanmar government. Still, reports continue of fighting, instances of forced labour and harassment of Mon villagers. Partly because of this, there remains much emigration to Thailand.

MOUNT KYAIKTIYO (GOLDEN ROCK)

ကျိုက်ထီးရိုး

☎ 057

Floating in clouds of atmosphere high above the coastal plains and, it seems, almost within touching distance of the heavens is the prayer- and wish-drenched balancing boulder stupa of Kyaiktiyo.

This sublime and magical monument is a major pilgrimage site for Burmese Buddhists, its image adorns many a local's car windscreen or family hearth and every good Buddhist dreams of the day they finally lay eyes on this holiest of shrines.

For a mere tourist this is a sight and an experience to rival the wonders of the Shwedagon Paya or the breathtaking beauty of Bagan. Like any proper pilgrimage a visit here involves a certain amount of hardship and nobody should approach this holy mountain lightly.

Legend states that the boulder maintains its precarious balance due to a precisely placed Buddha hair in the stupa. Apparently King Tissa received the Buddha hair in the 11th century from a hermit who had secreted the hair in his own topknot. The hermit instructed the king to search for a boulder whose shape resembled the hermit's head, and then enshrine the hair in a stupa on top. The king, who inherited supernatural powers as a result of his birth to a *zawgyi* (an accomplished alchemist) father and *naga* (dragon serpent) princess, found the rock at the bottom of the sea. Upon its miraculous arrival on the mountain top, the boat used to transport the rock then turned to stone. This stone can be seen approximately 270yd from the main boulder – it's known as the Kyaukthanban (Stone Boat Stupa).

The atmosphere surrounding Kyaiktiyo during the height of the pilgrimage season (from November to March) is charged with magic and devotion, especially when the glinting boulder is bathed in the purple, sometimes misty, light of dawn and dusk. Pilgrims chant, light candles and meditate all through the night. Men (only) are permitted to walk along a short causeway and over a bridge spanning a chasm to the boulder and affix gold leaf squares on the rock's surface.

From **Kinpun**, the base camp for the mountain, most people pile into one of the trucks that act as taxis and zoom up the road to Yatetaung bus terminal, a 'mere' one hour's walk from the shrine. On this walk you'll sweat, you'll pant and you'll curse the very day you thought of climbing this mountain but then, quite unexpectedly, the shrine will explode into view and the sweat and tears are forgotten.

The constructed plaza around Kyaiktiyo is the typical Myanmar mix of religious iconography and commercial development, monks and laypeople meditating in front of golden buddha statues while several yards away rosary beads and toy wooden rifles are for sale (these are especially popular with monks!). All but the fittest will probably have to take a breather at one of the drink stands clinging to the cliff sides on the road from Yatetaung to the stupa area.

The small stupa, just 24ft high, sits atop the golden rock, a massive, gold leafed boulder delicately balanced on the edge of a cliff at the top of Mt Kyaiktiyo. Like Shwedagon Paya

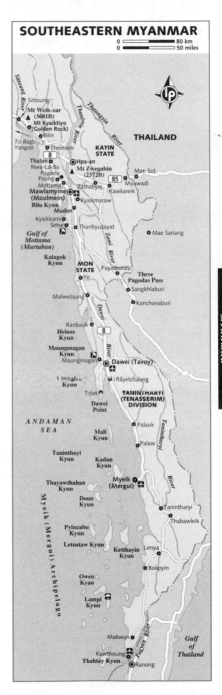

SOUTHEASTERN MYANMAR

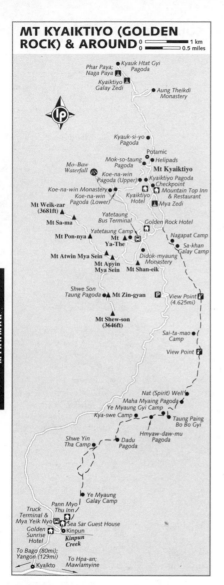

MT KYAIKTIYO (GOLDEN ROCK) & AROUND

trails, however, sometimes lead to unexpected views of the valleys below.

Further behind the pagoda plaza area, down a stairway, there is the Potamic village of restaurants, souvenir shops and guesthouses for Myanmar citizens. A government fee applies to Mt Kyaiktiyo visits.

Orientation & Information

Too many towns with similar-sounding names make orientation confusing. The town of Kyaikto is the least important. This is the town along the highway between Bago and places further south. There is no reason to get out here or to stay here. Buses turn off the highway and end their journeys in Kinpun at the base of the mountain, about 6 miles from the highway.

Kinpun is where you'll find most of the accommodation for foreigners – besides a few hotels near the top of the mountain itself. It's also the starting point for trips up the mountain to Kyaiktiyo. There is no internet access.

The Kyaiktiyo area was not in the direct path of Cyclone Nargis in May 2008 but was hit by strong winds. The minor damage to buildings was quickly repaired.

Hiking

If you have the time to extend your stay in the vicinity there are several other rewarding hikes, which take in gawping views and quiet religious meditation, originating from Kinpun, the Yatetaung bus terminal, and even the shrine itself.

From Kinpun the most obvious short hike is to **Maha Myaing Pagoda**, a miniature Kyaiktiyo, an hour's climb from Kinpun. Any of the Kinpun hotels can point you in the right direction. From Yatetaung bus terminal it's a 45-minute climb to the top of **Mt Ya-The**, a 30-minute walk down to **Mo-Baw Waterfall**, a 1½-hour walk to the **Sa-ma-taung paya and kyaung** (monastery). From Kyaiktiyo itself a trail continues along the crests of the surrounding peaks for another couple of hours to the **Kyauk-si-yo Pagoda** and **Kyaiktiyo Galay Zedi**.

Sleeping

Although Kyaiktiyo can be visited as a day trip from Bago and, in theory, Yangon, this isn't recommended; the advantage of staying near the shrine is that you can catch sunset and sunrise – the most magical times. Foreigners

in Yangon or Bahaman Paya in Mandalay, the Kyaiktiyo stupa is one of the most sacred Buddhist sites in Myanmar.

A new terrace allows devotees to view the boulder from below. There are several other stupas and shrines scattered on the ridge at the top of Mt Kyaiktiyo, though none is as impressive as Kyaiktiyo. The interconnecting aren't permitted to stay in one of the many *zayat* (rest shelters) for pilgrims at the top, nor are they permitted to camp in wooded areas on the mountain.

In the town of Kyaikto along the main road from Bago there are several guest-houses, none of them very appealing, and there really is no reason to stay here rather than in Kinpun.

Note, however, that the first truck up at the mountain from Kinpun leaves at 6am and the last one down leaves at 6pm. The truck ride takes at least 45 minutes and the walk to the summit a further 45 minutes. This means that if you choose to stay in Kinpun you will be unable to catch sunrise or sunset, which is frustrating. Therefore if perfect photographic light is important to you, you'll need to stay in one of the two overpriced hotels on the mountain itself.

ON THE MOUNTAIN

If you want to catch the best light and most enchanting atmosphere at the shrine (and yes, you do) then you simply have no choice but to stay at one of the two sister hotels near the top. This is unfortunate because, aside from the location, they represent such poor value for money that they are almost painful to recommend.

If you choose to stay at one of these (as most people do) then book in advance through a Yangon travel agency where you'll pay a slightly more realistic $45 a double.

Travellers keen to avoid government-owned hotels should stay well clear of the

---

SCALING THE HEIGHTS

A trip to Kyaiktiyo requires planning, enormous patience, endurance and strong legs. There is a $6 government entrance fee and $2 camera fee, payable at the checkpoint near the top, before the Kyaiktiyo Hotel. The ticket is valid for 30 days, so you may visit again without paying the government another $6.

In theory it is possible to reach the rock from Yangon, or Bago or elsewhere without ever setting one foot in front of the other: bus to truck to sedan chair and repeat in the other direction. But isn't the whole point of a pilgrimage, for aesthetic, intellectual or religious reasons, at least in part about the effort to get there?

There are two ways to the rock from the base camp in Kinpun. The first is to hike all the way there. This is approximately 7 miles and takes between four and six hours. The trail begins past the bazaar of souvenir shops in Kinpun and there are numerous 'rest camps' along the way where weary pilgrims can snack and rehydrate. Not many people, even the true devotees, choose to hike all the way up and back. The way down takes from three to four hours and should not be attempted in the dark even with a torch; it's too easy to stumble.

The second way to the rock, which most people do both ways, is to ride one of the large trucks (*lain-ka*) up the winding road to the Yatetaung bus terminal, the end point for all vehicle traffic. No cars, taxis, pick-ups or buses are allowed. The truck beds are lined with wooden slats for benches and seat 35 or so people (K1300). Five or so are allowed in the much more comfortable front seats (per person K2000 to K3000) but these are usually reserved in advance by groups or families. As an individual traveller it's difficult to secure a front seat, while a group of five has a better chance. Regardless, you could be in for a wait of an hour or more as trucks don't leave until they are completely packed to the brim. The ride to the top takes 45 minutes or so and usually includes a stop around halfway up to allow trucks coming from the opposite direction to pass. The first truck in the morning is at 6am and the last truck down is around 6pm, though you should try to be at the Yatetaung bus terminal earlier to avoid the risk of being stranded for the night.

From the terminal, nothing more than a dirt lot surrounded by snack and souvenir shops, it takes 45 minutes to an hour to hike up the remaining steep, paved switchback path. Those with accessibility concerns, or royal fantasies, might want to be carried the rest of the way in a sedan chair ($5 to $7 one way), a canvas litter held aloft by four perspiring Burmese men. Walking or reclining, you pass through an array of vendors along the way to the stupa area at the top. Men shouldn't wear shorts at the shrine and women should wear long skirts only – no trousers, miniskirts or skimpy tops.

Kyaiktiyo Hotel, along the ridge at the top of Mt Kyaiktiyo.

Golden Rock Hotel (☎ in Yangon 01-502 479; grtt@goldenrock.com.mm; s/d $60/80; meals $4-12; 🔊) The Golden Rock Hotel, just a few minutes up from the Yatetaung bus terminal, but at least 45 minutes from the shrine, is in a lovely spot and has larger and marginally more endearing rooms than the Mountain Top Inn, but its positioning, halfway between everywhere but not really anywhere, makes it of little use to anyone.

Mountain Top Inn & Restaurant (☎ in Yangon 01-502 479; grtt@goldenrock.com.mm; s/d $60/80; meals $4-12; 🔊) Rooms in the Mountain Top Inn are terrible value. However, situated right on the summit of the mountain and only a couple of moments' stroll to the shrine complex, its positioning is unbeatable.

KINPUN

Pann Myo Thu Inn (☎ 60285; s from $5, d from $7; 🔊) This green building full of green plants and lots of green, flowering orchids is another great choice. The cheap rooms are better value than the Sea Sar, but the pricier ones not quite as neat. It has a friendly home-away-from-home feel – probably because it is in fact the owners' home.

Sea Sar Guest House (☎ 60367; s $5-10, d $7-15; 🔊) In the heart of the town but set in spacious gardens a little way back from the pilgrimage noise, the more expensive rooms at the Sea Sar are memorable for all the right reasons. They're clean, with hot showers, silky soft beds and wooden floors – you can't really go far wrong. The cheaper rooms though are more disappointing and look like a crime scene. The staff are dialled into travellers' needs and can provide local maps with marked walks, taxi services and bus tickets. The attached restaurant has all the staples for K1500 to K2000.

Golden Sunrise Hotel (☎ in Yangon 01-701 027; gsunrise@myanmar.com.mm; s/d U$17/20; 🔊) A few minutes' walk outside the centre of Kinpun village in the direction of the highway, the Golden Sunrise is one of the best value hotels in southeastern Myanmar. There are eight bamboo-heavy bungalows with a touch of class. The spacious rooms are undisturbed by noise, immaculately clean and, for once, the bathrooms are a sheer delight to spend time in! The private verandas overlooking the secluded gardens are the perfect place to relax at the end of the day with a drink. The only

reason it hasn't been awarded an 'Our Pick' icon is that if you stay here you cannot catch the sunrise or sunset at the shrine.

Eating

Because Kinpun is the starting point for this popular Myanmar site, there are a number of good Chinese and Bamar restaurants running up and down the town's main street. Like all busy pilgrimage towns the restaurants are universally overpriced.

Mya Yeik Nyo (noodles with chicken K2000) This is the pick, and the one that all taxi drivers will recommend. It's very close to where the trucks depart for the mountain.

In addition to the food stalls at Kinpun and all along the footpaths, there is a veritable food court of restaurants at the summit past the shrines and plaza area and down the steps.

Getting There & Away

For individual travellers, Bago makes a better starting point for road trips to Kyaiktiyo than Yangon, as hotel staff there are adept at arranging inexpensive alternatives. A guide and driver to Kyaiktiyo can be hired through any of the central Bago hotels (see p150) for around $40. The same tour booked in Yangon costs more than double that.

BUS & PICK-UP

Buses that go straight from Yangon to Kyaiktiyo and Kinpun (K8000, 4½ hours) leave from Yangon's Aung Mingalar (highway) bus terminal (see p130) every 30 minutes or so from 7am to 1pm; other air-conditioned buses leave from Pansodan St in Yangon in the evening for the same price. It's virtually impossible to see Kyaiktiyo in one day on public transport from the capital.

There are large buses (K1700) and pick-ups from Kyaiktiyo to Bago (K1000, three hours).

Small pick-ups leave from Kinpun to Hpa-An (K5000, five hours) from 6am to 1pm or there is a more comfortable bus (K7000) which has a useful departure time of 1.30pm.

To Mawlamyine there is a bus at 8.30am and another at 11am (K7000, 4½ hours).

Pick-ups cruise the road between Kyaiktiyo and Kinpun every half an hour or so (K500).

TRAIN

There are a couple of trains a day to/from Yangon (via Bago) and Mawlamyine. Trains from Yangon continue to Mawlamyine after a 10- to 20-minute stop in Kyaiktiyo and trains from Mawlamyine continue to Bago and Yangon after a similar-duration stop.

Trains depart Yangon daily at 6.30am and 7.15am ($10 upper class, $4 ordinary class, five hours). Trains depart Mawlamyine at 6am and 10am ($8 upper class, $3 ordinary class, five hours). Trains leave Kyaiktiyo for Yangon and Bago at 11.10am and 3pm and for Mawlamyine at 11.30am and 12.15pm.

THATON

သထုံ

☎ 057

Long before the rise of Bagan, Thaton was the capital of a Mon kingdom that stretched from the Ayeyarwady (Irrawaddy) River delta to similar river deltas in Thailand, and possibly as far east as Cambodia. Early on, Thaton may have been known as Suvannabhumi, the 'Golden Land'. Legend says that Ashoka, the great Indian Buddhist emperor, sent a mission here in the 3rd century BC. Later it was called Dvaravati when it reached its dynastic peak between the 6th and 10th centuries AD. Shin Aran, a monk from Thaton, carried Theravada Buddhism north to the Burmese kingdom of Bagan, and in 1057 Thaton was conquered by King Anawrahta of Bagan.

Today Thaton sits on the main road and rail line that stretches from Bago to Mottama. Little of ancient Thaton is visible, as the modern town has been built over the old sites. The town's core is a leafy place, lining each side of the highway with colonial mansions and thatched-roof homes. A few older stupas dot the hillsides surrounding the town and a picturesque canal network irrigates rice paddies and fruit orchards.

Shwe Zayan Paya, on the northern side of the road, just beyond the clock tower, has an interesting monastery complex and a large stupa supposedly built during the early Mon period. A famous 10th-century standing buddha stele found at this paya was sculpted in the classic Mon style and shows strong similarities with Dvaravati period buddhas from central Thailand.

Thaton sits on the main road that stretches from Bago to Mottama. It avoided being seriously damaged by Cyclone Nargis and also quickly recovered from a flood in mid-June that submerged more than half the town.

MAWLAMYINE (MOULMEIN)

မော်လမြိုင်

☎ 057 / pop 300,000

Mawlamyine is the quintessential go-slow tropical town. As the town's clocks tick ever-so-slowly forward nothing much ever changes, except the vegetation, which becomes a little more riotous with each passing day. It surely won't be long until the inhabitants awake one morning to find that their entire town has been reclaimed by vines and palm trees.

With a ridge of stupa-capped hills on one side, the sea on the other and a centre filled with mildewed mosques, the stage is set for an attractive urban setting and one that is made only more charming by the general air of melancholy. As well as the delights of the town, the area around Mawlamyine has enough enthralling attractions to keep a visitor happy for several days.

Mawlamyine (some maps may show it as Mawlamyaing) served as the capital of British Burma from 1827 to 1852, during which time it developed as a major teak port. A great deal of coastal shipping still goes on, although Pathein and Yangon have superseded it as Myanmar's most important ports. The city is composed roughly of 75% Mon or some mixture of Mon, plus Kayin, Bamar, Indian, Chinese and other ethnic groups.

Largely escaping Cyclone Nargis, Mawlamyine suffered only minor damage from strong winds. Not long after the storm, everything returned to business as usual.

Information

A police station is located over the road from the government jetties. The post office is a couple of blocks further inland.

Thu Kha Zone (Htet Rd Magyi; 9am-9pm; per hr K1000) Decent internet connections are available at this wooden shack a little out of the town centre. Connections are often down in the daytime.

Sights & Activities

MON CULTURAL MUSEUM

မွန်ယဉ်ကျေးမှုပြတိုက်

This government-run, two-storey **museum** (cnr Baho & Dawei Jetty Rds; admission $2; 9.30am-4.30pm Sun-Fri) is dedicated to the Mon history of the region. It's on the corner of Baho Rd (formerly Dalhousie St). The museum's modest collection includes stelae with Mon inscriptions, 100-year-old wooden sculptures depicting

SOUTHEASTERN MYANMAR

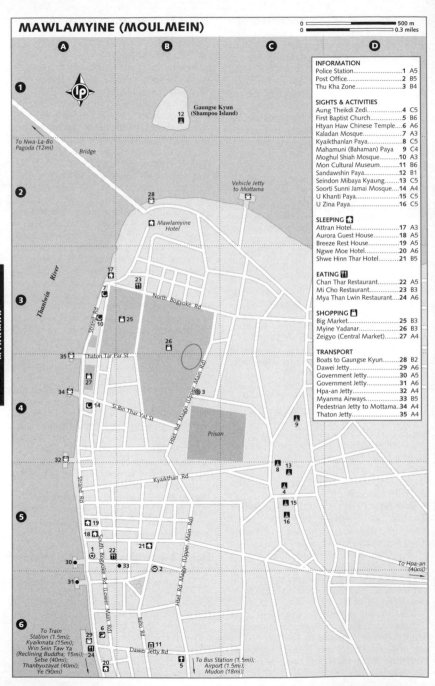

MAWLAMYINE (MOULMEIN)

0 ————————— 500 m
0 ————————— 0.3 miles

INFORMATION
Police Station..........................**1** A5
Post Office.............................**2** B5
Thu Kha Zone.......................**3** B4

SIGHTS & ACTIVITIES
Aung Theikdi Zedi..................**4** C5
First Baptist Church................**5** B6
Htyan Haw Chinese Temple...**6** A6
Kaladan Mosque.....................**7** A3
Kyaikthanlan Paya..................**8** C5
Mahamuni (Bahaman) Paya   **9** C4
Moghul Shiah Mosque...........**10** A3
Mon Cultural Museum............**11** B6
Sandawshin Paya...................**12** B1
Seindon Mibaya Kyaung.......**13** C5
Soorti Sunni Jamai Mosque....**14** A4
U Khanti Paya........................**15** C5
U Zina Paya...........................**16** C5

SLEEPING
Attran Hotel..........................**17** A3
Aurora Guest House................**18** A5
Breeze Rest House..................**19** A5
Ngwe Moe Hotel....................**20** A6
Shwe Hinn Thar Hotel............**21** B5

EATING
Chan Thar Restaurant............**22** A5
Mi Cho Restaurant.................**23** B3
Mya Than Lwin Restaurant....**24** A6

SHOPPING
Big Market............................**25** B3
Myine Yadanar.......................**26** B3
Zeigyo (Central Market)........**27** A4

TRANSPORT
Boats to Gaungse Kyun.........**28** B2
Dawei Jetty...........................**29** A6
Government Jetty...................**30** A5
Government Jetty...................**31** A6
Hpa-an Jetty.........................**32** A4
Myanma Airways...................**33** B5
Pedestrian Jetty to Mottama...**34** A4
Thaton Jetty..........................**35** A4

Gaungse Kyun
(Shampoo Island)

To Nwa-La-Bo
Pagoda (12mi)

Bridge

Thanlwin River

Vehicle Jetty
to Mottama

Mawlamyine
Hotel

North Bogyoke Rd

Strand Rd

Thaton Tar Par St

Si Bin Thar Yat St

Htet Rd, Magyi (Upper Main Rd)

Prison

Kyaikthan Rd

South Bogyoke Rd Lower Main Rd

Htet Rd, Magyi (Upper Main Rd)

To Hpa-an
(40mi)

To Train
Station (1.5mi);
Kyaikmata (15mi);
Win Sein Taw Ya
(Reclining Buddha; 15mi);
Setse (40mi);
Thanbyuzayat (40mi);
Ye (90mi)

Baho Rd

Dawei Jetty Rd

To Bus Station (1.5mi);
Airport (1.5mi);
Mudon (18mi);

SOUTHEASTERN MYANMAR

old age and sickness (used as *dhamma*-teaching devices in monasteries), ceramics, silver betel boxes, royal funerary urns, Mon musical instruments and wooden buddha altars.

This is all well and good, but unfortunately the collection is so poorly lit that many of the exhibits are actually impossible to see without a torch!

BUDDHIST MONUMENTS

Unknown Mawlamyine has inspired two of history's finest writers of the English language – George Orwell and Rudyard Kipling. Orwell lived here for some years, and generations of his family were born and bred here. Kipling's visit was shorter, just three days (the only three days he ever spent in Myanmar), but resulted in a few lines of prose that turned Burma into an oriental fantasy: 'By the old Moulmein Pagoda, lookin' lazy at the sea…' The spirit of the poem 'Mandalay', from which these words arise, lives on in Mawlamyine in the form of the golden poems of Buddhist stupas sprawled across the jungle ridge behind the town.

At the northern end of this ridge is **Mahamuni (Bahaman) Paya**, the largest temple complex and easily the most beautiful in Mawlamyine. It's built in the typical Mon style with covered brick walkways linking various shrines. The highlight is the Bahaman Paya itself, a jewel-box chamber shimmering with mirrors, rubies and diamonds and containing a century-old replica of its namesake in Mandalay (see p263).

Further south along the ridge stands **Kyaikthanlan Paya**, the city's tallest and most visible stupa. Impressive though the paya is, it didn't do much for Kipling, who was later to comment of it: 'I should better remember what the pagoda was like had I not fallen deeply and irrevocably in love with a Burmese girl at the foot of the first flight of steps. Only the fact of the steamer starting next noon prevented me from staying at Moulmein forever'. He was certainly not the last to think like that…

Just below the paya, a view looks over the city and is a favoured spot for watching the sunset.

Below Kyaikthanlan is the 100-year-old **Seindon Mibaya Kyaung**, a monastery where King Mindon Min's queen, Seindon, sought refuge after Myanmar's last monarch, King Thibaw Min, took power. On the next rise south stands the isolated silver-and-gold-plated **Aung Theikdi Zedi**.

U Khanti Paya was built to commemorate the hermit of Mandalay Hill fame; supposedly U Khanti spent some time on this hill as well. It's a rustic, airy sort of place centred around a large buddha image.

U Zina Paya, on the southern spur of the ridge, was named after a former monk who dreamt of finding gems at this spot, then dug them up and used the proceeds to build a temple on the site. One of the shrine buildings contains a very curvy, sensual-looking reclining buddha; there are also statues depicting Gautama Buddha's meeting with a sick man, old man, dead man and an ascetic – encounters which encouraged him to seek a meaning behind human suffering.

OTHER RELIGIOUS MONUMENTS

In the centre of town towards the waterfront, on South Bogyoke Rd, are three mosques built during the colonial era when many Indians arrived to work for the British. Since the Indian exodus of the 1970s, Muslim congregations have declined substantially, but the survival of these grand old buildings makes a walk here a fleeting exercise in nostalgia.

The most impressive building, **Kaladan Mosque**, is a green-and-turquoise structure designed by Sunni Muslims in an elaborate 'wedding-cake style'. Further south, on the same side of the street, is the smaller **Moghul Shiah Mosque**, a Shiite place of worship painted blue with austere Moorish arches. A couple of blocks further, south of the central market, the Sunni **Soorti Sunni Jamai Mosque** fills a similar space but presents a more brilliant turquoise-and-white facade.

Just up from Dawei jetty, on the eastern side of Strand Rd, the small but colourful **Htyan Haw Chinese temple** serves the local Chinese community. Of historic interest is the sturdy brick **First Baptist Church** (cnr Htet Lan Magyi & Dawei Jetty Rd), also known as the Judson Church; this was Myanmar's first Baptist church.

GAUNGSE KYUN (SHAMPOO ISLAND)

ေခါင်းေဆးကျွန်း

This picturesque little isle off Mawlamyine's northern end is so named because, during the Ava period, the yearly royal hair-washing ceremony customarily used water taken from a spring on the island.

You can hire a boat out to the island from in front of the Mawlamyine Hotel for K1500 return. Peace rather than sights are the reason for venturing out here, but you can visit **Sandawshin Paya**, a whitewash-and-silver *zedi* (stupa) said to contain hair relics, and a nearby Buddhist meditation centre. Many nuns, with a menagerie of pet dogs, live on the island.

Sleeping

Most of the accommodation is only a short trishaw ride from the central market and ferry landing.

BUDGET

Breeze Rest House (Lay Hnyin Tha; ☎ 21450; 6 Strand Rd; s $5-12, d $15; ✂) The rooms aren't much but the Breeze, an attractive, blue colonial-style villa on Strand Rd, produces its charms in other ways. The staff are quite simply priceless and are an endless source of information, pleasant conversation and superb guiding skills. The cheapest rooms are nothing more than small windowless prison cells (complete with viewing grills!) with shared bathroom. More expensive rooms, which are snapped up early in the day, are quite spacious and have large, modern bathrooms with air-con.

Aurora Guest House (☎ 22785; 277 Lower Main Rd; s $5-15, d $10-20) Not as friendly or suited to foreign travellers, nevertheless the Aurora is the only other budget option and to be honest has better rooms than the Breeze. More expensive rooms have private bathroom and air-con; others only have a fan and shared bathroom. Breakfast is not included.

MIDRANGE

Travellers keen to avoid government-owned hotels should stay clear of the Mawlamyine Hotel, in the northwestern corner of the city.

Shwe Hinn Thar Hotel (Baho Rd; s/d $15/20; ✂) For the 'luxury' backpacker this new hotel is the best place to stay. The rooms are cavernous and very clean with fancy extras like satellite TV. It's large enough to ensure that it normally has rooms available, but it doesn't have much character.

Attran Hotel (☎ 25764; www.attranhotel.com; Strand Rd; s/d $22/35; ✂) Overlooking the sultry river waters the Attran is suitably reminiscent of a beach resort. Tour groups like the series of orderly bungalows spread out across the green pastures. It's exceptionally friendly and helpful but there is no getting away from the fact that it's a little overpriced. The hotel restaurant, on a deck by the river and lit up at night, is a nice place to eat.

Ngwe Moe Hotel (☎ 24703; Strand Rd; s/d $27/36; ✂) The only place in Mawlamyine to look and act like a standard hotel, the three-storey Ngwe Moe on Strand Rd is frequented by groups and the rooms are fresh and comfortable but lack character. Pluses include reliable electricity and hot showers – a real rarity! Has a good Thai flavoured restaurant.

Eating

For a city of this size, the eating options are scarce. The Attran Hotel and Ngwe Moe Hotel have restaurants that serve lunch and dinner. Your best bet is to walk from the Breeze Rest House south along Strand Rd.

Mya Than Lwin Restaurant (☎ 25664; Dawei jetty, Strand Rd; fish K2000) This restaurant, in what appears to be a former warehouse, is now a popular hang-out. You can dine on the wooden planked floor outside and feel like you're on a boat at sea or in the smokier, and more bar-like, indoors. There's an extensive menu of soups, chicken and seafood, including about a hundred types of crab. For the lobster roast, order a day in advance.

Help Grandfather and Mother Restaurant (Strand Rd; noodles K500) Does what it says on the label; the money raised here goes to a charity helping the town's elderly. If that weren't reason enough to eat here, it's also a delightful waterfront restaurant in its own right and absolutely the place to watch the sunset with a cup of tea. The food is basic but does the job. The sign is written in Burmese only, but it's easy to see from the Breeze Rest House.

Mi Cho Restaurant (☎ 25495; North Bogyoke Rd; dishes K1500) This busy hole-in-the-wall place, just around the corner from the Attram Hotel (look for the green building with a sign in Burmese script), is widely regarded as the best Indian restaurant in town and its *biryani* (spiced rice) is truly deserving of the accolades.

ourpick Chan Thar Restaurant (☎ 21352; ☷ 10am-10pm; dishes K1500) You could easily mistake this restaurant for a cinema and walk right on past, but that would be missing out on the best place in town to eat. The sweet and sour is unusually good and the chef can even whip up a mean fruit salad. There's beer and

SOUTHEASTERN MYANMAR

conversations on tap and a TV tuned to the UK premiership.

Shopping

Mawlamyine has a number of bossy markets including the **zeigyo** (central market), the **Big Market** and the even bigger **Myine Yadanar** market. Though locals distinguish between all of them, you probably won't as they all virtually mould into one another and you'll be too engrossed in the melange of smells, sights and tastes to care anyway. The entire district is busiest in the early morning from 7am to 8am; by 9am business is considerably slower.

Getting There & Away

AIR

Myanma Airways used to have once weekly flights between Mawlamyine and Yangon but it hasn't been running them for quite some time now and it seems unlikely they will restart anytime soon.

BOAT

Double-decker ferries leave from the Hpa-an jetty in Mawlamyine at 6am on Mondays and Fridays for the trip up the Thanlwin River to Hpa-an on the river's eastern bank ($2, five hours). It's worth a trip to Hpa-an (p167) if only because this dirt-cheap riverboat cruise passes through stunning scenery of limestone mountains and sugarcane fields. It's not usually crowded and there are a few sun chairs, perfect front-row seats for the river show. Bring your own food and drinks.

Further south are two jetties reserved for government boats only, followed by the larger Dawei jetty for boats to Dawei and Myeik. These boats generally only carry cargo nowadays, but it doesn't hurt to enquire into whether or not the old passenger ferry service is running again.

BUS & PICK-UP

Mawlamyine's main bus station is a mile and a half out of town and very close to the train station. Two buses a day leave for Yangon (K13,000, eight hours) at 9am and 6pm. Tickets should be reserved in advance. Other northbound services include Bago (K13,000, seven hours) and Kyaiktiyo (K8000, four hours).

Note that if you are coming from Yangon on an evening or night bus you will have the sleepless pleasure of getting to the edge of the bridge linking Mawlamyine with the north only to find that you have to wait until dawn before being allowed to cross! If you happen to be reading this bit while you're on the night bus, well don't get disheartened – it's only another five hours until daybreak…

Around six buses a day bounce down the road to Hpa-an between 8am and 3pm (K1200, two hours). Buses leave Yangon for Mawlamyine between 7am and 8am, and 7pm and 8.30pm (K11,000 to K15,000).

TRAIN

Express trains run to Yangon at 6am and 10am daily. The 6am is the sweetest and fastest train (upper-class $18, nine hours). Tickets can be purchased at the train station in the south of town. All the trains make brief stops at Kyaiktiyo ($8, four to five hours) and Bago ($13, six hours). Occasionally foreigners manage to wrangle ordinary-class tickets from Mawlamyine. Prices for these are Yangon $9, Bago $5 and Kyaiktiyo $3.

Foreigners travelling south by train are only allowed as far as Ye, due to insurgency in the area.

Getting Around

Motorbike taxis and trishaws are the main form of public transport around the city. The highest concentration is on South Bogyoke Rd in front of the zeigyo. Because there are relatively few foreign visitors, local transport costs are low and the rates are probably not far off from what locals actually pay. The going rate is K500 for a short hop within the centre of town and as much as K800 for a ride up the ridge to Kyaikthanlan.

There are also a handful of wonderful old WWII-era American Chevy trucks that act as minibuses for the town and its environs. The most likely time you'll get to ride on one is from the train or bus station into town (K100).

AROUND MAWLAMYINE

The area around Mawlamyine contains a fascinating range of sights and experiences, which will keep even the most hard-to-please happy for a couple of days. Many people save themselves time and hassle by hiring a taxi (K50,000 per day) and guide ($10) for two or three days in order to explore fully. The best place to organise this is through the Breeze Rest House (opposite), where Mr Antony, a kindly old gentleman in the truest sense of the word, works both on the reception desk and acts as a highly informed and entertaining guide.

Bilu Kyun

ဘီလူးကျွန်း

Bilu Kyun (Ogre Island) isn't quite as scary as it sounds. Rather than a hideaway for nasty monsters it's a fascinating self-contained Mon island comprising 64 villages linked together by rutted dirt tracks full of adventures.

Some of the villages on this large island are involved in the production of coconut fibre-mats and even coconut-inspired and created cutlery and teapots. You can spend an interesting day exploring by taking the daily ferry at 9.45am and 10.45am ($1). Once on the island all local transport is by horse and cart, though the longer dots can be linked by one of the few rattling buses.

To get back to Mawlamyine you must be at Nut-Maw village by 3pm in order to catch the final ferry back to town. Foreigners are not allowed to stay overnight on the island (that's when the ogres come out to get you) and, in order to keep things running smoothly, it's a good idea to take a guide from the Breeze Rest House ($10, see p162).

North of Mawlamyine

NWA-LA-BO PAGODA

နွားလဘို့ ဘုရား

After you've travelled for some time in Myanmar you begin to realise that this is a land operating in two parallel worlds. One is the safe, scientific world of Myanmar that we all know and understand and the other is the alternate world of Burma, an ancient land of *nat* and gods, monsters and saints. Sometimes, in the glossy shops of Yangon or on the backside-bruising buses of the interior, this mystical world can be a little hard to see, but at other times this magic old world stares you straight in the face and demands that you believe in the unbelievable. In the jungle-cloaked hills to the north of Mawlamyine this Tolkienesque side of the country comes to life in an extraordinary fashion at the Nwa-la-bo Pagoda.

A local pilgrimage site, Nwa-la-bo is still relatively unknown outside of Mon State and currently very few foreigners make it out here. This is surprising because the pagoda is a smaller but, geologically at least, far more astonishing version of Kyaiktiyo. Unlike at that shrine, where just one huge boulder perches on the cliff ledge, Nwa-la-bo consists of three sausage-shaped **gold boulders** piled precariously atop one another and surmounted by a stupa. The result is lifted straight from the fairytale world of Middle Earth or could it possibly be that Middle Earth is actually lifted straight from the fairytale world of the Burma of old?

Getting There & Away

Getting to Nwa-la-bo is fairly easy and makes a perfect half-day trip from town. Try to go on a weekend when pilgrims will add more flair to the scene and transport is a little more regular.

From Mawlamyine take a bus or pick-up to Kyonka village (K600) around 12 miles north of town. From here clamber into the back of one of the pick-up trucks that crawl slowly up to the summit of the mountain (K1600 return) in around 45 minutes. Give yourself plenty of time as the trucks don't leave until beyond full and don't leave your descent back down the mountain too late in the day as transport becomes scarcer after 3pm.

South of Mawlamyine

PA-AUK-TAW-YA MONASTERY

ဖားအောက်တောရ ဘုန်းကြီးကျောင်း

Only 9 miles south of Mawlamyine is the **Pa-Auk-Taw-Ya Monastery** (www.paauk.org); at 500 acres it's one of the largest meditation centres in Myanmar. Foreigners can visit for the night or several days; sleeping and eating is gratis, meditation may be paid for by the sweat of your brow, but courses can be quite expensive. Venerable Pak Auk Sayadaw teaches *satipatthana vipassana* (insight-awareness meditation) using a penetrative and highly technical approach.

YADANA TAUNG, KYAUKTALON TAUNG & KANDAWGYI

ရတနာတောင် ကျောက်တစ်လုံးတောင် & ကန်တော်ကြီး

If you thought you'd seen some big old buddhas just wait till you get a load of this monster. Draped across a couple of green hillsides at Yadana Taung, and surrounded by a forest of other pagodas and shrines, is the recently constructed **Win Sein Taw Ya**, a 560ft-long reclining buddha, which makes it easily one of the largest such images in the world.

Many other stupas and standing buddhas dot the area, including 500 statues lining the road to the Win Sein Taw Ya. Aside from inflated buddhas the area affords some gentle walks with wonderful panoramas.

Every year around the first couple of days of February a crazy coloured **festival** takes place here to celebrate the birthday of the monk who constructed the buddha. As well as a host of itinerant traders, monks and nuns, magic men and the odd hermit or two, the festival often hosts a major kickboxing tournament, which leads to the slightly surreal sight of hundreds of cheering monks baying for blood in the ring!

Nearby is **Kyauktalon Taung**, a strangely shaped, sheer-sided crag rising out of the surrounding agricultural land and crowned with stupas. It's a sticky 20-minute climb to the summit. On the opposite side of the road is a similar but smaller outcropping surmounted by a Hindu temple.

Further south, and not far from Mudon is a turn-off east to **Azin Dam**, a water-storage and flood-control facility that's also used to irrigate local rubber plantations. A tidy recreation area at **Kandawgyi** – a lake formed by the dam – is a favourite picnic spot with locals. At the northern end of the lake stands the gilded stupa of **Kandawgyi Paya**.

Getting There & Away

For these sights hop on a bus or pick-up at Mawlamyine's market heading in the direction of Mudon (K500, 45 minutes) and ask to be dropped at the junctions for any of the above places (you will have to pay the full fare to Mudon).

THANBYUZAYAT

သံဖြူဇရပ်

Thanbyuzayat (Tin Shelter), 40 miles south of Mawlamyine, was the western terminus of the infamous Burma–Siam Railway, dubbed the 'Death Railway' by the thousands of Allied prisoners of war (POWs) and Asian coolies who were forced by the Japanese military to build it.

About a mile south of the town centre's clock tower, a locomotive and piece of track commemorating the railway are on display. There also used to be a WWII museum, but the government let it turn to ruin as, according to one local, 'They do not even want us to remember this history'.

Half a mile west of the clock tower towards Kyaikkami, on the southern side of the road, lies the **Thanbyuzayat War Cemetery**.

This lonely site contains 3771 graves of Allied POWs who died building the railway. Most of those buried were British but there are also markers for American, Dutch and Australian soldiers. As you walk around this simple memorial, maintained by the Commonwealth War Graves Commission, reading the heart-rending words inscribed on the grave stones it's impossible not to be moved to the brink of tears.

Some are simple and state only that 'One day we will understand', which of course we never did. Others are personal messages of love and remembrance, such as: 'I waited, but you did not come. Life was cruel to us. Dorothy' – GE Wright, died age 28.

Getting There & Away

Thanbyuzayat is easily reached by public pick-up or bus (K1000, two hours) from the Mawlamyine central market area; there are six departures, all before noon. As there is no legal lodging in Thanbyuzayat, start early so you can catch the last bus back to Mawlamyine at around 3pm. The road between the two towns passes through mile after mile of rubber and pineapple plantations. Women set up roadside stalls selling the sweetest pineapples you'll ever try.

KYAIKKAMI

ကျိုက္ခမိ

Located 5.5 miles northwest of Thanbyuzayat, Kyaikkami was a small coastal resort and missionary centre known as Amherst during the British era. Adoniram Judson (1788–1850), an American missionary and linguist who has practically attained sainthood among Myanmar Baptists, was sailing to India with his wife when their ship was blown off course, forcing them to land at Kyaikkami. Judson stayed on and established his first mission here; the original site is now a **Catholic school** on a small lane off the main road.

The main focus of Kyaikkami is **Yele Paya**, a metal-roofed Buddhist shrine complex perched over the sea and reached via a long two-level causeway; the lower level is submerged during high tide. Along with 11 Buddha hair relics, the shrine chamber beneath Yele Paya reportedly contains a buddha image that supposedly floated here on a raft from Sri Lanka in ancient times (see Thiho-shin Phondaw-pyi on p137 for more details on this legend). A display of 21

THE DEATH RAILWAY

The strategic objective of the 'Burma–Siam Railway' was to secure an alternative supply route for the Japanese conquest of Myanmar and other Asian countries to the west.

Construction on the railway began on 16 September 1942 at existing terminals in Thanbyuzayat and Nong Pladuk, Thailand. At the time, Japanese engineers estimated that it would take five years to link Thailand and Burma by rail, but the Japanese army forced the POWs to complete the 260-mile, 3.3ft-gauge railway in 13 months. Much of the railway was built in difficult terrain that required high bridges and deep mountain cuttings. The rails were finally joined 23 miles south of the town of Payathonzu (Three Pagodas Pass); a Japanese brothel train inaugurated the line. The railway was in use for 21 months before the Allies bombed it in 1945.

An estimated 16,000 POWs died as a result of brutal treatment by their captors, a story chronicled by Pierre Boulle's book *Bridge on the River Kwai* and popularised by a movie based on the book. The notorious bridge itself still stands in Kanchanaburi, Thailand. Only one POW is known to have escaped, a Briton who took refuge among pro-British Kayin guerrillas.

Although the statistics of the number of POWs who died during the Japanese occupation are horrifying, the figures for the labourers, many from Myanmar, Thailand, Malaysia and Indonesia, are even worse. It is thought that 80,000 Asians, 6540 British, 2830 Dutch, 2710 Australians and 356 Americans died in the area.

Mandalay-style buddha statues sits over the spot where the Sinhalese image is supposedly buried. Pilgrims standing at the water's edge place clay pots of flowers and milk into the sea in order to 'feed' the spirits.

Getting There & Away

During the early half of the day there are occasional pick-ups to Kyaikkami from Thanbyuzayat for K500 per person. From Mawlamyine it takes approximately 2½ hours to get there. The bus (K1500) leaves from the Thanbyuzayat stop near the market.

SETSE
စက်စဲ

Not a picture postcard beach by any stretch of the imagination, but as the grime of travel washes away you probably won't care. This low-key Gulf of Mottama beach is a very wide, brown-sand strip. The beach is lined with waving casuarina trees and has been a popular spot for outings since colonial times. Though a few locals stop by for a swim almost no foreigners visit this area and facilities are minimal. At low tide you can walk along the beach to the small temple on the rocks at the northern end.

You can stay at the privately owned **Ngwe Moe Guesthouse** (☎ 79375; s/d $10/16), which has spacious but run-down beach bungalows. A few modest restaurants offer fresh seafood including the Pyay Son Oo Restaurant, which is very close to the hotel.

Pick-ups run between Setse and Thanbyuzayat on a fairly frequent basis (K500). The last one leaves for Thanbyuzayat at 4pm.

East of Mawlamyine
KYAIKMARAW
ကျိုက်မရော

This small, charming town of wooden houses lined with flowering plants, 15 miles southeast of Mawlamyine, is the site of an impressive temple.

Kyaikmaraw Paya

The pride of the town is this temple of serene white-faced buddhas built by Queen Shin Saw Pu in 1455. Among the temple's many outstanding features are multicoloured glass windows set in the outside walls, an inner colonnade decorated in mirrored tiles, and beautiful ceramic tile floors. Painted reliefs appear on the exterior of several auxiliary buildings.

Covered brick **walkways** lead up to and around the main square sanctuary in typical 15th-century Mon style. The huge main buddha image sits in a 'European pose', with the legs hanging down as if sitting on a chair rather than in the much more common cross-legged manner. A number of smaller cross-legged buddhas surround the main image, and behind it are two reclining buddhas, one with eyes open, one with eyes closed. Another impressive feature is the carved and painted wooden ceiling.

A side room to the inner sanctuary contains sculptures depicting the Buddha in various stages of illness and death – other than the traditional *parinibbana* reclining posture, these are unusual motifs for Buddhist temples. Two images show the Buddha lying on his back with hands folded on his abdomen; another depicts an ill Buddha stooping over slightly with one hand clasped to his chest, the other hand against the wall as his disciples reach out to assist him.

Next to the main sanctuary is a small **museum** with buddha images, donated by the faithful, on the upper floor; other artefacts from the area are on the lower floor.

Getting There & Away
Buses nip between Mawlamyine bus station and market and Kyaikmaraw about every hour for K800.

KHA-YON CAVES
ခရုံဂူ

Spirited away in the back of the little known dark and dank Kha-Yon Caves, a short way along the road to Hpa-an, are rows of ghostly buddha statues and wall paintings that come lurching out of the dark as the light from a torch catches them. Close by is another, smaller, cave system. This one is more of an open cavern and contains further statues as well as a small cave-dwelling stupa. Bring a torch.

The statues and shrines in these caves make for a popular stop for local tourists and pilgrims alike. There is something unnerving about stumbling upon a meditating monk sitting in utter darkness at the foot of a cobweb stained shrine.

To get here from Mawlamyine take any bus towards Hpa-an (K1200, every hour until 3pm) and ask to be dropped at the junction for the caves.

KAYIN STATE
ကရင်ပြည်နယ်

The limestone escarpments and luminous paddy fields coupled with a fascinating ethnic mix would make Kayin State a Myanmar highlight but sadly, like so much of the nation's border regions, much of the area is very much off limits to foreign visitors.

Some parts are possible to visit though, including Hpa-an, the regional capital, an easy and highly recommended trip from Mawlamyine or Yangon. Kayin State itself, homeland to around a million Kayin, has probably received more foreign visitors, who have crossed over – unofficially – from Thailand, than from other parts of Myanmar. Many international volunteers have ventured into the frontier area to assist with refugee concerns.

Ever since Myanmar attained independence from the British in 1948, the Kayin have been embroiled in a fight for autonomy. The main insurgent body, the Karen National Union (KNU), controls much of the northern and eastern parts of the state, although recent Yangon military victories have left the KNU and its military component, the Karen National Liberation Army (KNLA), severely weakened. Rebel-held Kayin State is also the seat of the National Coalition Government of the Union of Burma (NCGUB), a 'parallel government' established by a group of National League for Democracy (NLD) members who won parliamentary seats in the ill-fated May 1990 national elections. By 2006 it was estimated that the number of KNLA recruits had dropped from a high of 20,000 in the '80s to 12,000 today.

Much of the state remains a potential battleground as sporadic fighting between Myanmar troops and the KNLA continues.

HPA-AN
ဘားအံ
☎ 058

Hpa-an (also known as Pa'an) is small-town Myanmar at its finest. Though this exceptionally friendly town has only a limited number of official tourist attractions, the atmosphere is energetic and the colours on the streets rich and vibrant. The real draw is in the surrounding countryside which contains cave-dwelling art galleries, sacred mountains, the gates of hell and cloud-scraping islands. In addition to this, the boat trip between Hpa-an and Mawlamyine is a gentle cruise through rural bliss.

Hpa-an escaped much of Cyclone Nargis. The minor damage that was caused to buildings by strong winds was quickly repaired.

Information
The post office is on a side road off Bogyoke St on the way to the highway bus station.
World Gate (Bogyoke St; ⏰ 10am-10pm; per hr K1500) Good internet connections with most websites available.

Sights & Activities

The town of Hpa-an itself is of limited interest, the vibrant market-filled streets are fun to walk around and the **Shweyinhmyaw Pagoda**, down by the waterfront, is a good place from which to watch the world sail on by. Some might also describe the central clock tower as a 'sight' at night when it's lit up like a gaudy lollipop – it's certainly memorable. For the real excitement see Around Hpa-an (right).

Sleeping

There are only two places that accept foreigners; neither offers breakfast, but to make up for that you'll be pleased to know that Hpa-an is about the only town in the entire country to have electricity 24 hours a day. This is thanks to the power demands of a nearby cement factory!

Soe Brothers Guesthouse (☎ 21372; 46 Thitsa Rd; s/d without bathroom $4/6, with bathroom $7/10) This is an excellent backpackers' choice and though the basic rooms here don't have much space in which to stretch, they are clean and cool and the communal bathrooms are kept shipshape. The 'luxury' rooms have more space and no queues for the toilet. The best asset though is the staff, they are a fountain of information on the area and will provide you with a detailed map of the town and region and organise great tours of the area.

Parami Hotel (☎ 21647; 304 Paya Rd, cnr Ohn Daw St; s/d $22/24) Large and comfortable rooms that come with satellite TV and hot-water bathrooms make this an ideal midrange rest stop. The friendly staff don't speak much English and aren't as foreigner savvy as the Soe Brothers. Nevertheless, in comparison to that hotel the Parami is the last word in luxury.

Eating

As with the hotels, the selection of restaurants is limited.

There are two nameless but good teahouses close to the Soe Brothers, one immediately to the left of the guesthouse and the other 100yd down the road on the right. Both serve fresh food including tasty fried potato, onion fritters and bean omelettes, which make for a filling breakfast. Near the guesthouses, Lucky Restaurant is a spit-and-sawdust bar with beer on tap.

our pick **San Ma Tau Myanmar Restaurant** (☎ 21802; 1/290 Bogyoke St; mains K1500) This is the best place to eat. A couple of thousand kyat wisely spent here will get you a feast of delectable curries – the eggplant curry is especially tasty. It's a cool and relaxed spot and they normally throw in a dessert for good measure.

Also recommended:

Diamond Restaurant (Bogyoke St; mains K2000) Rumour has it that this is the best Chinese restaurant in Hpa-an.

Khit-Thit Restaurant (New Age Restaurant; mains K1500) A typical mixed Bamar and Chinese menu in a quiet backstreet restaurant.

Getting There & Away

BOAT

See p163 for information on the double-decker ferries that travel the scenic route between Hpa-an and Mawlamyine. Boats leave Hpa-an at a very pleasant 5.45am on Mondays and Fridays ($2, four hours). The predawn departure means that you will actually miss the best of the scenery so though the journey from Mawlamyine is longer it's better to travel from there to Hpa-an by boat.

BUS & PICK-UP

Two buses a day leave for Yangon; one at 6.30am and the other at 5pm (K8000, eight hours). Tickets can be bought either at the highway bus station which is about a mile west of the town centre (K500 in a trishaw or motorbike) or from the ticket offices beside the clock tower in the town centre. Buses and pick-ups to Mawlamyine (K1200, two hours) leave every hour from 8am to 3pm. A single bus cruises to Kyaiktiyo (K3500, five hours) at 7am.

AROUND HPA-AN

The real highlights of the Hpa-an area are all scattered about the divine rural countryside out of town. While most of these sights are accessible by public transport you will need to devote several days to them and be prepared to give your leg muscles a work out. Therefore almost everyone takes a motorbike (or motorised trishaw) tour organised by the Soe Brothers Guesthouse (see left; it's no problem to join one of their tours if you're staying at the Parami Hotel). A full day tour costs K30,000.

Mt Zwegabin

ဇွကၟင်တောင်

Hpa-an is hemmed in by a wrinkled chain of limestone mountains. The tallest of these is

---

MONKEY MAGIC

In a country where, for many people, spirits live alongside the living and astrology dictates your path in life, it came as no surprise when we came across a market stall full of monkey skulls, 8in-long dried centipedes, powdered bones, a forest of herbs and roots, and an attractively laid out display of deer hooves. Fluttering in the breeze behind was a large cloth poster displaying the parts of the human body with their pressure points, possible ailments and certain cures. Cures that consisted almost entirely of the products displayed at this traditional healer's shop.

The 35-year-old healer with the perfect American film-star teeth explained how his chosen science was in the family blood and that his earliest exposure to the life of a travelling healer was through watching and learning from his father who was also a traditional healer.

After learning from his father, he went to Mandalay in 1994, where he attended a traditional medicine school for six months, studying for his certificate specialising in skin complaints. There he learnt the secrets of the plants, herbs and animals around him – where to find them and how to use them in conjunction with one another.

He sees us eyeing the more gory medicines and explains how the monkey skulls are rubbed over stones to grind them into a powder, which is then mixed with water to create the medicine, which in turn is rubbed over the wound. Apparently it's good for sores.

He tells us that business is good and that as many townsfolk as villagers use his services, but that the best money is to be made travelling from festival to festival. We're surprised by how much he charges – up to K2000 for the medicine using the monkey skull for home treatment, but this can vary depending on what disease it's being used to fight. In some other countries traditional healers use the power of the spirits to cure illnesses but in Myanmar apparently none of the treatments involve anything other than natural ingredients. And, unlike in some other countries, he doesn't claim to be able to cure all illnesses and diseases but just skin and bone complaints. In fact, that is all they are officially allowed to treat – for anything more serious the patient must be sent to a clinic in town.

Feeling confident with this last answer we roll up a trouser leg and show him a mysterious rash that has appeared in the last few days. He peers closely at it for some moments, tut-tutting under his breath, and announces that it's simply heat rash. What can be done about it? The corners of his mouth rise in an amused smile and his eyes flit to the dried centipedes and monkey skulls…

Mt Zwegabin, 7 miles south of town, which as well as being a respectable 2372ft is also a home of spirits and saintly souls.

It's a demanding two-hour hike to the summit – up more steps than you'd care to count, but once at the top the rewards are staggering views, a small monastery and a stupa containing, yes you guessed it, another hair from the Buddha. If you arrive at the top before noon you can take advantage of a complimentary lunch (rice, orange and tea) and the 11am monkey feeding – different primates, different menus.

The descent down the east side of the mountain takes around 1½ hours, and from the bottom it's another 2 miles to the main road from where you can catch a pick-up back to town. To get to the mountain, take the pick-up (K700) at 8am in the direction of Thamanya and get off at the Zwegabin junction; it's a 15-minute walk from here through a village to the base of the mountain on the west side past hundreds (1150 to be precise – don't believe us? Get counting!) of identical buddha statues lined up row after row. It's possible to overnight on the floor of the monastery compound on the summit (give a healthy donation), which means you can also appreciate the fantastic sunsets. Hiring your own transport – someone to drop you off on one side and pick you up on the other – makes everything run smoother.

Saddar Cave

သဒ္ဒရဂူ

How brave are you feeling today? Brave enough to journey into many people's idea of Hell? If so welcome to Saddar Cave!

This huge cave is simply breathtaking. As you enter the football stadium–sized cavern you'll be greeted by, what else but dozens of buddha statues, a couple of pagodas and some

SOUTHEASTERN MYANMAR

newer clay wall carvings, but the real treat lies beyond these relics. In absolute darkness (bring a good torch) you can scramble for 15 minutes through black chambers as high as a cathedral, truck-sized stalactites and, in places, walls of crystal.

To add to the general atmosphere thousands, possibly hundreds of thousands, of bats cling to the cave roof. In places the squealing from them is deafening and the ground underfoot becomes slippery with bat excrement!

Emerging at the cave's far side the wonders don't cease and the burst of sunlight reveals an idyllic secret **lake** full of ducks and flowering lilies hidden in a bowl of craggy peaks. There is another cave on the far side of the lake that is actually half flooded, but local fishers occasionally paddle through the cave for 10 minutes to yet another lake. You might be able to persuade one of them to take you along.

To get to Saddar Cave take a pick-up to Eindu village (K700), in the direction of Thamanyat monastery. From the village take a motorbike taxi for 2 miles to the cave.

Kawgun & Yathaypyan Caves
ကော့ကွမ်းဂူ & ရသေ့ပြန်ဂူ

Ferreted away in these remote southern hills is a secret gallery of Buddhist art and sculpture. The 7th-century artwork of the **Kawgun Cave** (admission K3000, camera K300) consists of thousands of tiny clay buddhas and carvings plastered all over the walls and roof of this open cavern.

Down at ground level newer buddha statues stand and recline in various lazy positions. This gallery was constructed by King Manuaha after he was defeated in battle and had to take sanctuary in these caves. Impressive as it is today you can only imagine what it was like a few years back, before a cement factory, in its quest for limestone, started dynamiting the nearby peaks – the vibrations caused great chunks of the art to crash to the floor and shatter.

Just over a mile away, and built by the same exiled king, is the **Yathaypyan Cave**, which is a proper cave rather than a cavern and contains several pagodas as well as a few more clay wall carvings. There is no public transport to anywhere in the vicinity of the caves – take a motorbike tour from Hpa-an.

Kyauk Kalap
ကျောက်ကလပ်

Standing proud in the middle of a small, artificial lake is Kyauk Kalap, a tall finger of sheer rock mounted by one of the most unlikely pagodas in Myanmar. It's certainly one of the more surreal sights in the area. To get to the island, which also contains a small monastery and numerous *nat* shrines, is easy as it's something of a pilgrimage site. Take a motorised trishaw from Hpa-an market area to Kawd Kyaik village for K500. From there it's an easy 10-minute walk.

Thamanyat Kyaung
သာမညကျောင်း

Hpa-an is famous among the people of Myanmar for the Buddhist village at Thamanyat Kyaung, where the highly respected monk U Winaya, whose solid support of democracy leader Aung San Suu Kyi is well known in Myanmar, resided. U Winaya passed away several years ago and his body is now entombed in a glass case around which, strangely, three circles appeared. People say this is an indication of his great powers.

Thamanyat monastery is about 25 miles southeast of Hpa-an, and there is a daily flow of small buses to this busy religious site. The bus fare from Hpa-an is K1000.

TANINTHARYI (TENASSERIM) DIVISION
တနင်္သာရီတိုင်း

Tanintharyi Division is one of the most alluring, exciting and little-known corners of Myanmar. Alluring thanks to an untouched archipelago of bridal white, cocktail coconut beaches; exciting thanks to an ethnic soup of exotic people, including the romantic sea gypsies; and unknown thanks to insurgents and government restrictions. A few years ago it looked as if parts of the region, including the thrilling Myeik Archipelago, were about to cast aside the veil of secrecy and flaunt their assets to the world, but since around late 2007 the doors suddenly and firmly swung shut again.

Known to the outside world as Tenasserim until 1989, Tanintharyi has a long history of trade with India, the Middle East and nations east of Myanmar's eastern mountain ranges. For many years, before the arrival of the British in the late 19th century, the Siamese either controlled the state or received annual tributes from its inhabitants.

Most of the people living in the division are of Bamar ethnicity, although splitting hairs one can easily identify Dawei and Myeik subgroups of the Bamar who enjoy their own dialect, cuisine and so on. Large numbers of Mon also live in the division, and in or near the larger towns you'll find Kayin (often Christian) and Indian (often Muslim) residents, as well as Thais and the sea gypsies, or Moken people (Salon in Burmese), who inhabit the islands of the coast. Pearl farms on islands in the area, established by the Ministry of Mines, are a major source of revenue for the region.

DAWEI (TAVOY)

ထား:ဝယ်

☎ 059

Despite the presence of a university, Dawei is still a sleepy, tropical seaside town. The thatch-roofed bungalows and colonial-style brick-and-stucco mansions of the town mingle with tall, slender palms, fruit trees and lots of hanging orchids. In spite of its remote location – or perhaps because of it – Dawei has become a significant Burmese Buddhist centre.

Hundreds of Tanintharyi Division residents fled to Thailand rather than work on the 100-mile-long Ye to Dawei railway completed, for the most part, in 1998. According to Amnesty International, refugees reported conditions approaching those described in chronicles of the Japanese army's 'Death Railway', though the government asserts the work was done by army personnel.

Dawei is also near the starting point of the massive 434-mile Yadana gas pipeline, which carries natural gas from fields in the Gulf of Mottama to Thailand's Ratchaburi Province. About 250 miles of the pipeline runs through Mon State and Tanintharyi Division. The Myanmar government relocated villages in the pipeline's path with little or no compensation for villagers. Civilians from the area filed lawsuits against the companies in charge of the pipeline in a Los Angeles court in 1996, accusing the companies of benefiting from the use of forced labour and of systematic destruction of village communities in the implementation of the project. Because of the pipeline's perceived strategic importance, there is a fairly heavy military presence around Dawei.

Sights & Activities
THEINWA KYAUNG (PAYAGYI)
သိမ်ဝကျောင်း (ဘုရားကြီး)
The main Buddhist monastery in town contains a complex of sizeable Mon-style *vihara*

(glittering cubes of reflective mosaics filled with gilded buddhas).

The best time to visit Theinwa Kyaung is in the early evening. In the period just after sunset, hordes of local residents come to make offerings and to meditate for an hour or two.

SHWETHALYAUNG DAW MU
ရွှေသာလျောင်း တော်မူ
Completed in 1931, one of the largest reclining buddhas in the country – 250ft long, 70ft high – is at the edge of town.

SHINMOKHTI PAYA
ရှင်လှမုထ္တီးဘုရား:
About 3 miles beyond Shwethalyaung Daw Mu on the same road, this paya is the most sacred of local religious monuments. Reportedly constructed in 1438, it's one of four shrines in the country housing a Sinhalese buddha image supposedly made with a composite of cement and pieces of the original Bodhi tree (see p137). During religious festivals, such as Thingyan, this is one of the liveliest spots in the district.

BEACHES & ISLANDS
Few foreigners have been permitted to visit the coastal areas around Dawei, so details are still sketchy. The best local beach, **Maungmagan** (also spelt Maungmakan), is around 11 miles west of Dawei. A very wide sand beach stretches along a large, pretty bay.

Opposite Maungmagan is a collection of three lovely island groups that were named the Middle Moscos Islands by the British – they are now known as **Maungmagan**, **Hienze** and **Launglon** (or collectively as the Maungmagan Islands). Due to a natural profusion of wild boar, barking deer, sambar and swiftlets (sea swallows), these islands are part of a marine sanctuary, originally established by the British in 1927.

Festivals & Events
During the annual **Thingyan** festival in April, Dawei's male residents don huge, 13ft bamboo-frame effigies and dance down the streets to the beat of the *kalakodaun*, an Indian long drum.

Sleeping & Eating
Most visitors to Dawei come on business and the guesthouses are not used to tourists.

SOUTHEASTERN MYANMAR

Garden Guest House (☎ 22116; 88 Yay St; s $6-10, d $8-18 🔀) The Garden offers fairly good value for money, especially if you can bag one of the air-con rooms. The staff are keen to please but it suffers from a bit of noise.

Pearl Akari Hotel (☎ 21980, 21780; 572 Ye Yeiqtha Rd; r with/without bathroom $30/20) A two-storey guesthouse in a relatively quiet part of town. It's the poshest place in town that will accept foreigners but still isn't great value for money.

Along Yodaya Rd, one of the main thoroughfares through town, are several small rice and teashops.

Getting There & Away

Technically Dawei, Myeik, Kawthoung and some of the Myeik (Mergui) Archipelago are open to foreign tourists, though access from Yangon is by air only. Ferry travel is possible between Dawei, Myeik and Kawthoung.

The reality on the ground though is worse and, for all intents and purposes, the whole area is off limits to foreign tourists. Published flight schedules might appear promising, with flights linking Dawei, Myeik, Kawthoung and Yangon several times a week. However, at the time of research the vast majority of flights were cancelled, leading to the very real chance of getting stranded down here for days, if not weeks.

In addition to this it has become very hard to find solid information on boat schedules and there is much debate about whether foreigners will now be allowed to travel around this area by ferry. The situation has become so unpredictable that almost every respectable Yangon travel agency advises against travelling in this area altogether.

However, don't lose faith entirely. With much patience, luck and a deep pocketful of money it is still possible to explore this area, though a visit to the highlight of the region, the Myeik Archipelago, is nowadays only really feasible by joining a live-aboard boat tour departing from Phuket in Thailand.

It is no longer possible to enter or leave Myanmar via the Kawthoung border crossing (though you can still visit Kawthoung from Thailand for a one-day visa run, see opposite).

AIR

Tay Za's **Air Bagan** (www.airbagan.com) flies out of Yangon stopping at Dawei, Myeik and Kawthoung and repeating the stops on the way back to Yangon on Monday, Wednesday and Saturday mornings. While **Yangon Airways** (www.yangonair.com) flies the same routes on Tuesdays, Fridays and Mondays.

Flight prices are:

- Dawei–Myeik $54
- Kawthoung–Yangon $136
- Myeik–Kawthoung $68
- Myeik–Yangon $115
- Yangon–Dawei $96

BOAT

Fortune Express and HiFi Express run erratic boats between Dawei and Kawthoung, calling at Myeik en route. Technically the boats run daily, in reality you may have to wait for several days and it's not certain that you will be allowed to travel in this manner.

The fare from Dawei to Myeik is $20 (6½ hours) and from Myeik to Kawthoung it's $25 (6½ hours).

There's no boat service from Yangon to Dawei.

BUS & TRAIN

Foreigners cannot travel to/from Dawei, Myeik or Kawthoung overland and the situation is unlikely to change soon.

MYEIK (MERGUI)

☎ 059

Myeik doesn't receive many foreign visitors, but those who do venture here will attract loads of friendly attention. Until recently, Myeik, which sits on a peninsula that juts out into the Andaman Sea, was a picturesque coastal city with a wide range of architectural styles lining the streets. Increased cash flow due to the export of seafood to Thailand caused a mini-boom in building during the 1990s, and many old buildings were replaced by modern ones. Then in 2001 a large portion of the remaining old architecture was razed by fire; the rebuilding effort has largely sacrificed style for utility.

Sights & Activities

The city's most venerated Buddhist temple, **Theindawgyi Paya**, sits on a ridge overlooking the city and harbour.

Pataw Padet Island, a five-minute boat ride from the harbour, is named after two prominent hills at either end of the island. Several religious buildings, stupas and sculp-

SOUTHEASTERN MYANMAR

tures have been constructed on the island. A large, hollow reclining 220ft-long buddha, **Atula Shwethalyaung**, lies at the foot of rocky, jungle-covered **Padet Hill** to the south.

ISLANDS

Boats to the nearby islands of the Myeik Archipelago can in theory be chartered from Myeik's harbour. However, for those seriously interested in visiting this offshore wonderland the easiest way of doing so is, strangely enough, from Phuket in Thailand where you can arrange expensive live-aboard boat charters around the islands as well as kayaking trips. For more on the islands see p174 or for more on visiting from Thailand see p338.

Sleeping

Accommodation in Myeik represents some of the worst value in the country. Travellers who wish to avoid Myanmar's government-owned hotels should stay clear of the Annawa Guest House, high on a ridge near Theindawgyi Paya.

Ban Gaba Guest House (r $10) Several cheap and ropey guesthouses can be found scattered around the town centre including this one near the jetty south of the market.

Dolphin Hotel (☎ 41523; 139 Kanphyar Rd; s/d $25/40) Owned as a joint venture with the Myanmar Fisheries Industry, the modern Dolphin is easily the nicest place in town; though staff members aren't especially friendly or helpful. Rooms in this two-storey building are dark wood with modern and clean bathrooms. It's on the road from the airport into town.

Eating

Seafood is abundant and inexpensive. One local speciality is *kat gyi kai* (scissor-cut noodles) – wheat noodles that have been cut into short strips and stir-fried with seafood and various spices. It's a delicious meal, usually eaten for breakfast or lunch.

Meik Set (U Myat Lay Rd, Kan Paya Quarter; ☺ 6am-5pm) An old wood-and-thatch teashop and restaurant with a dirt floor, this is one of the best places to try *kat gyi kai*.

Getting There & Away

For the full rundown on travel between towns in Tanintharyi Division see opposite.

KAWTHOUNG BORDER CROSSING

This is an open border. Boats to Kawthoung (250B, 40 minutes) from Thailand leave the Saphan Pla pier in Ranong, 6 miles away, regularly from around 8am till 6pm. After getting your passport stamped by Thai immigration, board one of the boats near the immigration office and you'll be taken to the Myanmar immigration office, where you must pay a fee of $10 for a permit. You cannot stay overnight in Myanmar – even with a valid 28 day Myanmar visa.

If you've been travelling elsewhere in Myanmar you will not be permitted to leave Myanmar for Thailand via this (or any other border) crossing. Entry and exit to Myanmar is by air only.

KAWTHOUNG
ကော့သောင်း
☎ 059

If coming here from within Myanmar, you're likely to be startled by the wacky sight of foreigners in bathing shorts and bikinis – day-trippers on visa runs from Ranong, Thailand. Travelling between the two countries at this point in time feels like teleporting 50 years. At the southernmost tip of mainland Myanmar – 500 miles from Yangon and 1240 miles from the country's northern tip – Kawthoung is only separated from Thailand by a broad estuary in the Pagyan River and, indeed from a tourist perspective, is more a part of Thailand than Myanmar.

The main business in town is trade with Thailand, followed by fishing, rubber and cashews.

At the moment it's very hard for a foreigner to visit Kawthoung from anywhere else in Myanmar.

Sights & Activities

Kawthoung's bustling **waterfront** is lined with teashops, moneychangers and shops selling Thai construction materials.

At the top of the hill overlooking the harbour is the **Pyi Taw Aye Paya**. Unlike many other temples, you can walk inside and under the main stupa. Originally built in 1949 to a height of only 16.5ft, it was later raised to its current stature of 70ft.

About 3 miles north of town, the fishing village of **Thirimyaing Lan** is known for its hilltop

---

MERMAIDS WITH GOGGLES

It wasn't so long ago that the Moken created their diving goggles by carving the eye pieces from wood and attaching the glass lenses, made from broken bottles they found washed up on the beaches, with sticky tree sap.

The Moken, sea gypsies, or Salon in Burmese, live a nomadic life drifting on the ocean winds around the Myeik Archipelago. Numbering around 2000 to 3000 individuals, scientists believe they have been floating around these islands since at least 2000 BC.

Totally at home on the water, the Moken spend almost all their time on wooden boats, called *kabang*, which are built from a single huge tree trunk. Each boat will provide a home to a single family. As the boys come of age they build their own boats and as the girls come of age and marry, they move away from their parents' boat.

Breathing through air hoses held above the water surface the Moken dive to depths of up to 200ft in search of shellfish. It has recently been discovered that the Moken spend so long underwater that Moken children can see twice as well underwater as European children and are able to spot shellfish that for most of us would be just a blur. Scientists believe that in order to do this the Moken are able to constrict their pupils and change the shape of their eyes lenses in order to obtain a sharper image underwater.

Like almost every ethnic minority in Myanmar the Moken have suffered greatly under the junta and reports from the late 1990s talk of how almost all Moken were subjected to forced relocations to onshore sites. If such practices continue it won't be long until the mermaid people of Southeast Asia no longer need to know how to make goggles from broken bottles.

Third Mile Pagoda, with good sea and island views. Another 7 miles is **Paker Beach**, reportedly the best nearby mainland beach.

Locals cool off in the waters flowing from the surrounding mountains at the **Ma Li Won rock pools**. To reach this bathing site involves a 24-mile drive through the beautiful Ma Li Won Valley north of Kawthoung.

MYEIK (MERGUI) ARCHIPELAGO

မြိတ်ကျွန်းစု

Comprising hundreds of shipwreck islands lying in a sea of jade, the stunning Myeik Archipelago may be Southeast Asia's most tantalising, drop-dead gorgeous beach destination. The virgin coral reefs, fluffy beaches and pristine environment are exactly the kind of thing you dream of running away to after every bad day at work.

The locals say there are over 4000 islands in the archipelago, though British surveyors recognised only 804. Most are uninhabited, though a few are home to the Moken, or 'sea gypsies', a nomadic seafaring people. It's thought they may have been the first ethnic group to have lived in what is today Myanmar.

A **sea-gypsy festival** is held during the second week of February at Ma-Kyon-Galet village on a small island near Lampi.

The Myeik Archipelago has remained a pristine dreamscape for so long for a reason.

These islands are incredibly hard to get to. A few years ago a flurry of activity indicated that Southeast Asia's least-known island group was about to open up to tourists, an exclusive resort was constructed and luxury boat tours from Thailand and mainland Myanmar began to plough the channels between the islands. But expense, bureaucracy and a general lack of infrastructure seems to have quietly killed off any such tourist aspirations. Perhaps this is all for the best – after all, the world needs somewhere beautiful that comes to us only in our dreams.

Tours

Technically you can get to the Myeik Archipelago by air from Yangon or boat from Kawthoung or Myeik, but at the time of writing that was, in reality, next to impossible. No Myanmar-based tour operators currently run trips to the islands (the flights from Yangon were cancelled with such frequency that tourists kept getting stuck either in the islands or in Yangon for days and even weeks waiting for their flights to leave).

If you really want to go there you have two options – one is to take an expensive liveaboard boat tour from Phuket in Thailand (see p338). The other is to charter a plane to take you to the exclusive Myanmar Andaman Resort; however, this very expensive resort has strong government links and so we will not review it.

Sleeping & Eating

Accommodation is limited and poor value. If coming on a visa run from Thailand you cannot stay the night here.

Kawthoung Motel (cnr Bogyoke Rd & Bosonpat St; r 800B; ✷) About a 450yd uphill walk from the jetty is the four-storey Kawthoung Motel – the classiest hotel in Kawthoung's town cen-

tre. Its simple, comfortable, carpeted, double rooms have private cold-water shower and satellite TV.

There are several teashops and restaurants along the waterfront.

Getting There & Around

See p173 for full details on hopping over from Thailand.

For the full rundown of travel between towns in Tanintharyi Division see p172.

SOUTHEASTERN
MYANMAR

Bagan & Central Myanmar

Traditionally the heart of Bamar culture, central Myanmar provides the rural countryside setting for road-tripping travellers getting about by bus, train or private car. Those coming through the bulk of this 'dry zone' are treated to some nice scenes out the window: ox carts, rice fields and rolling plains, all rimmed by the Shan Mountains visible to the east and the snaking Ayeyarwady (Irrawaddy) River to the west. But the majority of visitors treat much of the area as a 'fly-over zone' of sorts, rushing on to the region's clear highlight, Bagan (Pagan), or beyond to places like Mandalay, Kalaw or Inle Lake.

A destination making nearly all Myanmar itineraries, Bagan fills a 26-sq-mile plain of 4000-plus temples that date back centuries. It's one of Myanmar's most wondrous sights and rivals Cambodia's Angkor Wat in terms of scope and jaw-droppability. Its tallest and most majestic temples – made of brick and topped with gilded *hti* pinnacles – are awesome, mixing Hindu and Buddhist images with locally brewed *nat* (spirits) in nooks. Visiting is done over dirt paths by slow-going horse cârts or (more adventurously) by bikes. A few highlight temples like Ananda Pahto attract bigger crowds, including vendors, but it's easy to find space to yourself.

Apart from the temple-hop, nearby (extinct) volcano Mt Popa (visible from a number of temples) beckons day-trippers with its spiritual home of Myanmar's 37 *nat*. Elsewhere in central Myanmar are frequently fun highway cities not short on history. Taungoo and, particularly, riverside Pyay (Prome) are former capitals with a bit of ruins to see. Nay Pyi Taw, 3 miles off the Yangon–Mandalay highway, is Myanmar's latest capital – an expensive project in a nation without money to burn.

BAGAN & CENTRAL MYANMAR

HIGHLIGHTS

- Watch the **sun set** (or rise) over the hills around Bagan – most visitors pack onto Shwesandaw Paya (p213) before dusk but it's one of many options (see p215)

- Hit the **Ayeyarwady**: on a Bagan–Mandalay boat (*p183*), a half-day trip to nearby cave temples (p220) or a self-arranged sunset cruise at Old Bagan (p184)

- Pay respects to Myanmar's 37 *nat* at their spiritual home, the monkey-arama volcanic mountaintop temple at **Mt Popa** (p188)

- See the ancient Pyu city of **Thayekhittaya** (p200) at ox's pace

- Hang with elephants at a working camp outside **Taungoo** (p194)

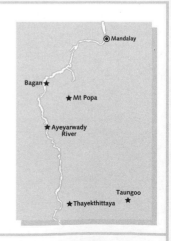

- HIGHEST POINT: MT POPA (2418FT)

HISTORY

Moving armies led by various people – the Pyu, the Mon, the Burmese – swish-swashed across this central plain, the 'heart of Myanmar', over the centuries. The area around Pyay served as the Pyu capital from the 5th to 9th centuries AD; some consider the Pyu as founders of Myanmar's 'first empire', though little remains known of this vanished group. Bagan's burst of energy ran two and a half centuries, beginning in 1047 and ending as the pounding footfall of Kublai Khan raiders approached in 1287. The latest empire to lodge in the area is the military junta, who founded a new capital at Nay Pyi Taw (Royal Capital), outside Pyinmana, in 2005.

See p203 for more on Bagan's history.

CLIMATE

This area comprises the bulk of the 'dry zone' of Myanmar, and it remains hot and dusty for much of the year. Most visitors come in winter (November to February), when daytime temperatures are a relatively chilly 30°C during the day and about 10°C at night. From March to May, the hottest season, daytime temperatures boil at up to 43°C. Rains peak in June and October but run throughout the months between.

GETTING THERE & AWAY

Nyaung U is the principal gateway for Bagan, with a train station, jetty and airport. Most visitors by boat come downriver from Mandalay. Despite being a major destination, most long-haul bus routes (eg Yangon–Mandalay) miss Bagan, instead stopping at Meiktila. But there are a few direct bus links between Bagan and Yangon, Mandalay and Inle Lake. Trains to the Bagan area are very slow and not very practical. Most people coming directly from Yangon by road do so via Pyay and Magwe by private taxi.

BAGAN

ပုဂံ

One of Myanmar's top attractions, the area known as Bagan (or, more bureaucratically, 'Bagan Archaeological Zone') occupies an impressive, 26-sq-mile area, 118 miles south of Mandalay and 429 miles north of Yangon. The zone is made up of several principal areas, including Nyaung U, Old Bagan and New Bagan.

This section includes sleeping, eating and transport options; see p203 for the history and descriptions of the temples themselves.

ORIENTATION

The Bagan Archaeological Zone is a massive area and isn't immediately a breeze to get to grips with. The Ayeyarwady drifts by its northern and western sides. Its most active town and chief transport hub is Nyaung U (p180), in the northeast corner. About 2.5 miles west, Old Bagan is the former site of the village that moved to New Bagan (2 miles south) in 1990. Between the two is Myinkaba, a village boasting a long-running lacquerware tradition.

Connecting the towns are paved roads making a 12-mile oval. The Bagan–Nyaung U Rd (to the north) and more-level Anawrahta Rd (to the south) connect Nyaung U and Old Bagan; the Bagan–Chauk Rd (the southern extension of the Bagan–Nyaung U Rd, sometimes just referred to as 'Main Rd' in the following Nyaung U listings) leads south from Old Bagan to Myinkaba and New Bagan; and the 'airport road' heads northeast from New Bagan, past the small villages of Pwasaw and Minnanthu, to the Nyaung U–Kyaukpadaung Rd, leading north to Nyaung U. Just east of the junction is the Nyaung U Airport, about 1 mile southeast of town. The train station is 1 mile south of the airport. See the map on p204 for the layout of Bagan.

In between it all, of course, is the bulk of Bagan action: the plain, featuring most of the temples, all connected with a vast network of bumpy dirt roads and trails. At times, you'll be about a mile from the nearest paved road.

Maps

In addition to the maps in this guide, you can purchase *The Map of Bagan* (K1000) at most hotels. It shows many of the paths, but isn't always 100% accurate.

INFORMATION

For travel information, try Nyaung U's Ever Sky Information Service (p180) or the government-run MTT office in New Bagan (p186).

Nyaung U has a post office. You can get online in Nyaung U and at select hotels.

Bagan used to have two area codes, and you may find dated listings with area code ☎ 02. A rare few still use ☎ 02, which we indicate,

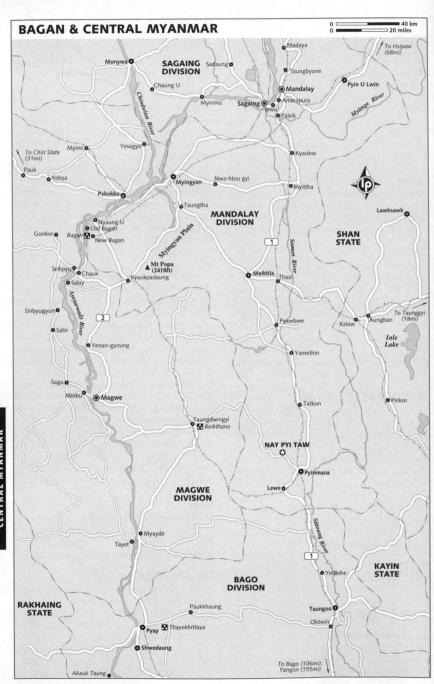

BAGAN & CENTRAL MYANMAR

BAGAN &
CENTRAL MYANMAR

but nearly all local numbers now use the area code ☎ 061.

ACTIVITIES
Boat Trips
Sunset chasing in Bagan isn't restricted to the tops of temples. An interesting alternative is a **dusk boat trip** (K8000) on the Ayeyarwady. The boat folk at the Old Bagan jetty tend to cater their hour-long tours for package tourists, but drop by to arrange your own ride.

You can also arrange an interesting boat/taxi side-trip to mountaintop **Tan Kyi** (off Map p204), one of four stupas that marked the original edges of the city. The boat trip across the river is about K15,000 return; taxis up the mountain and back are about K10,000.

See p220 for boat trips to temples north of Nyaung U.

Ballooning
One of the best ways to 'see' Bagan – to really get a sense of its size and sprawl – is aboard a thrilling ride over one of the world's most highly acclaimed ballooning spots. They only run from October to March and *if* there's space, any hotel or guesthouse can get you a ticket for the approximately 45-minute sunrise or sunset flight with **Balloons over Bagan** (Map p184; ☎ 061-60032; office in Bagan Hotel; www .balloonsoverbagan.com; per person $260).

The smooth, British-run operation has several balloons – which locals took to be blessed by the *nat* at Tharabar Gate – that usually fit eight passengers and a couple of pilots. You'll have coffee and snacks while watching the balloons fill with hot air, and champagne and snacks after you land. Locals often call out 'hello' as you drift over temples at up to 590ft. Note that balloon slots are often filled a month or more in advance.

GETTING THERE & AROUND
This section explains how to get around the sites (temples, towns, stations). See also the Getting There & Away/Around sections for Nyaung U (p183), Old Bagan (p186) or New Bagan (p188) for details on getting to Yangon, Inle Lake, Mandalay and other destinations.

To/From the Airport
Prices between Nyaung U Airport and hotels in Nyaung U, Old Bagan and New Bagan run K5000, K6000 and K7000 respectively. It's a

> **GOVERNMENT FEE**
>
> All foreign visitors to Bagan Archaeological Zone must pay a $10 entrance fee. If sellers don't find you when you arrive, your hotel will sell it to you.

bit cheaper from the Old Bagan or Nyaung jetties if you arrive by boat. Horse carts and taxis meet boats at the Old Bagan and Nyaung U jetty.

Bicycle
Bikes with baskets (and sometimes a bell) are widely available and can be an ideal way of getting around, despite the direct exposure to sun and some dirt roads that slow you up. Essentially all accommodation places rent bicycles: in Nyaung U it costs about K1000 or K1500 per day; in Old Bagan and New Bagan it's more like K3000 or K4000 per day.

Traffic is pretty light on all roads. Early-morning or late-afternoon rides along the sealed Bagan–Nyaung U Rd are particularly pleasant. It's worth planning ahead a little, as the bulk of the temples in the Central Plain (p212) are far away from much shade or lunch potential. The most convenient eating options are in Old Bagan (p185).

Many visitors have a 'greatest-hits temples' day on horse cart first, to get a sense of orientation, then follow it up checking more remote or lesser-known temples by bike.

Horse Cart
An understandably popular way of seeing the ruins is from the shaded, padded bed of one of the 240 horse carts around. Even if you're on a package trip – or especially so – it's a good idea to break away one day for a more intimate trip. Drivers speak some English (at least), know where to find the 'keymaster' to locked sites and can point out temples with few or no tourists around. (Some might stop by a shop with hopes for commission; it's OK to say 'no thanks'.) A cart works best for two people and the driver, but it's possible to go with three or (in a pinch) four.

In Nyaung U a day with a horse cart and driver runs about K10,000, a half-day is K5000 or K6000. It's about K5000 more if taken from Old Bagan or New Bagan.

Horse carts do mosey about though; you'll make a bit better time on a bicycle.

Pick-up

A pick-up (K200) runs regularly from outside the Nyaung U market, ending near the junction in New Bagan and passing Wetkyi-in, Old Bagan and Myinkaba on the way. This could be used to jump from one place to the next, then walk around the temples, particularly in the Northern Plain (p210) or within the old walls in Old Bagan (p207).

Taxi

Hiring a shared taxi for the day in Nyaung U costs about $20 to $25. An Old Bagan hotel will charge about $35. Hired taxis are also convenient ways of making day trips to Mt Popa (p190) and Salay (p191).

Trishaw

There's little trishaw activity outside Nyaung U, where you can get one at the jetty or bus station.

NYAUNG U

ညောင်ဦး

☎ 061

A bustling little river town with much more local flavour than you'll find elsewhere in Bagan, Nyaung U is where most independent travellers to Bagan hang their hat (or backpack). On the river about 3 miles northeast of Old Bagan, it's not a bad place to poke around.

Roaming the back roads towards the jetty or stopping at scrappy teashops will attract friendly wide-eyed looks, plus there are a handful of temples to see, including the Shwezigon Paya (p219) as well as the ominous, vacant HQ of the National League for Democracy on Main Rd. Visitors staying in New or Old Bagan tend to make it here, if not for the restaurant scene (the closest the Bagan area gets to nightlife) then for the transport links.

Guesthouses and roadside restaurants now push a couple of miles west, along the road to Old Bagan, reaching the small village of Wetkyi-in (Giant Pig). The town was named for a mythical pig that, per local legend, inhabited the lake there and killed a lot of people before being killed by a future king of Bagan.

Information

INTERNET ACCESS

Internet connections in all of Bagan are iffy to OK. You'll find a few internet places, particularly along 'Restaurant Row', offering connections (at times) for about K1500 per hour.

POST

Post office (Anawrahta Rd; ☼ 9.30am-7pm)

TELEPHONE

Stands around town follow the same set prices: it's $5 per minute to call Europe or Australia and $6 to call North America.

TOURIST INFORMATION

Ever Sky Information Service (☎ 60895; 5 Thiripyitsaya; ☼ 7.30am-9pm), on the restaurant strip, is a very friendly place with travel and transport information and a used bookshop. Staff can get share taxis (to Mt Popa, Kalaw, Salay, around Bagan) for the cheapest rates you'll find. A few copycats are also along Restaurant Row.

Activities

Part of the government-run Bagan Golf Resort, the Bagan Golf Course (☎ 60303; greens fee

---

WHERE TO STAY?

■ **Old Bagan** (p185) Closest to the big-time temples, most of Bagan's high-end hotels cluster in and around the riverside and the old palace walls. It's a good location (particularly for quick visits to Bagan), but rumours of government links reign and there's a lot less life. Doubles from $50.

■ **New Bagan** (p186) Not the most charming of villages but it's not the locals' fault (they were forcibly relocated here from Old Bagan in 1990). However, New Bagan has by far the best midrange choices, with excellent value rooms from $25, plus atmospheric riverside restaurants.

■ **Nyaung U** (opposite) The budget heart of Bagan, with the liveliest restaurant scene and the bulk of transport connections, Nyaung U is a real town, with guesthouses from $8. On the downside it's a 2-mile bike ride to the bulk of the temples.

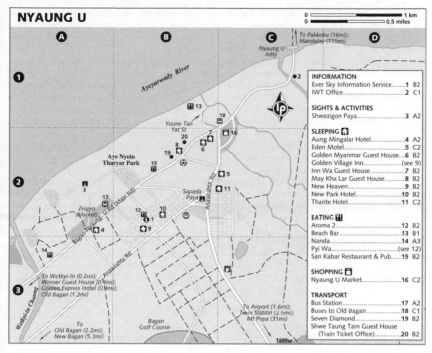

NYAUNG U

INFORMATION	
Ever Sky Information Service	1 B2
IWT Office	2 C1

SIGHTS & ACTIVITIES	
Shwezigon Paya	3 A2

SLEEPING	
Aung Mingalar Hotel	4 A2
Eden Motel	5 C2
Golden Myanmar Guest House	6 B2
Golden Village Inn	(see 9)
Inn Wa Guest House	7 B2
May Kha Lar Guest House	8 B2
New Heaven	9 B2
New Park Hotel	10 B2
Thante Hotel	11 C2

EATING	
Aroma 2	12 B2
Beach Bar	13 B1
Nanda	14 A3
Pyi Wa	(see 12)
San Kabar Restaurant & Pub	15 B2

SHOPPING	
Nyaung U Market	16 C2

TRANSPORT	
Bus Station	17 A2
Buses to Old Bagan	18 C1
Seven Diamond	19 B2
Shwe Taung Tarn Guest House (Train Ticket Office)	20 B2

incl caddy $35, club rental $10), just south of town, has about a half-dozen pagodas on its 18 holes. There's also a **swimming pool** (nonguest fee $5).

Sleeping

Nyaung U's main road has many more cheap, practically identical guesthouses than those that are listed here, which offer singles/doubles for about $5/8. For that price you can expect a boxy room with mint-green walls, a lazy ceiling fan, concrete or tiled floors and attached bath with (supposedly) hot water, and sometimes even an old air-con unit. Some are not really geared towards foreigners but will happily accept you. Many travellers prefer the quieter guesthouses off Restaurant Row.

All of the following come with free breakfast and most drop their prices a dollar or three off-season.

BUDGET

Inn Wa Guest House (☎ 60902, 60849; Main Rd; s/d $4/8; ❄) If you just need a cheap bed (and a little English), this three-floor, 16-room choice near the market should keep you happy: mini-golf green carpets in boxy rooms and simple attached bathrooms with hot water. Ask for rooms 206 or 306 for more window light (and less street noise). Breakfast is served on the open roof deck. Fan-cooled singles/doubles on the ground floor with shared bathroom are $3/6.

Golden Myanmar Guest House (☎ 60901, 02-70046; Main Rd; s/d $4/8; ❄) Part-time air-ticket agency, full-time guesthouse. The Golden Myanmar is more bare-bone than its neighbour Inn Wa. Go with room 108: it's got more light and is apart from the rest of the rooms.

Eden Motel (☎ 60815, 60812; Anawrahta Rd; s/d from $4/8; ❄) Split in two by the busy road towards the airport, Eden isn't exactly a garden party. The rooms in the newer Eden Motel II have bigger, tiled rooms and an over-touted bathtub, but we prefer the ones in the original – particularly the ones with all-bamboo walls and hardwood floors (from $6/8, but the 'satellite TV' sound will likely filter through the walls).

our pick New Heaven (☎ 60921; off Restaurant Row; s/d $5/8; ❄) The price is way right for these clean, compact rooms with small decks looking over the peaceful lawn. Floor tiles shine, as do the laminated waterfall photos on the walls.

Winner Guest House (☎ 60128; Main Rd, Wetkyi-in village; s/d $5/8; ✖) No-one stays out here (yet), but this little family-run guesthouse on the road to Old Bagan isn't a bad choice: it's nearer the temples, there are appealing roadside restaurants around, and the simple concrete-floor rooms with an air-con unit and tiled bathroom attached are just as good as the cheapies in town.

May Kha Lar Guest House (☎ 60306, 60907; Main Rd; s $7-8, d $8-14; ✖) The best kept of the main-road budget choices, the 35-room May Kha Lar's ground-floor, gaudy-tile rooms are compact, with air-con, ceiling fan and attached bath. It's worth shelling out another dollar or two for the upstairs options (which have wooden floors and TV).

Golden Village Inn (☎ 60921; off Restaurant Row; s $8-12, d $12-18; ✖) Behind New Heaven (and of the same ownership), the Village is another shady spot near the restaurant strip, with comfortable bungalow-style rooms. Higher-priced ones add TV, desk and tub.

MIDRANGE

New Park Hotel (☎ 60322, 60484, in Yangon 01-290073; www.newparkmyanmar.com; 4 Thiripyitsaya; s $10-18, d $15-25; ✖ ▢) Perhaps the best of the bunch on the leafy backstreets off Restaurant Row, the 24-room New Park has two classes. The older rooms, with bungalow-style front decks for afternoon journal writing, are comfortable, wood-floor jobbies, with spic-and-span bathrooms (a big upgrade from the main road choices). The recently opened new wing gets you more space, a fridge and a TV.

Aung Mingalar Hotel (☎ 60171, 60847; Main Rd; s $13-23, d $15-25; ✖) Popular as a 'midrange lite' choice, the Aung Mingalar complex is right across from several small pagodas and is spitting distance from the Shwezigon Paya. Its three types of rooms all have patios; those with TV have wood floors.

Golden Express Hotel (☎ 02-60034, 02-60381; www .goldenexpresstours.com; Bagan-Nyaung U Rd; s $17-28, d $21-34; ✖ ✖) With cartoon colours and some pagodas next door, this complex features four bright motel-style units. The best value of the four classes are the superior single/ double rooms ($23/28), with wood floors, a bit more space and tubs. There's a nice pool and a big buffet breakfast served on the grounds.

Thante Hotel (☎ 60315, in Yangon 01-664 424; nyaunguthante@mptmail.net.mm; Anawrahta Rd; s/d $30/35; ✖ ✖) South of the market, just off the main road, is the 37-room Thante Hotel. It offers roomy bungalows on shady grounds and has a decent swimming pool ($3 for nonguests). The rooms are starting to show a few nicks but they're spacious and come with satellite TV, twin beds, refrigerator, bathtub, wooden floor and deckchairs on the small porch. The hotel's staff members are very welcoming, plus there's a good bakery and restaurant on site.

TOP END

The only top-end choices in Nyaung U get some European tour groups, but we recommend avoiding both. The Bagan Golf Resort is run by the government, and the remarkable (and remarkably pricey) Aureum Palace, a mile or so southwest of town, is owned by Tay Za (p21). Its infamous Tower Restaurant – a blight on the Bagan plain – is overpriced but has views.

Eating
RESTAURANT ROW

Nyaung U's Restaurant Row (south of the main road, just east of the bus station) is a strip of atmospheric open-air eateries geared towards foreign visitors. Touristy? Maybe. But it's easily the hub(bub) of Bagan action. Many of the restaurants are copycats, with similar 'everything goes' menus (Chinese, Burmese, Thai, Indian, pizza, 'Western' options). Go and see what looks good.

Aroma 2 (Restaurant Row; dishes K2000-7000; ☺ 11am-9pm or 10pm) The best for Indian, by far. It serves veggie and meat curries on banana leaves (or plates) with an endless stream of hot chapattis and five dollops of condiments (including mango, garlic and tamarind sauces). Good stuff.

Pyi Wa (Restaurant Row; noodles & dishes K1500-3000; ☺ 7am-9pm or 10pm) Slightly less stylish than some, but Pyi Wa is the only one with a Bagan-era *zedi* (stupa) as a neighbour – staff light up its base at night. The best dishes are Chinese, but do start off with the 'potato cracken' (fried potato wedges that go particularly well with a bottle of Myanmar Beer).

ELSEWHERE

San Kabar Restaurant & Pub (Main Rd; pizza K4000-6000, salads K1500-2700; ☺ 7am-10pm) Famous as the

BAGAN &
CENTRAL MYANMAR

birthplace of Bagan pizza, the San Kabar's streetside candlelit courtyard is all about its thin-crusted pies and well-prepared salads.

Beach Bar (12 Youne Tan Yat; dishes K4000-8000; ◷ 7am-11pm) Signs lead past backstreets from the Nyaung U market to this slick, breezy spot with plenty of parking space for tour buses that may or may not come. The two-floor restaurant is on the river's edge, with good Thai, Chinese and Myanmar dishes and good views from wicker armchairs. Fine for a sunset martini (K3000) too; all drinks are 20% off from 4pm to 6pm.

Nanda (☎ 60096; Main Rd; set meals K6000; ◷ 9am-10pm) Tour groups go for Nanda, a pleasant open-air setting just west of town, with a 7.30pm puppet show and set meals of Myanmar or Chinese specialities.

Shopping
The main **market**, near the roundabout at the east end of the main road, has many traveller-oriented doodahs (woodcarvings, T-shirts, antique pieces) on its northern end.

Getting There & Away
See Mt Popa (p190) and Salay (p191) for transport details to those nearby attractions.

AIR
The Nyaung U Airport is about 2 miles southeast of the market. Flight schedules vary. Presently Air Mandalay, Bagan Air and Yangon Airways connect Bagan daily with Mandalay ($37), Heho ($54 to $56) and Yangon ($83 to $86). Flights to Thandwe (for Ngapali Beach) and other destinations must make connections in Yangon. The government-run Myanma Airways also has flights from Nyaung U.

Travel agencies sell tickets a bit cheaper than airline offices. Try **Seven Diamond** (☎ 60883; Main Rd; ◷ 8am-5.30pm Mon-Sat, 8am-4pm Sun) or at Golden Myanmar Guest House (p181).

BOAT
Boats to Mandalay go from either Nyaung U or Old Bagan, depending on water levels. The Nyaung U jetty is about half a mile northeast of the Nyaung U market. The IWT office, about 300yd inland from the jetty, sells tickets for Mandalay, Magwe and Pyay.

The most popular boat ride is to Mandalay ($13 to $20, 11 to 12 hours) aboard the *Shwei Kennery Express*, which leaves at 5.30am at least a few times a week. Most visitors take the journey from Mandalay but if you go the opposite way (to Mandalay from here), you get a discounted rate and it takes about the same amount of time.

The less practical government ferry (aka 'slow boat') headed to Mandalay only a couple of times weekly at research time, leaving Monday and Thursday at 4.30am ($10, two days) and overnighting near Pakokku. Meanwhile the south-bound government ferry left once weekly to Magwe ($5, two days) and Pyay ($9, three days).

From the Nyaung U jetty, small local boats leave for Pakokku (K3000, 2½ hours) a few times daily (at research time 6am, 9am and noon), the last returning to Nyaung U at 2pm. You can then catch a bus from Pakokku to Monywa. To charter a private boat to Pakokku and back costs about K50,000.

BUS
The main **bus station** serving Bagan is on the main road in Nyaung U.

During peak season, it's wise to book bus tickets for Mandalay, Taunggyi (for Inle Lake) and Yangon a couple of days in advance. You can call ☎ 60743 for information on the

BUS SERVICES
At research time, daily services included the following:

Destination	Price	Duration	Departure	Type
Magwe	K6500	4-5hr	7am	minibus (plus Yangon buses)
Mandalay	K8500	8hr	4am (from Nyaung U market), 7am & 9am	local (no air-con)
Kalaw	K10,500	9-10hr	4am	Taunggyi bus
Pyay	K15,000	9hr	3pm	Yangon buses
Taunggyi	K10,5000	12hr	4am	local
Yangon	K15,000	14-15hr	3pm	air-con & local

BAGAN &
CENTRAL MYANMAR

Magwe, Mandalay and Taunggyi buses, but it's better to drop by the office.

PICK-UP

The lone daily pick-up service to Mt Popa (K3000 each way, one hour) leaves at 8.30am and returns at 1pm. Half-hourly pick-ups go to Chauk (90 minutes), where you can connect via pick-up to Salay (one hour).

Pick-ups between Nyaung U, Old Bagan and New Bagan run along the main street, starting from the roundabout outside the Nyaung U market.

TAXI

As Bagan has limited (good) bus connections to other major destinations, many travellers hire share taxis – often quite old cars, some with open backs, most without air-con – to destinations around the country. Ask at Ever Sky (p180) or at your hotel.

Sample taxi fares:

Destination	Fare ($)	Duration
Inle Lake	$110-125	12hr
Kalaw	$110-125	9hr
Magwe	$100	5hr
Mt Popa	$23-25	1½hr
Salay	$45	2hr
Mt Popa & Salay	$45-50	

TRAIN

The Bagan train station is about 2.5 miles southeast of Nyaung U. **Shwe Taung Tarn Guest House** (☎ 60949; Main Rd) sells tickets. Presently a 7am train leaves for Mandalay (ordinary/

upper class, $5/10, eight hours). There's no direct train to Yangon, but one leaves at 8.45am for Pyinmana (ordinary class $5, 9½ hours).

OLD BAGAN

ပုဂံမြို့ဟောင်း

☎ 061

Although Old Bagan is no longer inhabited (except by hotel and government employees), it represents the core of the Bagan Archaeological Zone and contains several of the main temple sites, city walls and a museum. It's right on a bend of the Ayeyarwady River – sometime during your stay, wander down to the waterfront and watch the coming and going of the river trade.

Sights

Housed in an absurd, out-of-place, 19th-century-style temple, the government-run **Archaeological Museum** (Bagan-Chauk Rd; admission $5; ☿ 9am-4.30pm) was built in 1996 by the same people who redid the Mandalay Palace (p262). It features many fine pieces from Bagan (reclining buddhas, original images, inscribed stones and mural re-creations) and an unexpected room of modern-art renderings of the temples.

Near Tharabar Gate, the unnecessary **Palace Site** is a recent remake of a 'Bagan-style' palace. The red-walled compound is run by the government. At research time, it wasn't open to the public, but word is that it'll be accessible for $5.

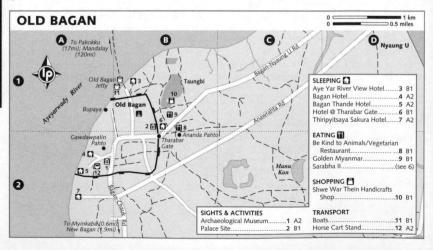

OLD BAGAN

0 _____ 1 km
0 _____ 0.5 miles

SLEEPING 🛏
Aye Yar River View Hotel.........3 B1
Bagan Hotel.............................4 A2
Bagan Thande Hotel..................5 A2
Hotel @ Tharabar Gate............6 B1
Thiripyitsaya Sakura Hotel.........7 A2

EATING 🍴
Be Kind to Animals/Vegetarian
    Restaurant.........................8 B1
Golden Myanmar....................9 B1
Sarabha II.........................(see 6)

SHOPPING 🛍
Shwe War Thein Handicrafts
    Shop.................................10 B1

SIGHTS & ACTIVITIES
Archaeological Museum.........1 A2
Palace Site...........................2 B1

TRANSPORT
Boats.................................11 B1
Horse Cart Stand................12 A2

See p203 for information on temples in Old Bagan.

Sleeping

Once you're past the views of the river, proximity to Bagan's temples and nice pool areas, you'll find that Old Bagan's handful of hotels don't necessarily offer much more comfort than you get at New Bagan's best hotels. With only a handful of choices, they can fill up months in advance of peak season.

All places listed here have restaurants, bars and pools, plus satellite TV and extras like a minibar in the room. Prices listed here are walk-in rates during peak season, and don't include the 10% service charge and 10% government tax. Yangon agents often arrange discounted rates.

Bagan Thande Hotel (☎ 60025, 60031; www.hotel baganthande.com; s $28-66, d $33-75; ✖ 🖭) Opened for King Edward VIII in 1922, this riverside hotel is a longstanding Bagan accommodation – and carries a bit of dated formality. The simple, but fine, midpriced 'superior' bungalows have decks looking over the pool and nearby Gadawpawlin Pahto. Best for views, though, are the riverfront deluxe rooms at the river's edge. Breakfast is served under tree shade with river views too.

Bagan Hotel (☎ 60032; www.bagan-hotel.com; r $75 & $95, ste $100, ✖ 🖭) More modern and stylish than Thande, this 108-room hotel has bungalows with teak floors in a nice setting, though the condition has drooped a bit since the hotel lost its German manager earlier this decade. Much of the complex – the 'night bazaar' up front and the great pool area – keeps focus away from limited river views, though breakfast's served on a lawn overlooking the water. Skip the overpriced 'river view' rooms ($160).

Thiripyitsaya Sakura Hotel (☎ 60048, 60049; www .bagan-thiripyitsaya-sakura-hotel.com; r $130-160; ✖ 🖭) The subtle, spread-out landscaping would probably work wonders in milder climates – say Kyoto – but it's hard to not wish for more midday shade in this nice Japanese joint-venture hotel on the river, about 500m south of the Old Bagan walls. There's a pool and rooms are away (mostly) from direct river views in four-room bungalow-style duplexes with covered decks.

Hotel@Tharabar Gate (☎ 60037, 60042; in Yangon 01-211 888; www.tharabargate.com; r $160-200; ste $300; 🅿 ✖ 🖳 🖭) If you can live without river views (or with a slightly awkward 'panhandle' layout), this 86-room hotel is Old Bagan's best option (particularly when you beat those rack rates). Lush gardens of tropical plants and bougainvillea line walkways to the roomy wood-floor bungalows with decks. The two-room suites at the far end go traditional, with gold-coloured ogres and *naga* spirits on the walls. An engaging Swiss manager keeps things clicking – perhaps he can get rid of that tacky '@' in the name.

Long run by the government, riverside Aye Yar River View Hotel is now supposedly run by a 'private business person'. Its huge makeover has made it nice, but there's still a bit of a formal air hanging over it.

Eating

With few or no eating options amid the temples, Old Bagan's restaurants (between the Ananda Pahto and Tharabar Gate) are a logical central point for lunch. The hotel restaurants (see Sleeping, left) add a little style (and kyat) to your meal.

Near the Ananda Pahto are a couple of eateries, including **Be Kind to Animals/Vegetarian Restaurant** (off Bagan-Nyaung U Rd; dishes from K1000; ⏰ 10am-9pm).

Sarabha II (dishes K1200-7000; ⏰ 11am-10pm) Of the two Sarabhas back-to-back by the Tharabar Gate, we like the one behind best, away from the road. It's a great midday resting point for shade and range of food (Chinese, Thai, Burmese, pizza). The food's good, and cheaper than hotel restaurants in the area, but best are the cold towels they hand out to wipe the dust off your face.

Golden Myanmar (Bagan-Nyaung U Rd; buffet K3000; ⏰ 10am-10pm) Keep-it-real seekers (and lots of horse-cart drivers) prefer this excellent roadside eatery with shaded seats on a brick floor. The 'buffet' (your pick of chicken, pork, fish or mutton curry) comes with the usual tableful of condiments. There's another location near Ananda Pahto.

Shopping

Just east of Tharabar Gate (and well signed off the Bagan–Nyaung U Rd), **Shwe War Thein Handicrafts Shop** (☎ 67032; shi@mptmail .net.mm; ⏰ 6am-10pm in peak season) is a popular treasure trove of Myanmar trinkets. The collection includes antique and new puppets, woodcarvings, chess sets, lacquerware and bronze pieces.

Lacquerware selections are bigger in Myinkaba (below) and New Bagan (p188).

Getting There & Away

Depending on water levels, boats from Mandalay arrive in Old Bagan near the Aye Yar Hotel. See p183 for more on boats leaving Nyaung U, the major gateway for buses, trains and planes out of Bagan.

MYINKABA
မြင်းကပါ

☎ 061

Like lacquerware? Bagan's most famous shopping zone comes in this otherwise ho-hum village, about half a mile south of Old Bagan, which has been home to family-run lacquerware workshops for generations. At least a dozen workshops and storefronts are located around the smattering of choice Early Bagan–period *pahto* (temples) and stupas (p214). And King Manuha, respectfully called the 'Captive King', built the poetic Manuha Paya while held here in the 11th century.

Shopping

Before pulling out your wallet, it's wise to stop at a handful of places to compare varying styles (and prices). Workshops (like the ones that follow) will show you the many stages of lacquerware-making, and how lacquer is applied in layers, dried and engraved. There's refreshingly little-to-no pressure to buy at any. But quality varies; often the best stuff is kept in air-conditioned rooms in the back. Most workshops and stores keep long hours (roughly 7am to 9pm during peak season).

Generally starting prices can go down by about 10% – and no more. We priced higher-quality 14-layer (or higher) vases for $35, full tea sets with tray for $110, tea cups or rice bowls for $15 to $25 and jewellery boxes from $12. Seven-layer pieces are cheaper.

A few places to check out:

Art Gallery of Bagan (☎ 60307; hlthantar@myanmar.com.mm) Two rooms and a busy workshop, on the road 200yd north of Mahamuni.

Family Lacquerware Work Shop (☎ 60770; Bagan-Chauk Rd) Smaller workshop off the east side of the road, with a few more modern styles.

Golden Cuckoo (☎ 60428; goldencuckoo@mandalay.net.mm) Just behind the Manuha Paya (p215), this family run workshop spans four generations and focuses on 'traditional' designs.

Getting There & Away

Pick-ups running between New Bagan, Old Bagan and Nyaung U stop here.

NEW BAGAN (BAGAN MYOTHIT)
ပုဂံမြို့သစ်

☎ 061

Far sleepier than Nyaung U, and feeling more remote (even though it's closer to the juicy temples), New Bagan only exists because the government forced locals from the Old Bagan area in 1990. Give the locals credit though: they've done the best to make the most of their new home, with a network of shady, dusty roads away from the river. It's way laid-back, and definitely the place for Bagan's best midrange accommodation choices and riverside restaurants.

Information

You'll find a couple of internet places and telephone stands along the main street.

Myanmar Travels & Tours (MTT; ☎ 60277; ⏰ 8.30am-4.30pm), the government-run tourist office (the only one in the Bagan area), is just north of town. It can help organise excursions (and getting permission via its Yangon office) to visit Chin State. It quoted us $88 per day for a jeep, $30 per day for an English-speaking MTT guide and a whopping $30 per day for accommodation. See p334 for more on the Chin State trip.

Exotissimo (☎ 60383; ⏰ 9am-6pm Mon-Fri, 9am-noon Sat) is a high-end agent, which can arrange Mt Popa tours ($65 including guide and car) or rent sturdy mountain bikes ($10 per day).

Sleeping

New Bagan has the area's best midrange options. All prices here include breakfast and all places claim to have hot water.

BUDGET

Bagan Central Hotel (☎ 60343; Main Rd; s/d $10/15; ❄) Bamboo-style rooms are compact and clean – no smoking! no shoes! – and great value for the price. Some have tubs. Breakfast is served under the courtyard tree.

Kyi Kyi Mya Guest House (☎ 60579; Main Rd; s/d $10/15; ❄) This simple complex with shade and an inviting pea-green paint job has straightforward rooms with new carpets laid atop concrete floors, an old air-con unit

NEW BAGAN (BAGAN MYOTHIT)

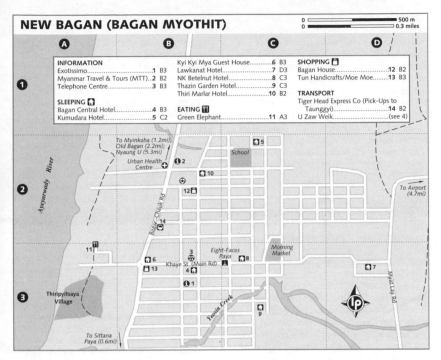

INFORMATION
Exotissimo.................................1 B3
Myanmar Travel & Tours (MTT)...2 B2
Telephone Centre.......................3 B3

SLEEPING
Bagan Central Hotel...................4 B3
Kumudara Hotel.........................5 C2

Kyi Kyi Mya Guest House............6 B3
Lawkanat Hotel.........................7 D3
NK Betelnut Hotel......................8 C3
Thazin Garden Hotel..................9 C3
Thiri Marlar Hotel....................10 B2

EATING
Green Elephant.........................11 A3

SHOPPING
Bagan House............................12 B2
Tun Handicrafts/Moe Moe.........13 B3

TRANSPORT
Tiger Head Express Co (Pick-Ups to
  Taunggyi)..............................14 B2
U Zaw Weik............................(see 4)

---

and attached bathroom. Still, it's roughly equivalent to the $8 doubles in Nyaung U, and there is a portrait of General Than Shwe under Buddha's in the reception.

MIDRANGE

You get satellite TV, working at various levels, at each of the following.

Lawkanat Hotel (☎ 60306; s/d $18/20; ✣) This small complex, just off the main road, has black-tiled decks leading to simple green-carpeted rooms with giant front windows, which look out over the peaceful gardens. It works.

NK Betelnut Hotel (☎ 60326; Main Rd; s/d $18/21; ✣) A bit overpriced for what you get, the Betelnut is nevertheless a funny group of cabin-style rooms with green carpet, a little TV and old tiled bathroom. There's no garden to speak of and you can find the same for $5 less in Nyuang U. But it's all clean and some rooms are in the 'betelnut log' cabins. That's neat.

ourpick Thiri Marlar Hotel (☎ 60312, 02-67370; thirimarlar@mptmail.net.mm; s/d $22/25; ✣) The teak walkways leading to the 21 lovely rooms are

wrapped around a small pagoda-style dining room, though most guests eat the free breakfast (or prearranged dinners) on the roof deck with temple views. Rooms are rather compact but inviting, with shiny wood floors and views of bougainvillea draping over the wall outside.

Kumudara Hotel (☎ 60965, in Yangon 01-295 472; www.kumudara-bagan.com; superior s/d $21/26, junior ste $31/36, ste $48; [P] ✣ [💻] [🛁]) No hotel boasts better balcony views of the mighty sprawl of red-brick temples than Kumudara, which now sports a stunning renovation for its junior suites and suites (skip the dated superior rooms until they get their update). The suites are in a green geometrical building that fits well with the arid, desert-like setting. Inside, rooms have a playful mix of wood panelling, modern art and retro-style safe boxes. There's a pool and restaurant, plus free internet.

TOP END

Thazin Garden Hotel (☎ 60052, 60302, in Yangon 01-512 715; www.thazingardenhotel.com; s $45-55, d $55-65; ✣ [🛁]) Set on a backstreet, this oasis of

BAGAN & CENTRAL MYANMAR

palms and flowers and shaded walkways is an irresistible choice. The deluxe 'bungalows' are built in a paya-style red-brick complex with a sea of dark luxurious teak inside and a balcony overlooking the hotel's private pagoda, where dinner's served. The 'superior' rooms are quite inviting, losing a little space (and TV size) but adding hanging paper umbrellas, a chess board and deck area. There's a pool (nonguests can swim for $5). It's owned by a Yangon entrepreneur.

We don't recommend staying at the Myanmar Treasure Resort, which is owned by Tay Za (p21).

Eating

New Bagan's Main Rd is lined with several Chinese and Burmese restaurants. Many foreigners grab a meal on the riverside, just west – there are several and at times you can either be lost amidst the tour groups or have the place to yourself.

Green Elephant (11am-4pm & 6-10pm) Probably the best choice, with small and large portions of many dishes (including local curries). The good-value and tasty Myanmar set meal (K7000) comes with a couple of curries, vegetable tempura, soup, dessert and coffee. The setting's the deal though, with shaded tables on a lawn overlooking the Ayeyarwady.

Shopping

Nearby Myinkaba village has more lacquerware factories and shops, but New Bagan has a few good options.

Tun Handicrafts/Moe Moe (60357; Main Rd; 9am-9pm) Large showroom with mix of traditional and modern lacquerware (exposed-bamboo tea cups for $4 and rice bowls from $7).

Bagan House (60767) Worth seeking out on the backstreets, this stylish showroom has a mix of cheap and higher-priced lacquerware.

Getting There & Around

See Nyaung U (p183) for most transport connections. **Tiger Head Express Co** (Bagan-Chauk Rd) sends daily pick-ups to Kalaw and Taunggyi (K9000, front seat K15,000) at the ungodly hour of 3am.

There are airline offices on Main Rd a block south. **U Zaw Weik** (60676; zawweik@myanmar.com .mm; Main Rd) helps with air tickets or can get you a taxi to Mt Popa ($40), Mt Popa and

Salay ($60), around Bagan ($30) or to Kalaw or Mandalay ($115).

Bicycle rental starts at K2500 per day; you can get a mountain bike at Exotissimo (see Information, p186). See p179 for more on getting around the Bagan site.

AROUND BAGAN

MT POPA
ပုပ္ပါးတောင်
☎ 02

Going on a day trip to Mt Popa without some sort of guide is like watching a foreign-language film without subtitles. Considered something of a Mt Olympus by locals, it's the spiritual HQ to Myanmar's infamous '37 nat', who boast an ever-confusing and fascinating history.

Distinctively Myanmar, Mt Popa – a lone 2418ft peak standing apart from higher forested mountains – looks like a tower. The mountain was forged out of a volcano that may have erupted some 250,000 years ago (some locals suggest 40 million years ago). One local told us: 'Popa is like the sun or moon, no-one can guess how old it is.'

Walking up along covered walkways occasionally smeared in monkey dung takes you to a host of temples devoted to some of the nat. Up top there are mammoth views back towards the Myingyan Plain and beyond. It's gorgeous, but only a few visitors come on a half-day trip from Bagan, shrug their shoulders a second, and move on, unfazed by one of the more fascinating sites in the country.

One revered guide to Mt Popa is **U Taung Hwin** (per day $20), a gentle old soul with good English and plenty of experience leading travellers around the culturally rich area. Ask for him by name at the Shwe Taung Tarn Guest House, on Nyaung U's main road (see p184).

Sights

MOTHER SPIRIT OF POPA & NAT SHRINE
Before you head up the mountain steps, look into this tiger-guarded **shrine**, at the foot of the mountain (just across from the steps guarded by elephant statues – there are loads of critters around here). Inside you'll find a display extending left and right from an inner hallway door of mannequinlike figures representing some of the 37 official nat, plus some Hindu

deities and a few necromancers (the figures with goatees to the right end).

There are also some of the many, many other *nat* who didn't make the '37', including three principal figures: the **Flower-Eating Ogress** (aka Mae Wunna, or 'Queen Mother of Popa') and her two sons (to her left and right) **Min Gyi** and **Min Lay** (see the boxed text, below). A few other interesting *nat* here caught our attention.

The plump Pyu goddess **Shin Nemi** (Little Lady) is a guardian for children, and gets toy offerings during school exam time. She's the cute little thing clutching a green umbrella and with a stuffed animal in her hand, midway down to the left.

There have been a few Kyawswas in Myanmar spirit history, but the most popular is the Popa-born **Lord Kyawswa** (aka Drunk Nat), who spent his few years cockfighting and drinking. He boasts: 'If you don't like me, avoid me. I admit I'm a drunkard.' He's the guardian of gamblers and drunks and sits on a horse decked in rum and whiskey bottles, to the right.

Locals pray to **Shwe Na Be** (Lady with Golden Sides) when a snake comes into their house. She's the woman holding a *naga* (serpent) near the corner to the left.

UP THE MOUNTAIN

Myanmar superstition says you shouldn't wear red or black on the mountain, nor should you curse, say bad things about other people or bring along any meat (especially pork). Any of these actions could offend the residing *nat* who might then retaliate with a spate of ill fortune. And no-one likes a mad *nat*.

Atop the impressive rocky crag clings a picturesque complex of monasteries, stupas and shrines that you can climb to via a winding, covered walkway, complete with misbehaving

monkeys. The 25-minute climb is steep and stiff, but it gets cooler as you get higher. Views are fantastic. You may be fortunate enough to spot one of the slow-walking hermit monks called *yeti*, who wear tall, peaked hats and come occasionally.

The higher mountain next to the pagoda-topped mountain is also considered 'Mt Popa', and there are **hiking trails** that lead up (it takes a couple of hours) to the rim of the volcano crater. The trek is best done with local guides. Ask at the turn-off, a mile or so back towards Bagan.

PETRIFIED FOREST

If you come by share taxi, ask the driver to point out bits of petrified forest, which are strewn along either side of the road west of Popa village.

Also present is much volcanic ash, which makes the surrounding plains fertile. The heights capture the moisture of passing clouds, causing rain to drop on the plateau and produce a profusion of trees, flowering plants and herbs. In fact, the word *popa* is derived from the Sanskrit word for flower.

Festivals & Events

Mt Popa hosts two huge **nat pwe** (spirit festivals) yearly, one beginning on the full moon of Nayon (May/June) and another on the full moon of Nadaw (November/December). Before King Anawrahta's time, thousands of animals were sacrificed to the *nat* during these festivals, but this practice has been prohibited since the Bagan era. Spirit possession and overall drunken ecstasy are still part of the celebration, however.

There are several other minor festivals, including ones held on the full moons of Wagaung (July/August) and Tagu (March/

NAT MORAL: FULFILL YOUR DUTIES!

Sometimes it's hard being a *nat*. The namesake figure of the Mother Spirit of Popa & Nat Shrine is Mae Wunna. She was famous for her love of Byat-ta, one of King Anawrahta's servants – a flower-gatherer Indian with superhuman powers – who neglected his duties and got executed for it.

Their two sons Min Gyi and Min Lay, supposedly born atop Mt Popa, followed their father's tradition. They became servants for the king (often going to China), grew neglectful of their duties, and then *they* got executed. King Anawrahta, however, ordered a shrine built at their execution site (at Taungbyone, north of Mandalay), now the site of a huge festival (see above). Many worshippers come to offer a blessing to these three. Mae Wunna and her sons are the central figures facing the entry to the shrine.

April), which celebrate the departure and return of the famous Taungbyone *nat* (Min Gyi and Min Lay). Once a year, the Taungbyone *nat* are believed to travel a spirit circuit that includes Mt Popa, Taungbyone (about 14 miles north of Mandalay) and China.

Sleeping

Most visitors find a couple of hours with Mt Popa's monkeys enough but, if needed, there are a couple of guesthouses in Popa village (rooms about $15).

Popa Mountain Resort (☎ 69169, in Yangon 01-202 101, ext 171; www.woodlandgroups.com; superior s/d $50/60, deluxe $100/110; ✖ ⛱) On the mountain overlooking Mt Popa, this lovely resort (a Singaporean joint venture) teems with sandalwood forest and views. It gets a bit lonely after hours, as most visitors only come for a dip in the pool (nonguest fee $3) or a meal while overlooking the pagodas atop Mt Popa. It's possible to begin hikes to the volcano crater (near the TV tower above) from here too.

Getting There & Away

Most travellers visit Mt Popa in half a day by share taxi or by organised tour from their hotel. In Nyaung U, guesthouses could get you a slot in a share taxi (without guide); a whole taxi is $24 and can fit four plus the driver.

At research time a lone daily pick-up left Nyaung U's bus station at 8.30am for Mt Popa (K3000, 90 minutes); it left Popa for Nyaung U at 1pm. Less conveniently, you could take an hourly pick-up from Nyaung U to Kyaukpadaung (90 minutes) and then another to Mt Popa (45 minutes). This would take up a full day.

SALAY

ဝင်လယ်

☎ 063

This Bagan-era village, 22 miles south of Bagan, is rooted in the 12th and 13th centuries, when Bagan's influence spread. It remains an active religious centre, with something like 50 monasteries for the 7000 or so residents! Day-trippers make it here to visit a few of the 19th-century wooden monasteries and some select Bagan-era shrines, and peek at more untouched British colonial buildings than you'll find in much of Myanmar.

It can be paired with Mt Popa on a full-day trip, though the two are in different directions from Bagan. Eating choices tend to be better in nearby Chauk, but you can get noodles in the Salay market. There are no hotels.

Sights

YOUQSON KYAUNG

ရုပ်စုံကျောင်း

Designed as a copy of the Crown Prince House in Mandalay, and built from 1882 to 1892, the huge **wooden monastery** (admission $3; ☾ 9am-4.30pm) is the best place to start a visit in Salay.

Along two of its exterior sides are detailed original carvings displaying 19th-century court life and scenes from the Jataka (stories of the Buddha's past lives) and Ramayana (one of India's best-known legends); sadly another side's pieces were looted in the 1980s. Inside, the 17th- to 19th-century pieces are behind glass cases, while the Bagan-era woodcarvings (including a massive throne backdrop) stand in open view.

The monastery was renovated twice in the 1990s and the government's Department of Archaeology runs the site; on-site staff can point you to other nearby sites in and outside town. For general information, try ☎ 40221.

BAGAN-ERA MONUMENTS

Little of the history of Salay's 103 ruins is known outside a small circle of Myanmar archaeologists working with limited funds. It is said that most of the monuments in Salay weren't royally sponsored but were built by the lower nobility or commoners – thus there are no structures on the grand scale of Bagan's biggest ones.

In the pagoda-filled area across from the Youqson Kyaung, you can see **Payathonzu** (Temples 18, 19 and 20), about 110yd east, which is a small trio of brick shrines with *sikhara* (Indian-style corncob-like temple finial) and some faded murals inside. The westernmost one (to the left if you come from the museum) has the most visible murals and also a narrow set of stairs leading to a small terrace. If it's locked, ask at Youqson Kyaung.

A more interesting feature is the modern makeover of the Bagan-era **Shinpinsarkyo Paya** (Temple 88), about 4 miles southwest of town via a dodgy road (and a couple of dodgy bridges). Inside the glass- and tile-filled pagoda, you'll find an original 13th-century wood Lokanat (Mahayana Bodhisattva guardian spirit).

The nearby northern entrance passageway features interesting 19th-century 3-D murals (some torture to see). Original woodcarvings abound, some of which are painted afresh in original design.

Another mile or so south (most taxis won't drive it, but it's an easy 15-minute walk) is **Temple 99**, an unassuming 13th-century shrine that features 578 painted Jataka scenes inside. The last 16 paintings to the left as you enter represent the '16 Dreams of King Kosala'.

OTHER SIGHTS

One of the most interesting aspects of Salay is the faded **colonial buildings** around town, many of which still feature the Royal Crown (look around the market area, about 220yd west of the museum). This is especially worth visiting as few buildings in Myanmar still sport the lion-guarded crown.

In the complex across from the museum (west of the Payathonzu), the **Nan Paya** (aka the Mann Paya) is a modern pagoda housing a 20ft gold buddha made of straw lacquer. As the story goes, the buddha image was originally located near Monywa and was washed downstream during an 1888 monsoon – all the way to Salay. Ask for a peek inside from the latched door out the back.

Just north of the Payathonzu, the monastery and meditation centre of **Sasanayaunggyi Kyaung** (a bit of a stop-off point for day-trippers) features a lovely 19th-century glass armoire with Jataka-painted panels and 400-year-old scripture in Pali inside. The monks are chatty and friendly, and will ask for a donation for their on-site school.

Getting There & Away

Salay is 22 miles south of Bagan on an often flood-damaged road. You pass through the larger town of Chauk on the way. From Chauk, another road goes east to Kyaukpadaung, with a turn-off for Magwe.

A hired taxi for a four- or five-hour trip to Salay from Nyaung U runs from $45. It's technically possible to come by pick-up from Nyaung U in three hours (not including a change in Chauk), but it's not advisable as sites in Salay are spread out.

PAKOKKU

ပခုက္ကူ

☎ 062

A transit point for wayward travellers on the west side of the Ayeyarwady River (about 16 miles north of Nyaung U), Pakokku was an appealing but quiet backwater until 2007, when it found itself front-and-centre in international headlines. Monks from the Myo Ma Ahle monastery here kick-started the nationwide protests against rising petrol prices.

It's an interesting place to see, even if you just have a couple of hours before catching a bus to Monywa (p286). But those hardy types who opt for a riverside homestay tend to rank the town amongst a trip's highlights.

Pakokku is famed for its tobacco and *thanakha* (logs that are ground into a face paste used cosmetically).

Sights

In town there's little in the way of attractions. About 17 miles northeast, on the way to Monywa, are the remains of **Pakhangyi**, a 19th-century wooden monastery. About 3 miles east (via the road behind the big modern pagoda) is the destroyed frame of **Pakhanngeh Kyaung**, which was once the country's largest wooden monastery, with 332 teak pillars. Many still stand, and the area – near the fork of the Ayeyarwady and Kaladan Rivers – makes for interesting exploration. A motorcycle taxi here from Pakokku is about $15.

If time is limited, you might get more out of Pakokku by seeing its **market** or just wandering its picturesquely decrepit, slightly tropical side streets, with old homes backing onto the Ayeyarwady.

One of the town's biggest *pwe* festivals, **Thihoshin**, is held during Nayon (May/June).

Sleeping

Mya Yatanar Inn (☎ 21457; 75 Lanmataw St; r per person K5000) A self-professed 'old place run by old people', Pakokku's main accommodation option is like no other in Myanmar. The managers are an outgoing English-speaking couple: a 70-something former boxing teacher and his Kachin wife. Conditions are homy but very basic. Electricity is mostly off here, as with all of Pakokku, and there's a shared bathroom. You'll either be squeamish over it or consider it the highlight of your trip. The pair accidentally started the business when they invited in a couple of backpackers sleeping in the street

BAGAN & CENTRAL MYANMAR

in 1980. They can help you find good food or get a taxi deal, or show you to local pagodas or where tattooing is done. The inn is on the river, a couple of blocks east of the market.

Tha Pye No Guest House (☎ 21166; Myoma Rd; s/d K10,000/20,000; ⊗) One room in this back-up option has private bathroom and air-con.

Getting There & Away

You can travel by local bus to and from Monywa (K1400, 4½ hours); at research time a few left daily, including at 10.30am and 2pm. The bus station is 2 miles south of the centre.

A handful of ferries go to Nyaung U (K3000, two to three hours), the last returning around 2pm.

MYINGYAN

မြင်းခြံ

☎ 066

Despite its Ayeyarwady River location 55 miles north of Nyaung U (towards Mandalay), sprawled-out Myingyan (sorta rhymes with 'engine') sees very few travellers, as major bus routes bypass the bumpier roads that come here. Some cycling groups pass through and occasionally long-distance boats stop at the Ayeyarwady docks, just west of town, but not the Mandalay–Bagan express boats. The town is famous for its big prison.

Sights

If you make it here, the two-storey **central market**, near a couple of Chinese-style restaurants, is a good starting point. About 1 mile east, accessed from the road just north of the train station, is the **Bodhi Dat Taw Taik** (meaning 'depository of Buddha's relics'), where (in the monastery just west) you can see Buddha relics (teeth, hair, bone and even skin) housed intriguingly in the former safe of a British colonial bank.

About 1 mile south of the market, via the north–south Mandalay–Meiktila Rd, is the **Soon Lu Kyaung**, an important monastery where you can see the remains of the well-known Soon Lu Sayadaw, draped in monastic robes. He died in 1951, though his body is (relatively) well preserved. An attendant said: 'He was a great man, very powerful. No chemicals on his body were used and he still is strong.'

Sleeping

One Star Drive In Inn (☎ 21389; Myo Pat St, 16th quarter; r per person K8000) This odd group of bungalows

on a side street is about half a mile southeast of the central market. Rooms are fan-cooled, mattresses are thin, attached bathrooms are a bit smelly and showers are cold.

Getting There & Away

Frequent buses and pick-ups leave from the street just east of the Myingyan–Meiktila road, a couple of blocks south of the market, for Meiktila (K4000, three hours). A lone daily pick-up goes to Nyaung U (two hours) at 4.30am.

The daily train between Mandalay and Bagan (p184) stops in Myingyan.

YANGON–MANDALAY HIGHWAY

This popular north–south route following the Yangon–Mandalay Hwy – some call it the 'high road', though it runs west of the Shan Hills – is often taken on overnight buses. It's not particularly gorgeous. Friendly Taungoo is the most popular stop-off, while a peek at (accessible) parts of a certain modern-day 'royal capital' (northwest of Pyinmana) plunges the deepest depths of bizarre.

TAUNGOO

တောင်ငူ

☎ 054

Little remains of Taungoo's glorious roots from its capital days in the 15th and 16th centuries. After much WWII bombing wrecked most of its Katumadi Palace (only a bit of the old walls and moat can still be seen), it's become more of a busy stop-and-go highway town. Most Mandalay or Inle-bound travellers with private cars overnight here; local truckers too. Off the highway there's more to suck you in for a couple of hours than any other town on the Yangon–Mandalay highway, and a great guesthouse makes it easy to stay an extra day.

The Karen hills to the east are famed for their vegetables and coffee. The area is also known for its bounteous areca (betel) palms. In Myanmar, when someone receives unexpected good fortune they are likened to a betel-lover receiving a paid trip to Taungoo.

Kayin State is less than 22 miles east, and Kayah State another 40 miles further east. Karen and Kayah insurgents have been

---

THREE-HOUR TAUNGOO BIKE TOUR

Most visitors in Taungoo leave without looking. Try to save a few morning hours to have a pedal around.

From the highway (presuming you stay at Beauty Guest House, p194), go north to where the billboard-rimmed road bends around the centre. Look for the small Zay St sign that leads west a few blocks to the **market**, where you'll pass teashops and piles of rice, bananas and clothing. Continue straight about half a mile west to reach the entrance to **Shwesandaw Paya** (below), guarded by two gold lions. After visiting it, go west 110yd till the street dead-ends at **Kandawgyi Lake**, dating from Taungoo's capital days (then known as Katumadi), when Bayin Naung ruled. It's lined with a few cafés – ask about local ghosts (supposedly many drowning victims linger here).

Turn right at the lake, then left on busy Mo Ma Phoe Kum St, and go straight. Just past the lake, you'll see a vegetated embankment, actually the ruins of the **old palace walls**. Just beyond is the **old moat**.

Continue 1 mile west on a nice countryside ride to reach **Kawmudaw Paya**, Taungoo's oldest religious site. In the southwest corner, you'll see a small pillar in a sandbox (with barefoot prints) – locals come here and walk around it to conquer personal problems.

Head back to the lake and turn right at its western edge, where you'll pass the Katumadi Hotel. Turn left on the lake's southern side (No 6 St, aka Kandaw St). Heading back towards the highway, go straight a few blocks to a dilapidated **mosque**. It was closed in recent years following struggles between area Muslims and Buddhists (we didn't see any pagodas or monasteries closed). Turn right for a couple blocks for a quick look at **Myasigon Paya** (below), then return to No 6 St and then the highway.

---

known to operate within these distances. A dry-weather road continues east all the way to Loikaw, but any travel beyond the Sittoung (Sittang) River a couple of miles to the east of Taungoo still requires special permission.

Information

In case of minor illnesses, **Dr Yee Yee Aye** (☎ 23270; Myanmar Beauty Guest House I), in town, runs a clinic and speaks good English.

Internet connections are iffy in Taungoo but **Net Star Computer** (Yangon–Mandalay Hwy), not far from the telecommunications tower, may have access.

Sights
SHWESANDAW PAYA
ရွှေဆံတော်ဘုရား

Situated in the centre of town, west of the main road, this is Taungoo's grandest pilgrimage spot. The central stupa, a standard-issue bell shape, is gilded and dates to 1597; local legend says an earlier stupa on the site was built centuries before and contains sacred-hair relics. Entering from the north, to your right is a display of Taungoo kings (and a rather busty queen), and a round building housing a reclining buddha surrounded by *devas* (celestial beings) and monastic disciples.

Nearby, on the western side of the stupa, there's a 12ft bronze, Mandalay-style sitting buddha, given to the paya in 1912 by a retired civil servant who donated his body weight in bronze and silver for the casting of the image. He died three years after the casting at age 72; his ashes are interred behind the image.

On the east side, there's a shrine to Thurathati, the Hindu-borrowed goddess, atop a mythical *hintha* bird. Fine-arts students come to pray to her before exams.

MYASIGON PAYA
မြစည်းဂုံဘုရား

Less famous than Shwesandaw, this pagoda has a few things worth seeing. Below its gold *zedi* the modern building features many glass mosaics. On the north side, an open building has a faded mural of Taungoo kings. A nearby squat white building with metal roof is actually a **museum** (ask in the pagoda to open it; they usually ask K1000), which has many bronze images of Erawan (the three-headed elephant who serves as Indra's mount) and assorted buddha images. It's more interesting for its random secular collection of British colonial-era memorabilia, including an ancient Kodak camera, 80-year-old plates and cream soda bottle, plus a rusty British cannon or two.

Just west of the pagoda is a small market.

ELEPHANT CAMPS

Taungoo is the starting point for visits to the nearby working **elephant camps** in a mountainous area of Karen villages and teakwood plantations, 35 miles northeast. Some Yangon-based agents arrange the trips, but it's easily done in Taungoo. Ask for **Dr Chan Aye** (chan_aye@yangon.net.mm) of the Myanmar Beauty Guest House (below), who can arrange a day-return trip for $40 to $45 per person for two or more people. The price includes the necessary permits, return transport, a walk into the forest, an elephant ride, a lunch of rice and curry, and plenty of bottled water. Bamboo rafting and motorbiking in the jungle can be added for an additional fee. Overnight trips with a stay in either Shwe Daung or Ngwe Daug, both Karen villages, cost $125 per person for three or four people. The doctor provides free medical service to villagers in the area.

A few travel agencies in Yangon book trips for about $100 a day, including Woodland Travel (p92).

Note: elephants work 6am to around 11am daily (later in the rainy and cool season) so an early start is essential if you want to see the elephants doing anything more than dreaming of other, very attractive, elephants.

Sleeping

our pick **Myanmar Beauty Guest House II, III & IV** (☎ 23270, 23527; Pauk Hla Gyi St; fourdoctors@mptmail.net.mm; r in III $10-15, s/d in IV $15/25; ❄) A three-part, 32-room rural complex at the edge of Taungoo is reason enough to stop in this town. Owned by two doctors, who delight in chit-chat, the Beauty has a grab-bag of rustic, all-wood, bungalow-style rooms. Don't get confused by the numbers – the higher the number, the nicer the room. The spacious IV ones face the fields and have air-con and a good hot shower; III is a step down, and II is usually used by drivers and guides. Staff are super, as is the wildly local breakfast, with samosas, sticky rice and exotic fruits – and lots of it. It's about 1.5 miles south of the central turn-offs and is a K1000 to K1500 trishaw ride from the centre. The original Myanmar Beauty Guest House I (☎ 23270; 7/134 Bo Hmu Pho Kun St; rooms $8 to $10), in town, isn't really worth considering.

Mother's House Hotel (☎ 24240, 24245; Yangon-Mandalay Hwy; s/d $15/20; ❄) If you need back-up to the Beauty, this 32-room bungalow hotel right on the highway grants you 24-hour electricity, satellite TV and clean and comfy bungalow-style rooms with wood floors and fudge-and-banana colour schemes.

Hotel Amazing Kaytu (☎ 23977; www.amazing-hotel.com; 8th St Ohtkyauttan; s/d $30/36; ❄) 'Hotel Dependable if a Little Overpriced & Generic Kaytu' is more apt. It's a bit north of the main turn-offs; its 18 rooms are perfectly fine – with round-the-clock electricity, satellite TV, plain tiled bathrooms, plus a clock for 'Spain' in the lobby.

At research time, a luxury hotel with pool and traditional palace-style design was under construction. The 62-room, lakeside **Royal Katumadi Hotel** (☎ 25147, in Yangon 01-553952; Kandawgyi Lake; s/d incl breakfast $70/80) is owned by a cooperative-bank exec from Yangon.

Eating

Around Taungoo's teashops, try asking for *yo yo* (normal coffee), which should get you a cup of 'Taungoo coffee' (actually it comes from the Karen mountains to the east). One good teashop, on the small island at the south side of the lake, is **Golden Lotus Café**. It doesn't have the local coffee, but there's good shade, a chatty manager and an impressive nursery.

At the **night market**, which convenes next to the central market, vendors specialise in chapattis and meat-stuffed *palata* (fried flatbread). On the highway, particularly to the south, are many Chinese and Myanmar restaurants; the restaurant at Mother's House Hotel (left) is particularly inviting.

Cozy Restaurant & Snack (Bo Hmu Pho Kun St; dishes K1000-1500) Across from a cinema, several blocks east of the lake, this great lil' restaurant gets serious on Chinese, with some spicy soups and an especially flavourful 'assorted vegetables' dish. Cozy's also a spic-and-span simple place, with some garden seats in back. Somehow a burger finds its way onto the menu too.

Getting There & Away

BUS

Most buses leaving Taungoo originated elsewhere. Generally stops are at private bus company offices scattered along the highway, just south of the turn-off to the 'centre'. It's easiest to have your local accommodation arrange a seat.

It tends to be easier to head south than north; many more local and 'express' buses head to Yangon (K4000 to K4200, six to seven hours), leaving at 6am, 9am, 9.30am, 2pm, 8pm, 9pm and 10pm. You pay the full fare only if you're heading to Bago (Pegu; three hours).

If you're heading to Mandalay, you can arrange a seat on Yangon–Mandalay express buses, but you have to pay the full fare (K8000 to K10,000, nine hours); buses come through at around 11pm. You can also jump on a Yangon–Taunggyi bus to reach Kalaw (K8000 to K12,000) at around 6pm or 7pm.

Private buses originating from Taungoo leave from offices along the highway near the centre, heading to Pyinmana and Nya Pyi Taw (K1800, three to four hours) at 7am, 8am, 10am, noon and 3pm.

CAR

If you have your own vehicle and are feeling adventurous, the 62-mile unpaved logging road from Oktwin (9 miles south of Taungoo) to Pakkaung provides a unique shortcut to Pyay. For the remaining 24 miles from Pakkaung to Pyay the road is sealed but not in good condition. This is a tiring, at least all-day trip; start early and bring at least one spare tyre, plus food and plenty of water. Dr Chan Aye (see opposite) can make this trip with you, including a one- or two-night stop in a village or jungle camp along the way ($500 to $760 for two to four people, including accommodation, meals and transport).

Any travel to the east, towards Loikaw, is restricted.

TRAIN

The Taungoo **train station** (☎ 23308) has a heavy military presence, following some Karen 'attacks' on passing trains in the night. If you go by to pick up a ticket, see how many rats you can count in the main ticket office (we saw two in 70 seconds).

Four express trains (*5 Up, 3 Up, 11 Up* and *29 Up*) for Mandalay (ordinary/upper class $15/26, about nine hours) leave daily; one at roughly 11.15am, two just after noon, and another at 6.50pm. It's $9/16 if you exit at Thazi, from where you can bus or taxi to Kalaw, Inle Lake or Meiktila. South-bound express trains (*4 Down, 6 Down, 12 Down* and *30 Down*) go to Yangon ($7/17, six to seven hours), also stopping in Bago ($4/11). These leave at roughly 7.30am and between 2pm and 3pm.

There are also slow trains to Mandalay ($7/20) and Thazi ($5/13).

PYINMANA

ပျဉ်းမနား

☎ 067

Dazed by the sudden appearance of an over-powering (and growing) neighbour in Nay Pyi Taw since 2005 (see below), Pyinmana keeps its head down and can feel a little less welcoming than some highway towns.

No hotels are licensed for foreigners, so a stop is pretty much limited to poking around the centre, where you'll find an Aung San statue facing the small **Shan Lake** (a couple of hundred yards east of the highway) and a street-spilling **market** in the walkable centre just beyond. Coconut palms are planted along the Ngalaik River, which passes through the town's north side. You can see the Shan Yoma and Aleh Yoma (Shan and Aleh mountain ranges) to the east and west.

Yan Naing Restaurant (☎ 21369; 1813 Bo Tauk Htain St; dishes from K1000; ☯ 7am-11pm), on the highway (about half a mile south of the centre turn-off), has friendly staff members who can help with area information, or just make you some tasty Chinese food.

The main bus station is about 1 mile north of the centre. Buses from Nay Pyi Taw stop here, en route to Mandalay. Also, trains between Yangon and Mandalay stop at the central train station.

NAY PYI TAW (ROYAL CAPITAL)

နေပြည်တော်

☎ 067

Any sense that the military junta running the country was opening up, embracing change or following the self-professed 'seven steps to democracy' seemed to take a few paces backwards in a move in 2005 that harked back to the 'royal' tradition of kings messily, expensively moving capitals to and fro. After consulting astrologers, and perhaps fearful of an Iraq-style invasion, the military relocated the capital to this arid, scrub-brush plain, about 3 miles west of Pyinmana.

It's a city built for SUVs, a spread-out money-sucker with six-lane lighted high-ways and zoned districts (shopping, government housing and hotels, plus closed-off zones for ministry buildings and generals' homes). The city's size dwarfs the (estimated) population of 20,000 of local workers, most of whom relocated here in hopes of work. One local told us that 10% of the built housing is vacated.

Outside of the roadblocks that stop traffic from the roads leading to generals' mansions or ministry buildings, it's surprisingly open. Particularly if you have a private driver, it's worth pulling over to get a surreal look at madness in the making, and put a dollar or two into the private economy.

We don't recommend overnighting here, as all hotels are government-owned or (very) government friendly – not to mention expensive. If you do stop for a couple hours, you'll find that most mall shops, teashops and restaurants are privately run.

Photography of official buildings or military officials is prohibited.

Orientation

Other than Google's (out-of-date) 'satellite map' of the area, no maps or road signs help orient the visitor. About 4 miles west of Pyinmana, the road reaches a lushly landscaped roundabout, a useful landmark. To the south (left, if approaching from Pyinmana) is the 'hotel zone'. A mile or so ahead (west) you'll pass a reservoir to your left and bus-ticket stands behind the small 'beer station' hill to your right. The roads north to mansions of military generals' homes and ministry buildings are closed-off.

Sights

In early 2008 the first 'tourist attraction' opened: the 200-acre **National Herbal Park** (about half a mile or so west of the roundabout), home to 8425 plants.

More interesting is just gawking at the modern mess and all the empty space (and pedestrians) between the spread-out buildings and services. About half a mile past the herbal park you'll see the **'beer station' hill** to the right. It's the best spot to get some barbecue, tea or beer, and just behind it is a huge market area

that bustles with life after dusk when the **night market** opens up.

Visible from the beer stations to the south is a sprawling reservoir before Singapore-style government housing. A road goes that way, winding its way to the fire-station tower, a school and a shimmering gold-topped **zedi**, from where you can get good views of the 'city'.

Just south, a road turns east and eventually passes the largely empty **'shopping zone'** of identical sky-blue or rose-coloured shops. About five of 180 identical column-fronted shops were in use when we dropped by. (You can find a Nay Pyi Taw souvenir shirt in a mall just southeast of the roundabout, about half a mile east of this zone.)

The giant **statues of three kings**, seen in some publicised photos of Nay Pyi Taw, are not accessible to the public.

Sleeping

If you get stuck in the area, you have no choice but to stay at one of the government-friendly hotels here. One, run by Tay Za (p21), is Aureum Palace (☎ 414114; room including breakfast $85), a 42-room hillside hotel with modern bungalows, an overpriced shop of pleated slacks and business shirts, and a restaurant.

Getting There & Away

It's possible to arrive by bus or train, get a taxi around Nay Pyi Taw, then catch a night bus out of town. Night buses leave from the bus station at 6pm and 7.30pm for Yangon (K4700 to K5000, nine to 10 hours) and Mandalay (K4700 to K5000, eight hours). There are also 5am buses to Taunggyi (11 hours) and Nyaung U (10 hours).

A motorcycle taxi from Pyinmana's centre costs about K3000.

MEIKTILA
မိတ္ထီလာ
☎ 064

A lakeside town on the crossroads between Yangon, Mandalay, Bagan and Inle Lake, Meiktila is a busy little trade centre with plenty of locals in uniform issued from the air-force bases outside town. It's not terribly exciting, but a bike ride around the lake can be fun – and you can peek at the old British officers' house where Aung San Suu Kyi and Michael Aris honeymooned.

BAGAN & CENTRAL MYANMAR

NIGHT MARKET SELLER

An out-of-work teacher from a 'dry zone' highway town to the north moved to the capital in hopes of work. He sells small appliances at the night market. He explains his new home: 'This town is very strange. Big distances and empty buildings. I don't like it much, but I had no choice. I had no job back home so I came here. But there's little money here too. The generals keep it all.'

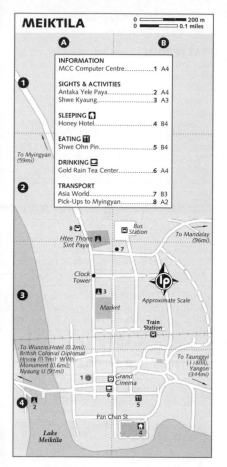

Legend goes that King Anawrahta, founder of Bagan, had a pond here broadened to the current lake that looms west of town. When he asked someone to see if it went to Mt Popa, the report came back: 'Lord, it doesn't go that far' ('Meiktila' is an abbreviation of the bad-news report).

In March 1945 the British surprised the Japanese based here and killed 20,000 Japanese soldiers over a few months in the final stand-off between Allied forces and the Japanese. Much of the city was flattened. Sadly that trend has continued: town-engulfing fires devastated the city in 1974 and 1991; another big one took out several buildings in 2003. One local warned: 'We have a fire every year. Better get fire insurance if you're planning to stay.'

Information

MCC Computer Centre (per hr K1000; 9am-9pm) occasionally gets a good connection if you need internet.

Sights

Lake Meiktila is the town's premier attraction. Though there are no boating options, you can cycle around some of it. From the bridge north of the centre, a dirt path leads away from the road; it starts just past the **Antaka Yele Paya**, a small island/pagoda reached by a wooden pier in the lake, and before the gold **Aung San statue** ahead.

About 270yd south of the bridge, the dark building to the east of the Wunzin Hotel (now housing its economy rooms) was once a **British colonial diplomat house**, and later was a fierce interrogation centre used by the Japanese in WWII. (Supposedly Aung San Suu Kyi and Michael Aris honeymooned here.)

Near the west end of the lake, **Shwe Kyaung** is a walled monastery on the inland side of the road with Japanese signs leading to a **WWII monument** that British and Japanese survivors put up in 1972. Monks will show you around. Just past the monument, a picturesque path leads between the lake and (usually) flooded rice fields.

Don't keep going to the south side of the lake, as the path leads into a no-go zone of a military compound.

Sleeping

Honey Hotel (25755; Pan Chan St; s with fan/air-con $5/10, d $8/15;) Right on the lake in town, this converted mansion is Meiktila's best bet. If available, opt for the rooms in the separate 'bungalows', particularly C-1 (right next to the water and covered gazebo where the free breakfast is served). Call ahead – it sometimes fills, and that can mean trouble.

Wunzin Hotel (23848, 23559; 49A Than Lwin Rd; economy/superior/deluxe s $8/24/30, d $12/30/36;) Formerly a government hotel (now leased to a private person apparently), the Wunzin shows its years, but the rather overpriced rooms do look over the lake from a quiet backstreet out of the centre. Staff are happy to join you for tennis on the scrappy court outside.

Eating & Drinking

Meiktila's not much for fancy eats.

Shwe Ohn Pin (Mandalay-Yangon Rd; dishes K1700-4000; 7am-10pm) This clean tiled restaurant, located in the centre, hands you an English menu for its tasty Chinese and Myanmar dishes.

The central blocks are something of a 'teashop district'. The bunker-style looking **Gold Rain Tea Center** (tea K200) is particularly popular.

Getting There & Away

BUS

Express buses zooming between Yangon and Mandalay stop on the road east of the clock tower (and not at the local bus station). Along this road you'll find half a dozen ticket-sales shops, including **Asia World** (☎ 24175), which sells tickets to Bagan (K3000, departing noon and 5.30pm).

The bus station is a couple of blocks north-east of the clock tower. Here, buses of various sizes and shapes leave regularly for Mandalay (K2000, three to four hours), 154km north.

Night buses to Yangon (K10,000, 10 to 12 hours) leave at 8pm, stopping in Taungoo and Bago for the same price.

A few minibuses go to Kalaw (K7000, about five hours) daily, leaving at 6.30am, 7.30am and 9.30am.

PICK-UP

From the bus station, pick-ups for Taunggyi (back/front K5000/10,000) leave regularly, stopping in Kalaw for the same price.

Pick-ups for Myingyan (K4000, 2½ hours) leave regularly from the main road in front of the Htee Thone Sint Paya, north of the clock tower.

TRAIN

There's a small train station in town, catching slow trains heading east–west. A more useful station is in Thazi, about 16 miles east, at the crossroads of the Yangon, Mandalay and Taunggyi lines.

YANGON–BAGAN HIGHWAY

Less traffic makes it to this western route north of Yangon. Sometimes called the 'low road', or 'Pyay Hwy', this route is debatably more attractive than the Yangon–Mandalay highway. It follows along the eastern bank of the Ayeyarwady River and rises over lovely hills and valleys north of Magwe. At Pyay,

connections to Thandwe (and Ngapali) head west over the mountains.

PYAY (PROME)
ပြည်

☎ 053

The most popular (and interesting) stop on the Yangon–Bagan highway, Pyay is richly historic – something not always evident in the bustle of the city centre. Pyay's glory comes from the partially excavated ancient Pyu capital of Thayekhittaya (p200), 5 miles east. But riverside Strand Rd is seeing a blip of a renaissance in recent years, with new hotels and a restaurant or two opening up with nice views of the passing Ayeyarwady.

Myanmar folk alternate the town's pronunciation between 'pyay' and 'pyi'. The Brits, apparently, couldn't deal with the confusion so called it Prome.

The current town site became an important trading centre during the Bagan era. The Mon controlled it when King Alaungpaya conquered it in 1754. Pyay boomed, along with the British Irrawaddy Flotilla Company in the 1890s. Today it's an important cargo town still, set at a trans-shipment point between northern and southern Myanmar.

Orientation & Information

Pyay's centre spills along the streets around the gold Aung San statue, at the corner of the Pyay–Yangon Rd and Bogyoke Rd. The bus station is a mile east.

For internet, try **Cybernet** (23 Tat St; per hr K1500; ☷ 9am-9pm).

Sights

SHWESANDAW PAYA & AROUND
ရွှေဆံတော်ဘုရား

Set on top of a hill in the centre, the stunning **Shwesandaw Paya** (and the surrounding pagodas and monasteries) is not only Pyay's biggest point of interest, but one of the country's biggest Buddhist pilgrimage sites. Just over 1yd taller than the main *zedi* at Yangon's Shwedagon, the Shwesandaw stupa follows the classic Bamar design seen at Bagan's Shwezigon (p219).

Legend goes that it was built in 589 BC, and that the golden *zedi* houses four strands of the Buddha's hair (the Golden Hair Relics).

Atop the *zedi* are two *hti* (umbrellalike pinnacles), unusual for Myanmar. The lower, bigger one dates from Pyay's days as a Mon city. The higher, smaller one was added by

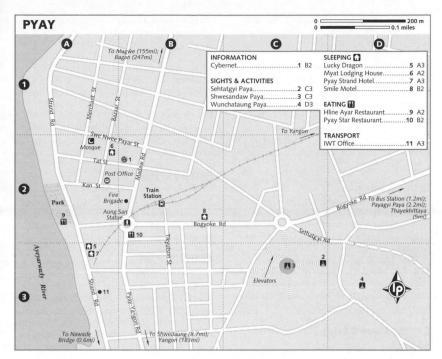

PYAY

INFORMATION	**SLEEPING**
Cybernet........................1 B2	Lucky Dragon....................5 A3
	Myat Lodging House..........6 A2
SIGHTS & ACTIVITIES	Pyay Strand Hotel.............7 A3
Sehtatgyi Paya................2 C3	Smile Motel.....................8 B2
Shwesandaw Paya............3 C3	
Wunchataung Paya..........4 D3	**EATING**
	Hline Ayar Restaurant........9 A2
	Pyay Star Restaurant.........10 B2
	TRANSPORT
	IWT Office........................11 A3

Alaungpaya as a symbol of peace between the Burmese and Mon, after brutally capturing the city in 1754. In the southwest corner of the complex, the **Sacred Tooth Hall** is said to house an original tooth from the Buddha. It's in the golden bell (locked) behind the glass. The locks come off once a year for the November full-moon festivities.

The panoramic views from the pagoda are pretty great too. To the east, you'll see the **Sehtatgyi Paya** (Big Ten Storey), a giant (maybe not 10 storeys though) seated buddha, eye-to-eye with the Shwesandaw and watching over it. The smaller gold stupa on the highest hill southeast of Shwesandaw is the **Wunchataung Paya** (Apology Mountain Pagoda), where people can say 'sorry' for misdeeds. They get the best view of Shwesandaw and the mountains across the river while they're at it. You can reach it via Sethatgyi Rd, east of the Shwesandaw.

PAYAGYI PAYA

ဘုရား:ကြီး:

Once marking one of Thayekhittaya's four corners, this towering **pagoda** is a mile east of the bus station. It likely dates from the 5th or 6th century AD. Three terraces encircle the slightly swollen, breastlike structure from its base; 'ladies' are not allowed on the upper one. The modern *hti* is lit up at night.

Sleeping

All of the following options include breakfast in the price.

Myat Lodging House (☎ 21361; 222 Bazaar St; s $6-12, d $10-14; ☒) This small backstreet guesthouse has well-loved but simple rooms (green carpet, writing desks) a block from the Pyay 'action'. The cheapest rooms have fan and shared bath (which are kept clean); only the highest priced rooms come with private bathroom. Friendly English-speaking staff give out maps of the Pyay and Thayekhittaya sites.

Smile Motel (☎ 22523, 25169; 10-11 Bogyoke Rd; s/d $15/20; ☒) If Myat is full, try Smile, which occupies a block building in the centre. The carpeted rooms go for a few extra dollars because of a refrigerator and TV in each. Staff are nice, if a bit surprised at your existence.

Pyay Strand Hotel (☎ 25846, 24874; Strand Rd; s $15-20, d $20-25; ☒) This hotel has 32 simple rooms

BAGAN & CENTRAL MYANMAR

with air-con, private bath and hot water, which are similar to Smile's. A key difference is that higher-priced ones get hot water and look out over the river.

Lucky Dragon (☎ 24222; luckydragon@mail4u.com .mm; Strand Rd; r $20-25; P 🔀) Still under construction (but looking promising) when we dropped by, the Lucky D is likely to take over Pyay's midrange incomers. It's a strip of modern, bungalow-style, wood-floor rooms across from the river, with a small pool on the premises. Supposedly guests will have internet access in the rooms.

Eating & Drinking

Pyay Star Restaurant (cnr Bogyoke Rd & Pyay-Yangon Rd; dishes from K1500) The Star is a great spot: a two-floor beer hall with plenty of buzz and a balcony to eat tasty Chinese fare and down that beer.

Hline Ayar (Strand Rd; dishes veg K1200, meat K2800-4000, fish K3000-6500; 🕑 9am-9pm) Over on the river, this live-house spot shows its years (plus cheesy pop singers at 7pm), but it has tables looking over the Ayeyarwady.

Getting There & Away

BOAT
Routes along the Ayeyarwady start and stop in Pyay, heading either north or south. Few foreigners use either service.

The **IWT office** (☎ 24503; Strand Rd; 🕑 9am-5pm Mon-Fri) is helpful on ever-changing times for slow-going government ferries. At research time, a ferry left at 5.30am on Wednesday for Mandalay (about five days), and another cargo boat left Tuesday night for Yangon (deck/cabin $9/18; about three days).

BUS
Pyay is located at the junction between Yangon, Bagan and Thandwe (for Ngapali Beach). The highway bus station, about a mile east of the centre (just off Bogyoke Rd), sends frequent buses to Yangon (K4050, six to seven hours) via a smooth two-lane road. Half a dozen companies make the trip throughout the day, including Asia Express (☎ 21759), New Generation, Yoma and Sun Moon. There are no direct buses north to Bagan from Pyay, but you can catch a bus that left from Yangon for the full Yangon–Bagan fare (K15,000 to K18,000, 12 to 13 hours). Or take the daily 8.30am bus to Magwe (K7000, six to seven hours), from where a 6am bus leaves for Bagan.

At research time, heading to Ngapali wasn't terribly convenient either – it's possible to get on a bus from Yangon to Thandwe (K22,000 to K25,000, 12 to 13 hours) in the evening, or to take a 6pm bus to Taunggok (K15,000, eight or nine hours), from where you can get a bus or pick-up to Thandwe, then onto Ngapali.

TRAIN
The train service is of little use to travellers, but a lone daily train leaves Pyay at 10pm for Yangon (eight hours).

Getting Around

Trishaws and blue bed-back taxis are the main ways of getting around. A trishaw ride to/from the bus station is around K1000, and K1500 by blue taxi. A regular pick-up service runs along Bogyoke Rd to the bus station (K200).

AROUND PYAY
Thayekhittaya
သရေခေတ္တရာ

It's no Bagan, but this ancient **site** (admission $5, incl museum $10; 🕑 8am-5pm), about 5 miles east of Pyay centre, can make for a fun few hours of laid-back exploration, often in isolation. Known to Pali-Sanskrit scholars as Sri Ksetra (Fabulous City), Thayekhittaya is an enormous Pyu city that ruled in the area from the 5th to 9th centuries AD. Local legend links its origin to the mythical King Duttabaung, who supposedly worked with ogres and other supernatural creatures to build the 'magical city' in 443 BC. The earliest Pali inscriptions found here date to the 5th or 6th centuries.

Seeing it means taking a three- or four-hour ox-cart loop to spaced-out temples (most just outside its oval city walls).

Little is known about the Pyu; one useful book is *The Ancient Pyu of Burma* by Janice Stargardt.

SIGHTS
Now that it's an extra $5, many visitors skip the small **museum**, with its posted map of the area and various artefacts from excavations (including Hindu deities, 6th-century buddha images and silver coins). From here you can arrange an ox cart for K3500, really the only way to make the 7.5-mile loop around the handful of sites. Walking is possible, but it's difficult to find your way without aid. Bicycles aren't permitted. Note that the site and museum fees go to the government.

Behind the museum to the south, the road soon follows the remains of the old palace walls. Ox-cart drivers – at a speed that ebbs and flows according to the mood of the ox – make a counterclockwise loop of the following sites.

After 2.5 miles or so, the road passes **Rahanta Gate**, where fragments of the overgrown brick gate run alongside the dirt road. Immediately south is the **Rahanta cave temple**, a small, quiet rebuilt temple with eight buddha images lined along the south wall.

About a mile south, the **Bawbawgyi Paya** is Thayekhittaya's most impressive site: a 50yd cylindrical stupa with a slightly banged-up golden *hti* on its top. It's among the oldest Pyu sights, the least obviously renovated, and the prototype of many Myanmar pagodas.

A couple of hundred yards northeast is the smaller cube-shaped **Bebe Paya**, with a cylindrical top and a few buddha images inside. Just north is the squat **Leimyethna Paya**, with a visible iron frame keeping it together. Inside four original buddha reliefs (a bit cracked, some faces missing) are visible. On either side of the roads around here, look out for long ruts in the ground, made from old canals.

A couple of hundred yards to the north is a fork in the road; to the right (north) is a tin-roofed **cemetery**; to the left (west), on the way to 'Thaungpye Mound', is the better (but bumpier) way back to the museum. After half a mile you'll pass by the old **city gate** along the overgrown trail and then, another mile further, through a booming farming village of thatch huts, with piles of radishes and other produce. Towards the north end of the village is the **East Zegu Paya**, a small four-sided temple with overgrown walls and (usually) locked doors. It's off the main road, but worth visiting for the walk past fields and farmers.

GETTING THERE & AWAY
The turn-off here is a couple of miles east of Payagyi Paya (p199). A return blue taxi should cost about K5000 or K6000. No direct pick-up connects the centre with the site. You can bike to the site, but not around it.

Shwedaung
ရွှေတောင်
This small town about 9 miles south of Pyay, via the road to Yangon, contains the famous **Shwemyetman Paya** (Paya of the Golden

Spectacles), a reference to the large, white-faced sitting buddha inside the main shrine. The buddha wears a gargantuan set of eyeglasses with gold-plated rims. Coming south from Pyay, the turn-off for Shwemyetman is located on the right-hand side of the road; a small green-and-white sign in English reads 'Shwemyethman Buddha Image – 1 Furlong'.

Spectacles were first added to the image during the Konbaung era, when a nobleman offered them to the temple in an attempt to stimulate local faith through curiosity. Word soon spread that the bespectacled buddha had the power to cure all ills, especially afflictions linked to the eyes. The first pair of spectacles was stolen at an early stage, and a second pair was made and enshrined inside the image to protect it from thieves.

An English officer stationed in Pyay during the colonial era had a third pair fitted over the buddha's eyes after his wife suffered from eye trouble and the abbot suggested such a donation. Naturally, as the story goes, she was cured. (This pair is now in a small shrine to the right of the image.)

One block south of the pagoda is a grand ol' 1925 **English home**. Another '20s beaut is two blocks south and two blocks east.

Another famous pagoda in town, south of Shwemyetman, is the **Shwenattaung Paya** (Golden Spirit Mountain), which reportedly dates back to the Thayekhittaya era. A large *paya pwe* (pagoda festival) is held here each year on the full moon of Tabaung (February/March).

To get here, you can hop on a pick-up headed towards Yangon, which leave frequently from the Pyay bus station and pass by the Aung San statue before hitting the highway.

Akauk Taung
အကောက်တောင်
Carved into cliffs overlooking the Ayeyarwady, about 19 miles downstream from Pyay, are dozens of buddha images at Akauk Taung (Tax Mountain). The mountain is named for the crafty toll-takers from the mid-19th century, who spent the hours between taxing boats by carving reclining and meditating buddhas in the steep cliffside.

To get there, you'll need to taxi across the Ayeyarwady to Htongo village, about 90 minutes by road from Pyay, then hire a boat (about K2500) for the 45-minute look. To do so, you must bring a copy of your passport or visa to show the *strict* immigration officers.

For some visitors, it's too much travel for minimal payoff. A return taxi to Htongo from Pyay (sometimes with Shwedaung thrown in) is about $20.

MAGWE

ပခွေး

☎ 063

Rather rough at the edges, with dilapidated buildings running along a confusing web of leafy streets and limited services, Magwe sees few visitors. About 155 miles north of Pyay and 93 miles south of Bagan, its locale on the Ayeyarwady River is nice enough, as is the remarkable 1.8-mile **Magwe Bridge**, which opened in 2002. If you're headed from, say, Bagan to Pyay there's no reason to blaze through without stopping – and if you bus south, you have time for the 'sights' before catching a Yangon- or Pyay-bound bus at 4.30pm.

Famously, the capital of Magwe Division sat out of the 1988 prodemocracy marches.

Sights

Magwe's chief pagoda, the 1929 **Mya Tha Lun Paya**, a mile north of the bridge, features a gilded stupa and occupies a hilltop site with great river views.

Just across the river, about the same distance north of the bridge, is Minbu and the fun **Nga Ka Pwe Taung** (Dragon Lake), a burping pool of butane gas and mud that has (over the years) built a few acres of lunar-like terrain with bubbling pools atop four odd mounds. The sludge isn't hot; if your toes slip in, wash them off below at a small pagoda. The largest mound is named Thu Sei Ta and the second-largest Nanda, for the mythical Dragon King's daughter and son, respectively. It's about a 30-minute ride here from the centre.

Sleeping & Eating

Rolex Guest House (☎ 23536; cnr Mya Than Lun Rd & Ayeyarwady Bridge; s/d $5/10; ❄) This basic guest-house, on the roundabout facing the bridge entry, seemed a bit 'dodgy' to us at last pass. It has simple concrete-floor rooms with cold-water bathrooms attached.

Sein San Hotel (☎ 23499; 234 17th St; s/d $20/35; ❄) Laughably overpriced but the best bet in Magwe. The Sein San has clean vinyl-floor rooms with generator-run air-con. It's on a quiet backstreet, a bit far from the centre by foot. It also has a guesthouse (single/double $10/15) a block away.

Monalizar 2 (dishes from K1500; ☉ 7am-10pm) On the river, just south of the bridge, this Chinese and Myanmar restaurant (and lively beer station) is clearly Magwe's hot spot. As the sun dips across the river, locals (mostly guys) hit the jars of beer as a crew of 15 start up the 7pm music/dance show.

Getting There & Around

Magwe's highway bus station is about 1.5 miles east of the central market. A minibus connects Magwe with Nyaung U (K2500, five to six hours), leaving at 6am from Nyaung U, or at 4.30am, 6am or 7.30am from Magwe. A 9am bus leaves for Pyay (K4000, five or six hours), a couple leave at 4.30pm for Yangon (K7500, 11 or 12 hours), which also stop in Pyay, and a 7pm bus goes to Mandalay (K6000, 12 or 13 hours).

IWT ferries between Pyay and Mandalay stop in Magwe. The **IWT office** (☎ 21503) is one block towards the river from the market's north side.

Motorised trishaws – with room for you and a few mates – tout their services at the bus station. A ride from the station to Nga Ka Pwe Taung and a stop at Monalizar 2 runs about K7000.

Temples of Bagan

Myanmar's greatest architectural site has as many red-brick temples on a plain the size of Manhattan island as Europe has medieval cathedrals. The kings of Bagan (Pagan), who introduced central Myanmar to Theravada Buddhism, were fond of making statements. Their building frenzy of over 4400 temples lasted only 230 years, fading before Mongols poured over the plains in 1287.

Today, temples like Ananda Pahto are stand-out highlights that no-one misses, while lesser-visited ones hide colourful murals and hidden stairways that lead to temple tops and wondrous views of the temple-spiked scene. If the vendor hassle at some of the more popular sites starts to wear on you, get a bike, a hat, some water and a torch, and take off for lesser-seen ones. Like travel anywhere, Bagan is what you make of it.

This section gives some background to Bagan's birth, and information on some of the highlights. For details of information, additional sights, accommodation, eating and transport options, see p176. Sites discussed in this chapter are shown on the map on p204.

Bagan's big, but no-one is sure how big. By the end of the 1200s, there were supposedly 4446 temples. Surveys in 1901 identified only 2157 still standing, yet a 1978 count found 2230, not including 1800 more brick mounds.

HISTORY

The extraordinary religious fervour that resulted in this unique collection of buildings lasted two and a half centuries. Although human habitation at Bagan dates back almost to the beginning of the Christian era, Bagan only entered its golden period with the conquest of Thaton in AD 1057. Bagan was already in decline by 1287 when it was overrun by the Mongols of Kublai Khan.

Over the years, neglect, looting, erosion, bat dung and, in particular, a massive 1975 earthquake have done their part to undermine a bit of the former majesty of Bagan. What's seen now are only religious structures, as none of the regular folk buildings – homes, markets, schools – remain. Many restoration projects, including several by Unesco, have rebuilt damaged temples from the 1975 earthquake.

King Anawrahta may have built the most Buddhist temples here, but monk Shin Arahan is more revered. He's responsible for converting Anawrahta to Buddhism.

ONE DAY TOUR

You can easily spend four or five days in Bagan (Pagan), leaving much unexplored. Many visitors stay just two days. If you only have one (and what a pity), go by horse cart or bicycle and try to hit the following sites.

Locals don't ride through the old city walls without getting a blessing from the nat (spirits) at **Tharabar Gate** (p209), a good place to start. Afterward, head south to Bagan's most popular temple, **Ananda Pahto** (p210), then head west to **Thatbyinnyu Pahto** (p208) and climb up the old city wall.

Just west is where King Anawrahta stored all the non-Buddhist images at **Nathlaung Kyaung** (p208). Back on the main road, pedal towards Tharabar Gate and detour on the gravel road for a river view from **Bupaya** (p210).

It makes sense to lunch while you're in this area (see p185 for eating options). Then head a mile south to visit lacquerware shops in **Myinkaba** (p186) and climb up the hidden stairs in modern **Manuha Paya** (p215) and see the bas-relief figures in **Nan Paya** (p215).

Bike north, then right on Anawrahta Rd for the turn-off (right again) to the 'bad luck temple' **Dhammayangyi Pahto** (p213), then take the paths east to the gorgeous **Sulamani Pahto** (p213) and escape the crowds at its neighbouring 'mini-me' version, **Thabeik Hmauk** (p214).

Then pick your sunset spot – **Shwesandaw Paya** (p213) is near Old Bagan, **Buledi** (p212) is northeast via crooked paths, or the **Pyathada Paya** (the more adventurous option, p214) is south on goat-herd trails.

TEMPLES OF BAGAN

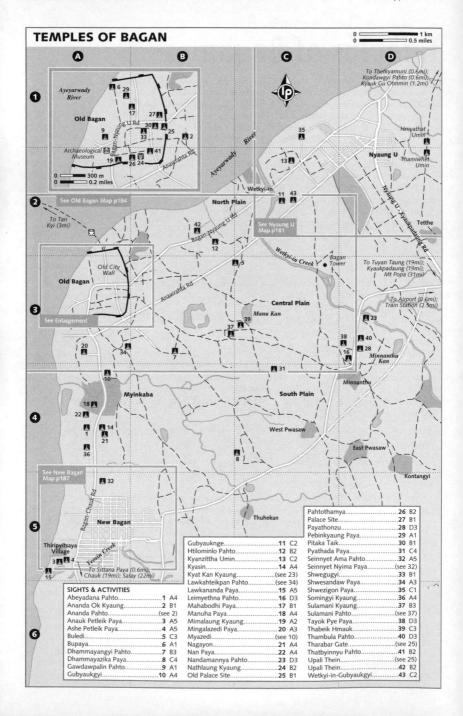

0 — 1 km
0 — 0.5 miles

A **B** **C** **D**

1
Ayeyarwady River
Old Bagan
6 29
17
27
30
25
9
33
2
Archaeological Museum
41
19
26 24
Anawrahta Rd
0 — 300 m
0 — 0.2 miles

To Thetkyamuni (0.6mi);
Kondawgyi Pahto (0.6mi);
Kyauk Gu Ohnmin (1.2mi)

Hmyathat Umin

Nyaung U

Thamiwhet Umin

35

13

Ayeyarwady River

Wetkyi-in

Tetthe

2
See Old Bagan Map p184

To Tan Kyi (3mi)

North Plain

11 43

See Nyaung U Map p181

42

12

Bagan-Nyaung U Rd

Wetkyi-in Creek

Bagan Tower

To Tuyan Taung (19mi);
Kyaukpadaung (19mi);
Mt Popa (31mi)

3
Old City Wall

Old Bagan

See Enlargement

5

Anawrahta Rd

Central Plain

Manu Kan

37 39

38
16
28

40

23

To Airport (0.6mi);
Train Station (2.5mi)

Minnanthu Kan

20

34

7

31

Minnanthu

4
10

Myinkaba

18

22

14
1 21

36

South Plain

West Pwasaw

8

East Pwasaw

Kontangyi

5
See New Bagan Map p187

32

Bagan-Chauk Rd

New Bagan

Thuhekan

6
Thiripyitsaya Village

3 4

15

Yeoin Creek

To Sittana Paya (0.6mi);
Chauk (19mi); Salay (22mi)

Bagan: the Prequel

Originally, this bend in the Ayeyarwady (Irrawaddy) River was occupied by a stable and thriving Pyu city-state. Excavations along the ruined city walls indicate that by 850 the city had reached complex proportions. The name Bagan may in fact derive from Pyugan, a name first written down by the Annamese of present-day Vietnam in the mid-11th century as Pukam. It became 'Bagan' by the 19th century, well after its glory days were past.

Glory Days

Bagan's rise coincided with the region's transition from Hindu and Mahayana Buddhist beliefs to the Theravada Buddhist beliefs that have since been characteristic of Myanmar. The main players were the monk Shin Arahan who came (sent by Manuha, the Mon king of Thaton; more on him in a bit) to convert Bamar King Anawrahta. To call his quest a success would be a landmark understatement. Inspired by his new faith, Anawrahta ordered Manuha to give him a number of sacred Buddhist texts and relics. When Manuha naturally refused, Anawrahta marched his army south and took everything worth carrying back to Bagan, including 32 sets of the Tripitaka (the classic Buddhist scriptures), the city's monks and scholars and, for good measure, King Manuha himself.

> Marco Polo described the towers of Bagan in his famous 1298 chronicle as being 'covered with gold a good finger in thickness…one of the finest sights in the world'.

Now quite self-assured, Anawrahta turned to architects to create something that befit Buddha. They built and built and built, and many of the greatest Bagan edifices date from their efforts, including Shwezigon Paya, considered a prototype for all later Myanmar stupas; the Pitaka Taik (Scripture Library), built to house the Pitaka (scriptures); and the elegant and distinctive Shwesandaw Paya, built immediately after the conquest of Thaton. Thus began what the Myanmar people call the 'First Burmese Empire', which became a pilgrimage point for Buddhists throughout Southeast Asia.

> Bagan scholar Paul Strachan argues in *Pagan: Art and Architecture of Old Burma* that the city was never abandoned at all.

King Anawrahta's successors, particularly Kyanzittha, Alaungsithu and Narapatisithu, continued scratching this phenomenal building itch, although the construction work must have been nonstop throughout the period of Bagan's glory.

Decline

Historians disagree on exactly what happened to cause Bagan's apparently rapid decline at the end of the 13th century. The popular Myanmar view is that millions of Mongols sent by Kublai Khan swept through the city, ransacking and looting. A more thoughtful take holds that the threat of invasion from China threw the last powerful ruler of Bagan into a panic.

BAGAN PERIODS

Most temples that you'll come across during your exploration of Bagan are divided into these three periods:

- **Early period** (c 850–1120) This period was influenced by Mon and late Pyu architecture, as seen in Pyay (Prome; p198), and is characterised by perforated windows and dimly lit interiors.

- **Middle period** (c 1100–70) Temples became bigger during this period and were better lit by broader windows, with more of an eye to vertical proportions than horizontal lines.

- **Late period** (c 1170–1300) The late period saw more intricate pyramidical spires or adorning tile work added to the buildings, with an increase of Indian influence, and (some say) a seeping in of Mahayana Buddhism influence.

After a great number of temples were torn down to build fortifications, the city was abandoned, in which case the Mongols merely took over an already deserted city.

Evidence suggests Bagan may have continued as an important religious and cultural centre into the 14th century, after which its decay can be blamed on the three-way struggle between the Shan, Mon and Bamar. Whatever happened, from the 14th to 18th centuries Bagan was considered a spooky region, riddled with bandits and *nat* (guardian spirits). The people only began moving back in some numbers after the British established a presence in the area.

It's hard to imagine Bagan as it once was because, like other Myanmar royal cities, only the major religious buildings were made of permanent materials. The kings' palaces were all constructed of wood, and even most *kyaung* (monasteries) were partly or wholly wooden. What remains is a frail shadow of Bagan at its peak.

Some locals like to suggest that the Pyu made it as far as the Americas a dozen or more centuries ago, and that 'Peru' derives from 'Pyu'.

1975 Earthquake

In 1975 Bagan was shaken by a powerful earthquake, registering 6.5 on the Richter scale. Many of the more important temples were badly damaged, but major reconstruction started almost immediately.

Since the renovation of these important religious monuments has been an ongoing project for many centuries, many were rebuilt using traditional means.

Unesco's recent restoration projects now support dozens of local artisans, and modern techniques are being employed as well. For example, Unesco engineers are reinforcing some of the monuments by inserting iron beams in the masonry in case of another earthquake.

Recent History

Myanmar authorities were so thorough in erasing all traces of the village that existed in Old Bagan that it's now hard to tell that one ever existed here.

Before the 1990 elections, the government forcibly relocated a village that had grown up in the 1970s in the middle of the walled area of 'Old Bagan'. Some claim the villagers had a week's notice for the move, others say it was longer and they put off the inevitable to the last minute. Either way there was certainly resistance to the uprooting of their homes and belongings for a new home in a peanut field, now developed as the village of New Bagan (Bagan Myothit; see p186).

BAGAN'S KINGS

There will be no test, but these are the main kings of Bagan's glory days and their major buildings. You'll hear their names from guides on occasion:

▪ Anawrahta (r 1044–77)	Shwesandaw Paya
▪ Sawlu (r 1077–84)	
▪ Kyanzittha (r 1084–1113)	Ananda Pahto, Shwezigon Paya
▪ Alaungsithu (r 1113–67)	Thatbyinnyu Pahto, Shwegugyi
▪ Narathu (r 1167–70)	Dhammayangyi Pahto
▪ Naratheinkha (r 1170–73)	
▪ Narapatisithu (r 1174–1211)	Sulamani Pahto, Dhammayazika Paya
▪ Nantaungmya (aka Htilominlo; r 1211–34)	Gawdawpalin Pahto, Mahabodhi Paya
▪ Kyaswa (r 1234–50)	
▪ Uzana (r 1250–55)	
▪ Narathihapati (r 1255–87)	Mingalazedi, Payathonzu

BAGAN VOCABULARY

A few terms used frequently around Bagan sites or features:

gu – cave temple

hti – umbrellalike decorated pinnacle atop stupa

Jataka – stories of Buddha's past lives

kyaung – monastery

oil painting – overly hawked souvenir

pahto – temple or shrine with hollow interior (some with one entrance to a windowless vault; others with four entrances and images around central cube); pronounced pah-TOE

paya – means 'holy one'; refers to pagodas, stupas, zedi or other Buddhist monuments, including statues

shwe – prefix meaning 'gold'

sikhara – Indian-style, corncoblike temple finial

stupa – zedi; solid hemispherical or cylindrical cone

thein – ordination hall

what country you come from? – standard greeting

zedi – stupa; solid hemispherical or cylindrical cone

The latest eyebrow-raising move was the construction of Aureum Palace's observation tower and upscale hotel in the east end of the central plain by Yangon entrepreneur Tay Za (p21). This broke the government's own zoning restrictions, which they overlooked again for a new palace site (p209), which was completed in 2008.

OLD BAGAN

ပုဂံမြို့ဟောင်း

The most practical part of Bagan to tour by foot (with water and a hat), this roughly counterclockwise 1-mile circuit takes in temples within the old city walls.

GAWDAWPALIN PAHTO

ဂေါ်တော်ပလ္လင်ပုထိုး

Just steps from a couple of Old Bagan hotels, on the road between Nyaung U and New Bagan, Gawdawpalin (197ft) is one of the largest and most imposing Bagan temples – though not necessarily the most inspiring, with its modernised altar and tile floors inside. Built during the reign of Narapatisithu and finished under that of Nantaungmya, it's considered the crowning achievement of the late period. Its name means 'Platform to which Homage is Paid'. The most recent homage was its heavy-duty reconstruction following terrific damage sustained in the 1975 earthquake (it stands near the quake's epicentre). The stairs to the top terrace are closed to visitors.

MIMALAUNG KYAUNG

မီးမလောင်ကျောင်း

A nice set of *chinthe* (half-lion/half-dragon mythical beasts) guards the stairway leading up this small, square monastery platform, constructed in 1174 by Narapatisithu. It's about 219yd south of Gawdawpalin, on the other side of the road. In front of the monastery is a brick-and-stucco Tripitaka library next to a large acacia tree. Atop the steps, a tiered roof (with a newer gold-capped *hti*, an umbrellalike decorated pinnacle) contains a large sitting buddha. Archaeologists discovered an intricately carved 2.5in votive tablet here that contained 78 sculpted figures.

If a temple gate or door is locked, ask for the 'keymaster'. Often they'll find you first. Many temples are attended to by keymasters (or their kids) who will open it for you. Sometimes a bit of 'tea money' is appreciated.

Probably the best way to get an overview of Bagan's scope is by balloon (p179) if there's an available space (and you can deal with the ticket price).

PAHTOTHAMYA
ပုထိုးသားများ

On the dirt road 160yd east towards the dominating Thatbyinnyu, the Pahtothamya (or Thamya Pahto) was probably built during the reign of Kyanzittha, around the turn of the 12th century, although it is popularly held to be one of five temples built by the little-known king Taunghthugyi (aka Sawrahan; r 931–64). The interior of this single-storey building is dimly lit, typical of the early type of Pyu-influenced temples, with their small, perforated stone windows. In its prominent vertical superstructure and reconstructed lotus-bud *sikhara* (corncoblike temple finial), however, the monument is clearly beginning to move forward from the early period.

Often kids with a torch will point out the super painting remnants along the interior passages, perhaps the earliest surviving murals in Bagan. Steps lead up to a roomy viewing platform.

NATHLAUNG KYAUNG
နတ်လှောင်ကျောင်း

Between Pahtothamya and Thatbyinnyu, this stubby temple has a fascinating history. Named 'Shrine Confining *Nat*', it's where King Anawrahta stored non-Buddhist images, particularly ones for local *nat*, as he tried to enforce Buddhism. The king himself described the temple as 'where the *nat* are kept prisoner'. It's actually the only Hindu temple remaining in Bagan. Severely damaged in the 1975 earthquake, only the temple's main hall and superstructure (with seven original Gupta-style reliefs) still stand.

A sign dates it to the early 11th century. Some say it was built in 931 by Taunghthugyi; if true, this was about a century before the southern school of Buddhism came to Bagan. The temple is dedicated to the Hindu god Vishnu.

The central square of brick supports the dome and crumbled *sikhara*, and once contained freestanding figures of Vishnu, as well as Vishnu reliefs on each of the four sides. The statues were stolen by a German oil engineer in the 1890s, but the badly damaged brick-and-stucco reliefs can still be seen.

THATBYINNYU PAHTO
သဗ္ဗညုပုထိုး

Named for 'omniscience', Bagan's highest temple (about 160yd east of Nathlaung and 220yd south of Shwegugyi) is built of two white-coloured boxy storeys, each with three diminishing terraces rimmed with spires and leading to a gold-tipped *sikhara*, 207ft up. Its monumental size and verticality make it a classic example of Bagan's middle period – and neatly provide a chronological link between early-period Ananda and late-period Gawdawpalin, both nearby. Built in 1144 by Alaungsithu, its terraces are encircled by indentations for 539 Jataka. Plaques were never added, leading some scholars to surmise that the monument was never consecrated.

TOP FIVE SITES

In terms of most-impressive structures, these stand out:
Ananda Pahto (p210)
Dhammayangyi Pahto (p213)
Pyathada Paya (p214)
Sulamani Pahto (p213)
Thatbyinnyu Pahto (above)

During the 1890s two enterprising Germans removed plaques, statues and murals from Bagan. You can see many of these at the Berlin Völkerkunde Museum or the Hamburg Ethnographical Museum.

Anawrahta tried to establish a 'pure' Theravada Buddhism in Bagan – dumping non-Buddhist images at Nathlaung Kyaung – but eventually gave in and placed shrines for 37 *nat* at Shwezigon Paya (p219).

The small 'tally *zedi*' just northeast of Thatbyinnyu Pahto was built using one brick for every 10,000 used in constructing the main temple.

Visitors are barred from climbing Thatbyinnyu's inner passages. There are some original murals near the west entrance.

A couple of hundred yards south you can climb up on the southeastern corner of the **old city wall**.

SHWEGUGYI

ေရွဂူကြီး

Built by Alaungsithu in 1131, this smaller but elegant *pahto* (temple or shrine), 220yd north of Thatbyinnyu, is an example of the middle period, a transition in architectural style from the dark and cloistered to the airy and light. Its name means 'Great Golden Cave' and its corncob *sikhara* is a scaled-down version of the one at Ananda (p210), while its reach marks a move towards verticality.

Inside you'll find fine stucco carvings, a teak buddha and stone slabs that retell (in Pali) its history, including that it took just seven months to build. Missing from the scripts are details of its builder's demise – Alaungsithu's son brought his sick father here in 1163 to smother him to death.

PITAKA TAIK

ပိဋကတ်တိုက်

Following the sacking of Thaton, King Anawrahta carted off some 30 elephant-loads of Buddhist scriptures in 1058 and built this library (just northeast of Shwegugyi) to house them. The square design follows the basic early Bagan *gu* (cave temple) plan, perfect for the preservation of light-sensitive palm-leaf scriptures. The old library is notable for the perforated stone windows, each carved from single stone slabs, and the plaster carvings on the roof, which are in imitation of Myanmar woodcarvings.

PALACE SITE

နန်းတော်ရာ

Word on the street: Tay Za built this sprawling reconstruction of the kings' old palace, just in from the Tharabar Gate, in return for the rights to build the controversial tower and overpriced Aureum Palace near Nyaung U (p196). It's meant to be a faithful replica, with red pavilion roofs akin to the re-creation of Mandalay Palace – never mind that the actual site is on the other side of the Bagan–Nyaung U Rd.

At research time it wasn't yet open; when it is, travellers will have to shell out a high $5 admission fee. Not recommended.

THARABAR GATE

သရပါတံခါး

Do stop on the east side of this former entrance of the original palace site. On either side of the arched gateway are two niches, not home to buddha images but to *nat* who guard the gate and who are treated with profound respect by locals. To the left is Lady Golden Face, and to the right her brother Lord Handsome.

Locals don't venture through the gate by motorbike, car or horse cart without first paying a one-time offering to the *nat* (usually a bunch of bananas and a couple of coconuts) to ensure protection against traffic accidents. Don't worry: bicycles are OK, blessing-free.

The gate is the best-preserved remains of the 9th-century wall, and the only gate still standing. Traces of old stucco can still be seen on the gateway.

A number of restaurants are past the former moat, about 220yd east.

Per Pali inscriptions found here, Bagan kings apparently flirted with a couple of different city names during its heyday: Arimaddanapura (City of the Enemy Crusher) and the less dramatic Tambadipa (Copper Land).

One local with a new motorbike neglected to make an offering to the *nat* at Tharabar Gate. 'Some people believe those old traditions, I never did! She had an accident a mile after her first time through. 'The next day I gave an offering and haven't had an accident since.'

Like most *nat*, Tharabar Gate's twosome had a tragic history. A king married Lady Golden Face to lure her brother Lord Handsome, whom he feared, out of hiding. When the king had Handsome burned at the stake, his sister jumped in too; only her face was saved from the fire.

MAHABODHI PAYA
မဟာဗောဓိဘုရား

The Mahabodhi Paya
features an unusual
pyramidal spire.

Unlike any other Bagan temple, this monument, located on the north side of the main road 380yd west of the gate, is modelled after the famous Mahabodhi temple in Bodhgaya, India, which commemorates the spot where the Buddha attained enlightenment. Built during the reign of Nantaungmya in 1215, the spire is richly coated in niches enclosing seated buddha figures, rising from a square block. The stairway to the top is closed.

Inside is a modern makeover – with tile floor and carpet. The ruined buildings just north feature some original glazed painting fragments.

BUPAYA
ဘူးဘုရား

On the bank of the Ayeyarwady (reached from the Nyaung U road, about 220yd northwest of the Mahabodhi Paya), this cylindrical Pyu-style stupa, named for *bu* (gourd), is said to date back further than any Bagan temple. Locals claim it dates to the 3rd century; most likely it was erected around the same time as the city walls (around 850). What's seen now – a gold stupa above a row of crenulated terraces leading down to the water – is a complete reconstruction; the 1975 earthquake demolished the original.

Off the road to the southeast is the **Pebinkyaung Paya**, a 12th-century pagoda built in a unique Sinhalese style.

ACROSS THE AYEYARWADY

Ananda is home to
Bagan's biggest festival,
a roughly two-week
event wrapping up at
the full moon of Pyatho
(December/January); it's
a time when hundreds
and hundreds of monks
come to collect alms from
merit-seeking locals.

From the Old Bagan jetty you can hire a private boat to reach Tan Kyi village, where you can arrange a taxi ride (or hike) up to **Tan Kyi Paya**, the gold stupa atop the mountain, visible from much of Bagan. Views are terrific and unique, looking back over the river to Bagan's mighty sprawl. A ride for three or four people, including wait time, is about K15,000. You'll need three or four hours.

NORTH PLAIN

The bulk of Bagan temples are out 'there' – in the vast, ruin-filled plains between Nyaung U, Old Bagan and New Bagan. This broad area runs between the Old Bagan walls and Nyaung U, and (mostly) between the two roads that connect the two. Sights are ordered (more or less) west to east.

ANANDA PAHTO
အာနန္ဒာပုထိုး

With its shimmering gold, 170ft-high, corncob-style *hti* shimmering across the plains, Ananda is one of the finest, largest, best-preserved and most revered of all Bagan souvenir stands, ur, we mean temples. Hawkers selling books and postcards and oil paintings surely know you'll be making it to this lovely terraced temple, but that shouldn't dissuade you from going.

It's roughly 490yd east of Thatbyinnyu, 550yd north of Shwesandaw and 1090yd northwest of Dhammayangyi Pahto. Most visitors access it from the northern side.

Like many paya around
Bagan, the Ananda Pahto
took a huge hit from the
1975 earthquake, but has
been totally restored.

Thought to have been built between 1090 and 1105 by King Kyanzittha, this perfectly proportioned temple heralds the stylistic end of the early Bagan period and the beginning of the middle period. In 1990, on its 900th anniversary, the temple spires were gilded. The remainder of the temple exterior is whitewashed from time to time.

The central square measures 58yd along each side. Upper floors are closed to visitors. The entranceways make the structure a perfect Greek cross; each

---

TOP FIVE MURALS

Much of Bagan is also famous for the fabulous murals that are found on the walls inside. These are our favourites.

- **Upali Thein** (below) Brightly painted frescoes from the late 17th or early 18th century.
- **Nandamannya Pahto** (p219) Vaguely Chinese- or Tibetan-looking murals.
- **Payathonzu** (p218) Similar to the murals at Nandamannya.
- **Ananda Ok Kyaung** (below) Paintings depict everyday scenes from the Bagan period.
- **Abeyadana Pahto** (p216) Has figures of Bodhisattvas and Hindu deities.

---

entrance is crowned with a stupa finial. The base and the terraces are decorated with 554 glazed tiles showing Jataka scenes, thought to be derived from Mon texts. Look back as you enter to see the huge carved teak doors that separate interior halls from cross passages on all four sides.

Facing outward from the centre of the cube are four 31ft standing buddha statues. Only the Bagan-style images facing north and south are original; both display the *dhammachakka mudra* (a hand position symbolising the Buddha teaching his first sermon). The other two images are replacements for figures destroyed by fire in the 1600s. All four have bodies of solid teak, though guides may claim the southern image is made of a bronze alloy. Guides like to point out that if you stand by the donation box in front of the original southern buddha, his face looks sad, while from a distance he tends to look mirthful.

The western and eastern standing buddha images are done in the later Konbaung, or Mandalay, style. If looked at from the right angle, the two lions at the eastern side resemble an ogre. A small, nutlike sphere held between the thumb and middle finger of the east-facing image is said to resemble a herbal pill, and may represent the buddha offering *dhamma* (Buddhist teachings) as a cure for suffering. Both arms hang at the image's sides with hands outstretched, a *mudra* (hand position) unknown to traditional Buddhist sculpture outside this temple.

The west-facing buddha features the *abhaya mudra* (the hands outstretched, in the gesture of no fear). At its feet sit two life-sized lacquer statues, said to represent King Kyanzittha and Shin Arahan, the Mon monk who initiated Anawrahta into Theravada Buddhism. Inside the western portico are two symbols on pedestals of the Buddha's footprints.

Don't leave without taking a brief walk around the outside of the temple, where you can see many glazed tiles and lovely views of the spires and terraced roofs (often away from vendor hassle too).

> Much of the mural work at Bagan is thought to be similar to how the interiors of Buddhist temples in northeastern India must have appeared before their destruction at the hands of Muslim invaders.

ANANDA OK KYAUNG
အာနန္ဒာအုတ်ကျောင်း

Just west of Ananda's northern entry, this small *vihara* (sanctuary or chapel) features some detailed 18th-century murals bursting with bright red and green, showing details of everyday life from the Bagan period. In the southeast corner, you can see Portuguese figures engaged in trade. Built in 1137, the temple's name means 'Ananda Brick Monastery'.

UPALI THEIN
ဥပါလိသိမ်

Just north of the Bagan–Nyaung U Rd, almost midway to Nyaung U, this squat mid-13th century ordination hall houses some brightly painted frescoes depicting big scenes on the walls and ceilings from the late 17th or early 18th century. Sadly many pieces crumbled in the 1975 earthquake. The building, named for a well-known monk from the 13th century, is often locked to protect the art. The roof battlements imitate Myanmar wooden architecture, and a small centre spire rises from the rooftop. It's often locked, but you can see in (a bit) from the three gated doorways if the 'keymaster' isn't around.

HTILOMINLO PAHTO

ထီးလို့မင်းလို့ပုထိုး

Across the road from Upali Thein, this 150ft-high temple (built in 1218) marks the spot where King Nantaungmya was chosen (by a leaning umbrella – that timeless decider), amongst five brothers, to be the crown prince. It's more impressive from the outside, with its terraced design, which is similar to Sulamani Pahto (opposite). Have a walk around the 140-sq-ft base to take in the fragments of the original fine plaster carvings, glazed sandstone decorations and nicely carved reliefs on the doorways. Inside are four buddhas on the lower and upper floors, though the stairways are closed. Traces of old murals are also still visible. Unfortunately it's vendor central.

BULEDI

ဘူးလယ်သီး

Great for its views, this steep-stepped, pyramid-style stupa looks ho-hum from afar, but the narrow terrace has become something of an alternative sunset spot. It's about 660yd south of the Htilominlo, across Anawrahta Rd. It's also known as 'Temple 394' (not correctly labelled on some maps).

If an oil-painting guy is getting to you, try the miniature version, **Temple 405**, with several glazed tiles visible, just east.

GUBYAUKNGE

ဂူပြောက်ငယ်

Off Anawrahta Rd, almost a mile east of Htilominlo, this early Bagan-period temple has some excellent stucco carvings on the outside walls (particularly on the north side) and some original paintings visible inside.

WETKYI-IN-GUBYAUKGYI

ဝက်ကြီးအင်းဂူပြောက်ကြီး

Just west of Nyaung U and about 100yd or so east of Gubyauknge, this off-the-main-circuit, detailed, 13th-century temple has an Indian-style spire, like the Mahabodhi Paya in Old Bagan. It is interesting for the fine frescoes of scenes from the Jataka but, unfortunately, in 1899 a German collector came by and surreptitiously removed many of the panels on which the frescoes were painted. Those that remain in the entry are in great shape. Steps inside lead to four buddha images and you can see Hindu figures engraved on the spire.

CENTRAL PLAIN

Extending from the edge of Old Bagan, this vast and lovely plain (roughly south of Anawrahta Rd between New Bagan and Nyaung U) is home to a few must-sees everyone gets to (eg Shwesandaw Paya, Dhammayangyi Pahto) and many pockets of temples that few ever see. It's great turf to follow your own whims, as you'll find goat herds and a bit of village life out here – but there is nothing in the way of restaurants or lunch options. Some temples are locked but a 'keymaster' should be in the area.

Bagan or Pagan? The British began calling the site Pagan until the previous name was restored by the Myanmar government a decade ago.

The Shwesandaw Paya offers the highest accessible points within the Bagan Archaeological Zone.

This list of well-worthy sites runs west to east (towards the clearly visible Bagan Tower construction site, near Nyaung U).

SHWESANDAW PAYA

ရွှေဆံတော်ဘုရား:

Bagan's most famous 'sunset pagoda', the Shwesandaw is the graceful white pyramid-style pagoda with steps leading past five terraces to the circular stupa top, with good 360-degree views. It's located roughly midway between Thatbyinnyu and Dhammayangyi. Its top terrace is roomy – and needs the space, considering the numbers of camera-toting travellers coming by taxi or bus before sunset. If you go during the day, you'll likely be alone.

Following his conquest of Thaton in 1057, King Anawrahta built this pagoda at the centre of his newly empowered kingdom. The terraces once bore terracotta plaques showing scenes from the Jataka but traces of these, and of other sculptures, were covered by rather heavy-handed renovations. The now-gilded *zedi* (stupa) bell rises from two octagonal bases, which top the five square terraces. This was the first Bagan monument to feature stairways leading from the square terraces to the round base of the stupa. This stupa supposedly enshrines a Buddha hair relic, brought back from Thaton.

The *hti*, which was toppled by the earthquake, can still be seen lying on the south side of the paya compound. A new one was fitted soon after the quake.

About 165yd north stands **Lawkahteikpan Pahto** – a small but interesting middle-period *gu* containing excellent frescoes and inscriptions in both Burmese and Mon.

The *nat* like tourists – or at least did during the 1975 earthquake. Explained one Nyaung U resident: 'The earthquake knocked the top off Shwesandaw Paya at 6.30pm in July. Normally people are up there for sunset, but no-one was there that day. Because of the *nat*!'

DHAMMAYANGYI PAHTO

ဓမ္မရံကြီးပုထိုး:

Visible from all parts of Bagan, this massive, walled, 12th-century temple (about 550yd east of Shwesandaw) is known locally as a 'bad luck temple'. Some believe this is because of the ruthless king Narathu who mandated that the mortarless brickwork fit together so tightly that even a pin couldn't pass between any two bricks. After he died – by assassination in 1170 – the inner encircling ambulatory was filled with brick rubble – as 'payback', most say. (Others quietly argue the temple dates from the earlier reign of Alaungsithu, which would refute all this fun legend stuff.)

The plan here is similar to Ananda, with projecting porticoes and receding terraces, though its *sikhara* is reduced to a stub nowadays. Walking around the outer ambulatory, under ceilings so high you can only hear the squeaks of bats circling in the dark, you can see some intact stucco reliefs and paintings, suggesting the work had been completed. The mystery goes on.

Three out of the four buddha sanctums were also filled with bricks. The remaining western shrine features two original side-by-side images of Gautama and Maitreya, the historical and future buddhas (it's the only Bagan site with two side-by-side buddhas). Perhaps someday, when Myanmar's archaeological department, or Unesco or some other party, clears out all the brick rubble, one of the great architectural mysteries of Bagan will be solved.

The top terraces are closed to visitors.

The west entrance of Dhammayangyi Pahto (aka the 'bad luck temple') is considered particularly evil; just inside, note the stones with arm-sized grooves. Apparently workers not able to lay brick tight enough had an arm chopped off here.

SULAMANI PAHTO

စူဠာမဏိပုထိုး:

About half a mile east of Dhammayangyi, this broad two-storey temple is one of Bagan's most attractive, with lush grounds (and ample vendors) behind the surrounding walls. It's a prime example of later, more sophisticated temple styles, with better internal lighting.

Entered from five doorways, this temple, known as the Crowning Jewel, was constructed around 1181 by Narapatisithu. Combining the early period's horizontal planes with the vertical lines of the middle period, the receding terraces create a pyramid effect. The brickwork throughout is considered some of the best in Bagan. The gilded *sikhara* is a reconstruction; the original was destroyed in the 1975 earthquake. The interior face of the wall was once lined with 100 monastic cells, a feature unique among Bagan's ancient monasteries.

There's much to see inside. Carved stucco on mouldings, pediments and pilasters represents some of Bagan's finest ornamental work and is in fairly good condition. Glazed plaques around the base and terraces are also still visible, as are many big and small murals.

Buddha images face the four directions from the ground floor; the image at the main eastern entrance sits in a recess built into the wall. The interior passage around the base is painted with quite big frescoes from the Konbaung period, and there are traces of earlier frescoes. The stairways to the top are closed.

> Thabeik Hmauk means 'Boycott Temple', as it was made in response to the similarly designed Sulamani, which was ordered by the brutal king Narapatisithu.

THABEIK HMAUK
သပိတ်မှောက်

Facing Sulamani from 150yd east, and well worth visiting, this *sikhara*-topped temple looks like a miniature version of its more famous neighbour but sees far fewer visitors (or vendors). Much of its interior was damaged by the 1975 earthquake, but there are multiple stairways up to a wrap-around meditation chamber with little light (and a few bats). There are two outside terraces, reached by narrow stairs, with superb views.

PYATHADA PAYA
ပြဿဒါးဘုရား

About half a mile southeast of Sulamani, reached by dirt roads that sometimes get obscured in goat fields, this huge, impressive pagoda is a superb sunset-viewing spot, with a giant open terrace (Bagan's largest) atop the steps, and another small deck further up. Many days, visitors have it to themselves; on others a lone group may be here. Note how the top stupa isn't centred on the top platform.

> The Mingalazedi Paya represents the final flowering of Bagan's architectural outburst.

MYINKABA AREA
မြင်းကပါ

The sites north and south of Myinkaba village are all just off the main road and are easy to access. These are listed in order from north to south.

MINGALAZEDI PAYA
မင်္ဂလာစေတီ

Close to the riverbank, towards Myinkaba from the Thiripyitsaya Sakura Hotel (Map p184), Mingalazedi Paya (Blessing Stupa) is noted also for its enormous bell-like dome and for the beautiful glazed Jataka tiles around each terrace. Although many of the 1061 original tiles have been damaged or stolen, there are still 561 left. The smaller square building in the *zedi* grounds is one of the few Tripitaka libraries made of brick.

> King Narathihapati shrugged off a local prophecy that when the Mingalazedi Paya, the last of the large late-period monuments, was finished, Bagan would fall. Ten years after its completion, in 1274, Mongols invaded – and Bagan's prominence fell.

Mingalazedi used to be a great sunrise spot, but its steps are now closed.

GUBYAUKGYI
ဂူပြောက်ကြီး

Situated just to the left of the road as you enter Myinkaba, Gubyaukgyi (Great Painted Cave Temple) sees a lot of visitors, drawn by its well-

---

BEST SUNSET & SUNRISE TEMPLES

Each dusk at Bagan is marked with a frantic sunset chase, with scurrying tourists carrying cameras up pagoda stairways to watch the Bagan sprawl turn all shades of tangerine, lavender and rust. Many leave once the sun dips behind the mountains, though colours only start their show at that point. By all means do witness the scene, from different spots, short and tall. Some temples teem with tourists, while hundreds of lesser-known ones (including dozens and dozens of good choices not in this section) stand empty.

Yeah, but what's 'the best' place to witness sunsets and sunrises? OK, **Shwesandaw Paya** (p213) is the long-standing favourite at dusk. Near Bagan's belly, **Buledi** (p212) is a newcomer 'alternative' favourite, while another wonderful spot, way out in the central plain, **Pyathada Paya** (opposite), has a sprawling viewing deck, which is sometimes empty.

---

preserved, richly coloured paintings inside. These are thought to date from the temple's original construction in 1113, when Kyanzittha's son Rajakumar built it following his father's death. In Indian style, the monument consists of a large vestibule attached to a smaller antechamber. The fine stuccowork on its exterior walls is in particularly good condition.

Perforated, Pyu-style windows mean you'll need a powerful torch to see the ceiling paintings clearly. If it's locked during off-season, ask in the village for the keymaster.

Next to the monument stands the gilded Myazedi (Emerald Stupa). A four-sided pillar in a cage between the two monuments bears an inscription consecrating Gubyaukgyi and written in four languages – Pyu, Mon, Old Burmese and Pali. Its linguistic and historical significance is great, since it establishes the Pyu as an important cultural influence in early Bagan and relates the chronology of the Bagan kings.

MANUHA PAYA
မနူဟာဘုရား

In Myinkaba village, about a third of a mile south of Gubyaukgyi, stands this active (and rather modern-looking) pagoda, named after the Mon king from Thaton, who was held captive here by King Anawrahta.

In the front of the building are three seated buddhas; in the back is a huge reclining buddha. All seem too large for their enclosures – supposedly representing the stress and discomfort the king had to endure. However, these features are not unique in Bagan.

It is said that only the reclining buddha, in the act of entering *parinibbana* (final passing away), has a smile on its face, showing that for Manuha, only death was a release from his suffering. But if you climb to the top of this paya via the stairs in the back (ask for keys if it's locked), you can see the face of the sitting buddha through a window – from up here you'll realise that the gigantic face, so grim from below, has an equally gigantic smile.

Devotees of Manuha Paya celebrate a large *paya pwe* on the full moon of Tabaung (February/March).

NAN PAYA
နန်းဘုရား

Just south of the Manuha Paya by dirt road, this shrine is said to have been used as Manuha's prison, although there is little evidence supporting the legend. In this story the shrine was originally Hindu, and captors thought using it as a prison would be easier than converting it to a Buddhist temple. It's worth visiting for its interior masonry work – sandstone block

Legend says that Manuha, the captured Mon king, built the Bagan temple that bears his name in 1059, and that the design represents his displeasure with captivity. (At least he wasn't executed.)

Aung San Suu Kyi described the Bagan rulers' respect for the captive king Manuha as 'one of the most admirable parts of Burmese history...unstinting respect for a noble enemy'.

facings over a brick core, certainly some of Bagan's finest detailed sculpture. Perforated stone windows are typical of earlier Bagan architecture – in fact it was probably Bagan's first *gu*-style shrine.

In the central sanctuary the four stone pillars have finely carved sandstone bas-relief figures of three-faced Brahma. The creator deity is holding lotus flowers, thought to be offerings to a freestanding buddha image once situated in the shrine's centre, a theory that dispels the idea that this was ever a Hindu shrine. The sides of the pillars feature ogrelike *kala-ate* heads with open mouths streaming with flowers. Legend goes that Shiva employed such creatures to protect temples, but they proved too ferocious so Shiva tricked them into eating their bodies, then fed them flowers to keep their minds off snacking on worshippers. In the centre of the four pillars is an altar, on which once stood a standing buddha or (some locals believe) a Hindu god.

Ask at Manuha if the temple is locked.

ABEYADANA PAHTO
အပယ်ရတနာပုထိုး

About 440yd south of the Manuha, this 11th-century temple with a Sinhalese-style stupa was supposedly built by Kyanzittha's Bengali wife Abeyadana, who waited for him here as he hid for his life from his predecessor King Sawlu. It's famed for its original frescoes, which were cleaned in recent years by Unesco staff. With a torch, you can make out many figures that Abeyadana, believed to be a Mahayanist, would likely have asked for: Bodhisattvas such as Avalokitesvara, and Hindu deities Brahma, Vishnu, Shiva and Indra.

The inner shrine contains a large, brick, seated buddha (partly restored); surrounding walls are lined with niches, most now empty. Inside the front wall are many Jataka scenes.

Ask at the caretaker's house to the south if the temple is locked.

Some visitors enjoy the sunset at the often-overlooked **Kyasin** across the road.

NAGAYON
နဂါးရုံ

Slightly south of Abeyadana and across the road, this elegant and well-preserved temple was built by Kyanzittha. The main buddha image is twice life size and shelters under the hood of a huge *naga* (dragon serpent). This reflects the legend that in 1192 Kyanzittha built the temple on the spot where he was sheltered while fleeing from his angry brother and predecessor Sawlu – an activity he had to indulge in on more than one occasion.

Paintings also decorate the corridor walls. The central shrine has two smaller standing buddhas as well as the large one. The temple itself – with corncob *sikhara,* which some believe to be the Ananda prototype – can be climbed via tight stairs.

SOMINGYI KYAUNG
စိုးမင်းကြီးကျောင်း

Named after the woman who supposedly sponsored its construction, this typical late-Bagan brick monastery (about 220yd southwest of Nagayon) is thought to have been built in 1204. A *zedi* to the north and *gu* to the south are also ascribed to Somingyi. Many brick monasteries in Bagan were single-block structures; Somingyi is unique in that it has monastic cells clustered around a courtyard.

NEW BAGAN AREA

ပုဂံမြို့သစ်

Sights are a little scarcer heading south of New Bagan towards the outskirts of the Bagan area.

SEINNYET NYIMA PAYA & SEINNYET AMA PAHTO

စိမ်းညှက်ညီမ နှင့် & စိမ်းညှက်အမပုထိုး

This stupa and shrine stand side by side (about 270yd north of New Bagan) and are traditionally ascribed to Queen Seinnyet in the 11th century, although the architecture clearly points to a period two centuries later. The *zedi* rests on three terraces and is topped by a beautiful stylised umbrella.

LAWKANANDA PAYA

လောကနန္ဒာဘုရား

At the height of Bagan's power, boats from the Mon region, Rakhaing (Arakan) and even Sri Lanka would anchor by this riverside pagoda (about 270yd southeast of the New Bagan crossroads – a sign in Burmese points the way) with its distinctive elongated cylindrical dome. It was built in 1059 by Anawrahta. It is still used as an everyday place of worship and is thought to house an important Buddha tooth replica. There are lots of benches for wide-open views of the Ayeyarwady, but it's sometimes hard to enjoy hassle-free.

ASHE (EAST) & ANAUK (WEST) PETLEIK PAYA

အရှေ့ နှင့် အနောက် ပက်လိပ်ဘုရား

Just inland to the northeast from Lawkananda Paya are the excavated remains of these twin 11th-century paya. Found in 1905, the lower parts of the pagodas are ho-hum from the outside but feature hundreds of terracotta Jataka lining the vaulted corridors (particularly impressive in Anauk Petleik Paya). A keymaster usually appears to unlock the door and turn on the fluorescent lights.

SITTANA PAYA

စစ်တနာဘုရား

About half a mile further south, this large, 13th-century bell-shaped stupa is New Bagan's most impressive structure. Built by Htilominlo, and showing some Hindu influences, it's set on four square terraces, each fronted by a standing buddha image in brick and stucco. A rather rickety stairway leads up the stupa's southern side to the terraces, where you can circle the structure. At the southwestern corner is a chamber leading into an inner sanctum (closed recently by the Department of Archaeology).

SOUTH PLAIN

This rural area, along Bagan's southern reaches, follows the main road between New Bagan and Nyaung U Airport, passing Pwasaw and Minnanthu villages on the way. Other than a few places, such as Payathonzu, most sights see few tourists. Many horse-cart drivers will take in the cluster of sights north of Minnanthu and go via dirt paths towards Central Plain sights, such as Sulamani Pahto (p213). Views west from some temples here rival any other in Bagan in terms of scope of the site.

The following sites are listed in order from west to east.

After Bamar King Anawrahta conquered the Mon kingdom of Thaton, he had 30,000 Mon prisoners of war brought back to Bagan.

DHAMMAYAZIKA PAYA

ဓမ္မရာဇိကဘုရား

Watch out for ghosts at Dhammayazika! Supposedly the stupa's construction began under a general who died before its completion. His likeness is said to appear in many photos of the site, including a fairly recent one of government officials.

About 2 miles east of the New Bagan crossroads, and standing north of the main road, this pentagonal *zedi* is similar to the Shwezigon (opposite) but with a more unusual design. Set in the south-central end of Bagan, it also has lovely views from its highest terrace.

Sitting in lush garden grounds with a gilded bell, the Dhammayazika dates from 1196. An outer wall has five gateways. Up top, five small temples, each containing a buddha image, encircle the terraces; some of them bear interior murals added during the Konbaung era.

It's possible, with perseverance, to cycle the thrilling dirt roads here from Dhammayangyi Pahto, a mile north.

LEIMYETHNA PAHTO

လေးမျက်နှာဘုရား

Built in 1222, this east-facing, whitewashed temple near Minnanthu village (almost 2 miles east of Dhammayazika on the north side of the road) stands on a raised platform and has interior walls decorated with well-preserved frescoes. It is topped by a gilded Indian-style spire like that on Ananda. The jarlike structures out the front were pillars of a building toppled by the 1975 earthquake.

TAYOK PYE PAYA

တရုတ်ပြေးဘုရား

Four temples (each with Buddha tooth relics) were built to mark the borders of Bagan: Shwezigon Paya, Lawkananda Paya in New Bagan, Tan Kyi (the gold stupa across the Ayeyarwady from Old Bagan) and Tuyan Taung (a hilltop stupa 20 miles east).

A couple of hundred yards north of Leimyethna by dirt road, this spired temple gets attention for the views from its upper reaches (though its top level is now closed).

PAYATHONZU

ဘုရားသုံးဆူ

Across the main road from Tayok, this complex of three interconnected shrines (the name means Three Stupas) is worth seeing for its 13th-century murals close up. It was abandoned shortly before its construction was complete – possibly due to the invasion of Kublai Khan. Each square cubicle is topped by a fat *sikhara;* a similar structure appears only at Salay (p190). The design is remarkably like Khmer Buddhist ruins in Thailand.

You enter the middle shrine. To the right (south) are scratched-up, whitewashed walls. The other two shrines (particularly the northernmost one) are home to lovely, vaguely Chinese- or Tibetan-looking mural paintings that contain Bodhisattva figures. Whether these indicate possible Mahayana or Tantric influence is a hotly debated issue among art historians. Some drawings are rather crudely touched up.

Many horse-cart tours begin by heading south then west on the New Bagan road from Nyaung U, passing the tacky Aureum Palace tower (admission $5) and stopping at sites like Payathonzu, then crossing to the Central Plain.

The three-shrine design hints at links with the Hindu Trimurti (triad) of Vishnu, Shiva and Brahma, a triumvirate also associated with Tantric Buddhism. One might just as easily say it represents the Triple Gems of Buddhism (buddha, *dhamma* and *sangha*), except that such a design is uncommon in Asian Buddhist archaeology, although it does appear in the Hindu shrines of India and Nepal.

THAMBULA PAHTO

သမ္ဘုလပုထိုး

This square temple, surrounded by crumbling walls just north of Payathonzu, is decorated with faded Jataka frescoes and was built in 1255 by Thambula, the wife of King Uzana. It's often locked, but go to the (shaded at midday) doors and peek through the gate to see into wall and ceiling murals. A mural of a boat race can be seen from the southern entrance; good ceiling murals are seen from the north side.

NANDAMANNYA PAHTO
နန္ဒာမညာ

Dating from the mid-13th century, this small, single-chambered temple has very fine frescoes and a ruined seated buddha image. It's about 220yd north of Thambula; a sign leads down a short dirt road. (It's the one to the right.)

Nandamannya earns its reputation from its mural of the 'Temptation of Mara', in which nubile young females (vainly) attempt to distract the Buddha from the meditation session that led to his enlightenment. The undressed nature of the females shocked French epigraphist Charles Duroiselle, who wrote in 1916 that they were 'so vulgarly erotic and revolting that they can neither be reproduced or described'. Times change: the topless women can be seen, without blushing, on the back left wall.

The murals' similarity with those at Payathonzu has led some art historians to suggest they were painted by the same hand.

Just behind the temple is the **Kyat Kan Kyaung**, a working underground monastery dating from the 11th century. Mats on the tunnel floors are used for meditation.

> In recent years a monk at Nandamannya Pahto died while meditating. His body was left for days, as everyone thought he was still in meditation.

NYAUNG U AREA
ညောင်ဦး

The main site in this area is the superb Shwezigon Paya.

SHWEZIGON PAYA
ရွှေစည်းခုံဘုရား

At the west end of Nyaung U, this big and beautiful *zedi* is the town's main religious site, and is most famous for its link with the 37 *nat*.

The gilded *zedi* – lit up impressively at dusk – sits on three rising terraces. Enamelled plaques in panels around the base of the *zedi* illustrate scenes from the Jataka. At the cardinal points, facing the terrace stairways, are four shrines, each of which houses a 13ft-high bronze standing buddha. Gupta-inspired and cast in 1102, these are Bagan's largest surviving bronze buddhas.

> The 12th-century original *nat* figures of the Shwezigon were spirited away by a collector and are now reportedly somewhere in Italy.

OWL KILLER IN BIG PIG VILLAGE

Bagan's heavily set on the travel circuit but customs and traditional beliefs live everywhere. While researching this book, we noticed a young man in a Pink (the singer) T-shirt, poking a pole at a tree outside a road stand at 'Big Pig Village' (Wetkyi-in), and stopped to chat.

What are you doing? There's an evil owl up there. I'm trying to get it out.

Is it alive? Not anymore. I shot it with my catapult.

Why? It made my mother sick. With its singing. If an owl doesn't make a sound, it's OK. But when they make noise, it makes people sick.

How do you know? A couple years ago one made a young girl sick nearby. I couldn't shoot it and the next day the girl died.

We stopped by the next day, and Mum was fine and the owl buried nearby. 'There were three more owls up there. They don't sing so they can stay. But if they start singing, I'll kill them too.'

A 4in circular indentation in a stone slab, before the upwards-heading eastern steps, was filled with water to allow former Myanmar monarchs to look at the reflection of the *hti* without tipping their heads backwards (which might have caused them to lose their crowns).

The most important site here is the small yellow compound called **37 Nat** (in English) on the southeast side of the site. Inside are figures of all the 37 pre-Buddhist *nat* that were officially endorsed by Bamar monarchy in a compromising gesture towards a public reluctant to give up all their beliefs for Buddhism. Ask around if the compound is locked. At one end stands an original stone figure of Thagyamin, king of the *nat* and a direct appropriation of the Hindu god Indra. This is the oldest known freestanding Thagyamin figure in Myanmar.

The site was started by Anawrahta but not completed until the reign of Kyanzittha. The latter is thought to have built his palace nearby.

A path on the north side leads down to the riverbank, where you can get some interesting views.

KYANZITTHA UMIN
ကျန်စစ်သား:ဥမင်

Although officially credited to Kyanzittha, this cave temple may actually date back to Anawrahta. Built into a cliff face 270yd southwest of Shwezigon, the long, dimly lit corridors are decorated with frescoes, some of which are thought to have been painted by Bagan's Tartar invaders during the period of the Mongol occupation after 1287. An attendant usually will greet you with a torch to lend and keys to unlock the doors. It's *very* quiet in there, and you can actually see the 700-year-old brush strokes.

NORTH OF NYAUNG U

From the Nyaung U jetty you can negotiate a fun boat trip to see three temples just off the Ayeyarwady riverbank. Half a mile north, you can find the 13th-century **Thetkyamuni**, with a few murals inside (hard to make out) and tight, dark steps leading up to a small terrace up top. On the hill nearby is the same-era **Kondawgyi Pahto**, with better preserved murals and views from the surrounding platform.

Another kilometre or so north is the 11th- and 12th-century **Kyauk Gu Ohnmin** cave temple, built in the side of a ravine. The inside tunnels lead about 55yd to blocked-off rubble. Some locals say the tunnel was intended to go, ahem, to Pindaya Cave near Inle Lake. You can climb on top of the temple from the new steps to the right.

These sights are accessible, with more difficulty, by road. A boat trip takes about two or three hours, and your driver will show you the temples. It costs about K10,000 for three or four people.

Not just a gilded blob: the Shwezigon Paya *zedi's* graceful bell shape has been the prototype for virtually all later stupas around Myanmar.

During WWII, Japanese soldiers hid out in Kyauk Gu Ohnmin.

Eastern Myanmar

Back in the days when Myanmar was only open to package tourists, Inle Lake was one of the four areas that foreign visitors were free to explore. The lake, and the rolling hills between Mandalay and the Thai border, are still an established part of the traveller circuit – hotels are plentiful, famous sights abound and flights drop in daily from all over Myanmar to the tiny airstrip at Heho. That said, it's easy to escape the crowds, particularly if you go trekking from Kalaw or Kengtung.

Travel routes in Myanmar are dictated by road conditions and the shifting government restrictions on the roads travellers are allowed to use. Most of the towns in the eastern half of Shan State are accessible via the pitted highway or the slow but picturesque railway line from Thazi to Taunggyi. Travellers are only allowed to continue to Kengtung by air – which will involve using a government-linked airline – or overland across the Thai border on a two-week entry permit.

The highlight of eastern Myanmar has to be Inle Lake – despite the crowds, speeding through a maze of marshes and stilt houses on a motorised canoe is one of the definitive Myanmar experiences – and nearby Kalaw offers some of the best trekking in the country. Because of the logistical difficulties of getting to Kengtung, the border region sees far fewer visitors, but it's worth making the effort to reach this intriguing enclave of hill-tribe culture. As well as treks to hill-tribe areas, you can soak up the uniquely Thai atmosphere of the area.

HIGHLIGHTS

- Drift around the backwaters of **Inle Lake** (p232) to ruined stupas, tribal markets and workshops run by the industrious Intha

- Sample medicinal herbs and learn the local folklore as you trek to hill-tribe villages around **Kalaw** (p224)

- Gasp at the sight of 8000 golden buddhas in the atmospheric cave pagoda at **Pindaya** (p229)

- Go pagoda hopping then trip out to traditional hill-tribe villages in **Kengtung** (p247), the gateway to the Golden Triangle

- HIGHEST POINT: SHAN PLATEAU (UP TO 8600FT)

CLIMATE

The hilly topography of eastern Myanmar produces a markedly cooler climate compared to the sweltering heat of the plains. Even during the hot season (March to June), daytime temperatures are refreshingly bearable, and night-time temperatures can plummet to near zero in December and January. At any time of year, it's wise to bring a coat or blanket to keep out the early morning or evening chill.

PEOPLE

Eastern Myanmar is the heartland of the Buddhist Shan tribe, who have strong cultural links to the Tai peoples of northern Thailand. Many of the towns in eastern and northern Myanmar were once ruled by hereditary Shan chieftains known as *sao pha* (sky lords). With their strong sense of cultural identity and separatist leanings, the Shan have long been perceived as a threat by the central government, and clashes with rebels are not uncommon.

The Shan dominate the cities of eastern Myanmar – particularly Kengtung – but the surrounding villages are home to dozens of smaller tribes, each with their own languages and traditions. Many tribal villages can be visited on treks from Kalaw, Inle Lake and Kengtung (see p226, p242 and p250 respectively).

DANGERS & ANNOYANCES

There are still pockets of insurgency in eastern Myanmar, particularly in the far south and the so-called Golden Triangle, the remote hilly region bordering Laos, China and Thailand. However, travellers are unlikely to be able to visit any of the affected areas because of government restrictions on travel.

GETTING THERE & AWAY

Although tourists can move freely through most of eastern Myanmar, restrictions have been tightened in recent years. In particular, tourists entering Myanmar from Thailand via Tachileik are now only permitted to travel as far as Kengtung and Mong La. Heading in the other direction, they can only leave Myanmar at Tachileik with a government permit from Myanmar Travel & Tours (MTT) in Yangon (p91). If you do not have this permit, you will not be allowed to leave the plane at Tachileik.

Most places between Taunggyi and Thazi are open to foreigners, but the only way to reach Kengtung from inside Myanmar is by air. All of Kayah State and the far south of Shan State are off limits, allegedly because of problems with insurgents. Bear in mind that flying or travelling by state-owned trains and boats puts money directly into the pockets of the junta.

See under individual towns for more information on travel restrictions.

THAZI TO INLE LAKE

The rolling hills between Mandalay and Inle Lake have attracted travellers ever since Myanmar first opened up to international visitors. From the junction town of Thazi, a pitted highway cuts east across a series of mountainous ridges, divided by broad valleys covered in a multicoloured patchwork of fields, villages and hedges. After Yangon and Bagan, this is probably the most visited part of Myanmar – not least because of the enduring appeal of Inle Lake.

The Shan Plateau is heavily farmed for oranges, maize, soya, corn and christophines (a

MAJOR GROUPS IN EASTERN MYANMAR

Tribe	Area	Religion
Akha	Kengtung	Animism/Christianity
Danaw	Kalaw/Inle Lake	Animism/Buddhism
Danu	Kalaw/Inle Lake	Buddhism
Eng	Kengtung	Animism
Intha	Inle Lake	Buddhism
Lahu	Kengtung	Animism
Pa-O	Kalaw/Inle Lake	Buddhism
Paduang	Kayah State/Inle Lake	Buddhism/Animism
Palaung	Kalaw/Kengtung	Animism/Buddhism
Taung Yo	Kalaw/Pindaya	Buddhism
Wa	Northeast Shan State/Yúnnán (China)	Animism

EASTERN MYANMAR

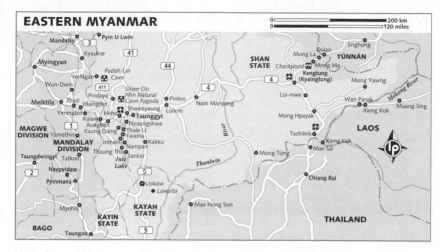

EASTERN MYANMAR

kind of squash) but areas of higher ground are still densely forested, providing shelter for many of eastern Myanmar's indigenous hill tribes. However, the forests are getting less dense every day – enormous trucks piled high with tree trunks roll downhill to the plains in a constant stream.

THAZI

☏ 064

Thazi crops up on travellers' itineraries for one reason only – the town marks the intersection of the Mandalay–Yangon rail line and the highway towards Inle Lake and the Thai border. There isn't much to see or do, but the town guesthouse is a pleasant spot to break the journey east.

Sleeping & Eating

Moon-Light Rest House (☏ 69056; Thazi-Taunggyi Hwy; s/d with shared bathroom $3/6, d with air-con $10; 🆒) On the main road to Taunggyi, this simple guesthouse is run by the delightful Htun family. The simple rooms are clean, the atmosphere is wholesome, the welcome is genuine and the attached restaurant serves good food. Staff can help out with travel arrangements.

Getting There & Away

Most people arrive in Thazi by train – the station is about 300yd north of the main road. Buses leave from an informal stand on the main road just east of the railway crossing.

BUS

To reach Thazi from Mandalay, take a bus to Meiktila (K3000, three hours) from the highway bus station, then a pick-up from Meiktila to Thazi (K500, one hour). Bus drivers on this route routinely double the fare for foreign passengers; wait to see what other passengers pay before you hand over your fare.

Heading east from Thazi, several buses leave between 7am and 11am daily bound for Kalaw (K3000, four hours) and Taunggyi (K6000, seven hours). Again, fares are often hiked for foreigners. To ride on one of the more comfortable express buses between Mandalay and Taunggyi, you'll need to make an advance reservation – the staff at the Moon-light Rest House can help.

PICK-UP & TAXI

Pick-ups for Kalaw (K3000, four hours) leave every few hours throughout the day, but it's a slow bumpy ride. A few pick-ups continue to Shwenyaung (for Inle Lake; K6000, six hours) and Taunggyi (K6000, seven hours).

A few long-distance taxis loiter around the station in Thazi charging $40 to Kalaw and $60 to Nyaungshwe (Inle Lake). You'll need to bargain hard for a fair price.

TRAIN

Thazi is an important stop on the rail route between Yangon and Mandalay. From Mandalay to Thazi (ordinary/upper class $3/8, three hours), there are trains at 5am, 5.30am, 6am and 10.30pm. Trains to Yangon (ordinary/

upper class $32/12, 11–12 hours) leave Thazi at 7.45am, 8am, 9am and 1am. See p367 for trains from Yangon to Thazi.

Slow trains rumble uphill on the scenic mountain line to Kalaw (ordinary/upper class $3/5, six hours) and Shwenyaung ($3/7, nine hours) at 5am and 8am.

A horse cart from the station to the bus stand will cost around K1000.

KALAW

ကလော

☎ 081 / elev 4356ft

Founded as a hill station by British civil servants fleeing the heat of the plains, Kalaw still feels like a holiday resort in the hills. We mean this in a good way – the air is cool, the atmosphere is calm, the streets are leafy and green, and the surrounding hills offer some of the best trekking in Myanmar. The town sprawls along a ridge on the western edge of the Shan Plateau, 43 miles from Thazi and a similar distance from Taunggyi, making this a logical place to break the journey east to Inle Lake.

Most visitors to Kalaw these days are Western backpackers and international tour groups, with the occasional Chinese and Thai tourist thrown in for good measure. For locals, the main point of interest is the huge military university on the edge of town. Kalaw has a significant population of Nepali Gurkhas and Indian Hindus, Sikhs and Muslims, who came here to build the roads and railway line during the British period.

Sights

Right in the centre of Kalaw, just west of the market is **Aung Chan Thar Zedi**, a glittery stupa (Buddhist ceremonial tower), covered in gold- and silver-coloured glass mosaics. South of the market, the myriad stupas of **Hsu Taung Pye Paya** were restored from ruins using donations from visiting pilgrims. For a good view over the market area, take the steps on the north side of the highway to **Thein Taung Paya**, a modest Buddhist monastery with a small congregation of friendly monks.

There are more Buddhist monuments on the outskirts of Kalaw. A little over a mile southwest of the market, **Nee Paya** (also called Hnin Paya) contains a 500-year-old, gold-lacquered bamboo Buddha.

Set inside a natural cave dripping with golden Buddha statues (and also just dripping – watch your footing on the slippery marble pathways) the atmospheric **Shwe Oo Min Paya** (Oo Min Rd) is about half a mile southwest of the market.

About a mile south of the market, **Christ the King Church** (University Rd) was run by the same Italian priest from 1931 to 2000. His successor, Father Paul, presides over an enthusiastic daily mass at 6.30am and a well-attended Sunday service at 8am and 4pm.

The town **market** (Merchant Rd; 6am-5pm) is also worth a browse – several stalls sell dried fruit and local liqueurs. Every five days, the market is swelled by traders from hill-tribe villages around Kalaw.

Activities

TREKKING

The main reason people visit Kalaw is to go trekking (see boxed text, p226). There are numerous trekking agencies in Kalaw, and most hotels have their own resident guides. Trekking without a guide is not recommended – the trails are confusing, the terrain challenging and few people in the hills speak English.

On single-day treks, the only equipment you need is a pair of good walking shoes and some drinking water, plus a coat or blanket to keep out the evening chill. For overnight trips, guides provide sleeping bags and mosquito nets. Meals are usually included in the price of the trek, but you should buy and carry your own drinking water. Trekking goes on year-round, but expect muddy conditions during the rainy season (May/June to November).

The going rate for a half/full day trek is $4/7; overnight treks start at $8 per day, including accommodation and basic meals. Reliable trekking guides include Harri and Rambo Singh at the Golden Lily Guest House (see p226) and **Sam Trekking Guide** (☎ 50237) on the north side of the market. If you don't feel up to the challenge of tramping on foot, horse treks can be arranged for around K15,000 per person per day. Check with your guide to see if transport to the trailheads is included.

Sleeping

Kalaw has a generous spread of hotels and guesthouses, many set up specifically for budget travellers. None of the hotels offer air-con – in this climate they don't need to – and most places offer discounts in the low season (May to October).

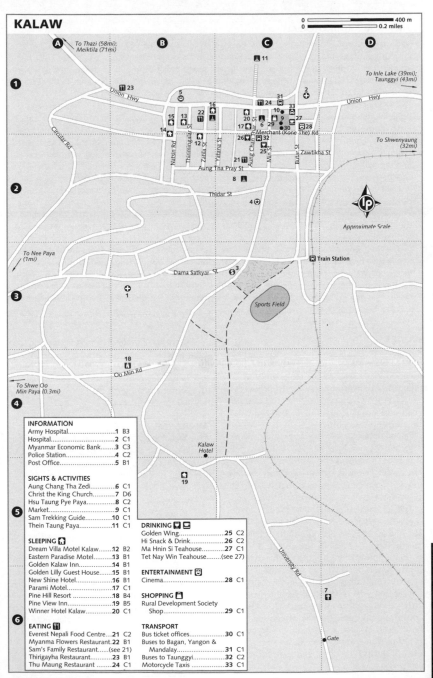

KALAW

TREKKING AROUND KALAW

Almost everyone who comes to Kalaw goes trekking in the hills. The town is surrounded by Buddhist pagodas, hilltop viewpoints and the peaceful villages of the Palaung, Danu, Pa-O, Taung Yo and Danaw tribes, all set in a gorgeous landscape of forest-capped hills. Guides in Kalaw are experts on the culture and customs of the hill tribes – as you walk along, you may find yourself sampling medicinal herbs and learning about tribal legends and animist customs.

The level of development varies as you move from village to village. Some tribes wear traditional clothing and live without electricity or running water, while their immediate neighbours watch European football on satellite TV. The standard of living for tribal people across the region has been raised by development projects run by the UN and other international NGOs. Most villagers depend primarily on farming, but some subsidise their income by making handicrafts and providing meals and accommodation for visiting trekkers.

Where you go on a trek will depend on how much time you have, and to an extent, on the interests and experience of your guide (see p224). Popular destinations for a single-day trek include the Myin Ma Hit Cave, the Pa-O villages south of Lamaing, and the Pa-O, Danu and Taung Yo villages near Myin Dike train station. Another popular route runs southwest from Kalaw to the Palaung villages of Ywa Thit and Tar Yaw and 'The Viewpoint', a rustic, Nepali-run restaurant with sweeping views over the hills.

The most popular longer trek is the two- to three-day hike to Inle Lake. There are four routes to the lakeshore, ending at Inthein, Tone Le, Thandaung or Kaung Daing. Guides can arrange to have your bags transported to a hotel in Nyaungshwe (p236), so you only carry what you need for the walk. Note that begging can be a problem on the trail to Kaung Daing because of tour groups handing out money, sweets and pens in the past – see the boxed text p228 for better ways to help local people.

BUDGET

Golden Kalaw Inn (☎ 50311; 5/92 Natsin Rd; s/d with shared bathroom $3/6, s/d with bathroom $5/8) There are good views over Kalaw from this simple, village-style guesthouse behind the Golden Lily. The wood-floored rooms are plain but clean and the balcony and front yard catch the afternoon sunshine.

Parami Motel (☎ 50027; Merchant Rd; s/d with shared bathroom $3/6, s/d with bathroom $6/12) Set in two pale blue blocks behind the Winner Hotel, the Parami has friendly owners and modest but inexpensive rooms. Rooms with private bathrooms have the benefit of windows and TVs.

our pick Golden Lily Guest House (☎ 50108; golden lily@mandalay.net.mm; 5/88 Natsin Rd; s/d from $5/10; 🖳) A chalet mood pervades at this friendly guesthouse just west of the centre. Owned by the delightful Singh family, who came to Kalaw generations ago to build the Thazi– Shwenyaung railroad, the guesthouse offers several floors of tidy, wood-panelled rooms with private bathrooms and wide shared verandas that soak up the afternoon sun. Slow internet access is available for K3000 for 30 minutes. Harri and Rambo Singh are some of the best trekking guides in town (see also p228).

Eastern Paradise Motel (☎ 50315; 5 Thirimingalar St; s/d from $6/12) A cheerful, chintzy mood infuses this family-run motel two blocks west of the market. The rooms upstairs are better than the rooms opening off the lobby, but all have bathrooms and carpets.

MIDRANGE

Pine View Inn (☎ 50185; University Rd; s/d $10/15) If you'd rather stay in the leafy part of town, this quiet hotel offers rooms in a new bungalow block or an older wooden house on the road to Christ the King church. Inside, rooms are quite modern and tasteful, and rates include a hearty breakfast.

Winner Hotel Kalaw (☎ 50025; Union Hwy; s/d from $10/20; 🖳) A large, modern Chinese-style hotel on the main road, the Winner holds few surprises, but rooms are large, uncluttered and clean. The top-floor breakfast room has good views of town, and the owner can organise treks and transport.

New Shine Hotel (☎ 50028; newshine@myanmar.com .mm; 21 Union Hwy; s/d $16/20, with bathtub & TV $18/25) Targeting travellers on organised tours, the New Shine is cosier in than out. Rooms get lots of light and all have large bathrooms; for some reason, the rear-facing standard rooms are cosier than the deluxe rooms with TVs and tubs.

Dream Villa Motel Kalaw (☎ 50144; 5 Zatila St; dreamvilla@myanmar.com.mm; s/d $20/24, deluxe s/d $25/36) A cut above your average Myanmar hotel, the Dream Villa calls out to tour groups with tasteful wood-panelled rooms and lots of potted greenery. More expensive rooms have tubs, TVs and minibars and some have hill views.

TOP END

Several flashy resort hotels have recently opened up around Kalaw, but all are joint ventures with the Myanmar government, as is the sprawling British-era Kalaw Hotel on University Rd.

Pine Hill Resort (☎ 50079; www.kalawpinehill.com; 151 Oo Min Rd; s/d bungalow from $40/50) Set around an original colonial bungalow, this sophisticated modern hotel has rooms in wooden cottages sprawling through immaculate gardens. All the rooms have balconies and meals are served in a wooden pavilion with a huge open terrace. Beware of locals freewheeling downhill on their bikes as you walk up Oo Min Rd.

Eating

Kalaw has some excellent places to chow down, many serving food with a distinctive Indian or Nepali flavour. Unless otherwise stated, the following restaurants open for breakfast, lunch and dinner.

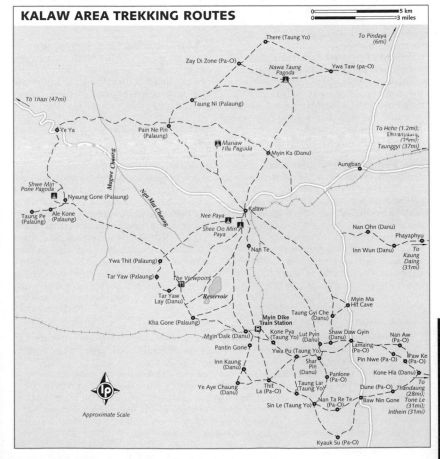

KALAW AREA TREKKING ROUTES

Sam's Family Restaurant (Aung Chan Thar St; dishes K1000-2000) Run by the same family as Sam Trekking Guide, this cosy little place serves good Shan and Chinese standards and old-fashioned backpacker breakfasts.

Everest Nepali Food Centre (Aung Chan Thar St; dishes K1000-2500) Relive memories of trekking in Nepal with a plate of *dhal baht* at this convivial eatery run by a Nepali family who originally came to Myanmar from Pokhara.

Myanma Flowers Restaurant (Zatila St; dishes K1500) West of the market, this traveller-oriented restaurant does its best to recreate the rock-and-roll mood of Happy Days. The menu features a good selection of Bamar, Chinese, Indian and Western food.

Thu Maung Restaurant (Union Hwy; meals K2000) Probably the best Burmese restaurant in town, Thu Maung serves tasty chicken, pork and fish dishes with all the usual Myanmar salads, pickles and trimmings.

Thirigayha Restaurant (Seven Sisters; ☎ 50216; Union Hwy; meals from K5000; ☺ till 10pm) If you want a romantic dinner, there's really only one choice in town. The menu runs from Shan traditional meals to beef stroganoff, noodle soups and Indian curries and there's often a guitarist serenading diners.

Drinking

Golden Wing (Min Rd; ☺ 9am-8pm) South of the market, this typical Chinese beer station has Dagon and Skol beer on draught.

Hi Snack & Drink (Merchant Rd; ☺ 10am-10pm) A real hole-in-the-wall bar behind the market, owned by fans of the band Iron Cross. It's tiny, but good fun when it gets busy.

Teashops around the market open from early morning to late evening. A snack breakfast should set you back less than K1000. Try the following:

Ma Hnin Si Teashop (Butar Rd) This Indian-style teashop on the east side of the market has no English sign but you can't miss it – just look for the crowds of locals enjoying plates of *pakoda* (vegetables fried in lentil-flour batter).

Tet Nay Win Teahouse (Butar Rd) An Indian-style teashop serving samosas, chapattis, *channa puri* (fried bread with chickpea curry) and other treats from the subcontinent.

Entertainment

Kalaw is an early to bed, early to rise kind of town, but the town **cinema** (Merchant Rd) screens entertaining Myanmar action movies.

Shopping

Numerous art galleries around the market sell paintings of monks, tribal people and mountain scenery, some ordinary and others very good.

Rural Development Society Shop (wt_aungthwin@ lissamail.com.mm; ☺ 8.30am-6.30pm) On the west side of the market, this charitable enterprise sells fabrics, clothing and handmade paper produced by local tribes. Profits go towards development projects in local Shan and Pa-O villages.

Getting There & Away
BUS

Several bus ticket offices around the market book seats on the long-distance buses between Yangon and Mandalay and Taunggyi. Buses to Yangon (K15,000, 15 hours) leave around 2.30pm. Mandalay buses (K8000 to K12,000, nine hours) leave between 7.30pm and 9pm, and there's normally a single bus to Bagan (K10,000, nine hours) around 7.30am. These buses stop on the main road, in front of the market.

Small local buses for Taunggyi (K2000; three hours) leave in the morning from a stop

---

HARRI SINGH

Many trekkers carry gifts to improve the lives of local villagers, but handing out money, pens and sweets to children can have the opposite effect to that intended. Trekking guide Harri Singh gave us the following advice:

'If you want to help local people, make a donation to the headman or the village monastery or school. Most villages need clothing and medicines as well as toothpaste and toothbrushes – there is no tradition of keeping teeth clean in the hills and few village people can afford to visit a dentist. For the same reason, sweets are not the best gifts to give to children! Notebooks and pens are much more useful but always give these to parents or teachers – otherwise children will expect presents from everyone who comes into the village.'

behind the Aung Chang Tha Zedi. These buses will drop you in Shwenyaung or Aungban (the junction for Pindaya) for the same fare.

Buses to Thazi (K3000, four hours) or Meiktila (K4000, five hours) stop periodically on the highway – however, pick-ups are more frequent.

PICK-UP & TAXI

Pick-ups run frequently from the highway to Thazi (K3000, four hours) and Taunggyi (K3000, three hours). Taunggyi-bound pick-ups will drop you in Shwenyaung or Aungban for the same fare. Services tend to slow down to a trickle by mid-afternoon.

You can charter taxis from Kalaw to Pindaya ($30, two hours), Nyaungshwe ($30), Taunggyi ($40) and Thazi ($50).

TRAIN

Slow trains rattle along the winding railway line from Thazi to Kalaw (ordinary/upper class $3/5, six hours) twice daily, continuing to Shwenyaung ($1/3, three hours). Stunning scenery makes up for the slow journey time and frequent delays.

Heading from Kalaw to Shwenyaung, the *143 Up* leaves around 11.30am and the *141 Up* leaves around 12.30pm. From Kalaw to Thazi, the *142 Down* leaves around 11.30am and the *144 Down* leaves around 2pm. However, trains often leave hours behind the official departure times. See p223 for train times from Thazi.

Getting Around

Most people choose to walk around town but motorcycles at the northeast corner of the market can run you to Nee Paya or the Shwe Oo Min caves and back for around K2000.

Guesthouses can arrange bike hire for K3000 to K3500 per day.

AUNGBAN
အောင်ပန်း
☎ 081

The typical, dusty highway town is the junction for the road north to Pindaya. There isn't much here to delay the traveller, but the town **market** (held on a five-day cycle) attracts traders from across the Shan Plateau.

The **Mikhine Restaurant** (meals K1300) by the junction is the best place to wait for transport – taxis loiter out front and pick-ups and buses heading east and west stop nearby.

KAYAH STATE

Wedged between Shan State to the north and west, Kayin (Karen) State to the west and south, and Thailand to the east, tiny Kayah State is home to numerous tribal groups, including the Padaung, Yinbaw, Bre, Kayin (Karen) and Karenni (Red Karen). Unfortunately, foreigners are prohibited from travelling anywhere in Kayah State because of ongoing violence between government forces and rebels fighting for an independent Kayin homeland. Reliable information on the current political situation in Kayah State is hard to come by, but human rights groups report ongoing abuses by government forces, including forced labour, forced relocations and the conscription of civilians for the clearing of landmines.

Getting There & Away

Local buses and pick-ups heading east from Kalaw can drop you in Aungban, or transport you on to Shwenyaung or Taunggyi; the Kalaw–Aungban fare is K1000. A few local buses and pick-ups head from Aungban to Pindaya (K1500, two hours) in the afternoon, returning the next morning.

If you want to visit Pindaya as a day trip, taxis waiting by the junction will take you to the caves and back for K30,000. The same taxis charge K25,000 to Nyaungshwe and K6000 to Kalaw.

PINDAYA
ပင်းတယ
☎ 081

The road north from Aungban to Pindaya cuts across the top of the Shan Plateau. This is one of the most densely farmed areas in Myanmar – at first glance, the patchwork of fields and hedges could almost be a landscape from central Europe or middle America. Along the way, you'll pass buffalo carts and groups of toiling farmers in black Danu tunics and checked Pa-O headscarves. The main reason to make this appealing journey is to visit the famous Shew Oo Min Cave, a massive limestone cavern filled with thousands of gilded buddha statues. You could easily spend several days here exploring the cave shrines and dozens of smaller pagodas strung out along the ridge.

Sights & Activities
SHWE OO MIN NATURAL CAVE PAGODA
ပင်းတယဂူ

There are several 'Golden Cave' temples in Shan State, but Pindaya's **Shwe Oo Min Pagoda** (admission $3, camera fee K300; ☉ 6am-6pm) is by far the most impressive. Set high on a limestone ridge above Pone Ta Loke Lake, this winding complex of natural caves and tunnels is filled to bursting point with buddha images in an astonishing variety of shapes, sizes and materials, many gaudily daubed with gold paint.

At the latest count, the caves contained more than 8090 statues, some left centuries ago by Burmese pilgrims and others newly installed by Buddhist organisations from as far afield as Singapore, the Netherlands and the USA. The collection of alabaster, teak, marble, brick, lacquer and cement images is still growing – pilgrims arrive in a slow but steady stream, installing new images and meditating in tiny meditation chambers formed by natural cavities in the cave walls.

A series of covered stairways climb the ridge to the cave entrance. Most people arrive via the long stairway that starts near the gleaming white *zedi* (stupas) of **Nget Pyaw Taw pagoda**, just south of the Conqueror Hotel. You can skip the last 130 steps to the cave mouth by taking the **lift** (admission free; ☉ 9am-noon & 1-4pm).

Two more covered stairways lead north from the lift pavilion. One descends gently back to Pindaya, while the other climbs to a second **cave pavilion** containing a monumental 40ft-high, gilded, Shan-style sitting buddha. The steps continue along the ridge to a third chamber with a large **reclining buddha** and more shrines and pagodas along the hilltop.

The easiest way to reach the caves is to walk along the tarmac road past the Golden Cave and Conqueror Hotels, but an easy-to-follow track runs straight to the cave complex from the western shore of Pone Ta Loke Lake – just follow the road along the lakeshore and turn right after the Pindaya Hotel; the path to the caves branches off to the left over a small bridge. A horse cart from the market to the Nget Pyaw Taw pagoda entrance will cost K2000.

OTHER STUPAS
Downhill from the main cave on the dirt path to the lake, the gorgeous **Sing Kyaung monastery** was constructed from carved teak panels in the late 19th century. The steps to the main cave start just beyond the *kyaung* (monastery) – the path is lined with ancient crumbling *zedi*.

At the north end of Pone Ta Loke Lake, the **Kan Tau Monastery** features some heavily restored stupas and a fine teak *kyaung* with a large collection of antique buddha images on ornate plinths.

PADAH-LIN CAVES
ပုဒါးလင်းဂူ

About 31 miles northwest of Pindaya, near the village of Ye-Ngan, Padah-Lin is the most important prehistoric site in Myanmar. The caves here are decorated with Neolithic paintings of animals and human figures that date back 11,000 years. Unfortunately, access to the caves is currently restricted – check locally with travel agents in Kalaw or Nyaungshwe to see if anyone is running trips to the caves.

TREKS
Day and overnight treks to Danu, Pa-O, Palaung and Taung Yo villages around Pindaya can be organised at the Golden Cave Hotel (opposite) or the Conqueror Hotel (opposite) for about $10 per person per day.

Festivals & Events
The main annual **paya pwe** (pagoda festival) at Shwe Oo Min takes place on the full moon of Tabaung (February/March). Expect all the

---

ALONG CAME A SPIDER
As you enter Pindaya, keep an eye out for the official town symbol – an archer and a giant spider. According to legend, seven princesses took refuge in Shwe Oo Min cave during a storm, and were imprisoned by an evil *nat* (spirit being) in the form of a giant spider. Lucky for them, Prince Kummabhaya of Nyaungshwe (Yaunghwe) was strolling nearby – hearing their pleas for help, the heroic prince killed the spider with an arrow and freed the princesses from the cave. You can see some Disney-esque sculptures of the spider and prince by the entrance to the Shwe Oo Min cave complex.

usual singing, dancing and hand-operated fairground rides.

Sleeping

The only cheap options are in the town itself, a long walk from the caves.

Myit Phyar Zaw Gji Hotel (☎ 21785; 106 Zaytan Quarter; s/d $10/15) Next to the market and close to the lake shore, this is the closest Pindaya has to budget accommodation. It's a bit faded but OK value for money. All rooms have bathrooms and some face the lake.

Golden Cave Hotel (☎ 40227; r from $20, r with TV & fridge $25) A warm welcome awaits at this unassuming midrange hotel about 150yd from the start of the steps to the Shwe Oo Min cave. The smarter superior rooms in the annexe have balconies looking towards the caves. The owners are outstandingly helpful and the restaurant serves good Chinese and international food.

Pindaya Inle Inn (☎ in Yangon 01-448 1311; inleinnp@myanmar.com.mm; Mahabandoola Rd; s/d $35/40, chalets $70; ▣) A surprisingly sophisticated place to stay for a small town like Pindaya. Rooms are set in tasteful bamboo or stone cottages in a lovingly tended garden centred on a longhouse-style restaurant and bar. It's worth paying extra for the 'chalet rooms' with fireplace, TV and appealing local bric-a-brac on the walls.

ourpick Conqueror Hotel (☎ 448 1211, Yangon 01-256 623; s/d from $55/65; ▣ ▣) There isn't a blade of grass out of place at this immaculately maintained resort hotel near the main entrance to the caves. Rooms are set in cottages around a central restaurant and a large, inviting pool. Set in bamboo villas, wooden stilt houses or stone chalets, the rooms are luxuriously appointed, with TV, minibar and stylish bathroom. You can rent bikes here for $3 per day.

Eating

There are several basic local restaurants around the market, but the offerings tend to be fairly basic.

Kyan Lite Restaurant (dishes K1000; ☯ 6am-9pm) On the lakeshore close to the market, Kyan Lite serves cold beers and a familiar menu of Myanmar Chinese dishes, as well as boxes of Shan tea.

To dine in more salubrious surroundings, visit the restaurants at the Pindaya Inle Inn, Golden Cave Hotel or Conqueror Hotel (see above).

Getting There & Away

There is only limited public transport to Pindaya so most people stay at least one night. Coming from Taunggyi, local buses leave for Pindaya (K2500, four hours) at around 1pm, returning to Taunggyi between 5.30am and 6am the following morning.

Starting from Kalaw or Shwenyaung, your best bet is to take a bus or pick-up to Aungban (p229), and change there. Infrequent pick-ups run between Aungban and Pindaya (K1500, two hours) but schedules are erratic; there is normally a guaranteed service from Pindaya to Aungban at 8.30am.

It is much easier, though much more expensive, to complete the journey from Aungban to Pindaya by taxi. Drivers loiter on the highway in Aungban charging K25,000 for a drop-off in Pindaya and K30,000 for a return trip to the caves.

HEHO

ဟဲဟိုး

☎ 081

The quiet highway town of Heho has the main airstrip in the Inle Lake area. Hundreds of travellers visit daily, but few stay longer than it takes to charter a taxi or flag down a pick-up to Kalaw, Taunggyi or Nyaungshwe (for Inle Lake). Apart from the airport, there is little to see in town; there is no licensed accommodation and most people head straight to the airport by taxi from Taunggyi or Nyaungshwe.

Getting There & Away

AIR

There are frequent flights to and from Heho with Bagan Air, Air Mandalay and Yangon Airways, as well as the ageing aircraft of government-run Myanma Airways. The airlines all have offices in Heho, but most people make bookings in Taunggyi or Nyaungshwe. Be sure to check-in early – schedules are erratic, and it is not unheard of for flights to leave early without warning.

All the airlines have flights to Mandalay ($45, 30 minutes) and Yangon ($98, one to two hours, some flights go via Mandalay). **Air Bagan** (www.airbagan.com), **Air Mandalay** (www.airmandalay.com) and **Yangon Airways** (www.yangonair.com) also fly to Nyaung U (Bagan; $71 to $90; 1¼ hours) with a stop in Mandalay.

Air Bagan, Air Mandalay and Yangon Airways have several flights a week to Tachileik ($76 to $128, two hours, via

Mandalay) and Kengtung ($76 to $128, 2½ hours, via Mandalay and Tachileik). Note that you need a government permit to fly into Tachileik – see p254.

There are also daily flights to Thandwe ($101 to $198, one hour) and two weekly flights to Pathein ($95, one hour) with Air Bagan.

BUS & PICK-UP

Taxis at Heho airport charge high fares; a cheaper option is to hike 200yd to the highway and wait for a pick-up or bus to Taunggyi (K2000, 1½ hours) or Shwenyaung (K1500, one hour), where you can change for Nyaungshwe. Bear in mind that you may face a long wait for a ride in either direction.

TAXI

Taxis waiting at the airport charge around K30,000 to Kalaw (1½ hours), K35,000 to Nyaungshwe (1½ hours) and K25,000 to Taunggyi (1½ hours).

SHWENYAUNG

ရွှေညောင်

☎ 081

The village of Shwenyaung marks the junction of the Kalaw–Taunggyi highway and the road to Nyaungshwe and Inle Lake, but there's no reason to linger here longer than it takes to change pick-ups or charter a taxi to the lake or Heho airport.

The Pan Za Lat Teashop, situated right at the Heho–Nyaungshwe–Taunggyi junction, is a convenient place to wait for transport and escape the taxi and hotel touts, who'll descend upon you as soon as you arrive.

Getting There & Away
BUS & PICK-UP

Any bus travelling from Mandalay or Yangon to Taunggyi can drop you at Shwenyaung for the full Taunggyi fare (see p246 for details). Buses heading west from Taunggyi are normally full by the time they reach Shwenyaung. To secure a seat, make an advance booking with a travel agent in Nyaungshwe (p234) or directly with the bus companies in Taunggyi.

Pick-ups pass through Shwenyaung regularly bound for Kalaw (K2000; 1½ hours) and Taunggyi (K700, 40 minutes).

TAXI

Taxis hover around the main junction, charging K5000 to K6000 for the 20-minute jour-

ney between Shwenyaung and Nyaungshwe. Guesthouses in Nyaungshwe can arrange taxis in the opposite direction for a similar fare. After dark, fares soar to K9000 or more.

Motorcycle taxis charge around K3000 for the trip, but you don't get a helmet and there isn't much room for baggage.

TRAIN

Slow trains rumble through the hills between Thazi and Shwenyaung twice daily – the journey takes at least nine hours but the scenery en route is stunning. Heading downhill from Shwenyaung, the *142 Down* leaves at 8am and the *144 Down* leaves at 9.30am. The fare is $3/7 for ordinary/upper class. Both trains pass through Kalaw ($1/3, three hours).

For train times from Thazi to Mandalay or Yangon see p223.

INLE LAKE

အင်းလေးအိုင်

Placid Inle Lake ranks among Myanmar's top five tourist attractions, which ensures that visitors come here in droves. The once-sleepy village of Nyaungshwe at the north end of the lake has grown into a bustling traveller centre, with dozens of guesthouses and hotels, a surfeit of restaurants serving pancakes and pasta and a pleasantly relaxed traveller vibe. If Myanmar could be said to have a backpacker scene at all, it can be found here.

Every day, dozens of motorised long-boats skitter along the reed-lined channel that connects Nyaungshwe to the main body of the lake, transporting visitors to tribal villages, floating pagodas, and the inevitable craft workshops and souvenir shops. Anywhere else, this kind of development would feel oppressively commercial, but this is Myanmar – visitors are vastly outnumbered by locals and tourism manages to coexist quite happily with traditional village life.

On paper Inle Lake is 13.5 miles long and 7 miles wide but up close it's hard to tell where the lake finishes and the marshes start. Looking down over the lake from the Taunggyi road, Inle sits like a puddle on an enormous carpet of greenery. The lake doesn't really have a shoreline – the water gets shallower and the tangled reed and hy-

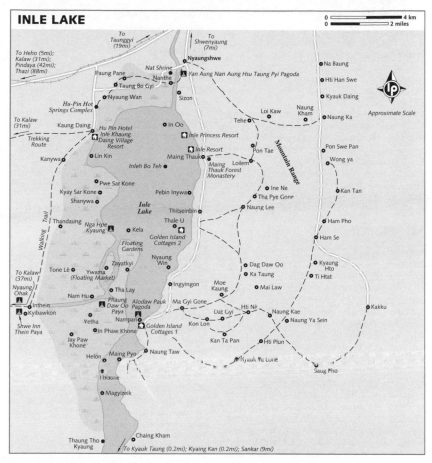

INLE LAKE

acinth beds get denser until you suddenly find yourself on dry land.

Dotted around the lake are the stilt-house villages and floating gardens of the Intha tribe (see boxed text, p236). You may also encounter Shan, Pa-O, Taung Yo, Danu, Kayah and Danaw tribal people at the markets that hopscotch around the lake on a five-day cycle.

Boats are the main means of transport around the lake – travellers tend to explore on motorised canoes (a little like Thai long-tail boats) but most Intha people get around using traditional flat-bottomed skiffs propelled by a single wooden paddle. The Intha technique of leg-rowing – where one leg is wrapped around the paddle to drive the blade

through the water in a snake-like motion – is unique. The silhouette of a leg-rower on a canoe piled with Intha nets is probably the definitive photo opportunity on the lake.

The waters cool the surrounding air considerably. A pall of mist hangs over the lake before sunrise and morning, and evenings can be surprisingly cold. Bring a coat or buy a blanket in the market to keep off the windchill on boat tours around the lake.

INFORMATION

There is a compulsory $3 government fee to enter the Inle Lake area, which you must pay on arrival at the small **permit booth** (🕑 6am-9pm) by the bridge at the entrance to Nyaungshwe.

EASTERN MYANMAR

FESTIVALS & EVENTS

Inle comes alive during late September or early October for the **Phaung Daw Oo Paya Festival** at Phaung Daw Oo Paya (p240). The four revered golden buddha images from the pagoda are ferried around the lake in a gilded barge shaped like a *hintha* (the golden swan of Burmese legend) visiting all the pagodas in the area. The festival lasts for 18 days and locals carry out energetic leg-rowing races on the channels between the villages.

The pagoda festival is closely followed by **Thadingyut**, which marks the end of Waso (Buddhist Lent). The custom of lighting oil lamps in windows and doorways suggests a link between this festival and the Hindu festival of Diwali.

NYAUNGSHWE

ညောင်ရွှေ

☎ 081

The main traveller centre for the Inle Lake area, Nyaungshwe is a neat grid of streets next to the main channel leading down to the north end of the lake. Originally known by the Shan name Yaunghwe, the town was renamed Nyaungshwe (Golden Banyan) by the Bamar-dominated authorities after Independence. Until the 1960s, this was the official home of the last Shan *sao pha* (shy lord), Sao Shwe Thaike.

On one level, Nyaungshwe is a tourist town, with dozens of hotels, guesthouses, traveller-oriented restaurants, and all sorts of activities laid on for visitors. On the other hand, Nyaungshwe still functions as a trading hub for the villages on the lake, with a busy market and dozens of warehouses where crafts and produce from the lake are packaged for shipment around the country.

Besides Kalaw, this town is one of the few places in the country to exude a backpacker vibe – there's plenty to do and lots of good places to stay and eat. Many travellers spend several days here exploring the lake and relaxing after the rigours of travel elsewhere in Myanmar.

Information

Any guesthouse in town can arrange tours, boat trips, flights and bus tickets. Some hotels are willing to change US dollars into kyat for guests.

See p233 for information on the permit fee.

Comet Travel & Internet Café (☎ 29126; Yone Gyi Rd; ☷ 8am-8pm) Books flights and buses and has a few internet terminals.

Cyber Café (Kann Nar Rd; per hr K4000; ☷ 8am-7pm) Close to the boat jetty, above Mini Mart, with decent connections and a full drinks menu.

Golden Island Cottages (GIC; ☎ in Taunggyi 081-23136; Phaung Daw Seiq Rd; ☷ 8am-6pm) Come here to arrange guides to Kakku and Sankar.

Inle Blooms Global Online Information Bar (Phaung Daw Pyan Rd; per hr K3000; ☷ 8am-11pm) The best and fastest internet café in Nyaungshwe; international email accounts can be accessed via proxy servers.

Sights & Activities

YADANA MAN AUNG PAYA

The oldest and most important Buddhist shrine in Nyaungshwe, this handsome gilded **stupa** (donations appropriate; ☷ 6am-10pm) is hidden away inside a square compound south of the market. The stepped stupa is unique in Myanmar, and the surrounding pavilion contains a museum of treasures amassed by the monks over the centuries, including carvings, lacquerware and dance costumes.

BUDDHA MUSEUM

Formerly the Museum of Shan Chiefs, this sprawling government-run **museum** (Museum Rd (Haw St); admission $2; ☷ 9.30am-3.30pm Tue-Sun) has fallen victim to the government crackdown on symbols of Shan ethnic identity (see p302). Today the museum displays antique buddha images rather than any objects that might suggest a distinct Shan history and culture. It's still worth coming here to see the stately brick-and-teak *haw* (palace) of the 33rd and last Shan *sao pha*, Sao Shwe Thaike, who briefly served as the first president of Independent Burma, before the junta seized control.

OTHER RELIGIOUS MONUMENTS

There are stupas and monasteries all over Nyaungshwe. Most of the monasteries are clustered around the Mong Li Canal southeast

---

WARNING

Touting for commissions is alive and well in Nyaungshwe. Taxi drivers and self-appointed guides may try to steer you towards a hotel where they earn a commission, using the usual excuses – your hotel is closed, the owner died etc. Be firm about where you want to go and check in by yourself, or you'll end up paying over the odds.

of the market – all welcome visitors but try not to disturb the novices during their classes. Monks start their morning rounds for alms at around 6.30am.

Hlaing Gu Kyaung (off Yone Gyi Rd) has around 100 resident monks and an interesting collection of antique Buddha images. Nearby,

Shwe Gu Kyaung (Myawady Rd) has 130 novices and a huge central hall that echoes with the sound of synchronised chanting. A block further south, **Kan Gyi Kyaung** (Myawady Rd) is the largest monastery in Nyaungshwe; listening to 250 monks of all ages reciting the scriptures is quite an experience.

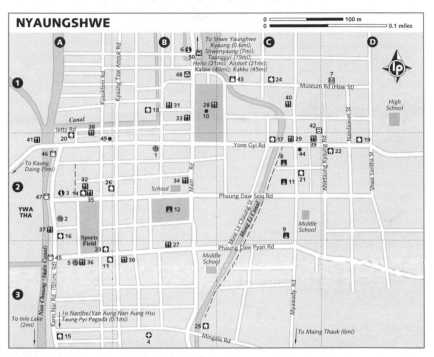

NYAUNGSHWE

EASTERN MYANMAR

THE INTHA OF INLE LAKE

Although they follow Buddhism and wear modern Burmese costume, the Intha people of Inle Lake are culturally quite distinct from their Shan neighbours. The ancestors of the Intha are thought to have migrated to Inle from Dawei in southern Myanmar. According to the most popular legend, two brothers from Dawei came to Yaunghwe (the original name for Nyaungshwe) in 1359 to serve the local Shan *sao pha* (sky lord). The chieftain was so pleased with the hardworking Dawei brothers that he invited 36 more families from Dawei; purportedly, all the Intha around Inle Lake are descended from these migrant families. A more likely theory is that the Intha fled southern Myanmar in the 18th century to escape wars between the Thais and Bamar.

About 450yd north of town on the road to Shwenyaung, **Shwe Yaunghwe Kyaung** (Shwe Yan Pyay) is probably the most photographed monastery in Nyaungshwe; the unique oval windows in the ancient teak *thein* (ordination hall) create a perfect frame for portraits of the novices.

South of town in the village of Nanthe, **Yan Aung Nan Aung Hsu Taung Pyi Pagoda** (what a mouthful!) features a 26ft-high sitting buddha, surrounded by stucco *deva* (celestial beings) and *chinthe* (half-lion, half-dragon guardians). Although heavily restored, the statue is said to be more than 700 years old.

MINGALA MARKET

The busy *zei* (market) at the entrance to town is flooded with locals every morning, when traders from the lake bring in fresh fish and produce from the floating gardens. A few stalls sell local handicrafts but the focus is on day-to-day objects used by local people – food, begging bowls, machetes, fishing spears, you name it.

BOAT TRIPS

Every hotel in town can arrange boat trips around the lake, and freelance boat drivers will approach you in the street. The going rate for a whole-day trip around the lake is K12,000. You can also rent canoes for paddles closer to Nyaungshwe for around K2000 per hour. See p242 for details.

TREKKING

Hotels and guesthouses can arrange day treks for $10 and multiday treks from $15 per day. See p242 for some suggested destinations.

Sleeping

Nyaungshwe has dozens of hotels and guesthouses, ranging from basic backpacker hang-outs to comfortable midrange hotels. Most places offer low-season discounts from March to October, but rates are open to negotiation most of the time because of the intense competition.

Almost all rooms have bathrooms with hot showers, but few places offer air-con because of the natural cooling effect of the breeze passing over the lake. All room rates include breakfast.

BUDGET

Gypsy Inn (☎ 29084; Kann Nar Rd; s/d in old bldg from $3/6, new bldg from $6/12; 🖳) Handy for the canal leading to the lake, this place has an old block containing budget rooms with shared or private bathrooms, and a much more appealing new block of rooms with private bath. The bright, wood-floored rooms upstairs have TVs and fridges.

our pick Aquarius Inn (☎ 29352; aquarius352@gmail .com; 2 Phaung Daw Pyan Rd; s/d $4/8, with private bathroom $7/12) Charming owners make this small, family-run guesthouse a real home away from home. The cosy rooms contain an intriguing collection of local bric-a-brac and guests are treated to plates of fresh fruit and Chinese tea. There are tables and chairs in the plant-filled yard where you can sit and chat in the evenings.

Joy Hotel (☎ 29083; Jetty Rd; s/d $5/8, with bathroom $7/10) Set on the canal used by market traders delivering goods to Mingala Market, Joy has more of a local feel than the other budget guesthouses. The cheaper rooms with shared bathrooms are small and boxy but there are better rooms with private bathrooms and hot showers.

Bright Hotel (☎ 29137; 53 Phaung Daw Seiq Rd; s/d from $5/10, superior r from $15) The price is the draw-card rather than the atmosphere at this big white place near the boat jetty. The standard rooms are fairly typical for this kind of hotel but the more inviting superior rooms have tub, TV and mini-bar.

Nawng Kham – Little Inn (☎ 29195; Phaung Daw Pyan Rd; s/d $5/10) Opposite the Aquarius Inn,

EASTERN MYANMAR

this small but perfectly formed guesthouse has just seven rooms with fans, bathrooms and hot showers, set in a peaceful garden. Considering the number of rooms, it's a good idea to book ahead.

May Guest House (☎ 29417; 85 Myawady Rd; s/d/tr $6/12/16) Wagon wheels mounted in the front wall set the tone at this village-style guesthouse in the monastery quarter. The simple square rooms have fans and bathrooms and the breakfast is one of the best in town.

Teakwood Guest House (☎ 29150; teakwoodhtl@ myanmar.com.mm; Kyaung Taw Anouk Rd; s/d in old bldg from $6/10, new bldg from $15/20; 🖳) Straddling the divide between budget and midrange, this attractive guesthouse is popular with older independent travellers. The best rooms are in the new block – big windows let in lots of light and the bathrooms are finished with small pebbles. The communal areas are great, but be ready for some assertive sales pitches from the owner for boat trips and excursions.

Four Sisters Inn (☎ 29190; 105 Nan Pan Quarter; s/d $7/12) Away from the other guesthouses on the way to Yan Aung Nan Aung Hsu Taung Pyi Pagoda, this quiet place consists of small bamboo matt-lined rooms around an old village house with a cosy restaurant. Rooms have chintzy bedspreads but reliably hot showers.

Primrose Hotel (☎ 29150; 40 Mingala Rd; s/d $10/15) Better inside than out, this complex of wooden chalets is an OK choice in a quiet part of town. The large wood-lined rooms have bathroom and verandas but some get more sun than others.

Inle Inn (☎ 29016; Yone Gyi Rd; s/d from $12/15) Potted plants and trellises create a pleasing cocoon of vegetation at this village inn on the eastern side of town. Rooms are arranged around a shady sitting area and restaurant. It's worth paying more for one of the larger, brighter, superior rooms.

MIDRANGE

Nanda Wunn Hotel (☎ 22540; nandawunn@myanmar .com.mm; 80 Yone Gyi Rd; bungalows $15-20, s/d $20/25; 🖳) In a residential part of Nyaungshwe east of the market, this place follows the standard midrange pattern in Nyaungshwe – cabins in the grounds and a big hotel block at the back. You can pay extra for air-con and a tub.

Paradise Hotel & Restaurant (☎ 29321; 40 Museum Rd; s/d from $25/30; 🖳) Paradise is probably overstating it, but this large chalet-style hotel near the museum is still a good choice. Take your pick from standard Chinese-style rooms in the main hotel block or a row of appealing wooden bungalows with big verandas in the garden. All rooms have hot showers, fridges, TVs and air-con.

Hu Pin Hotel Nyaungshwe (☎ 29291; hupin@ myanmar.com.mm; 66 Kan Tha Quarter; s/d from $30/36; 🖳) Asian tour groups make a beeline for this behemoth of a hotel just west of the market. The Chinese-style rooms won't win any prizes for interior design, but everything is spotlessly clean, hot water is reliable and the hotel has its own boats for trips around the lake.

ourpick **Hotel Amazing Nyaung Shwe** (☎ 29079; www.amazing-hotel.com; Yone Gyi Rd; s/d $32/38, suite $57-94) A league apart from the other hotels in Nyaungshwe, this immaculate boutique hotel has gorgeous rooms decorated with murals and cultural artefacts and an open-air breakfast pavilion on a bridge over the canal.

Eating

Nyaungshwe is awash with traveller-oriented restaurants, all serving broadly identical menus of Chinese, Indian, Burmese and Western food. For some reason, many places advertise pizzas but only a few places actually serve them. Unless otherwise stated, the following restaurants are open for breakfast, lunch and dinner.

Kaung Su Lwin Teashop (Main Rd; snacks from K100) The best and busiest teashop in Nyaungshwe, serving hot drinks and snacks to crowds of locals daily.

Inle Pancake Kingdom (off Phaung Daw Seiq Rd; pancakes from K1000) Choose from a huge range of filled pancakes and toasted sandwiches at this cute little cabin on a narrow alley north of the sports field. Follow the signs from Phaung Daw Seiq Rd.

Smiling Moon Restaurant (Yone Gyi Rd; dishes from K1000) A laid-back terrace restaurant serving Inle regional dishes, hill tribe food and the traveller holy trinity of Chinese, pasta and pancakes.

Miss Nyaungshwe Restaurant (Phaung Daw Seiq Rd; pastas K1000) Travellers gather at this cute bamboo-fronted restaurant for inexpensive Chinese and Bamar curries, plus pancakes, pasta and bottled beers. The doors close when the last diners leave.

Shanland Restaurant (Jetty Rd; meals from K1500) A rustic Shan-style restaurant on the narrow canal north of Yone Gyi Rd. The menu includes some interesting Shan and Intha dishes, including river fish cooked in banana leaves.

Unique Superb Food House (3 Myawady Rd; fish dishes from K1500) This simple restaurant in a village house serves all sorts of dishes prepared with freshly caught fish from the lake.

Nyaungshwe Restaurant (Kann Nar Rd; mains from K1500) Housed in a big, wooden building overlooking the water, this old-fashioned beer hall has a decent selection of Chinese, Myanmar and European dishes and cold beer on tap.

Kaung Kaung Restaurant (Main Rd; mains from K1500) One of the few restaurants in town to pull in a mainly local crowd, this Chinese beer hall serves good, inexpensive Chinese food. If you've eaten at any other Chinese restaurant in Myanmar, you'll know what to expect.

Hu Pin Restaurant (Kan Tha Quarter; dishes from K1500) Close to the Hu Pin Hotel and run by the same team, this bright Chinese canteen has an English menu of tasty Chinese soups and fried favourites like sweet and sour pork. It gets very busy with tour groups at lunch time – come early or late for lunch or face a long wait.

Golden Kite Restaurant (Yone Gyi Rd; dishes from K2000) A step up from the other traveller restaurants in town, Golden Kite serves delicious Chinese, Burmese and Western food in a large, inviting wooden dining room.

Teakwood Restaurant (Kyaung Taw Anouk Rd; mains from K2000) The balcony restaurant at the Teakwood Guesthouse is open to non-guests; the menu is limited but the Chinese, Burmese and Western food is good and the atmosphere relaxing.

our pick **Viewpoint Restaurant** (☎ 29062; Taik Nan Bridge; mains K2000-7000) Just across the bridge over the main canal, this stucco-fronted restaurant looks like a wine bar from a resort town in the Mediterranean. It is not only the most stylish choice in Nyaungshwe, it also has a menu that features local wines and modern interpretations of traditional Shan dishes.

Some of the cheapest – and tastiest – food available in Nyaungshwe is sold at the **food stalls** (meals K1000) in Mingala Market. Local specialities include Shan *kauq-sweh* (noodle-soup), *maung jeut* (round, flat rice crisps) and *tofu thoke* (Shan tofu salad), prepared using yellow split-pea tofu, chilli, coriander and sesame oil. There are more rustic food stalls along the canal that traders use to deliver goods to market.

There are several other traveller restaurants that serve decent fare. Try the following:
Exodus Restaurant (Phaung Daw Pyan Rd)
Htoo Htoo Aung Chinese & Shan Food (Phaung Daw Pyan Rd)
Mr Cook (Phaung Daw Pyan Rd)

Entertainment

Kaung Kaung Restaurant (Main Rd) The residents of Nyaungshwe get their heads down early – this restaurant doubles as the town pub, with Myanmar beer and ABC stout on tap.

Aung Puppet Show (Ahletaung Kyaung Rd; ☺ 7pm & 8.30pm) Down the road opposite the Nanda Wunn Hotel, this place has a nightly show of traditional Burmese puppetry.

Shopping

On any trip onto Inle Lake, you will be approached by dozens of vendors in canoes selling crafts objects and curios, so there isn't any great need to buy souvenirs in Nyaungshwe.

Lilypad (☎ 29256; off Museum Rd; ☺ 8am-6pm) Run by a charity that produces natural clay filters for drinking water for local villages, this cute café and shop sells handicrafts, coffee and cakes. You can purchase school books and medical soap to donate to schools and families in villages when you go trekking.

Getting There & Away

By far the easiest way to reach the Inle Lake region is to fly. Most long-distance road transport starts or finishes in Taunggyi – to reach Nyaungshwe, you'll have to change at the junction town of Shwenyaung (see p232) on the highway between Taunggyi and Heho.

AIR

The main airport for the Inle region is at Heho, 25.5 miles northwest of Nyaungshwe on the way to Kalaw – see p231 for details. There are no official airline offices, but hotels and private travel agents in Nyaungshwe can make bookings – see p234.

The one-hour taxi ride between Heho airport and Nyaungshwe costs K15,000.

BUS & PICK-UP

Any bus or pick-up travelling between Taunggyi and the plains can drop you by the junction of the road to Nyaungshwe in Shwenyaung. Hotels and travel agents in Nyaungshwe can book seats but be sure to be at the junction in Shwenyaung early so you don't miss the bus.

EASTERN MYANMAR

THE PADUANG – LONG NECKS BUT FEW PROSPECTS

Originally from Kayah state on the Thai border south of Inle Lake, the Paduang tribe – Myanmar's famous 'giraffe women' – have become a victim of their own traditions. The ancient custom of fitting young girls with brass neck-rings has made the Paduang a major tourist attraction – and a major target for exploitation on both sides of the border.

Originally intended to make Paduang women less attractive to raiding parties from neighbouring tribes, the application of heavy brass neck-rings causes deformation of the collar bone and upper ribs, pushing the shoulders away from the head. Many Paduang women reach a stage where they are unable to carry the weight of their own heads without the rings as additional support.

These days, the rings are applied with a different purpose – to provide women from impoverished hill villages with the means to make a living posing for photographs. Many Paduang women are ferried across the border to Thailand and kept in virtual slavery to provide a photo opportunity for visiting tour groups. The UN has compared the treatment of Paduang women to the treatment of animals in a zoo.

Many souvenir shops on Inle Lake employ Paduang women to lure passing tourist boats, which leaves travellers with an ethical dilemma. If you want to help the Paduang, purchase handloom fabrics and other Paduang crafts rather than taking pictures of 'long-necked women' to save another generation of young women from ending up as exhibits in a human freak show.

Shwenyaung & Taunggyi

Pick-ups run regularly through the day to Shwenyaung (K500, 30 minutes) and Taunggyi (K700, one hour) from 5am to around 6pm. The **pick-up stand** (Yone Gyi Rd) is west of the market but pick-ups also stop near the bridge north of Mingala Market. Coming from Taunggyi, look for the sign of a leg-rower on top of the pick-ups.

Kalaw, Thazi & Meiktila

To reach Kalaw, Thazi or Meiktila, you must first take a pick-up or taxi to Shwenyaung. Once you reach the highway junction, you can flag down local buses and pick-ups heading west – see p232 for details.

Bagan

Hotels and travel agents can book seats on the non-air-con buses from Taunggyi to Nyaung U (K13,000, 12 hours). The bus passes the Shwenyaung junction at around 5am.

Mandalay

Buses to Mandalay start in Taunggyi but hotels and agents in Nyaungshwe can book tickets for K10,000. Mandalay-bound buses reach the junction in Shwenyaung at around 6pm, arriving in Mandalay around 12 hours later.

Yangon

Overnight buses from Taunggyi to Yangon reach the junction in Shwenyaung between noon and 1pm, arriving at Yangon's highway bus terminal 16 to 20 hours later. Agents and hotels in Nyaungshwe can book seats for around K14,000.

TAXI

The easiest way to find a taxi in Nyaungshwe is to ask at your hotel; whole taxis fares include Shwenyaung (K7000), Heho (K15,000), Taunggyi (K16,000) and Kalaw (K40,000) and taxis have room for three or four passengers.

Motorcycle taxis near the market can transfer you to Shwenyaung for K2000.

Getting Around

Dirt tracks run through the marshes in all directions from Nyaungshwe – several shops on Yone Gyi Rd and Phaung Daw Pyan Rd rent out clunky Chinese bicycles for exploring for K1000 per day.

Motorcycle taxis (near the market) can take you to Kaung Daing hot springs for K4000 return.

THE LAKE

☎ 081

Almost every visitor to Nyaungshwe takes a boat trip on Inle Lake, but the lake is so large and the villages so spread out that Inle never feels too crowded with foreigners. The exception is when the traditional five-day market rotation comes to Ywama or Inthein; every tour boat and souvenir vendor in the Inle region heads straight for the market and tourists jostle for space with tribal people trying to do their weekly shopping.

Sights

KAUNG DAING

ခေါင်းလ္လွတိုင်လ္လွ

Set on dry land on the northwestern shore of the lake, about 5 miles from Nyaungshwe, this Intha village is known for its tofu, prepared using split yellow peas instead of soybeans. The main attraction here is the **Hu-Pin Hot Springs Complex** (☎ 29296; swimming pool $4, private bathhouse $8, mixed hot pool $5; ◷ 5am-6pm), just over a mile north of the village. The steaming hot water from the natural springs has been channelled into a swimming pool and a series of private bathhouses for men and women. The special pools for mixed bathing are only open to foreigners. You can rent a *longyi* (sarong-style garment) for K500.

Getting There & Away

You can reach Kaung Daing and the hot springs by boat or by road. Boat operators charge around K2000 each way for the 30-minute trip across the lake. Motorcycle taxis at Mingala market will ferry you to the springs and back for K4000, including a couple of hours waiting time.

To reach the springs on foot or by bicycle, cross the bridge over the channel leading to the lake and follow the bone-shaking dirt track through the marshes until you reach the sealed road, then turn left. The trip to the springs will take around 40 minutes by bicycle or two hours on foot.

The springs are also the start or end point of several trekking routes between Kalaw and Inle Lake – see p226 and p242 for details.

NGA HPE KYAUNG (JUMPING CAT MONASTERY)

ငါးဖယ်ချောင်း

On the eastern side of the lake, the Nga Hpe Kyaung is famous for its jumping cats, trained to leap through hoops by the monks during the slow hours between scripture recitals. The monks seem happy to put on a cat-jumping show for visiting tourists and the cats get treats for their efforts, so they seem fairly happy too. However, don't expect a show when the monks are eating or medi-

tating. A better reason to visit the pagoda is to see the collection of ancient buddha images. Constructed four years before Mandalay Palace, the huge wooden meditation hall has statues in the Shan, Tibetan, Bagan and Inwa (Ava) styles displayed on hugely ornate wood and mosaic pedestals.

YWAMA

ရွာမ

Ywama was the first village to be developed for tourism, and as a result, it has the greatest number of souvenir shops and restaurants. It's still a very pretty village, with winding channels lined with tall teak houses, but the charm is diminished by the crowds of tourist boats and paddling souvenir vendors.

The main attraction at Ywama is the famous **floating market**, though this has also been a victim of its own success. Held once every five days, the market is a traffic jam of tourist boats and souvenir hawkers, with a few local farmers peddling vegetables in among the crowds.

Luckily, the market moves on to quieter destinations during the week. To see a floating market without the crowds, visit one of the other villages on the five-day circuit – hotels and guesthouses can advise you where the market will be heading next.

A land-based five-day market rotates among the lakeshore villages of Kaung Daing, Maing Thauk, Nampan, Inthein and Than Taung. This market is arguably more interesting than the floating market as tribal people come down from the hills to trade livestock and produce.

PHAUNG DAW OO PAYA

ဖောင်တော်ဦးဘုရား

A wide channel leads south from Ywama to the village of Tha Ley and **Phaung Daw Oo Paya** (camera/video fee K200/300), the holiest religious site in southern Shan State. Enshrined within the huge tiered pagoda are four ancient buddha images that have been transformed into amorphous blobs by the sheer volume of gold leaf applied by devotees. During the annual Phaung Daw Oo festival (see p234), the images are paraded around the lake in an ornate barge shaped like a *hintha*.

At other times of the year, the images are displayed with a fifth golden relic in a pavilion inside the paya, while the boat is stored in a nearby boathouse. Local families often bring their children here as part of the ordination rites for the *sangha* (Buddhist brotherhood) – a fascinating spectacle if you happen to be there at the right time.

NAMPAN

South of Ywama, the peaceful village of Nampan is built on stilts over the water. It's off the main tourist circuit, but the **Alodaw Pauk Pagoda** is one of the oldest shrines on the lake. Built on stilts over the water, the whitewashed stupa enshrines a fabulous gem-encrusted, Shan-style buddha. Nampan has several small **cheroot factories** and there are some good restaurants on the edge of the village.

IN PHAW KHONE

This tidy village of teak stilt houses is famous for its **weaving workshops**. Buildings across the village vibrate with the clatter of shuttles and the click-clack of shifting loom frames. The workshops are a popular stop on the tourist circuit, but it's fascinating to see the skill of the weavers as they produce ornate, multi-coloured fabrics on looms made from bamboo poles lashed together with rope.

The workshops produce some fine shawls, scarves and *longyi* in silk, cotton and threads drawn from the stems of lotus plants – lotus-fibre shawls cost $30 or more because of the limited availability of the raw material.

FLOATING GARDENS

North of Nampan are these famous gardens, where Intha farmers raise flowers, tomatoes, squash and other fruit and vegetables on long wooden trellises supported on floating mats of vegetation. In the morning and afternoon, farmers paddle up and down between the rows tending their crops. It's a bucolic scene made all the more photogenic by the watery setting.

INTHEIN

အင်းတိမ်

West of Ywama, a narrow, foliage-cloaked canal winds through the reeds to the lakeshore village of Inthein (Indein). As the channel leaves the reed beds, the jungle grows denser and denser on either side, before the village appears suddenly among the vegetation. The *Apocalypse Now* ambience evaporates somewhat when you see the waiting tourist boats, but no matter – the ruined pagodas on the hilltop are still incredibly atmospheric despite the crowds.

The first group of ruined stupas is immediately behind the village. Known as **Nyaung Ohak** ('Under the Shade of Banyan Trees'), the crumbling stupas are choked in greenery but you can still discern some ornate stucco carvings of animals, *deva* and *chinthe*.

From Nyaung Ohak, a covered stairway climbs the hill, flanked by stalls selling lacquerware, puppets and other souvenirs – quality is high but so are the prices. At the top is **Shwe Inn Thein Paya**, a complex of 1054 weather-beaten *zedi*, most constructed in the 17th and 18th centuries. Some of the *zedi* lean at crazy angles while others have been reconstructed using donations from local Buddhists, which may ultimately be the fate of the whole complex. From the pagoda, there are great views across the lake and valley. For even better views, there are two more **ruined stupas** on conical hills just north of the village, reached via a dirt path behind Nyaung Ohak.

Part of the five-day inshore circuit, the **market** in Inthein is one of the biggest and liveliest in the area. Numerous Pa-O and Danu tribal people come down from the hills, and villagers engage in non-lethal cockfights and lively football and *chinlon* (a Myanmar ball sport) matches. The village is one possible starting point for **treks** to Kalaw – see p242 for more information.

MAING THAUK

မိုင်းသောက်

On the eastern side of the lake, the village of Maing Thauk has a split personality – half the village is set on dry land, while the other half sits on stilts over the water, linked to the shore by a 450yd wooden bridge.

Inland from the main road through the village, a few crumbling gravestones near the orphanage mark the location of the colonial-era **Fort Steadman**.

You can continue walking uphill to a peaceful **forest monastery** for good views over the lake. Maing Thauk is accessible by boat and by road – you can cycle to Maing Thauk in an hour or so along a dirt track leading southeast from Nyaungshwe.

SOUTHERN END OF THE LAKE

At the southern end of the lake, the village of **Thaung Tho Kyaung** holds an important tribal market every five days. This market sees far fewer visitors than the one at Inthein, and a long walkway leads uphill from town to a complex of whitewashed **Shan stupas**. There are more interesting stops in this part of the lake; the village of **Kyauk Taung** is devoted to pottery-making, while nearby **Kyaing Kan** specialises in weaving robes using lotus threads.

A long canal at the bottom of Inle Lake winds south through peaceful countryside to a second lake ringed by Shan, Intha and Pa-O villages. It takes around three hours to reach the largest village, **Sankar** (Samka), once the seat of a Shan hereditary prince. On the opposite side of the lake is **Tharkong Pagoda**, a collection of crumbling *zedi* and stucco sculptures that date back at least 500 years. The main attraction here is the almost total absence of other tourists – visits to this area have only been permitted since 2003 and foreigners must still be accompanied by a Pa-O guide. Guided boat trips to Sankar should be arranged through Golden Island Cottages (opposite) in Nampan, Thale U or Nyaungshwe; guides cost $10 and there's a permit fee of $5.

Activities
MOTORBOAT TRIPS
It is *de rigueur* to take at least one boat trip on the lake during a visit to Inle. Every morning, a flotilla of slender wooden canoes fitted with long-tailed outboard motors surges out into the lake, transporting visitors to famous sights like the Phaung Daw Oo Paya in Tha Ley, the Nga Hpe Kyaung in Nga Phe village, the ruined *zedi* at Inthein and the floating gardens.

Almost every trip involves at least one visit to a souvenir emporium and stops at workshops producing textiles, silverware and other crafts. The quality of crafts on offer is actually very high, and there isn't too much hard sell, though the floating vendors who stalk tourist boats in Ywama can get a little tiresome. There are plenty of restaurants out on the lake serving Chinese, Shan and Bamar food so tell your driver to stop whenever you feel hungry.

The lake itself is rich in wildlife, especially waterfowl. The area around the lake has been protected as the Inle Wetland Bird Sanctuary, an official bird sanctuary, since 1985 and you'll see herons, warblers, cormorants, wild ducks and egrets as you zip along the channels between the villages. However, you won't hear them – or the comments of fellow passengers for that matter – over the thunder of the boat's motor. Bring ear plugs or sit right at the front, away from the thundering pistons.

Every hotel and guesthouse in Nyaungshwe can arrange motorboat trips or you can make your own arrangements directly with the boat drivers. Prices for day-long boat trips start at around K12,000, which covers the entire boat; drivers will carry five or more passengers in a single boatload. A half-day trip costs K6000 but you'll only have time to visit the northern half of the lake. Passengers get a seat on deck – with a cushion on more expensive boats – and all the boats carry life jackets.

It's important to remember that you call the shots. If somewhere doesn't interest you, tell the driver to move on; if you want to stop somewhere all day, let the driver know.

Drivers are happy to stop along the way for photos but make sure to keep an eye on the time – once the sun falls behind the Shan hills, the lake becomes dank and cold and the journey back to Nyaungshwe can take an age in the dark.

CANOE TRIPS
Travel agents and guesthouses in Nyaungshwe can rent you a canoe for around K2000 per hour. Foreigners are not allowed to canoe onto the main body of the lake but there are several old paya and teak *kyaung* (monasteries) accessible via small channels leading off the main canal. One place that can only be visited by canoe is the large **nat shrine** in the middle of a swampy banyan-tree jungle opposite Nanthe village on the main channel.

TREKKING
Inle Lake is the end point for several trekking routes from Kalaw. Trails run west from Kalaw through the villages of the Shan, Intha, Pa-O, Danu, Palaung and Danaw tribes, ending at villages on the western lakeshore. These treks can be walked in either direction, though most people walk from Kalaw to Inle as the final stages are mainly downhill.

The most popular start/end point for treks is Kaung Daing, but begging has become a problem on this route because of tour groups handing out sweets and money to children. More interesting places to start or end the walk to Kalaw include Inthein, Tone Lé and Thandaung.

There are also some interesting extended walks north and south of Nyaungshwe, passing through rice paddies dotted with Shan stupa ruins. Trails into the hills east of town lead to Pa-O villages with panoramic views over the lake. Guides can talk you through the various treks and itineraries.

Guided hikes can be arranged at most guesthouses and hotels in Nyaungshwe for around $10 a day, which includes a basic lunch of rice and curry (carry your own bottled or purified water). The only overnight trips currently encouraged are to Kalaw, though other trips may be possible depending on the current whim of the authorities.

SWIMMING
The lake waters are very clear so a swim looks inviting, but the channels around the villages are shallow and full of weeds. The best place for a swim is out on the main body of the lake, though you need to be wary of speeding riverboats. One safe spot for a swim is the disused teak mansion known as **Inleh Bo Teh**, near the mouth of the channel leading to Nyaungshwe.

Sleeping
Although many travellers choose to stay in Nyaungshwe, there are also a number of upmarket resorts built on stilts over the lake. The sensation of sleeping over the water is very atmospheric and all of the resorts have their own boats and drivers, but the resorts are all somewhat isolated, so most people eat where they stay.

Reservations are recommended in the high season, and discounts are often available for advance bookings. All rates include breakfast. All of the hotels arrange pick-ups and return boat trips to/from Nyaungshwe for around K8000. None of the following hotels appear to have government links.

Golden Island Cottages I (Nampan) & II (Thale U) (GIC; ☎ in Nampan 29390, in Thale U 29389, in Yangon 01-549 019; www.gicmyanmar.com; r $50-70; 🖳) Owned by a cooperative of Pa-O tribal people, the Golden Island Cottages resorts provide some of the best accommodation on the lake. The Nampan resort has a great location over open water while the Thale U resort is closer to shore. Both resorts offer attractive raised cottages linked by wooden walkways, arranged around a central restaurant serving good Chinese, Pa-O and Shan dishes. The owners can arrange treks and boat trips to Kakku and Sankar – they have an office in Nyaungshwe at the Diamond Star Guesthouse on Phaung Daw Seiq Rd.

Hu Pin Hotel Inle Khaung Daing Village Resort (☎ 29291; hupin@myanmar.com.mm; Kaung Daing; s/d $60/70, cottage $70/80, ste $150) Owned by the same people as the Hu Pin Hotel in Nyaungshwe (p237), this resort sits on dry land facing out onto the lake. The wooden bungalows are comfortable and well cared for and the Hu-Pin hot springs complex is just down the road.

Inle Resort (☎ 29722, in Yangon 01-3331444; www.inleresort.com; cottages $60-105) Opened in 2005, this handsome resort is centred on a palatial wooden restaurant and lobby. The stylish cottages feature huge picture windows and private sun decks facing onto the lake and the location on the east shore near Maing Thauk ensures plenty of afternoon sunshine. The health spa is a unique feature on the lake.

ourpick Inle Princess Resort (☎ 29055; www.inleprincessresort.com; bungalows $160-250) Head and shoulders above the other resorts on the lake, the Inle Princess is honeymoon material. The stylish wooden cottages would not look out of place in an Asian design magazine, with handmade furniture, luxurious fabrics, potted plants and ethnic artefacts on the walls. The more expensive bungalows have plant-filled sun-decks facing the lake.

Eating
As well as the resorts, there are numerous floating restaurants in stilt houses on the lake that offer good Chinese and Shan food, cold beers and English-language menus. Your boat driver will almost certainly steer you towards a restaurant where he earns a commission, but you can tell the driver to stop at any restaurant that looks appealing. The greatest concentration of restaurants is in Ywama, but there are also some good choices around Nampan.

AROUND INLE LAKE
Taunggyi
ေတာင္ႀကီး

☎ 081 / elev 4980ft

Although travellers make a beeline for Nyaungshwe, Taunggyi is the administrative capital for the whole of Shan State. It's a busy trading post and the town markets are piled high with Chinese and Thai goods, freighted in daily via the border crossings at Mong La and Tachileik. Needless to say, the black market in luxury goods is flourishing.

Taunggyi is primarily set up for locals rather than tourists, but the town has some interesting pagodas and a museum devoted to

EASTERN MYANMAR

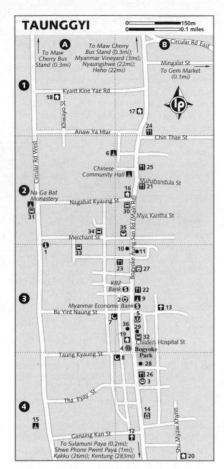

preserving Shan culture and heritage, something that has come under increasing threat from the central government in recent years. Most residents are Shan, Bamar or Chinese, but there are also sizeable populations of Sikhs, Muslims and Hindus from India and Nepal, reflecting the town's colonial past.

INFORMATION

There is no tourist office, but hotels can advise on tours and transport.

Golden Island Cottages (☎ 23136; 18 Circular Rd West; ☺ 6am-5pm) Arranges Pa-O guides for trips to Kakku and Sankar.

Public Internet Access Centre (Bogyoke Aung San Rd; per hr K500; ☺ 8.30am-9pm) Fast access; near Bogyoke Park.

SIGHTS
Markets

The focal point of Taunggyi is the market area on the main road through town. The **Old Market** is dominated by foodstuffs and household goods while the **New Market** has clothes and black-market goods. Every five days the old market ground hosts a busy **tribal market** that attracts lots of traders from the hills – it moves in a circuit from Taunggyi to Pwehla, Kalaw, Pindaya, Heho and back to Taunggyi.

Northeast of the centre, off the main road to Kalaw, the daily **gem market** (Mingalar St; ☺ noon-4pm) bustles with traders dealing in jade, rubies and sapphires. This is one of the

EASTERN MYANMAR

few places in the country where you can see the gem traders at work, but bear in mind that stones cannot be taken out of the country without an export licence.

Shan State Cultural Museum & Library

At the southern end of town, the **Shan State Cultural Museum & Library** (Bogyoke Aung San Rd; admission $2; 🕑 9.30am-3.30pm Tue-Sun) has displays of colourful tribal costumes, weapons, musical instruments, jewellery, old photos and displays on the peace treaty signed between Shan rebels and the government. Thus far, the museum has escaped the government crackdown on Shan cultural identity, but for how long remains to be seen.

Religious Monuments

The main downtown pagoda is the **Mya Le Dhamma Yon** (Bogyoke Aung San Rd) near the market and nearby is the huge **gurdwara** (Sikh temple) used by Taunggyi's Sikh population. Taunggyi has a number of historic **churches** and there are several Burmese-style **mosques** on the alleyways southwest of the market.

Set amongst the pines above Circular Rd West, the **Yat Taw Mu Pagoda** contains a 33ft-high standing buddha, constructed using donations from Japanese Buddhists. Just north of the Empire Hotel, **Min Kyaung** features gaudy statuary and a pagoda styled after the Mahabodhi temple at Bodhgaya in India.

On the outskirts of town in the direction of Kengtung, the huge white **Sulamuni Paya** has a gilded corncob stupa that pays tribute to the Ananda Pahto in Bagan. You can continue uphill to the ridge-top paya of **Shwe Phone Pwint Paya** for dizzying views over Taunggyi and Inle Lake.

FESTIVALS & EVENTS

As part of the full-moon celebrations during Tazaungmon (the eighth month of the Burmese lunar calendar), the city holds a huge **fire-balloon festival**, when hundreds of hot-air balloons in a kaleidoscope of colours and shapes are released into the sky to carry away sins. The three-day festival takes place in October or November and accommodation can be very hard to find in Taunggyi at this time.

SLEEPING

Hotels in Taunggyi cater primarily to visiting traders so there are few bargains to be had. Note that hotels are frequently booked solid during the balloon festival (see left). Rooms at the following hotels have bathrooms and fans.

Muse Hotel (☎ 22567; 6 Bogyoke Aung San Rd; s/d from $7/12) The closest Taunggyi has to budget accommodation, this faded block at the north end of town has large concrete rooms with rudimentary furnishings. It's worth paying a little more for one of the rooms with wood or tiled floors.

Hotel Empire (☎ 23737; 31 Bogyoke Aung San Rd; s/d $15/24) Another substantial Chinese business-style hotel, the Empire has modern rooms with TVs and bathrooms with reliably hot showers. Staff here are more used to dealing with foreign visitors than at the other hotels in town.

Paradise Hotel (☎ 22009; 157 Khwayo St; s/d from $24/30) This modern, four-storey Chinese-style place benefits from a quiet location away from the main road. The décor tests the eye, but rooms are comfortable and service attentive. The hotel is on the corner of Kyant Kine Yae St.

Taunggyi Hotel (☎ 21127; Shu Myaw Khynn St; s/d from $24/30) Set in a peaceful wooded area in the old British enclave, this former government hotel now has private owners. The woodland setting is the main attraction – rooms are institutional, rectangular boxes with squeaky plastic-wrapped mattresses,

---

A VERY BURMESE VINEYARD

Myanmar probably isn't the first place that comes to mind when you think of fine wine, but all that may be set to change with the increasingly robust vintages coming out of the **Myanmar Vineyard** (☎ 081-24536; www.myanmar-vineyard.com) at Aythaya, 3 miles west of Taunggyi. Founded in 1999 by German entrepreneur Bert Morsbach, the vineyard sits at an elevation of 4290ft on well-watered, limestone-rich soils, providing good growing conditions for Shiraz, Cabernet Sauvignon, Sauvignon Blanc, Chenin Blanc and Moscato grapes. Aythaya wines are now sold all over Myanmar, and the vineyard is open daily for tours and tastings – see the website for details. You can reach the vineyard by taxi, or on any pick-up travelling between Taunggyi and Shwenyaung.

but all have TV, mini-bar and a hot shower or tub.

Also recommended:

Sunnmin Hotel (☎ 22353; 137 Bogyoke Aung San Rd; s/d from $15/30;))

EATING

Unless otherwise stated, the following restaurants are open from 8am to 9pm.

Shwe Min Thu Café (Bogyoke Aung San Rd; snacks K300) Near the post office, this humble teashop has posters of London on the walls and hot tea, coffee and cakes to warm your belly on cold mornings.

Saung Oo (Chin Thae St; noodles from K1000; ⏰ 6am-3pm) North of the centre on a lane off the main drag, this popular noodle house serves hearty bowls of noodle soup with a choice of toppings. It's only open for breakfast and lunch.

Lyan You (Bogyoke Aung San Rd; meals from K2000) The best of several boisterous beer halls on the main road, Lyan You has Skol and Dagon beer on tap and above average Chinese food – we recommend the special assorted noodles and sweet and sour ribs.

Sein Restaurant (Bogyoke Aung San Rd; meals K2000) Locals crowd into this busy restaurant on the northern highway for tasty Chinese food and Myanmar set meals with all the trimmings. The fried snakehead fish goes down a treat.

The Old Market has a number of inexpensive **food stalls** (meals K1500; ⏰ 6.30am-5pm) serving *kauq-sweh* (Shan noodle soup) and other local staples. There's also a good night market on the street south of the New Market. A good place for breakfast is **7 Donuts** (Bogyoke Aung San Rd) – it sells, you guessed it, doughnuts and coffee.

ENTERTAINMENT

There are several cinemas along Bogyoke Aung San Rd, such as Myoma Cinema, screening Myanmar blockbusters. All the films are in Burmese but the plots are normally easy to work out from the dramatic music.

Dynasty Melody & Restaurant (Bogyoke Aung San Rd; ⏰ till 10pm) Upstairs in an arcade near the Myoma Cinema, this grungy beer hall has periodic live bands, karaoke singers and other stage shows.

GETTING THERE & AWAY

Air

The airport at Heho, about 22 miles west of Taunggyi, has regular flights to Yangon, Mandalay, Bagan and other cities – see p231.

Yangon Airways (☎ 23995), **Air Mandalay** (☎ 21330) and **Air Bagan** (☎ 24737) all have offices on Bogyoke Aung San Rd. A taxi from Heho to Taunggyi costs around K20,000.

Bus

Buses leave from several stands around town. The offices of companies running long-haul services to Mandalay (K10,000, 12 hours), Yangon (K14,000, 16 to 20 hours) and Nyaung U (Bagan; K13,000, 12 hours) are strung out along the main road. **Eastern State Express** (☎ 22722, Bogyoke Aung San Rd) runs reliable express buses to Yangon at 12.30pm and Mandalay at 5.30pm. Bagan buses leave around 4am.

Buses to Kalaw (K3000, three hours) leave every afternoon from the **Maw Cherry bus stand** (Circular Rd West), about a mile north of the centre. This bus stand also has a single daily service to Pindaya (K2500, four hours) at 1pm. Any of these buses can drop you in Shwenyaung or Heho. To get to the Maw Cherry bus stand, charter a pick-up taxi at the market for around K1500.

Small local buses to Meiktila (K6000, eight hours) and Thazi (K6000, seven hours) leave from a stand on Circular Rd West, near the Na Ga Bat Monastery.

Pick-up

Pick-ups leave regularly from a stand just north of the New Market to Nyaungshwe (K700, one hour) between 6am and 4pm. Pick-ups to Meiktila (K6000, eight hours) leave from a separate stand one block west of the New Market; the fare is K2000 to Heho and K3000 to Kalaw.

Taxi

Taxis loiter in front of the Hotel Empire, offering charter rides to Nyaungshwe (K20,000), Heho airport (K20,000) and Kakku (K35,000 return).

Share taxis to Mandalay (K21,000 per person) leave early in the morning from offices near the Hotel Empire.

Kakku

ကက္ကူ

Arranged in neat rows sprawling over the hillside, the 2478 stupas at Kakku (Kekku) are one of the most remarkable sights in Shan State. According to local legend, the stupa garden was founded by the Buddhist missionaries of the Indian emperor Ashoka in the 3rd century BC. The stupas at Kakku were built in a bewildering variety of styles, marking the prevailing architectural styles when they were constructed. Some are simple and unadorned while others are covered in a riot of stucco deities and mythical beasts. Among the tall Shan-style stupas are a number of small square 'monastery style' stupas that are unique to this region.

Like ancient sites across the country, Kakku is slowly being restored and modernised using donations from pilgrims – the stupa garden still has a palpable sense of antiquity but don't expect an Indiana Jones–style ruin in the jungle. The annual **Kakku Paya Pwe**, held on the full-moon day of the lunar month of Tabaung (March), attracts Pa-O pilgrims from across Shan State.

Kakku is surrounded by Pa-O villages and the site can only be visited with a Pa-O guide, arranged through **Golden Island Cottages** (☎ in Taunggyi 081-23136; 18 Circular Rd East, Taunggyi; ☽ 6am-5pm). There's a $3 entry fee for the site and a $5 fee for the guide and you must also arrange a taxi to the site – around K35,000 from Taunggyi, including a few hours waiting at the stupas.

So far there isn't any accommodation at Kakku, but you can get a good meal at the **Hlaing Konn Restaurant** (☽ lunch & dinner) overlooking the site.

KENGTUNG & BORDER AREAS

Beyond Taunggyi, the landscape rucks up into great folds, cloaked in dense forest and cut by rushing mountain rivers. This is the heartland of the Golden Triangle, where insurgent armies battled for most of the last century to gain control of the opium trade between Myanmar, China, Laos and Thailand. Ceasefires with the main rebel groups have allowed the region to finally move out of the shadow of civil war but drug trafficking and other illegal activities are common and travel to the border areas is still subject to government restrictions.

Kengtung is only accessible by air from inside Myanmar and travellers entering Myanmar overland from Thailand cannot travel to the rest of the country.

KENGTUNG

ကျိုင်းတုံ

☎ 084

The second-biggest city in Shan State, Kengtung (Kyaing Tong), pronounced 'Cheng Dong', is the capital of the Golden Triangle region and one of the most attractive towns in Myanmar. In culture and appearance, it feels closer to the hill towns of northern Thailand and southern China than to anywhere else on this side of the border. Kengtung rose to prominence in the 13th century as the capital of a Shan kingdom that once extended as far east as Chiang Rai and Chiang Mai. The last *sao pha* of Kengtung, Sao Sai Luang, died in Yangon in 1997, but more than 80% of inhabitants still define themselves as Tai Khün – the local name for the Shan.

For years, Kengtung was caught in the crossfire between rival drug lords, but peace has returned to the quiet, pagoda-lined streets. However, restrictions on travel remain – Kengtung can only be reached by air from inside Myanmar and travellers visiting from Thailand are banned from travelling deeper into Myanmar. The rugged terrain of eastern Shan State contributes to the sense of isolation – Kengtung is an outpost of development in a sea of forested mountains, where Wa, Eng, Shan, Akha and Lahu tribal people follow a way of life that has changed little in centuries. Needless to say, treks to hill-tribe villages are a major attraction.

Information

Travel agents and hotels can book flights and bus tickets. The website www.kengtung.net has some interesting information on the city. Moneychangers in the market exchange kyat, US dollars, Thai baht and Chinese yuan.

Immigration Office (☽ 24hr) Down an alley north of the Paleng gate; issues permits for travel to Mong La and Tachileik.

Shining Star (☎ 21568; 58 Airport Rd; per hr K1000; ☽ 9am-9pm) Reliable internet access on the way to the airport.

Sunfar Travels (☎ 22626; 65 Loi Mwe Rd) Sells tickets for all the private airlines.

Sunflower Travel & Tours (☎ 21833; 16 Kyaing Ngarm 1st St) Reliable agent just east of the central market.

Sights & Activities

The **central market** draws people from all over the Kengtung district, including tribal people from the hills. The market has lots of stalls selling food and household items, including

EASTERN MYANMAR

THE OPIUM KING

Every region has a local hero, but Khun Sa has to be one of the most unlikely. Born in Shan State in 1934, the man who would one day control a quarter of the world's heroin production cut his teeth fighting with Chiang Kai-shek's nationalist Kuomintang army along the border between Burma and Yúnnán.

In 1963, Khun Sa formed his own private army, fighting for, and later against, the Burmese government, to gain control of eastern Shan State and the thriving drug trade in the Golden Triangle – the lawless border area between Myanmar, China, Laos and Thailand. To achieve this end, Khun Sa assembled a rag-tag force of 20,000 men and women – the Mok Tai Army – which waged a heroin-funded separatist war against the Myanmar authorities for more than 20 years.

Khun Sa's stranglehold on the Golden Triangle region started to unravel in the early 1990s, when he began to lose control of his own forces. Khun Sa finally surrendered in 1996 and the United Wa State Army took control of the heroin and methamphetamine trade. Many expected Khun Sa to face trial for drug trafficking, but instead the veteran drug lord lived out the rest of his days in genteel retirement, passing away at his mansion home in Yangon at the ripe old age of 74. Even today, the people of Shan State are split as to whether Khun Sa was a great freedom fighter or simply a very successful criminal.

the coins, buttons, beads and threads used to decorate tribal costumes. Twice a week, there's a **water-buffalo market** on the road leading to Taunggyi. You probably won't be able to fit a buffalo into your backpack but it's interesting to watch the traders haggling for the best price on a used beast of burden.

The old British enclave in Kengtung was centred on the small **Naung Tung** lake. The lakeshore is a popular spot for morning and evening strolls and there are several decaying colonial buildings above the lake shore, including the handsome **Colony House** (Mine Yen Rd). On the road leading towards Taunggyi, the **Roman Catholic Mission** and **Immaculate Heart Cathedral** have been providing an education for hill-tribe orphans since colonial times.

MONASTERIES & TEMPLES

If there were many more Buddhist monasteries in Kengtung people would have nowhere left to live. The town's many monasteries are called *wat* rather than *kyaung*, and local monks wear both orange and red robes, reflecting the close cultural links to Thailand.

The gilded stupa of **Wat Jong Kham** (Zom Kham) rises majestically above the centre of town. Legend dates the *wat* to a visit by Gautama Buddha but a more likely date for the stupa is the 13th-century migration from Chiang Mai. In the middle of the traffic roundabout below Wat Jong Kham, **Wat Mahamuni** (Maha Myat Muni) is a classic Thai-style *wat* with a richly painted interior. Just north of Airport Rd, **Wat In** contains a

stunning collection of ancient gilded wooden buddha images in all shapes, sizes and positions. Chinese residents of Kengtung worship at the appealing **Chinese Buddhist temple** near the immigration office.

Pointing dramatically towards the mountains on a ridge overlooking Naung Tung lake, the 60ft-high standing buddha statue known as **Ya Taw Mu** is probably the most distinctive landmark in Kengtung. Next to the statue is a small **Cultural Museum** (admission $1) with costumes, farming implements and other tribal objects, some inexplicably painted silver. It's open daily but there are no fixed hours – you must find the man with the key at the adjacent monastery.

The most impressive sights in Kengtung used to be the palace of the Kengtung *sao pha* but the government demolished the palace in 1991 in one of its many campaigns against Shan nationalists; the ugly Kyaing Tong Hotel now sits in its place. You can see the dome-shaped stone **mausoleums of the Tai Khün princes** opposite Wat Chiang Jan.

HOT SPRINGS

Reached via a bumpy dirt track off the road to Tachileik, the bubbling **Mya Shwe Ye Hot Springs** (s/d bathhouse K1500/2000, family bathhouse K3000; ☼ 6am-8pm) are hot enough to cook eggs, and that's exactly what locals do, before relaxing in a warm bath in the adjacent bathhouse. Bathers get a private room with a tub and piped cold water to dilute the boiling spring water to a bearable temperature. Several roadhouse

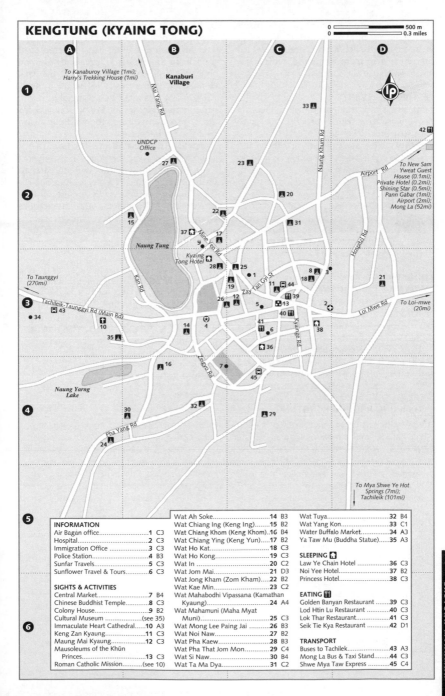

KENGTUNG (KYAING TONG)

0   500 m
0   0.3 miles

EASTERN MYANMAR

restaurants around the springs serve meals and cold beers but you'll need to bring your own *longyi* or towel. Taxis charge K5000 for the return trip from Kengtung, with a few hours waiting at the springs.

FESTIVALS & EVENTS

Kengtung's Chinese community celebrate the Chinese New Year in early February with the usual firecracker-charged festivities. For Buddhists, the big calendar event is the Water Festival in April, when everyone gets a dousing, including visitors.

Sleeping

Unless otherwise stated, rooms at the following hotels have TV and bathroom, and rates include breakfast. Note that rooms are scarce during the Chinese New Year festivities and during the Water Festival (see above).

BUDGET

Noi Yee Hotel (☎ 21144; 5 Mine Yen St; s/d $5/10) A former royal residence, the Noi Yee has fallen on hard times. The faded colonial charm ends at reception – rooms are grungy and the shared bathrooms need some serious TLC.

ourpick **Harry's Trekking House** (☎ 21418; 132 Mai Yang Rd; r $5-15) Although, sadly, Harry passed away a few years back (the business is now run by his wife), this backpacker-oriented hotel is still the best choice for budget travellers. The guesthouse is about half a mile north of the lake in Kanaburoy village. Guests have a choice of simple wooden rooms at the back or smarter doubles with TV in the annexe. All sorts of treks can be arranged and you can rent motorcycles for $10 per day. Ask for a receipt when you pay to avoid confusion over the bill later.

New Sam Yweat Guest House (☎ 21643; 21 Airport Rd; s/d from $8/16) Near the pond on the airport road, this guesthouse was built to cater to visiting tour groups. It looks flashier outside than in, but rooms are OK for the money. The creaky old wooden rooms have more character than the plain modern rooms above reception.

MIDRANGE

The poshest option in town, the Kyaing Tong Hotel by the lake, is government owned.

Private Hotel (☎ 21438; www.privatehotelmyanmar .com; 5 Airport Rd; s/d from $18/25) Away from the centre on the airport road, this place offers plenty of creature comforts. The eccentric owner makes every effort to please and there's a cute lawn with benches where you can soak up the sun. Rooms have TVs, mini-bars and 24-hour hot water.

TREKKING AROUND KENGTUNG

The forested hills of eastern Shan State are dotted with the villages of the Eng, Lahu Akha, Palaung, Loi, Lishaw, Shan and Wa tribes, many of which can be visited on guided treks from Kengtung. Modernity is slowly coming to the hills in the form of electricity and modern building materials, but most villages are made up of timber-framed stilt houses with thatched roofs. Ingenious irrigation systems made from hollow tree trunks channel in water for drinking and washing.

Although some tribes have converted to Christianity, others still follow Buddhism or ancient animist beliefs. Traditional costume is widespread – the Akha are famous for their embroidered tunics and headdresses covered in coins and hammered metal disks, while the Eng wear neat black tunics and metal armlets and blacken their teeth with betel nut and black dye.

Each village is governed by a headman or shaman, and villagers work together to build new houses – usually an excuse for feasting and lots of drinking. Almost all the tribes raise pigs and chickens and some cultivate tea, maize, pumpkins, betel nut, peanuts and bananas. Dog meat is a local delicacy, but this is rarely offered to visitors.

Most hotels in Kengtung can arrange day treks to local villages, with lunch at a village home; the treks organised by Harry's Trekking House (see above) get good reports. Producing arts and crafts to sell to trekkers has become an important cottage industry – buying crafts and donating useful items to the village headman is a better way to help the villagers than randomly handing out pens, sweets and money to children.

Overnight trips are currently discouraged, but you can easily see the villages of several different tribes in a single day. Guide fees start at $10 per day, including lunch. You will also have to factor in the cost of getting to the trailheads by taxi or rented motorcycle – a further $10 to $20.

Princess Hotel (☎ 21319; kengtung@mail4u.com .mm; s $20-25, d $28-35; ⚒) The most popular midrange choice in town, the Princess has a great location near the market and very polished service. Staff are used to dealing with tour groups and the rooms have TVs, aircon, fridges and phones. There isn't much to choose between the big superior rooms at the front and the small but brighter standard rooms at the back.

Law Ye Chain Hotel (☎ 21114; Kyaing Lan Rd; r from $25; 🖵) Above a Chinese bakery just south of the market, Law Ye Chain opened in late 2007 so everything is brand new. The smart rooms have air-con, TV and carpet, and immaculate bathrooms with hot showers.

Eating

Kengtung has some excellent places to eat and many dishes have a distinctively Thai flavour. Because of paranoia about bird flu, chicken is periodically unavailable in Kengtung. The following restaurants are open for breakfast, lunch and dinner.

Seik Tie Kya Restaurant (☎ 21387; Airport Rd; dishes from K1500) This recommended Chinese restaurant has a cosy dining room at the back and tables under an awning in the yard. The spicy beancurd hotpot is big enough for two.

Lok Thar Restaurant (meals from K1500) One block northeast of the market, this large, open-plan restaurant has bottled beers in the cooler and a top-notch menu of Chinese and Thai favourites. The Thai-style pork with green beans is delicious.

Lod Htin Lu Restaurant (Kyainge Rd; meals K1500-3000) Downhill from the mausoleums of the Khün princes, this is another Chinese banquet restaurant with private tables for families screened off by partitions at the back. The menu features noodle soups, pork with cashews and other Chinese classics.

Golden Banyan Restaurant (meals K2000) Yet another Chinese-style restaurant near the mausoleums of the Khün princes. Food is pretty standard for this kind of restaurant but the outdoor tables beneath a huge banyan tree create atmosphere.

Pann Gabar (Airport Rd; meals from K2000) If you fancy a break from Chinese food, this popular roadhouse by the bridge on the airport road has indoor and outdoor seating and good Thai food – the chef doesn't scrimp on the spices.

> ### CROSSING THE BORDER TO LAOS
>
> About 12 miles northeast of Tachileik on the highway to Kengtung, a small road branches east to the tiny town of Wan Pasak on the Mekong River, which marks the border between Laos and Myanmar. From Wan Pasak there are regular boats to Xieng Kok in Laos. Although locals use this border crossing regularly, foreigners are not currently permitted to cross the river between the two countries. However, it's always worth enquiring locally to see if the regulations have been relaxed.

Getting There & Away

The only way to reach Kengtung from inside Myanmar is by air, but road travel is permitted to Tachileik and Mong La with a permit from the immigration office (p247).

AIR

Air Bagan (☎ 22300; www.airbagan.com; 13B Zay Tan Gyi St) and **Yangon Airways** (www.yangonair.com) operate several weekly flights to Kengtung from Mandalay ($90, two hours), Heho ($76, 2½ hours) and from Tachileik ($43, 25 minutes). To fly from Kengtung to Tachileik, you will need a permit from the MTT in Yangon (p91). Air Bagan's office is near Wat Pha Jao Lung.

The airport is just a small shed and a couple of teashops. Trishaws charge K2500 to K3000 for the 20-minute trip into town.

BUS & PICK-UP

Foreigners can travel by road to Mong La and Tachileik but the 280-mile road between Kengtung and Taunggyi is completely off-limits. Officials blame banditry and fighting between the government and Shan, Wa and Pa-O rebel groups, but the ban probably has more to do with the smuggling of opium and methamphetamines through the Golden Triangle.

Tachileik

If you want to visit Tachileik by bus from Kengtung, you must first visit the immigration office (p247). Depending on the prevailing political wind, staff may be willing to issue you a free permit on the spot. However, you must leave your passport with the immigration officer so you don't feel tempted to cross into Thailand. Once you get the permit, you must make five photocopies to hand out at checkpoints along the way. The same procedure must be carried out at the Tachileik immigration office to return to Kengtung. In practice, it usually helps to get someone from your hotel to help with these arrangements.

Buses to Tachileik (K9000, four hours) leave from a stand on the Taunggyi road at around 10am. Share taxis from the same stand charge K20,000 per seat. **Shwe Mya Taw Express** (☎ 23145) runs daily buses to Tachileik from the market at 8am and noon; the fare is K9000.

In the other direction, you may be encouraged to buy a ticket from the small tourist office next to the immigration checkpoint, but you can also buy tickets at the offices at the bus stand. The standard rate is 300B, payable in baht or dollars at a poor conversion rate. Shared taxis charge 500/700B for a front/back seat.

Mong La

The bus and taxi stand for Mong La is down a lane next to Keng Zan Kyaung; the fare for the three- to four-hour journey is K7000 by bus and K12,000 by shared taxi, but you need permission from the Kengtung immigration office (p247) to make the trip. In practice, it is easier to do this journey by shared taxi as drivers know the ropes and will take you to the immigration office to sort out the paperwork. If you travel by bus, you will have to find the office yourself and make five photocopies of the permit for the driver to hand out at the various checkpoints along the way.

The free permit is issued in about 20 minutes, but you will be expected to leave your passport – or the permit allowing you to enter Myanmar from Thailand – at the immigration office until you return. Before you leave Kengtung, be sure to visit the market to change some dollars into yuan to pay the Y36 entry fee for Mong La. When you are ready to return to Kengtung, you must take your permit to the immigration office in Mong La and get a second document to facilitate your return to Kengtung.

Getting Around

Drivers of motorcycle taxis and trishaws wear coloured bibs. The going rate for a downtown trip is around K1000. A trishaw from the airport to town costs around K3000.

Some hotels hire out motorcycles for around $10 per day – insist on a helmet as the condition of the roads is terrible. Taxis can be rented for longer trips through your hotel; bank on $25 to $30 for a half-day trip.

AROUND KENGTUNG
Local Villages

The floodplain of the Khün River is dotted with small villages containing ancient *wat* and friendly locals who are still surprised by the sight of foreigners. If you rent a motorcycle or a trishaw for the day, you can roam around at your leisure. If you want to get deeper into the hills to the villages of the Eng, Lahu Akha, Palaung, Shan and Wa tribes, it's best to go with a guide from Kengtung (see p250).

Loi-mwe
လွိုင်မွယ်

Although it lies outside the official permit zone, no-one seems to care if you visit Loi-

---

EVERY CLOUD HAS A SILVER LINING...

When the Chinese government banned travel to Mong La in 2005, locals braced themselves for an economic catastrophe. The storm came, but the effects were less severe than many had predicted, largely down to the entrepreneurial wizardry of Sai Leun (Sai Lin; opposite), the warlord leader of Special Region #4.

When gamblers stopped crossing the border, the gambling industry shifted its attention to online gambling. Secretive online casinos were created in small villages like Mong Ma and Wan Hsieo, with live video feeds transferring the action on the card tables straight into living rooms across China.

The physical playing of games of chance is carried out using agents and mobile phones, and winnings are electronically transferred to bank accounts in China or physically smuggled across the border. Foreigners are welcome to visit the casinos at Mong Ma to take a flutter on the card tables, but note that the minimum stake is Y10 to Y50.

CROSSING THE BORDER TO THAILAND

The government has tightened the regulations at the border crossing between Tachileik and Mae Sai, making it much more difficult to cross between Myanmar and Thailand. As with so much else in Myanmar, the following information is liable to change, so check the situation locally before you travel.

Myanmar to Thailand

At the time of writing, travellers were only permitted to cross into Thailand at Tachileik with a permit from the MTT in Yangon (see p91). This permit is also required to fly into Tachileik, even if you do not intend to leave the country. Permits are issued in around two weeks but you may be required to book your flights and a taxi to the border through MTT. If you do obtain permission to cross into Thailand, the Thai authorities will issue you a 30-day Thai visa on arrival, or you can enter with a Thai visa obtained overseas.

Thailand to Myanmar

At the time of writing, tourists were allowed to cross from Mae Sai to Tachileik with a 14-day entry permit issued at the border. This entitles you to visit Tachileik, Kengtung and Mong La, but you cannot travel anywhere else in Myanmar, even if you have a full Myanmar visa. The permit costs 500B (or the equivalent in US dollars) and immigration officials will hold on to your passport until you leave the country.

---

mwe, 20 miles southeast of Kengtung. The town functioned as a second-tier hill station in the British era and you can still see a number of fading **colonial buildings** and a 100-year-old Catholic **church**. The main attraction though is the drive up here through a classically Asian landscape of dense forests and terraced rice fields. You'll have to hire a car or motorcycle to reach Loi mwe as there is no scheduled transport.

Mong La

 မိုင်းလား

About 53 miles north of Kengtung, Mong La (Mengla) straddles the border between Myanmar and China. Until recently, the town was Myanmar's answer to Las Vegas, with dozens of casinos, luxury hotels and hostess KTV bars catering to a steady stream of 'vice tourists' crossing the border from Yúnnán. The bubble burst in 2005 when the Chinese government banned its citizens from visiting Mong La to prevent the laundering of millions of yuan by Chinese crime syndicates. Most of the glitzy casinos and hotels closed down and the gambling cartels shifted their investments to new online casinos in the villages south of town.

On the surface, Mong La seems completely Chinese – the yuan is the local currency, the street signs are in Mandarin and the markets are piled high with Chinese cigarettes and rice wine – but most of the population are actually Tai Khün. Security for the town is provided by the private militia of Sai Leun (Sai Lin), a one-time communist insurgent and drug lord who signed a treaty with the Myanmar government and swapped opium poppies and rifles for gambling machines!

Since the closure of the big casinos, the main sights in town are the huge and busy **central market** and the towering **Shwedagon Pagoda**, which offers great views over the town and Chinese border post.

Nearby is a **Drug Eradication Museum** (free admission; ☼ sunrise-sunset) built by Sai Leun to back up his claim that Mong La was an 'opium-free zone'. Note the cautionary diorama showing long-haired, heavy metal–loving drug users being rehabilitated as upstanding Myanmar citizens. If you fancy a game of baccarat or Pai-Gow poker, head to the new complex of casinos just outside town at **Mong Ma** (see the box, opposite).

Foreigners cannot cross the border into China but visits to Mong La are easy to arrange with a permit from Kengtung – see opposite for details. Before you return to Kengtung, you must visit the immigration office on the outskirts of Mong La to complete the paperwork for the return journey – ask directions from a local as the office is hard to find on your own.

Before visiting, you'll need to change some dollars into yuan at the Kengtung market to cover meals and accommodation and the Y36 entry fee at the checkpoint just outside town. The road between Mong La and Kengtung passes through some dramatic countryside – look out for hill-tribe villagers in traditional costume along the roadside.

SLEEPING & EATING

There are several modern hotels in Mong La, none accustomed to dealing with English-speaking tourists. Try the business-like **Haung Faun Hotel** (r Y60) beside the market or the flashy-looking **Powerlong Hotel** (r Y150) by the river. Both are owned by Chinese businesspeople.

The best place to eat is the Central Market – there are dozens of stalls here piled high with fresh vegetables displayed in neat plastic baskets. Just pick any ingredients that take your fancy and they will be cooked up into delicious soups, grills and stir-fries in minutes.

GETTING THERE & AWAY

To visit Mong La from Kengtung you must obtain a permit from the immigration office in Kengtung – see p252 for details. The bus and taxi stand in Mong La is near the market.

Tachileik
တာ ချီလိတ်
☎ 084

Facing the town of Mae Sai across the Thai–Myanmar border, this nondescript town is like border towns all over Asia – a border post, a market for black-market goods and a handful of hotels catering to travellers en route somewhere else. Since the tightening of the border restrictions, the number of

visitors to Tachileik has slowed to a trickle – most travellers who come here today are entering Myanmar from Thailand on a 14-day pass, or returning to Thailand after exploring Kengtung and Mong La. Like other towns in the Golden Triangle, Tachileik has a double life – Thai tourists come here to escape the ban on gambling in Thailand and bet big stakes at the casinos by the Mekong River.

SLEEPING

If crossing the border into Thailand is an option, you'll find the accommodation there better in every respect. Hotels in Tachileik prefer payment in Thai baht, but some places will accept US dollars.

Dream Flower Hotel (☎ 51318; 1st St; r 250B) A 10-minute walk south from the border post, this hotel has clean rooms with attached bathroom and large communal balconies.

With more money to spend, there are decent air-con rooms at the **Mya Shwe Ye Hotel** (☎ 51792; 3/52 Mya Shwe Ye St; r 600B; ✂) and **Mekong River Hotel** (☎ 51912; Bogyoke Rd; r 1500B; ✂).

In Mae Sai, on the Thai side of the border, the Mae Sai Guesthouse on the river is recommended.

GETTING THERE & AWAY

Air Bagan (www.airbagan.com) and **Yangon Airways** (www.yangonair.com) fly between Mandalay and Tachileik $76 (one hour) daily except Saturday. Four days a week, flights continue to Kengtung ($43, 25 minutes). Note that you cannot board flights to Tachileik without a permit – see the boxed text, p253, for details.

For details of road travel to/from Kengtung, see p251.

EASTERN MYANMAR

Mandalay

မန္တလေး

For those who've not been – and that list includes *The Road to Mandalay* author Rudyard Kipling – the mention of 'Mandalay' conjures the most peaceful and serene settings imaginable: Asia at its most traditional, timeless and alluring. But those who go see what it really is – a rather scruffy, booming city on a wide bend of the Ayeyarwady (Irrawaddy) River, still an infant at 150 years old, with a sizeable makeover as a 'Chinese town' with many uninspired modern buildings. That said, Mandalay easily earns its place as a Myanmar attraction for its sunset views from Mandalay Hill, the powerful buddha image at Mahamuni Paya, an evening walk around the downtown market, nightly traditional music performances like the famously dissident Moustache Brothers, and superb attractions outside town (see p276).

Despite the energy and thriving business, Mandalay still 'lives like a village', as at least one Yangon resident told us mockingly. Locals cherish that reputation. They walk along the old king's moat in the evenings, and before the September 2007 protests about 60% of Myanmar's monks lived in the leafy villagelike area southwest of downtown. (Some were 'encouraged' to return to countryside homes.)

It's sometimes easy to get worn out by rich locals beeping in their low-riding jeeps, but just wait. Mandalay is at its most endearing as dusk settles to dark, and all that ugly traffic goes home.

HIGHLIGHTS

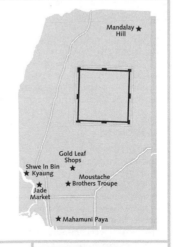

- Climb **Mandalay Hill** (p258) for the city's best vantage point from the spot where, the story goes, Buddha pointed out the setting of the future capital

- Witness a rarity in Myanmar: a dissenting voice, told with a smirk and a funny hat, at the **Moustache Brothers Troupe** (p270)

- Bypass the government's $10 combo ticket (p261) with a visit to the teak monastery at **Shwe In Bin Kyaung** (p263)

- Wake up at **Mahamuni Paya** (p263) as attendants brush the teeth of the country's most famous buddha image at 4am

- Shop like a demon – the wild **Jade Market** (p272) is best for people-watching, but you can pick up a puppet or edible gold-leaf sheet (!) at the **Gold Leaf Shops** (p271) on 36th St

| ■ TELEPHONE CODE: 02 | ■ POPULATION: 927,000 | ■ ELEVATION: 244FT |

HISTORY

Despite references to the contrary, Mandalay is a comparatively young city, and its time as the capital of the last Burmese kingdom was short. Only a few of its temples predate the 19th century. For centuries, though, this area of Myanmar was the site of the capitals of the Burmese kingdoms; from Mandalay you can easily visit four former royal cities – all now deserted.

King Mindon Min, penultimate ruler in the Konbaung dynasty, founded the city in 1857. The capital moved here from Amarapura in 1861. In true Myanmar tradition, the new palace was mainly constructed from the dismantled wooden buildings of the previous palace at Amarapura. Mandalay's period of glory was short – Mindon was succeeded by the disastrous Thibaw Min and, in 1885, Mandalay was taken by the British. Thibaw and his notorious queen were exiled and 'the centre of the universe' or 'the golden city' (as it was known) became just another outpost of the British Empire.

For years after independence in 1947, Mandalay slumbered like the rest of the country, particularly through the socialist mismanagement of Ne Win and company. However, with the reopening of the Burma Road through Lashio to China, the city has been undergoing an economic boom since the 1990s. The money fuelling this boom is generated by three trades – rubies, jade and heroin – and supposedly controlled by Kachin, Wa, Shan, Kokang and Chinese syndicates.

The population is nearing a million, with new townships springing up along the edges of the city, many inhabited by former squatters once at home in the city's central area. The Chinese presence has grown by a great deal since the easing of foreign trade restrictions with Myanmar's northerly neighbour.

Many new office buildings, 10-storey hotels and department stores have flourished along downtown blocks.

ORIENTATION

The hill with the huge grounds of old Mandalay Palace at its base is the natural focus of Mandalay. The bulk of the city sprawls to the south and west of the fort, bounded further west by the Ayeyarwady River.

The city centre – called 'downtown' on signs and by English-speaking locals – runs roughly from 21st St to 35th St, between 80th St and 87th St or 88th St. Cutting it in half, east–west 26th St divides south downtown (home to many Indians and Nepalis) from north downtown (where there's a notable Shan community).

The city streets are laid out on a grid system and numbered from north to south and east to west. For moving across the city quickly, 35th St serves as the main east–west thoroughfare, while 80th St is the main north–south street. The two major business thoroughfares are 26th and 84th Sts. It's also worth remembering that, between 35th and 26th Sts, the major thoroughfares of 81st and 83rd Sts are northbound one-way streets, and 82nd street is a southbound one-way street.

INFORMATION

Internet Access

Net Com (Map p259; 25th St, 82/83; per hr K1000; ☺ 8am-10pm)

Net Forever (Map p257; 29th St, 70/71; per hr K600; ☺ 9am-10pm)

Medical Services

Main Hospital (Map p257; 30th St, 74/77)

Nandaw Clinic (Palace Clinic; Map p257; ☎ 36128, 60443; cnr 29th & 71st Sts) Private clinic with a good reputation.

1885 OMENS

Burma's strength was waning when Britain conquered it in three decisive swoops in the 19th century, finishing with the humiliation of dragging the last king, Thibaw, onto the streets in Mandalay in 1885. Apparently it took hours for Thibaw's procession to find its way to the river!

It's something that led to a sense of defeat for much of the population suddenly ruled by a foreign, non-Buddhist power. But it's not something they didn't see coming.

Always superstitious, the Burmese noted two terrible signs before Mandalay's fall. A few days before, Thibaw's white elephant died and the sky at night was filled with thousands of shooting stars and meteors (this Andromeda shower was one of modern history's biggest meteor storms), which locals saw as a dark forecast.

MANDALAY

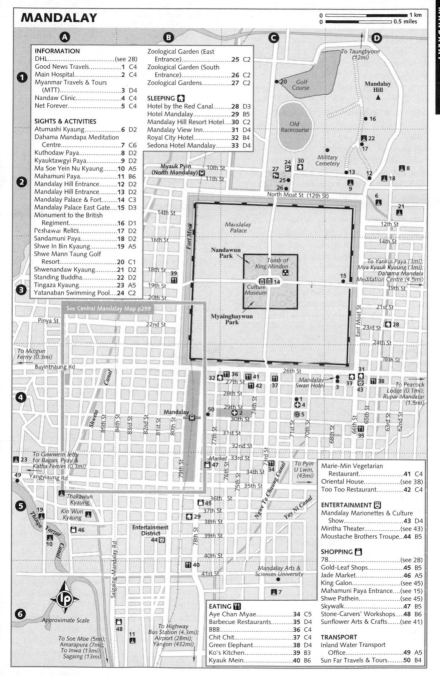

0 _____ 1 km
0 _____ 0.5 miles

INFORMATION
DHL...(see 28)
Good News Travels..................**1** C4
Main Hospital..........................**2** C4
Myanmar Travels & Tours
   (MTT)..................................**3** D4
Nandaw Clinic.........................**4** C4
Net Forever.............................**5** C4

SIGHTS & ACTIVITIES
Atumashi Kyaung.....................**6** D2
Dahama Mandapa Meditation
   Centre.................................**7** C6
Kuthodaw Paya.......................**8** D2
Kyauktawgyi Paya...................**9** D2
Ma Soe Yein Nu Kyaung.........**10** A5
Mahamuni Paya......................**11** B6
Mandalay Hill Entrance...........**12** D2
Mandalay Hill Entrance...........**13** D2
Mandalay Palace & Fort..........**14** C3
Mandalay Palace East Gate.....**15** D3
Monument to the British
   Regiment.............................**16** D1
Peshawar Relics......................**17** D2
Sandamuni Paya.....................**18** D2
Shwe In Bin Kyaung...............**19** A5
Shwe Mann Taung Golf
   Resort.................................**20** C1
Shwenandaw Kyaung..............**21** D2
Standing Buddha.....................**22** D2
Tingaza Kyaung......................**23** A5
Yatanaban Swimming Pool......**24** C2

Zoological Garden (East
   Entrance)............................**25** C2
Zoological Garden (South
   Entrance)............................**26** C2
Zoological Gardens.................**27** C2

SLEEPING
Hotel by the Red Canal..........**28** D3
Hotel Mandalay......................**29** B5
Mandalay Hill Resort Hotel.....**30** C2
Mandalay View Inn.................**31** D4
Royal City Hotel.....................**32** B4
Sedona Hotel Mandalay..........**33** D4

EATING
Aye Chan Myae.....................**34** C5
Barbecue Restaurants.............**35** D4
BBB.......................................**36** C4
Chit Chit................................**37** C4
Green Elephant......................**38** D4
Ko's Kitchen..........................**39** B3
Kyauk Mein...........................**40** B6
Marie-Min Vegetarian
   Restaurant..........................**41** C4
Oriental House.......................(see 38)
Too Too Restaurant...............**42** C4

ENTERTAINMENT
Mandalay Marionettes & Culture
   Show..................................**43** D4
Mintha Theater......................(see 43)
Moustache Brothers Troupe....**44** B5

SHOPPING
78...(see 28)
Gold-Leaf Shops....................**45** B5
Jade Market...........................**46** A5
King Galon.............................(see 45)
Mahamuni Paya Entrance.......(see 15)
Shwe Pathein........................(see 45)
Skywalk.................................**47** B5
Stone-Carvers' Workshops.....**48** B6
Sunflower Arts & Crafts.........(see 41)

TRANSPORT
Inland Water Transport
   Office.................................**49** A5
Sun Far Travels & Tours.........**50** B4

To Taungbyone (12mi)
Golf Course
Mandalay Hill
Old Racecourse
Military Cemetery
Myauk Pyin (North Mandalay)
10th St
11th St
North Moat St (12th St)
Mandalay Palace
Nandawun Park
Tomb of King Mindon
Culture Museum
Myainghaywun Park
See Central Mandalay Map p259
Fort Moat
14th St
16th St
18th St
19th St
20th St
Pinya St
22nd St
To Mingun Ferry (0.3mi)
Bayintnaung Rd
Shweta Canal
85th St
84th St
83rd St
82nd St
81st St
80th St
79th St
Mandalay
To Gawwein Jetty for Bagan, Pyay & Katha Ferries (0.3mi)
Yangylaung Rd
Thakawun Kyaung
Kin Wun Kyaung
Thinge Yamar Canal
To Soe Moe (5mi); Amarapura (7mi); To Inwa (13mi); Sagaing (13mi)
Approximate Scale
East Moat St
12th St
14th St
To Yankin Paya (3mi); Mya Kyauk Kyaung (3mi); Dahama Mandala Meditation Centre (4.5mi)
19th St
21st St
23rd St
24th St
75th St
26th St
Mandalay Swan Hotel
27th St
28th St
29th St
30th St
31st St
32nd St
Market 33rd St
34th St
35th St
36th St
37th St
38th St
39th St
40th St
41st St
77th St
78th St
76th St
75th St
73rd St
74th St
71st St
70th St
68th St
66th St
65th St
63rd St
62nd St
To Pyin U Lwin (43mi)
Ngwe Ta Chaung Canal
Yay Ni Canal
Mandalay Arts & Sciences University
Entertainment District
Saigaing Mandalay Rd
To Highway Bus Station (4.3mi); Airport (28mi); Yangon (432mi)
To Peacock Lodge (0.1mi); Rupar Mandalar (1.5mi)

MANDALAY

Money

If you're out of dollars and need a room, the Mandalay View Inn (p267) and the Hotel by the Red Canal (p267) accept credit cards at 10% commission, while the Sedona (p268) accepts them at 4.5% commission.

Kyaw Kyaw Aung Email/Central Hotel (Map p259; 27th St, 80/81; ☯ 9am-6pm) There's no internet, but they can cash credit cards for a 27% commission.

Post

DHL (Map p257; Hotel Mandalay, 652 78th St, 37/38; ☯ 8.30am-5.30pm Mon-Fri, 8.30am-12.30pm Sat)
Main post office (Map p259; 22nd St, 80/81; ☯ 10.30am-4pm) A postcard sent overseas is K30; domestic mail is free if you're blind.

Telephone

Local calls can be made for K200 from street stands all over Mandalay. Some offer black-market international calls for about K2500 per minute.

Central Telephone & Telegraph (CTT; Map p259; 26th St, 80/81; calls to Europe/North America per min $4/5; ☯ 7am-8.30pm) Make expensive international calls at this official-looking, unsigned building set back from the street.

Travel Agencies

A number of Yangon-based travel agents have locations in Mandalay, here for appearance and housekeeping. They tend to be much less help for independent travellers popping in with questions.

Good News Travels (Map p257; ☎ 73571; www.myanmargoodnewstravel.com; No B6 71st St, 28/29) Well-run Yangon agent can get you a good private-car service.

Myanmar Travels & Tours (MTT; Map p257; ☎ 60356; cnr 68th & 27th Sts; ☯ 9am-5pm) The government-run tourist office, behind the Mandalay Swan Hotel, can book package

---

MANDALAY ADDRESSES

A street address that reads 66th (26/27) means the place is located on 66th St between 26th and 27th Sts. Some of the longer east–west streets take names once they cross the Shweta Chaung (Shweta Canal) heading west. Hence 19th St becomes Inwa St, 22nd St becomes Pinya St, 26th St becomes Bayintnaung Rd and 35th St becomes Yangyiaung Rd.

---

trips in mid-January to Khamti (aka Naga Land) from $1200! Trips are to witness the Naga people's New Year celebrations on January 15. You can't go on your own. You'll need to talk with the Yangon office to arrange trips to Mt Victoria in Chin State (p334). Staff members speak English.

SIGHTS

Also see p264 for a downtown walking tour.

Around Mandalay Hill
MANDALAY HILL

မန္တလေးတောင်

Many people begin a Mandalay stay at the one place that breaks out of Mandalay's pancake-flat sprawl – 760ft-high **Mandalay Hill** (Map p257). Visitors can taxi halfway up along a switchback road (allegedly built with the aid of forced labour), where an escalator leads to the top and a lift goes back down (it's too steep for trishaw drivers). Alternatively, you can make the half-hour barefoot climb that takes in numerous buddha and *nat* (spirit being) shrines; there are many pleasant places to stop for a rest or a drink.

At the top the reward is a full panoramic view – the hazy blue outline of the Shan hills to the east, the Mandalay Palace (and city sprawl) to the south and the Ayeyarwady to the west.

Sometimes attendants will ask for your $10 combo ticket (see p261) – if you don't want to pay it, say 'no thanks' and head to the stairs.

Those walking the whole way will likely sweat off some of the previous night's chapattis. But the trek's not that hard. You can start at either of two entrances on the south side (which wind their way up and meet halfway to the top), or make a steeper ascent from the west. Two immense carved lions guard the southwest entrance to the hill, and the **Bobokyi Nat** (Bobokyi spirit) watches over the southeast entrance. For most of the year it makes most sense to climb before 10am or after 4pm to avoid the midday heat.

The first shrine you come to, halfway up the hill, contains the so-called **Peshawar Relics**, three bones of the Buddha. The relics were originally sent to Peshawar, now in Pakistan, by the great Indian king Asoka.

The stupa (Buddhist religious monument) into which they were built was destroyed in the 11th century, but in 1908 the curator of

CENTRAL MANDALAY

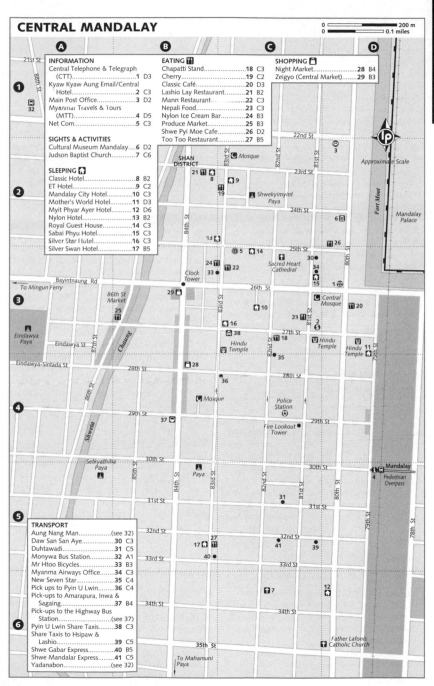

0   200 m
0   0.1 miles

INFORMATION
Central Telephone & Telegraph
(CTT)..1 D3
Kyaw Kyaw Aung Email/Central
Hotel..2 C3
Main Post Office..............................3 D2
Myanmar Travels & Tours
(MTT)..4 D5
Net Com..5 C3

SIGHTS & ACTIVITIES
Cultural Museum Mandalay....6 D2
Judson Baptist Church.............7 C6

SLEEPING
Classic Hotel.................................8 B2
ET Hotel..9 C2
Mandalay City Hotel................10 D3
Mother's World Hotel.............11 D3
Myit Phyar Ayer Hotel............12 D6
Nylon Hotel...............................13 B2
Royal Guest House...................14 C3
Sabai Phyu Hotel......................15 C3
Silver Star Hotel........................16 C3
Silver Swan Hotel.....................17 B5

EATING
Chapatti Stand...........................18 C3
Cherry..19 C2
Classic Café..................................20 D3
Lashio Lay Restaurant.............21 B2
Mann Restaurant......................22 C3
Nepali Food..................................23 C3
Nylon Ice Cream Bar................24 B3
Produce Market..........................25 B3
Shwe Pyi Moe Cafe...................26 D2
Too Too Restaurant..................27 B5

SHOPPING
Night Market...............................28 B4
Zeigyo (Central Market)........29 B3

TRANSPORT
Aung Nang Man..................(see 32)
Daw San San Aye.....................30 C3
Duhtawadi....................................31 C5
Monywa Bus Station................32 A1
Mr Htoo Bicycles.......................33 B3
Myanma Airways Office.........34 C3
New Seven Star...........................35 C4
Pick ups to Pyin U Lwin..........36 C4
Pick-ups to Amarapura, Inwa &
Sagaing.....................................37 B4
Pick-ups to the Highway Bus
Station...................................(see 37)
Pyin U Lwin Share Taxis.........38 C3
Share Taxis to Hsipaw &
Lashio...39 C5
Shwe Gabar Express................40 B5
Shwe Mandalar Express........41 C5
Yadanabon............................(see 32)

Approximate Scale

Mandalay
Palace

SHAN
DISTRICT

Mosque

Shwekyimyint
Paya

Fort Moat

Clock
Tower

Sacred Heart
Cathedral

Bayintnaung Rd
To Mingun Ferry

86th St
Market

Central
Mosque

Eindawya
Paya

Chaung

Eindawya St

Eindawya-Sintada St

Hindu
Temple

Hindu
Temple

Hindu
Temple

Mosque

Police
Station

Fire Lookout
Tower

Mandalay
Pedestrian
Overpass

Setkyathika
Paya

Paya

To Mahamuni
Paya

Father Lafonis
Catholic Church

the Peshawar Museum discovered the actual relic casket during excavations. Although Peshawar had once been a great Buddhist centre, it had by that time been Muslim for many centuries; therefore, the British government presented these important relics to the Burmese Buddhist Society.

Close to the top of the hill is a huge **standing buddha** (Map p257) image that looks out towards the royal palace with its outstretched hand pointing in that direction. It points to where the Buddha prophesised the location of the future capital.

According to legend, the Buddha, accompanied by his disciple Ananda, climbed Mandalay Hill while on one of his visits to Myanmar. There he prophesied that, in the 2400th year of his faith, a great city would be founded below the hill. By our calendar that 2400th year was 1857 – the year King Mindon Min decreed the move from Amarapura to Mandalay.

Those interested in military history can also find a **monument to the British regiment** that retook the hill from the Japanese in 1945. The monument is in a small building attached to one of the shrines at the top of a wide, steep flight of steps.

SANDAMUNI PAYA
စန္ဒာမုဏိဘုရား

Just off the road east of the northeast corner of the Mandalay Palace moat, and near the road up to Mandalay Hill, is the **Sandamuni Paya** (Map p257; admission free). Built as an 'extension' to nearby Kuthodaw (right), the Sandamuni features a cluster of slender whitewashed stupas built on the site of King Mindon's temporary palace while the new Mandalay Palace was under construction.

King Mindon had come to power after the successful overthrow of King Pagan Min, an operation in which he had been assisted by

his younger brother Prince Kanaung. Mindon tended to concentrate on religious matters and leave the niceties of secular rule to his brother, but in 1866 Prince Kanaung was assassinated in an unsuccessful revolt inspired by Prince Myingun. The Sandamuni Paya was built as a memorial to Prince Kanaung on the spot where he was killed.

The paya enshrines an iron image of the Buddha cast in 1802 by Bodawpaya and transported here from Amarapura in 1874. Around the stupa lies a collection of 1774 marble slabs inscribed with commentaries on the Tripitaka (Buddhist canon). Another project of the venerable U Khanti, they were erected in 1913.

KUTHODAW PAYA
ကုသိုလ်တော်ဘုရား

Frequently dubbed 'the world's biggest book' for its surrounding 729 marble slabs (apparently far fewer than Sandamuni's count, but why fuss over details?), the **Kuthodaw Paya** (Maha Lawka Marazein Paya; Map p257; admission $10 combo ticket) – behind Sandamuni (past the pond) – sees a lot of worship, and tourists. The entire 15 books of the Tripitaka are inscribed on the slabs, each of which is housed in its own small stupa. Building of the paya commenced in 1857, the same year work began on the royal palace. Kuthodaw was modelled on the Shwezigon Paya at Nyaung U, Bagan (see p219).

It took an editorial committee of over 200 to produce the original slabs. It has been estimated that, reading for eight hours a day, one person would take 450 days to read the complete 'book'. King Mindon convened the 5th Buddhist Synod and used a team of 2400 monks to read the whole book in a nonstop relay lasting nearly six months! In 1900 a paper edition of the stone original was printed in 38 volumes, each with about 400 pages. A 730th slab in the corner of the inner enclosure tells of the construction.

ATUMASHI KYAUNG
အတုမရှိကျောင်း

More impressive for its history than its present convict-built reconstruction, the **Atumashi Kyaung** (Map p257; admission $10 combo ticket) stands a couple of hundred metres south of Kuthodaw. Originally built by King Mindon in 1857, at the same time as Kuthodaw, this *kyaung* (Burmese Buddhist monastery) features the traditional

---

OUR CUSTOMER SERVICE AWARD…

…Goes to Mandalay's post office's 'information desk' for posting several inspirational quotes, including this gem from Karl Albrect/Ron Zembke [sic]: 'Understanding the perceptions of the customers is crucial to service success.' Yes! Make that *two* postcard stamps please!

HOW TO DODGE THE $10 COMBO TICKET

Since 2002 several of the Mandalay area's key sites have been linked to a $10 combo ticket, which apparently lasts the length of your stay. It's very unlikely that it goes towards restoration of the sites covered. Sights that require the ticket include Mandalay Palace, Kuthodaw Paya, Atumashi Kyaung, Shwenandaw Kyaung, Cultural Museum Mandalay and, occasionally, Mandalay Hill.

If you're planning to go to Inwa outside town, or the Mandalay Palace, Atumashi Kyaung and Shwenandaw Kyaung in town, you won't have a shot without paying. No one checks at Mahamuni Paya, but a few other sites require some trickery to beat the fee. Consider the following:

■ The south entrance (not west) of **Kuthodaw Paya** (opposite) has ticket checkers, who sit at a table and chat away until they leave work at 5pm. If avoiding them seems too 007 for you, the similarly designed adjoining **Sandamuni Paya** (opposite) is free and features even more marble slabs housed in individual white stupas.

■ Skip the **Atumashi Kyaung** (opposite), which is mostly modern, and get a glimpse of the teak **Shwenandaw Kyaung** (below) with your zoom from outside the unobtrusive fence (otherwise a ticket booth will check for your ticket, or sell one, at the entry). South of the centre, the zone-free 'teak monastery' **Shwe In Bin** (p263) is equally impressive.

■ Roving folks atop **Mandalay Hill** (p258) sometimes irritatingly check tickets. **Yankin Paya** (p264), 3 miles east, sees stunning sunsets too (and almost no foreigners).

Burmese monastic construction – a masonry base topped by a wooden building – but instead of the usual multi-roofed design it has graduated rectangular terraces.

Atumashi was once home to a famous buddha image clothed in king's silk clothing and with a huge diamond set on its forehead, but the image was stolen following the British takeover of the city in 1885. Five years later, a fire gutted the monastery and destroyed its contents (including four complete sets of the Tripitaka in teak boxes).

SHWENANDAW KYAUNG

ရွှေနန်းတော်ကျောင်း

Just east of Atumashi Kyaung stands the wooden **Shwenandaw Kyaung** (Golden Palace Monastery; Map p257; admission $10 combo ticket). This monastery is of great interest, not only as a fine example of a traditional Burmese wooden monastery, but also as a fragile reminder of the old Mandalay Palace. It was once part of the palace complex – King Mindon lived here, and in fact died in the building. Afterwards, King Thibaw Min had the building dismantled and reassembled outside the walls; it became a monastery in 1880. It's a good thing he did, as all the other royal buildings were lost to WWII bombs. It's said that Thibaw used the building for meditation.

The building is covered inside and out with carved panels, but unfortunately many of the exterior panels have weathered badly, some have been removed and some replaced.

At one time the building was gilded and decorated with glass mosaics. The carved panels inside are still in excellent condition, particularly the 10 Jataka (past-life stories of the Buddha).

KYAUKTAWGYI PAYA

ကျောက်တော်ကြီးဘုရား

Directly south of Mandalay Hill (across 66th St from the previous sights) stands the **Kyauktawgyi Paya** (Map p257; admission free), built over a 25-year period that ended in 1878. The pagoda's nice enough, but its fame comes from its central occupant: an 26ft, 900-tonne buddha, carved from a single block of marble. The marble block (from the mines of nearby Sagyin) was so colossal, it's said, that 10,000 men spent 13 days transporting it from a canal to the current site. Ornamented with royal attire, the image was completed and dedicated in 1865.

Around the shrine are figures of the Buddha's 80 *arahats* (enlightened disciples). In a building in the southeast of the compound are a giant alms bowl and colourful renderings of King Mindon's visit here in 1865.

Originally this paya, like its namesake in Amarapura, would have been modelled on the famous Ananda Pahto of Bagan (p210), but due to a palace rebellion this grand plan was not carried through.

Mandalay's biggest festival is held at Kyauktawgyi Paya for seven days in early to mid-October to commemorate Thadingyut (see p30).

ZOOLOGICAL GARDENS

တိရစ္ဆာန်ဥယျာဉ်

Built in 1989, purposely on top of a site used during the 1988 demonstrations, the leafy **Zoological Gardens** (Map p257; admission K2000; 8am-6pm) is better than you'd expect.

The hilarious hoots of the gibbons from their central island serenade the area (including guests of nearby Mandalay Hill Resort), and you can pay K500 to feed Asiatic black bears by hand (you're definitely not in Kansas anymore!). There are many shady areas where locals like to picnic. The zoo can be entered from the south (north of the palace walls) or from the east, near the Mandalay Hill Resort.

Mandalay Palace & Fort

မန္တလေးနန်းတော် & ကျုံး

If you get busted for the $10 combo ticket, you might as well see this centrepiece of Mandalay, the **palace compound** (Map p257; admission $10 combo ticket; 7.30am-5pm), sprawling south of Mandalay Hill. The original was destroyed in WWII, but you get a sense of the spot where Burma's last two kings (before the current ones anyway) lived. It's a leafy complex with rebuilt crimson-and-gold palace buildings in the heart of immense fort walls that are 2 miles long, 26ft high and guarded by a 230ft-wide moat.

Visitors can enter at the east gate only (by trishaw, taxi, bicycle etc), where a road passes off-road army barracks before arriving at the royal palace site, surrounded by an internal ring road in the centre.

Many choose not to come, as the site was built by forced local labour in the late '90s. It's easy to admire the scale of the palace from **moat-side walkways** outside the walls, as many locals do in the afternoons.

HISTORY

The original palace was more than just royal living quarters; it was a walled city within Mandalay. It served as the home to two Burmese kings: King Mindon Min (who built the palace in 1857) and King Thibaw (who lived here until British forces seized the city in 1885 and unglamorously sent him into the Mandalay streets, bound for a 'house prison' in India).

Afterwards, the British used the palace as the colony's government house and British Club.

The Japanese held Mandalay for much of WWII. In March 1945, amid fierce fighting from advancing British and Indian troops, the royal palace caught fire and was destroyed. Only the huge walls and moat, the base on which the reconstructed palace buildings stand, and a few masonry buildings and tombs remain of the original palace. Beyond, in the restricted areas around the palace, Myanmar soldiers live in meagre barracks.

THE SITE

Visitors are allowed to tour the central oval-shaped site, which is surrounded by a ring road, and a couple of sites in the field immediately northeast of the entrance. In the oval area, several crimson and gold pavilions loom ahead. Within the **palace compound** (to the left of the Mye Nan Pyathat temple, where the $10 combo ticket is asked for, or sold), just west of the 'Hall of Victory', is the so-called **Glass Palace** (aka Central Palace), where the kings lived.

Just south is the 110ft **Nan Myint Saung watchtower**, where you can climb the spiral stairs to get views of the city, the compound and the peeling paint atop the temples' corrugated metal roofs.

Do continue past the many buildings west to reach the back side of the Queen's Audience Hall It houses the **Culture Museum**, which includes some great vintage photos, King Thibaw's glass bed and 13 life-size models of former cabinet members in traditional attire; signs in English tell their tale. One cabinet member, Prince Kanaung, is given props for being 'very clever' as he 'sent young scholars to Western countries to study'.

As you head back to the palace wall gate, look left (north) to see the (restricted to travellers) **tomb of King Mindon**, just past giant open sheds that contain over 600 stone slabs collected by King Bodawpaya (r 1782–1819) and later moved here.

South of the Centre

While in the area of Mahamuni Paya (opposite), be sure to drop by the Jade Market (p272).

MAHAMUNI PAYA

မဟာမုကိုဘုရား

In southwest Mandalay, off the road towards Amarapura, stands the **Mahamuni Paya** (Map p257), one of Myanmar's more famous Buddhist sites (it's also known as Payagyi, Big Paya, or the Rakhaing Paya). The gold-and-crimson site was originally built by King Bodawpaya in 1784, when a brick road was constructed from his palace to the paya's eastern gate. You can still find traces of this royal highway. In 1884 the shrine was destroyed by fire; the current one is comparatively recent.

The paya's fame comes from its shrine centrepiece, the highly venerated **Mahamuni buddha image**, which was seized from Mrauk U in Rakhaing State in 1784. It was believed to be of great age at that time and it may even have been cast during the 1st century AD (though many in Rakhaing believe it to have been made in the likeness of the Buddha during his legendary visit in 554 BC).

The 13ft-high seated image is cast in bronze, but over the years thousands of devout Buddhists have completely covered the figure in a 6in-thick layer of gold leaf. Only men are permitted to walk up to the Mahamuni buddha image and apply gold leaf.

It's always the centre of much activity, especially during festivals, when you can see locals bowing before TV screens installed to allow locals to pay respects to the Mahamuni's video image at other parts of the packed complex. Each morning at 4am a team of monks washes the buddha's face and even brushes its teeth.

In the northwestern corner of the outer courtyard, a small building houses **six bronze Khmer figures** brought back from Rakhaing State, along with the Mahamuni buddha. Three are lions (the heads of which have been replaced with ones in the Burmese style), two are images of the Hindu god Shiva, and one is Airavata, the three-headed elephant. Originally, these figures were enshrined at Angkor Wat in Cambodia; they were taken from Angkor by the Thais in 1431. King Bayinnaung subsequently looted them from Ayuthaya in 1564 and brought them to Bago, where in 1663 they were nabbed by King Razagyi of Rakhaing. According to legend, rubbing a part of the image will cure any affliction on the corresponding part of your own body. Local legend has it that there were once many more Khmer figures

WOMEN & MAHAMUNI

Visiting Mahamuni, you'll see groups of women kneeling from outside the inner chamber where Mahamuni sits – only men are allowed in. Some women believe desegregation is overdue. One local grandmother told us, 'Lord Buddha never said anything like this, and I'd so much like to put gold leaf on the Buddha image at Mahamuni!'

here, but they were melted by order of King Thibaw to cast cannons for the defence of the Mandalay Palace.

In the northeastern corner, there's a **museum** with giant 1950s-era paintings that chronologically tell the tale of the Mahamuni image.

In the southeastern corner of the courtyard are **inscription stones** collected by King Bodawpaya, who appears to have had quite a thing for this pursuit.

There are many interesting **shop stalls** and palm readers at the entrance to the shrine (though the little stone elephants are cheaper from the stone carvers to the west, see p272; and see p349 for information on the trade in precious stones before you buy).

SHWE IN BIN KYAUNG

ရွှေအင်ပင်ကျောင်း

On the lip of a rivulet, this large, elegant, quite peaceful, wooden **monastery** (Map p257; cnr 89th & 38th Sts) dates from 1895, when a pair of wealthy Chinese jade merchants commissioned it. Called simply 'the teak monastery' by many locals, the central building stands on tall poles, and its balustrades and roof cornices are covered in detailed engravings. It's seldom crowded.

The surrounding villagelike neighbourhood is something of a **'monk's district'**, with many robed monks and nuns walking to and from smaller monasteries on the leafy lanes, or playing football. (Numbers have diminished in the aftermath of the 2007 protests, as many younger monks were encouraged to return to their homes.) One of the other more currently active monasteries, **Ma Soe Yein Nu Kyaung** (Map p257), is just across the bridge to the south from Shwe In Bin.

Also nearby, and fascinating to visit, is the **Tingaza Kyaung** (Map p257; 48th St, 34/35), a largely dilapidated but lived-in wood monastery on a back street 500yd northwest. Here you

MANDALAY

HERE'S TO INTELLIGENCE: VERY GOOD WATER

Near Yankin Paya, **Mya Kyauk Kyaung** (☎ 88732) is a modern monastery famed for its alkaline-rich mineral water, which – it is claimed – can 'promote your IQ', plus help with ailments like diabetes, constipation, gout and morning sickness. Apparently a Japanese company offered to distribute the water (collected from springs here), but the monastery's Sayadaw Bhadanta Khemar Sarya refused. Do drop by and offer a small donation for a bottle or two – the water is the tastiest and smoothest we've ever tried.

---

can walk along elevated planks around the teak monastery, and monks will show you the woodwork details inside. To get there from Shwe In Bin, go to 35th St, go west two blocks and turn north (right), then take the first left.

CHURCHES

It's not all pagodas! Mandalay has several churches and mosques among the many temples, including the **Judson Baptist Church** (Map p259; 82nd St, 33/34), named for the American missionary who has virtually become a saint in Myanmar. Other key churches and mosques are marked on the map.

Yankin Paya
ရန်ကင်း ဘုရား

About 3 miles east of Mandalay Palace, the quiet and relaxed Yankin Paya is on a pagoda-dotted hillside overlooking Mandalay, and with far fewer visitors (and certainly no pesky $10 combo ticket checkers). Up the steep steps from where the road from Mandalay dead ends, you reach a pagoda, with deer to feed (for merit) and nice views of the mountains just behind. Follow the pagoda walkways to the right (south), where after a couple of hundred yards steps lead down into a cave altar with gold fish at the feet of a buddha image.

Be sure to get a bottle of water at the nearby Mya Kyauk Kyaung, about 200yd back towards Mandalay (see the boxed text, above).

It's a pleasant bike ride out. Cars can take a back road up to the top of Yankin Hill.

ACTIVITIES

Other than paying $5 to jump into a high-end hotel's pool, the outdoor **Yatanaban Swimming Pool** (Map p257; admission K500; ☼ 5am-6pm), next to the east entrance to the Zoological Gardens, is the best bet for a cheap dip. A restaurant, bumper cars and a karaoke club surround the

Olympic-sized pool, which is generally pretty quiet during the heat of the day.

Shwe Mann Taung Golf Resort (Map p257; ☎ 60570; nine-/18-hole $15/30, gear rental $10) is a lovely course at the west base of Mandalay Hill. There's a driving range nearby.

DOWNTOWN WALKING TOUR

Not much of Mandalay can be seen on foot, but this loose tour takes in some (mostly) secondary sights and the city's most interesting street life in a few hours.

Start a block from the Mandalay Palace moat with tea at the **Shwe Pyi Moe Cafe** (1; p269); if the desire strikes, take a cultural chaser a block north at the **Cultural Museum Mandalay** (2; ☎ 24603; cnr 24th & 80th Sts; admission $10 combo ticket or K1000; ☼ 10am-4pm). Staff will be delighted to see you, perhaps flicking the light switch with a shrug to show the electricity's out. Exhibits show a bit of past kingdoms (with coins and pots and iron knick-knacks from various capitals), plus various handicrafts and buddha images. Most displays are subtitled in English. There's also an aerial shot of Mandalay from 1958 ('made by German', staff told us), but you may need a torch to make it out. The top-floor library has a small collection of Burmese and English books – and a bit of a palace view from the window.

Afterwards, head west a couple of blocks to see the lushly shaded and peaceful **Shwekyimyint Paya** (3; btwn 23rd & 24th, 82nd & 83rd Sts), which considerably predates Mandalay itself. Prince Minshinzaw (the exiled son of King Alaungsithu) founded it in 1167, dur-

---

WALK FACTS

▪ **Start** Shwe Pyi Moe Cafe

▪ **Finish** Night Market

▪ **Distance** 1.4 miles

▪ **Duration** About two hours

ing the Bagan period. The shrine is notable because it contains the original buddha image consecrated by the prince, as well as many images collected by later Myanmar kings and relocated here from Mandalay Palace after the British occupied it. These images are only shown to the public on important religious occasions.

Afterwards, take 83rd St south, perhaps stopping at **Nylon Ice Cream Bar** (**4**; p269), then turn right onto busy 26th St. Looming ahead is a clock tower, standing smack-dab in the middle of 26th and 84th Sts on the northern side of the relocated **zeigyo** (**5**; central market, see p271). The original market, designed in 1903 by Count Caldari (the Italian first secretary of the Mandalay Municipality), was dismantled – much to the dismay of locals – around 1990 and moved here to these two three-storey buildings done in Communist Chinese style. Less atmospheric, for sure, but the market still represents a fascinating collection of stalls.

Squeeze past vendors on 27th St to the west, then detour onto brick Eindawya St (where shops sell monk gear) to reach the nicely proportioned but slightly scruffy

Eindawya Paya (**6**). Built in 1847 by King Pagan Min, Eindawya was the site of one of Myanmar's many small battles for independence. In 1919 a group of Europeans who defied the Buddhist ban on shoe-wearing within Eindawya were forcibly evicted by outraged monks. Four monks were convicted by a colonial court, and one, U Kettaya, received a life sentence. (So please take your shoes off.)

OK, one more paya. Roam south to 30th St and head a block east to reach the elevated **Setkyathiha Paya** (**7**; 30th St; admission free). It was badly damaged during WWII, but was subsequently repaired. Its main point of interest is the impressive 17ft-high seated buddha image, cast in bronze by King Bagyidaw in Inwa in 1823, just before the First Anglo-Burmese War broke out. Since then it's been moved to Amarapura in 1849 (during the Second Anglo-Burmese War) and then returned to Mandalay in 1884 (just before British troops overtook the city). Reclining buddha images can be seen in the paya courtyard, along with a sacred bodhi tree planted by U Nu, a former prime minister of Myanmar.

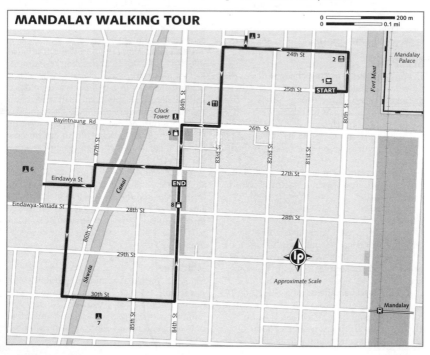

MANDALAY WALKING TOUR

MANDALAY

From here, take a trishaw or walk back via the **night market** (**8**; p271) on 84th St.

COURSES

Dahama Mandapa Meditation Centre (Map p257; ☎ 39694; cnr 73rd & 42nd Sts) has regular one- to 20-day courses geared for foreigners.

Its newer location at **Dahama Mandala Meditation Centre** (☎ 57655), near Yankin Paya (3 miles east of Mandalay Palace), has modern accommodation and a very peaceful locale.

FESTIVALS & EVENTS

Traditional *pwe* (small or massive) happen all the time, for weddings, birthdays, funerals, holidays and so on. You'll see them in side streets and at paya. Ask a trishaw driver if they've passed one.

Mahamuni Paya pwe This happens in early February, when thousands of people from nearby districts make pilgrimages to Mahamuni (see p263).

Taungbyone About 12 miles north in Taungbyone, this major festival has been held each August (more specifically for six days up to and including the full moon of Wagaung, the fifth lunar month) since Anawrahta's reign; the festival honours the so-called Muslim Brothers, Byat-wi and Byat-ta, two of the most famous *nat* from the Bagan era.

Thadingyut Mandalay's biggest festival is held in early- to mid-October at Kyauktawgyi Paya (p261) for seven days.

SLEEPING

If you're looking to stay cheap, stick with downtown. Aside from those listed here, there are many other Chinese-type hotels in the blocks south of 27th St that offer predictable rooms without much style.

From April to October it's likely that all places will have empty rooms waiting for you.

All room rates include breakfast and have private bathrooms with hot water unless otherwise stated.

Budget

Don't be surprised if your air-con or hot water's not working. Several guesthouses tout it, but have it linked with the government-provided power source, not their humming generators.

ourpick **Royal Guest House** (Map p259; ☎ 65697; No 41 25th St, 82/83; s $4-8, d $7-12; ✗) Putting a lot of effort into little space, the Royal is the cheapie that fills first. The clean rooms ooze character, with endearing details like raised

hallways going to bathrooms and Mondrian-style tile jobs. The cheapest rooms have shared bathroom. Room 202 (single/double $8/12) has a balcony with some sunset potential. Everything's quite compact though, including the miniscule 'can I join you?' dining room.

Nylon Hotel (Map p259; ☎ 66550, 60757; nylon@mandalay.net.mm; cnr 25th & 83rd Sts; s $5-6, d $10-12; ✗ 💻) A modern building above a generator shop, the Nylon's rooms tend to get better the higher up the five floors you go. Room 401 is a good cheapie up top. Free breakfast is served in the upstairs dining area. Some visitors have complained about over-charging on taxis.

Sabai Phyu Hotel (Map p259; ☎ 32297, 39997; No 58 81st St, 25/26; s/d $6/12; ✗) This 20-room back-up to the others has slightly musty rooms in a four-floor walk-up. Free breakfast's served on the top floor (good views), rooms have putt-putt green carpets and ceiling-less bathroom cubes in the corner. Air-con, supposedly, is on 5pm to 5am.

ET Hotel (Map p259; ☎ 65006, 66547; tmchomdy@mandalay.net.mm; No 129A 83rd St, 23/24; s $8-10, d $10-12; ✗ 💻) The only thing extra-terrestrial in the 27-room ET is the glow of the lone fluorescent bulb against the mint green walls in the compact and clean but dated rooms. An extra $2 gets you air-con and satellite TV. There's a roof deck and lobby internet.

Classic Hotel (Map p259; ☎ 32841, 61891; No 59 23rd St, 83/84; s/d $9/15; ✗) Near the Shan restaurants, the six-floor Classic's 34 rooms have *just* enough space to fit a bed or two, an old TV with satellite access and a small attached bathroom. Higher floors get a peek of Mandalay Hill from out the pea-green curtains. If you left your suitcase in Pyin U Lwin, no worries: there's a small *longyi* (sarong) and pyjama store on the 1st floor.

Mother's World Hotel (Map p259; ☎ 33627, 33880; No 58 79th St, 27/28; s/d $15/22; ✗) The street's a little trashy and the hotel feels a little sad. It's certainly overpriced for what you get (dated pieces, ruffled spreads), but the single rooms – particularly 506 – get some nice views of Mandalay Hill.

Midrange

Many of Mandalay's midrange hotels don't reward the extra dollars and seem to run off the same template: a 10-storey Chinese-style building with doorperson, elevator and rather unloved clean rooms. Here are some that rise above the norm.

Royal City Hotel (Map p257; ☎ 31805, 28299; city mdy@mptmail.net.mm; No 130 27th St, 76/77; s $15-18, d $20-25; 🟦) Owned by the Royal Guest House folks, the Royal City is a block south of the palace between downtown's frantic energy and Mandalay Hill's pagodas. Its 19 big, rather long rooms are nice enough, with satellite TV, phone and some serious views to the east, but not all nicks are being tended to. Breakfast's served in the mezzanine dining area or the super outdoor/indoor roof garden.

our pick **Peacock Lodge** (off Map p257; ☎ 61429, 09-204 2059; peacocklodge@gmail.com; No 5 60th St, 25/26; s/d $16/20; 🟦) One of Myanmar's great homestay-style inns, the Peacock hosts will treat you like part of the family, beginning by showing you old family photos and phonebooks from the British era. Rooms are in the family's 1960s-built home, or in bungalow-style rooms off the garden, where you find tables for nicely prepared breakfasts. It's comfy if not posh, and well worth the extra hike from the centre if you don't mind a few minutes' extra commute.

Silver Swan Hotel (Map p259; ☎ 36333, 39820; www .silverswanhotel.com; No 400 83rd St, 32/33; s $17-22, d $22-27; 🟦 🖥) One of a few midrange choices freckling the streets south of downtown that justify the dollars or distance, the eight-storey Swan has wood-floor rooms with wood chairs that look out over Mandalay. Perhaps the modern razzamatazz recently done in the cool lobby, where cheery staff greet you, will move up to the rather dated rooms.

Silver Star Hotel (Map p259; ☎ 33394, 68222; silverstar@mandalay.net.mm; cnr 27th & 83rd Sts; s $18-25, d $25-28; 🟦 🖥) This perfectly comfortable 48-room high-rise hotel downtown is perfectly forgettable too. Everything's sit-on-the-floor spotless. The corner rooms, with two windows, are higher priced. There's a lift and a headachey white 1st-floor dining room for breakfast. Some group tours check in.

Myit Phyar Ayer Hotel (Map p259; ☎ 35210, 71404; No 568 80th St, 33/34; s $20 & $25, d $25 & $30; 🟦) One of many Chinese-style hotels looming in the blocks south and southeast of downtown, this friendly 40-room job may put a bit more care into its lobby and soft-lit hallways (filled with giant wood sculptures) than its more ordinary rooms, with wood floors and old air-con units. Roomier 'superior' rooms are worth the extra $5. It has a lift.

Mandalay View Inn (Map p257; ☎ 61119; mandalay .viewinn@mptmail.net.mm; No 17B 66th St, 26/27; s $25-30,

d $30-35; 🟦) Though near the palace moat, the view from the small front garden or a couple of the rooms' balconies is limited to the Sedona Hotel Mandalay across the street, but this nicely kept up, modern hotel keeps its dozen compact rooms clean and inviting. All have air-con, satellite TV and a bit of woodwork for flair. The extra $5 gets you more bathroom elbow space (and a tub). Best, you can pay by credit card (for a 10% commission).

Top End
Mandalay's high-end hotels can't compare with the standards of Yangon's.

Hotel Mandalay (Map p257; ☎ 71582, 71585; www .hotel-mandalay.com; No 652 78th St, 37/38; r $35, $45 & $65; 🟦) Done up like a big business hotel on a busy street, with elaborate lobby pillars and hell-loads of woodwork in the rooms, the relatively new, seven-floor Hotel Mandalay (run by a local entrepreneur) tends not to make use of its higher-priced rooms' space: $65 suites have room dividers, but hardwood chairs will mean you tune into the satellite TV from the bed anyway. There's a gym.

Mandalay City Hotel (Map p259; ☎ 61700, 61704; www.mandalaycityhotel.com; 26th St 82/83; s $50 & $60, d $55 & $65; 🟦 🖥 🟦) The poshest spot downtown must have tickled rival hoteliers as construction got under way in 2004. Set at the old bus station (in a lot walled by dreary downtown buildings – listen for bus ghosts moaning at night), the hotel (run by local entrepreneurs) somehow works. Lush, view-blocking landscaping, an entry pond, a pool and private *zedi* (stupa) do wonders to distract from the locale. And it gets you downtown, with 24-hour electricity. Comfortable L-shaped rooms in mint/chocolate colours and wood floors envelope rather small bathrooms. Stick with the cheaper rooms, the others essentially only add a tiny for-two dining table.

Hotel by the Red Canal (Map p257; ☎ 61177, www .hotelredcanal.com; No 417 cnr 22nd & 63rd Sts; r $66-90; 🟦 🖥 🟦) An intriguing new high-end deal in the backroads east of the palace, the 25-room faux palace-style hotel – built near the namesake canal – offers more intimacy than other high-end hotels. Rooms aren't particularly big, but local flourishes play off four themes: some Shan villas have small balconies overlooking the small pool (others in back are roomy, good-value choices for $66); Chin villas have private decks alongside a 'waterfall'. It's run by the same local family who run the

Mandalay View Inn. Credit cards accepted with 10% commission.

Mandalay Hill Resort Hotel (Map p257; ☎ 35688; www.mandalayhillresorthotel.com; 10th St; s/d from $100/120; 🄫 🄬) This former French-run Novotel (now a Thai joint venture) sits impressively between the north end of the Palace and Mandalay Hill. Up from the bejewelled lobby pillars, the 207 rooms run the modern resort template – comfy, with disappointingly fake wood floors, embroidered bed throws and rather tight bathrooms. Bonus points come for the back garden, with a lovely pool, the town's only disco (Gem Club), a couple of tennis courts and an outdoor restaurant with nightly puppet-show meals ($20 per person). Plus that mountain.

Sedona Hotel Mandalay (Map p257; ☎ 36488; www.sedonahotels.com.sg; cnr 26th & 66th Sts; superior r $108, deluxe r $120; 🄫 🄬) This palatial Singaporean joint venture faces the southeastern corner of the palace. Rooms are a bit standard for the price and the tennis court needs a makeover, but the pool sprawls and the deluxe views of the Palace moat and far-off Mandalay Hill can't be beat. The Sedona accepts credit cards at 4.5% commission.

Rupar Mandalar (off Map p257; ☎ 61555; www.ruparmandalarresort.com; No A-15 53rd St, at 30th St; r $200; 🄫 🄭 🄬) A stunning new complex, almost lost in the fringes of Mandalay's eastern outskirts, this hotel is done up in a self-described Burmese/Indonesian/Thai style – but thoroughly modern. Its luxurious teak-wood rooms are easily Mandalay's swankest. There are thoughtful gardens leading back to a pool, tennis court and spa. The local owners made their millions from jade.

EATING

Those looking for stylish, high-end meals will be mostly disappointed in Mandalay. The 'nicest' restaurants, outside the hotels, are in the 'tour-bus restaurant ghetto' (as we call it), a collection of big, open-air restaurants near the Sedona Hotel with big parking lots – the food's fine, but independent travellers often feel either lost in the crowd or empty in a gymnasium at such places (see Green Elephant, right).

For fresh goods go to the **produce market** (Map p259; 86th St, 26/28) off the canal between 26th and 28th Sts.

Bamar

Chit Chit (Map p257; cnr 72nd & 27th Sts; 🕑 6am-5pm) A big corner teashop, run by the Peacock Lodge

family, is a good spot to sit over tea and some tasty 'Mandalay noodles' (egg noodles with shredded chicken, scallion and spice; K500) or creative pancake desserts.

ourpick Too Too Restaurant 26th St (Map p257; ☎ 66451; No 79, 27th St, 74/75; dishes K1000; 🕑 10am-9pm); 83rd St (Map p259; No 39, 83rd St, 32/33) The place for homestyle Burmese fare – even visitors from Yangon and around the country come for it. There's a couple of sitting areas (air-con ones in back), but start in the front pointing at fresh pots of mutton curry, sautéed sardines, prawns and mushrooms with watercress. Meals come with rice and a tableful of condiments. There's a newer location in Central Mandalay.

Green Elephant (Map p257; ☎ 61237; No 3H 27th St; dishes from K4500, soups K1500-2000; 🕑 10am-9pm) One of a handful of big, open-air restaurants in the 'tour-bus restaurant ghetto', Green Elephant is the most inviting, occupying a colonial-era building with bamboo-covered areas in the garden and period relics in the air-conditioned rooms inside. Plenty of Burmese dishes, plus Chinese and Thai.

Good for outside dinners (and beer drinking) is the string of hopping **barbecue restaurants** (Map p257; 30th St, 65/66) southeast of the palace. Each has open-air and inside seats with fans. Out the front, pick the skewers of meat (pork, chicken, whole fish) or a couple of veggie options (lady fingers, spiced bean curd) and hand to the cooks. A full meal plus a beer or two runs to around K4000.

Shan

Particularly inviting at night, the 'Shan district', around 84th and 23rd Sts has several inviting noodle and barbecue restaurants – some geared to beer drinkers, some to families.

Aye Chan Myae (Map p257; cnr 33rd & 73rd Sts; buffet K600) Students and workers file past the 40 or so pots of Shan-style curries in this barebones place; you pick four (a meat and three veggies) and get rice for K600.

Lashio Lay Restaurant (Map p259; No 65 23rd St, 83/84; dishes from K600; 🕑 8am-10pm) One of a couple of great Shan restaurants downtown, this two-floor spot is constantly crammed. Two dozen Shan dishes (mostly curries with rice, plus several vegetarian options daily) are on offer, served under blazing fans.

Indian & Nepali

ourpick Chapatti Stand (Map p259; cnr 27th & 82nd Sts; dishes K800-1200; 🕑 5-9pm) For people-watching, price and taste, it's hard to beat a sidewalk spot where a diverse group of folks with turbans, *longyi*, skullcaps or backpacks mingle for freshly made chapattis (K150 each) served with veggie and meat curries. Recent popularity has seen price increases though.

Nepali Food (Map p259; 81st St, 26/27; dishes K1000; ⏰ 7am-9.30pm) This Nepali-run spot serves a mean *thali* (curry meal), with dollops of veggie curry served on banana leaves or metal plate. No meat, no eggs, no alcohol.

Marie-Min Vegetarian Restaurant (Map p257; 27th St, 74/75; dishes K1500-3000; ⏰ 7am-9pm, closed May) A long-time popular Indian restaurant south of the palace, Marie-Min only sees foreigner diners – and prices its curries and chapatti dishes accordingly. It's certainly good, and it's all vegetarian (the sign out front says, 'be kind to animals by not eating them'). Lassis made with purified water are K1500. Much attention is directed to its sprawling antiques shop Sunflower (see p271).

Chinese

Oriental House (Map p257; ☎ 61143; cnr 27th & 64th Sts; dim sum per piece from K400; ⏰ dim sum 6.30am-2pm, dinner 5-9pm) This big banquet hall is best for its midday dim sum.

Kyauk Mein (Map p257; 78th St, 40/41; dishes K800-1800; ⏰ 8am-9pm) Out towards Mahamuni Paya and the Moustache Brothers, this basic eatery is all vegetarian. Best are the 'Taiwan-style fake meat' (ask for *kong baung kyaw*) with fake mutton, chicken and duck dishes with rice. No beer. The restaurant is named for a famous Myanmar actor.

Mann Restaurant (Map p259; 83rd St; dishes K1500-2000; ⏰ 7am-10pm) A crusty Mandalay classic, the Mann serves up pretty good Chinese dishes for a mix of red-faced local men and a few guidebook-toting foreigners. Plenty of squashed deer heads and assorted horns overlook the bare concrete floor, and there's usually a Ms Dagon rep ready to pour your beer.

Cherry (Map p259; No 138, 83rd St, 23/24; dishes K1500-5000; ⏰ 7am-9pm) Far more wholesome than Mann, Cherry is a simple family run place with no beer or red-faced locals.

Thai

our pick **Ko's Kitchen** (Map p257; ☎ 69576; cnr 19th & 80th Sts; soups & dishes K1400-5000; ⏰ 11.30am-2.30pm & 5.30-10pm) The most reliable place to eat with a little snazziness and not feel like you're in a custom-built-for-tourism restaurant, Ko's cooks a diverse selection of Thai dishes, including northern Thai specialities, the usual curries and noodles, plus a particularly tasty crispy catfish salad with mango and cashews (K3200).

Western

BBB (Map p257; ☎ 25623; No 292 76th St, 26/27; dishes K1800-5000; ⏰ 8.30am-11pm) Geared up for all things West, the BBB (Barman Beer Bar) has a ski-lodge atmosphere with Native American chiefs on the walls and BBC or ESPN on the telly. Food's fine – if you go for a burger (K1800), be sure to specify beef or sardine (!?). Also pastas, barbecue and pizza.

Teashops

Shwe Pyi Moe Cafe (Map p259; 25th St, 80/81; tea K100; ⏰ 5.30am-5.30pm) Downtown's busiest teashop, Shwe Pyi Moe makes top-quality teas, boils up fresh *ei-kya-kwe* (long, deep-fried pastries, known as *you tio* in Chinese) in the giant wok up the front, and fries pancakes with banana (K500).

Classic Café (Map p259; 80th St, 26/27; noodles K500) Popular with a younger crowd, the Classic puts on local rock music and serves good tea or Shan noodles (and a host of other snacks) at its *palapa*-style shaded tables.

Dessert

Nylon Ice Cream Bar (Map p259; No 173 83rd St, 25/26; snacks from K1000; ⏰ 8.30am-9.30pm) The de-facto meeting place for locals and downtown-based travellers, the Nylon has outside tables (the shade starts in the afternoon). It's worth lingering in the evening for an OK ice cream, shake, lassi or a beer.

DRINKING

A couple of buzzing eating places good to sit over a beer at are the barbecue restaurants (opposite) on 30th St, and the Nylon Ice Cream Bar (above) downtown. Hotel-wise, the Gem Club and Kipling's Lounge at the Mandalay Hill Resort Hotel (opposite) are nice, if a little stuffy. The latter has live music nightly and you can order drinks by the pool too.

Small shops around Mandalay sell cold beer for about K1700 per bottle of Myanmar Beer, the local Mandalay Beer (a bit watery) or Tiger Beer, which you can take to your hotel (best if it has a roof terrace). Shops often sell locally made rum too.

MANDALAY

MOUSTACHE BROTHERS – FROM SLAPSTICK TO SATIRE

A Moustache Brothers show is not just a glimpse of a traditional *a-nyeint pwe* (a vaudeville folk opera with dance, music, jokes and silly walks); it's about artists brave enough to continue their work in a country where a joke can get you jailed – or worse.

Two of the 'brothers' know this all too well. In 1996 after telling politically tinged jokes about Myanmar generals at an Independence Day celebration at Aung San Suu Kyi's compound in Yangon, Par Par Lay and his bare-faced cousin Lu Zaw (two-thirds of the troupe) were seized by police and sentenced to seven years' hard labour. Initially they worked amid violent criminals, breaking rocks for roads and digging ditches, and were unable to receive visits from their family.

In 1997 several Hollywood comedians (including Rob Reiner and political comedian Bill Maher) wrote to the government in protest. Meanwhile, Par Par Lay's brother, the outgoing Lu Maw, kept up the show here with his wife.

After serving five years of their seven-year sentence, Par Par Lay and Lu Zaw were released in 2002. The Moustache Brothers remain 'blacklisted' from playing at outside events (marriages, funerals, festivals and so on) and continue to be off the government's lists of artists that locals can legally hire. So the brothers celebrated the occasion at home with a series of gala performances, attended – inevitably – by government agents with video cameras.

The regional commander soon summoned Par Par Lay and told him not to perform at home any more. When he got home, some Westerners had already gathered for that night's show, and he and his family cleverly decided to perform without costumes and makeup. Thus the show went on for the tourists (and the 'KGB' people – Lu Maw's nickname for Myanmar's military intelligence). They explained they were merely 'demonstrating' a performance since they couldn't do a 'real' one without costumes. Somehow, it worked.

'They've ordered us to stop six times', Lu Maw told us. 'It goes in one ear and out the other. That's our job!'

Their job has become exclusively for foreign eyes only, as their performances are limited to English – and locals who would want to attend would very likely be followed by police. Tourists get no backlash for attending.

Following the September 2007 demonstrations, Lu Maw was mistaken for Par Par Lay and briefly detained by police, before Par Par Lay was arrested and jailed for a month. The shows, during his jail time and after his release, have never stopped.

Historically, Par Par Lay was the famous one. But as the only English speaker, tireless bundle of energy Lu Maw has become the clear spokesperson for the group now that the shows are limited to English.

ENTERTAINMENT

The neighbourhood surrounding the house of the Moustache Brothers – Mandalay's 'West End', as Moustache Brother Lu Maw jokes – is home to many *pwe* troupes (not banned by the government), which practise their craft during June and July from 10am to 4pm daily. Visitors are welcome to wander and watch for free (donations are appreciated). You'll see traditional *pwe* (see p266) in side streets and paya.

Moustache Brothers Troupe (Map p257; 39th St, 80/81; donation K8000; ☾ 8.30pm) Performed in the home of the banned Moustache Brothers, this famous, colourful troupe has celebrated traditional Myanmar folk opera for over three decades. The show is quite in-your-face, and pretty cornball, as it's relayed from atop a mini wood-crate stage, with a dozen or so plastic chairs a yard away. Not all visitors come away bowled over, but it's stunning to see such open dissent, and presented by such traditional comedy as this. The one-time famous troupe is now banished from public performances, and its original *schtick* in Burmese has shifted to English. The only English-speaker, Lu Maw, kneels over an antique microphone stand and jokes through a minispeaker, as the night meanders through slapstick, political satire, Myanmar history, traditional dance and music, and how to tie up your *longyi*. Lu Maw's English is pretty good, though if you speak English as a second language you might struggle a bit. He retells the story of their woes (even showing a clip from the Hugh Grant film *About a Boy,* which mentions his brother, and troupe leader, Par Par Lay). It's a good idea to bone up on some Myanmar factoids (eg Ne Win, 1988, Aung San; see the History chapter, p36) before attending and you can drop by any time to chat. T-shirts are K5000. See also the boxed text, opposite.

Mintha Theater (Map p257; ☎ 72029; 27th St, 65/66; admission K6000; ⏰ 8.30pm) Around the corner from the Sedona, this relatively new theatre performs a similar show to the more-famous puppet show (below), but it's actually more rewarding seeing some of the same themes performed by uniformed dancers to the tunes of the live traditional orchestra. Plus it's cheaper.

Mandalay Marionettes & Culture Show (Map p257; ☎ 34446; www.mandalaymarionettes.com; 66th St, 26/27; admission $8; ⏰ 8.30pm) A bit touristy now, this troupe's hour-long show mixes big-time puppetry and live traditional music – with musicians playing drums set in circles and the distinctive *hneh* (an oboe-like instrument) from the floor. The musicians introduce traditional dancers and puppeteers, who recreate tales of *zat pwe* (Buddhist Jataka tales) and Yamazat (tales from the Indian epic Ramayana) traditions. The catch is the price – it's nearly tripled recently, possibly due to the troupe's international stints (a scorecard of shows comes with the brochure). This troupe (though based on tourism, and puppet sales) is the most serious among several around the country about preserving the folk art.

SHOPPING
Arts & Crafts
Mandalay is a major crafts centre, and probably the best place in the country for traditional puppets (antique or new) and hand-woven *kalaga* (embroidered tapestries) designed in the style of Myanmar's royal days.

If you enter without a tout or a driver, you can get (slightly) better deals, as touts usually get commissions. Some 'antiques' are new pieces scuffed up to look aged.

Handicrafts are available at a few vendor stalls in the *zeigyo* (central market, Map p259) or at the Mahamuni Paya (Map p257) entrance. You'll find puppets everywhere. The Moustache Brothers (opposite) and Mandalay Marionettes (above) sell new puppets during the day or at their nightly shows.

Sunflower Arts & Crafts (Map p257; 27th St, 74/75; ⏰ 7am-9pm) This store is part of the Marie-Min Vegetarian Restaurant and fills two expansive showrooms on either side of the alley with new and old bronze and wood doodads, such as anatomically correct puppets.

Shwe Pathein (Map p257; No 108 36th St, 77/78) Gold leaf street (below) now has many crafts shops and the most intriguing is this workshop that sells cotton and bamboo Pathein-style sun umbrellas ($3 to $6) and other crafts including bark portraits of lions and birds (about $6).

Soe Moe (off Map p257; ☎ 70558; soemoe@mandalay .net.mm; No 496 84th St, Chan Mya Thar Si Township) On the way to Amarapura, this wholesaler is packed with statues, puppets and other pieces (new and old – or new disguised as old) for very good prices. If you don't want to tote your purchases around the rest of your trip, they can ship what you get to a Yangon hotel for about K5000.

Gold Leaf Shops
Most of the hammer-pounded thin gold leaf sheets you see worshippers putting onto ever-shining buddha images around the country come from Mandalay's 70 or so workshops, centred on 36th St between 77th and 78th Sts.

King Galon (Map p257; No 143 36th St, 77/78; ⏰ 7am-7pm) Places like this aren't just touristy bus-tour stops – drop by one and get a pressure-free walk-through of the traditional techniques employed by a couple dozen workers. When we dropped by one of the sledgehammer wielders had a bandaged toe from a slipped shot, ow! You can get 10 small sheets – something like 0.00005in thick – for about K3500.

Markets
Zeigyo (Map p259; 84th St, 26/28) This downtown market offers wall-to-wall stands selling just about everything Myanmar in two large modern buildings and in stalls spilling out onto the footpaths.

Night market (Map p259; 84th St, 26/29) Vendors selling food, music, army hats and Chinese

---

EAT THAT GOLD

Gold leaf shops sell their sheets of gold not just to put on buddha images, but to eat. One seller told us: 'It's good for your heart to eat. But don't eat it plain. It's better if you put it on a banana or some chocolate.'

imported clothes block off the street as dusk approaches – a worthy wander.

Malls

78 (Map p257; 78th St, 37/38) This modern four-floor mall with escalators, grocery store and top-floor eateries includes a fake KFC-style chicken shop and a Japanese coffeehouse.

Skywalk (Map p257; 78th St, 33/34) If you're into mall exploration, go to Skywalk. The ground floor is a typical crusty market with produce and reams of *longyi*; up the escalator is an air-conditioned maze of boutiques ($25 Thai imported shirts etc), and up the betel-spit stairs are dark hallways, awkward nightclubs and English-language schools.

Stones & Sculpture

Jade market (Map p257; 87 St, 38/39; ⊙ 7am-5pm) Near Shwe In Bin Kyaung, this is an all-timer of a lively market, with shoulder-to-shoulder locals carrying green jade items on pieces of paper, trying to trade with side-by-side sellers on the crammed walkways. It's a rather sketchy feeling place, and foreigners (if not locals) who do come to pick up some stones get ripped off (we've heard of someone paying $2000 for fakes). However, much of it is genuine (and unlicensed), if not all of equal quality. Outside the market you can see workers cutting and polishing jade pieces. There are plenty of teashops here, plus billiards tables (and tattoos!).

Stone-carvers' workshops (Map p257; cnr 45th & 84th Sts) Just across from the west entrance of the Mahamuni Paya is a whole series of workshops around the corner of 45th and 84th Sts. You can see workers blast slabs of rock, chip them into shapes (buddhas, small elephants, etc) and polish them. Interesting to see, and you can pick up small elephants or buddhas for a couple of thousand kyat.

GETTING THERE & AWAY

Check schedules and prices for outgoing transport when you arrive, as it's likely many of the following will have changed.

Air

Mandalay's huge, gleaming airport – a staggering 28 miles south of the centre – sends and receives daily flights around the country via Air Mandalay (AM), Yangon Airways (YA), Bagan Air (BA) and the government's puny Myanma Airways (MA).

Flights to Chiang Mai come direct, but fly back through Yangon.

Sample rates for one-way flights with peak-season schedules follow; prices are for airlines other than MA unless MA is the only airline offering the route:

Destination	Price	Frequency	Airlines
Bhamo	$115-120	Sun	MA
Heho	$37-40	daily	AM, BA, YA
Kalaymyo	$95-105	Mon, Thu, Sat	MA
Kengtung	$80-85	Tue, Thu, Sun	BA, YA
Monywa	$20-25	Tue	MA
Myitkyina	$80-83	Sun, Tue, Thu, Fri	BA
Nyaung U (Bagan)	$40-43	daily	AM, BA, YA
Tachileik	$80-85	Mon-Sat	BA, YA
Yangon	$90-93	daily	AM, BA, YA

Flights to Thandwe (for Ngapali) go via Yangon.

Travel agencies offer cheaper rates than airlines themselves, so we've included reliable ones to pick up tickets from. Bring US dollars to buy a ticket.

Daw San San Aye (Map p259; ☎ 73441; 81st St, 25/26; ⊙ 9am-5pm)

New Seven Star (Map p259; ☎ 60990; No 269 82nd St, 27/28; ⊙ 9am-5pm Mon-Fri, 9am-noon Sat)

Sun Far Travels & Tours (Map p257; ☎ 69712; No H, 30th St, 77/78; ⊙ 9am-5pm Mon-Fri, 9am-noon Sat & Sun)

The office of the government-run **Myanma Airways** (Map p259; ☎ 36221, 87458; 81st St, 25/26; ⊙ 9am-2pm) has, eerily, a Yangon Airways poster ('You're safe with us') behind the front desk.

Boat

A popular way out of Mandalay is on a private boat service that glides down the wide Ayeyarwady to Bagan ($27, nine hours), leaving around 7am and taking most of a full day. The best of two options is the two-deck *Shwei Kennery*, with outside decks. It goes at least five times weekly from September through January. The return trip from Bagan is slightly cheaper. Another option is the *Malikha* express boat, which lacks outdoor decks to take in the scenery. Your hotel can arrange tickets, or book directly through **Sun Far Travel & Tours** (Map p257; ☎ 69712; No H, 30th St, 77/78; ⊙ 9am-5pm Mon-Fri, 9am-noon Sat & Sun). Many visitors with a short trip to Myanmar fill a day on this journey; debatably, the 40-minute flight to Bagan for $40 is a better use of your time.

The government-owned **Inland Water Transport office** (IWT; Map p257; ☎ 36035; 35th St; ☻ 9am-4pm Mon-Fri), at the western end of Yangyiaung Rd (35th St), sells tickets for the 'slow boat' ferry down the Ayeyarwady including Bagan ($10, 15 hours) and up river to Katha (deck/cabin $9/51, one to two days) or Bhamo (also $9/51, two-three days). This schedule is likely to change. It's easier to have your hotel get the tickets or stop by an MTT office (p258). It's sometimes said that you need to buy tickets a few days in advance, but often it's OK to buy them one day beforehand. IWT generally accepts US dollars only. The service to Mandalay has no reserved seats, but deck chairs are available for rent.

Boats leave from various points along the river, depending on the water level. Your accommodation (or taxi) will know where to go.

Bus

HIGHWAY BUS STATION

Most buses leaving or arriving in Mandalay en route to destinations to the south and southeast operate from the highway bus station, a giant dusty lot 4 miles south of the centre with a mind-numbing array of bus companies, often selling tickets to the same places leaving at the same time.

Schedules are prone to constant change, so take the following sample of fares and schedules from the highway bus station as a loose guide only. Local buses have no air-conditioning and some are 32-seaters.

Bagan

The government-run Nyaung U Mann company sends buses to Nyaung U (K8500, eight hours) at 9am and 2pm.

Kalaw & Inle Lake

Several bus companies head on Taunggyi-bound night buses to Kalaw and Inle Lake, including **Taung Paw Ya** (☎ 71304, 88339), which sends an air-con bus at 6pm, stopping in Kalaw (K10,000, eight hours) and Taunggyi (K10,000, 10 to 12 hours). **Shwe Chin Thae** (☎ 80154) is the only day-time departure for Kalaw or Taunggyi, leaving at 5.30am.

Yangon

Several companies leave Mandalay at 5pm or 6pm on an overnight bus to Yangon (K13,000, 12 to 15 hours). Ticket agents south of downtown include **Shwe Gabar Express** (☎ 88507, 33899; cnr 83rd & 33rd Sts) and **Shwe Mandalar Express** (32nd St, 81/82).

Other Destinations

Frequent local buses head for Meiktila (K2000, three hours) from the highway bus station. You can also get direct service, if you should want it, to Pyay or Magwe. See Monywa bus station, p274, for other towns to the northwest.

If you're heading up to the Shan hills to the northeast (between Pyin U Lwin and Lashio), there are several options from the highway bus station. **Duhtawadi** (Map p259; ☎ 61938; 31st St, 81/82), which has a central ticket office, leaves for Hsipaw (K4000, six or seven hours) at 6am. They also arrange share taxis (K12,000, five hours). There are also buses to Kyaukme (K3500, five hours) and Lashio (K6000, eight

---

LOCAL VOICES: TRISHAW DRIVER

Blue taxis, taxis and new-fangled jeeps with TVs on the dashboard are noticeably taking over the Mandalay streets, previously famous for their bicycle-only, pedal-squeak quiet. We thought we'd talk with one of the 13,000 or so trishaw drivers still eking out a living here.

Do you own or rent your trishaw? I own it. It cost about K10,000 when I bought it in 1996 – now they're worth more than $100. I'm lucky. About 70% of trishaw drivers rent them for about K500 per day.

How much do you make a day? About K2000. I do many things – move electronic supplies or construction supplies for some businesses. Particularly out of tourist season.

How much does your family need a day? Well, K4000 is ideal. That means me, my wife and four children can have a bit of meat. But we're OK with just K1000.

Do you enjoy driving a trishaw? I do like it. I'll never forget it. It's my benefactor. And I've been able to meet so many people because of it! And I now can speak English!

MANDALAY

hours). Times change often. A couple of companies to ask about are Shwe Mandalar Express and Mandalar May Express.

MONYWA BUS STATION

To reach Shwebo or Monywa to the west and northwest by bus, the small **Monywa bus station** (Map p259; off 88th St, 21/22) sends frequent local buses to both. It takes three hours to either town. At research time, some drivers were reluctant to allow foreigners on the bus. A company that allows foreigners to go to Monywa, **Yadanabon** (Map p259; ☎ 61500), facing outward on the south side of the central building, sends buses hourly from 7.30pm to 4.30pm (1800K). A couple of doors down is **Aung Nang Man** (Map p259; ☎ 72193), which does the same for Shwebo (1700K), five times daily beginning at 11am. Both take reservations for seats by phone.

At research time, foreigners were not allowed to bus north to Bhamo from this station.

Taxi & Pick-Up

Hotels in Mandalay can arrange share taxis to Pyin U Lwin, or you can get one downtown (back/front seat K5000/6000, two hours); check at the corner of 27th and 83rd Sts (Map p259). Or call **Shwe Mann May** (☎ 38685). Pick-ups to Pyin U Lwin leave from the corner of 28th and 83rd St.

Duhtawadi (Map p259; ☎ 61938; 31 St, 81/82) arranges share taxis to Hsipaw (K12,000, six hours); a full car is K50,000. There are also share taxis for Hsipaw (per person K11,000 to K13,000) and Lashio (per person K15,000, eight hours) – these leave from along 32nd St, 80/81. Another option that some travellers take up is a share taxi to Hsipaw, then the lovely train ride to Lashio.

Your hotel or guesthouse should be able to help you rent a car with driver, for a day or long-term, for about $60 per day.

Pick-ups to Amarapura and Sagaing (which pass near the boat to Inwa island) leave from along 84th St, south of the market in the centre. A one-way ride costs K200. For more information on taking taxis or pick-ups to nearby towns, see Amarapura (p280), Inwa (p281) and Sagaing (p284).

Train

The newish (largely bare) **train station** (Map p259; 30th St, 78/79) is a mostly unused, modern, multi-storey building with four drive-up ramps, elevated taxi stands and escalators leading to waiting areas with TVs. Meanwhile it's generally the same ol' poky, packed trains that ferry mostly locals on slow-going trips back home.

All train lines are government run. Just inside the main entrance downstairs is an **MTT office** (Map p259; ☎ 35140; ☉ 9.30am-6pm), which can sell tickets at 10% commission.

Sample fares (ordinary/upper class/sleeper) and schedule follow:

Destination	Price	Duration	Departure
Hsipaw	$4/7/-	10hr	4.35am
Lashio	$6/12/-	14¼hr	4.35am
Myitkyina	$11/36/40	20-22hr	noon, 1.30pm, 4pm
Naba (near Katha)	$-/21/23	12-14hr	noon, 1.30pm, 4pm
Nyaung U (Bagan)	$4/10/-	8hr	9pm
Pyin U Lwin	$3/5/-	4hr	4.35am
Yangon	$15/35/40	14-16hr	4am, 5am, 5.30am, 8am

GETTING AROUND
To/From the Airport & Stations

A small 'blue taxi' to the airport (a one-hour ride) runs to K10,000, a car taxi is about K12,000. It's less reliable trying to jump in a share taxi, but you can try **Shwe Airport Taxi** (Map p259; 83rd St, 23/24), which can also arrange a car taxi for K12,000.

A taxi between downtown and the highway bus station is about K2500 or K3000. Pick-ups to the highway bus station (K1000) troll central streets – try just south of the market on 84th St.

Note that trishaws are discouraged from hanging out at the train station and aren't allowed on the entry ramps on the west side.

Bicycle & Motorcycle

Several bicycle-rental shops stand on footpaths downtown, including the ever-helpful **Mr Htoo Bicycles** (Map p259; 83rd St, 25/26; hire per day K1500; ☉ 8am-7pm). Mr Htoo has an English-speaking buddy who rents a motorbike for $10 per day (either with or without him driving); petrol is extra. Most hotels and guesthouses can get you either bicycle or motobike from around the same rates (not including guide or petrol).

Bus & Pick-Up

Mandalay's buses and pick-ups are virtually always crowded, particularly during the 7am to 9am and 4pm to 5pm rush hours. It can be fun, even if you never get where you want to get. The best place to find one is just west of the clock tower near the *zeigyo* along 26th St (Map p259), where unmarked pick-ups and some (Myanmar) numbered buses depart from. Ask, ask, ask. You should be able to jump on bus 7 or a pick-up to Mahamuni Paya, a pick-up to Mandalay Hill, or bus 5 or a pick-up to Yankin Paya.

No city buses or pick-ups go to the airport.

Taxi

Taxis and 'blue taxis' (teeny blue Mazda pick-ups with room for four or so in the covered cab) whisk people around Mandalay most hours. They're easy to find downtown. Prices are negotiable. A ride from downtown to the Bagan jetty is about K2000. You can hire a blue taxi on a full-day trip to Amarapura, Inwa and Sagaing for about K18,000 to K20,000; a regular taxi is about K8000 to K15,000 more.

Trishaw

About 13,000 trishaws still ply Mandalay streets, and you can get to and fro for K1000 or so on most trips around the centre.

Around Mandalay

What puts Mandalay on most travellers' maps looms outside its doors – former capitals with battered stupas and palace walls lost in palm-rimmed rice fields where locals scoot by in slow-moving horse carts. Most of it is easy day-trip potential.

In Amarapura, for-hire rowboats drift by a three-quarter-mile teak-pole bridge used by hundreds of monks and fishers carrying their day's catch home. At the canal-made island capital of Inwa (Ava), a flatbed ferry then a horse cart leads visitors to a handful of ancient sites surrounded by village life. In Mingun – a boat ride up the Ayeyarwady (Irrawaddy) from Mandalay – steps lead up a battered stupa more massive than any other...and yet only a third finished. At one of Myanmar's most religious destinations, Sagaing's temple-studded hills offer room to explore, space to meditate and views of the Ayeyarwady.

Further out of town, northwest of Mandalay in Sagaing District, are a couple of towns – real ones, the kind where wide-eyed locals sometimes slip into approving laughter at your mere presence – that require overnight stays. Four hours west of Mandalay, Monywa is near a carnivalesque pagoda and hundreds of cave temples carved from a buddha-shaped mountain; further east, Shwebo is further off the travelways, a stupa-filled town where Myanmar's last dynasty kicked off; nearby is Kyaukmyaung, a riverside town devoted to pottery, where you can snoop about pottery factories.

HIGHLIGHTS

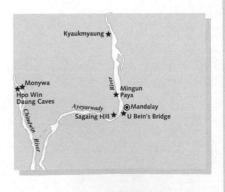

- Join the monk parade crossing the world's longest teak bridge, Amarapura's stunning **U Bein's Bridge** (p278)

- Look over hundreds of pagodas and the Ayeyarwady River from atop **Sagaing Hill** (p283), one of Myanmar's more important religious sites

- Climb **Mingun Paya** (p284), an unfinished, but still king-sized, stupa reached by a boat ride from Mandalay

- Go to Bagan the back way – via **Monywa** (p286), where you can join monkeys in admiring the **Hpo Win Daung Caves** (p289)

- Peek into ancient pottery traditions at **Kyaukmyaung** (p292), a rarely visited riverside village lined with giant pots bound for delta villages

HISTORY

From the fall of Bagan (Pagan) to the end of the third and last Anglo-Burmese War in 1885, the capitals of Myanmar played musical chairs in the area around Mandalay. At first, new kings sought to build their legacy by breaking new ground (and often the bricks and wood from old palace buildings) to build a new capital.

By the late 18th century, kings turned to astrological forces to pick a site. Generally, when a new reign began, the royal entourage of the new king took much of the construction materials from an old capital and left the area to farming villagers.

In the chaos after the fall of Bagan, it was Sagaing that first rose to prominence (in the early 14th century), but in 1364 Inwa succeeded it. Alaungpaya appointed himself a royal in 1752, and the capital was briefly stationed in his home town of Shwebo (then called Mokesebo).

In 1760 the capital shifted back across the river to Sagaing, where it remained for just four years. Inwa only regained its pre-eminent position from 1764 to 1783, after which time Amarapura became the capital. In 1823 Inwa was again the capital but, following the terrible earthquake of 1838, which caused considerable damage to all these cities, the capital was moved back to Amarapura in 1841. Then in 1860 the seat of power was transferred to Mandalay, where it remained until the end of the British conquest of Myanmar 25 years later.

CLIMATE

As in Mandalay, it's hot here, sometimes reaching 40°C (104°F), and April and May bake. Dust cakes the trees (and the back of your throat) any time it's not raining.

GETTING THERE & AROUND

All of these destinations are best reached via Mandalay (p255). Three of the ancient cities (Amarapura, Inwa and Sagaing) outside Mandalay's door are reached by pick-ups, but most visitors go on day trips by taxi (see p278). Monywa and Shwebo are a few hours west and north of Mandalay by bus; Monywa also has air and slow-train connections with Mandalay and a useful bus connection with Pakokku (p191) en route to Bagan. See the Getting There & Away sections in individual destinations for more details.

ANCIENT CITIES

Mandalay's real claims to fame are its day trips to some distinct ancient cities, which you can visit by boat, horse cart or foot – Amarapura, Inwa and Sagaing, as well as the Snake Pagoda at Paleik; upriver to the north is Mingun. You'll need to pick up Mandalay's 'Archaeological Zone' $10 combo ticket (government-bound; see p261) to visit Inwa's main sites, or the Sagaing/Mingun $3 ticket to visit Mingun and Sagaing (if you cross the old Ava Bridge). No-one checks for tickets at the other sites.

AMARAPURA

အမရပူရ

☎ 02

Myanmar's penultimate royal capital, the now-modern town of Amarapura (pronounced amuRA-puRA), 7 miles south of Mandalay, is well known by the many day-trippers for its 1849 pedestrian bridge built of over 1000 teak posts. The setting on the wide Taungthaman Lake is gorgeous too, and there's much more to see, though most sites are scattered (and sometimes not easy to find). Allow time and energy for walking if

---

LOCAL FESTIVAL LOWDOWN

- **Mingun Nat Festival** Mingun, p285
- **Inwa Nat Pwe** Inwa, p281
- **Paleik Festival** Paleik, p282
- **Waso Festival** Kaunghmudaw Paya, near Sagaing, p283
- **Irinaku Festival** (Yadanagu) South of Amarapura, p280
- **Festival of Lights** Amarapura's Kyauktawgyi Paya hosts this *paya pwe* (pagoda festival), p279
- **Hpo Win Daung Festival** West of Monywa, p289

PLANNING DAY TRIPS

You can't visit all the ancient cities in one day. Mingun is a bit more than a half-day trip by boat. With a taxi driver, it's possible to visit Amarapura, Inwa and Sagaing in one busy day (and many visitors do), but many travellers prefer saving Sagaing for another day.

At research time, a 'blue taxi' from Mandalay (see p275) for the three sites cost about $15, a regular taxi from $55 or a van from $80, while renting a motorcycle (with/without driver) is about $15/10, not including petrol. Most guesthouses and hotels can arrange cars. If you want to be sure of a good quality car with air-con, contact **Good News Travels** (Map p257; ☎ 02-73571; www.myanmargoodnewstravel.com; No B6 71st St, 28/29).

Packed pick-ups leaving from the corner of 29th and 84th Sts in Mandalay (Map p259) stop by Amarapura (30 minutes) and the Inwa junction (40 minutes), before reaching Sagaing (45 minutes). It's K200. Considering how far apart many sights are, even many shoestringers spring for a full-day taxi, which is the only way to link them up with Paleik.

Note that the popular dining time for monks at the Maha Ganayon Kyaung (below) in Amarapura and the snake-feeding time at Paleik (see p282) is 11am daily.

Other transport details are listed at the end of each section.

you don't have a driver. Technically U Bein's Bridge is part of Mandalay's $10 combo ticket (see p261), but no-one here checks for it.

Amarapura means 'City of Immortality', though its period as capital was relatively brief. It was founded by Bodawpaya as his new capital in 1783. In 1857 Mindon Min decided to make Mandalay the capital, and the changeover was completed in 1860.

Today little remains of the old Amarapura palace area. The city walls were torn down to make quarry material, while most of the wooden palace buildings were dismantled and taken to Mandalay.

There is no licensed accommodation in Amarapura.

Sights

U BEIN'S BRIDGE

ဦးပိန်လျှတံတား

Amarapura's biggest draw – and easily one of Myanmar's most photographed sites – is this remarkable 1300yd-long teak footbridge leading across the shallow **Taungthaman Lake** (which is named for an ogre who supposedly came looking for Buddha here). Still strong after 200 years, the world's longest teak span sees a lot of life: fishers casting a line into the water, locals walking their bicycles home to Taungthaman village across the lake, and monks in saffron robes carrying alms bowls between the monasteries on both sides.

The best times to visit the bridge are just after sunrise or just before sunset (most visitors come at this time), when hundreds of villagers commute back and forth across it. A popular

sunset activity is hiring boats (about K2500) from owners at the western end of the bridge to get close-up looks of the 1060-post bridge from the water. In the dry season the lake dwindles greatly in size; in June or July the water levels sometimes rise above the walkway.

The bridge's name is usually attributed to the 'mayor' of Amarapura when the capital moved here from Inwa in 1841, but some say it was named for a Muslim servant of the king who built the bridge. Most of the posts are original, though some have been replaced by concrete blocks. The bridge curves to better withstand the wind.

There are five shaded rest areas on the bridge, including (at times) a couple of places to sample fresh palm toddy.

AROUND THE BRIDGE

Near the start of the bridge are a few food stalls where you can buy noodles, tea or beer and enjoy the view.

Just west from the start of the bridge is the **Maha Ganayon Kyaung**, home to several thousand young monks. If you visit at about 11am, you can watch the whole monastery eating silently. (Try to refrain from thrusting cameras into monks' faces, as many visitors do.) It was founded around 1914 and is renowned as a centre for monastic study and strict religious discipline.

Kyauktawgyi Paya

ကျောက်တော်ကြီးဘုရား

If you cross U Bein's Bridge, you'll come to **Taungthaman village** and Kyauktawgyi Paya (about 180yd from the bridge). Constructed in 1847 by Pagan Min, this paya is said to have been modelled on the larger Ananda Pahto at Bagan (p210), but its five-tiered roof gives it more the look of a Tibetan or Nepali temple.

While the paya doesn't have the perfectly vaulted roofs or the finer decorations of the original, it does have an excellent seated buddha image and well-preserved frescoes. Check the entry ceiling murals to see some suspiciously English-looking figures in bamboo hats, looking a little bossy despite the smiles.

The *paya pwe* (pagoda festival), known as the **Festival of Lights**, marks the end of Buddhist Lent, when pagodas and homes are lit up by strings of lights or candles. It takes place here during Thadingyut (October).

The atmosphere around Kyauktawgyi is very peaceful and shady, and this is a good alternative place to hang around at sunset. There are several smaller overgrown stupas to be seen in the vicinity, including a unique honeycomb-shaped stupa covered with buddha niches. There are a couple of traditional outdoor teashops.

You can also catch a boat back across the lake.

SHWE-KYET-KYA & SHWE-KYET-YET
ရွှေကြက်ကျ & ရွှေကြက်ယက်

On the bank of the Ayeyarwady, about a mile west of Amarapura, stand two 12th-century paya – the Shwe-kyet-kya and the Shwe-kyet-yet, or Golden Fowl's Run, a string of stupa ruins cascading from a high bluff. If the river isn't too high, you can get someone to take you out in a local *hgnet* (swallow-tailed boat) for a view of the paya, the Sagaing hills and the sun setting behind the Ava Bridge.

PAHTODAWGYI
ပုထိုးတော်ကြီး

Built by King Bagyidaw in 1820, this well-preserved paya, about 1.25 miles north of the bridge, stood outside the old city walls. The lower terraces have marble slabs illustrating scenes from the Jataka (stories of the Buddha's past lives). There's a fine view over the surrounding countryside from the upper terrace. An inscription stone within the temple precinct details the history of the monument's construction.

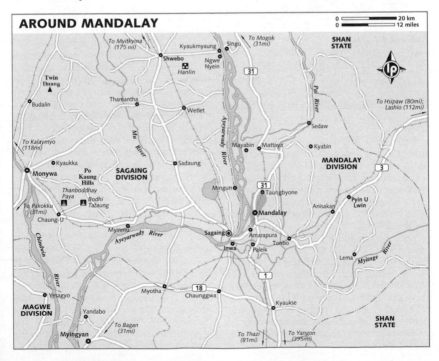

AROUND MANDALAY

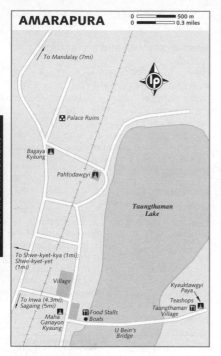

AMARAPURA

0 —— 500 m
0 —— 0.3 miles

To Mandalay (7mi)

🏛 Palace Ruins

Bagaya 🏛
Kyaung

Pahtodawgyi 🏛

Taungthaman Lake

To Shwe-kyet-kya (1mi);
Shwe-kyet-yet (1mi)

Village

Kyauktawgyi Paya 🏛

To Inwa (4.3mi);
Sagaing (5mi)

🏛 Food Stalls
● Boats

Teashops
Taungthaman Village 🏛

Maha Ganayon Kyaung

U Bein's Bridge

AROUND MANDALAY

BAGAYA KYAUNG

ဘားကရာကျောင်း

The history of the Bagaya Kyaung, now a government-built reconstruction dating from 1996 and a **museum** (⏰ various), goes back two centuries. Admission is free but it is customary to give the 'keymaster' about K100.

Based on a still-standing predecessor in Inwa, the first version of the Bagaya Kyaung dates from when King Bodawpaya built the monastery after moving the capital to Amarapura, but it was destroyed by fire in 1821. A second version, built in 1847, was again burned down in 1866, leaving only eight brick stairways.

These were gradually overgrown until the Hsinbyume Paya *sayadaw* (master teacher) built a two-storey brick building in 1951, in which he deposited 500 buddha images and 5000 sets of *pe-sa* (palm-leaf manuscripts) from throughout Myanmar. The project to rebuild it was based on ground plans and drawings found at the Kyauktawgyi Paya.

Ask the caretaker to open the museum; it's usually locked.

Bagaya Kyaung is located just off the Mandalay road, about half a mile northeast of Pahtodawgyi.

Festivals & Events

In August, a week after the end of the Taungbyone *nat pwe* (p266) and the full moon of Wagaung, Myanmar's *nat* (spirit being) worshippers move to the **Irinaku Festival** (Yadanagu), just south of Amarapura, and to the east of the road. The festival celebrates Popa Medaw, the mother of the Taungbyone brothers.

Getting There & Away

If arriving by pick-up, the best access point to U Bein's Bridge is just after you see a big sign on the left-hand side of the road. It's easier to just tell the driver where you're headed beforehand. See p278 for day-trip info.

Touring by bicycle from Mandalay is another alternative (see p274). Pedalling to Amarapura should take an hour.

INWA (AVA)

အင်းဝ

☎ 02

Cut off from roads by rivers and canals, the ancient city of **Inwa** (admission $10 combo ticket) served as capital of the Burmese kingdom for nearly 400 years, longer than any other city. Nowadays, it's both an ultra-raw place where rural life reigns, and a rather touristy heist (beginning with the government's combo ticket, see p261, and continuing with a K1000 boat ride and K4000 horse cart). Nearly all visitors get around on a pre-priced horse-cart system that whisks you to the same few sights (where souvenir vendors greet you), passing many other atmospheric, ruined pagodas lost in palm-lined rice fields. Adventurer types should consider going by motorbike (see p274), and making up your own itinerary; also, if you skip the wood monastery site you won't need the $10 combo ticket. (See the boxed text, p282, for some directions.)

Inwa – known as Ava to the outside world until relatively recently – is reached by ferry, from near the Mandalay side of the Ava Bridge, 4 miles southwest of Amarapura. On its south side, the Myittha Chaung (Myittha Canal) connects the Myitnge and Ayeyarwady Rivers, making Inwa an 'island'.

The **Inwa Nat Pwe** celebrates Thon Ban Hla from the 10th day of the waxing moon through to the full moon of Tabaung (February/March).

A horse-cart loop takes a few hours. There's a garden restaurant near the boat jetty, but no places to stay.

History

Inwa's classical Pali name was Ratnapura (City of Gems), Tadanabon in Burmese. In 1364, when the capital Sagaing fell to the Shan, the capital moved to Inwa (Mouth of the Lake), and Bamar kings here quickly set about re-establishing Bamar supremacy, which had been in decline since the fall of Bagan. Save for an interlude or three (it fell to Taungoo in 1555 and the Mon in 1752), it served as the Burmese capital till 1841 (when northern Myanmar was called the Kingdom of Ava). The capital moved to Amarapura in 1841.

Sights

BAGAYA KYAUNG

ဘာ:ကရာကျောင်:

Probably Inwa's finest attraction is the teak Bagaya Kyaung, which dates from 1834. The entire monastery is supported by 267 teak posts (the largest measures 60ft in height and 9ft in circumference). The cool and dark interior feels old and inviting (though you may catch your bare foot on a raised nail or two).

On the outside, look for the **Keinayi peacock** – half bird and half woman. How long this pristine wooden structure will escape the heavy hand of renovation is not certain, but visit it while you can.

There are a few interesting **temples** in the fields surrounding the monastery. Some horse-cart drivers will get mad if you linger long, but you could breeze through Bagaya and walk out to them – no postcard vendors out there.

NANMYIN

အင်:ဝငမျှာ်စင်

The 90ft-high masonry watchtower Nan-myin –the 'leaning tower of Inwa' – is all that remains of the palace built by Bagyidaw. The upper portion was shattered by the 1838 earthquake and the rest has taken on a pre-carious tilt that is clearly noticeable when you're climbing the steps. It's not a reli-gious site so you can keep your shoes on. Visible up the top, across the Ayeyarwady, is the hemisphere-shaped Kaunghmudaw Paya (p283).

MAHA AUNGMYE BONZAN

မဟာ အောငမျှ မြဘုံ စံ

Also known as the Ok Kyaung or the Me Nu Ok Kyaung, this is a brick-and-stucco monastery built by Meh Nu, the chief queen of Bagyidaw, for her royal abbot U Bok (Nyaunggan *say-adaw*) in 1822. Monasteries were generally built of wood and were prone to deteriora-tion from the elements or destruction by fire. This monastery's masonry construction has ensured its long life. The 1838 earthquake badly damaged it, but it was restored in 1872 by one of King Mindon's queens.

Located nearby, the **Htilaingshin Paya** dates back to the Bagan period; in a shed in the compound an inscription records the con-struction of the wooden palace during the first Inwa dynasty.

BRIDGES

Visible from the tower and from the ferry are two bridges. The first one is the British-engineered, 16-span **Ava Bridge**, which leads to Sagaing and dates from 1934.

In 1942 the British demolished two spans of the bridge to deny passage to the advancing Japanese. Not until 1954 was it repaired and put back into operation.

Just beyond is **Sagaing Bridge**, a modern four-lane bridge completed in 2005.

OTHER SIGHTS

Shortly after leaving the village, you'll pass the best preserved remnants of the massive **old city walls** near the northern gate, facing the Ayeyarwady (northwest of the Maha Aungmye Bonzan). This gate was also known as the **Gaung Say Daga** (Hair-Washing Gate), where kings apparently went for a shampoo.

Other sights aren't normally included on a horse cart tour – ask if you can visit them. On the southern side of the city stand the remains of the huge four-storey **Le-htat-gyi Paya**. There is also the **Lawkatharaphu Paya**, while to the south of the city stands the **Singyone Fort**.

Getting There & Around

If you're not coming by taxi, pick-ups will drop off passengers near the Ava Bridge, half a mile to the ferry. (In the rainy season the ferry

AROUND MANDALAY

DIY INWA TOUR

If you bring a motorbike to Inwa, and don't see any horse carts to follow to the sites, you could easily miss them. Follow the road in from the village, which bends left. After a couple hundred yards, take the first right and go straight (past a left turn, then a right turn, then several faded white stupas to the left). Continue straight through a brick gate and over a small wooden bridge to the crossroads in a small village; take a right, then your first left, and continue past rice fields and a brick temple. A bit ahead is a tree-lined road to the left, which leads to Bagaya Kyaung. Retrace your way, back through the village and brick gate, then take the left turn (near the white stupas), which bends past Nanmyin and the nearby Maha Aungmye Bonzan and through the city gate back to the boat jetty.

---

leaves from near Ava Bridge at the Thabyedan Fort, just below the bridge to the south.)

A horse cart tour of the three main sites is K4000 (for one or two people) and takes about three hours. A motorcycle or bicycle can easily board the ferry (passenger without/with motorcycle K1000/1500) to Inwa.

PALEIK
ပလိပ်

☎ 02

Most visitors on the ancient cities circuit miss Paleik's Yadana Labamuni Hsu-taung-pye Paya, better known as the **Snake Pagoda** (Hmwe Paya). It's named after the three giant pythons that sleep curled around the bud-dha images and that are tenderly washed and fed at 11am daily. The modest temple, dating alternatively to the early 11th century or the 15th century, received little notice until 1974, when three pythons appeared from the nearby forest. Now daily revellers (including a scared baby or two) pose for photographs with the snakes, which are led by attendants to the main buddha image.

Paleik is surrounded by an estimated 325 stupas and paya in varying states of repair, many from the Konbaung period – it's something like a mini-Bagan.

The big **Paleik Festival** takes place in the two weeks following the full moon of Waso (June or July).

Paleik is about 12 miles south of Mandalay (about 45 minutes) on the highway to Meiktila and Yangon (Rangoon). Nearly everyone who comes does so by taxi, but Meiktila-bound buses from Mandalay's highway bus station stop here. A lovely tree-lined back road leads 6 miles east to Inwa (no public transport is available); it's possible to arrive for the 11am event and reach Inwa by noon.

SAGAING
စစ်ကိုင်း

☎ 072

Home to 500 stupas, even more monasteries and nunneries, and some 6000 monks and nuns, lovely Sagaing is where Buddhists in Myanmar go when they're stressed. Set on a riverbank across the Ayeyarwady from Inwa, its peaceful pace – led by a *lot* of local meditation – is welcome to visitors as well.

Those also trying to cram in Amarapura and Inwa in the same day usually get only a whirlwind look at Sagaing in 90 minutes. Considering the town's massive network of leafy paths connecting hilltop stupa to riverside stupa, and with licensed accommodation here, there's much to explore for those willing to linger. If you're unable to temple-hop in Bagan, Sagaing may provide an interesting substitute.

Named for the trees hanging over the river, Sagaing became the capital of an independent Shan kingdom around 1315, after the fall of Bagan had thrown central Myanmar into chaos. Its period of importance was short, for in 1364 the founder's grandson, Thado Minbya, hop-scotched the capital to Inwa. For four years, from 1760 to 1764, Sagaing was once again the capital, but the historic importance of this period is comparatively minor.

Devotion is the name of the game these days. In addition to the many sites, there's a major monastic hospital here. During the full moon of Tazaungmon (October/November), devotees from Mandalay and beyond flock to Sagaing to offer robes. Kyaswa Kyaung holds a 'foreign yogis retreat' in December or January (foreigners are welcome), and visitors are sometimes invited to stay in monasteries around Sagaing Hill by friendly monks.

Sagaing is also famous for its acoustic guitars.

Sights

SAGAING HILL

စစ်လျက်ကိုလ္လေးတောငလ္လ

If you have limited time in Sagaing, come to this **hill** (admission Sagaing/Mingun $3 ticket). The government ticket is valid for five days and includes admission to the nearby town of Mingun. Trees hang over stone steps that lead past stupas, monasteries and nunneries to a glorious top, where you can take in many of Sagaing's 500 stupas and views of the river back towards Mandalay. There are several ways up, not all of which have government ticket stands en route; trishaw drivers (if not taxi drivers) will know where to go.

Tilawkaguru, near the southwest base of the hill, is an impressive mural-filled cave temple that dates from 1672. Though much was damaged by fire 80 years ago (and frisky bats hang out in some chambers), a walk-through can be superb. Monks from the outside monastery may turn on the electricity, but it's best by the (provided) candlelight, where colourful murals slowly reveal themselves in the dark hallways.

Other sights around the hill include **Padamya Zedi** (a stupa which dates from 1300); **Umin Thounzeh** (30 Caves), which has 45 buddha images in a crescent-shaped colonnade; and the 97ft-high **Soon U Ponya Shin Paya**, built in 1312 and home to large bronze frogs on wheels that serve as collection boxes.

If you don't want to go up the hill, you can still soak up Sagaing's atmosphere by roaming along the pathways that cover the hillsides and link up the hundreds of *tazaung* (shrine buildings) down to Thayetpin jetty.

On the way back to the market, your taxi driver will likely stop off at one of the **silver shops**, where you can see artisans bang away at various pieces.

SOUTH OF AVA BRIDGE

Buddhist Sites

Heading along Strand Rd, following the water south of the bridge, you can drop by a couple of interesting pagodas. About 450yd south is the **Tupayon Paya**, built in 1444, which has an unusual style for Myanmar. It consists of three circular storeys each encircled by arched niches. The 1838 earthquake toppled the superstructure, and it's never been completely reconstructed.

Another few hundred yards to the south, Strand Rd passes the entrance to the sandstone **Aungmyelawka Paya**, built in 1783 by Bodawpaya in imitation of the Shwezigon Paya in Bagan (see p219).

Forts

Overlooking the Ayeyarwady are three forts, built by an Italian engineer as a last-ditch defence by the Myanmar people in the Third Anglo-Burmese War. About half a mile south of Aungmyelawka Paya is the most easily accessed, the riverside **Asekhan Fort** (Fort Savage). Follow Strand Rd south (to its end) and then continue on side roads about 180yd further south.

Once the site of a minor 1886 battle, the fort now is mostly home to grazing cows ('they match the intelligence of our army now', one local joked). Just north, under a large tree, is a small walled cemetery with three tombstones of British soldiers.

From the riverside wall you can just make out the other forts across the river. **Thabyedan Fort** is amid the trees, just south of the Ava Bridge.

To the south (in Inwa, maybe 180yd south of Lawgtharaphu Paya) are the barely visible remains of a concrete wall (low, with much vegetation), where **Singyone Fort** once stood.

KAUNGHMUDAW PAYA

ကောင်းမူတော်ဘုရား

The best known of the Sagaing stupas, actually 6 miles west towards Monywa, is the Kaunghmudaw Paya. The enormous white dome rises 150ft and was modelled after the Mahaceti (Great Stupa) in Sri Lanka. A local joke is that the king agonised over how to shape the stupa, and his queen (tired of his indecisiveness) ripped open her blouse and said 'make it like this!' and pointed to her breast. Also known by its Pali name, Rajamanisula, the stupa was built in 1636 to commemorate Inwa's establishment as the royal capital of Myanmar. The pagoda's big **Waso Festival** is held during the full moon of Waso (June/July).

Around the base of the structure are 812 stone pillars, each 3ft to 5ft high and with a small hollow for an oil lamp. Images of *nat* can be seen in the 120 niches that also circle the base. A nearly 10ft-high polished marble slab stands in a corner of the paya grounds (it's in a small gold building, back to the right as you enter); its 86 lines on both sides record details of the monument's construction.

AROUND MANDALAY

Many vendors here sell *thanakha* (sandalwood-like logs used for skin paste), brought from Shwebo and Pakokku.

You'll need to hire a taxi in Sagaing to get here.

Sleeping

Happy Hotel (☎ 21692, 21693; s $8-20, d $15-$30; 🅿)
This simple hotel, a couple of blocks from the market, has simple clean rooms in a two-part complex. Cheaper, fan-cooled rooms have shared bathroom; the best options are the midpriced rooms (single/double $15/25), which are air-conditioned with tile floor, TV and private bathroom – roughly equivalent to a $12 Mandalay room. Coming from Mandalay, turn right at the market, then take the second right.

Getting There & Away

Sagaing is about 12 miles southwest of Mandalay and is reached by a road that crosses the Ayeyarwady via the Ava Bridge. Mandalay-bound pick-ups stop on the main road just after the bridge; hired 'blue taxis' from Mandalay usually take the new Sagaing Bridge.

Sometimes authorities check the Sagaing/Mingun $3 ticket at the old Ava Bridge, but not the new Sagaing Bridge.

MINGUN

မင်းကွန်း

☎ 72

Home to several unique pagodas – including an unfinished, earthquake-cracked one with a flat top that offers some of the country's best Ayeyarwady views – **Mingun** (admission Sagaing/Mingun $3 ticket) makes for a rather relaxed half-day trip 7 miles upriver from Mandalay. Reached most easily by boat, the site is famous for Mingun Paya, which would have been the world's largest (if King Bodawpaya hadn't died before it was finished in 1819). Some visitors love it, others leave complaining it's 'too touristy' due to the dozens of oil-painting and T-shirt vendors along the way.

Boats arrive at different locations, depending on water levels. Sites are scattered along the river. Avoid the hordes by walking to the north end and walking back. (Or come by private boat in the afternoon when you'll have the sites to yourself.)

It's sometimes possible to bypass the government fee, if you're sly at the Mandalay jetty (see Getting There & Away, opposite).

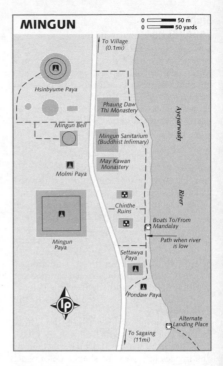

MINGUN

To Village (0.1mi)

Hsinbyume Paya

Phaung Daw Thi Monastery

Mingun Bell

Mingun Sanitarium (Buddhist Infirmary)

May Kawan Monastery

Molmi Paya

Ayeyarwady River

Chinthe Ruins

Boats To/From Mandalay

Path when river is low

Mingun Paya

Settawya Paya

Pondaw Paya

Alternate Landing Place

To Sagaing (11mi)

Sights

PONDAW PAYA

ပုံတော်ဘုရား

On the southern end of the site, this unassuming structure, a 16ft-high white pagoda, is a working model for the gigantic, unfinished Mingun Paya, 90yd north.

SETTAWYA PAYA

စကြုတော်လျှရာဘုရား

On the river immediately north of the Pondaw Paya is the Settawya Paya, a hollow, vaulted shrine containing a footprint of the Buddha. King Bodawpaya brought the footprint to Mingun when the relic chamber in the base of his huge *pahto* (temple) was sealed up. Settawya Paya was built in 1811.

MINGUN PAYA

မင်းကွန်းဘုရား

Looming high and wide on the inland side of the road, the Mingun Paya is actually just the cracked brick base of the original plan. The grandiose pagoda King Bodawpaya had in mind was set to reach 500ft (three times the paya's present size). Construction began in 1790 with a labour force of thousands of slaves and prisoners of war. Bodawpaya often supervised construction from a set-up residence on an island offshore. Work halted in 1819 when Bodawpaya died.

An earthquake split the monument in 1838 and reduced it to partial rubble – it's possibly the world's largest pile of bricks. But what a pile! Each side of the enormous base measures 240ft, and the lowest terrace measures 460ft. There are projecting four-layer lintels over the porticoes on each of the four sides. Beautiful glazed tiles in brown, pale brown, cream and green were intended to be set in panels around the terrace; some of these tiles can be seen in the small building in front of the enormous ruin.

Despite its dilapidated state, you must go barefoot if you intend to climb the base. From the flat top you have a fine view of the Hsinbyume Paya, Mingun village and the river.

It's worth walking around the back – some locals climb up the huge crack on the southwestern corner.

Across the road towards the river is a pair of large **chinthe** (half-lion, half-dragon guardian deities). Apparently after the earthquake cracked it, as many as 10 people lived in their mouths!

MINGUN BELL
မင်းကွန်းခေါင်းလောင်း

In 1808 Bodawpaya had a gigantic bronze bell cast to go with his gigantic stupa. Weighing 55,555 *viss* (90 tonnes), the bell is claimed to be the largest hung, uncracked bell in the world. (A larger bell in Moscow is cracked.)

The 1838 earthquake that shook the *zedi* (stupa) base also destroyed the bell's teak supports, so it was hung in a new *tazaung* (shrine building) close to the riverboat landing, with new British-made iron supports. The bell is about 13ft high and over 16ft across at the lip. You can scramble right inside it, and some helpful bystander will give it a good thump so that you can hear the ring from the interior.

An alternate path to/from Hsinbyume Paya is just behind the bell (and avoids many vendors). Go up to the path, turn right (past a German English-language school), then left on a sidewalk. This area used to be a village cemetery, until a recent Mingun village split (over arguments about property lines), and many relocated here. The two headstones in the middle of the path pay tribute to the two people who created the Mingun Sanitarium. Beyond it turn right to reach Hsinbyume.

HSINBYUME PAYA
ဆင်ဖြူမယ်ဘုရား:

Also known as Myatheindan, and built by King Bagyidaw in 1816, three years before he succeeded Bodawpaya as king, this unusual stupa has a couple of stories behind it.

Some say it was constructed in memory of the king's senior wife, the Hsinbyume princess; others claim Bodawpaya's daughter built it with unused (and outright pilfered) materials from the Mingun Paya. It's supposedly a representation of the Sulamani Paya, which, according to the Buddhist plan of the cosmos, stands atop Mt Meru (the mountain that stands at the centre of the universe).

The seven whitewashed wavy terraces around the stupa represent the seven mountain ranges around Mt Meru, while the five kinds of mythical monsters can be found in niches on each terrace level. At the top, note the presence of a buddha sitting directly behind another; the small one behind was beheaded by raiders looking for gold; when it was fixed, locals worried the buddha's head was tilted too low, so they made another.

The pagoda was badly damaged by the 1838 quake, but was restored in 1874.

MINGUN SANITARIUM
Also called the Buddhist Infirmary, this nursing home for the family-less elderly is worth checking out. The friendly head nurse here is Thwe Thwe Aye, who speaks excellent English (and likens herself to 'J-Lo' on occasion). She does good work here. Drop by and offer a donation for medicines – or bring some (they need Amlodipin for hyper-tension or Super Glucocard II test strips for insulin tests).

Festivals & Events
The **Mingun Nat Festival** takes place between the fifth and 10th days of the waxing moon of Tabaung (February/March). This celebration pays homage to the brother and sister of the Teak Tree, who drowned in the river while clinging to a trunk.

Getting There & Away
Government-run riverboats to Mingun (K3000 return, about one hour) depart at 9am

from the western end of 26th St in Mandalay (off Map p257), and leave Mingun at 1pm to make the return journey. It's possible to buy tickets in advance from your hotel or from the jetty office. At the jetty, look for the small blue sign near the water, inside you'll see two tables – the one to the right sells the boat tickets. Some visitors, and Lonely Planet researchers, have successfully bypassed the government's Sagaing/Mingun $3 ticket, sold at the left table. Inland Water Transport ferries going up and down the Ayeyarwady don't stop in Mingun.

It's also possible to arrange a small private boat to take you (about K15,000 return). If you do so, go in the afternoon, perhaps timing it for sunset atop the Mingun Paya – you'll have no crowds and very little vendor hassle.

You could technically ride by motorbike to Sagaing then to Mingun on the rough road in about three hours (one way). Also, a pick-up goes from Sagaing to Mingun at 11am, and returns at 1.30pm.

NORTH OF MANDALAY

Further from Mandalay are a number of attractions in Sagaing District that usually require an overnight stay. Few tourists visit here, which is part of its appeal. Monywa (right) is near some top-shelf attractions; historically key Shwebo (p290) kicked off Myanmar's last dynasty. Much further north, near the Indian border and only reachable by air, Kalaymyo is covered in the Western Myanmar chapter (p334).

About two hours up into the Shan hills from Mandalay, Pyin U Lwin (Maymyo, p294), covered in the Northeastern Myanmar chapter, offers a breath of fresh (and cooler) air from Mandalay.

It's not recommended, but government-run MTT in Mandalay (p258) offers government trips way north to Khamti ('Naga Land') in January for a laughable $1200 per person.

During the 17th century, when the Portuguese adventurer (and soon to be impaled) Philip de Brito was defeated at Thanlyin, all the Portuguese and Eurasians living at de Brito's 13-year-old colony were exiled to areas around Monywa and Shwebo (notably the villages of Monhla and Chantha near Monywa). Called *bayingyis*, rare fair-haired residents may occasionally be seen, although no linguistic or cultural legacies remain.

MONYWA

မုံရွာ

☎ 071

Offering many more wide-eyed looks than at most of Myanmar's highlights or along the main Mandalay–Yangon highway, your trip four hours north of Mandalay brings you to this engaging, slightly scrappy trade town poised on the eastern bank of the lovely Chindwin River. There's not much to do in town – wander and see where random meetings take you – but there's no dissing the interesting attractions nearby (p288), which can fill a couple days.

In WWII Monywa found itself between the British and Japanese forces twice; it was flattened by bombs in 1942 and 1945. The area – particularly west of the river – was for many postwar years a centre for the Burmese Communist Party.

Monywa sees a lot of trade to and from India. Agricultural products and hardwoods (including teak) come into town across the Chindwin Bridge, opened in 2004 to ease transport to/from India. (The road in that direction is restricted for foreigners.)

Orientation & Information

Monywa's centre revolves around Shwezigon Paya, north of the old market, with the clock tower on Bogyoke St to its southeast, and the Bogyoke roundabout (with a statue of Aung San on horseback) to its northeast. There's a **clinic**, just west of Shwezigon Paya.

Monywa e-Business Group Internet (Station Rd; per hr K500; ☻ 8am-9pm) On the 1st floor of an official-looking building.

Sights

Monywa's best attraction is the way it embraces its river, unlike so many cities in Myanmar. Go for sunrise or sunset along **Strand Rd**, a two-level road alongside the lovely Chindwin River, where locals stroll and sit as the sun dips over the mountains just west.

Also it's worth wandering around the centre's lanes, where you can find atmospheric monasteries on village-like dirt roads. A key *zedi* is **Su Taung Pye Zedi**, a popular wish-fulfilling spot for locals.

The central **Shwezigon Paya** is worth a look (particularly when it lights up at night), but

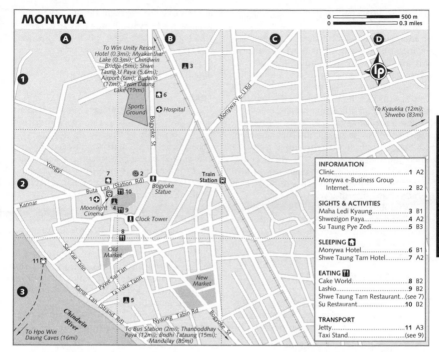

MONYWA

0 — 500 m
0 — 0.3 miles

AROUND MANDALAY

INFORMATION
Clinic..1 A2
Monywa e-Business Group
   Internet....................................2 B2

SIGHTS & ACTIVITIES
Maha Ledi Kyaung.....................3 B1
Shwezigon Paya.........................4 A2
Su Taung Pye Zedi.....................5 B3

SLEEPING
Monywa Hotel.............................6 B1
Shwe Taung Tarn Hotel............7 A2

EATING
Cake World....................................8 B2
Lashio...9 B2
Shwe Taung Tarn Restaurant....(see 7)
Su Restaurant..............................10 B2

TRANSPORT
Jetty..11 A3
Taxi Stand...............................(see 9)

Monywa's primary religious site is the **Maha Ledi Kyaung**, about half a mile northeast of the Bogyoke roundabout (on the other side of the train tracks). Built in 1886 by order of renowned Pali scholar Ledi Sayadaw, this monastery has 806 stone slabs inscribed with Buddhist scriptures.

About half a mile north of the centre, **Myakanthar Lake** (Beautiful Lake) isn't aptly named, but there's a roly-poly wood bridge leading to a small island where locals like to sit and watch couples drift by in rowboats.

Sleeping

Shwe Taung Tarn Hotel (☎ 21478; 70 Station Rd; r per person $5 & $8; ✸) It's best skipping on the front building's $5 rooms, and walk through the dodgy ground-floor hallway and back garden to the surprisingly comfy, bunga-low-style buildings in the back. Rooms show some wear, but are arranged nicely with wood floors, a local TV channel to watch and private bathroom. Free breakfast is served on the roof deck of its great restaurant.

Monywa Hotel (☎ 21581, 21549; Bogyoke St; s $15-20, d $20-25; ✸) Apparently leased from the govern-ment to a private businessperson, the midrange Monywa has cabin-style bungalows with dated but kept-up furnishings in a leafy, faintly bar-rack-style complex about 250yd north of the Aung San statue. All get 24-hour electricity, hot water and air-con; the smaller, cheaper rooms don't have chairs on the deck.

Win Unity Resort Hotel (☎ 22438, 22013; in Yangon 01-227 389; tintinmoe@mptmaill.net.mm; Bogyoke Rd; s $30-42, d $38-54; ✸ 🖳 🏊) Right on the lake, half a mile north of the centre, privately run Win Unity brings in some tour groups with its nice bungalow-style rooms with wood floors and modern comfort (easily the 'swankiest' Monywa gets). Opened in 2004, there's still a bit to go – with a lack of landscaping, plus a pool and business centre still in the works at last pass. The restaurant serves $5 Chinese and Thai set meals. There are also nine econo rooms (singe/double $20/24).

Eating

As sun sets, street vendors open appealing stalls on the south side of Shwezigon Paya, where you can get cheap noodles, eggs-and-rice or snacks. The best spot for *hmi shei* (Shan noodles) is **Lashio** (an all-day restaurant signed in Burmese).

Su Restaurant (Station Rd; buffet K1700; 9am-9pm) Just east of the northern Shwezigon Paya entrance, this great, popular family-style Myanmar restaurant is a pick-and-point eater, where your choice of curry (goat, fish, prawn) comes with 10 condiments and rice. Look for the English sign 'Myanmar restaurant'.

Shwe Taung Tarn Restaurant (21478; 70 Station Rd; dishes K1500-2500) The budget hotel has a bustling Chinese restaurant with three eating areas – under the trellises outside (men with beer and noodles), in the fluorescent-bulb dining room (families) or on the rather chic rooftop (rich locals – staff will usher you here).

A couple of blocks south of Shwezigon, **Cake World** has plenty of cakes and dough-nuts, plus a creative hamburger (K800), with twice-split buns and fried chicken coated in mayonnaise stripes.

Getting There & Away

AIR

The airport is a 30-minute ride north of town. The government's Myanma Airways con-nects Monywa with Mandalay ($20 to $25) on Tuesday.

BOAT

Word at research time was that high-end boat trips would begin traversing the lovely Chindwin River (p363). Otherwise, its ferry services have long been restricted for for-eigners, but some Yangon travel agents can arrange permission on private boats from south of Homilin (aka Homalin, over 100 miles north of Kalaymyo, p334) in northern Myanmar near the India border.

Sadly, there is no boat service downriver to Pakokku.

BUS

Monywa's bus station, off the highway to-wards Mandalay 2 miles south of the clock tower, has no English signs.

Hourly 28-seater buses connect Monywa with Mandalay from 5am (K1800, four hours) and similarly sized ones with Shwebo (K1100, 3½ hours) from 5am to 2.30pm. Note that buses *to* (not from) Monywa from Mandalay tend to be reluctant to take foreigners.

Seven daily buses (presently leaving at 6.30am, 8am, 8.30am, 10.30am, 12.30pm, 2pm

and 3pm) go to Pakokku (K1400, 4½ hours) to catch the ferry to Nyaung U (Bagan, p180), which goes at 1pm, 2pm and 4pm. A lone bus to Yangon (K12,000) leaves at 1pm.

See Around Monywa (below) for transport details for sites around Monywa.

TRAIN

Don't do it. The Mandalay–Budalin branch goes slower than bus or car, and train ticket sellers won't know what to do if you try to book a ticket to Mandalay (six to seven hours). We've seen passengers pushing a faulty car-riage to another track here, three hours behind departure time. Then again, it could be a real bonding experience with locals.

Getting Around

Motor-trishaws – actually a four-seat cab strapped on the back of a motorcycle – make up Monywa's chief public transport. A ride to the centre from the bus station is K1500. Ride fares are set for nearby sites. For getting around town, you probably won't need more than a regular ol' trishaw.

Also, higher-priced, white, plain-clothes taxis linger on Station Rd, near the northern Shwezigon Paya entrance.

AROUND MONYWA

There's something to do in all directions out of this place. If you have only a full day, you can fit in the Hpo Win Daung caves and Bodhi Tataung.

South of Monywa

These two sites are generally combined on a visit by motor-trishaw (K7000) or taxi (K20,000). Many people time a three-hour trip to end at sunset. It's about 45 minutes to Bodhi Tataung from Monywa.

THANBODDHAY PAYA

သမ္ဗုဒ္ဓေဘုရား:

The magnificent, carnivalesque **Thanboddhay Paya** (admission $3; 6am-5pm), 12 miles south of Monywa (just east of the Mandalay road), bursts with pink, orange, yellow and blue spikes, and has so many buddha images in the inside nooks and crannies in halls and archways – one tally makes it 582,363 – that it feels like you're walking through a bud-dha house of mirrors. Some compare the building to Borobudur in Indonesia, though Thanboddhay is smaller. It's certainly unique for Myanmar. It was built from 1939 to 1958.

Supposedly the fee revenue (collected by the government) stays on the premises (it's certainly a hefty price for a religious site).

BODHI TATAUNG
ဗောဓိတစ်ထောင်

Another 3 miles east from Thanboddhay, this outrageous buddha-rama complex (the name means 1000 buddhas, but that number was long ago surpassed) at the western edge of the Po Khaung Hills is the one that makes the souvenir T-shirts. From the highway, you'll see the glimmering 423ft **standing buddha**, in progress since 1994; it's open but a few marble tiles have yet to be laid around the base. You can go up inside it – supposedly a lift will take you up, but it wasn't working when we dropped by.

Before you reach the standing buddha, there are a couple of sites to walk past. The first is the gold 430ft **Aung Setkya Paya**, surrounded by 1060 smaller stupas and with particularly lovely views from its rim, which you can reach from an inner passageway.

Just beyond, past a host of vendors who may ask you jokingly to take their child, is a 312ft **reclining buddha**, with several (dark) altars inside (the entrance is behind).

Carry your sandals to save some gravel dents on your feet on connecting roads.

West of Monywa
HPO WIN DAUNG CAVES
ဖိုးဝင်းတောင်ဂူ

The real reason most of the few visitors that bounce north from Mandalay come here is this complex of 492 cave temples built inside the limestone cliffs of the long Hpo Win Daung mountain, shaped – locals say, convincingly – like a reclining buddha.

Across the Chindwin River and 16 miles west of Monywa, the **Hpo Win Daung caves** (admission $2), built between the 14th and 18th centuries, sprawl up and down the west side (along the 'Buddha head') of the mountain, and are packed with 2588 buddhas and some boldly coloured murals. Prepare yourself for being startled a time or two by **snack-seeking monkeys** that aren't afraid to shake your pants leg.

The hills here were named for *zawgyi* (alchemist) hermit Hpo Win a millennium ago. He pranced about the hills with a magic stick, used to ease ills, plant medicine trees and solve

problems – you see his (rather jolly and a bit poncey) likeness next to the entry sign.

From the starting point, the main caves lead up and left (west). A guide (available at the jetty or at the site for about K5000) is not a bad idea, as some caves aren't easy to find.

The cave chambers vary in condition. In some there are giant reclining buddhas; others are packed with smaller buddhas and have streams of light shining in from holes in the walls. Many murals are painted '3-D' – what's above the eye level is far, what's below is near. In one mural, you can see 'Portuguese-looking persons' burning in hell. Sadly, relic smugglers have feasted on some statues, but much remains intact and evocatively unrestored.

If you're not caved out, the facing hill to the south, **Shwe Ba Taung**, features 46 more caves.

The week-long **Hpo Win Daung Festival**, the year's biggest here, takes place in November. The area has 12 monasteries.

To the southwest of the long-inhabited hills lies the Pondaung-pon-nya mountain range, where the fossilised remains of **Pondaung Man** (a primate ancestor who may have lived 30 million years ago) were found.

If you visit Hpo Win Daung by taxi or motor-trishaw via the Monywa Bridge (an extra 9 miles), you can stop off at **Shwe Taung U Paya**, a meditation centre just across the bridge (5 miles north of Monywa centre). There are a couple of caves and gorgeous Chindwin River views from its hilltop locale. Note that the caves fee goes to the government.

GETTING THERE & AWAY
It's a bit of a scam coming here. The same simple ferry boats that locals take across the river for a few kyat to Nyaungbingyi village cost foreigners an outrageous K3000 each way. Boats run from 6am to 8pm daily from the jetty on Strand Rd.

Once across, a troop of jeeps offer to take you the rest of the way (45 minutes) for a set K12,000.

Motor-trishaws in Monywa will be bugging you about going before you get to your hotel. The ride (K17,000) includes a look at Shwe Taung U Paya and some copper-mining villages, but takes about 100 minutes one-way. It's quicker, and more expensive, by taxi (K35,000).

AROUND MANDALAY

North of Monywa

TWIN DAUNG LAKE

တွင်းေတာင်

This lake doesn't quite look like the fountain of youth – more a green-water lake set in a volcanic cone – but much of Myanmar believes it is. Spirulina Beer, made from the moss-substance on the lake in a factory here, about 19 miles north of town, is marketed as the anti-ageing beer. You can visit – and see if you can look around the factory – by motorcycle or taxi only (motor-trishaws can't deal with the rough 3-mile road off the highway).

East of Monywa

Set along a tamarind tree–lined road about 12 miles east of town, **Kyaukka** is a simple village famed for the pre–Chiang Mai style **lacquerware** it's been making since the Konbaung era. Some of the pieces seen in household factories are more basic and utilitarian than some Bagan shops – and many of these pieces end up going to Bagan anyway. There are also some shops outside the interesting 14th-century **Shwe Gu Ni Paya** (famous for its wish-fulfilling powers), about half a mile west of town.

Motor-trishaws make this trip for K7000. You can pick up a pick-up to Kyaukka at various points, including near Monywa's bus station.

SHWEBO

ေရွှဘို

☏ 075

So off-the-radar, yet so close to Mandalay, Shwebo is a fairly messy and dusty former capital, but one rightly proud of its historical role. King Alaungpaya (p39) kicked off Myanmar's third empire here, and the area has been settled since at least the 4th century AD. Those willing to hoof about the market and over to the moat will likely be detoured by a local mix of folk entirely unused to outside interest.

Occupying the flat (and hot) plain between the Mu and Ayeyarwady Rivers, Shwebo has a Bamar majority, and sizeable Muslim and Christian communities. The local economy depends on the trade of nuts, pulses, rice and sesame cultivated on surrounding farms.

Apparently another claim to fame is snakes; as a Monywan warned us, 'You're going to Shwebo? Watch out for cobras, brother.' Nevertheless, many Myanmar folk reach for the dirt when coming to Shwebo. It's considered good luck to take home some earth from 'Victory Land' (as Shwebo's reputation goes).

There's no internet access in Shwebo.

Sights

Several pagodas in the blocks south of the market give Shwebo's centre a gold-studded backdrop. The biggest, **Shwe Daza Paya**, is said to have been built by King Narapatisithu over 500 years ago. **Maw Daw Myin Tha Paya**, about 1 mile north of the market, is the city's most important Buddhist site and a peaceful enough place. Alaungpaya is said to have built it. Take Aung Zeya St north, past the train tracks, where an English sign points to it, about 90yd east.

As the capital, Shwebo was an enormous walled city. Remnants include bits of the walls and the **moat** (the most visible legacy of Alaungpaya's original plan); the moat is best seen from **Yan Gyi Aung Park**, northeast of the centre.

The British built a jail on the **Alaungpaya Palace grounds** (admission K50, camera fee K200), which the government moved and rebuilt as the palace (the above fee goes to the government). You can see a few red-and-gold structures, similar in form to the Mandalay Palace (but less complete), around a grassy lot. It's pretty

---

SHWEBO THANAKHA

If you make it to Shwebo, be sure to pick up a few logs of locally grown *thanakha* (sandalwood-like paste) – considered to be the country's sweetest-smelling and best-value *thanakha*. Ground into a yellowish paste – and used, with imagination, as a sun block and skin moisturiser by women across Myanmar, no *thanakha* tree is more famous than Shwebo's, the subject of a famous folk song 'Shwebo Thanakha'. (See if the women selling it in the Shwebo market will sing it for you – they might; they certainly are a lively bunch.)

If you can, take some to hand out around Myanmar. You'll win huge points with your guest-house grandmas by offering a bit of Shwebo *thanakha* – something very hard to find the further south you go.

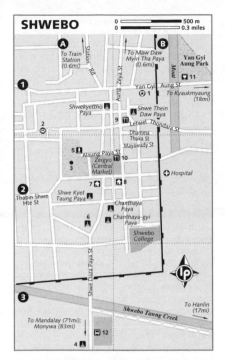

SHWEBO

AROUND MANDALAY

Myo Ma (☎ 21259; r per person K18,000) A laughably overpriced guesthouse will fumble a bit over your passport in a pinch, but generally can get you into one of its dark, tiny rooms.

Eating & Drinking

Open-air noodle stands start brewing their cauldrons outside the market at dusk. You'll find a few restaurants along Aung Zeya St, north and south of the market too, and a beer station over by the old moat.

Eden Culinary Garden (Aung Zeya St; dishes K450-900; 6am-10pm) An English menu (and English sign) makes Eden a go-to spot for many visitors. Food's fine – noodles, typical Chinese fare, plus a small European list including fried eggs and an untested hamburger. There's inside dining, but it's more atmospheric to sit at the little tables in the courtyard, with local guys sitting over Tiger beer. There's a bakery in front.

Getting There & Away

BOAT

Ferries heading up and down the Ayeyarwady River between Mandalay and Katha stop at Kyaukmyaung (p292), 18 miles to the east; pick-ups regularly run half-hourly between Kyaukmyaung and Shwebo's bus station (K500, one hour).

BUS

The Shwebo bus station is about half a mile south of the centre. A few bus companies head out hourly during the day on the 71-mile route between Shwebo and Mandalay (K1700, three hours).

quiet – a few nappers and couples hanging out in a re-made home for the king. At the gate is the **King Alaungpaya Memorial**, where his body was burned following his death in 1760.

Aung Mye Hsu Taung (aka 'Army Pagoda'), near the bus station, is supposedly the spot used by King Alaungpaya as a staging point before going into battle, and it remains the city's wishing ground (for military too). A 15-ministupa maze up the front has glass-spiked 3ft-high walls to deter cheats.

Sleeping

Win Guest House (☎ 22049, 22107; Aung Zeya St; r per person $6-12;) So superior is spic-and-span Win (opened in 2007) to the 'competition' (dank, dark, dated guesthouses) you should call ahead as soon as you know your dates. Cheap rooms are boxy, but clean, with twin beds and a fan, and spotless bathroom down the hall. Best are the top-floor rooms, tiled beauties with private bathroom, satellite TV and phone in the room. Staff speak (some) English and are accustomed to dealing with foreigners; other guesthouses aren't licensed and will likely turn you away.

Hourly buses also connect Shwebo with Monywa – via a quiet 1.5-lane road (K1100, 3½ hours).

TRAIN

Few travellers reach Shwebo by train, though daily trains between Mandalay and Myitkyina stop here. It takes about five hours to reach Mandalay – longer and more expensive than the bus.

Getting Around

Trishaws (and a few horse carts) are the main modes of public transport. A trishaw ride from either station to the centre is K500 or so. There are no taxis, but jeeps are sometimes for hire.

AROUND SHWEBO
Kyaukmyaung

ကျောက်မြောင်း

The nearest Ayeyarwady River jetty to Shwebo, Kyaukmyaung (18 miles east) is worth visiting for a half day even if you're not headed onto the river. The town is a typical river town with a scrubby market and a few *zedi* to see, but the claim to fame is half a mile south at **Ngwe Nyein**, a stunning pottery village that dates back centuries.

Walking along the riverside path, you'll see pots in piles waiting to be shipped south and homes doubling as storefronts, where you can pick up ready-for-export glazed vases (the yellow ones get their colour from old batteries apparently) for a few thousand kyat. A few blocks inland is where the factories are – wondrous 60-person operations, where workers chop up piles of clay, let it dry, sculpt big and small pots on foot-powered urns, dry them in the sun and cook them in giant kilns. They're masters at work – so few tourists come they'll be happy to have you snoop around.

Neither Kyaukmyaung nor Ngwe Nyein have licensed accommodation.

The southbound ferry from Bhamo to Mandalay (about five hours) supposedly stops here at 2pm daily. Less exciting, but more dependable, options are the pick-ups that regularly go to Shwebo (K500, one hour), where you can get buses to Mandalay.

A ride with a motorbike driver from Shwebo is about K12,000 return.

Hanlin

ဟန်လင်း

About 16 butt-kicking miles southeast of Shwebo, the town of Halingyi is set just south of the architectural remains of Hanlin (also called Halin), a massive 2 mile by 1 mile walled city from the Pyu kingdom (which existed between the 4th and 9th centuries). Little is left, but locals can point out overgrown gates to the wall. In another part of town is a monastery with a small **museum**, which has some pots and other artefacts excavated from the 'old city'.

Halingyi village is interesting in that it's set atop a network of **hot springs**; the water is collected in stone cauldrons and pools for bathing and washing clothes.

You may be asked to show your passport and keep notes of what you see and when. Locals will most assuredly lead you around.

To get here, you can either try to hire a jeep (if you find one), or get a motorcycle with driver (K13,000). And it's helpful to have a local figure out where to go. It's perhaps possible to bike (with a soft seat!), but it's a hard full-day trip. The road to Halingyi begins south of the aqueduct next to the bus station. After about 6 miles you'll see a big pagoda across the water. At the next village (the biggest you'll see), turn left over the bridge; you're halfway there.

Northern Myanmar

The region formed by Kachin State and northern Shan State is only tenuously connected to the rest of Myanmar. Few roads cross this rugged and undeveloped area and the main conduit for freight and passenger transport is the mighty Ayeyarwady (Irrawaddy) River, which snakes south across the plain from Myitkyina to Mandalay. Beyond Myitkyina lie the so-called Ice Mountains – the snow-capped peaks of the Myanmar Himalaya, which can only be visited on organised tours to Putao.

The most visited places in northern Myanmar are the towns strung out along the highway to Lashio though these are still sleepy backwaters, even by Myanmar standards. Hsipaw remains one of the most idyllic getaways in Southeast Asia, and growing numbers of adventurers are visiting the rolling hills around Kyaukme and Namhsan in search of an even more utopian vision of Myanmar.

Foreigners travel to Myitkyina with one objective in mind – the slow, mesmerising journey south along the churning, mud-yellow Ayeyarwady River. Depending on how much time you have, you can ride the river all the way to Mandalay or break the trip south at the laid-back riverbank towns of Bhamo and Katha. The most important thing to remember is that travel in this region is time consuming – buses are infrequent, boats and trains move more slowly than Galapagos tortoises, and airlines fly only a few days each week.

NORTHERN MYANMAR

HIGHLIGHTS

- Promenade in the cool mountain air at **Pyin U Lwin** (p294), the old British summer capital of Myanmar

- Spend lazy days drifting down the mighty Ayeyarwady River from **Myitkyina** (p307), **Bhamo** (p309) or **Katha** (p312)

- Let your hair down in **Hsipaw** (p300), a laid-back mountain village with something going on down every side street

- If money allows, head north to the land of ice and snow – **Putao** (p313) is the gateway to the Myanmar Himalaya

- Escape from it all at tranquil **Indawgyi Lake** (p310), a rarely explored gem in the west of Kachin State.

- HIGHEST POINT: HKAKABO RAZI (19,295FT)

Climate

The area northeast of Mandalay experiences similar climatic conditions to the rest of the Shan plateau, ie moderately warm days and cold nights, particularly in December and January. North of Myitkyina, rugged foothills climb to the snowy peaks of the Myanmar Himalaya. Putao has a similar climate to towns on the Shan Plateau, but bring serious mountain trekking gear for walks above the snowline.

Dangers & Annoyances

Clashes between the government-backed United Wa State Army (UWSA) and Shan rebels are not uncommon in the northern part of Shan State, including the area east of Lashio. Check the security situation before travelling off the beaten track in this area.

People

The largest tribe in Shan State is the Shan (p61), the remnants of a tribal nation that once stretched across Myanmar, Laos, northern Thailand and southern China. Several groups of Shan rebels are involved in an ongoing separatist struggle against the government and its allies from the Wa tribe.

Across the state border in Kachin State, the Tibeto-Burman Kachin people (p59) are fighting for their own independent homeland in the far north of Myanmar. See www.kachin state.com for more information. Many Kachin have converted from animism to Christianity under the influence of Western missionaries.

You may also see Lisu, Rawang, Drung, Daru, Nung, Naga and Tibetan tribal people on treks through the hills around Putao. Villagers from the Taron tribe, the only known pygmy group in Asia, are occasionally seen in the remote region around Mt Hkakabo Razi.

Getting There & Away

Visitors are free to visit the towns along the Mandalay–Lashio highway, but travel from Lashio to Mu-se is prohibited. However, it is possible to enter Myanmar from China at Mu-se and continue by road to Lashio with a permit – see p307 for details.

Most people visit Myitkyina and the towns of southern Kachin State for the express reason of riding the river boats back to Mandalay – see p308 for more information. The only way to reach Putao in the far north is by air, with a permit from Myanmar Travels & Tours (MTT; see p315 for details). Bear in mind that a portion of what you pay to fly or travel by state-owned trains and boats goes directly to the junta.

PYIN U LWIN TO LASHIO

From the dusty plains around Mandalay, the road to Lashio climbs steeply into the green hills of the Shan Plateau. It passes through a string of quiet country towns, which offer a taste of rural life that is a million miles from the commercialism of Inle Lake or Bagan. The only way to reach the northern part of the state is through Mandalay – there are no direct road links and no direct flights linking the north and south.

PYIN U LWIN

ပြင်ဦးလွင်

☎ 085 / elev 3445ft

The British generally left only a light mark on the culture of Myanmar but Pyin U Lwin is a notable exception to this rule. The town was founded in 1896, on the site of a small Danu village, as a hill station where the colonial government could come to escape the heat of the plains. It was originally called Maymyo (May-town), after Colonel May of the 5th Bengal Infantry. After the construction of the railroad from Mandalay, Pyin U Lwin became the summer capital for the British colonial administration, a role it held until the end of British rule in 1948.

The name was changed after the British departed but the colonial buildings remain. So too do the descendents of the Indian and Nepali workers who came here to lay the railway line and construct the road to Lashio.

The main way to get around town is by horse and cart, which adds an extra layer of nostalgia to the mix. For locals, Pyin is famous for its fruit and vegetables – and jams and fruit wines – and for its huge military academies, which train the soldiers of the Tatmadaw (the Myanmar Army).

Information

Hotels can advise you on things to do in the area. Alternatively, point your browser towards www.pyinoolwin.info.

Shwe Htay Internet (share-taxi stand, Mandalay-Lashio Rd; per hr K800; ☷ 8am-8pm) Fast internet connections (with proxy servers) and international calls from K2000 per minute.

NORTHERN MYANMAR

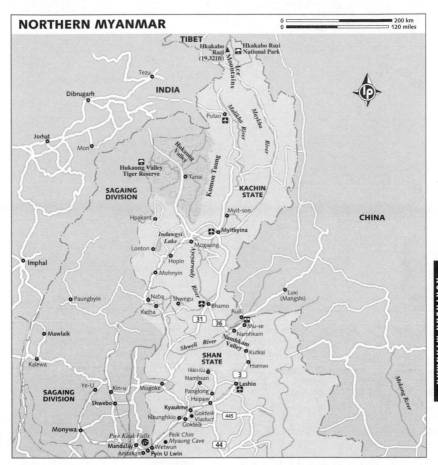

NORTHERN MYANMAR

NORTHERN MYANMAR

Sights

NATIONAL KANDAWGYI GARDENS

အမျိုးသားကန်တော်ကြီးဥယျာဉ်

Founded in 1915 by the English botanist
Alex Rodgers, this 176-hectare **botanic garden**
(☎ 22130; admission $4, camera/video fee K1000/K3000;
🕒 8am-6pm) is now lovingly maintained by a
Singaporean company. It features more than
480 species of flowers, shrubs and trees, including the ginkgo tree, a living fossil, which
only grows wild in one tiny area in China.
Nearby, a new 'culture garden' is under
construction, with tacky representations of
famous landmarks from around Myanmar.

Admission to the garden includes use of the
inviting swimming pool near the entrance.
You must pay an additional $1 to take the
lift to the top of the **Nan Myint Tower** for panoramic views over Pyin U Lwin. Elephant rides
around the gardens cost $10.

The gardens are a 1-mile walk or a K2000
horse-cart ride south of the main road.

TEMPLES & MOSQUES

The pretty **Maha Aung Mye Bon Thar Pagoda**, next
to the central market, is covered in a shimmering mirror mosaic. The most important
pagoda in town is the **Shwezigone Pagoda**, close
to the sports field east of the market. On the
western outskirts of town, the huge, gilded
Kyauk Taung Pagoda offers views over the parade
ground for the Defence Services Academy –
taking photos of this secretive institution is
probably not a good idea.

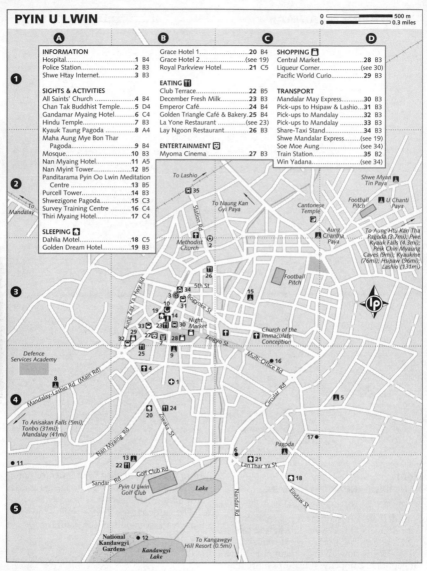

PYIN U LWIN

INFORMATION	
Hospital	1 B4
Police Station	2 B3
Shwe Htay Internet	3 B4

SIGHTS & ACTIVITIES	
All Saints' Church	4 B4
Chan Tak Buddhist Temple	5 D4
Gandamar Myaing Hotel	6 C4
Hindu Temple	7 B3
Kyauk Taung Pagoda	8 A4
Maha Aung Mye Bon Thar Pagoda	9 B4
Mosque	10 B3
Nan Myaing Hotel	11 A5
Nan Myint Tower	12 B5
Panditarama Pyin Oo Lwin Meditation Centre	13 B5
Purcell Tower	14 B3
Shwezigone Pagoda	15 C3
Survey Training Centre	16 C4
Thiri Myaing Hotel	17 C4

SLEEPING	
Dahlia Motel	18 C5
Golden Dream Hotel	19 B3
Grace Hotel 1	20 B4
Grace Hotel 2	(see 19)
Royal Parkview Hotel	21 C5

EATING	
Club Terrace	22 B5
December Fresh Milk	23 B4
Emperor Café	24 B4
Golden Triangle Café & Bakery	25 B4
La Yone Restaurant	(see 23)
Lay Ngoon Restaurant	26 B3

ENTERTAINMENT	
Myoma Cinema	27 B3

SHOPPING	
Central Market	28 B3
Liqueur Corner	(see 30)
Pacific World Curio	29 B3

TRANSPORT	
Mandalar May Express	30 B3
Pick-ups to Hsipaw & Lashio	31 B3
Pick-ups to Mandalay	32 B3
Pick-ups to Mandalay	33 B3
Share-Taxi Stand	34 B3
Shwe Mandalar Express	(see 19)
Soe Moe Aung	(see 34)
Train Station	35 B2
Win Yadana	(see 34)

Pyin U Lwin's Chinese Buddhist community worship at the huge **Chan Tak Buddhist temple** (off Lan Thar Ya St), east of Circular Rd, founded by migrants from Yúnnán. It's a classic Chinese temple with ornate stucco dragons, rock gardens, landscaped ponds and a six-storey pagoda. Catering to the significant population of Hindus and Muslims in Pyin U Lwin are several ornate **Hindu temples** and **mosques** on the main road through town.

HISTORIC BUILDINGS

The **Purcell Tower**, just north of the central market, was a present from Queen Victoria, who made a habit of handing out these things to the colonies (there are similar towers in Cape Town and the Seychelles). The tower's chime is said to copy Big Ben, playing 16 notes before the hour.

Just south of the main road is the tin-roofed **All Saint's Church** (Ziwaka St; ⏲ services 8.30am Sun, 7am Wed), constructed as the regimental church for Maymyo in 1912. The guest book is full of signatures from British visitors chasing up family members buried in the town cemetery.

The main colonial district is southeast of the centre. Multi-Office Rd is lined with grand colonial administrative buildings, many taken over by schools or bureaucratic bodies from the Myanmar government. Check out the St Trinian's–like **Survey Training Centre** (Multi-Office Rd).

A number of old British mansions have been converted into hotels but most are government owned (staying in these establishments will contribute directly to the military regime). Architecture fans should take a peek at the **Thiri Myaing Hotel** (originally called Candacraig; immortalised in Paul Theroux's *The Great Railway Bazaar*), the **Gandamar Myaing Hotel** (formerly Croxton) and the **Nan Myaing Hotel** (originally Craddock Court).

Activities

On the southern edge of town, the 18-hole **Pyin U Lwin Golf Club** (☎ 22382; Golf Club Rd; green fee $10, caddy $2, club hire $5, shoe hire $1; ⏲ 6am-6pm) is one of Myanmar's better golf courses but it's government run. It hosts the annual Water Festival Golf Cup in April.

Sleeping

Many of Pyin's cheaper hotels are not licensed to accommodate foreigners. Unless otherwise stated, rates at the following hotels include breakfast.

BUDGET

Budget hotels in Pyin U Lwin are mainly strung out along the main road.

Golden Dream Hotel (☎ 21302; 42/43 Mandalay-Lashio Rd; s/d $4/8, with shared bathroom $3/6) Run by an Indian family, the Golden Dream is perched on top of a knitwear shop. The tiled rooms are pretty modest, but you can't fault the price.

Grace Hotel 2 (☎ 22081; 46/48 Mandalay-Lashio Rd; s/d $4/8, with shared bathroom $3/6) The second Grace Hotel lacks the charm of Grace 1, but it's right in the thick of things near the Purcell Tower. All rooms have hot showers and front-facing rooms have the luxury of a balcony.

Grace Hotel 1 (☎ 21230; 114A Nan Myaing Rd; s/d $7/14) A lovely garden, charming owners and a quiet location away from the noisy main drag raise Grace I above the pack. The cosy tiled rooms with fan, TV and bathrooms with hot showers are good for the price and you can rent bikes for K2000 per day.

Dahlia Motel (☎ 22255, 165 Eidaw Rd; s/d from $8/12) In a peaceful location down a tree-lined lane east of the golf club, the Dahlia is a good choice for light sleepers. It's spread over several buildings that were built at various times so some rooms are smarter than others, but all have TV, fridge and reliable hot water.

MIDRANGE & TOP END

Those keen on avoiding government-run hotels should bypass the heritage-style Thiri Myaing Hotel, Gandamar Myaing Hotel and Nan Myaing Hotel.

Royal Parkview Hotel (☎ 22647; www.pyinoolwin -royalparkview.com; 107 Lan Thar Ya St; s/d from $25/30; 🍴 🖳) Spread over several bungalows in a tidy garden, the Royal caters mainly to package groups. The attractive wood-finished rooms all have TV, fridge and a small terrace. The bar and restaurant serves a familiar menu of Myanmar, Chinese and European dishes.

Kandawgyi Hill Resort (☎ 21839, in Yangon ☎ 01-202 071; www.woodland-resorts.com; Nandar Rd; bungalows s/d $40/50, ste s/d $50/60) Run by the same team as the Kandawgyi Gardens, this is the only heritage property in Pyin that is not directly run by the government. The main lodge was constructed in 1921 and the enormous rooms have tasteful wood and wicker furniture. Some rooms are set in appealing bungalows in the garden.

Eating

All the dining options in Pyin U Lwin are open for breakfast, lunch and dinner.

Golden Triangle Café & Bakery (☎ 24288; Mandalay-Lashio Rd; cakes, sandwiches & pizzas K500-2000; ⏲ 6.30am-10pm) You won't find many places like Golden Triangle in all of Myanmar. This upbeat café in a stately colonial building on the main road serves real espresso, yummy cakes, and sandwiches prepared with freshly baked bread. Sit indoors in the calm, cool lounge or pull up a wicker chair on the front deck.

NORTHERN MYANMAR

Lay Ngoon Restaurant (4 Mandalay-Lashio Rd; dishes K1500) North of the market near the train station, Lay Ngoon is your typical Chinese-style restaurant. Wooden booths make the place feel cosier than most of the competition and the Chinese and Bamar food is worth the trip out here.

La Yone Restaurant (off Mandalay-Lashio Rd; dishes K2000) This tourist-oriented place by the market is heavily overpriced, but the Chinese food is good and there's an English-language menu.

Club Terrace (☎ 22612; 25 Golf Club Rd; mains K3500; ☼ from 11am) A genuinely classy place to eat, this upmarket Thai restaurant by the golf club occupies a gorgeous colonial bungalow with a lovely open terrace that is lit up by lanterns at night. The red and green curries and Thai stir fries are blisteringly authentic.

There are numerous teashops dotted around town serving tea, coffee, cakes, fried dough, samosas and fried rice. The **Emperor Café** (Ziwaka St; snacks from K300) gets busy in the evenings. A more unusual choice is **December Fresh Milk** (near Central Market; snacks from K300), which seems to exist mainly to market iced milk to local students.

Entertainment

Pyin U Lwin goes to bed early. The best place for a late-night drink and chat is the Golden Triangle Café & Bakery (see p297).

Myoma Cinema (Mandalay-Lashio Rd; tickets K200) The best of several cinemas in town, this place screens Myanmar romances and Indian musicals – entertaining even if you can't understand the dialogue.

Shopping

The **central market** (Zeigyo Rd; ☼ 7am-5pm) is the place to come to sample some of the fruits produced around Pyin U Lwin. Strawberries, damsons, plums, passion fruit, grapes, pineapples and other fruit are fermented into fruit wines, boiled into jams, or dried to create natural sweets. A jar of local jam will set you back about K250. Just north of the market, **Liqueur Corner** (☼ 7am-8pm) sells local fruit wines (from K1000) and wines from the Aythaya Vineyard near Taunggyi (K9000).

Organic coffee from the Shan Hills is sold at the Golden Triangle Café & Bakery (p297): Café Fino costs K2500 for 200g, Misty Mountain costs K350 for 35g.

There are several stores in the area around the market selling local arts and crafts –

far and away the best stock is at **Pacific World Curio** (75 Mandalay-Lashio Rd; ☼ 8am-6pm).

Getting There & Away

BUS & PICK-UP

Pyin U Lwin has no bus station, and buses between Mandalay and places further east are generally full by the time they reach town. **Mandalar May Express** (☎ 21993) and **Shwe Mandalar Express** (☎ 22515; Mandalay-Lashio Rd) have daily buses to Yangon (K12,000, 14 hours) via Mandalay (K3000, two hours), leaving around 2pm.

Pick-ups run by MMTA and HMV depart very regularly to Mandalay (K1500, two hours) from 5am to 7pm. They leave from or near the main road, just west of the central market. Pick-ups going to Lashio, Hsipaw or Kyaukme (K4000, four hours) leave at 5.30am from a small stand opposite the share-taxi stand.

TAXI

By far the easiest way to travel from Pyin U Lwin is by taxi. **Win Yadana** (☎ 22490; Mandalay-Lashio Rd) and **Soe Moe Aung** (☎ 21500; Mandalay-Lashio Rd) run shared taxis from the share-taxi stand. Taxis to Lashio, Hsipaw or Kyaukme (back/front seat K14,000/16,000) leave between 6am and 8am; taxis for Mandalay (back/front seat K5000/5500) leave periodically throughout the day.

TRAIN

Pyin U Lwin's tiny red-brick train station is north of the centre. The slow *132 Down* to Mandalay (ordinary/upper class $2/4) leaves at 5.40pm daily, arriving four to six hours later. The *131 Up* to Lashio ($4/8) leaves at 8.50am, reaching Lashio 10 hours later. This latter train crosses the dramatic Gokteik Viaduct and stops at Kyaukme ($2/4, four hours) and Hsipaw ($2/4, six hours). Note that trains frequently run late and sometimes fail to run at all.

Getting Around

The most popular way to get around Pyin U Lwin is by wagon. The horse-pulled carts are lavishly decorated and highly photogenic. Drivers bump up the price for foreigners: bank on K2000 for a short trip across town.

Miniature pick-ups provide a local taxi service, or there are dozens of motorcycle taxis, most of whom will provide a helmet for passengers. A return trip to the Kandawgyi

Gardens or the waterfalls outside town will cost around K2000.

If you'd rather get around under your own steam, hotels can arrange bicycle rental for K2000 per day.

AROUND PYIN U LWIN
Anisakan Falls

အနီး:စခန်း ရေတံခွန်

About 6 miles south of Pyin U Lwin, in the village of Anisakan, the gorgeous **Dat Taw Gyaik Falls** (admission free) thunder through trees into a shady splash pool beside a small pagoda. To get here, follow the signposted road off the Mandalay–Pyin U Lwin highway, then take the right fork at the first large pagoda. The falls are reached via a 45-minute trek through the forest below the village. The trail to the falls begins at a cluster of basic restaurants at the end of the tarmac road, about 1.5 miles from the highway.

To get to Anisakan village, you can jump on any pick-up bound for Mandalay. A chartered pick-up taxi or motorcycle taxi costs K5000 return, including a few hours waiting time.

Pwe Kauk Falls

ပွေးကောက်ရေတံခွန်

Called Hampshire Falls in British times, **Pwe Kauk Falls** (admission K500, camera fee K300) rumble over several small cataracts in a forest glade below the road to Hsipaw, about 5 miles northeast of Pyin U Lwin. Locals swim – fully clothed, in case you were thinking of stripping down – in several splash pools, and there's a water-powered merry-go-round for children.

A few shared-taxis and pick-ups run this way early in the morning, but it's much easier to come here by bicycle or by motorcycle taxi – a return trip on the latter including waiting time at the falls will set you back K3000. On the way, you can detour to the famous **Aung Htu Kan Tha Pagoda** (see the box, below).

Peik Chin Myaung Cave

ပိတ်ချင်းမြောင်ဂူ

About 12 miles northeast of Pyin U Lwin, near the village of Wetwun, this natural limestone cave features some dramatic cascades of stalactites and stalagmites. Like other caves in Myanmar, the site is used as a Buddhist shrine, with numerous buddha images left by devotees. To get here, charter a pick-up taxi or motorcycle taxi from Pyin U Lwin for around K4000.

KYAUKME

ကျောကလျှမဲ

☎ 082

On the main road between Pyin U Lwin and Hsipaw, the market town of Kyaukme (pronounced 'Chao May') is another slice of rural Myanmar waiting to be discovered by those willing to step off the beaten track. People come here to experience the easy pace of country life, rather than ticking off any must-see sights.

At the end of Kantkaw St, a few blocks south of the market, a set of covered steps climbs the ridge to **Shwe Kyin Thait Monastery**, which offers great views over town. Come here to plan a walking route to other pagodas in the vicinity. On the main road through town is a colourful **Chinese Buddhist temple** decked out with gaudy statuary.

Trekking in the hills around Kyaukme is neither prohibited nor officially sanctioned, but it isn't hard to find a local guide. Contact Nelson at the A Yone Oo Guest House (see p300) for advice on arranging treks. Possible destinations include the traditional Palaung village of **Lwe Sar** (7 miles from Kyaukme) and the small town of **Pan Kwan** (22 miles from Kyaukme), which is famous for its pickled tea.

The gem-mining town of **Mogoke** is now completely off limits to foreigners – if you travel too far along the road running north from Kyaukme, you *will* be turned back.

NORTHERN MYANMAR

THIS BUDDHA IS GOING NOWHERE...

On the Pyin U Lwin–Lashio highway near the turn-off to Pwe Kauk Falls, the **Aung Htu Kan Tha Pagoda** contains an enormous 17-ton marble buddha statue that fell off a truck bound for China in April 1997. After attempts to retrieve the buddha failed, it was decided that the statue 'had decided to stay in Myanmar' and a new pagoda was built to enshrine the statue where it fell. The stricken image has since been raised upright in a vast chamber filled with golden murals. Ask your driver to stop at the pagoda on the way back to Pyin U Lwin from the falls.

THE GOKTEIK VIADUCT

About 34 miles northeast of Pyin U Lwin, the landscape plunges suddenly into the Gokteik Gorge, a densely-forested ravine that seems almost bottomless from the top of the plateau. Crossing the gorge has always been an obstacle to easy travel between Lashio and Mandalay – the road switches back a dozen times as it descends towards the Myitnge River, with numerous blind corners where trucks and buses meet head-on in an alarming game of chicken. The British solution to the problem was to go straight across the ravine – the mighty **Gokteik Viaduct** was constructed in 1901 by contractors from the Pennsylvania Steel Company to carry the railway line to Lashio.

At 318ft high and 2257ft across, the viaduct was the second-highest railway bridge in the world when it was constructed, and it survived the next 100 years with almost no maintenance. It's the oldest and longest railway bridge in Myanmar, and its age shows: trains slow to a crawl when crossing the viaduct to avoid putting undue stress on the superstructure. Much needed renovation work was carried out in the 1990s but the viaduct still creaks ominously as trains edge their way across the chasm.

The best way to see the bridge is from above on the Mandalay–Lashio train. Before crossing the bridge, the train stops for a few minutes to down-gear, giving passengers enough time to step off the train and admire the precarious-looking structure they are about to cross. Taking photographs of the viaduct is banned for 'security reasons', but the ban is laxly enforced.

SLEEPING & EATING

There are three guesthouses in town, all offering similar facilities.

Northern Rock (☎ 40340; 52/4 Shwe Phi Oo Rd; s/d per person K5000) North of the market, Northern Rock has modest but clean rooms with bathrooms and it accepts payment in kyat. We assume that the guesthouse was named before the collapse of the British bank of the same name.

A Yone Oo Guest House (☎ 40183; Shwe Phi Oo Rd; s/d $8/12, with shared bathroom $4/8) The longest-established guesthouse in town, A Yone Oo offers a choice of clean wooden rooms in the main house or posher en suite rooms in comfortable bungalows in the grounds.

San Ngwe Yaung (☎ 40380; 234A Aung San Rd; s/d $8/16, with shared bathroom $4/8) Easy to find on the main road through town, this village-style place has simple concrete-floored rooms arranged off a central corridor.

For meals, there are several teashops around the market, or **Café Ayo** (Shwe Phi Oo Rd; meals K2000) can prepare you a convincing cappuccino or a filling Shan meal.

Getting There & Away

BUS & PICK-UP

From the highway bus station in Mandalay, there are direct buses to Kyaukme (K3500, five hours) at 6am. In the opposite direction, buses leave Kyaukme at 5.30am. Heading northeast, several buses leave from near the market to Lashio (K2000, three hours) via

Hsipaw (K1000, one hour) between 5am and 6.30am.

You can flag down pick-ups heading north or south on the highway, but expect to pay at least K4000 to Mandalay or Pyin U Lwin and K1500 to Hsipaw.

TRAIN

The train station is a 10-minute walk northwest of the market and guesthouses. The *131 Up* leaves Kyaukme at 1.50pm for Hsipaw (ordinary/upper class $2/4, two hours) and Lashio ($2/4, six hours). The *132 Down* leaves Kyaukme for Mandalay ($3/6, 10 hours) at 11.25am.

HSIPAW

သီပေါ

☎ 082

Pronounced 'See Paw', this small country town has become a popular stop on the traveller circuit as much for its laid-back atmosphere as for any must-see attractions. This is a place to settle down for a couple of days, strolling to cheroot factories and ruined monasteries in the surrounding villages. There's a traveller scene here but it's very low key – just three guesthouses and a handful of restaurants with English menus. Hsipaw is a much more attractive base for exploring northern Shan State than Lashio is and the bucolic pace of life here encourages people to linger – quite a few travellers come for a day and end up staying a week.

Information

You can get reliable advice about things to do and see at Mr Charles Guest House (p302). Another good source of local information is Ko Zaw Tun, known locally as Mr Book – he runs a small bookshop on Namtu Rd (Main Rd). Note that locals have become much more circumspect about chatting to foreigners since the wave of local arrests in 2005 (see p302).

Sights & Activities

Hsipaw's large **central market** (☿ 5am-5pm) is best visited early in the morning, when Shan and other tribal people come from nearby villages to trade. There's an interesting **produce market** (☿ 5am-noon) further south on the riverbank. If you come early, you'll see villagers unload-ing produce from their canoes. Down by the river at the southern end of the central market are some handsome 19th-century **godowns** (warehouses) and a **banyan tree** worshipped by locals as a *nat* (spirit) shrine. The Dokhtawady River is clean and clear, but the currents are dangerous and locals tell tales of a malevolent *nat* luring swimmers to their deaths.

South of the centre, **Mahamyatmuni Paya** (Namtu Rd) is the biggest and grandest pagoda in town. The huge brass buddha image here was inspired by the famous Mahamuni buddha (p263) in Mandalay. Further north on Namtu Road is a smaller **pagoda** covered in a mosaic of mirrored tiles.

Near the police station at the north end of town, a small road runs down to the riverbank,

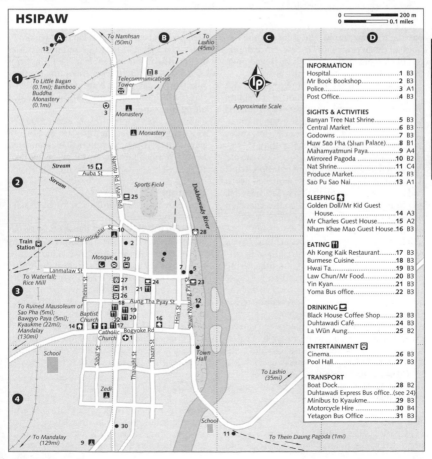

HSIPAW

INFORMATION	
Hospital	**1** B3
Mr Book Bookshop	**2** B3
Police	**3** A1
Post Office	**4** B3

SIGHTS & ACTIVITIES	
Banyan Tree Nat Shrine	**5** B3
Central Market	**6** B3
Godowns	**7** B3
Haw Sao Pha (Shan Palace)	**8** B1
Mahamyatmuni Paya	**9** A4
Mirrored Pagoda	**10** B2
Nat Shrine	**11** C4
Produce Market	**12** B3
Sao Pu Sao Nai	**13** A1

SLEEPING ⌂	
Golden Doll/Mr Kid Guest House	**14** A3
Mr Charles Guest House	**15** A2
Nham Khae Mao Guest House	**16** B3

EATING ⊞	
Ah Kong Kaik Restaurant	**17** B3
Burmese Cuisine	**18** B3
Hwai Ta	**19** B3
Law Chun/Mr Food	**20** B3
Yin Kyan	**21** B3
Yoma Bus office	**22** B3

DRINKING ⊟	
Black House Coffee Shop	**23** B3
Duhtawadi Café	**24** B3
La Wün Aung	**25** B2

ENTERTAINMENT ⊡	
Cinema	**26** B3
Pool Hall	**27** B3

TRANSPORT	
Boat Dock	**28** B2
Duhtawadi Express Bus office	(see 24)
Minibus to Kyaukme	**29** B3
Motorcycle Hire	**30** B4
Yetagon Bus Office	**31** B3

NORTHERN MYANMAR

THE VANISHING SHAN

One of the most interesting experiences in Hsipaw used to be a visit to the fading Shan palace at the north end of town in the company of the charming Mr Donald (the nephew of Sao Kya Seng, who was the last *sawbwa* (Shan prince) of Hsipaw. Sao Kya Seng vanished during the military takeover in 1962 – an event powerfully described by his wife, Inge Sargent, in the book *Twilight over Burma: My Life as a Shan Princess*.

History in Myanmar has a habit of repeating itself – Mr Donald was himself arrested and imprisoned in 2005 on dubious charges of 'operating as an unlicensed tour guide and defaming the State'.

This was not an isolated incident. More than 30 Shan leaders were arrested across Shan State as part of an orchestrated crackdown on tribal leaders who were opposed to the reconvening of the National Convention. The convention was charged with the task of creating a constitution for Myanmar after the annulled elections in 1990. In response to the crackdown, at least one faction of the Shan State Army (SSA) has resumed its armed struggle against the government. Thus far, the resumption of hostilities has had only a minor effect on travel, but the situation could change at any time, so check locally before heading off the beaten track. The website www.shanland.org is a reliable source of information.

passing the **haw sao pha**, the palace of the last *sawbwa* (Shan prince) of Hsipaw. Since the arrest of Dr Donald, the palace is no longer open to visitors (see the boxed text, above).

Probably the most interesting sight around Hsipaw is **Little Bagan**, a collection of crumbling Shan-style brick and stucco stupas surrounded by fields of African daisies just north of town. In the same area, ruins sprawl for miles around the **Bamboo Buddha Monastery** (Maha Nanda Kantha), which contains a 150-year-old lacquered buddha made from bamboo strips. To reach Little Bagan, follow Namtu St north and look for the sign on the left to **Sao Pu Sao Nai**, a colourful shrine dedicated to the guardian *nat* of Hsipaw. The trail to the ruins branches off to the left, just before the *nat* shrine.

There are various **factories** around town, where you can see locals carrying out cottage industries like weaving, manufacturing noodles, dipping candles, hand-rolling cheroots and even popping popcorn. All these are marked on the map in the reception at Mr Charles Guest House (see right).

For a stunning sunset view over Hsipaw, cross the bridge on the highway to Lashio (east of town) and look for the obvious path on your right. A 1-mile walk will lead you to **Thein Daung Pagoda** (also known as Five Buddha Hill), which offers sweeping views over Hsipaw and the river.

Hiking

Mr Charles Guest House (right) runs a variety of guided walks, treks and excursions around

Hsipaw, visiting Shan and Palaung tribal villages, waterfalls, hot springs and monasteries in the hills around town. Half-/full-day trips cost $3/8. Overnight trips, including the two-night/three-day trek to Namhsan, cost $10 per day, with basic accommodation in villages along the route.

Be wary of people offering to arrange private trips to a 'village festival' for an upfront payment. Several travellers have reported being scammed into paying for expensive taxis to see celebrations that fail to materialise.

Sleeping

There are just a few choices in town; all rates include breakfast.

Golden Doll/Mr Kid Guest House (☎ 80066; 124 Bogyoke Rd; s/d $4/8, with shared bathroom $3/6) On the highway in the direction of Kyaukme, this rickety village guesthouse is cheap but fairly grungy. The owners are friendly, but the rooms need the attentions of a handyperson.

Nam Khae Mao Guest House (☎ 80077; nkmao@ myanmar.com.mm; 134 Bogyoke Rd; s/d from $6/8, with shared bathroom $3/5) This village-style guesthouse offers good value for your dollar. Rooms are simple wooden boxes, but all are clean and those with bathrooms have the bonus of a window.

ourpick **Mr Charles Guest House** (☎ 80105; 105 Auba St; s/d from $6/12, with shared bathroom $4/7, air-con ste $35) Travellers congregate at this expanding guesthouse on the north edge of Hsipaw for one simple reason – it's the best place in town. The friendly owners can arrange transport, treks and tours and there's a communal upstairs balcony where guests swap travel stories late into the evening. The more expensive rooms in the new annexe are brighter and more comfortable than those in the old village house.

Eating

Most of the dining options are strung out along Namtu Rd. The following restaurants are open for breakfast, lunch and dinner.

Burmese Cuisine (Namtu Rd; dishes K500) Opposite the more famous Law Chun. This simple Burmese canteen has a tiny dining room and a tiny menu of Burmese curries that changes depending on what was available in the market. Dishes come with soup, rice and an intriguing spread of salads, condiments and pickles.

Law Chun (Mr Food; Namtu Rd; meals from K1000) Part of the 'Mr' craze sweeping through Hsipaw, 'Mr Food' is the first place most visitors eat at...and many end up eating nowhere else. The menu treads familiar waters, but the food is satisfying and you can enjoy a draught Dagon beer with your meal. Similar food is served at Hwai Ta next door.

Yin Kyan (Thazin St; soups from K1000) A few doors south of the market, this hole-in-the-wall eatery serves the best Shan noodle soup in town. There's no English menu but you can order by pointing to the various toppings.

Ah Kong Kaik Restaurant (Mandalay-Lashio Rd; meals from K1800) A big roadhouse-style place on the highway serving filling Burmese lunches and Chinese staples like hot-and-sour pork. Passing buses and pick-ups often stop here for lunch.

Drinking & Entertainment

Law Chun (see above) is the most popular place for a drink of an evening – it has excellent fruit juices and Dagon beer on tap. Other nightlife options include the **cinema** (Namtu Rd; seats K200) and the adjacent **pool hall** (Namtu Rd; per game K500; ☺ 9am-midnight).

La Wün Aung (Namtu St; snacks K300; ☺ 6am-10pm) North of town, near Mr Charles Guesthouse, this is the most popular teashop in town – partly because it screens international football matches.

Duhtawadi Café (Lanmataw St; snacks K300; ☺ 7am-8pm) Another reliable teashop opposite the market; this is also the departure point for the Duhtawadi bus to Mandalay.

Black House Coffee Shop (23 Shwe Nyaung Pin St; coffee from K1000; ☺ 8am-5.30pm) Run by the energetic Maureen, who came to Hsipaw from Australia, this coffeeshop is housed in a stately teak mansion just south of the market. Bring a book and settle down with a cappuccino on the rear deck overlooking the river.

Getting There & Away
BUS & PICK-UP

Three bus companies run services to the highway bus stand in Mandalay (K3800 to K4000, six hours) via Pyin U Lwin (K3500, four hours). If there are spare seats, these buses will take you to Kyaukme (one hour) for K1000. Buses depart between 5.30am and 6am daily. The Duhtawadi Express leaves from in front of the Duhtawadi Café by the market, the Yetagon (Yedakhun) bus leaves from near the cinema on Namtu Rd and the Yoma bus leaves from opposite Law Chun (Mr Food) on Namtu Rd. Daily buses to Lashio (K1500, two hours) leave from all the above stands between 5.30am and 8am.

A minibus runs to Kyaukme (K1000) at 7.30am from the corner opposite the post office on Namtu Rd. You may be able to flag down pick-ups bound for Mandalay (K4000) or Lashio (K1500) on the highway near the Ah Kong Kaik restaurant.

TAXI

Shared taxis run from the Duhtawadi Café to Mandalay (front/back seat K13,000/11,000) at around 7am. The whole taxi fare is K45,000 to Mandalay or Lashio, and K25,000 to Kyaukme.

TRAIN

Hsipaw's tiny train station is down a dirt track beginning near the mirrored pagoda on Namtu Rd. The *131 Up* leaves Mandalay at 4.30am and arrives in Hsipaw around 3pm (ordinary/upper class $3/6). The same train leaves Hsipaw at 3.25pm bound for Lashio ($2/4, 4½ hours). Heading down to the plains, the *132 Down* leaves Hsipaw for Mandalay at 9.40am.

Getting Around

Most places in town are within easy walking distance, but Mr Charles (opposite) rents out bicycles for K2000 per day. Trishaws waiting by the market charge around K500 to any of the guesthouses in town.

NORTHERN MYANMAR

A small motorcycle shop on the road to the Mahamyatmuni paya rents out 125CC motorcycles for K8000 per day. Make sure the bike is mechanically sound before attempting the road to Namhsan.

Around Hsipaw

BAWGYO

ဘော်ကျိ

Five miles southwest of town, off the Mandalay–Lashio highway, the Shan-style **Bawgyo Paya** is the most revered paya in northern Shan State – equivalent to Inle Lake's Phaung Daw Oo Paya (p240) in the south. The original Shan stupa was replaced by a geometric modern pagoda in 1995, but the four wooden buddha statues enshrined within are at least 800 years old. The images are only displayed once a year during the annual **Bawgyo Paya Pwe**, held from the 10th day of the waxing moon to the full moon of Tabaung (February/March).

Any bus or pick-up heading southwest from Hsipaw can drop you at Bawgyo. Alternatively, you can come by rented bike, though the journey has steep uphill sections in both directions.

NAMHSAN

နမ့်စမ်

elev 5249ft

Once the capital of an ancient Shan kingdom, Namhsan is a sleepy cluster of timber houses with rusted tin roofs. But what a view! The town looks out over a sea of rucked-up mountain ridges and plunging ravines. The surrounding hills are covered by tea plantations and, more discreetly, by plantations of opium poppies. A cobbled track leads uphill behind the town to the green, shady reservoir that supplies Namhsan with water. If you continue uphill through the small Palaung villages above Namhsan, you'll reach **Taung Yo** monastery, a small pagoda on an exposed hilltop with amazing views over the surrounding countryside.

There are no permit restrictions for visiting Namhsan town and hiking to nearby villages, but the shocking condition of the road and the unreliable transport links deter all but the most dedicated travellers.

Most of the inhabitants are Shwe (Golden) Palaung and the tea industry is the main local employer. During the annual harvest (April to August) the road to Namhsan can be blocked

for days by overloaded tea trucks that have dug themselves into the mud.

Sleeping & Eating

When you arrive in Namhsan, you will be steered towards the town **guesthouse** (per person K4000), which offers basic accommodation in rooms with shared bathrooms. Reportedly this place is government run. Locals Daw May Saw Nu and U Shwe Tun have put up foreigners in their houses in the past and may do so again if they can obtain the necessary paperwork – ask at Mr Charles Guest House in Hsipaw (p302) for the latest information.

For meals, there are several Chinese restaurants along the narrow main street, serving all the usual Myanmar-Chinese dishes for the usual prices.

Getting There & Away

In theory, there is a daily bus to Namhsan (K5000) from near Mr Charles Guest House on Namtu Rd in Hsipaw, but the departure time is completely random. Sometimes the bus leaves early in the morning; other times it fails to leave at all. The best thing to do is contact Mr Charles (p302) and find out when the bus will next be running. If drivers are willing, you may be able to do the journey by chartered jeep for around U$40. Either way, the journey can take six hours, or more if the road is blocked by tea trucks.

A few brave souls come here by bike or motorcycle, but the road is long, the route confusing and you may have to break the journey overnight. Start by following Namtu Rd north out of Hsipaw; the turn-off to Namhsan is about 17 miles along, at the town of Panglong. A third alternative is to trek here from Hsipaw with a guide from Mr Charles Guest House, staying in Shan and Palaung villages along the way.

LASHIO

လား:ရှိ:

☎ 082 / elev 2805ft

The last major city before the Chinese border at Mu-se, Lashio (pronounced 'Lar Show') is a typical northern market town with a significant Chinese population. Once the seat of an important Shan *sao pha* (sky lord), the town played a pivotal role in the fight against the Japanese in WWII. It was the starting point of the Burma Road, which supplied food and arms to Chiang Kai-shek's Kuomintang army.

Not much evidence of either historical period remains today, though a few interesting pagodas survive amongst the modern houses and hotels.

Lashio was ostensibly off limits to foreigners until the early 1990s because of skirmishes between government forces and rebels from the Shan State Army (SSA) and Kachin Independence Army (KIA). Even today, foreigners are banned from travelling north from Lashio to Mu-se and the Chinese border – though, perversely, tourists are allowed to enter Myanmar from China at Mu-se and travel south to Lashio with a special permit (see p307).

Orientation

Lashio is divided into two main districts – the main town is known as Lashio Lay (Little Lashio), but the airport and bus stand are downhill on the way to Lashio Gyi (Big Lashio).

Sights & Activities

The busy **central market** (cnr Bogyoke & Theinni Rds; ☯ 5am-5pm) is full of local produce but don't expect to see many tribal people. More interesting is the **night market** (5-9pm), which sprawls east from the market after dark. It's particularly atmospheric when the power fails (which happens regularly) and the stalls are lit by candles.

There are numerous pagodas in town. Just north of the market are the gaudy **Mahamyatmuni Paya** (La Ma Daw St) and the ornate pagoda-style **Sasana Beikman** (La Ma Daw St) – a kind of Buddhist community hall. Continuing downhill, you'll come to **Nannhaewon Park**, a peaceful open space with a small **roller rink** (per hr K1000; ☯ 8am-10pm) where teenagers pass the time of day.

The most interesting Buddhist monument in town is the enormous **Quan Yin Temple**, hidden away in the backstreets about a mile south of the market. The principal place of worship for Lashio's Chinese community, the temple is a riot of stucco sculptures, coiling dragons and step-roofed pagodas. A pick-up taxi to the temple from the market will cost about K2000 return.

There are more pagodas on the outskirts of town. Just north of the bus stand (accessible via the shared pick-ups to Lashio Gyi), the gold and stucco **Mansu Paya** is said to be over 250 years old. If you follow the road beside Nannhaewon Park and turn left along Pagoda St, you'll reach the covered wooden stairway leading to **Thatana (Sasana) 2500-Year Paya**, reportedly built by Sao Hon Phan, the last Shan *sao pha* in the area. It's a serene spot with good views over town.

Sleeping

There are now only two choices open to foreigners, apart from the government-owned Lashio Motel. Room rates in Lashio do not include breakfast.

Ya Htaik Hotel (☎ 22655; Bogyoke Rd; s/d from $15/25, with shared bathroom $5/10; ✇) The best choice in town, this four-storey Chinese-style place has a lift shaft but no lift. Skip the cheaper rooms with basic shared bathrooms for the comfortable en suite rooms with TV and views.

Thi Da Aye Hotel (☎ 22165; 218 Thiri Rd; r from $15, s/d with shared bathroom $5/10; ✇) Run by the same owners, this place offers more of the same – plain concrete rooms with shared bathrooms or better rooms with en suite.

Eating

All the restaurants in Lashio open for breakfast, lunch and dinner.

Palace Gardens Café (Kutkhaing Rd; snacks K300) Local men gather to sip tea and chat about the weather in this partly open-air teashop in Nannhaewon Park.

Sun Moon Café (Theinni Rd; dishes from K1000) On the main road leading downhill from the market, this place achieves a kind of Hawaiian chic, with cascades of plastic flowers and fruit hanging in the windows. Come here for good ice cream, coffee and fast food.

Lashio Restaurant (San Kyaung St; meals K1500) A typical Myanmar restaurant, serving decent Bamar and Chinese food. Burmese-style meals come with various salads and sides.

Jupiter Restaurant (San Kaung St; meals from K1500; ☯ from 11am) Downhill from the market, this large beer hall serves the same Chinese dishes as every other Chinese restaurant in the country, but does them well. The bar serves Tiger beer and local rum and whiskey by the peg.

One of the best places to eat in the evening is the bustling **night market** on the road leading downhill from the southeast corner of the day market. Stalls here stock lots of Shan specialities, including pig-organ hotpots, Shan noodle soup and savoury cakes made from steamed purple sticky rice and sesame seeds.

NORTHERN MYANMAR

There are several **Myanmar canteens** with no English signs on San Kaung St, which serve tasty Bamar dishes from huge aluminium pots. Ordering is a case of peeking into the pots and picking whatever takes your fancy – a meal of rice with three or four toppings will cost around K2000.

Getting There & Away

AIR
Air Bagan has two or three weekly flights from Mandalay ($57, 40 minutes) to the tiny airport just north of Lashio. You can connect to Lashio from Yangon for $123, but you may face a long wait at Mandalay.

BUS & PICK-UP
The main bus stand is about one mile north of the centre on Theinni Rd, on the way to Lashio Gyi. Buses leave daily for the highway bus stand in Mandalay (K6000, eight hours) at 7am and 1pm. These buses will drop you in Pyin U Lwin (K3000, six hours) or Kyaukme (K3000, three hours).

Buses to Hsipaw (K1500, two hours) and Kyaukme (K2000, three hours) leave from the Hsipaw Ma bus stand, about a mile south of the market on the back road to Hsipaw; there are several services between 7am and 1pm. A pick-up taxi from the market will cost about K1500. Infrequent and overloaded pick-ups from Lashio to Mandalay (K5000) leave from near the main bus stand.

See opposite for information on travel between Mu-se and Lashio.

TAXI
Shared taxis run from the back of the main bus stand to Mandalay (per person K15,000, eight hours) via Pyin U Lwin (K13,000, six hours). You'll pay around K10,000 as far as Hsipaw (two hours) or Kyaukme (three hours).

TRAIN
Lashio's miniature train station is 2 miles north of the market (follow La Ma Daw St north and cross the intersection onto Station Rd). The *131 Up* rumbles up through the hills from Mandalay at 4.30am daily. The scenery on the way is wonderful, particularly around the Gokteik Viaduct (p300), but the train takes an age to reach Lashio (ordinary/upper class $6/12, 16 hours). In the other direction, the *132 Down* leaves Lashio at 5am. The fare from Lashio to Hsipaw is $2/4 (five hours); to Pyin U Lwin it's $4/8 (10 hours).

Getting Around
Miniature pick-up taxis charge K1500 for the trip from the central market to the train station, the airport or the Quan Yin temple. These taxis also provide a regular shuttle service between Lashio Lay and the bus stand for K100.

MU-SE
မူဆယ်
☎ 082
Northern Myanmar meets Yúnnán China at the town of Mu-se on the Shweli (Ruili) River. Few visitors get to see this part of the country, as foreigners are banned from travelling to Mu-se from Lashio. However, it is possible to cross the border at Mu-Se from China and travel south to Lashio by road with advance permission from the Myanmar authorities (see the boxed text, opposite).

If you do get to visit Mu-se, you'll find a typical bustling border town, with a surprisingly high level of development, which reflects the relative wealth of China compared to Myanmar. Predictably, the border also acts as a conduit for the movement of Golden Triangle heroin and methamphetamines to markets in China, Myanmar and the rest of Asia.

Sleeping & Eating
There are plenty of hotels in Mu-se but only a few have a licence for foreign guests. Many tour groups stay at the Muse Hotel but this is government owned.

Shwe Thiri Hotel (☎ 50768; Phi Daung Su Rd; s/d $15/20) Less plush than the Muse Hotel, this privately owned place offers decent Chinese-style rooms with private bathrooms. It's not bad for the money.

Getting There & Away
Buses and shared taxis run regularly along the legendary Burma Road between Mu-se and Lashio – a 109-mile journey that takes at least five hours. However, the means of transport that you must use to reach Lashio will be specified in your permit. In most cases the tour operator will have a chartered vehicle waiting when you cross the border.

MYANMAR-CHINA BORDER

The border crossing between Mu-se and Ruili in China is nominally open to travellers heading from China to Myanmar but closed to those heading in the opposite direction. To enter Myanmar from China, you must make arrangements through a travel agency, either in Kunming, China, or with an international agency that specialises in travel in this region. In Kunming, the **Myanmar consulate** (☎ 0871-360 3477; www.mcg-kunming.com; Room A504, Long Yuan Hao Zhai, 166 Wei Yuan Jie; ☻ 8.30am-noon & 1-2pm Mon-Fri) can arrange a standard Myanmar visa, but you must find a travel agent to sort out the paperwork for the border crossing and onward travel to Lashio. Expect to pay around Y1400 ($200) for the whole package, including a taxi from Mu-se to Lashio. Travellers have recommended the travel agency at the **Kunming Camelia Hotel** (☎ 0871-317 6607; ww.kmcamelliahotel.com; 154 East Dong Feng Rd, Kunming).

MYITKYINA TO KATHA

The mighty Ayeyarwady River snakes across Kachin State like a fat yellow python on its way from the mountains to the plains, providing the main transport route in this under-developed part of the country. Although infrastructure is limited, growing numbers of travellers brave the discomfort to ride the riverboats of the Inland Water Transport (IWT) company back to Mandalay. However, these boats are government owned. If you'd rather not use government transport, you can complete some sections of the route on small private boats.

This is one case where the journey is definitely the destination – the ancient ferries take days to complete the journey, passing through a landscape of rolling fields and forest-cloaked gorges. Every few hours, the ferries dock at small villages to be greeted by a flotilla of local women selling packaged meals from canoes piled high with cooking pots. It's a remarkable spectacle.

Unlike the river journey from Mandalay to Bagan, the boats from Myitkyina to Mandalay are mainly used by locals. The slow days chugging on the river provide an opportunity to interact with local people in a way that would be impossible on dry land.

MYITKYINA
မြစ်ကြီးနား
☎ 074

The capital of Kachin State, Myitkyina is a sleepy northern town tucked into a bend of the Ayeyarwady River. For most visitors, the main reason for visiting Myitkyina is to start the slow but atmospheric boat ride back down the Ayeyarwady River to Mandalay. The ferries that ply the Ayeyarwady offer an unparalleled window onto rural life in Myanmar, but when we say slow, we mean *slow*. The trip to Bhamo by local ferry takes two days and the big boats of the Inland Water Transport company take a further two days to travel downriver from Bhamo to Mandalay. Hotels in town can arrange trips to Kachin villages and tranquil Indawgyi Lake (see the boxed text, p310).

Information
Snowland Tours (☎ 23499; snowland@mptmail.net .mm; Wai Maw St) Southwest of the market, this agency can book flights and arrange customised tours.
YMCA (☎ 23010; NE 12 Myothit Quarter; per hr K1500; ☻ 9am-noon & 1-5pm Mon-Fri) Slow internet access and a free map of Myitkyina.

Sights & Activities
Like most towns in Myanmar, Myitkyina is centred on a large and busy **market**. Numerous stalls sell embroidered Kachin bags, shoes and shawls, along with tribal jewellery and ceremonial swords. Missionaries have been very successful in converting the Kachin to Christianity and there are around 15 Baptist, Methodist and Catholic churches in Myitkyina. About 9 miles north of town is the so-called **Praying Mountain**, a sacred site for Kachin and Lisu Baptists.

Myitkyina also has an interesting collection of pagodas. Probably the most eye-catching is the gilded 'wish-fulfilling' **Hsu Taung Pye Zedidaw** on the banks of the Ayeyarwady River in the northern part of town. A large wooden pavilion opposite the stupa contains a 98ft-long reclining buddha, constructed using donations from Japanese Buddhists. A short stroll west from the YMCA is the large **An Daw Shin Paya**, which boasts a silver-plated stupa said to contain tooth relics. On the road to the airport, **Aung Ze Yan Aung Pagoda** is noteworthy for hundreds of buddha statues, lined up in neat rows to face the rising sun.

On a quiet street a mile north of the YMCA, the government-owned **Kachin State Cultural Museum** (Yonn Gyi St; admission $2, camera fee K1000; ☻ 10am-3.30pm Tue-Sun) displays Kachin and Shan costumes and the usual assortment of instruments, farming tools and ethnological artefacts.

Festivals & Events

On **Kachin State Day** (10 January), Myitkyina bursts into life for the annual **Manao Festival**, held to propitiate the local *nat*. Costumed dances are performed in front of a pavilion made up of painted totem poles, and 29 cows or buffaloes are sacrificed: one for each of the 28 *nat* plus one dedicated to all of them. Observers get into the festival mood by drinking copious quantities of *churu* (rice beer).

Sleeping

our pick **YMCA** (☎ 23010; mka-ymca@myanmar.com.mm; NE 12 Myothit Quarter; s/d $10/14, with shared bathroom $6/8; ❄ 🖳) By far the most traveller-friendly and savvy place to stay in Myitkyina, the 'Y' has a thoroughly wholesome atmosphere and large clean rooms with crisp bed linen. Internet access is available at the attached communications centre, international phone calls are possible from reception (from $1 per minute) and the genial and well-informed staff can answer all your questions about local sightseeing and transport. Breakfast is not included but there are several nearby teashops.

Pantsun Hotel (☎ 22748; pantsunmka@myanmar .com.mm; 36/7 Myothit Quarter; s/d from $18/24; ❄) Cleaners work tirelessly to keep the rooms at this modern Chinese-style hotel clean and inviting. Some rooms are better than others, so look at a few before you decide. More expensive rooms have TV, air-con, fridge and balcony.

Two Dragons Hotel (☎ 23490; Zay Gyi St; s/d $20/25; ❄) West of the market, this place offers comfortable, tidy rooms that aren't quite as grand as the glitzy reception.

Xing Xian Hotel (☎ 22281; xingxianhotel@mptmail .net.mm; 127 Shan Su North; s/d $20/30; ❄) Visiting NGOs choose this quiet modern hotel, four blocks south of the market between Wai Maw St and Yadana Gone Yi St. Rooms have those three important indicators of comfort – TV, fridge and air-con.

The large Nanthida Hotel by the river has links to the government.

Eating

Restaurants in Myitkyina are open for breakfast, lunch and dinner.

Swem Htet Tha Café (Pyi Htaung Su Rd; dim sum K1000) This popular teashop two blocks north of the YMCA serves steamers of tasty dim sum at lunch time and other Myanmar and Chinese snacks till late. The attached beer bar attracts a crowd in the evenings.

Kashmir Restaurant (Myothit Quarter; curries K1500) Close to where the road crosses the railway tracks near the YMCA, this Indian-Muslim place serves delicious fish, mutton and chicken curries and wonderfully spicy dhal (lentil soup).

Bamboo Field Restaurant (313 Pyi Htaung Su Rd; dishes K2000-4000) A short walk north from the YMCA, Bamboo Field is a modern 'restobar' that serves excellent Kachin and Yúnnánese food. Every evening from 6.30pm, local girls sing along to a cheesy organ soundtrack in a surreal beauty pageant – winners are rewarded with different coloured tinsel boas.

Every evening from around 4.30pm, the junction of Aung San Rd and Wai Maw St is the setting for a busy **night market** (meals from K1000), with stalls selling all sorts of Kachin and Shan dishes.

Getting There & Away

The journey to Myitkyina by train or boat is tortuously slow. Most people fly in and then work their way south to Mandalay along the Ayeyarwady River.

AIR

Air Bagan flies several times a week from Mandalay to Myitkyina ($90, one hour). Twice a week, the flight continues to Putao ($52, 40 minutes), but you can only travel on this route if you arranged a permit in Yangon – see p315 for more information. Once a week the government's Myanma Airways flies from Myitkyina to Bhamo ($25, 25 minutes) but the schedule is extremely erratic – a bit like the maintenance of their aircraft…

BOAT

The large passenger ferries of the Inland Water Transport company don't travel between Myitkyina and Bhamo because the river is too shallow to navigate safely.

However, a small local boat weaves between the sandbars to the tiny village of Sinbo, where you can board a second local ferry to Bhamo. If the water level is high enough, the boat will leave the same day; if not, it will leave the following morning. If the river is really low, the boat won't leave at all.

Assuming things are running smoothly, the daily boat to Sinbo leaves Myitkyina's Talawgyi pier at around 8.30am (K8000, five hours). If you have to stay overnight in Sinbo, there's a basic government-owned guesthouse that charges K2000 per person. The trip downriver from Sinbo to Bhamo takes eight hours and costs K8000.

The government has banned foreigners from travelling on these boats in the past but at the time of writing there seemed to be no problems. Ask at the YMCA (opposite) for the latest information.

BUS & PICK-UP

The only bus route open to foreigners is the daily service to Bhamo (K10,000, six hours) which leaves at 8.30am from the dusty bus stand, just north of the centre, off Tha Khin Net Phay Rd. Pick-ups cover the same route for K10,000/8000 (front/back seat).

To travel on this route, you must prepare five photocopies of the visa and ID pages from your passport to hand out at the various checkpoints between Myitkyina and Bhamo. Without these papers, drivers will not let you board.

TRAIN

A British-era railway line connects Mandalay to Myitkyina, via Naba near Katha, but delays and cancellations are routine and there have been accidents on this route. Daily government trains run from Mandalay to Myitkyina (ordinary/upper class $11/35) at noon *(37 Up)*, 1.30pm *(55 Up)* and 5pm *(41 Up)*. The journey can take anything from 22 to 36 hours. The *37 Up* has a sleeper compartment (per person $40) but you must reserve well in advance to secure a berth.

Trains return from Myitkyina at 5am *(42 Down)*, 7am *(56 Down)* and noon *(38 Down,* sleeper). The fare to Naba is $4/13 (ordinary/upper class, eight hours plus). The trains provide a great opportunity to meet ordinary people away from the eyes of the authorities but you may wish to avoid ordi-

nary class unless you enjoy being crammed in like a sardine and shaken like a martini.

If you want to minimise the money that you give to the government, there's also a private train, the *Mandalar Express,* which runs several days a week on the same route (check the current schedule with your guesthouse). The train normally leaves Mandalay around 4pm, returning from Myitkyina around 3.30pm; reclining seats in upper class cost $25.

Getting Around

Motorised three-wheelers called *thonbeecars* (*thon* is three and *bee* is wheel) are everywhere in Myitkyina. The journey from the airport into town costs K1000. Taxis can be chartered at the airport and around the market for trips further afield (such as to Indawgyi Lake).

The YMCA and motorcycle repair shops rent ageing 125CC motorcycles for around K20,000 per day. These are fine for getting around town and to nearby villages, but they are not really up to the challenges of longer trips.

If you just want to explore the villages across the river, there are frequent cross-river ferries (K200) from the Waingmaw pier in the middle of town.

Around Myitkyina
MYIT-SON & HPAKANT

မြစ်ဆုံ

About 27 miles north of Myitkyina, Myit-Son marks the point where the Mayhka and Malikha Rivers come together to form the Ayeyarwady. It's a popular beauty spot and prospectors pan for gold along the riverbanks close to town. The return taxi fare from Myitkyina to Myit-Son is anywhere from K30,000 to K50,000, depending on your negotiating skills. It's about an hour each way over a very rough road.

Until recently, it was possible to visit the jade-mining town of **Hpakant**, 92 miles west of Myitkyina, on expensive organised tours, but the town has dropped off the approved list. Contact hotels to see if tours are possible when you visit.

BHAMO
ဗန်းမော်

☎ 074

For most people, Bhamo, or Banmaw (pronounced 'ba-more'), is just a staging post on the river journey to Myitkyina or Mandalay, but it's an attractive town with some of the best accommodation between Mandalay and Putao.

Sights

The main activity in town is watching the comings and goings along the riverfront. Close to the jetty where the fast boats to Katha come and go is an open area where clay-pots in an astonishing array of shapes and sizes are sold from old fishing boats hauled up onto the shore. Just inland from the river, the **daily market** (5am-4pm) draws Lisu, Kachin and Shan tribal people from the surrounding villages.

East of the Friendship Hotel on the road to Bhamo's tiny airport, **Theindawgyi Paya** features a striking bell-shaped gilded stupa. North of the market is the **Yunnan Chinese Temple** with the usual Chinese religious statuary in super-saturated colours.

About 3 miles north of town, beyond the military enclave, the Shwe Kyina Pagoda marks the site of the 5th-century Shan city of **Sampanago**. Little remains of the old city, but the pagoda features a number of ancient pavilions, one containing a 33ft-long reclining buddha. A horse cart or rickshaw from the market will cost around K3000 return; tell the driver to go to Bhamo Myo Haung (Old City of Bhamo).

For guided trips to Kachin villages around Bhamo, ask at the reception of the Friendship Hotel (see right). The manager should be able to put you in touch with Sein Win, an ec-centric English-speaking guide who claims to have built his own helicopter (we haven't seen it ourselves, so can't verify the claim).

Sleeping & Eating

Friendship Hotel (50095; Mingone Quarter; s/d $7/14, with air-con $20/25;) This large, modern and comfortable hotel is a welcome sight when you step off the boat after two days on the Ayeyarwady. The spic-and-span rooms have TV, fridge and bathroom with sizzling hot showers. The manager, Moe Naing, is extremely helpful and can book boat trips and flights. Ask for a photocopied map of Bhamo.

Grand Hotel (50317; Post Office Rd; s/d from $10/15;) Grand-looking from the outside, this place is more down-to-earth inside, though the rooms are as clean as a newly washed sheet. Perks include TV, fridge and air-con.

There are several places to eat on the street behind the Friendship Hotel that are open for breakfast, lunch and dinner.

Heaven Tea Shop (dim sum from K300) This smart-looking teashop serves tasty steamed dumplings stuffed with meat, fish and vegetables.

Shamie Restaurant (curries K1000) A few doors down from Heaven, this Muslim canteen serves satisfyingly spicy Indian curries. No alcohol is available but you can quench your thirst after dinner at the nearby Sky Beer Station (the name says it all).

INDAWGYI LAKE

About 110 miles southwest of Myitkyina, placid Indawgyi is the largest natural lake in Myanmar. The lakeshore is ringed by rarely visited Shan villages, and the surrounding Indawgyi Wetland Wildlife Sanctuary provides a habitat for more than 120 species of birds, including shelducks, pintails, kingfishers, herons, egrets and the Myanmar peacock.

Linked to the shore by a curving causeway, the serene **Shwe Myitsu Pagoda** seems to float on the surface of the lake. Surrounded by white-washed *zedi*, the gilded stupa was constructed in 1869 to enshrine Buddha relics transported here from Yangon. Pilgrims visit in droves for the Shwe Myitsu Pwe, held from the 8th day of the waxing moon to the full moon in the lunar month of Tabaung (February/March). There is also a working **elephant camp** just inland from the lake.

The village of Lonton has the only licensed guesthouse (per person $10) but it is owned by a military family. Boat drivers charge a steep K45,000 for day trips around the lake, or K15,000 for a return trip to the pagoda. Land-based tours around the lakeshore are much cheaper – locals will guide you for around K5000.

To reach the lake from Myitkyina, take the 7am train *(56 Down)* to the village of Hopin (ordinary/upper class $2/4, four hours), then board a local pick-up for the 26-mile trip to Lonton (K3000, two hours). Trains from Hopin to Myitkyina leave at 6am and 2pm. Considering the unreliable nature of train services in upper Myanmar, you may prefer to charter a taxi for a day trip from Myitkyina for around K50,000 return.

IRRAWADDY DOLPHINS

The Irrawaddy dolphin is one of Myanmar's most endangered animals. Still found in small numbers on the upper stretches of the Ayeyarwady, this small cetacean has a short, rounded snout like a beluga whale and hunts using sonar in the turgid waters of lakes and rivers. In the past, dolphins and humans were able to coexist quite peacefully – there are even reports of dolphins deliberately herding fish into nets – but the use of gill nets and the poisonous run-off from gold mining on the upper stretches of the Ayeyarwady has driven the dolphin onto the critically endangered list. The latest survey in 2003 estimated a population of just 37 dolphins.

Without urgent action, the Irrawaddy dolphin may be destined to go the same way as the Yangtze dolphin, which was declared functionally extinct in 2006. Keep your eyes peeled as you travel between Bhamo and Katha but be aware than any dolphins you see may well be the last of their species.

Blue Sea (dishes K1500) Probably the best Chinese restaurant in town, Blue Sea is one block back from the river, behind the market. Ordering can be a challenge as little English is spoken, but the food is excellent and there's Myanmar beer on tap.

Getting There & Away

AIR

The clunky aircraft of Myanma Airways are supposed to fly between Bhamo and Mandalay ($45, one hour) once a week on Sunday. However, everything about this flight is subject to change. Assuming the flight is running, the plane continues from Bhamo to Myitkyina ($25, 25 minutes).

BOAT

At the north end of town, near the Tat Twin Kyaung monastery, **Inland Water Transport** (IWT; ☎ 50117; Strand Rd) issues tickets for the slow government ferries to Katha and then Mandalay. The three-storey riverboats drift out of Bhamo at around 7am on Monday, Wednesday and Friday. Return boats leave Mandalay at around 6am on Monday, Thursday and Saturday.

The journey takes at least 1.5 days (2 days going upriver to Bhamo) so pick a spot on deck and settle down to watch the passage of life in the tiny villages along the riverbanks. The scenery along the upper reaches of the Ayeyarwady is particularly impressive, especially north of Shwegu, where the boat passes through a steep rocky gorge. Rare Irrawaddy dolphins (see above) are occasionally spotted in the murky waters and gibbons can sometimes be heard calling from the thick jungle.

Deck class tickets cost $9, which entitles you to a space on the lower deck. No chairs are provided and the deck is cold metal so wear some warm clothes and bring a blanket or a roll-up grass mat. For more comfort, go for cabin class: $54 gets a private two-bed cabin with a washbasin, fan and reading light, and keys to the superior toilets on the upper deck. There's a kitchen on board serving noodles, fried rice, soups and other meals, along with various soft and 'hard' drinks. An impromptu meal service in the form of villagers with food-laden canoes greets the boats at every stop.

Boats to Mandalay stop along the way at Katha (deck class $4), arriving sometime in the late afternoon.

Depending on how much time you have available, you may prefer to take the privately run 'fast ferry' (K18,000, around eight hours), a long, overloaded passenger ferry that seems to float just an inch above the waterline. From Bhamo, the fast boat leaves at around 8.30am from a dock just south of the clay-pot market on Strand Rd.

Small local boats navigate the heavily silted stretches of the Ayeyarwady north of Bhamo, but the ferries may not run if the water levels are too low. Heading to Myitkyina, you'll have to change boats – and possibly stop for the night – at Sinbo (see p308). The ferry from Bhamo to Sinbo leaves at around 10am from a jetty at the south end of Strand Rd; tickets cost K8000.

BUS

The only bus route open to foreigners is the daily bus service to Myitkyina (K10,000, six hours). The bus leaves Bhamo at 7am. Ask your guesthouse to make a booking the day before and prepare five photocopies of the visa and ID pages from your passport to hand out at the various checkpoints between Myitkyina and Bhamo.

Getting Around

Horse carts and rickshaws loiter near the market. Expect to pay K3000 to Bhamo Myo Haung (the old city) or K5000 to the airport.

KATHA

သကသ

☎ 074

A popular embarkation or disembarkation point for the IWT ferry, Katha is another rural town where life moves as slowly as the silt-laden waters of the Ayeyarwady. The town sees even fewer visitors than Myitkyina or Bhamo – what action there is in this sleepy settlement takes place along the riverbank when the ferries from Bhamo and Mandalay drift into town.

Sights

It might be hard to believe today, but Katha was once an important outpost of the British Empire. Eric Blair – better known by his pen name, George Orwell – was stationed here as a colonial police officer from 1926 to 1927, and he used the town as the setting for his novel *Burmese Days*. You can still see several buildings that featured in the book, including the police station, the jail, the hospital and the old **British Club**.

Strand Rd – the main road along the riverbank – is bookended by the **Myauk Kyaung** and **Maha La Tak Chaung** pagodas, two riverfront pagodas with friendly resident novices who are happy to show visitors around. For a close encounter with a working jumbo, head to the **elephant camp**, 6 miles west of Katha on the road to Naba. The best way to get here is by taxi from Katha (K30,000 return, or K8000 return by motorcycle taxi).

Sleeping & Eating

There are two guesthouses in town that accept foreigners, but don't expect too many luxuries. Breakfast is not included in the following rates.

Ayarwady Guest House (☎ 25140; Strand Rd; per person K5000) The better of the two, the Ayarwady is right in front of the boat jetty and the owners are a good source of local information. It's an old wooden rooming house and the rooms, which are clean, share a basic but clean toilet and shower.

Annawah Guest House (☎ 25146; Strand Rd; s/d K5000/8000) Simpler and plainer than the competition, this place has modest rooms with shared bathrooms. Skip the gloomy downstairs rooms for the better ones upstairs. The two front rooms have windows and views of the river.

Katha has a lively **night market** with several noodle stands. The best place for a formal meal is the beer-hall style **Sein Restaurant** (Chinese dishes K3000; ☉ 8am-8pm), three streets inland from the Ayarwady Guest House.

Getting There & Away

The bus service between Katha and Mandalay has been suspended so the only way out of Katha is by train (through Naba) or by boat.

BOAT

Opposite the main jetty, the **Inland Water Transport office** (IWT; ☎ 25057; Strand Rd) handles bookings for the slow government ferries to Bhamo and Mandalay. Ferries bound for Mandalay leave Katha at around 9.30pm on Monday, Wednesday and Friday. The journey takes at least 24 hours (28 hours coming upriver from Mandalay). Tickets to Mandalay cost $7/42 in deck/cabin class. Heading upriver to Bhamo, boats leave on Monday, Thursday and Saturday. You'll pay $4 in deck class, but this trip can take 12 hours or more, depending on the level of the river. See p311 for more on the IWT ferry service on this stretch of the Ayeyarwady.

A slightly faster route to Bhamo is the privately operated 'fast ferry' – an elongated freight and passenger boat that completes the journey in around eight hours; it leaves the Bhamo jetty at around 8.30am and tickets cost K18,000.

TRAIN

Trains between Mandalay and Myitkyina stop at Naba, approximately 16 miles west of Katha. A branch line goes from Naba to Katha, but it's usually more convenient to take a local bus between the two towns (K1000, one hour). Buses run to meet the arriving trains (ask at your guesthouse for the current schedule), or you can charter a taxi for K30,000. A rickshaw to the bus stand will cost around K500.

Government trains pass through Naba bound for Mandalay (ordinary/upper class $10/27, 19 hours) at around 4am, 6pm and 8pm, however, these times are approximate as the trains are invariably late. The privately owned *Mandalar Express* runs several times a week on the same route (ask at your guesthouse for the schedule).

THE FAR NORTH

The 'Ice Mountains' surrounding Putao are the easternmost spur of the mighty Himalayan mountain range, which stretches right across the top of Asia through Pakistan, India, Nepal, Tibet and Bhutan. The landscape here is the same glorious terrain found in the Indian state of Arunachal Pradesh and Bhutan – ridges of rocky peaks bursting through the snow-line and deep valleys carved by fast-flowing mountain rivers.

The small villages between the peaks are occupied by a diverse population of tribal people. The Kachin dominate Putao and other large settlements, but elsewhere, you may encounter smaller groups like the Lisu and Rawang. Farming is the main industry, though many tribal people make a living from gold panning, gem mining and hunting. Many of the tribes converted from animism and Buddhism to Christianity under the influence of missionaries from Europe and America.

The Putao highlands are one of the most pristine Himalayan environments in Asia and the region could become a major destination for ecotourism if it were ever made more accessible to foreigners. There seems to be no chance of this happening soon – at the time of writing, the only way to visit Putao was with a permit from the MTT in Yangon, arranged as part of an expensive tour (see right).

PUTAO

ပူတာအို

☎ 074 / pop 10,000 / elev 1320ft

The only settlement of any size in the Myanmar Himalaya, Putao is a quaint and picturesque township set in a wide valley. During the British colonial era the town was known as Fort Hertz, but it reverted to its Kachin name after independence. Putao was an outpost then and it remains an outpost today – road travel to Putao is only possible in the dry season and foreigners are only permitted to visit by air, on expensive organised tours from Mandalay or Yangon.

Most of the population are Kachin and Lisu, with small numbers of Bamar, Shan, Rawang and various other smaller tribal groups. The main industries in the area are

---

PUTAO & THE NORTH

Brett Melzer, the owner of Balloons over Bagan (p179), gave us this summary of the appeal of the far north:

'Compared to the rest of Myanmar, Putao seems like another country. The whole feel of the place is different – the weather, the landscapes, the vegetation and of course the people. The Lisu and Rawang are largely Christian, which breaks down some of the barriers between locals and visitors. If you come at Christmas you'll see tribal people celebrating in full traditional costume, accompanied by music with a definite country twang – a clear sign of missionary influence. The main sensation you get from a visit to Putao is of isolation and peace. You definitely feel cut off from the rest of the world.'

---

farming, gold-panning and gathering medicinal herbs. Added to this is hunting and trade in animal parts for Chinese traditional medicine, with predictable consequences for rare and endangered species. The mercury used by gold-panners to separate gold from sediment is also having a worrying effect on aquatic ecosystems downstream.

Information

The only way to reach Putao is to fly and permission to travel must be arranged at least two weeks in advance through the MTT in Yangon or with one of three approved private travel agencies (see below). In either case, some of the money will inevitably end up in government hands. The permit is normally issued as part of a package that includes return flights, transfers, accommodation in Putao and activities once you arrive. Rates for a standard four-day/three-night package (to coincide with flights) start from around $300 per day.

The best time to visit is from October to April, when daytime temperatures are quite pleasant and nights are cold but rarely freezing.

TRAVEL AGENCIES

The following travel agencies in Yangon can arrange trips to Putao:

Ayeyarwaddy Expeditions (☎ 01-652 809; www .easternsafaris.com; Suite 03-06, Sedona Hotel, 1 Kaba Aye Pagoda Rd) Run by the same team as the Malikha Lodge

NORTHERN MYANMAR

(see right) and Balloons over Bagan. At the Sedona Hotel (Map p93).

Myanmar Himalaya Trekking (Map p93; ☎ 01-227 978; www.myanmar-explore.com; Room 215, Summit Parkview hotel, 350 Ahlone Rd)

Snow Land Travels & Tours (☎ 01-572 588; snow land@mptmail.net.mm; 139/1 Thanthumar Rd, Thuwunna)

Sights

Putao is centred on the **Myoma Market**, which has the usual crush of stalls selling produce, household goods, wooden handicrafts and medicines made from local plants. Reflecting the success of Christian missionaries, there are numerous small **churches** in town and in the surrounding villages.

Just outside the main town, in Ho Kho village, the teak-panelled **Mahamuni Paya** has a chime bell made from the propeller of a wrecked WWII aircraft. South of the airstrip, the Lisu village of **Mulashidi** has a famous suspension bridge stretching over the crystal clear Mula River.

Activities

TREKKING

Although the mountains call out to trekkers, don't overlook the floodplain around Putao. Trails lead out from the town in all directions to villages of thatched stilt houses occupied by the Lisu and Rawang tribes. One popular short itinerary is the four-day circuit to the Wanglai Dam and Ziya Dam, which offers glorious views towards the mountains.

For more committed trekkers, there are many longer routes leading up towards the snowline. Expect empty trails, villages full of friendly locals who seem faintly bemused by the sight of foreigners, and numerous river crossings over wobbly bamboo suspension bridges. Keep an eye out for Himalayan black bears and red pandas while you walk.

The most popular longer trek is the 10-night, 11-day hike to the peak of 11,926ft **Mt Phon Kan Razi**, a stunning viewpoint over the Myanmar Himalaya and the Mishimi Hills of neighbouring Arunachal Pradesh. Another peak calling out to mountaineers is **Hkakabo Razi** (19,295ft), the highest peak in Myanmar. After two failed attempts, the peak was finally conquered in 1996 by Takeshi Ozaki of Japan and U Nama Johnson of Myanmar.

Climbing Hkakabo Razi is beyond the reach of most visitors, but it is possible to trek to **Tahaungdam**, the last village before

Hkakabo Razi, in around 35 days. On the way, you'll pass through **Hkakabo Razi National Park**, founded in 1998 after a long campaign by Alan Rabinowitz of the New York–based Wildlife Conservation Society (www.wcs .org). Rabinowitz also worked to create the **Hukuang Valley Tiger Reserve** (about 60 miles southwest of Putao), which, at 5220 square miles, is larger than all of India's tiger reserves put together.

If you visit Putao on a trekking expedition, everything you need will be provided, including food supplies, camping gear, porters and guides. For most treks, there are additional permit fees which must be paid when you make the original booking – it is very difficult to make arrangements for treks after you arrive. Expect to pay upwards of $1400 for the 10-night, 11-day trek to Mt Phon Kan Razi, plus the cost of flights.

RAFTING

The rivers slicing down from the Myanmar Himalaya provide some fantastic opportunities for white-water rafting. In conjunction with **Ultimate Descents** (www.ultimatedescents.com) the Malikha Lodge (see below) runs a variety of rafting trips on the Class 3 and Class 4 waters of the Nam Lang River and the even wilder Mayhka River. The best season for rafting is November to March (contact the lodge or see the Ultimate Descents website for more details).

OTHER ACTIVITIES

Ayeyarwaddy Expeditions (see p313) can arrange **elephant treks** and **mountain biking tours** as part of their Putao packages – contact them for details.

Sleeping & Eating

The travel agencies that run trips to Putao arrange meals and accommodation for guests, normally in camping sites or the government-owned Rest House (which you may wish to avoid). Assuming you have deep pockets, Ayeyarwaddy Expeditions offers accommodation in the stunning **Malikha Lodge** (☎ in Yangon 01-652 809; www.easternsafaris.com; per person $450 incl activities) in Putao. With an open lounge warmed by a real log fire and a private deck overlooking the Nam Lang River, the lodge is almost unmatched in Myanmar. Electricity comes from solar power, the luxurious bamboo bungalows have deep teak bathtubs, and staff can arrange treks, elephant safaris and rafting trips.

Getting There & Away

The only way to reach Putao is by air, and you must obtain permission to travel from the MTT in Yangon before you fly or you will be turned back at the airport. Most people leave all the arrangements to a private travel agent (see p313 for a list).

Now that Air Bagan flies from Yangon to Putao ($188 one way, four hours) via Mandalay (Mandalay to Putao $111, two hours) and Myitkyina (Myitkyina to Putao $52, 40 minutes) twice weekly, there's no need to gamble on the ancient aircraft of Myanma Airways. At the time of printing, flights ran on Tuesdays and Fridays but this could change so contact the airline for the latest schedule.

Western Myanmar

Visiting Myanmar's feisty Rakhaing (Arakan) State almost feels like entering a new country. Locals speak Rakhaing language – linked with Burmese at varying levels, depending on your viewpoint – the food comes with more chilli, and conversations quickly lead to 300-year-old events that bring out serious opinions. Traditionally the Rakhaing have looked more towards the sea than inland to the Bamar, and it still feels a bit that way – though they're unlikely to benefit much from the multimillion-dollar oil wells found just 37 miles offshore.

The 370-mile tall Rakhaing State borders Bangladesh and is often a lovely area, though travel is restricted to a few, relatively hard-to-reach spots. Many visitors limit a visit to a trip-ending cleansing in the turquoise waters of Ngapali Beach, Myanmar's top midrange beach resort, with snorkel trips and lots of free space to sprawl out on the sand. Few reach it by the gruelling bus ride over the Arakan Mountains from Pyay or Yangon (Rangoon), but zip here on a flight from Yangon. More rewarding is continuing – either by an eight-hour boat ride from nearby Taunggok or 30-minute flight – to Sittwe, where you can make boat trips to the ancient Rakhaing capital of Mrauk U, an archaeological site of 700 temples that remains embedded in thrilling-to-see, often-untouched village life.

Looming to the north is the bigger, elusive Chin State, a richly traditional area only visited with government permits. Some visitors get a taste of Chin life at Chin villages in Rakhaing State, reached on easily arranged boat trips from Mrauk U.

WESTERN MYANMAR

HIGHLIGHTS

- Bike between some of the 700 temples in timeless **Mrauk U** (p327), the last proud Rakhaing capital
- Savour the squid on the sand at **Ngapali Beach** (p319), Myanmar's top beach destination
- Boat to **Chin villages** (p333) outside Mrauk U, where tattoo-faced women lead you around by the arm
- Wander about one of Myanmar's most exotic scenes: Sittwe's morning **fish market** (p324)
- Skip the flight and try one of Myanmar's **roughest bus rides** (p322) – from Ngapali to Pyay

Chin Villages

★ Mrauk U

Fish ★ Market

Roughest Bus Rides ★

★ Ngapali Beach

- POPULATION: RAKHAING & CHIN STATES ABOUT 3.13 MILLION
- HIGHEST POINT: MT WEIK-ZAR (3681FT)

PEOPLE
Rakhaing

Much of Western Myanmar is home to the fascinating Rakhaing ethnic group, which is in itself a controversial topic – are the Rakhaing actually Bamar (Burmans) with Indian blood, Indians with Bamar characteristics or a separate race (as is claimed locally)?

Although the first inhabitants of the region were a dark-skinned Negrito tribe known as the Bilu, later migrants from the eastern Indian subcontinent developed the first Hindu-Buddhist kingdoms in Myanmar before the first Christian millennium. These kingdoms flourished before the invasion of the Tibeto-Burmans from the north and east in the 9th and 18th centuries. The current inhabitants of the state may thus be mixed descendants of all three groups: Bilu, Bengali and Bamar.

The Rakhaing proudly speak 'Arakan', a language they claim birthed Bamar (and it's certainly related).

Rohingya

The Myanmar government denies the existence of a Rohingya minority, a group of anywhere between 750,000 and 1.5 million Muslims separate from another local Muslim group called the 'Rahking Muslims'.

Many of the Rohingya – who speak a Bengali dialect – have been subjected to much Bamar persecution (including arbitrary taxes, forced labour, forced relocation, rape and murder, according to Amnesty International). The Rohingya must seek permission just to travel to the next village.

Between 1978 and the mid-'90s, half a million Rohingya people fled to Bangladesh, though many were repatriated to Myanmar following agreements between the two national governments. Similarly in the past few years, refugee camps in Thailand – where Rohingya had escaped, seeking exile in Thailand or Malaysia – were seeing deportations back to Myanmar.

CLIMATE

Those wishing to risk the heat or rains outside the high season (about October to March) will find that downpours or jellyfish will discourage much fun at Ngapali Beach. Sittwe and Mrauk U receive more rain than most of the country – about 200in per year. Sudden rainstorms during the monsoon (mid-May to mid-September) season are dangerous if travelling by boat to Mrauk U, or between Sittwe and Taunggok. Cyclones and tropical storms tend to occur just before and after the rainy season.

DANGERS & ANNOYANCES

Malaria precautions should be taken during monsoon season. Seven people were killed when their boat was hit by a chance storm in late 2004, while heading from Sittwe to Mrauk U (see p326).

Both Sittwe and Mrauk U saw many locals march during the nationwide protests in September 2007, but there were no shootings.

GETTING THERE & AROUND

Thandwe (Sandoway) is the major access point for visitors heading to Ngapali Beach. Most arrive by air from Yangon. Two long bus routes from Yangon go to Thandwe too, one via Pyay (Prome), and the other via Gwa in the south; both take 18 hours and may require vomit bags. See p322 for more details.

Sittwe is the necessary access point to Mrauk U. It's possible to reach it by plane from Thandwe or Yangon, or by boat from Taunggok (p323), four or so hours north of Thandwe.

Overland routes between Thandwe and Sittwe, or Taunggok and Pyay, are restricted unless you have a government permit.

RAKHAING OR ARAKAN?

The interchangeable terms Rakhaing and Arakan are frequently used and refer to the people, the state or the local language. Arakan, actually, is a version of Rakhaing muddled up by foreigners. As it harkens to the era when Mrauk U was a regional powerhouse, English-speaking locals often use the term with a particular pride.

Either term gets a bit touchy with the government, which officially uses Rakhaing but supposedly forbids study of the Rakhaing script. In 2007 the planned Mrauk U Princess Hotel in Mrauk U, apparently, had to change its name from Rakhaing Princess, per government orders.

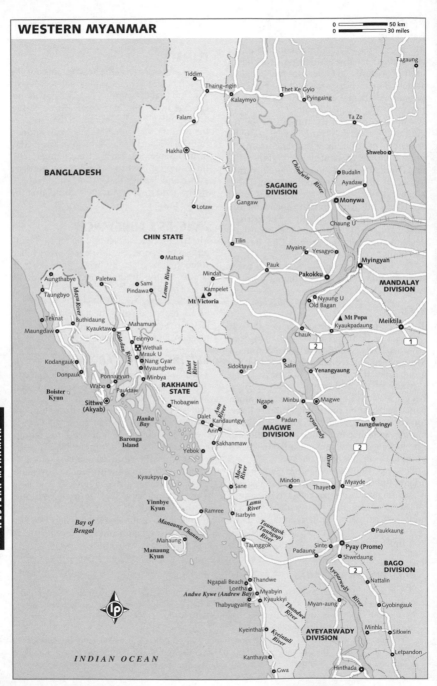

WESTERN MYANMAR

0 — 50 km
0 — 30 miles

BANGLADESH

Tagaung

Tiddim
Thaing-ngin
Kalaymyo
Thet Ke Gyio
Pyingaing
Falam
Ta Ze
Shwebo

Hakha

SAGAING
DIVISION

Chindwin River

Budalin
Ayadaw
Monywa
Chaung U

Lotaw
Gangaw

CHIN STATE

Tilin
Myaing
Yesagyo
Myingyan

Matupi
Pauk
Pakokku

Aungthabye
Paletwa
Mindat
Kampelet
Mt Victoria
MANDALAY
DIVISION

Sami
Pindawa

Taungbyo

Nyaung U
Old Bagan
Mt Popa
Kyaukpadaung
Meiktila

Teknat
Buthidaung
Mahamuni
Chauk

Maungdaw
Kyauktaw
Teinnyo
Wethali
Mrauk U
Nang Gyar
Myaungbwe
Sidoktaya
Salin
Yenangyaung

Kodangauk
Donpauk
Ponnagyun
Minbya
RAKHAING
STATE
Ngape
Minbu
Magwe

Boister
Kyun
Wabo
Pauktaw
Thobagwin
Padan
Taungdwingyi

Sittwe
(Akyab)
Hanka
Bay
Dalet
Kandauntgyi
MAGWE
DIVISION

Baronga
Island
Ann
Sakhanmaw

Yebok
Mindon
Thayet
Myayde

Kyaukpyu
Sane

Yinnbye
Kyun
Ramree
Isarbyin

Bay of
Bengal
Manaung Channel
Manaung
Taunggok
Padaung
Sinte
Pyay (Prome)
Paukkaung

Manaung
Kyun
Shwedaung
BAGO
DIVISION

Ngapali Beach
Thandwe
Nattalin

Lontha
Andwe Kywe (Andrew Bay)
Myabyin
Kyaukkyi
Thabyugyaing
Myan-aung
Gyobingauk

Kyeinthali
Kyeintali
River
AYEYARWADY
DIVISION
Minhla
Sitkwin

Kanthaya
Hinthada
Letpandon

INDIAN OCEAN
Gwa

WESTERN MYANMAR

SOUTHERN RAKHAING

This part of slender Rakhaing State boasts some of Myanmar's best beaches and, unsurprisingly, sees most of the visitors who do make it to the region. It's the only part of the state with bus connections, in addition to air.

NGAPALI BEACH

ငပလီ

☎ 43

It feels weird to think about 'getting away from it all' while in Myanmar, but Ngapali's lovely palm-lined beach serves as the country's beach hotspot for a deep-pocketed jet-set crew of (mostly) Europeans and rich locals. With lovely white sands on the Bay of Bengal's blue water, Ngapali – some say named by a wayward Italian reminiscing about his Napoli years ago – still holds onto its fishing-village roots. You'll see ox-cart tracks on the beach, as locals find the sand-ways a smoother ride than the rough one-lane road. And only a dozen bungalow-style resorts over 2 miles gives a lot of space on the beach.

During peak season (from November to March), hotels can be booked way ahead. Things get qu-i-et in rainy season (mid-May to mid-September).

Orientation

Ngapali Beach is a 2-mile stretch paralleled by (the unsignposted) Ngapali Rd, with hotels spread along its curve. Ngapali village is about 2 miles further north, located at the 'Thandwe junction', where a road goes 4.3 miles inland to Thandwe and 2 miles further north to the airport.

Services are limited. Bayview Beach Resort accepts Visa and MasterCard. A hotel is your best bet for help for travellers' info or money exchange.

Information

EMERGENCIES

Ngapali Dispensary (☎ Sandoway Resort 42233)
This is a 24-hour charity-built clinic across from Sandoway Resort with English-speaking staff.

INTERNET

Web connections go painstakingly slow, or not at all. Upscale hotels allow nonguests to use their internet (per 30 minutes/hour $3/6).
Ngapali Beach Hotel (per 15 mins/hr $1/4) Offers a good deal.

NGAPALI BEACH

INFORMATION	
Ngapali Dispensary	1 B4
Ngapali Beach Hotel	(see 8)
Telephone Centre	(see 12)
Wathon Myay	2 B3
SIGHTS & ACTIVITIES	
Ngapali Golf Course	3 A3
SLEEPING 🏠	
Amata Resort & Spa	4 B4
Bayview Beach Resort	5 B3
Laguna Lodge	6 B4
Lin Thar Oo Lodge	7 B4
Ngapali Beach Hotel	8 B4
Sandoway Resort	9 B4
Silver Beach Hotel	10 B3
EATING 🍴	
Amata Resort Restaurant	(see 4)
Laguna Lodge/Lili's Bar	(see 6)
Mingalabar	(see 5)
Moonlight	11 B4
Paradise Restaurant	12 B3
Smile Restaurant	13 B4
Two Brothers Restaurant	14 B4
TRANSPORT	
Air Mandalay/Caravan Tours	15 A2

TELEPHONE

Most hotels can place international calls ($6 per minute), or you can use the telephone centre outside the Silver Beach Hotel.

TOURIST INFORMATION

Wathon Myay (☎ 42544; www.wathonmyaytravel.com; ⏰ 8am-5pm) Ask here about boat trips, plus a few tours not offered by hotels, including to Zalon village ($40 for two people, including transport and guide) to see a crafts market and the undecomposed body of a monk who died in 1984.

Sights

FISHING VILLAGES

With a bicycle you can tour several of the fishing villages. South of the hotels, and easily reached barefoot by the beach, is the interesting fishing village of **Jade Taw**, where fish dry on bamboo mats across the beach.

Even further south is the bigger village of **Lontha** and an inlet of the same name, backed by a sweeping curve of mangrove and sand facing south. It's said that Rudyard Kipling wrote his first draft of *The Jungle Book* from a bungalow around here – and that the bay is sometimes called 'Kipling's Bay' (though don't expect locals to give a hoot about the guy).

On a bayside hill east of Lontha is a modest white **stupa**. It's worth seeing for its glorious panoramic views – and for the adventure to reach it. To get there, turn left at the town junction (near the market). The road parallels the boat-filled bay and quickly degenerates into a path too sandy to ride on; if on a bike, leave it with a local. About five minutes or so after passing a small bridge, you reach the hill steps to the stupa.

Activities

Four-hour **snorkelling trips** (per person incl boat, mask & snorkel K15,000), arranged by any hotel, usually go at 7am or 8am to catch the clearest water. Most trips take in a few spots around (private) 'Pearl Island' off the south end of the beach. The coral's not super – there are some towering cones to swim around – but there are plenty of bright red and blue fish to follow. Some bring along fishing rods to drop a line.

Boat guys troll the beach (tenderly). Ask one if you can go out for a few hours at dusk as the squid fishers turn on their lights to catch the next day's meal. One quote was K12,000 for two hours out.

Though few visitors tend to go, another possible boat trip is to the so-called **Pirate Beach**, a full-day trip to an isolated beach an hour south; trips should include a barbecue lunch there. It's about $30 to $40 per person. If you like, Wathon Myay Travel (see p319) can arrange 'treasure hunts' around the beach.

The government-run **Ngapali Golf Course** (green fee $10) has nine of 18 holes in use. Clubs are available. Upscale hotels offer golfing outings for about $30.

Sleeping

If you're travelling cheap, brace yourself for Ngapali. The one-time budget scene is gone, and potentially cheap, haggard guesthouses around the Thandwe junction are overpriced

or unlicensed for foreigners. The 'Top End' here covers rooms for $100 and over.

If you're travelling in high season – when nearly all Ngapali visitors come – note that many hotels are booked out (sometimes way in advance); call ahead.

All hotels here offer free airport transfer and breakfast.

MIDRANGE

These hotels keep their generators on from roughly 6pm to midnight, then an hour or so in the morning.

Lin Thar Oo Lodge (☎ 42333, Yangon 01-229 928; www.linntharoo-ngapali.com; r $20-45; 🐾) Those looking for private decks facing the sea for not too much have an easy answer: Lin Thar Oo's shady 270yd strip of 41 bungalows on the beach's north stretch. Best of the confusing array of price levels are the two $45 bungalows (with air-con and TV) or the six $30 fan-cooled bungalows – both come with hot water. The cheapest are in an unappealing motel-style strip away from the water. The beach here is a little rocky but there is plenty of room to use the hotel's innertubes.

our pick **Royal Beach Motel** (☎ 42411, Yangon 01-243 880; www.royalbeachngapali.com; r $25 & $40) Near the south end of the beach, the Royal is an excellent midranger that feels a bit more cosy and personable than the others. The complex's wood-floor rooms have lounge chairs on the deck, a bell 'doorbell' for when staff bring a bucket of hot water, and a great restaurant, where the free breakfast buffet's served. Unlike most hotels, it's set a bit back from the beach, with a forest of palms providing easy-breezy day-round shade. Higher-priced rooms face the water.

Pleasant View Resort (☎ 42511, Yangon 01-393 086; r $40 & $75; 🐾) At 12 rooms, 'resort' is a stretch, and it's situated *just* as the palms start to thin out at the beach's south end, but the higher-priced duplex bungalows get some high-end style (ie glass-ceiling bathrooms, satellite TV, lush woodwork) for a lot less. It was just opening when we came by: the $40 room was a bit thrown together, and the generator wasn't yet clicked-on all day, but the restaurant was already super.

Laguna Lodge (☎ 43122, Yangon 01-501 123; r $45-65) For a 'house on the beach' feel, the six-room Laguna goes rustic (with dark-wood, open-shuttered windows – meaning mosquitoes later on). By far the best is upstairs No 1 – with a sunken bed area facing the water. It's open from mid-October to May.

Ngapali Beach Hotel (☎ 42200, Yangon 01-211 888; www.ngapalihotel.com; r $55-95; ❌ 💻) This former government-run hotel (leased to private operators since 1999) has noticed the style of incoming resorts, and half tried to keep up, adding wood floors, lush gardens and some local décor – but it still comes off a bit stiff.

Silver Beach Hotel (☎ Yangon 01-381 898; sbh01@ goldenbrothers.com.mm; bungalows $75 & 100; ❌ 💻) At the beach's north end, Silver Beach is the cheapest way to go for 24-hour electricity and air-con. At first, things look appealing, but the awkward layouts have zero style for the price.

TOP END

These hotels are designed to compete as 'international resorts' with the best in Thailand. Debate for best remains between Amata and Sandoway. All have 24-hour generators for electricity.

Bayview Beach Resort (☎ 42299, Yangon 01-504 471; www.bayview-myanmar.com; garden-/sea-view bungalows $150/160; ❌ 💻 🛜) This luxurious German-Myanmar joint venture occupies a nice strip of beach, with a rare on-the-beach bar. The 33 swank bungalows have an inviting, basic layout – with peach-coloured bedspreads and four lounge chairs on the private deck. There are windsurfers, kayaks and catamarans to use.

Amata Resort & Spa (☎ 42177, Yangon 01-542 535; www.amataresort.com; r $120-140, cabana cottage/sea-view villa $180/420; ❌ 💻 🛜) Owned by a Yangon entrepreneur, this swish complex of gorgeous two-storey cabanas (the cottage is a steal compared to the sea-view villa cost) is reached by a long open-air hallway that looks like a giant inverted Viking ship (you have to see it) and pool sandwiched between the bar and beach. Ngapali's lone tennis court is next to the 'cybercafe'.

Sandoway Resort (☎ 42244, Yangon 01-294 612; www.sandowayresort.com; deluxe $180, garden-view/sea-view cottages $240/300, villas $300-340; ❌ 💻 🛜) Lushly shaded in palms, with evocative walkways leading past gardens and ponds (and a lizard or two), this Italian-Myanmar joint venture is one part villa, one part cottage 'resort'. Two-storey bungalows are lovely, with lofty ceilings and round-stone 'ottomans' before a sea-facing sofa. You get no TV, but there's a massive screening room with padded armchairs

for movies. A mezzanine library is above a bar, next to a giant pool. Supposedly wi-fi access will be available before you arrive too.

Aureum Palace welcomes some tour groups, but isn't recommended as it's owned by Tay Za (p21). Also, some tour groups check into the nice, privately run Amazing Ngapali Resort, but it's on a less appealing beach near the airport.

Eating & Drinking

Cheap, fresh and plentiful, Ngapali's seafood (particularly fresh squid dunked in spiced ginger-and-garlic sauce) ranks easily among Myanmar's best dining. The long lights that line the western horizon offshore at dusk are fishing boats using bulbs to attract squid.

MAIN ROAD RESTAURANTS

A dozen take-your-pick open-air restaurants cleverly cluster outside the gates of hotels and their higher-priced restaurants. These have practically identical menus (posted in English) and practically identical prices. A dish of crab, squid or barracuda runs about K2000 or K2500, barbecued tiger prawn is K3500 to K5000, and lobster is K15,000 and up.

A few good choices:

Mingalabar (Ngapali Rd) Outside Sandoway Resort

Moonlight (Ngapali Rd; ⏰ 7.30am-10pm Oct-Apr) Outside Amata

Paradise Restaurant (Ngapali Rd) Outside Bayview and Silver Beach

Seagull (Ngapali Rd) Near Royal Beach Hotel

Smile Restaurant (Ngapali Rd) Outside Ngapali Beach Hotel

Two Brothers Restaurant (Ngapali Rd) Outside Amata

HOTEL RESTAURANTS

All things said, food tends to be a bit more nicely prepared inside the hotels – though you pay more for it. A few stand-outs include the following:

Laguna Lodge/Lili's Bar A cute spot in the palm-shaded sand with a lazy dog or two, fake turtles and $2 *mojitos* or $4 plates of pasta.

ourpick Pleasant View Restaurant (near Pleasant View Resort; dishes K4000-K10,000) Set on a rocky islet at the beach's south end (you often have to wade through knee-deep surf to get to it), this stylish eatery serves very tasty seafood for less than most hotels; there are also K5000 margaritas.

Catch/Sunset Bar (Bayview Beach Resort; dishes $5-24) Though Bayview's actual restaurant is away from the beach, everyone eats from the Catch's menu at seaside Sunset Bar. It's good for fillets of barracuda, burgers and pizzas.

Amata Resort Restaurant (dishes $8-20; ☺ 7-10am, 11am-2pm & 6.30-10.30pm) This hotel restaurant overlooks the pool and beach. It serves pretty good pizzas ($8 to $10) and a real-deal beef burger ($8), plus pricier fare.

Getting There & Away
AIR
Thandwe airport is named for the town 4.3 miles inland, but is closer to Ngapali village, about 2 miles north of the 'Thandwe junction'. Hotel buses meet planes offering free transport to Ngapali Beach, reservations or not.

Presently **Air Bagan** (☎ 44299), 180yd north of 'Thandwe junction' and **Air Mandalay** (Caravan Tours; ☎ 44044), on the southeast corner of 'Thandwe junction', serve Yangon ($65 to $68) daily, with almost daily flights to Sittwe ($60 to $65). Direct flights with Nyaung U/ Bagan and Heho/Inle Lake were suspended in late 2007, but may resume. Connections are less frequent from May through September.

Government-run Myanma Airways (MA) also has some flights to Sittwe and Yangon.

BOAT
See Taunggok (opposite) for info on the boat service to Sittwe.

BUS
The 17- or 18-hour route between Thandwe and Yangon via Pyay (about 12 hours), run by **Aung Thit Sar** (☎ 65363) costs K15,500 for either destination. Tickets are sold by hotels, and the bus will pick you up there. The road – particularly between Taunggok and Pyay – has the reputation of being one of Myanmar's hardest, bounciest, most stomach-churning trips, not helped by aisle-stuffed bags of dried fish. Some buses hand out vomit bags. Bring warm clothes, as the ride over the Arakan Mountains at night gets cold. But, really, it's not that bad. On the cargo bus, we found seats one to three (on the front row) and five (second row, with no seat before it) particularly good to keep an eye on the road. Also, a hearty dose of garlic beforehand seems to help neutralise the fish odour.

There are no longer day buses from Taunggok to Pyay, but they may resume. Previously it was necessary to overnight in Taunggok to take one, which would save you an overnighter on the bus at least.

The other just-as-rough option to Yangon (K15,500; 17 to 18 hours), via Gwa (supposedly eight hours), was suspended at research time due to the travel restrictions in the Ayeyarwady Delta following Cyclone Nargis. Previously you could bus this way and stop off at Kanthaya for the full fare.

Getting Around
A pick-up from Thandwe to Ngapali Beach and on to Lontha village (K400, one hour) runs frequently. Catch one in either direction on the main road.

Bicycles can be rented from most hotels for about K2500 per day; and a few motorbikes are available for about K15,000.

THANDWE
သံတွဲ
☎ 43
Though your air- or bus-ticket stub will read 'Thandwe', this inland town plays a third fiddle to Ngapali in terms of travel appeal. Located about 4 miles inland to the northeast of Ngapali Beach, Thandwe is home to some 50,000 residents and nicely fills a hilly valley with its low-key streets.

Thandwe has been a key Rakhaing centre for many centuries. When the British stationed a garrison here around the turn of the 20th century, they twisted the name into Sandoway.

Sights
MARKET & AROUND
Housed in a former British jail in the centre of town, the **Thandwe market** is where a handful of guests from upscale beach resorts on day trips go seeking a 'real deal market'. It is kinda real deal actually. Vendors sell medicinal herbs, clothes, textiles, some souvenirs, hardware and free-market consumer goods.

Across the street on the north side is the **Suni Mosque**, Thandwe's largest of five.

HILL PAGODAS
Three golden (and rhyming) stupas stand on hilltops at four points around Thandwe. None are spectacular in themselves, but each offers excellent viewpoints of the town's tin roofs peeking out of a sea of palms and hills.

The tallest, **Nandaw Paya**, a mile west of the market, was supposedly erected in AD 761 by

King Minbra to enshrine a piece of a rib of the Buddha. The long shrine facing the stupa to the south houses some nice wood-carving reliefs of Buddha's life.

Just east of town, right across a small river about half a mile from the market, the **Sandaw Paya** was supposedly built in AD 784 by Rakhaing King Minyokin to house a Buddha hair, and was rebuilt by the Burmese in 1876.

Across the river north (past the bus station and east on a stone road about 1.3 miles from the market), the **Andaw Paya** is the lowest, but has revealing looks at the river's fork from the hills east. It claims to house a Buddha molar relic and dates from AD 763.

Sleeping & Eating

Thandwe has no licensed places to stay. You can find some noodles around the market, and a couple of rice-'n'-curry restaurants on side streets a block north and south.

Getting There & Away

The pick-up truck from Ngapali runs every 30 minutes at least (K400; one hour). It's possible to get a pick-up to Taunggok (four or five hours) several times daily from a small station a couple of hundred yards north of the bus station (across the river).

KANTHAYA

ကမ်းသာယာ

☎ 43

Waiting in the wings as a potential new beach town, this small Rakhaing coastal town, stranded on bad roads 80 miles south of Thandwe and 16 miles north of Gwa, has a ways to go. The lone licensed-for-foreigners military-run guesthouse closed up shop – and it's a good thing (we've heard tales of extremely decrepit conditions). It's about five to six hours south of Thandwe – but be sure you have a place you can stay before jumping off the bus to Yangon.

TAUNGGOK

တောင်ကုတ်

☎ 43

This surprisingly hopping lil' town 50 miles or so north of Thandwe is a stopping-off point for travellers between Pyay and Thandwe by bus, or for catching a boat to Sittwe.

The **Royal Guest House** (☎ 61088; r K6000) supposedly lets foreigners stay. It's a couple of blocks north of the bus station.

Malikha Express (☎ 60127) sends fast boats to Sittwe ($40, eight hours) at 7am on Monday, Wednesday and Saturday.

The Yangon-bound bus via Pyay comes through from Thandwe around 4pm or 5pm. Morning buses to Pyay were cancelled when fuel prices rose in 2007; they may resume at some point.

NORTHERN RAKHAING

This area, brushing against the Bangladesh border, can be reached only by air or boat.

SITTWE

စစ်တွေ

☎ 43 / pop 200,000

Scrappy and seemingly several time zones away from anywhere, once-booming Sittwe (pronounced 'Sit-TWAY' by Burmese, 'Sigh-TWAY' by Rakhaing) is still a source of pride for its mix of locals – Rakhaing, Muslims, Indian Hindus, Burmese – if not the foreign travellers who skedaddle to Mrauk U as soon as possible. Those willing to look will find a lot to like.

The town sits in an incredible spot – where the wide tidal Kaladan River mouth kisses the big fat Bay of Bengal. There's good dusk sunset viewing, plus a wild fish market that's one of Myanmar's more fascinating, and you're likely to be swarmed by chatty monks at one of the Buddhist museums in town.

Sittwe's economy and legend underwent a boom when the British moved the capital here from Mrauk U in the early 19th century. Incoming wealth from cargo trade with Calcutta fuelled the construction of some fine colonial mansions, but much of the grace was lost under heavy WWII raids.

In September 2007, less-reported protests stormed the streets of Sittwe, with some 2000 locals (including some Muslims) surrounding City Hall. No shots were fired.

Ask around about the colourful nicknames many locals get – we've heard of names like 'Destroy the Drum', 'King of the Hell' (sic) and 'Noodle-Eater'.

Orientation & Information

Most of Sittwe's action runs along the almost north-south Main Rd, which parallels the Kaladan River. The airport is about 1.5

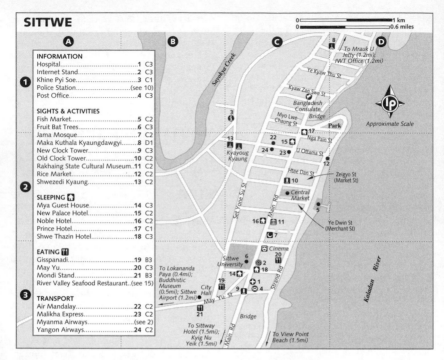

SITTWE

miles southwest of the centre; the main boat jetty is about 2 miles north.

The main hospital and post office are near the new clock tower, south of the centre (where you'll find the old steel clock tower, erected by the Dutch in the 18th century).

A pudgy local (often called 'the fat man' by locals) *will* meet you however you arrive and try to get commissions on whatever you do (eg boats to Mrauk U, hotels in Sittwe). He's harmless, but pesky enough to annoy some travellers.

Outside the generator-run midrange hotels, electricity runs generally from 6pm to 11pm only. In the rainy season, clouds can sometimes cut telephone communication.

EMERGENCIES

Hospital (☎ 21511, 21522; Main Rd) In case of emergency, Sittwe's hospital offers far better services than Mrauk U's does.

INTERNET ACCESS

Internet stand (Main Rd; per 30 min K2500; ☒ 7.30am-9pm) In a central spot.

TRAVEL AGENCIES

Khine Pyi Soe (☎ 23159; aungmrakyaw@mail4u.com .mm; 25 Mill Rd) This local out-of-the-way travel agency, housed in the home of a former karate teacher, can arrange boats to Mrauk U (K140,000 return with three nights waiting) and Baronga Island as a day trip from Sittwe (about K60,000).

Sights
WATERFRONT

Sittwe's greatest attraction is the morning **fish market**, which kicks off in the central market around 6am and is worth popping by before your boat or plane leaves. From the main road, follow the road two blocks north of the Rakhaing State Cultural Museum, straight past vegetable stands to the fish area, where sting rays and de-gutted eels and drying sharks make quite a scene.

While you're in the area, a few blocks north is the **rice market**, with tiny lanes between the water and Strand Rd filled with simple wood homes hawking brown and sticky rice – some bound for Bangladesh.

The riverside Strand Rd leads about 1.3 miles south to a smashing location called the

WESTERN MYANMAR

View Point (camera/video fee K1000/2000), where you can eat or sip on a beer or fresh coconut as the sun sets over the Bay of Bengal. Just west, in front of a closed naval base, is a grey-brown sand **beach** that has a tricky undertow, where a few swimmers lose their lives each year.

RAKHAING STATE CULTURAL MUSEUM

The government-run **Rakhaing State Cultural Museum** (Main Rd; admission $2; ☼ 10am-4pm Tue-Sat) features two floors of Rakhaing cultural goodies that benefit from just enough English subtitles. On the ground floor, diagrams, artefacts and signs in English detail Rakhaing's origins around 3000 BC and four key periods (Dhanyawadi, Vesali, Lemro and Mrauk U), compelete with useful renderings and models.

Upstairs are displays on local customs (eg models showing off some of the 64 Mrauk U royal hairstyles), the 'auspicious comb' used in weddings, and drawings illustrating key moves you may need if you should try traditional Rakhaing wrestling.

BUDDHIST SITES

Sittwe monk U Bhaddanta Wannita spent 49 years collecting old coins and buddha images from monasteries to protect them from thieves, and their whereabouts has resulted in some tug-of-war between his former monastery and a government-opened museum.

His former monastery, the **Maka Kuthala Kyaungdawgyi** (Large Monastery of Great Merit; Main Rd; admission free), is housed in (of all things) a grand, century-old British colonial mansion north of the centre. The modest museum upstairs contains cases of 'Union of Burma' notes, buddhas and votives and coins from the Mrauk U and other ancient periods, plus many bone relics of head monks, kept in small tins. Plenty of friendly English-speaking monks will follow you around. It's a great time.

A less satisfying collection, forcibly borrowed from U Bhaddanta Wannita, as many locals tell it, is at the government-run **Buddhistic Museum** (Baw Dhi St; admission $5). The big pagoda between this museum and the centre is the **Lokananda Paya**, put up by General Than Shwe himself in 1997. Just north is a small ordination hall, which houses the **Sachamuni image**, a 5ft bronze buddha pock-marked with mini-buddhas. Apparently the image dates from 24 BC and was found by Mrauk U fishers in recent years. It was moved from Mrauk U

by the government in 1997. Rakhaing State Day is staged here, see below.

Some locals are more keen about **Shwezedi Kyaung**, a monastery in a brilliant English-era building on a backstreet. The 2007 protests began daily from under the bodhi tree outside its gates.

OTHER SIGHTS

Hundreds of **fruit bats** slumber during the day in the trees around Sittwe University, then head off at dusk. Next to the Rakhaing State Cultural Museum, the **Jama Mosque** (1859) is one of Sittwe's most impressive buildings.

Festivals & Events

The **Rakhaing State Day** (a Saturday in mid-December) is staged at Lokananda Paya, with traditional wrestling, bamboo pole climbing and tug-of-war – it's well worth delaying a departure to see it. Locals may tell you the real Rakhaing day is December 31, 'when Mrauk U fell – it's more a day to grieve'.

Sleeping

All hotels offer free breakfast.

BUDGET

The three shoestring options could use a little more love. Electricity runs from about 6pm to 11pm.

Prince Hotel (☎ 24075, Yangon 09-501-9114; www.mraukuprincehotel.com; 27 Main Rd; s/d $6/12) A cute courtyard, English-speaking staff and a bit of travellers' advice make up a bit for the rather dingy rooms (small, with fan and mosquito net and coil) and shared bathrooms you'll want to wear sandals in. Check a few rooms before choosing – some are better than others. There's also a lone 'family room' with private bath and air-con from 7pm to 11pm for about $20.

Mya Guest House (☎ 22358; Bowdhi Rd; r $10) A bit off Main Rd, this curious complex is made from a century-old, blue-and-red mansion once home to a British lawyer who put the first Mercedes on Sittwe streets. The main building is dingy and now houses students, but a few new private 'bungalows' with simple tiled rooms, fan and private bath nearby make OK budget choices.

New Palace Hotel (☎ 21996; 5 Main Rd; s/d $10/16) Is everything else full? Not much is new about the Palace but the sign and a tiny TV in the room. Rooms are rundown and a bit depressing.

MIDRANGE

These far more comfy options include round-the-clock generators and air-con.

The seaside Sittway Hotel is government run and not recommended.

our pick Noble Hotel (☎ 23558; 45 Main Rd; noble@myanmar.com.mm; s/d $25/35; 🔀) Across from the Rakhaing State Cultural Museum, the modern Noble has small but clean carpeted rooms with a desk, a teapot and satellite TV with a few movie channels. Nothing fancy, but in all the best deal for recovering from the boat ride back from Mrauk U.

Shwe Thazin Hotel (☎ 23579; stz@myanmar.com.mm; 250 Main Rd; s/d $30/35; 🔀) A bit more polished than Noble, the Shwe Thazin is proud of a 5th-floor restaurant, and (higher up) lookout deck, good for glimpses of those fruit bats at dusk. Rooms are clean and modern, if not overly stylish.

Eating

our pick Mondi stand (bowl K200; 🕑 6am-6pm) *Mondi* is the Rakhaing-style fish noodle soup downed by locals for breakfast. It's similar to *mohinga* but comes with chillies not peanuts, and often eel not fish. Sittwe's best – many claim – is served at the small *mondi* stand facing the city hall. If you're feeling frisky ask for the ultra spicy *abu shabu*. Beware: students pour in for lunch.

Gisspanadi (dishes K1000-2500; 🕑 6am-10pm) This friendly family Chinese/Burmese restaurant – along a strip of eateries, just east of city hall – is a standard spot, busy with local men sitting over tables of fried fish fingers (better than they sound), grilled prawns and Myanmar beer bottles.

River Valley Seafood Restaurant (5 Main Rd; set meals K4500-7000; 🕑 7am-10.30pm) Popular with many foreigner visitors, the River Valley has ample open-air space, wall murals and African safari photos (!?); the style was 'inspired by my dreams', said the jovial ponytailed and moustached owner. Plenty of seafood, plus a handful of spicy Rakhaing-style dishes. Some waiters wear bowties.

There are also a few waterfront places worth considering:

Kyig Nu Yeik (Main Rd & Seaside) Tables on the sand, 1.5 miles south from the new cloth tower; good for beer and K800 noodles as the sun sets.

May Yu (Strand Rd) Seafood spot done up like a Caribbean shack, with a blue-and-green wood house and plank-board deck facing water.

View Point (see p325) Simple restaurant on Bay of Bengal, 1.5 miles south of the centre via Strand Rd.

Getting There & Away

Overland routes between Sittwe and Yangon (as well as to Mrauk U) are presently closed to foreigners.

AIR

Before leaving Sittwe, you must reconfirm your booking – your hotel should be able to help. Sittwe's airport is about 1.5 miles west of the centre. Taxis (K2500 to K3000) and trishaws (K1500) await flights.

In peak season (between October and April), daily flights go to and from Yangon ($85 to $88) and (at research time) there were flights six days a week to and from Thandwe ($60 to $65).

See map locations for the offices of **Air Mandalay** (☎ 21638; 🕑 9am-5pm) and **Yangon Airways** (☎ 24102; 🕑 9am-5pm), both of whom help with Air Bagan tickets. The government-run Myanma Airways has an office off the Main Rd.

BOAT
To Mrauk U

The only way to/from Mrauk U for foreigners at present is by boat. There are a couple of speeds to go by.

Most visitors used to go straight from the airport to the jetty to take a 'private boat', a simple tarp-covered boat with flat deck, a few plastic chairs and often no WC. The government suspended afternoon departures in early 2008, due to the potential danger of after-dark travels (in 2004, five tourists were killed when a boat capsized during a sudden storm). This means you'll likely have to overnight in Sittwe before taking a morning boat to Mrauk U.

You will have offers for such a 'private boat' before you can get out of the airport. Generally a boat can fit four to six easily and runs $100 to $120 return, with the driver waiting two or three nights. Ask ahead about the cost if you decide to stay another day in Mrauk U, which often happens.

The two-level ferry to Mrauk U ($4, six to seven hours) is run by the government's Inland Water Transport (IWT), which has an office 90yd west of the Mrauk U jetty, though there's no need to buy tickets in advance. Following petrol price hikes, IWT cut back its service to once weekly (leaving Sittwe at 7am on Tuesday, leaving Mrauk U on Wednesday). At some point over this book's life, it's likely the ferries will resume their past schedule, departing Sittwe Tuesday, Thursday and Saturday, and returning from Mrauk U on Wednesday, Friday and Sunday. Deck chairs are available for rent (K500) and there's a stall serving basic food.

Suspended at research time, the eight-seater 'fast boat' of **Shwe Pyi Ohe** (☎ 24141) previously offered zippy 90-minute rides to Mrauk U for a whopping $300 or so, and it may resume again.

To Taunggok

Malikha Express (☎ 24248; Main Rd; ☺ 9am-5pm) sells tickets for the 130-person fast boat (enclosed with windows) for Taunggok ($40, eight hours), which departs at 7am on Monday, Thursday and Saturday. The boat stops in the island port town of Kyaukpyu for 30 or 40 minutes for lunch. See Taunggok (p323) for schedule times to Sittwe.

AROUND SITTWE

With a day to spare, one of the two most appealing day trips is to the weaving village **Wabo**, reached by a 90-minute boat ride from Sittwe, where you can see where Rakhaing-style *longyi* are made. Khine Pyi Soe (p324) can arrange the trip for K50,000, with the option of an English-speaking guide for $20. Bring food for lunch.

Another tempting option is a ride over to **Baronga Island**, to see a fishing village on the hilly island visible across the wide Kaladan River. Typically a boat for the day is about K60,000 or more, ask at Khine Pyi Soe.

MRAUK U
မြောက်ဦး
☎ 043

'Little Bagan?' Not by a long shot. Myanmar's second-most-famous archaeological site, Mrauk U (pronounced 'mraw-oo') – reached by a flight or long boat ride to Sittwe, then a long 40-mile boat ride up the Kaladan River – is an ancient city of 700 or so temples that remains very much alive. The temples – previously mistaken for forts due to thick bunker-style walls built against the fierce Rakhaing winds – are smaller and younger than Bagan's. Being here is as much about seeing temples in the gorgeous scenery of

rounded hillocks as about mingling with the goat shepherds and vegetable farmers who remain very much a part of the temple areas (unlike Bagan). It's a Myanmar highlight yet, in a good year, only about 3500 to 4000 foreign visitors come.

Much daily activity seems to be taken up with water trips. Instead of the usual clay pots or rectangular oil cans, Mrauk U residents carry shiny aluminium water pots (imported from Bangladesh) on their hips.

For visitors coming on pre-arranged private boats, it's necessary to let the driver know how much time you'll need in Mrauk U (though it can often be changed, with an extra charge). Most visitors come for two or three full days. Consider if you'll want to take a day trip to the Chin villages – and how much you want to explore on your own after you've seen the greatest hits.

History

Mrauk U served as the last great Rakhaing capital for 354 years from 1430 to 1784. In its heyday, it served as a free port trading with the Middle East, Asia, Holland, Portugal and Spain. A Dutch bloke who visited in the 16th century called it one of the richest cities in Asia, comparable to London or Amsterdam. Little remains of the European quarter Daingri Kan, just across from the jetty southwest of town.

The Mrauk U dynasty was much feared by the peoples of the Indian subcontinent and central Myanmar. Mrauk U kings even hired some Japanese samurai as bodyguards against assassination. At Mrauk U's peak, King Minbin (1531–53) created a naval fleet of some 10,000 war boats that dominated the Bay of Bengal and Gulf of Martaban. Many of Mrauk U's finest temples (Shitthaung, Dukkanthein, Laymyetnha and Shwetaung) were built during his reign.

In the late 18th century, the Konbaung dynasty asserted its power over the region and Mrauk U was integrated into the Bamar kingdoms centred around Mandalay.

After the First Anglo-Burmese War of 1824–26, the British Raj annexed Rakhaing and set up its administrative headquarters in Sittwe, thus turning Mrauk U into a political backwater virtually overnight.

During the September 2007 protests many locals marched in the centre (by the market). We heard that numbers from '3000' to an exaggerated '20,000' marched over four days.

WESTERN MYANMAR

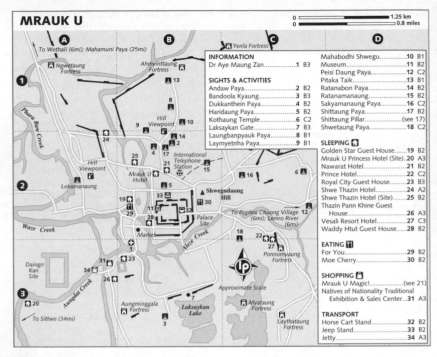

MRAUK U

INFORMATION		
Dr Aye Maung Zan	1	B3

SIGHTS & ACTIVITIES		
Andaw Paya	2	B2
Bandoola Kyaung	3	B3
Dukkanthein Paya	4	B2
Haridaung Paya	5	B2
Kothaung Temple	6	C2
Laksaykan Gate	7	B3
Laungbanpyauk Paya	8	B1
Laymyetnha Paya	9	B1

Mahabodhi Shwegu	10	B1
Museum	11	B2
Peisi Daung Paya	12	C2
Pitaka Taik	13	B1
Ratanabon Paya	14	B2
Ratanamanaung	15	B2
Sakyamanaung Paya	16	C2
Shittaung Paya	17	B2
Shittaung Pillar	(see 17)	
Shwetaung Paya	18	C2

SLEEPING		
Golden Star Guest House	19	B2
Mrauk U Princess Hotel (Site)	20	A3
Nawarat Hotel	21	B2
Prince Hotel	22	C2
Royal City Guest House	23	B3
Shwe Thazin Hotel	24	A2
Shwe Thazin Hotel (Site)	25	B2
Thazin Pann Khine Guest House	26	A3
Vesali Resort Hotel	27	C3
Waddy Htut Guest House	28	B2

EATING		
For You	29	B2
Moe Cherry	30	B2

SHOPPING		
Mrauk U Magic!	(see 21)	
Natives of Nationality Traditional Exhibition & Sales Center	31	A3

TRANSPORT		
Horse Cart Stand	32	B2
Jeep Stand	33	B2
Jetty	34	A3

Orientation

The original site covers 45 sq km, though the town proper and bulk of the temples to visit cover a 7-sq-km area. The boat jetty is about half a mile southwest of the central market; just east is the central Palace Site.

Information

There are a couple of useful books on Rakhaing history and Mrauk U, but at research time you needed to buy them beforehand in Yangon (try bookshops on Bogyoke Aung San or Bagan Bookshop, p89).

Myar Aung's stylish publication *Famous Monuments of Mrauk-U* (2007) is the newest and most portable. Older books include Tun Shwe Khine's artful *A Guide to Mrauk U* (1993) and U Shwe Zan's more detailed *The Golden Mrauk U: An Ancient Capital of Rakhine* (1997).

In case of an emergency, the hospital at Sittwe (p324) is your best bet. For minor bruises and stomach upsets, friendly **Dr Aye Maung Zan** (☎ 24200, ext 50032; Main Rd), south of the market, speaks English. There is no internet connection in Mrauk U.

The town of around 250 subscribers share five telephone lines, so all local numbers add on an extension; access operates only 8am to 8pm. For international calls, the only choice is the government-run Mrauk U Hotel.

Sights

The Mrauk U area is home to about 700 temples, some unexcavated. With a bike, a packed lunch and the heart of exploration, you could take any path for DIY adventures. Climb random hills and who knows what you'll find.

PALACE SITE & AROUND

Just east of the main strip of Mrauk U village, the one-time royal palace of Mrauk U now is mostly crumbling walls (though the outer walls still stand 11.5ft high). It's a good place to get your bearings though. Haridaung is just north, golden Shwetaung on the hill to the southeast.

According to the legend, King Minbun's astrologers advised a move here in 1429 after the palace at Launggret had been invaded by 'poisonous snakes and evil birds'. His representatives witnessed some strange things at

WESTERN MYANMAR

this spot – an old guy playing a flute pointed to a cat-chasing rat and then a snake-biting frog – apparently suggesting its soil as being worthy of a king. Construction began in 1430 (though some sources say it didn't start until 1553); the palace layout is roughly based on the Mahamuni Paya (p333) to the north.

Just inside the palace's western walls is the government-run Department of Archaeology's **museum** (admission $5; 9am-4pm Mon-Fri). The fee keeps some visitors away; if you go, you can see buddha images, inscribed stone slabs (a 15th-century one features ancient Arabic writing), cannons, Wethali-era coins and a helpful model of the Mrauk U site. Old photos on the walls include a before-restoration shot of Ratanabon's (p330) crack. Items are signed in English. If you come on a weekend, ask next door for the key.

Off the road just north of the Palace walls, steps lead up to hilltop **Haridaung Paya** (built around 1750), a small white paya with particularly good westward views.

NORTH GROUP

For many, this area is the pick of the litter for Mrauk U, with all sites within walking distance. There are a couple of food stalls and a gift shop below Shittaung.

Shittaung Paya

The usual starting point is at Mrauk U's most complex temple, the Shittaung (Sittaung in Burmese), where the $5 zone fee and K3000 'light fee' is collected (see boxed text, right). King Minbin, the most powerful of Rakhaing's kings, built it in 1535. It's a frenzy of stupas of various sizes; some 26 surround a central stupa. Shittaung means 'Shrine of the 80,000 Images', a reference to the number of holy images inside (the actual tally is more like 84,000, though some have since been stolen). Thick walls, with windows and nooks, surround the two-tiered structure.

Outside the southwest entrance stairway, and inside a locked mint-green building, is the much-studied **Shittaung Pillar**, a 10ft sandstone obelisk brought here from Wethali by King Minbin. Considered the 'oldest history book in Myanmar' (by the Rakhaing at least), three of the obelisk's four sides are inscribed in faded Sanskrit. The east-facing side likely dates from the end of the 5th century. The western face displays a list dating from the 8th century outlining

GOVERNMENT FEES

All foreign visitors to Mrauk U are asked to pay a one-time visit fee of $5, even if you're not planning to visit any temples. We're told the money goes to the government, not upkeep of the site. The palace site museum (left) charges an additional $5 for entry, and sometimes foreigners are asked to pay a K3000 'donation fee' for lighting at temples – this happens at the Shittaung Paya (left).

Rakhaing kings from 638 BC to AD 729 (King Anandacandra).

Lying on its back next to the pillar is a cracked, 12ft-long **sandstone slab** featuring an engraved lotus flower (a Buddhist motif) growing from a wavy line of water (Brahman motif) and touching an intricately engraved *dhammachakka* (Wheel of the Law).

Inside the temple's **prayer hall** you'll see several doors ahead. Two lead to passageways that encircle the main buddha image in the cave hall (which is seen straight ahead).

The far left (southwest) doorway leads to the **outer chamber**, a 310ft passageway with sandstone slabs cut into six tiers. Over 1000 sculptures (perhaps over-illuminated) show a lot of detail of Rakhaing customs (eg traditionally dressed dancers, boxers and acrobats), beasts of burden, and hundreds of Jataka (scenes from Buddha's past 550 lives). At each corner are bigger figures, including the maker King Minbin and his queens at the southwest corner. The passage opens in the front, where you can step out for views.

Next to the outer chamber entry is a coiling **inner chamber** leading past dozens of buddha images in niches, passing a Buddha footprint where – it's said – Buddha walked during his post-enlightenment. Once you get to the dead end, double back to the hall, and see if you can feel the passageway becoming cooler. Some claim it does, symbolising the 'cooling effect' of Buddhist teachings.

Along the **outer walls**, several reliefs can be seen engraved (some are hard to reach); a few on the south side are rather pornographic.

Andaw Paya

Immediately northeast of Shittaung stands a smaller, eight-sided monument with a

---

'ONLY GUARDIAN OF BUDDHA WISDOM'

Mrauk U is home to a couple of harmless English-speaking characters that will find you. Let them. One, the 'Literature Man' (aka 'Mr Radio'), is a shaved-headed ex-teacher who is fond of talking to foreigners about books read or things heard on the radio he carries around. An interesting partner at tea-time.

Another is a deeply sun-tanned, middle-aged man, who always seems to find you around Mrauk U, often keeping his distance but mumbling things in English. I've seen him – or rather he's quickly found me – every time I've been in Mrauk U. For this edition, I managed a rather sprawling, unruly sit-down 'interview' (many long tangents about ancient hermits, globalisation and German commanders have been edited out).

What's your name? Oh, so many! The town calls me 'mad man', but only because their slow minds cannot keep up with my thoughts. I am Simple Human Being. I am Only Guardian of Buddha Wisdom.

What do you think of Mrauk U? It's like a shanty. It's deserted. I'm so sorry.

What's your dream for it? No freedom like East Timor! [Laughs] My dream? Golden suns and full moons and one million gold pagodas.

Are you married? No. Don't want to be. A woman wouldn't let me wander around.

Robert Reid

---

similar linear layout: rectangular prayer hall to the east, multispired sanctuary to the west. Sixteen *zedi* (stupas) are aligned in a square-cornered U-shape around the southern, northern and western platforms. As at Shittaung, small windows admit light and ventilation, but here the fluorescent glare is dimmer. Two concentric passageways are lined with buddha niches; in the centre of the shrine, an eight-sided pillar supports the roof.

The original construction of the shrine is ascribed to King Minhlaraza in 1521. King Minrazagyi then rebuilt Andaw in 1596 to enshrine a piece of the tooth relic supposedly brought from Sri Lanka by King Minbin in the early 16th century.

Ratanabon Paya

This massive stupa (sometimes called Yadanapon), just north of Andaw Paya, is ringed by 24 smaller stupas. It was apparently built by Queen Shin Htway in 1612. During WWII a bomb nailed it, but it had already been picked at by treasure hunters attracted by the name, which means 'accumulation of treasure'. Recent renovations repaired the enormous bomb-made crack and reinserted the tall *chattra* (spire).

Dukkanthein Paya

Across the road to the west of Shittaung, the Dukkanthein (the name loosely means 'ordination hall that spiritually reinforces the

town') smacks of a bunker (with stupas). Wide stone steps lead up the south and east side; take the latter to reach the entrance. Many consider this to be Mrauk U's most interesting pagoda.

Built by King Minphalaung in 1571, Dukkanthein's interior features spiralling cloisters lined with images of buddhas and common people (eg landlords, governors, officials and their spouses) sporting all of **Mrauk U's 64 traditional hairstyles**. The passageway nearly encircles the centre three times before reaching the sun-drenched buddha image, now lit by Christmas-style lights too.

The **Laymyetnha Paya**, 90yd north, looks a bit like a squashed-up version of the Dukkanthein, but was actually built 140 years earlier.

North of Ratanabon

Around the hillock northeast of the Ratanabon are a few worthy sites in an even quieter area, with fewer villagers (and visitors). The squat hilltop **Mahabodhi Shwegu** (built in 1448) is above to the right (past two gold hilltop *zedi* and a covered water well below). Its narrow passageway leads to a 6ft central buddha and four buddhas in niches. The best are the 280 Jataka scenes, acrobats, worshippers, and animal love scenes (!) engraved onto either side of the arched entry walls.

Back on the road, and 100yd north, is the octagonal **Laungbanpyauk Paya**, a slightly leaning *zedi* built by King Minkhaungraza in 1525.

Some locals call it the 'Plate Pagoda', as its outer wall is still adorned with glazed platelike tiles in bright colours.

At the end of the road, 180yd north, the compact, highly ornate **Pitaka Taik** is the last remaining of the 48 libraries that were in Mrauk U. Now dominated by a blue-and-maroon shelter, it was built in 1591 by King Minphalaung as a repository for the Tripitaka (Three Baskets; the Buddhist canon), which was received from Sri Lanka in the 1640s. It's wee – only 13ft long and 9ft high. The old city walls are just beyond.

EAST GROUP
Starting east of the palace walls, this area stretches a mile or so east.

Sakyamanaung Paya
Roughly half a mile northeast of the palace walls, and behind Shwegudaung hill, this graceful *zedi* was erected in 1629 by King Thirithudhammaraza. At this later stage, stupas were built more vertically and ornately than before (an absorption of Bamar and Shan styles).

The lower half of the well-preserved 280ft *zedi* features a multitiered octagonal shape as at Laungbanpyauk Paya, but beyond this the bells revert to a layered circular shape mounted by a decorative *hti* (umbrellalike top). You'll see half-kneeling giants at the west gate.

Looking over Shwegudaung (back to the west) **Ratanamanaung** offers fine views. From the path off the road, villagers will likely walk with you up on the overgrown path.

Kothaung Temple
One of Mrauk U's highlights, this temple (finishing up several years' of restoration at research time) is a mile or so east of the palace. At 230ft by 250ft, it's Mrauk U's largest temple. Built in 1553 by King Minbun's son, King Mintaikkha, to outdo his pop's Shittaung by 10,000 images ('Kothaung' means 'Shrine of 90,000 Images'), much of it was found in fragments. Legends vary – that lightning or an earthquake in 1776 destroyed it, jewel-seekers overturned walls, or that it was built with inferior stones by a superstitious king bent on beating a six-month timeline.

The outer passageway is lined with thousands of bas reliefs on the walls and buddha images (some headless). Stairways lead up to a top terrace, once dotted with 108 stupas.

Get here either on the winding road to Sakyamanaung (just north of Moe Cherry), veering right at one fork, or from the east–west road from the market, veering left before the bridge.

Immediately south of Kothaung, back on the road from the market, an overgrown hill is topped with a buddha figure. Go up to find **Peisi Daung Paya**, a thrillingly unexcavated four-door pagoda, with four images, lots of cobwebs, and wondrous views from the top. A few locals even insisted that it has the honour of keeping testicle relics of the Buddha.

SOUTH GROUP
South of the palace site and across the river are evocative, easy-to-lose-your-way back lanes through thatched-hut villages and a host of pagodas.

About half a mile south, the **Laksaykan Gate** leads to the eponymous lake, a source of clean water.

To the west is the interesting hilltop **Bandoola Kyaung**, a monastery where many worshippers climb the steps to see several buddha images in covered areas.

Southwest of the palace, the **Shwetaung Paya** (Golden Hill Pagoda) is the highest in Mrauk U; you can see it for nearly half the trip from Sittwe. Built by King Minbin in 1553, it's accessed by a few trails largely lost under thick vegetation.

Festivals & Events
One of the most interesting times to visit Mrauk U is during the huge weeklong **paya pwe** (pagoda festival) held near Dukkanthein Paya (opposite) in mid-May.

Sleeping
For the first time in a handful of years, Mrauk U is seeing a hotel construction boom of sorts – with three new projects that may eclipse all those below in terms of comfort.

Some guesthouses supplement the town's power source (roughly 6.45pm to 8.45pm) with generators. Generators add power from 5pm to 10pm or so, unless otherwise noted.

All hotels offer free breakfast.

BUDGET
Golden Star Guest House (☎ 24200, ext 50175; per person $5) This newcomer, 180yd north of market across from a small reservoir, is Mrauk

U's best cheap deal, with little Rakhaing-style figurines and private cold-water bathrooms in most of the 13 basic rooms. The English-speaking manager goes out of his way to help – sometimes adding a free lunch for long stayers. At research time, two 'traditional house' rooms in back were in the works, with windows looking out into a palm forest (these will be $15). We like the clocks in the front: 'Myanmar', 'Bangkok' and 'Arakan'.

Thazin Pann Khine Guest House (groupstar@myanmar.com.mm; r per person $5) Basic and a bit funny, this six-room guesthouse near the jetty goes for its own style: checkerboard vinyl floors and aqua green walls. It's a ways from the centre and has no phone, but staff speak English.

Waddy Htut Guest House (☎ 24200, ext 50240; r $5-30) Sometimes pushed by a certain legendary Sittwe tout, this modern-style two-floor house has an OK mix of options – basic rooms with shared bath ($5), a well-lit 'family room' with sofa, a few beds and a balcony ($30, but negotiable). It's across from the palace site, 90yd northeast of the market.

Prince Hotel (☎ 24200, ext 50174, Yangon 09-501 9114; www.mraukuprincehotel.com; r $15 & 25) Half a mile southeast of the market, this leafy complex of nine bungalows sits below a hill in a gorgeous leafy garden. The bungalows are certainly rustic, but a bit aged for the price. The $15 rooms are slightly smaller and have wood floors.

MIDRANGE

Royal City Guest House (☎ 24200, ext 50257; s/d about $20/30) This traditional-style complex of five 'bungalow' rooms, between the jetty and the market, was undergoing a serious (and overdue) renovation at research time.

Vesali Resort Hotel (☎ 24200, ext 50008, Yangon 01-526 593; myathiri@mptmail.net.mm; s/d $30/35) Though removed from the bulk of the temples and town, Vesali's snazzy bungalows – with dark-wood floors, vaulted bamboo ceilings, private decks and a shockingly modern bathroom – remain Mrauk U's best choice for the time being. Rooms come with battery-powered lamps. There's an inviting café/restaurant up front, and behind is a path up to Shwetaung Paya.

TOP END

Nawarat Hotel (☎ 24200, ext 50077, Yangon 01-578 786; s $38-46, d $46-60; ❄) If you need all-night electricity, the Nawarat's 30-room motel-style complex, a short walk from the (out of sight) Shittaung Paya, has long been the only choice, but it suffers a bit in atmosphere. Across from the government-run Mrauk U Hotel, the walled-off compound consists of simple boxy bungalow rooms with air-con, satellite TV, glow-in-the-dark stars on some ceilings, and that glorious 24-hour generator. Identical, cheaper rooms get power 6pm to 6am only.

At research time, construction for the Shwe Thazin Hotel, run by the Sittwe hotel of the same name, was underway along a canal. And by the time you arrive, the Mrauk U Princess Hotel, a high-end complex of monastery-style modern bungalows a few hundred yards south of the jetty, should be open. Expect high prices and group tours.

Eating

The midrange hotels have dependable restaurants. There are a few local restaurants facing the market to the west of the Mrauk U market, serving basic Chinese food.

For You (dishes K1000) Two blocks north of the market (via the road from the jetty), this plain concrete-floor restaurant serves good noodles (with an egg on top) and cans of Myanmar beer at the ground floor of a traditional wood house.

our pick Moe Cherry (☎ 24200, ext 50177; dishes K1000-2000, beer K1500) This friendly, traveller-focused, two-storey restaurant, east of the palace walls, serves a few meals and what's on offer changes nightly. There's a deliciously Rakhaing edge to the chicken curry, prawn and veggie dishes (cauliflower's the best). They're open 'anytime: this is our home' and the restaurant also arranges area tours.

Shopping

A few teashops outside the Shittaung Paya sell some souvenirs. A few other choices:

Mrauk U Magic! (Nawarat Hotel; ⏰ 7am-5.45pm) Small – but magical! – shop sells a K2000 Mrauk U T-shirt and art pieces.

Natives of Nationality Traditional Exhibition & Sales Center (⏰ 10am-7pm) A simple wood house 90yd north of the jetty sells traditional Rakhaing and Khumi fabrics, made by village weavers.

Getting There & Away

For information on the difference between the boat services to Mrauk U, see p326.

The Mrauk U jetty is about half a mile south of the market. If you don't want to get back by government ferry, it's often possible to jump aboard a fellow traveller's boat and share costs for the ride. Negotiating a one-way 'private boat' ride may be possible too (about $60).

Getting Around

A horse cart around the temples costs about K10,000 per day (the stand is just southeast of the palace site). Usually fitting four plus a driver, a jeep (arranged by your hotel or from the stand on the north side of the palace site) should be about K18,000 around Mrauk U, or K30,000 to the Lemro River or Mahamuni Paya.

A trishaw ride between the jetty and hotels is about K1000, a jeep ride is K4000. Hotels can get you a bicycle for K2000 or K3000.

AROUND MRAUK U

The temples are really only a part of the area's attractions. The lovely boat ride to Chin villages is a Myanmar highlight, and a couple of sites north of Mrauk U are of particular pride for locals.

Chin Villages

A popular day trip to assorted Chin villages on the nearby Lemro River doesn't quite reach the elusive Chin State, but visitors can witness the famous Chin 'tattooed faces' on elder women (the practice of tattooing girls' faces ended a couple of generations ago) on the clear waters of the Lemro, northeast of Mrauk U. It's a nicer boat ride than the one to Mrauk U from Sittwe, and if you ask your boat drivers, you can usually stop off at one of the peanut, chilli or bean farms on islands or the riverside that you pass on the way for a short visit.

Typical trips begin at 7am or 8am and include a two- to three-hour boat ride each way, and an hour or so at a couple of villages. Your guesthouse or hotel can help arrange a boat, permission to travel there, and transport to the Lemro River, about 6 miles east. Most hotels and guesthouses charge about K55,000 for the trip (if you go by jeep) or K35,000 (if you go by bike).

It's well worth taking an English-speaking guide (about $15 per day), who should be able to help you communicate with the friendly locals and understand some of the customs you'll see.

Many visitors go to the river jetty by jeep, which begins at Nang Gyar village, southeast of Mrauk U a mile or two further from the villages on the river. A cheaper, and more fun, way of doing it is beginning by bicycling directly to the river, on a rough but gorgeous ride, past the Kothaung temple 6 miles or so east to the Lemro River at Pophru Chuong village. It's best to have a boat driver or a guide go with you to help show the way. (Even if you don't take a trip, a bike ride on this road is great fun, particularly just before sunset.)

Be sure to pack what you need for lunch and the amount of water you'll need. There's not much to buy in Chin villages.

DONATIONS

There is no actual charge to visit the several Chin villages in the area, but you should plan on donating a few thousand kyat to the town leader, which in the past has been used to build schools. Also consider bringing simple medicines like tiger balm or pain medicines.

Wethali

ဝေသာလီ

Almost 6 miles north of Mrauk U are the remains of the kingdom of Wethali (aka Vesali, or Waithali in local parlance). According to the Rakhaing chronicles, Wethali was founded in AD 327 by King Mahataing Chandra. Archaeologists believe that this kingdom lasted until the 8th century. Little remains of the oval-shaped city (and apparently some buildings were damaged purposely for road-building materials in recent years). The walls of the 1650ft by 990ft central palace site are reasonably well preserved; its prayer hall is now used as an irrigation tank during the rainy season.

The main attraction for visitors en route to Mahamuni Paya is the so-called **Great Image of Hsu Taung Pre** (Pye), home to a 16.5ft Rakhaing-style sitting buddha. It's said to be carved from a single piece of stone and date to AD 327 (but most visitors argue the features look more modern).

Regular transport is rare. It's possible to reach here by bicycle (take the sign that says 'VSL' and 'you are here' east from the main road).

Mahamuni Paya

မဟာမုက်ဘုရား:

Many local Rakhaing recount, with fresh, fiery passion, how the Bamar King Bodawpaya sent soldiers to dismantle and remove the

WESTERN MYANMAR

Mahamuni buddha in 1784. Originally housed here at the Mahamuni Paya, 25 miles north of Mrauk U and just north of the former ancient capital of Dhanyawady, the image is one of the country's most famous and venerated. Still, it's fascinating to visit the site.

Some Rakhaing believe the image was cast when Buddha visited the area in 554 BC. Others say the Bamar unknowingly took a counterfeit back to Amarapura (it now resides in Mandalay; p263) and the true one rests under the banyan tree at the site's southwest corner. The Rakhaing don't let go easily.

The current Konbaung-style shrine dates from the 18th or 19th centuries, as earlier ones were destroyed by fire. The Mahamuni buddha is gone, but 'Mahamuni's brother' is now one of three fine golden images resting inside. Down the steps, near the south walls of the shrine, is a **museum** with a couple of dozen relics and engraved stones.

The hilltop golden stupas visible (barely) to the east mark **Salagiri Hill**, the fabled site Buddha visited in 554 BC. The area is closed to foreigners.

The easiest way to get to the site is by hired jeep (about K30,000 from Mrauk U, including a stop at Wethali). It takes about three hours from Mrauk U.

CHIN STATE

ချင်းပြည်နယ်

At research time, much of Chin State remained a question mark for travellers. It's possible to visit Mt Victoria (west of Bagan) with a licensed guide. A couple of options to mingle with Chin people just outside Chin State don't require government permits: villages near Mrauk U in Rakhaing State (p333) and a flight from Mandalay to Kalaymyo, a half Chin town just northeast of Chin State (see right).

TOURS & PERMISSION

You won't be able to roam Chin State on your own. All visits require both permission from the government and the presence of a licensed guide – something that will take two to four weeks.

The most popular trip to Chin State, and one not that hard to arrange, is to **Mt Victoria**. With KS Elephant (see right), it's about $500 per person from Nyaung U (Bagan) for a three-night trip including car, driver, guide, accommodation (minimum two people per trip). The loop from Nyaung U starts with a seven-hour ride to Mindat town – across the Ayeyarwady (Irrawaddy) on rough roads. The next day it's seven more hours to Kampelet at the foot of the mountain, where you trek up (3 miles one way). Bird-watching possibilities abound, and it's possible to camp overnight on the mountain. It's an eight-hour ride back to Nyaung U from Kampelet.

The government's MTT offers trips too. A four-night trip is $910/1040/1310 for one/two/three to five people including guide, transport, accommodation and permits from Nyaung U.

You can only get permission from the Yangon office of government-run Myanmar Travel & Tours (p91), though the Bagan office (p186) may be able to help. Either way, you're better off finding a Yangon-based independent, more travel-oriented agency that specialises in far-flung tours to do it for you. Their guides tend to be better too. One dependable guide is Mr Saw at **KS Elephant Travels & Tours** (☎ 01-666 202; www.kselephanttravels .com; Bldg 2, Eight Mile Junction, Rm 40, Mayangone, Yangon), who can arrange permits. Also ask about possible trips to Paletwa, in southwestern Chin State, on the Kaladan River.

KALAYMYO

ကလေးမြို့

☎ 073

It's remote, and not particularly exciting, but travellers with up-for-grabs expectations and hopes to mingle with Chin folk can fly to Kalaymyo without special government permission. Part of Sagaing Division (near the northern border of Chin State), the town, about 62 miles from the India border, doesn't have much to do, but it's interesting for the make-up of its population (half Burmese, half Chin) and its slender setting, ringed by far-off lush mountains (the town is 9 miles long and rarely more than two blocks wide).

GOVERNMENT PERMIT

It's impossible to visit Chin State without paying for a government permit and taking a guide. It is, however, possible to go with a private guide to places like Mt Victoria or Paletwa.

THE CHIN

In hilly and sparsely populated Chin State, the people and culture exhibit a mixture of native, Bengali and Indian influences similar to that found among the Rakhaing, with a much lower Burman presence. As in Rakhaing State, there have been clear governmental efforts in recent years to promote Burmese culture at the expense of Chin culture, and many Chin have fled west to Bangladesh and India.

Of Tibeto-Burman ancestry, the Chin people call themselves Zo-mi or Lai-mi (both terms mean 'mountain people'), and share a culture, food and language with the Zo of the adjacent state of Mizoram in India. Outsiders name the different subgroups around the state according to the district in which they live, eg Tidam Chin, Falam Chin and Haka Chin.

Traditionally the Chin practise *swidden* (slash-and-burn) agriculture. They are also skilled hunters, and animal sacrifice plays a role in important animistic ceremonies. Currently, Chin State has the largest proportion of animists of any state in Myanmar. Between Christian missionaries (including the Chin Christianity in One Century Project) and the government's Buddhist missions, the traditional Zo or Chin groups are fading fast.

The **Chin National Front** (www.chinland.org), a nonviolent nationalist movement active on both sides of the India-Myanmar border, would like to create a sovereign 'Chinland' to be divided into the states of East Zoram (the current Chin State in Myanmar), West Zoram (part of southeastern Bangladesh plus Tripura in, India), Central Zoram (the state of Mizoram in India) and North Zoram (Manipur in India). This was a unified area before the British came along.

Most foreign faces who do make it here belong to Christian missionary types, who donate time and money to the Chin population (who are 95% Christian; no women have tattooed faces here), who live in the western half of town. The Chin folk sometimes refer to Kalaymyo as 'Zomi'. There's some local debate on who lived here first, Bamar or Chin.

Sights

Foreigners are restricted to staying within town. The **downtown (Burmese) market**, in and around the roundabout about 450yd east of the airport, is worth a look. Many locals pluck on guitars around town; you can get your own guitar here for K3000 or so.

The principal Chin district, **Tahan**, is 2 miles west of downtown and has a market too. Just before the sign, turn south on Taung Za Lat Rd to reach the local **golf course**, set below a small mountain with a **pagoda** you can reach by foot.

About 9 miles west of the airport, in the Chin Hills (and into restricted areas), is **Shukintha** (aka Mt Zion View Point), where a local can usually take you if you ask at the unsigned police stand near the Kalaymyo University, about 6 miles west of airport.

Sleeping & Eating

Taung Za Lat Hotel (☎ 21463; Bogyoke Rd; s $15 & $20, d $20 & $35) The lone hotel licensed for foreigners is directly across the street from the airport. There are slightly grubby but doable rooms and balconies, fans, screened windows and squashed 'squitoes left on the walls. The Chin staff speak some English. More expensive rooms are slightly bigger but not really worth it.

Thein Shwe Restaurant (☎ 21313; Bogyoke Rd; dishes K800; ⏱ 9am-9pm) You'll find some eateries in Tahan and around the downtown market. The best is this one, about 90yd west of the roundabout. It's run by a welcoming English-speaking, Burmese-Chinese woman who provides good local information.

Getting There & Around

Boat and bus journeys here from Monywa are off limits for foreigners. Government-run Myanma Airways flies three times weekly from Mandalay ($95 to $105) on Monday, Thursday and Saturday. The MA ticket office is halfway between the airport and the downtown market; arrange to buy a ticket (with passport and dollars in hand) at 9am the day before your flight.

WESTERN MYANMAR

Directory

CONTENTS

ACCOMMODATION

This guidebook lists many of Myanmar's 600 or so licensed, privately run hotels and guesthouses. Many are simple family-run guesthouses or minihotels, sometimes just with bubbly vinyl flooring laid over concrete, a mosquito net, a fan that turns off at midnight (when the generator does) and a cold shower down the hall. In particularly popular destinations (eg Yangon, Bagan, Inle Lake, Mandalay, Ngapali Beach), you'll find high-end affairs akin to luxury resorts in Thailand, with bungalow-style rooms, swimming pools, tennis courts and restaurants with European chefs. In between (but closer to budget in quality) are many, many modern, hit-or-miss Chinese-style hotels that follow familiar templates: tiled rooms with air-con, a private bath with hot water and a refrigerator in a corner.

Essentially all accommodation choices provide free breakfast (usually eggs and toast, but sometimes quite sprawling breakfasts that include local dishes like *mohinga,* a spicy fish noodle soup). Staff at most can also change money, arrange for laundry service (starting at K1000 per load at budget guesthouses), rent bikes, arrange taxis, sell transport tickets, and find you local English-speaking guides.

Restrictions

Foreigners are only allowed to stay at 'licensed' hotels and guesthouses, which supposedly must keep at least five rooms and reach a certain standard. In the past some owners bent the rules in less-visited towns, but that seems to be waning. Staff will often say 'we have no rooms' instead of owning up that they lack the licence.

At night, all hotels and other accommodation options must fill in police forms on behalf of all guests, which include the details of your visa and your passport number. Hotels will not have to keep your passport.

Types of Hotels

This guidebook tries to include only hotels run by private owners. When considering where to stay, consider this (informal) breakdown of the choices.

FAMILY-RUN GUESTHOUSES

Often with just five or so rooms and a TV lounge to share with three or four generations of a family living in-house, these budget-level guesthouses can be a highlight of a trip, of-

---

BOOK YOUR STAY ONLINE

For more accommodation reviews and recommendations by Lonely Planet authors, check out the online booking service at www.lonelyplanet.com/hotels. You'll find the true, insider lowdown on the best places to stay. Reviews are thorough and independent. Best of all, you can book online.

PRACTICALITIES

- **Electricity** When it's working: 230V, 50Hz AC electricity. Most power outlets have two-pronged round or flat sockets. Many hotels have generators (some run at night only) – local power sources in many towns are scheduled for just two to three hours daily.

- **Emergencies** Outside Yangon, no-one in Myanmar calls an ambulance in an emergency; they go to the hospital. You could call top-end hotels in a crisis and ask about English-language doctors.

- **Newspapers** Yangon publishes two English-language newspapers: *Myanmar Times,* which offers some useful travel and entertainment information, and the government mouthpiece *New Light of Myanmar.*

- **Radio & TV** All national radio and TV broadcasts are state-controlled. Many locals listen to short-wave radios for BBC and VOA broadcasts. Satellite TV has brought some dramatic changes in recent years, with CNN, MTV Asia, BBC World Service and – *sacré bleu!* – Fashion TV all piping in.

- **Video** The standard video system in Myanmar is NTSC, but many people also own PAL models, which are compatible with Thailand, Australia and most of Europe.

- **Weights & Measures** 1 Burmese *viss* or 100 *ticals* = 3.5lb; 1 *gaig* = 36in; petrol is sold by the gallon; distances are in miles, not kilometres.

---

fering quick connections with local life and cheap deals (often $10 to $15 for a double). Most come with fan or some sort of air-con unit, though electricity frequently cuts out after midnight. Some are better than others, however, and, like budget hotels, you'll find some with squashed mosquitoes left on the walls.

BUDGET HOTELS
In many towns your only options will be a couple of four-floor, modern, 'Chinese-style' hotels. In some there are dark cell-like rooms with shared bathroom on the ground floor (usually for locals only), and two types of nicer rooms on upper floors. Some have lifts; some have doorstaff; some keep their generators on 24 hours, others just for a few hours at night and in the morning. Most run $15 to $30 for a double. Have a look before taking the higher-priced 'deluxe' rooms; often it's an extra $10 for a refrigerator and writing desk you may not use. Others get more space, nicer flooring and maybe a satellite TV.

GOVERNMENT HOTELS
We advise against using any hotels run by the government's Ministry of Hotels & Tourism (MHT). All money is directly put into the government's hands *and* they're generally dated, empty and poorly cared for. These hotels are generally easy to identify: they are often named

for the town they're located in (eg Sittwe Hotel in Sittwe), fly a lone Myanmar flag out front – and the staff are often quite upfront about it if you ask! 'Government hotels' have been dwindling in number in recent years; some being leased out to 'private' owners. Throughout this book we point out government hotels so you can avoid them if you choose.

JOINT-VENTURE HOTELS
A number of foreign hotel groups operate hotels – technically maintaining their hotel grounds via a 30-year lease with the government. These are all top-end, electricity-all-day hotels, sometimes costing $450 per night, and are often the nicest options.

Though these work on the whole as private hotels, it's unclear how much beyond an approximate 10% or 12% tax, and whatever 'licence' fee is settled on, goes to the government. Because of this murkiness, some travellers opt to skip joint ventures. On the other hand, they are known to pool some of their profits into community projects, such as building clinics, and are known for paying a slightly higher salary than average.

OTHER PRIVATE HOTELS
It's hardest to peg where the money goes for receipts from this category – upper mid-range and top-end hotels that are owned and run by various local entrepreneurs. Some

DIRECTORY

ACCOMMODATION: WHERE THE MONEY GOES

Those who support a tourism boycott of Myanmar frequently cite hotels as a major source of revenue for the government. The situation has actually changed a lot since the mid '90s, when the government controlled most options for tourists. There are now an estimated 600 private choices, which we focus on in this book. There is a catch, however, regarding how 'private' these hotels are, as some are run by government cronies or family members (see p337 for more on this).

Also note that *all* hotels pay approximately 12% of the room price to the government, and have to acquire government licences to serve foreigners.

Those wanting to ensure that a minimum of their money goes to the government can consider math. The 12% room tax on a $300 room is $36; on a $15 room it's $1.80 – for many travellers it's a compelling case to go with more budget choices than they would usually. But maths isn't the only factor. Some high-end hotels, particularly joint-venture hotels, use their higher room rate to employ many more locals (at slightly higher-than-average salaries) and put money back into community projects.

---

are former government hotels now leased to local owners. Some owners are legit, part of Myanmar's tiny middle class; others can be linked with the government, as either generals' family or cronies. One example is the Aureum Palace chain owned by Tay Za (p21). We avoid recommending known 'crony' hotels, or try to identify who the owners are.

Prices

Hotels and guesthouses licensed for foreigners quote prices in US dollars. Typically you can pay in kyat too, but the price quoted may be at a slightly unfavourable rate so it's worth keeping dollars ready for accommodation expenses. Prices quoted at budget and midrange hotels include all taxes; usually top-end hotel quotes don't include up to 20% in tax and service charges. A few top-end hotels in Myanmar accept credit cards.

Listings in this book are ordered by budget. Where helpful, we break down accommodation into three groups: budget (doubles under $16), midrange (doubles $16 to $35), top end (over $35). Note that most hotels have a two-tier pricing system (for foreigners and locals).

It's possible to bargain a little at most hotels, especially during the low season (March to October). Most people checking in early – say those arriving on an overnight bus that gets in at around 6am or 7am – are only charged for the following night.

ACTIVITIES

See p35 for an activities-based map of Myanmar.

Ballooning

It's expensive to do, but Bagan (p179) is considered one of the world's most ideal ballooning spots.

Bird-Watching

The nation's best bird-watching is found on the hike up Mt Victoria in Chin State (see p334), which requires a government permit to visit. You can also see some 125 species at the Moeyungyi Wetlands (p152), near Bago.

Cycling

Most of Myanmar gets around on self-propelled two-wheeled contraptions called bicycles. Some cycling groups come on tours, making full loops from Yangon through Bagan to Mandalay and back again. More adventurous riders take to the hills on routes such as Kalaw to Inle Lake, or from Mandalay to Hsipaw or Lashio. For more on bike travel and routes, see p362.

Diving & Snorkelling

It's not world-class coral, but there are plenty of snorkelling opportunities at beach resorts Ngapali Beach (p319) and Chaung Tha Beach (p140).

The best diving, by far, is at the Mergui (Myeik) Archipelago in southwestern Myanmar, which is only accessible by group tour from Phuket, Thailand. **South East Asia Liveaboards Co** (http://seal-asia.com) offers six- and seven-night trips on a yacht from November through April (from about $2200 per person). Another Phuket-based operator offering trips to Mergui is **Faraway Sail & Dive** (www.far-away.net).

Golf

Nearly all golf courses are government-run and are found all over Myanmar. Pyin U Lwin (p297) hosts a tournament in April.

Rafting

Ultimate Descents (www.ultimatedescents.com) offers trips down some key tributaries of the Ayeyarwady River in northern Kachin State, at the foothills of the Himalaya.

Check the website for scheduling or contact the Yangon office of privately run **Malikha Lodge** (☎ 01-652 809; thelisu@myanmar.com.mm; Suite 03-06, Sedona Hotel, Yangon) to set up a trip (p314). Four-day trips (with two days' trekking) on the Nam Lang River start at $1600 per person (in December, including two nights at the Malikha Lodge).

Very serious and experienced rafters can consider arranging an intense three-week descent of the Mayhka River (Mother River; aka 'the Everest of Rivers'); ask the office.

Trekking

Great hiking potential abounds, particularly in northern and eastern Myanmar. Restrictions against overnight treks have been loosened in recent years, though some places still only allow day hikes. Wherever you trek, it's recommended you take along a guide. It's hard to know where to go, and in early 2008 a foreign tourist was arrested and deported after (wilfully, we understand) venturing into restricted areas in the Shan hills. It's about $8 to take a guide on an overnight trek from Kalaw, and about $10 in Kengtung.

Here are some popular hikes:

Hkakabo Razi National Park (p314) Costly permits and tours are required to wander this remote park outside Putao in the far north.

Hsipaw area (p302) A great hiking hub with good day-hike potential to villages and waterfalls, five hours northeast of Mandalay. Guides can offer insight on multi-day hikes to minority villages, often en route to Inle Lake.

Kalaw to Inle Lake (p224) Kalaw is Myanmar's top hiking hub, with guided one-way, multi-day treks to Inle Lake, staying in minority village longhouses that freckle the mountain tops.

Kengtung Area (p250) A more remote pocket of Shan State, with day trips to Wa villages.

Mt Victoria (p334) Bird-watching haven in Chin State; requires a government permit.

Namhsan (p304) North of Hsipaw; guided hikes in a far-flung area.

Pindaya area (p230) Near Inle Lake; overnight trek potential.

BUSINESS HOURS

Most government offices – including post offices and official telephone centres – are open Monday to Friday from 9.30am to 4.30pm. Don't arrive at a government office at 4pm expecting to get anything done, though; most government workers start drifting to the local teashops after 3.30pm.

Private shops are generally open Monday to Saturday, from 9am or 9.30am to 6pm or later, but sometimes for a half-day on Saturday. Most restaurants – even ones without many breakfast visitors – open at 7am or 8am and close late, at 9pm or 10pm. Internet cafés, where they exist, tend to keep shorter hours.

RESPONSIBLE DIVING & SNORKELLING

If you want to enjoy Myanmar's underwater realm, remember these simple rules to minimise your impact.

- Don't use anchors on a reef and ask your operators not to either.
- Be conscious of your fins or your body dragging across fragile reef ecosystems – both parties can be hurt.
- Take out all rubbish or litter, including what you find; plastic in particular can wreak havoc on marine life.
- Don't feed fish; it disturbs their normal eating habits and can prompt aggressive behaviour.
- If you're diving in the Myeik Peninsula, be sure that you possess a current diving certification card.
- Be aware that underwater conditions vary significantly from one region to the next – dive only within the limits of your experience.

SAFETY GUIDELINES FOR HIKING

We've heard about some travellers finding new paths and staying in the hills for a week or more. Most, however, stick with day trips. Here are a few points to consider before lacing up the boots.

■ Hike with at least one companion; in most cases it's best to hire a guide.

■ Do not venture by foot into areas restricted to foreigners; ask around before taking off.

■ Camping in the hills is not technically legal, as foreigners must be registered nightly with local authorities by owners of 'licensed accommodation'.

■ Trail conditions can get slippery and dangerous, especially in the rainy season.

■ Walk only in regions within your capabilities – you're not going to find a trishaw out there to bring you back.

CHILDREN

As in many places in Southeast Asia, travelling with children in Myanmar can be very rewarding as long as you come well prepared with the right attitude, the physical requirements and the usual parental patience. Lonely Planet's *Travel with Children,* by Cathy Lanigan, contains useful advice on how to cope with kids on the road and what to bring along to make things go more smoothly. Special attention is paid to travel in developing countries.

People in Myanmar love children – dote on them actually – and in many instances will shower attention on your offspring, who will find ready playmates among their local counterparts and an impromptu nanny service at practically every stop. However, it may be confusing for some children seeing young children working at restaurants and teashops.

Due to Myanmar's overall low level of public sanitation, parents ought to lay down a few ground rules with regard to maintaining their children's health – such as regular hand-washing – to head off potential medical problems. All the usual health precautions apply (see the Health chapter, p370); children should especially be warned not to play with animals they encounter, as a precaution against rabies.

Nappies (diapers) are hard to come by outside Yangon, and it's wise to bring all the nappies or formula you'll need for the trip from home. Most high-end hotels and restaurants will have highchairs available.

When travelling with children, it may be more comfortable getting about by private car (p365).

Sights & Activities

Kids, like adults, often get a thrill from little things such as rides on trishaws, motorised canoes and horse carts. While in Bagan, give your driver (if you have one) the day off and take a horse cart around by yourselves (p179). Inle Lake's famous boat trips (p242) are in dugout canoes, and the ancient cities outside Mandalay offer fun, brief boat trips. Options include rowing boats in the lake by Amarapura's U Bein's Bridge (p278), a flat-bed ferry and then a horse-cart loop around Inwa (p280), and a boat ride up the Ayeyarwady to Mingun (p284).

Big Buddhist sights and ancient ruins can make for good gawking and learning experiences, including Yangon's Shwedagon Paya (p92), the reclining buddhas in Bago (Pegu; see p147) or the 10-storey buddha in Pyay (Prome; see p199). You can climb into the back of the lacquered buddha image at Nan Paya in Salay (p215).

Some kids might dig ruins of old palace walls and moats, which you can see at places like Bagan and Mrauk U (see p328). Some kids may enjoy trying on *thanakha* (yellow sandalwood-like paste) on their faces; this is sold and applied from sidewalk stands around the country. Taunggyyi's fire-balloon festival (p245), in October or November, is quite a spectacle of floating animals near Inle Lake.

Consider asking about a local orphanage – there are many – so your children can play with kids their own age for a bit. The local kids would love it.

CLIMATE CHARTS

Myanmar has three seasons, which follow the classic 'dry and hot, wet and hot, dry and less

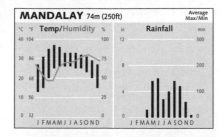

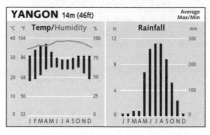

hot' pattern common to other parts of mainland Southeast Asia. Rain falls mostly from mid-May to October. In most places temperatures fall from November to February, then rise from March through to May. See p27 for more information on the best times to visit.

COURSES
Meditation

For foreigners interested in meditation, Yangon provides the most opportunities for the study and practice of *satipatthana vipassana,* or insight-awareness meditation. This is based on instructions in the Maha Satipatthana Sutta of the Theravada Buddhist canon, and instruction at most places is in English. Many Westerners have come to Myanmar to practise at the various centres for periods ranging from 10 days to more than a year. Visitors typically attach themselves to a respected *sayadaw* (master teacher) in the Buddhist tradition for the duration.

Food and lodging are generally provided for no charge at the centres, but meditators must follow eight precepts, which include abstaining from food after noon and forgoing music, dancing, jewellery, perfume and high or luxurious beds (or bedding down with fellow meditators). Daily schedules are rigorous and may involve nearly continuous practice from 3am till 11pm. Westerners who have undergone the training say it is not recommended for people with no previous meditation experience.

Myanmar embassies no longer issue 'meditation visas', as they did in the past. You can come for meditation courses with a regular tourist visa (p352).

For details on meditation courses in Yangon, Mandalay and south of Mawlamyine, see p115, p266 and p164. Meditation centres can also be found in other areas, like Sagaing (p282), which is Myanmar's principal monastic centre in terms of numbers of monks, nuns, monasteries and nunneries.

CUSTOMS

For the vast majority of visitors, clearing customs is a breeze, but it's important to be aware of the restrictions. Any foreign currency in excess of $2000 must be declared upon entry (you're unlikely to need that much, though we've met humanitarian-oriented travellers who have failed to declare larger amounts and have not had problems). Besides personal effects, visitors are permitted to bring in the following items duty free: 400 cigarettes, 100 cigars, 250g of tobacco, 2L of liquor and 0.5L of perfume. Telecommunication equipment (including mobile phones) can be brought in but must be declared. You cannot bring in antiques, pornographic materials or narcotic drugs (obviously). It's not a problem to bring a camera, video camera or laptop.

See p351 for a list of items that cannot be taken out of the country.

DANGERS & ANNOYANCES

Considering all the bad news that trickles out of Myanmar, it may sound like a rather unsafe country to visit. For the vast majority of visitors, the truth is quite the opposite.

ONLINE TRAVEL ADVISORIES

Governments' advisory websites for people travelling to Myanmar:

- **Australia** (www.smarttraveller.gov.au)
- **Canada** (www.voyage.gc.ca)
- **UK** (☎ 0845 850 2829; www.fco.gov.uk) The most comprehensive; click on Travel Advice and select Burma.
- **USA** (travel.state.gov) See the Consular Information Sheet for Burma.

DIRECTORY

Air Travel

Government-operated Myanma Airways (MA) has a sketchy safety record, and there are reports that some MA aircraft have been used by Air Bagan. In February 2008 an Air Bagan flight out of Putao was damaged after missing the runway; a month later engine trouble on a Yangon–Thandwe Air Bagan flight required the plane to return to Yangon. This pales in comparison to past problems. In 1994 a flight missed the runway at Kawthoung, killing 16; in 1998 it took authorities 24 hours to realise one of its planes had crash-landed near Tachileik; while another flight crashed en route from Thandwe (Sandoway) to Sittwe, killing 10 passengers.

Bugs, Snakes, Rats & Monkeys

Mosquitoes, if allowed, can have a field day with you. As a Burmese character in George Orwell's *Burmese Days* says: 'At night, master too drunk to notice mosquitoes; in the morning, mosquitoes too drunk to notice master.' As alcohol won't help, bring repellent from home, as the good stuff (other than mosquito coils) is hard to come by here. Also, some guesthouses and hotels don't have mosquito nets. See also entries on malaria (p373) and dengue fever (p372).

Myanmar has one of the highest incidences of death from snakebite in the world. Watch your step in brush, forest and grasses. See p378 for information on what to do if you're bitten.

Rats aren't all that rampant. Family-run guesthouses, like regular homes, might have a rodent or two. Wash your hands before sleeping (we've seriously heard of happy rats licking cake-covered fingers clean at night) and try to keep food out of your room. If you trek in Shan State and stay in local accommodation, you may hear little footsteps at night.

A guide outside Monywa pointed out natural medicines for 'not shitting', 'shitting' and 'snakebite', but said there's nothing for monkey bites. 'Monkey bite is no problem,' he said. In a few sites, such as Hpo Win Daung Caves, near Monywa (p289) or Mt Popa (p188), you'll have monkeys begging for snacks. It's more spooky than dangerous, but bites are possible. See p374 for precautions against rabies.

Crime

All over Myanmar, police stations have English signs up that ask: 'May I help you?' It's easy to smirk at, but supposedly some of the restrictions to travel around Myanmar are based on the government's desire to keep foreigners out of harm's way. One local told me: 'No-one will steal from a foreigner. If I take your camera, I could get five years' hard labour in prison!' Most travellers' memories of locals grabbing their money are of someone chasing them down to return a K500 note they dropped. If someone grabs your bag at a bus station, it's almost certainly just a trishaw driver hoping for a fare.

There are, however, occasional reports of street crime, particularly in Yangon, which include burglaries of some expats' homes. But the high gates around some of the finer homes in north Yangon are more for show; as one Yangon residents says, 'the higher the fence, the more money you have'.

Electricity, or Lack Thereof

Power outages occur everywhere, Yangon and Mandalay included. Many smaller towns have short scheduled periods for electricity, such as a few hours in the afternoon (or in the evening if Myanmar TV is airing a premiership game). Many hotels and shops run generators 24 hours, others keep them on only a few hours (eg 6pm to midnight, and a few hours in the morning).

Insurgents & Bombs

As this book goes to press, the threat of more protests (and potentially more military crackdowns) looms. In the aftermath of 2007's protests, there were a few bombings, though none targeted foreigners. One at the Pyinmana railroad station, near the capital at Nay Pyi Taw, reportedly went off accidentally while a Karen rebel was trying to set it; in January 2008 a small bomb exploded at a Yangon train station bathroom (no-one was killed). The government blamed Karen insurgents but many locals believe the government planted both bombs.

POWER PLEASE!

If you can't handle uncertainty about when or if you're losing power (or can't afford hotels that keep generators running all night), Hpa-An (p167) is the only town in Myanmar with regular 24-hour electricity (the cement factory requires it).

A few past incidents have been linked with insurgent groups. In May 2005 three bombs at two Yangon shopping centres and a Thai trade expo killed up to 20 people and injured several hundred. During the previous month a bomb killed at least three at a Mandalay market. In December 2004 a small bomb went off at a central Yangon restaurant, injuring one person. The Vigorous Burmese Student Warriors supposedly claimed responsibility for the latter act.

A few other explosions in Yangon were reported, without injuries, in mid-2004 and mid-2003. An explosion in May 2003 in a cinema in Pyu, near Bago, killed one person and injured 47 others.

Despite treaties between the government and most insurgent groups, signed in the late 1990s, which give limited autonomy to many areas, violent incidents on the Myanmar-Thai border could erupt at any time, particularly in and around Tachileik. Land mines on the Myanmar side of the border are another threat. Most travel advisories warn against travel in this area, most of which is restricted to foreigners.

In Kayin State, splintered Kayin groups live in a potential battleground between the Karen National Liberation Army and government troops. The section of the Myanmar border in a restricted area of Kayin between Um Phang and Mae Sariang occasionally receives shelling from Myanmar troops in pursuit of Kayin (also known as Karen) or Mon rebels.

The presence of Shan and Wa armies along the Myanmar-Thai border in northern Mae Hong Son makes this area dangerous. Although the Wa have reportedly sworn off drug production, there's still plenty of amphetamines and opium crossing some border areas.

In the past there have been reports of bandits holding up vehicles at night, most commonly in the Tanintharyi (Tenasserim) division in southeastern Myanmar, but also near Taungoo. We've not heard of foreigners being targeted.

Some 'revolutionaries' maintain the sympathy of most locals. In the aftermath of the 1990 election controversy (see p47), a group of student protestors hijacked a plane from Bangkok to get worldwide attention, and tearfully handed out snacks with apologies to the inconvenienced passengers.

Politics

Talking politics can get not only you, but also the locals you're speaking with, into trouble. Let them introduce the subject and proceed to talk with discretion. Human rights activist James Mawdsley was arrested in 1999 after handing out political leaflets; he was freed after 415 days. (He describes the experience in his 2002 book *The Iron Road: A Stand for Truth and Democracy in Burma*.) Following the 10th anniversary of the 1988 democracy demonstrations, 18 foreigners were arrested for handing out leaflets. In January 2005 another Westerner was arrested for handing out leaflets outside Yangon's City Hall.

Be aware that if you're interested in seeing Aung San Suu Kyi's house in Yangon, or are dropping by an NLD office, you not only risk trouble (possible deportation) but you implicate your taxi driver too.

Guides, trishaw drivers, vendors and hotel staff are often able to talk at length with foreigners without suspicion due to their day-to-day contact with foreigners. Some can be surprisingly frank in their views. Teahouses carry the reputation as being open-discussion forums for some locals – but not all. Again, let the locals lead the conversation in that direction.

Restricted Roads

Many overland roads are closed to foreigners. And access to the Ayeyarwady Delta, including towns like Twante, Pathein and Chaung Tha Beach, were restricted to foreign travellers after Cyclone Nargis in May 2008. However, in places you can enter there are surprising levels of freedom to stop and look around where you want. The map on p360 shows the main routes that are openly accessible, though this can change.

Scams & Hassle

Myanmar touts are pretty minor league in comparison with those in India or the *tuk-tuk* drivers in Bangkok. Most hassle is due to commissions. These small behind-the-scenes payments are made, like it or not, for a taxi or trishaw driver or guide who takes you to a hotel, to buy a puppet or even to eat some rice. Often it doesn't affect the price you pay.

When arriving at a bus station, you're likely to be quickly surrounded by touts, some of whom will try to steer you to a particular hotel that offers them a commission. Be wary of claims that your chosen place is 'no good', though in some cases we found that trishaw drivers who had warned us that 'foreigners can't stay there' ended up being correct. If you know where you want to go (and it's a good idea to pretend to, even if you don't), persist and they'll take you.

Be wary of offers of fanciful jade or other gems (Myanmar has rich mines for these precious stones) as some are filled with worthless rock or concrete mixture.

Many people may approach to say 'hello' on the street. In some cases, they're just curious or want to practise some English. In other cases the conversation switches from 'what country you from?' to 'buy some postcards?' or 'where you need to go?' It's all pretty harmless.

You'll be asked to change money frequently. See p347 for tips on doing so with caution.

Spies

At some point on your trip – and you may likely never know it – the authorities (or the 'KGB' as the Moustache Brothers in Mandalay joke) will be watching you. This is even more likely to happen when you go to more off-the-beaten-track places, where authorities are less used to seeing foreigners (or are bored). In Shwebo, for example, a guesthouse told us, 'We need to see your bus ticket here. We have to report *everything* you do to the police!' Also, our pedalling about Taungoo led to police suspicions – they asked what we were doing at the guesthouse – and were satisfied to hear we were just 'travelling around the country'.

DISCOUNT CARDS

Neither student nor senior-citizen cards will get you any discounts.

EMBASSIES & CONSULATES

The generals moved the capital from Yangon to Nay Pyi Taw in 2005, but foreign embassies and consulates stayed behind in Yangon. Check the government's **Ministry of Foreign Affairs** (www.mofa.gov.mm) for more information.

Australia (Map p102; ☎ 01-251 810, 01-251 809; fax 01-246 159; 88 Strand Rd)

Bangladesh (Map p93; ☎ 01-515 272; 11B Thanlwin Rd, Kamaryut Township)

Cambodia (Map p93; ☎ 01-549 609; 25 New University Ave Rd, B3/4B)

Canada Affairs handled by Australian embassy or Canadian embassy in Bangkok (☎ +66 (0)2 6360540)

China (Map p98; ☎ 01-221 281; 1 Pyidaungsu Yeiktha Rd, Dagon)

France (Map p98; ☎ 01-212 523, 01-212 532; 102 Pyidaungsu Yeiktha Rd, Dagon)

Germany (Map p93; ☎ 01-548 951; fax 01-548 899; 9 Bogyoke Aung San Museum Rd)

India (Map p102; ☎ 01-243 972, 01-391 219; 545-547 Merchant St) Wins our coveted award for 'friendliest embassy'; they'll let you keep your passport for travel in Myanmar while processing a visa for India.

Indonesia (Map p98; ☎ 01-254 465, 01-254 469; 100 Pyidaungsu Yeiktha Rd)

Israel (Map p90; ☎ 01-515 155; fax 01-515 116; 15 Kabaung Rd, Hlaing Township)

Italy (Map p93; ☎ 01 527 100; 3 Inya Myaing Rd)

Japan (Map p93; ☎ 01-549 644; 100 Nat Mauk Rd)

Korea (Map p93; ☎ 01-527 142; 97 University Ave Rd, Bahan)

Laos (Map p98; ☎ 01-222 482; A1 Diplomatic Quarters, Taw Win St)

Malaysia (Map p98; ☎ 01-220 249; 82 Pyidaungsu Yeiktha Rd)

Nepal (Map p93; ☎ 01-545 880; fax 01-549 803; 16 Nat Mauk Rd)

Netherlands Affairs handled by German embassy or Netherlands embassy in Bangkok (☎ +66 (0)2 3095200)

New Zealand Affairs handled by UK embassy

Pakistan (Map p98; ☎ 01-222 881; 4A Pyay Rd)

Philippines (Map p90; ☎ 01-558 149; 50 Sayasan St)

Singapore (Map p93; ☎ 01-559 001; 238 Dhama Zedi Rd)

Sri Lanka (Map p98; ☎ 01-222 812; 34 Taw Win St)

Sweden Affairs handled by UK embassy or the Swedish embassy in Bangkok (☎ +66 (0)2 2637200)

Switzerland Affairs handled by German embassy or the Swiss embassy in Bangkok (☎ +66 (0)2 2530156)

Thailand (☎ 01-226 721; 94 Pyay Rd, Dagon)

UK (Map p102; ☎ 01-256 438, 01-370 863; fax 01-380 322; 80 Strand Rd)

USA (Map p93; ☎ 01-536 509, 01-535 756; fax 01-650 306; 110 University Ave, Kamayut)

Vietnam (☎ 01-524 656; 72 Thanlwin Rd, Bahan)

FOOD

Most restaurants are cheap (around $1 or $2 per person, not including beer). This book orders them by budget except in the Yangon and Mandalay chapters, where they are arranged by cuisine type and then budget. See p73 for more on the types of food and restaurants you'll find in Myanmar. A 10% government tax is added to upmarket restaurant bills in Yangon and in top-end hotel restaurants.

GAY & LESBIAN TRAVELLERS

Contrary to some outside reports, there is no law against homosexuality in Myanmar and we've not heard of any arrests for homosexual behaviour. Generally a local woman walking with a foreign man will raise more eyebrows than two same-sex travellers sharing a room.

As elsewhere, it can be seen as a bit of a cultural taboo, though most of Myanmar's ethnic groups are known to be tolerant of homosexuality, both male and female. Some Buddhists, however, believe that those who committed sexual misconducts (such as adultery) in a previous life become gay or lesbian in this one. Muslim and Christian Myanmar communities may object to homosexuality but, as they form relatively small minorities, they rarely foist their world perspectives on people of other faiths. Public displays of affection, whether heterosexual or homosexual, are frowned upon.

Check **Utopia-Asia** (www.utopia-asia.com) for some Yangon scene reports; they also publish a gay guide to Southeast Asia, including Myanmar.

A few foreign travel agencies specialise in 'gay tours' – meaning a standard tour on which gay or lesbian travellers can feel comfortable they'll check into gay-friendly hotels. (Many of the guides are openly gay too.) Agencies with trips to Myanmar include **Purple Dragon** (www.purpledrag.com) and **Mandalay Travel** (www.mandalaytravel.com).

HOLIDAYS

Major public holidays include Independence Day (January 4), Union Day (February 12), Peasants' Day (March 2), Armed Forces Day (March 27), Workers' Day (May 1), National Day (late November or early December) and Christmas (December 25). Government offices grab just about any excuse for taking the day off, though many private businesses remain open. For a broader list of festivals and events see p30.

INSURANCE

A travel-insurance policy to cover theft, loss and medical problems is a very wise idea, though not all companies cover travel to Myanmar.

There is a wide variety of policies and your travel agent will have recommendations. A couple of companies that offer insurance are **World Nomads** (www.worldnomads.com) and **Access America** (www.accessamerica.com).

See p370 for advice on health insurance.

INTERNET ACCESS

Getting online in Myanmar remains a question mark for the future. Before the 2007 protests, as many as 1000 internet cafés operated around Myanmar without the official government licence, and despite some outsider reports that the government reads every email, it didn't appear to be true. This may change, however.

At the peak of tension, when locals were sending out photos and blog entries to the outside world, the government cut the nation's internet access full stop (only the second time a government has done this; the first happened in Nepal in 2005). After turning it back on a few days later, the government required internet cafés to make a screen shot of each computer every five minutes. In February 2008 the government announced it would track down illegal cafés and make all acquire a new permit.

In the past proxy sites such as www.01proxy.com have been required to bypass blocks and access Yahoo or Gmail accounts, much less the BBC (or Lonely Planet!) site.

At research time, internet cafés were abundant in Yangon and Mandalay, and less available everywhere else. Most access was limited to painfully slow dial-up connections. In the town-specific information sections in this book we indicate the status of the internet system at research time – but this may change.

For more on internet and news sources, see p62. Some fine sources of online information can be found on p29.

LEGAL MATTERS

The Myanmar government includes no judiciary branch separate from the executive powers vested, by force of totalitarian rule, in the Tatmadaw (military). So you have absolutely no legal recourse in case of arrest or detainment by the authorities, regardless of the charge. Foreign visitors engaging in political activism (such as James Mawdsley; see p343) risk deportation or imprisonment. If you were arrested you would most likely be permitted to contact your consular agent in Myanmar for possible assistance.

If you purchase gems or jewellery from persons or shops that are not licensed by the government, you run the risk of having them confiscated if customs officials find them in your baggage when you're exiting the country.

DIRECTORY

Journalists often claim a different profession in order to get a visa, and they risk deportation if authorities suspect that they're researching a political exposé while in the country. Forming public assemblies is illegal.

Drugs are another area where you must be very careful. We know of a French traveller arrested for possession of opium or heroin in Kengtung and held for several weeks before he was able to bribe his way out. Drug trafficking crimes are punishable by death.

Many foreigners (like Jonathan Rambo in a certain eponymous film) foolishly enter Myanmar illegally from northern Thailand, but not all succeed in avoiding arrest. In late 1998 three Western motorcyclists crossed illegally from Thailand's Mae Hong Son Province into Shan State. They were held for three months before being released and deported.

MAPS

If you want a map before you go, the best available is the 1:2,000,000 Periplus Editions *Myanmar Travel Map,* a folded map with plans for Mandalay, Yangon and the Bagan area, or the ITMB 1:1,350,000 *Myanmar (Burma).* Another choice is the 1:1,500,000 Nelles *Myanmar,* a folded map on coated stock. Good places to buy maps online include **Travel Maps and Books** (www.itmb.com) and **MapLink** (www.maplink.com).

The Myanmar company **Design Printing Services** (DPS; www.dpsmap.com) prints useful tourist maps of Myanmar, Yangon, Mandalay and Bagan – get a free one online. Sometimes these maps are sold locally for about K1000.

In Yangon you can pick up the full-colour, folded *Tourist Map of Myanmar,* published on coated stock by DPS, from many hotels and bookshops. Sometimes you can grab one free at the Yangon Airport arrival hall.

The Myanmar government's Survey Department publishes a very good paper sheet map of the country, simply entitled *Myanmar,* which has a scale of 1:2,000,000. It's big and the uncoated paper decays rapidly. You can find it on Bogyoke Aung San Rd in Yangon, just east of the market.

MONEY

Myanmar's national currency, the kyat (pronounced chat, and abbreviated K) is divided into the following banknotes: K1, K5, K10, K20, K50, K100, K200, K500 and K1000. See the inside front cover for black-market exchange rates as this book was going to press (official rates are much less favourable). Considering the economy's freefall, and rising inflation, rates are likely to change.

See p27 for details on costs in Myanmar and p24 for tips on spreading your budget through the private sector rather than giving it to the government.

ATMs

Myanmar has no ATMs (automatic teller machines).

Banks

Myanmar's banking system is still reeling from the mass emigration of foreign banks that followed the 2003 sanctions by the EU and USA. The few national banks that remain are of little use to travellers, as official exchange rates massively overvalue the kyat. So there's really no reason to exchange money at a bank.

Cash

Most guesthouses and hotels quote prices in US dollars. These places usually accept kyat, but at a slightly disadvantageous rate (perhaps a difference of K50 or K100 to the dollar). Some hotels, shops and government ferry clerks give change in kyat or with torn US bills that you can't use elsewhere in Myanmar. If you're counting pennies, bring lots of small dollar bills – ones, fives and 10s – and use them to pay for your hotel.

Government-run services (such as archaeological sites, museums and ferries) and flights are paid for in US dollars or FEC notes (see opposite), not euros.

Items such as meals, bus tickets, trishaw or taxi rides, bottles of water or beer and market items are usually quoted in kyat.

BRING NEW BILLS!

Don't expect to change any rumpled, torn US dollar bills. Moneychangers accept only crisp, clean (and mostly uncreased) bills, and tend to only take the 'new' US dollar bills (with the larger full-frame heads). We've heard that $100 bills starting with the serial number 'CB' have been turned down.

Any amounts over $2000 per person are supposed to be declared upon arrival.

Credit Cards & Travellers Cheques

At research time, credit cards and travellers cheques were essentially useless in Myanmar. Surprised tourists in Yangon found themselves helpless when trying to use them. It's not likely to change in the near future. However, a couple of high-end hotels in Yangon (p91) and Mandalay (p258) are able to accept credit cards, and sometimes give cash back. This is done via a processing system linked outside the country, usually in Singapore, and is at the mercy of internet connections.

Moneychangers

Avoid the official exchange counters, which undercut black-market rates substantially (K450 per dollar, rather than K12,000). In fact, the official exchanger at the Yangon airport told us to go outside for better rates.

You will be asked to 'change money' many times on your trip. Technically, the only reasonable way to buy kyat is through the 'black market' – meaning from shops, hotels, travel agents, restaurants or less reliable guys on the street. You can change US dollars or euros in Yangon, but generally only US dollars elsewhere.

The $100 bill gets a slightly better exchange rate than a $50 or $20, and so on. And supposedly the exchange rate is marginally better early in the week (Monday or Tuesday). We've also been told that exchange rates sometimes fluctuate with poppy season too!

It's safest to change money in hotels or shops, rather than on the street. The moneychangers standing around just east of the Mahabandoola Garden in Yangon have a reputation for short-changing new arrivals of several thousand kyat.

Never hand over your money until you've received the kyat and counted them. Honest moneychangers will expect you do this. Considering that K1000 is the highest denomination (roughly $0.90), you'll get a lot of notes. Moneychangers give ready-made, rubber-banded stacks of a hundred K1000 bills. It's a good idea to check each note individually. Often you'll find one or two (or more) with a cut corner or taped together, neither of which anyone will accept. We heard from some travellers that Yangon moneychangers have asked for a 'commission'.

KYAT & DOLLARS

Prices in this book alternate between kyat (K) and US dollars ($), depending on the currency in which prices are quoted. Be careful to keep some US dollars with you in case you're turned back by a strict and unbending museum cashier who will not take kyat. For more information, see opposite.

Many travellers do the bulk of their exchanging in Yangon, where you can get about K100 more per dollar than elsewhere, then carry the stacks of kyat for a couple of weeks around the country. Considering the relative safety from theft, it's not a bad idea, but you *can* exchange money elsewhere.

Also, when paying for rooms and services in US dollars, check your change carefully. Locals like to unload slightly torn $5 bills that work fine in New York, but will be meaningless for the rest of your trip.

FECs

Previously, all travellers entering the country had to exchange $200 into FEC (Foreign Exchange Certificates); one of the government's primary ways of acquiring dollars from tourists. This requirement was suspended indefinitely in August 2003, though some government businesses, such as Myanma Airways and museums, may still quote prices in FEC. Technically they can still be used anywhere but most private shops prefer foreign currency. One FEC is equal to $1.

Tipping, Donations & Bribes

Tipping as known in the West is not customary in Myanmar, though little extra 'presents' are sometimes expected (even if they're not asked for) in exchange for a service (such as unlocking a locked temple at Bagan, helping move a bag at the airport or showing you around the 'sights' of a village).

It's a good idea to keep some small notes (K50, K100, K200) when visiting a religious temple or monastery, as donations may be asked for. Also, you may wish to leave a donation.

In the past, many travellers have offered a little 'tea money' to officials in order to help expedite bureaucratic services such as visa extensions or getting a seat on a 'sold out' flight. You shouldn't have to do this. If you overstay your visa, you'll often pay a $3 'fee' for the paperwork, in addition to the $3 per day penalty. See p354 for more details.

See also p343 for details on the 'commissions' paid to guides and drivers, and p22 for ideas on gifts you should and shouldn't give in Myanmar.

PHOTOGRAPHY & VIDEO

There should be no problem bringing a camera or video camera into Myanmar, although a huge contraption that looks like a portable movie set *will* attract attention. Some internet cafés can burn digital photos onto a CD, but you should have your own adapter. Colour film – Fuji and Kodak – is widely available. Photo-supply shops don't often sell cameras, but they can develop film.

Avoid taking photographs of military facilities, uniformed individuals, road blocks and bridges. Aung Sang Suu Kyi's home is absolutely off limits to all photographers. We've heard that some travellers who took photos of the house have had their film confiscated.

Most locals are not at all unhappy about being photographed, but ask first. If you have a digital camera with a display screen, some locals (kids, monks, anyone) will be overjoyed to see their image.

Some sights, including some paya and other religious sites, charge a camera fee of K100 or so. Usually a video camera fee is a little more.

For tips on how to shoot photos, pick up Lonely Planet's *Travel Photography: A Guide to Taking Better Pictures*.

POST

Most mail out of Myanmar seems to get to its destination quite efficiently. International-postage rates are a bargain: a postcard, including registration, is K30. If you're blind, you can send mail for free.

Officially, post offices all over Myanmar are supposed to be open from 9.30am to 4.30pm Monday to Friday.

DHL Worldwide Express Mandalay (Map p257; ☎ 02-39274; Hotel Mandalay, 652 78th Rd, 37/38; ☽ 8.30am-5.30pm Mon-Fri, 8.30am-12.30pm Sat); Yangon (☎ 01-251 751; 7A Kaba Aye Pagoda Rd; ☽ 8am-6pm Mon-Sat) is a more reliable way of sending out bigger packages (though you can send only documents to the USA because of sanctions). Packages begin at $78 (1.1lb/0.5kg); documents at $72.

Marine Transport Service (☎ 01-256 628; mts@yangon.net.mm; MGW Centre, 170/176 Bo Aungkyaw Rd) can ship freight boxes if you end up going nuts on puppets.

SHOPPING

There are some good bargains to be had in Myanmar, particularly for textiles and handicrafts. It's a good idea to seek out local artisans and buy handicrafts directly from them, rather than directing profits towards government-owned shops. See p28 for a list of top souvenirs.

In larger towns and cities, bargains are usually found in the public markets, called *zei* or *zay* in Burmese. The main market is often called *zeigyo* (also spelt *zei-gyo* or *zay-cho*).

Though the Bogyoke Aung San Market in Yangon (p128) offers many arts and crafts from around the country, it's not a bad idea to buy items where they are made. Some regional specialities are not widespread (eg cotton and silk shirts at Inle Lake, best-quality parasols at Pindaya and Pathein, regional *longyi* styles, and Bagan's lacquerware selection).

The big hotel shops, the large air-con handicrafts emporiums and the shops in the departure lounge at Yangon airport are very expensive.

Outside the hotel shops, haggling is generally in full force, and very few things have marked prices. Often the acceptable selling price is about half of what is originally offered. Cheaper items, such as T-shirts, are less likely to drop that much.

Antiques
SCALES

Although they're not all as ancient as they're made out to be, *a-le* (opium weights) are popular things to collect. These are the little animal shapes in descending sizes that are traditionally used for weighing opium, gems and other precious goods.

The older system of scales used a series of nine weights; the newer system uses six

---

DIY SHOPPING

If touts, taxis or trishaw drivers take you to shops, they'll get a commission – and often that means your quoted price is jacked-up. You'll often save a little money if you take yourself to souvenir shops.

weights. Production of the traditional zoomorphic weights came to a halt once the British colonial administration standardised the system of weights and measures in 1885. The pre-1885 weights were made of bronze; reproductions made for the tourist trade are usually brass. The most common animal figures are *to-aung* (a creature that looks like a cross between a bull and a lion), *hintha* (a swan-like bird) and *karaweik* (the Myanmar crane).

KAMMAWA & PARABAIK

Kammawa (from the Pali *kammavacha*) are narrow, rectangular slats painted with extracts from the Pali Vinaya (the Pitaka) concerned with monastic discipline; specifically, extracts to do with clerical affairs. The core of a *kammawa* page may be a thin slat of wood, lacquered cloth, thatched cane or thin brass, which is then layered with red, black and gold lacquer to form the script and decorations.

The *parabaik* (Buddhist palm-leaf manuscript) is a similarly horizontal 'book', this time folded accordion-style, like a road map. The pages are made of heavy paper covered with black ink on which the letters are engraved.

Both *kammawa* and *parabaik* are among the items prohibited for export – though it's difficult to say how well this is enforced.

Books

Bookshops are plentiful but Yangon's Bagan Bookshop (p89) is by far the best place to dig up old Myanmar-related English-language books (and those in some other foreign languages), including regional-based books on sites such as Mrauk U (which aren't available outside Yangon). You can find many interesting old books and magazines along Bogyoke Aung San St, across from the market. Yangon is also the best place to pick up English-language magazines such as *Newsweek* and *Time*.

Clothing & Shoes
LONGYI

Myanmar is the only country in Southeast Asia where the majority of the population wear non-Western clothes as part of their everyday dress. Native fabrics are for the most part limited to the *longyi*.

Men wear ankle-length patterns of checks, plaids or stripes. To tie them they gather the

---

> **YANGON PICK-UP**
>
> Shipping goods abroad from Myanmar is very expensive (and impossible if you live in the US, due to sanctions). If you want a few puppets, but are worried about breaking them along the way, many shops around the country will package your gifts and arrange to deliver them to a Yangon hotel by bus for a minimal fee.

---

front of the *longyi* to create two short lengths of material, then twist them into a half-knot, tucking one end in at the waist while allowing the other to protrude from the knot. Any kind of shirt, from a T-shirt to the formal mandarin-collar *eingyi*, may be worn with a man's *longyi*. On very formal occasions such as weddings, the *gaung baung* (Bamar turban) is added to the outfit.

Local women favour calf-length *longyi* in solid colours, stripes or flower prints, topped off by a form-fitting, waist-length blouse. A black waistband is stitched along the waist end, which is folded in front to form a wide pleat, then tucked behind the waistband to one side. The most expensive designs tend to feature wavy or zigzag *acheiq* patterns, the rarest of which are woven using a hundred or more spools of thread and called *lun-taya* (hundred-spool) *acheiq*.

OTHER ITEMS

Simple flip-flops with leather soles and velvet thongs are the most common footwear for both men and women. If you need them big, some shops can have them tailor-made for you in about three days.

Tailoring in Myanmar is very inexpensive compared with just about anywhere else in the world, with many good choices in Yangon (p129).

Trousers, of the same cut as those sold in Thailand as 'fisherman's pants', can be found in Shan State, particularly around Inle Lake but also in Hsipaw.

Yangon's malls are the best place to find the biggest selection of Western-style imports (mostly from Thailand).

Jewellery & Precious Stones

Myanmar generates considerable income from the mining of precious stones, including rubies, jade and sapphire. There is

DIRECTORY

controversy surrounding their mining, with reports of forced labour. Mining areas are not open to foreigners, including Mogok (Sagaing Division), Pyinlon (Shan State), Maingshu (Shan State), Myaduang (Kayah State) and parts of Kachin State. Following the September 2007 protests, the EU added sanctions specifically against the purchase of gems and precious stones.

There are many tales of visitors buying cheap gems and selling them for huge profits in the West. Beware of scams (we've heard of a foreigner spending $2000 on worthless stones hawked as jade in Mandalay).

Precious stones are supposed to be a government monopoly, and the government is very unhappy about visitors buying stones from anywhere other than licensed retail shops.

The finer imperial-jade or pigeon-blood rubies can only be purchased at exclusive special dealer sessions during the government-sponsored Myanmar Gems, Jade & Pearl Emporium held each year in October, December and February in Yangon.

Still, many visitors manage to buy stones from unlicensed dealers, who far outnumber those who are licensed. The government turns a blind eye to most domestic trade; Mandalay's jade market (p272) is an example.

If *any* stones are found when your baggage is checked on departure, they may be confiscated unless you can present a receipt showing that they were purchased from a government-licensed dealer.

Lacquerware

Probably the most popular purchase in Myanmar is lacquerware. You'll find bowls, trays, boxes, containers, cups, vases and other everyday items (including tables!) on sale in the main markets of Yangon and Mandalay; in the entrance walks to Mahamuni Paya in Mandalay; and particularly in Bagan, where most of the lacquerware is made.

If you purchase large lacquerware items, most shops will wrap and crate them for you for easier shipping.

HISTORY

The earliest lacquerware found in Myanmar can be dated to the 11th century and sported a very Chinese style. The techniques used today are known as *yun*, the old Bamar word for the people of Chiang Mai, from where the techniques were imported in the 16th century

(along with some captured artisans) by King Bayinnaung. An older style of applying gold or silver to a black background dates back to, perhaps, the Pyay era (5th to 9th centuries) and is kept alive by artisans in Kyaukka (p290), near Monywa.

HOW IT'S MADE & WHAT TO LOOK FOR

Many lacquerware shops – in Kyaukka, Myinkaba (p186) and New Bagan (Bagan Myothit; p188) – include active workshops, where you can see the long-winded process involved in making the bowls, trays and other objects. The craftsperson first weaves a frame (the best-quality wares have a bamboo frame tied together with horse or donkey hairs; lesser pieces are made wholly from bamboo). The lacquer is then coated over the framework and allowed to dry. After several days it is sanded down with ash from rice husks and another coating of lacquer is applied. A high-quality item may have seven to 15 layers altogether.

The lacquerware is engraved and painted, then polished to remove the paint from everywhere except from within the engravings. Multicoloured lacquerware is produced by repeated engraving, painting and polishing. From start to finish it can take up to five or six months to produce a high-quality piece of lacquerware, which may have as many as five colours. A top-quality bowl can have its rim squeezed together until the sides meet without suffering any damage or permanent distortion.

Parasols

The graceful and beautifully painted little parasols you see around Myanmar are cheap and a product of the port of Pathein (p139) – in fact they're known in Myanmar as *Pathein hti* (Pathein umbrellas). Everyday parasols have wooden handles, and the more ceremonial ones have handles of silver.

Tapestries

Along with lacquerware, tapestries (*kalaga*) are one of the better bargains in Myanmar. They consist of pieces of coloured cloth of various sizes heavily embroidered with silver- or gold-coloured thread, metal sequins and glass beads, and feature mythological Myanmar figures in padded relief. The greatest variety is found in Mandalay, where most tapestries are produced. You can also purchase tapestries in Yangon's Bogyoke Aung San Market (p128).

Good-quality *kalaga* are tightly woven and don't skimp on sequins, which may be sewn in overlapping lines, rather than spaced side by side, as a sign of embroidery skill. The metals used should shine, even in older pieces; tarnishing means lower-quality materials. Prices vary according to size and quality, from $5 to $100.

Woodcarving & Puppets
You can still find some pleasantly carved new buddha images and other items from workshops in Mandalay or in the corridors leading to Shwedagon Paya in Yangon, but in general you won't see much woodcarving on sale.

Older items from the Amarapura, Yadanapon and Mandalay periods are plentiful, but you can't be sure that Myanmar customs will allow them out of the country (it's not a good idea to remove historical items for your personal use anyway). Some high-end antique shops in Bangkok and Chiang Mai seem to have an endless supply of pieces that once graced Burmese *kyaung*.

Wooden puppets, old and new (cheapies go for as little as $3 or $4 in Mandalay and Yangon), are other popular items.

Export Restrictions
The following items cannot legally be taken out of the country: prehistoric implements and artefacts; fossils; old coins; bronze or brass weights (including opium weights); bronze or clay pipes; *kammawa* or *parabaik;* inscribed stones; inscribed gold or silver; historical documents; religious images; sculptures or carvings in bronze, stone, stucco or wood; frescoes (even fragments); pottery; and national regalia and paraphernalia. Technically you have to show approval from various government agencies to bring out videotapes or books, though this is very unlikely to be enforced.

SOLO TRAVELLERS
The already hospitable locals are even more so if you're travelling alone. But unaccompanied travellers will be questioned about why they're going solo, sometimes with an endearing dose of pity.

Nearly all accommodation options have reduced rates for single rooms. However, some side trips (which require you to hire a boat, taxi or big horse cart) will mean extra expenses that could otherwise be shared. Generally, outside budget guesthouses in bigger destinations, the easiest way to meet fellow travellers is on transport where you can roam a bit, such as boat rides.

TELEPHONE

'Approach the telephone with a prayer.'
Aung San Suu Kyi

Most business cards in Myanmar purposely list a couple of phone numbers, and a mobile (cell) phone number, as lines frequently go dead and calls just don't go through.

Local call stands – as part of a shop, or sometimes just a table with a phone or two on a sidewalk – are marked by a drawing of a phone and can be found all over Myanmar. A local call should be K100 per minute.

Official telephone (call) centres (like the ones in Mandalay, p258, and Ngapali Beach, p319) are sometimes the only way to call overseas, though sometimes this can be done on the street too.

Generally, it costs about $5 per minute to call Australia or Europe and $6 per minute to phone North America. You'll usually be asked to pay in US dollars.

In August 2008, the government unexpectedly allowed local mobile-phone users to send international text messages through E-Trade Myanmar Company.

Like electronic devices, all mobile phones must be declared upon arrival (see the box on p352 for more info on mobile phones).

CALLING MYANMAR

■ To call Myanmar from abroad, dial your country's international access code, then ☎ 95 (Myanmar's country code), the area code (minus the '0'), and the five- or six-digit number. Area codes are listed below town headings throughout the book.

■ To dial long distance within Myanmar, dial the area code (including the '0') and the number.

DIRECTORY

MOBILE PHONES & STATUS

There's no international roaming in Myanmar, so your mobile (cell) phone will be useless here. You'll see a fair share of them in use though. Apparently some 300,000 locals have them, up from essentially zero not many years ago. This is a serious status symbol (even without a Beyoncé ringtone), considering the SIM card alone costs about $1000!

   If you come with a mobile phone it must be declared upon arrival.

Mobile-phone numbers in Myanmar begin with ☎ 09.

A useful resource is the **Myanmar Yellow Pages** (www.myanmaryellowpages.biz).

TIME

The local Myanmar Standard Time (MST) is 6½ hours ahead of Greenwich Mean Time (GMT/UTC). When coming in from Thailand, turn your watch back half an hour; coming from India, put your watch forward an hour. The 24-hour clock is often used for train times (eg 16.00 instead of 4pm).

TOILETS

Toilets, when you need them most (at bus stops or off the highway), are often at their worst. Outside most guesthouses, hotels and upscale restaurants, squat toilets are the norm. Most of these are located down a dirt path behind a house. Usually next to the toilet is a cement reservoir filled with water, and a plastic bowl lying nearby. This has two functions: as a flush and for people to clean their nether regions while still squatting over the toilet. Toilet paper is available at shops all over the country, but not often at toilets. Some places charge a nominal fee to use the toilet.

Note that, other than at top-end hotels, the plumbing in flush, sit-down toilets is not equipped to flush paper. Usually there's a small waste basket nearby to deposit used toilet paper.

It's perfectly acceptable for men (less so for women) to go behind a tree or bush (or at the roadside) when nature calls.

Note that buses and smaller boats usually don't have toilets.

TOURIST INFORMATION

Government-operated **Myanmar Travels & Tours** (MTT; www.myanmars.net/mtt) is part of the Ministry of Hotels & Tourism and the main 'tourist information' service in the country. Those who want to avoid using government services should avoid the tours and services offered here, including train or plane ticket sales. MTT offices are located in Yangon (p91), Mandalay (p258), New Bagan (p186) and Inle Lake (p232). Other than at Yangon, these offices are pretty quiet, and often the staff have sketchy knowledge on restricted areas.

There are no MTT offices abroad. Try www.myanmar.com for (often useful) travel information provided by the government.

Much of the tourist industry in Myanmar is now privatised. Travellers who want to arrange a driver, or have hotel reservations awaiting them, would do well to arrange a trip with the help of private travel agents in Yangon (p92). Many Myanmar 'travel agents' outside Yangon only sell air tickets.

TRAVELLERS WITH DISABILITIES

With its lack of paved roads or footpaths (even when present the latter are often uneven) Myanmar presents many physical obstacles for the mobility-impaired. Rarely do public buildings (or transport) feature ramps or other access points for wheelchairs, and hotels make inconsistent efforts to provide access to the handicapped (exceptions include the Strand Hotel and the Traders Hotel in Yangon, which both have some ramping).

For wheelchair travellers, any trip to Myanmar will require a good deal of planning. A few useful USA-based organisations you can contact are **Accessible Journeys** (www.disabilitytravel .com), which has a Thailand tour that reaches the Myanmar border; **Mobility International USA** (www.miusa.org) and the **Society for Accessible Travel & Hospitality** (www.sath.org), which publishes the magazine *Open World*.

VISAS

Passport holders from Asean countries, China, Bangladesh and Russia do not need to apply for visas to visit Myanmar. All other nationalities do. A tourist visa's validity expires 90 days after issue and only allows a 28-day, single-entry visit. It officially costs $20 but sometimes runs to €25 in Western Europe.

You'll need three passport-sized photos for the process.

There are also 28-day business visas ($30) and 28-day special visas ($30) for former Myanmar citizens (these visas can be extended for three to six months once in Yangon). A multiple-entry business visa is $150. There is no longer an e-visa service or 'meditation visa' available.

At research time, Bangkok travel agents, particularly on Khao San Rd, specialised in getting quick tourist visas for Myanmar. Rates depended on turnaround times, which aren't always met. One agent quoted us a three-day turn-around time for B1700 ($54), including B500 fee.

See p358 for more information on entering Myanmar overland from Thailand or China, which includes details of short-term visas (with very limited access to Myanmar) available at the borders. Special permission is required to leave the country overland from Tachileik to Thailand.

Note that Myanmar doesn't recognise dual nationalities.

Applications

Following the September 2007 protests, Myanmar mandated that visa applicants apply *in person*, meaning that, say, Kansas City residents would have to book a flight to Washington, DC or New York City to apply. Here's hoping this will change before your trip. For what it's worth, Thai tour agents told us this was not the case in Bangkok at research time.

Myanmar's embassies and consulates abroad scrupulously check out the background of anyone applying for a tourist visa. In particular, writers and journalists may have a difficult time obtaining visas. Therefore, it's probably not a good idea to list your occupation as any of the following: journalist, photographer, editor, publisher, motion-picture director or producer, cameraperson, videographer or writer. Of course, plenty of journalists and photographers do get into the country – by declaring a different profession on the visa application.

Myanmar foreign missions may also be suspicious of anyone whose passport shows

---

LIVING ON MYANMAR TIME

That bus may roll in late, but much of Myanmar actually does work on a different time system. Most Myanmar Buddhists use an eight-day week in which Thursday to Tuesday conform to the Western calendar but Wednesday is divided into two 12-hour days. Midnight to noon is 'Bohdahu' (the day Buddha was born), while noon to midnight is 'Yahu' (Rahu, a Hindu god/planet). It's rare that the week's unique structure causes any communication problems, however.

The traditional Myanmar calendar features 12 28-day lunar months that run out of sync with the months of the solar Gregorian calendar. To stay in sync with the solar year, Myanmar inserts a second Waso lunar month every few years – somewhat like the leap-year day added to the Gregorian February. The lunar months of Myanmar:

Tagu March/April	**Thadingyut** September/October
Kason April/May	**Tazaungmon** October/November
Nayon May/June	**Nadaw** November/December
Waso June/July	**Pyatho** December/January
Wagaung July/August	**Tabodwe** January/February
Tawthalin August/September	**Tabaung** February/March

Most traditional festivals take place according to the lunar calendar, making it difficult to calculate festival dates using the fixed-date Gregorian calendar. Ask most Buddhist villagers when a *pwe* is scheduled and you may hear something like, 'It's on Pyatho, 8th day of the waning moon.' OK, see you there!

Traditionally, Burmese kings subscribed to various year counts. The main one in current use, the *thekkayit*, begins in April and is 638 years behind the Christian year count. Therefore, the Christian year of 2009 is equivalent to the *thekkayit* of 1371. If an ancient temple you see sounds way too old, it may be because locals are using the *thekkayit*.

Another calendar in use follows the Buddhist era (BE), as used in Thailand, which counts from 543 BC, the date that Buddha achieved *nibbana*. Hence AD 2009 is 2552 BE.

two or more previous visits to Myanmar in a five-year period. Obviously the government can't believe anyone would want to visit Myanmar more than once or twice! In cases such as these you'll need more of a reason than simply 'tourism' for receiving another visa. Be creative.

Extensions & Overstaying Your Visa

At research time, it was apparently no longer possible to extend a tourist visa. However, overstaying your visa is possible. At research time, Yangon Airport's immigration allowed visitors to overstay their visa for a charge of $3 per day, plus a $3 'registration fee'. We were told it's OK 'up to 90 days' but it's probably wise to not push it more than 10 or 14 days. Many local travel agents and ex-pats shrug their shoulders on whether there's an official policy. We've not heard of anyone having problems for short overstays. Have exact change ready (they're not likely to change your $100 bill and they won't take kyat) and arrive early enough to fill out a few forms in a nearby office (after which they may tell you 'see you next time').

Note, however, that once you've overstayed your visa, you may have difficulties with airport immigration if you're planning domestic flights, particularly in far-flung airports (like Sittwe or Myitkyina). It's wise to stick with land routes.

VOLUNTEERING

Official opportunities to volunteer are greatly limited. A list of NGOs that may have volunteering opportunities can be found on www .ngoinmyanmar.org, although mostly their postings are for specific experienced workers (often in medicine). Don't let this sway you. Everyone in Myanmar wants to learn English, and few can afford to. Ask in towns or villages to sit in at an English class.

One or two smaller operations have wrangled past the government- and sanction-inspired red tape and set up low-key projects to improve lives. The following two are able to accept both skilled and unskilled volunteers, but give them as much advance notice as possible.

Trained and untrained teachers and builders and handypeople are needed by Swiss-run project **Growing Together School** (gt.camp@gmail.com), which has two schools based in and around Yangon. They generally require volunteers for at least six weeks. **The Eden Centre for Disabled Children** (☎ 640 399; www.edencentre.org) is the first Myanmar-run NGO working to better the lives of disabled children in the city.

Also see p25 for suggestions on volunteering and responsible travel in Myanmar.

WOMEN TRAVELLERS

As in most Buddhist countries, foreign women travelling in Myanmar are rarely hassled on the road as they might be in India, Malaysia or Indonesia. However, we have heard a few reports of sexual harassment. Dressing modestly should help reduce this risk: wear a local *longyi* instead of a skirt above the knee, and any old T-shirt instead of a spaghetti-strap top.

No Myanmar woman would even consider travelling without at least one female companion, so women travelling alone are regarded as slightly peculiar by the locals. Lone women being seen off on boats and trains by local friends may find the latter trying to find a suitably responsible older woman to keep them company on the trip.

If you didn't bring tampons, one good place to find them is Yangon's City Mart Supermarket (p91).

'Ladies' (per the posted signs in certain areas) cannot go up some altars or onto decks around stupas, including the one affording a close-up look at the famous Golden Rock at Kyaiktiyo (p154), or to apply gold leaf on the Buddha image at Mandalay's Mahamuni Paya (p263). Also, women are never supposed to touch a monk. If you're handing something to a monk, place the object within reach of him, not directly into his hands.

Most locals tend to visit teashops, restaurants or shops with members of the same sex. Asian women, even from other countries, travelling with a Western man may encounter rude comments.

See p67 for some background on the role of local women in society.

Transport

CONTENTS

GETTING THERE & AWAY

ENTERING THE COUNTRY

If you're arriving by air, and have your visa ready (see p352) and valid passport in hand, you should have no trouble entering Myanmar.

Arriving by land is not very practical. You can cross from Ruili (China) to Mu-se, but not leave that way. From Mae Sai (Thailand) you can cross to Tachileik, but can only go as far as Kengtung. Those in Thailand on a visa run can cross to Kawthoung but cannot venture further into Myanmar.

There is no way that foreigners can reach Myanmar by land or sea from Bangladesh, India or Laos. (See p358 for more on border crossings.)

Overland links could change at some point in the future. Most of Myanmar's neighbours actively covet Myanmar ports and are planning on investing for infrastructure projects to eventually criss-cross Myanmar by road. This may mean connections from Danang, Vietnam (through Laos and Thailand) to Mawlamyine, and up through central Myanmar, across the India border at Morei (open already to traffic, but not foreigners) to New Delhi.

There is no requirement for you to show an onward ticket out of the country in order to enter Myanmar.

Passport

You will need to have a passport that has at least six months of validity from the time of entry.

AIR
Airports & Airlines

All international flights arrive at Yangon (Rangoon) airport (RGN), except a lone Thursday flight from Chiang Mai (Thailand)

WARNING – THINGS CHANGE

The information in this chapter is particularly vulnerable to change, and this is especially so in Myanmar. The 500% inflation in gas prices Myanmar suffered in late 2007 affected transport costs greatly, and Cyclone Nargis in May 2008 had lasting effects on road conditions and timetables in much of the delta region around Yangon.

In terms of international travel, prices are volatile, routes are introduced and cancelled, schedules change, special deals come and go, and rules and visa requirements are amended. Airlines and governments seem to take a perverse pleasure in making price structures and regulations as complicated as possible. You should check directly with the airline or a travel agent to make sure you understand how a fare (and ticket you may buy) works. In addition, the travel industry is highly competitive, and there are many lurks and perks.

The upshot of this is that you should get opinions, quotes and advice from as many airlines and travel agents as possible before you part with your hard-earned cash. The details given in this chapter should be regarded as pointers and are not a substitute for your own careful, up-to-date research.

to Mandalay airport (MDL). Both airports can land DC10s and 747s.

The most common route to Yangon is via Bangkok, though flights also connect Yangon with Calcutta, Kuala Lumpur, Singapore and Kunming (China). Flights to Dhaka, Bangladesh and Hong Kong have been discontinued, but may resume at some point.

Airlines with offices in Yangon and regular international links with Myanmar follow:

Air China (☎ 01-500 054; www.fly-airchina.com; airline code CA; B13/23 Narnattaw Rd, Kamayut Township) Flies to/from Kunming twice weekly.

Air Mandalay (Map p93; ☎ 01-525 488; www.airmandalay.com; airline code 6T; 146 Dhama Zedi Rd) Flight from Chiang Mai to Mandalay on Thursday, to Yangon on Sunday; from Yangon to Chiang Mai on Thursday and Sunday.

Bangkok Airways (Map p102; ☎ 01-255 122; www.bangkokair.com; airline code PG; Sakura Tower, 339 Bogyoke Aung San Rd) Flies to/from Bangkok four times weekly.

Indian Airlines (Map p102; ☎ 01-253 598; http://indian-airlines.nic.in; airline code IC; 127 Sule Paya Rd) Flies to/from Calcutta on Monday and Friday.

Malaysia Airlines (Map p102; ☎ 01-241 007; www.malaysiaairlines.com; airline code MH; 335/337 Bogyoke Aung San Rd) Flies daily (except Thursday) to/from Kuala Lumpur.

Mandarin Airlines (☎ 01-245 484; www.mandarin-airlines.com/en; airline code AE; 353/355 Bo Aung Kyaw St, Kyauktada) Flies Tuesday, Thursday and Sunday to/from Taipei.

Myanmar Airways International (MAI; Map p102; ☎ 01-255 440; www.maiair.com; airline code 8M; Sakura Tower, 339 Bogyoke Aung San Rd) This international line is not affiliated with the government's Myanma Airways. Flies to/from Bangkok, Delhi, Kuala Lumpur and Singapore.

Silk Air (Map p102; ☎ 01-255 287; www.silkair.com; airline code MI; Sakura Tower, 339 Bogyoke Aung San Rd) Flies daily to/from Singapore.

Thai Air Asia (Map p98; ☎ 01-251-885; www.airasia.com; airline code FD; Park Royal Hotel, 33 Ah Lan Paya Pagoda Rd, Dagon) Flies daily to/from Bangkok.

Thai Airways (Thai; Map p102; ☎ 01-255 499; www.thaiair.com; airline code TG; 1st fl, Sakura Tower, 339 Bogyoke Aung San Rd) Flies daily to/from Bangkok.

A few airlines keep Yangon representatives despite not offering direct services to Myanmar, including the following:

All Nippon Airways (ANA; Map p102; ☎ 01-255 412; www.ana.co.jp/eng; airline code NH; 339 Bogyoke Aung San Rd, Sakura Tower)

China Airlines (☎ 01-245 484; www.china-airlines.com; airline code CI; 353 Bo Aung Kyaw St, Kyauktada)

Japan Airlines (JAL; Map p102; ☎ 01-240 400; www.jal.co.jp; airline code JL; FMI Bldg, 380 Bogyoke Aung San Rd)

Korean Air (☎ 01-677 410; www.koreanair.com; airline code KE; 2B Sae Myaung Ave, 8 Mile Junction)

CLIMATE CHANGE & TRAVEL

Climate change is a serious threat to the ecosystems that humans rely upon, and air travel is the fastest-growing contributor to the problem. Lonely Planet regards travel, overall, as a global benefit, but believes we all have a responsibility to limit our personal impact on global warming.

Flying & Climate Change

Pretty much every form of motorised travel generates CO_2 (the main cause of human-induced climate change) but planes are far and away the worst offenders, not just because of the sheer distances they allow us to travel, but because they release greenhouse gases high into the atmosphere. The statistics are frightening: two people taking a return flight between Europe and the US will contribute as much to climate change as an average household's gas and electricity consumption over a whole year.

Carbon Offset Schemes

Climatecare.org and other websites use 'carbon calculators' that allow travellers to offset the level of greenhouse gases they are responsible for with financial contributions to sustainable travel schemes that reduce global warming – including projects in India, Honduras, Kazakhstan and Uganda.

Lonely Planet, together with Rough Guides and other concerned partners in the travel industry, support the carbon offset scheme run by climatecare.org. Lonely Planet offsets all of its staff and author travel.

For more information check out our website: www.lonelyplanet.com.

Air Bagan's service to Singapore was suspended following sanctions directed towards Air Bagan's owner Tay Za (p21) in late 2007. See p361 for a list of domestic carriers.

Tickets

The lack of many services to Myanmar means discounted fares are hard to come by. Sometimes buying two tickets – one to Bangkok, and another to Yangon – ends up cheaper than a one-ticket fare to Yangon from your home country.

If you have a little wiggle room in your itinerary, compare costs of flying return between Bangkok and Yangon (about $300 return, while a one way ticket to Bangkok bought in Yangon is about $120). If your London–Yangon or New York–Yangon flight is more than that extra from a Bangkok ticket, you could book separate tickets and save. Sample fares to Yangon from London run from £650 (about £150 more than Bangkok), from New York $1600 (about $450 more than Bangkok).

A one-way ticket bought in Yangon for Singapore is about $300.

Once in Myanmar you can only buy international tickets from travel agents or airline offices in Yangon.

AIR PASSES

The **Visit Asean AirPass** (www.visitasean.travel) covers six Southeast Asian countries including Myanmar. You pre-buy three to five 'coupons' for set prices.

INTERCONTINENTAL (RTW) TICKETS

Round-the-world (RTW) tickets only go as near as Bangkok. Here are a few online companies that can help with tickets:

Airstop & Go (www.airstop.be)
Airtreks (www.airtreks.com)
Air Brokers International (www.airbrokers.com)
Around the Worlds (www.aroundtheworlds.com)

DEPARTURE TAX

Myanmar locals pay K500, but foreigners pay $10 departure tax, not included with your air ticket. Have the US dollars in hand when leaving the country. You pay at the window in the entrance hall, before you check in. Kyat are not accepted. There is no departure tax for domestic flights.

Reconfirming Tickets

It's important to reconfirm your outgoing tickets from Myanmar a few days in advance for all airlines other than Thai Airways and Silk Air. If you've forgotten what time your flight is, the inside back page of the *Myanmar Times* lists the week's international flight schedule.

Asia

STA Travel (www.statravel.com) often has good deals. It has branches in China, Hong Kong, Indonesia, Japan, Malaysia, the Philippines, Singapore, Taiwan and Thailand.

Some other locally based agents that can help with tickets:

China Four Seas Travel (☎ Hong Kong 2200 7777; www.fourseastravel.com)
India STIC Travels (☎ Delhi 011-2335-7468; www.stictravel.com)
Japan No 1 Travel (☎ Tokyo 03-3205 6073; www.no1-travel.com)
Thailand Traveller 2000 (☎ Bangkok 662-652-2569; www.traveller2000.com; 86 Soi Langsuan, Ploenchit, Pathumwan) Helps get visas or flight tickets.

Australia

STA Travel (☎ 134 782; www.statravel.com.au) and **Flight Centre** (☎ 133 133; www.flightcentre.com.au) have offices throughout Australia. An online booking agent is www.travel.com.au. A return fare from Sydney to Yangon runs about A$1300, including tax.

Canada

Travel Cuts (☎ 866-246-9762; www.travelcuts.com) is Canada's national student-travel agency. For online bookings, try www.expedia.ca and www.travelocity.ca.

Continental Europe
FRANCE

Sample fares from Paris to Yangon run about €800. Recommended travel agencies:

Anyway (☎ 08 92 30 23 01; www.anyway.fr)
Nouvelles Frontières (☎ 08 25 00 07 47; www.nouvelles-frontieres.fr)
Voyageurs du Monde (☎ 08 92 23 56 56; www.vdm.com)

GERMANY

Find fares at these online agencies:

Expedia (www.expedia.de)
Just Travel (☎ 089 747 3330; www.justtravel.de)
Last Minute (☎ 01805 284 366; www.lastminute.de)
STA Travel (☎ 069 743 032 92; www.statravel.de)

TRANSPORT

TRANSPORT

ITALY
CTS Viaggi (☎ 199 50 11 50; www.cts.it) Specialises in student and youth travel.

NETHERLANDS
Airfair (☎ 0 900 7717 717; www.airfair.nl)

SPAIN
Barcelo Viajes (www.barceloviajes.com)

New Zealand
Flight Centre (☎ 0800 24 35 44; www.flightcentre.co.nz) and **STA Travel** (☎ 0800 474 400; www.statravel.co.nz) have many branches.

UK
Return tickets to Yangon, usually through Bangkok (or Singapore or Kuala Lumpur), run from £650 including taxes. Discount air-travel ads appear in *Time Out,* the *Evening Standard* and in the free magazine *TNT.*

Recommended travel agencies include the following:
Flight Centre (☎ 0870 499 0040; www.flightcentre.co.uk)
Ebookers (☎ 0871 223 5000; www.ebookers.com)
Quest Travel (☎ 0845 263 6963; www.questtravel.com)
STA Travel (☎ 0871 230 0040; www.statravel.co.uk) Popular with travellers under 26, but sells tickets to all. Branches throughout the UK.
Trailfinders (☎ 0845 058 5858; www.trailfinders.co.uk)
Travel Bag (☎ 0800 804 8911; www.travelbag.co.uk)

USA
Unlike many Asian destinations, airfares to Yangon tend to be the same from the West or East Coast (about $1600 to $2000 return). Discount travel agents – or 'consolidators' – can be found in San Francisco especially, but also Los Angeles and New York.

Berkeley-based **Avia Travel** (☎ 800-950-2842, 510-558-2150; www.aviatravel.com) specialises in custom-designed RTW fares and a few Myanmar tours. Travellers aged under 26, including students, should check with **STA Travel** (☎ 800 781-4040; www.statravel.com) for discount fares.

Check the following recommended agencies' websites for making online bookings: www.cheaptickets.com, www.expedia.com, www.itn.net, www.lowestfare.com, www.orbitz.com, www.travelocity.com.

LAND
Border Crossings
You're probably going to fly in. Borders tend to open and close, mostly the latter of late.

The only border you can cross into Myanmar to continue a trip throughout the country is via Ruili (China). The other borders reach closed-off areas. No bus or train service connects Myanmar with another country, nor can you travel by car or motorcycle across the border – you must walk across. Have your visa before you get to the border (see p352).

In addition to the following there's a border crossing with Morei (India) at Tamu, but it's closed to foreigners.

TO/FROM MAE SAI, THAILAND
North of Chiang Rai it's possible to cross to dreary Tachileik (p253). Travellers are issued a 14-day entry permit, not a visa, at the border for B500. You can travel to Kengtung, but cannot continue anywhere else (even if you have a regular tourist visa).

Travellers wanting to exit Myanmar here can do so with the 14-day permit mentioned above, or if they have a permit from MTT in Yangon (p91).

TO/FROM RANONG, THAILAND
This exit has been closed for out-going tourists, though it's possible to cross into Myanmar from Thailand on a 'visa run'. A day permit is $10, and visitors cannot spend overnight in Myanmar. See p173 for more.

TO/FROM RUILI, CHINA
At the time of research, you could come into Myanmar from China, but not leave Myanmar from this border. You can arrange a regular 28-day tourist visa in a day or two in Kunming (see p307).

To cross overland at Ruili it's necessary to book a multiday 'visa-and-package trip' – you can't go on your own – to cross the border at Mu-Se and on to Lashio. It's about Y1400 ($200). Ruili is about 20 hours from Kunming by road, and Lashio is a five-hour trip from the border, but you can stay in Mu-Se if necessary.

RIVER & SEA
It is not possible for foreigners to go to/from Myanmar by sea or river.

TOURS
Many foreign-run companies book package tours to Myanmar. We're not recommending them as, in most instances, more money will reach the local people if you travel on

---

RESTRICTED AREAS

Some sites require government fees (p20), but the following areas are only accessible via previously arranged government permits from the MTT office in Yangon (p91) or a government-run trip.

The **Ayeyarwady Delta** area was closed to foreigners after Cyclone Nargis (see p133).

- **Khamti**, aka Naga Land (p286) The government's group tour in January costs $1200!
- **Mong La**, Shan State (p253) The permit is free at least, but you need to arrange one in Kengtung.
- **Mt Victoria**, Chin State (p334) Bypass the government guide by going with a private one, but you'll still need a permit.
- **Putao**, Kachin State (p313)
- **Tachileik**, Shan State (p254) If you're travelling around central Myanmar, you need a permit to visit Tachileik and exit to Thailand by land.

---

your own or arrange a driver and guide from a locally based agent. See p92 for tips on arranging your own tour in Yangon.

Travel agents along Bangkok's Khao San Rd offer a host of short-term package trips to Myanmar, some of which are geared more to midrange, locally run hotels than top-end, joint-venture hotels.

GETTING AROUND

Much of the mountainous areas of Myanmar near the borders are closed, due to conflicts with minority groups or sometimes due to dodgy infrastructure. We highlight these places in the text but situations could change, with routes opening (or closing).

Another big factor, of course, is weather. After Cyclone Nargis hit in 2008, roads heading into the washed-out Ayeyarwady Delta region, south of Yangon, were barred to foreign visitors and remained so as this book went to press. It's likely to change during the life of this book, particularly as the restrictions have isolated unaffected tourist destinations like Pathein and Chaung Tha Beach. All other transport services rebounded shortly after the storm.

In the places you can openly visit in Myanmar, travel methods are remarkably open to visitors. No set itineraries are required (unlike places like North Korea or the old USSR) and you can pick and choose how you go as you go – taking a bus, plane or train, or crammed pick-up, or hopping into a giant ferry that drifts at ox-like speed.

Speaking of which, local transport also comes ped-powered, often with trishaws

and horse carts greeting you for rides around town, and rental bikes awaiting you at nearly all accommodation.

It's worth trying to go by land in Myanmar. Airlines have higher fares – thus more tax money that reaches the government – than a bus, not to mention higher carbon emissions.

Many places that are restricted actually *can* be visited with permits provided by the government's Myanmar Travels & Tours (MTT) and a guide. Sometimes this takes several months of advance planning. So don't expect to cross Chin State's rough highways by showing up and asking (see p334).

The bulk of this book, of course, focuses on places you can go on your own without any pre-planning. See the map on p360 for transport routes that were open at research time. Reaching some isolated towns such as Kengtung or Sittwe requires jumps by air or boat.

AIR

Popular with many travellers getting between Yangon, Mandalay, Inle Lake and Bagan, Myanmar's tiny private domestic air service features only seven planes (the government has five more), meaning that overworked planes have busy days, sometimes landing at an airport, leaving the engine on, unloading and loading, and taking off in 20 minutes! This doesn't yield a spot-free safety record (see p342).

There are 66 airstrips around the country, of which about 20 are served by regular flights. Between the main destinations you'll

TRANSPORT

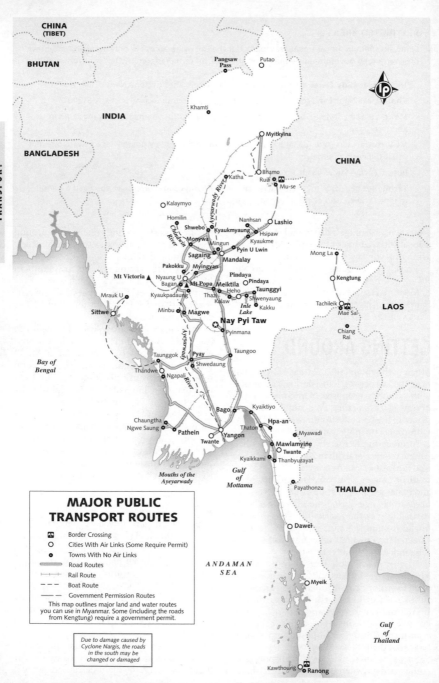

MAJOR PUBLIC TRANSPORT ROUTES

- Border Crossing
- ○ Cities With Air Links (Some Require Permit)
- ◉ Towns With No Air Links
- Road Routes
- Rail Route
- Boat Route
- Government Permission Routes

This map outlines major land and water routes you can use in Myanmar. Some (including the roads from Kengtung) require a government permit.

Due to damage caused by Cyclone Nargis, the roads in the south may be changed or damaged

AIRPORT CODES

Many posted flight schedules around the country only use domestic airport codes.

Bhamo	BMO
Dawei (Tavoy)	TVY
Heho (Inle Lake)	HEH
Kawthoung	KAW
Kengtung	KET
Mandalay	MDL
Myeik	MGZ
Myitkyina	MYT
Nyaung U (Bagan)	NYU
Sittwe	AKY
Tachileik	THL
Thandwe (Ngapali Beach)	SNY
Yangon	RGN

find daily connections. In many other places, there are new, spotless, largely unused airports serving, well, no flights other than visiting dignitaries on occasion. As one Magwe resident told us, 'Our airport? It's for show. We don't get flights here'.

As with international flights, domestic flights involve immigration and customs checks.

In the wake of Visit Myanmar Year in 1996, forced labour was reportedly used to ready new airstrips. Many travellers avoid air travel.

Airlines in Myanmar

While three of the four airlines in Myanmar are 'private' (on paper), rumours about some level of government links hover over all – at least in licensing and administration fees being increased from government, as one insider put it, 'because the government didn't feel they were making enough from tourism'. Tay Za (p21) owns Air Bagan, and has been targeted directly by some outside sanctions. Apparently in 2007, Air Mandalay was refused parts from a Canadian company for reported connections with Air Bagan too.

If you fly, we advise avoiding Myanma Airways in particular – it's not only government-run but its Fokkers are antiques with the worst reputation for upkeep.

Following is the contact information for the offices in Yangon for the four airlines; the regional offices are listed in the respective chapters.

Air Bagan (☎ 01-513 322, 01-513 422; www.airbagan .com; airline code AB; 56 Shwe Taung Gyar St, Bahan) Often

linked to the government, but tends to have best reputation for service.

Air Mandalay (Map p93; ☎ 01-501 500, 01-501 520; www.airmandalay.com; airline code 6T; 146 Dhama Zedi Rd) Running since 1994, this is a Singapore-Malaysia joint venture.

Myanma Airways (MA; Map p102; ☎ 01-374 874, 01-373 828; www.mot.gov.mm/ma; airline code UB; 104 Strand Rd) Government airline.

Yangon Airways (Map p102; ☎ 01-383 101, 01-383 106; www.yangonair.com; airline code HK; MMB Tower, Level 5, 166 Pansodan St) A private Myanmar-run airline operating since 1996, with a cute flying-elephant logo; their slogan 'you're safe with us' is a poke at government-run Myanma Airways' safety record.

Schedules

One Yangon agent told us 'in Myanmar, air routes change in the air'. They're not joking. It's particularly true of MA flights, where dates and departure times are often not written on your ticket, so the airline doesn't have to honour the days and hours for which reservations were originally made. (In some cases, if officials are flying somewhere – say to Lashio – seats may suddenly open to the public.) Schedules are more reliable on the other three airlines, and between main destinations during the high season.

Peak-season is dry season, and sometimes that means renovations on runways. In 2006, Thandwe airport's runway was closed for five days weekly, nearly cutting off travel to Ngapali; in 2007, Kengtung's runway was closed, meaning flights landed a tough three-hour drive away.

Tickets

Because travel agents sell flight tickets at a slightly discounted rate, it makes little sense to buy directly from the airlines. One-way fares are half a return fare, and can usually be bought a day in advance. To buy a ticket, you'll need to pay with US dollars or FEC (see p347), and bring your passport to the travel agent or airline office. It's sometimes difficult to buy a ticket that departs from a town other than the one you are in.

There is no domestic departure tax.

SAMPLE AIRFARES

Here are some one-way airfare quotes during peak season for key routes in Myanmar.

Air Mandalay is generally a few dollars cheaper than Yangon Airways or Air Bagan.

MA tickets are generally a bit cheaper than the other airlines'. You have to go to MA or the government's MTT office to purchase tickets on that airline.

Fares during the off-season (roughly March through October) are about $4 or $5 cheaper.

From	To	Price
Mandalay	Heho (Inle Lake)	$41-5
Mandalay	Nyaung U (Bagan)	$40-3
Nyaung U (Bagan)	Heho (Inle Lake)	from $54
Thandwe	Sittwe	$60-5
Yangon	Heho (Inle Lake)	$98
Yangon	Mandalay	$90-3
Yangon	Nyaung U (Bagan)	$81-7
Yangon	Thandwe (Ngapali)	$65-8

BICYCLE

You'll sure see a lot: bicycles are clearly the number-one means for locals to get around. Bikes can easily be hired around the country, but they're best for getting around a town rather than for use on long-haul trips.

Around Town

In places such as Mandalay, Bagan and Inle Lake you'll see 'bike rental' signs; rates start at K1000 per day; top-end hotels and occasionally more far-flung places charge up to K4000. Most guesthouses in such places keep a few bikes on hand; if not, staff can track one down. Note the condition of the bike before hiring; check the brakes and pedals in particular. Many rental bikes have baskets or bells.

Sturdier Indian, Chinese or Thai imports are around – from $100 – if you'd rather buy one. Some tours provide bikes, so you may be able to rent better quality ones from agents (eg Exotissimo in New Bagan, see p186).

Apart from in Yangon and Mandalay, vehicular traffic is quite light.

Long-Distance

A few visitors bring their own touring bikes into Myanmar. There doesn't seem to be any problem with customs as long as you make the proper declarations upon entering the country.

Gradients in most parts of Myanmar open to tourism are moderate. Frontier regions, on the other hand – particularly Shan, Kayin, Kayah and Chin States – tend to be mountainous. You'll find plenty of opportunity everywhere for dirt-road and off-road pedalling.

Especially in the north, where main roads can resemble secondary roads elsewhere, a sturdy mountain bike would make a good alternative to a touring rig.

Some of the key routes around Myanmar:

- Thazi to Inle Lake via Kalaw
- Pyin U Lwin (Maymyo) to Lashio via Hsipaw
- Mandalay to Bagan via Myingyan
- Mandalay to either Monywa, Pyin U Lwin, Sagaing, Inwa (Ava) or Amarapura

November to February is the best time to cycle in terms of the weather.

If you're bringing your bike, bring the spare parts you need. There are (at least) basic bicycle shops in most towns, but they usually have only locally or Chinese-made parts to equip single-speed bikes. You can also buy lower-quality motorcycle helmets here; many are disturbingly adorned with swastikas – a fad, not a political alliance. Bring reflective clothing and plenty of insurance. Don't ride at night.

Travellers on a bike may end up needing to sleep in towns few travellers make it to, and a lack of licensed accommodation may be an issue. Technically, you will need permission from local immigration to stay at such places. Be patient. Most cyclists get permission from local authorities to stay one night, but the paperwork (coming with some frowns) may take an hour to arrange.

It's possible to store your bicycle in the undercarriage storage on buses. You may have to pay a little extra, though. On smaller buses it's possible you'll be asked to buy a 'seat' for your bike.

Some bike tours connect the dots of Myanmar's greatest hits – going, for example, up the Pyay highway to Bagan then Mandalay, and back to Yangon via Meiktila and Taungoo. It's more rough going, but nicer riding, to reach some mountainous areas, like Inle Lake. One that does is offered from **Spice Roads** (www .spiceroads.com), whose 14-day bike tour costs $1800 per person.

BOAT

A huge fleet of riverboats, remnants of the old '20s-era Irrawaddy Flotilla Company (IFC), still ply Myanmar's major rivers, where the bulk of traveller-oriented boat travel gets done. Some boats are ramshackle (but certainly lively) government ferries; some date from the British era and oth-

TRANSPORT

ers are old-style IFC liners that run luxury cruises. The main drawback is speed. Boat trips for many routes are loosely scheduled in terms of days, not hours.

There are 5000 miles of navigable river in Myanmar, with the most important river being the Ayeyarwady (Irrawaddy). Even in the dry season, boats can travel from the delta region (dodging exposed sandbars) all the way north to Bhamo, and in the wet they can reach Myitkyina.

Other important rivers include the Twante Chaung (Twante Chanel), which links the Ayeyarwady to Yangon, and the Chindwin River, which joins the Ayeyarwady a little above Bagan. The Thanlwin River in the east is only navigable for about 125 miles from its mouth at Mawlamyine, though the five-hour trip to Hpa-an is one of the country's most scenic waterway journeys (see p163).

It takes great expertise to navigate Myanmar's waterways. Rapidly changing sandbanks and shallow water during the dry season mean the captains and pilots have to keep in constant touch with the changing pattern of the river flows. For example, seven pilots are used on the stretch from Mandalay to Pyay (Prome). Each is an expert on their own particular segment of the river.

In addition to the rivers, it's possible to travel along the Bay of Bengal between Sittwe and Taunggok (north of Ngapali Beach); see p323.

Cargo Ships

Although the obstacles standing in your way are daunting, it may be possible to travel along Myanmar's coastline via Myanma Five Star Line (p129), the country's government-owned ocean transport enterprise. Technically it's only cargo now, but you can try to see about jumping on a boat to Thandwe, Taunggok or Sittwe, or south to

Dawei, Myeik or Kawthoung, at some point in the future.

Ferries & Private Boats

Most ferry services are government-run, particularly the Inland Water Transport (IWT; p129). The IWT has over 500 boats totalling nearly 1.5 million tonnes and supposedly carrying 14 million passengers annually. Today most of the IWT boats are rather run-down and ramshackle, but provide remarkable glimpses into local river life. Many of the passengers on the long-distance ferries are traders who make stops along the way to pick up or deliver goods.

Along the heavily travelled 262-mile-long Yangon–Pyay–Mandalay route, there are 28 ferry landings, where merchants can ply their trade. IWT offices are usually near the jetty. They can offer information, schedules and fare details, and usually tickets. IWT offices, officially, accept US dollars and FEC (see p347) only.

Some short trips – eg between Bagan and Pakokku – are handled with small covered wood-boat ferries that fit about 25 people. Often there are smaller, private boats you can negotiate to use with the driver. We include private boat services whenever possible. However, because of their size it's not always as safe riding with private boats compared with bigger government ferries. In 2004, a small private boat between Sittwe and Mrauk U capsized during a storm and several Italian tourists were killed.

Only a few riverboat routes are regularly used by visitors. Key routes:

- Mandalay to Bagan (see p272) On the IWT or private boats such as the *Shwei Kennery Express*
- Myitkyina to Mandalay via Bhamo and Katha (see p308) A few private fast-boat services, but mostly done on the IWT

OPENING THE CHINDWIN?

By 2009, river routes on the Chindwin River, northeast of Monywa, will reportedly open the long-restricted river-way to some foreign-operated group tours. Either way, it can be possible to get a government permit with a knowledgeable local guide and make the trip on your own from Homilin to Monywa. Unlike the Ayeyarwady it's a narrow river with oodles of local life to dip into. Mr Saw at Yangon's **KS Elephant Travels & Tours** (☎ 01-666-202; www.kselephanttravels .com; Bldg 2, Eight Mile Junction, Rm 40, Mayangone, Yangon) has heaps of experience with this trip. Two people could make it in six days for about $900 (including flight up, meals, accommodation, boat and permit).

- Mawlamyine to Hpa-an (see p163) Daily government ferries
- Sittwe to Mrauk U (see p326) Small private boats or government ferry

There is no direct service between Yangon and Mandalay: you'd need to change boats in Pyay – and the IWT offices seemed to frown on taking passengers on this route. If you make it, take a book or two: it's about two days by boat between Mandalay and Bagan, three more to Pyay, and two more to Yangon. A more feasible long journey, and a more attractive one, is south from Myitkyina.

Luxury Boats

Be aware that the higher-priced cruises are either privately run boats on lease from the government or a joint-venture operation. You can book services with travel agents in Yangon, but keep in mind that many trips are booked out by tour groups.

Several luxury ferries travel the upper and lower reaches of the Ayeyarwady River. Cyclone Nargis put an end to the luxury boat run by the joint-venture operation **Road to Mandalay** (www.orient-express.com), but it's expected to be in operation by late 2009. In past seasons, the company has offered three-, four-, seven- and 11-day trips (from $1780 to $3610 per person for three nights, or $2320 to $4810 for seven nights), which centre on Mandalay.

Pandaw Cruises (www.pandaw.com) Yangon (☎ 01-727 029, Dusit Inya Lake Hotel); Mandalay (☎ 02-244 256, 14 Strand Rd, 35/37) Offers various high-end cruises aboard a replica of the teak-and-brass IFC fleet such as a popular two-night trip between Bagan and Mandalay (about $584 per cabin, all inclusive) and a 14-night trip between Yangon and Mandalay (from $2700 per cabin, all-inclusive).

Similar trips are offered by **Pandaw 1947** (☎ 01-380 877; www.pandaw1947.com), run by the private owner of *Shwei Kennery* (whose boats connect Mandalay and Bagan).

At research time, the **Delta Queen** (www.myanmar-rivercruises.com) had suspended its cruises between Yangon and Pathein.

BUS

Almost always faster and cheaper than trains, Myanmar buses come in different sizes. Options include luxury air-con express buses, less luxurious but nice buses (without air-con), local buses, and mini 32-seaters. Most are operated by private companies (unlike the train).

Note that gas prices went up by 500% in late 2007, and bus fares around the country were up by two or three times from a few years before. No other typical tourist daily expenditure has seen more of a rise in price in recent years. This may change, perhaps meaning considerably cheaper fares than quoted in this book.

See the section on pick-up trucks, p367, for other transport options.

Classes & Conditions

Many long-haul trips, such as from Yangon to Mandalay, allow the greatest comfort, with new(ish) air-con express buses – some of which are quite nice. A lot of bus activity happens at night, with buses leaving from 4pm to 10pm or later, and arriving at the final destination in the wee hours (often 5am or 6am).

If you want extra air-con comfort but don't want to go the whole way on one of these routes, you usually have to pay the full fare (eg going from Mandalay to Taungoo you pay the

---

HOW TO SKIP OVERNIGHT BUSES

There's not one obvious way to travel by bus between Myanmar's big four – Yangon, Bagan, Inle Lake and Mandalay. Most travellers just bus to Mandalay one night, then pick between Inle Lake or Bagan next. But this requires at least a couple of overnight buses.

If you like being able to see scenery out the window, or sleeping in beds, you can manage it all without one overnighter. But it takes pre-planning and a bit more time.

Bus to Mandalay, by going first to Taungoo (p192) for a night, then to Meiktila (p196) for another; there are many buses to Mandalay from Meiktila.

There's currently a lone morning bus from Mandalay to Kalaw (p224) or Taunggyi (p243; near Inle Lake). Head west on a 4am bus out of Taunggyi to Bagan (p180) by day. Return to Yangon in two days. The first, bus to Magwe (p202), have a couple of hours to look around, and catch an afternoon bus to Pyay (p198). There are many bus connections to Yangon from here.

> **GOVERNMENT BUSES**
>
> Formerly, many buses were operated by the government's Road Transport Enterprise (RTE). Now RTE buses are almost exclusively used for cargo, while nearly all passenger buses are privately run.

full fare to Yangon) and will have to deal with middle-of-the-night arrival time. Similarly, by paying the full fare for the route, you can jump on a bus at a stop along the way, eg catch the Mandalay to Yangon bus at Meiktila. Staff at your guesthouse or hotel should be able to help with this.

A bottle of water is often handed out on better-quality buses. There are usually no bathrooms on the bus, but frequent toilet-and-soup stops perforate the night – frustrating if you've *just* got to sleep and the bus stops at 3am for 'breakfast'. Often the TV blares for much of the trip – usually sticking with Myanmar-made concerts or movies detailing things such as, oh, protagonists dying bloody deaths in car crashes, but the occasional *Raiders of the Lost Ark* slips in.

Be aware that temperatures can drop substantially at night. Take a jacket or blanket (preferably both).

Similar sized but older buses, with no air-con, make shorter-haul trips, such as direct links from Yangon to Pyay or Taungoo to Yangon.

Local buses, or 32-seat minibuses, bounce along the highways too. These tend to use the aisles, if not for blokes, for bags of rice, veggies or (worst) dried fish. Sometimes the floor in front of you is filled too, so you'll find your knees to your chin for some bouncy hours. Getting up to stretch your legs while moving just isn't an option. (Try to sit in the front couple of rows, which sometimes have fewer bags stored, and better visibility.)

Trip durations for all forms of public road transportation are very elastic. We hear of travellers on the nicest buses who were stopped for hours on the Yangon–Mandalay highway. (The authors of this book had no such troubles.)

Myanmar superstition says that when you're on a journey you shouldn't ask anyone 'How much longer?', or 'Brother, when will we arrive?', as this is only tempting fate. Note how some local passengers hold their breath whenever a bus passes a particularly dodgy looking bridge.

Buses of all types do break down sometimes. Older buses often stop to hose down a hot engine. Some roads – one-lane, mangled deals (read: *very* rough) – don't help matters, and tyre punctures occur too.

Costs

Unlike for train, plane and most boat tickets, you can pay kyat for all bus fares. But, similarly, foreigners will pay more than locals – and on occasion the price is 'set' on the spot. Generally minibuses, local 32-seaters, express buses with no air-con, and air-con luxury jobbies charge roughly the same on overlapping routes. Sample foreigner fares and trip times:

From	To	Price	Duration
Bagan	Pyay	K15,000	9hr
Bagan	Taunggyi	K10,500	12hr
Mandalay	Bagan	K8500	8hr
Mandalay	Hsipaw	K4000	6hr
Mandalay	Taunggyi	K10,000	12hr
Pyay	Taunggok	K15,000	8-9hr
Yangon	Bagan	K20,000	16hr
Yangon	Bago (Pegu)	K6000	2hr
Yangon	Chaungtha	K8000	6-7hr
Yangon	Kyaiktiyo	K8000	4½hr
Yangon	Mandalay	K10,000	12-15hr
Yangon	Pyay	K4000-6000	6hr
Yangon	Taunggyi	K15,000	17hr
Yangon	Thandwe	K12,000	17-18hr

Reservations

From November to February, it's wise to pre-book buses a couple of days in advance for key routes, such as Bagan–Inle Lake. Seat reservations are made for all buses. Ask to see the bus ahead of time to choose the seat you'd like.

Restricted Roads

Foreigners are permitted to buy bus tickets of any class, using kyat, to any destination within or near the main Yangon–Bagan–Mandalay–Taunggyi quadrangle. We also found that buses were easily boarded in most other places in the country, except for a couple of tricky areas, like travel towards the Thai border, or – of all things – the Mandalay–Monywa trip.

CAR & MOTORCYCLE

Visitors not wanting to take planes, or endure overnight-bus bumps, frequently hire a car and driver for the bulk or entirety of a trip. It's

TRANSPORT

a good way to go, though not always cheap. To drive one yourself is difficult to arrange, but permission must be arranged via the government-run MTT and Road Transport Administration Department (RTAD; ☎ 01-252-035), *and* you must be accompanied by a local at all times. (Some expats bypass this with registration from the RTAD.)

Driving conditions can be poor but often better than on many roads in Vietnam, Cambodia or Laos – and traffic is comparatively light compared to Thai or Vietnamese roads. Of the 15,000 miles of roads in Myanmar, about half are paved; the remainder are graded gravel, unimproved dirt or simple vehicle tracks.

Hiring a Car & Driver

The best place to arrange a driver, perhaps for a full trip, is in Yangon, but it's possible to track down a 'taxi' or 'private car' from most travel agencies or guesthouses around the country, particularly in popular destinations like Bagan, Mandalay and Inle Lake.

When trying to find a car with driver, consider there are three unofficial types of cars:

- **Tourist cars** – these are reasonably new, air-conditioned cars run by a company that provides back-up or repairs in the event they break down. These are the most comfortable – and that air-con is handy when it's dusty and hot out – but the most expensive, running to about $80 to $100 a day, depending on the length of the trip. This price includes petrol for up to 12 hours' driving per day and all of the driver's expenses.
- **Airport taxis** – a midrange option are the so-called 'airport taxis' – often yellow taxis that will be offering you their service for your trip before you leave the Yangon airport. These are older, may or may not have working air-con, and run to about $50 to $60 per day.
- **Private cars** – the cheapest option are 'private cars,' run by entrepreneur drivers.

These go with windows down (ie no air-con), vary in condition and price dramatically – and there's less of a chance that you'll have any sort of replacement in case the engine goes out midway between Bago and Taungoo. They can be found for as little as $40 or $50 per day. Some travellers tell us of great experiences at this level, others have problems.

There are no car-rental agencies per se, but most travel agencies in Yangon, Mandalay or Bagan – as well as guesthouses and hotels elsewhere – can arrange cars and drivers.

Among the most popular and reliable rental cars in the country are second-hand, reconditioned Toyota Corona hatchbacks imported from Japan from 1988. Such a car can cost a staggering $40,000. A slightly better quality car are Toyota Chasers (from 1990 to 1992). Myanmar also assembles its own Mazda jeeps – MJs – using 85% local parts. Though mostly a government monopoly, these jeeps make decent off-road vehicles. The old US-made, WWII-era Willys Jeeps that once characterised outback Myanmar travel are becoming few and far between.

Petrol is rationed (four gallons per week) to vehicle owners – not nearly enough for most drivers. The supply is rationed (two gallons per car, at K2500 per gallon) with black-market outlets that run makeshift stands everywhere. Prices rise and fall, but black-market petrol is usually twice as expensive (about K6000 per gallon, up from K2000 in the past several years). When Myanmar vehicle owners make an upcountry 'road trip' (the Burmese-English term for any driving out of Yangon), they have to buy fuel on the black market or carry along numerous jerry cans of petrol.

Another small cost to consider when travelling by car is the customary K50 or K100 'toll' collected upon entering many towns and villages throughout Myanmar. Many drivers are adept at handing these to the toll collectors while barely slowing down.

ROAD RULES: TO THE RIGHT!

All Myanmar traffic goes on the right-hand side of the road. This wasn't always so. In an effort to distance itself from the British colonial period, the military government instigated an overnight switch from the left to the right in 1970. By far, most cars either date from before 1970, or are low-cost Japanese models, so steering wheels are perilously found on the right-hand side – this becomes particularly dicey when a driver blindly zooms to the left to pass a car!

**T
R
A
N
S
P
O
R
T**

Motorcycle

It's occasionally possible to rent a motorbike, though few locals advertise this. In Mandalay, for example, it's about $10 per day to rent a motorbike, while one in Myitkyina goes for about $17. Unlike cyclists, you're required to wear a helmet in most towns.

HITCHING

Hitching is never entirely safe in any country in the world, and we don't recommend it. Travellers who decide to hitch should understand that they are taking a small but potentially serious risk. People who do choose to hitch will be safer if they travel in pairs and let someone know where they are planning to go.

One extra reason to avoid hitching in Myanmar is that local drivers may not know which areas are off limits to foreigners and may unwittingly transport them into such areas. In such cases the driver will probably be punished.

LOCAL TRANSPORT

Larger towns in Myanmar offer a variety of city buses *(ka)*, bicycle rickshaws or trishaws *(saiq-ka*, for sidecar), horse carts *(myint hlei)*, ox carts, vintage taxis *(taxi)*, more modern little three-wheelers somewhat akin to Thai *tuk-tuks (thoun bein*, meaning 'three wheels'), tiny four-wheeled 'blue taxi' Mazdas *(lei bein*, meaning 'four wheels') and modern Japanese pick-up trucks *(lain ka*, meaning 'line car'; see below).

Small towns rely heavily on horse carts and trishaws as the main mode of local transport. However, in the five largest cities (Yangon, Mandalay, Pathein, Mawlamyine and Taunggyi) public buses take regular routes along the main avenues for a fixed per-person rate, usually K25 to K100.

Standard rates for taxis, trishaws and horse carts are sometimes 'boosted' for foreigners. A little bargaining may be in order. Generally a ride from the bus station to a central hotel – often a distance of 1.25 miles or more – is about K1000 or K1500. Rides around the centre can be arranged for K500 or K800. You may need to bargain a bit. Sometimes first time offers are several times higher than the going rate.

Pick-Up Trucks

Japanese-made pick-up trucks feature three rows of bench seats in the covered back. Most pick-ups connect short-distance destinations, making many stops along the way to pick up people or cargo. They are often packed (yet somehow never 'full' according to the driver). Pick-ups trace some useful or necessary routes, such as from Mandalay to Amarapura, from Myingyan to Meiktila, from Bagan to Mt Popa, and up to the Golden Rock at Kyaiktiyo. Unlike buses, they go regularly during the day.

Fares are not necessarily cheaper than those charged for local bus trips of the same length, and prices often go up more after dark. You can, however, pay 25% to 50% extra for a seat up the front. It's often worth the extra expense, if you don't want to do scrunch duty. Sometimes you may share your spot with a monk riding for free; usually you get exactly what you pay for ('the whole front'), unlike in some other parts of Southeast Asia.

Pick-ups often start from the bus station (in some towns they linger under a big banyan tree in the centre) and then, unlike many buses, make rounds through the central streets to snare more passengers.

TOURS

Many high-end hotels offer expensive day tours. If you want to have your trip planned out, you can still do it and keep your money in the private sector. We list many sources for private guides throughout this book. Also see p22 for tips on organising a 'DIY package trip'.

TRAIN

'You don't need a disco in Myanmar. Just listen to techno and sit on a train – it'll do the dancing for you.'

Mandalay local

The first thing the British did anywhere they colonised was stick a railroad in. In Myanmar, it's often the same old train on the same old tracks. There are as many opinions of Myanmar's oft-maligned train service as there are people riding it. For some train ride on narrow-gauge tracks is like going by horse, with the old carriages rocking back and forth and bouncing everyone lucky enough to have a seat on the hard chairs; others dig it, as some routes get to areas not reached by road. One local said, 'It's not as bad as some people say, not as good as you hope'. What's known for sure is that train trips along the same routes as buses mean extra travel time.

They also mean extra expense. A 1st-class seat between Yangon and Mandalay is $35; a bus ticket on an air-conditioned bus is about $8.50.

Long-distance trains have dining cars accessible to passengers in 1st, upper and sleeper class. The food isn't bad – fried rice and noodles. Attendants can also take your order and bring food to your seat. Trains stop pretty often too, with vendors on platforms offering all sorts of snacks. Bathrooms are basic; there are also sinks to wash hands and brush teeth. Attendants sometimes hire out bamboo mats to spread on the floor in aisles or under seats if you can't sleep upright. It can get cold at night, so bring a jacket and/or a blanket.

To guarantee a seat on most trains with upper and sleeper cars, book three days or more in advance. Smaller stations sometimes require some perseverance to get a ticket, as agents aren't used to foreigners climbing on.

Major train routes tend to require payment in US dollars or FEC (see p347).

Private Railways

All trains are now government run.

Myanma Railways

Myanmar maintains 2900 miles of 1m-gauge railway track – much of which is now open to foreign tourists – and 550 train stations.

The 400-mile-long trip from Yangon to Mandalay is the only train trip most visitors take – though there are plenty more routes for the adventurous. Others worth considering are the Mandalay (or Pyin U Lwin) train to Lashio (or Hsipaw), which takes in hilly terrain the roads miss (Paul Theroux managed to do this back when foreigners weren't supposed to, in his book *The Great Railway Bazaar*), and the Yangon to Mawlamyine route.

On the Yangon to Mandalay route there are reserved carriages on express trains, where you can be sure of getting a seat. One way to tell what type an approaching train is, is to check the engine colour: express engines are generally painted yellow; local ones blue.

The express trains are far superior to the general run of Myanmar trains. Other trains are late, almost by rule – taking one 12-hour train trip that ends up running as much as 15 hours late is enough for most travellers. The Mandalay to Myitkyina route, though scheduled to take around 24 hours, can take up to 40 hours. In 1995 this train derailed, killing 120 people, and in 2001 a bridge collapsed, killing an equal number. Even on the far-more-travelled Yangon–Mandalay route, delays are common. In recent years, late-night robberies (allegedly) by insurgents near Taungoo prompted the government to shift the starting time of the overnight train from Yangon to pass Taungoo just before dark.

Apart from the straightforward Yangon–Bago–Pyinmana–Thazi–Mandalay route, you can also take the poke-along line from Pyinmana to Kyaukpadaung (31 miles south of Bagan) or the Thazi-to-Shwenyaung branch (7 miles north of Inle Lake). From Yangon lines also run northwest to Pyay, with a branch to Pathein; from Bago there's a branch southeast to Kyaiktiyo (the jumping-off point for the Golden Rock; see p154) and on to Mottawa, a short ferry ride from Mawlamyine.

An express line now runs between Bagan/Nyaung U and Mandalay (though this was built with forced labour in the mid-1990s). At Mandalay there are three branch lines: one running slightly northwest across the Ava

---

GOVERNMENT'S TRAIN FARES

Something to consider: foreigner fares on trains are skies above the local fare (Yangon–Mandalay upper class foreigner $35, local K8000), sometimes inflated by 550%. Considering the trains are government run, you could argue that, percentage-wise, train service fares are more tilted towards the generals' pockets than private airfares (and certainly more than the tax culled from cheaper private-bus companies).

Transport	Ticket price	Amount to government
Yangon–Mandalay train (1st class)	$35	$35
Yangon–Mandalay flight	$90	perhaps $11 (12% tax)
Yangon–Mandalay bus	$8.50	perhaps $1 (12% tax)

TRAIN COSTS

Following are sample fares and scheduled times as quoted in Yangon. Each of these stop in Thazi (at the crossroads for Inle Lake to the east, or Bagan to the west). Thazi is about 11 or 12 hours north of Yangon, or three hours south of Mandalay.

Yangon to Mandalay

Train	Departure	To Mandalay	Ordinary/upper/sleeper
29 Up	4.30am	6.30pm	$15/35/40
05 Up	5am	8.10pm	$11/30/33
03 Up	5.30am	9.30pm	$11/30/33
33 Up	12.45pm	3am	$15/35/40

Mandalay to Yangon

Train	Departure	To Yangon	Ordinary/upper/sleeper
30 Down	4am	6pm	$15/35/40
06 Down	5am	8.10pm	$11/30/33
04 Down	5.30am	9.30pm	$11/30/33
34 Down	8am	10.15pm	$15/35/40

Bridge and up to Ye-U, one directly north to Myitkyina in Kachin State and one northeast through Pyin U Lwin to Lashio in the northern part of Shan State.

Note also that Myanmar trains are classified by a number and the suffix 'Up' for northbound trains or 'Down' for southbound trains. Train numbers are not always used when purchasing tickets.

Classes

Express trains offer two classes of passage, upper class and ordinary class, while many trains also offer sleepers. The main differences between ordinary and upper are that the seats recline and can be reserved in the latter, while ordinary class features hard upright seats that can't be reserved. Some trains also offer another class of service called 1st class, which is a step down from upper in comfort.

Reservations

For government-run services along the Yangon–Mandalay line, all foreigners are sup-posed to purchase tickets from the MTT (p91) or from the train station. MTT sets aside seats for foreigners, which means that they often have seats when the booking office or station window says that the train is full. A day's notice is usually enough to book a seat.

If you want to try your luck at getting a coveted sleeper, you'll need at least a couple of days' notice – longer during the high season (November to March), when berths are sometimes booked weeks in advance. If you hold a seat on a train pulling a sleeper car, you can try to upgrade to a berth after you board by paying the additional fare directly to the conductor.

To buy tickets at other train stations you can use the same ticket windows as the locals.

If you're having trouble buying a ticket or making yourself understood at a train station, try seeking out the stationmaster – the person at the station who is most likely to speak English and most inclined to help you get a seat.

Health Dr Trish Batchelor

CONTENTS

Health issues and the quality of medical facilities vary enormously depending on where and how you travel in Myanmar. Many of the major cities are very well developed, although travel to rural areas can expose you to a variety of health risks and inadequate medical care.

Travellers tend to worry about contracting infectious diseases when in the tropics, but infections are a rare cause of serious illness or death in travellers. Pre-existing medical conditions such as heart disease, and accidental injury (especially traffic accidents), account for most life-threatening problems. However, becoming ill in some way is relatively common. Fortunately, most common illnesses can either be prevented with some common-sense behaviour or be treated easily with a well-stocked traveller's medical kit.

The following advice is a general guide only and does not replace the advice of a doctor trained in travel medicine.

BEFORE YOU GO

Pack medications in their original, clearly labelled, containers. A signed and dated letter from your physician describing your medical conditions and medications, including generic names, is also a good idea. If carrying syringes or needles, be sure to have a physician's letter documenting their medical necessity. If you have a heart condition, bring a copy of your ECG taken just prior to travelling.

If you take any regular medication, bring double your needs in case of loss or theft.

INSURANCE

Even if you are fit and healthy, don't travel without health insurance – accidents do happen. If your health insurance doesn't cover you for medical expenses abroad, consider getting extra insurance. Declare any existing medical conditions – the insurance company *will* check if your problem is pre-existing and will not cover you if it is undeclared. You may require extra cover for adventure activities such as rock climbing. If you're uninsured, emergency evacuation is expensive – bills of over $100,000 are not uncommon. Some policies offer lower and higher medical-expense options; the higher ones are chiefly for countries that have extremely high medical costs, such as the USA.

Find out in advance if your insurance plan will make payments directly to providers or reimburse you later for overseas health expenditures. (In many countries doctors will expect payment in cash.) You may prefer a policy that pays doctors or hospitals directly rather than you having to pay on the spot and claim later. If you have to claim later, make sure you keep all documentation. Some policies ask you to call (reverse charges) a centre

Dr Trish Batchelor wrote the Health chapter. She is a general practitioner and travel medicine specialist who works at the Ciwec Clinic in Kathmandu, Nepal. She is also a medical advisor to the Travel Doctor New Zealand clinics. Trish teaches travel medicine through the University of Otago and is interested in underwater and high-altitude medicine, and in the impact of tourism on host countries. She has travelled extensively through Southeast and East Asia, and particularly loves high-altitude trekking in the Himalaya.

in your home country, where an immediate assessment of your problem is made.

RECOMMENDED VACCINATIONS

Specialised travel-medicine clinics are your best source of information; they stock all available vaccines and will be able to give specific recommendations for you and your trip. The doctors will take into account factors such as past vaccination history, the length of your trip, activities you may be undertaking and underlying medical conditions, such as pregnancy.

Most vaccines don't produce immunity until at least two weeks after they're given, so visit a doctor four to eight weeks before departure. Ask your doctor for an International Certificate of Vaccination (otherwise known as the yellow booklet), which will list all the vaccinations you've received.

MEDICAL CHECKLIST

Recommended items for a personal medical kit:

- antifungal cream, eg Clotrimazole
- antibacterial cream, eg Muciprocin
- antibiotic for possible skin infections, eg Amoxicillin/Clavulanate or Cephalexin
- antibiotics for diarrhoea, such as Norfloxacin or Ciprofloxacin; for bacterial diarrhoea, such as Azithromycin; and for giardiasis or amoebic dysentery, such as Tinidazole
- antihistamine – there are many options, eg Cetirizine for daytime and Promethazine for night
- antiseptic, eg Betadine
- antispasmodic for stomach cramps, eg Buscopan
- contraceptive method
- decongestant, eg Pseudoephedrine
- DEET-based insect repellent
- diarrhoea treatment – consider an oral rehydration solution (eg Gastrolyte), diarrhoea 'stopper' (eg Loperamide) and anti-nausea medication (eg Prochlorperazine)
- first-aid items such as scissors, Band-Aids, bandages, gauze, thermometer (but not mercury), sterile needles and syringes, safety pins and tweezers
- Ibuprofen or another anti-inflammatory
- indigestion tablets, such as Quick Eze or Mylanta
- iodine tablets (unless you are pregnant or have a thyroid problem) to purify water

HEALTH ADVISORIES

It's usually a good idea to consult your government's travel-health website before departure, if one is available:

Australia (www.dfat.gov.au/travel)
Canada (www.travelhealth.gc.ca)
New Zealand (www.mfat.govt.nz/travel)
UK (www.doh.gov.uk/traveladvice)
USA (www.cdc.gov/travel)

- laxative, eg Coloxyl
- migraine medicine – sufferers should take their personal medicine
- paracetamol
- Permethrin to impregnate clothing and mosquito nets
- steroid cream for allergic/itchy rashes, eg 1% to 2% hydrocortisone
- sunscreen and hat
- throat lozenges
- thrush (vaginal yeast infection) treatment, eg Clotrimazole pessaries or Diflucan tablet
- Ural or an equivalent if prone to urine infections

INTERNET RESOURCES

There is a wealth of travel-health advice on the internet. For more information, **Lonely Planet** (www.lonelyplanet.com) is a good place to start. The **World Health Organization** (WHO; www.who.int/ith/) publishes a fine book, *International Travel & Health*, which is revised annually and is available online at no cost. Another website of interest is **MD Travel Health** (www.mdtravelhealth.com), which provides complete travel-health recommendations for every country and is updated daily. The **Centers for Disease Control and Prevention** (CDC; www.cdc.gov) website also has good general information.

FURTHER READING

Lonely Planet's *Healthy Travel – Asia & India* is a handy pocket size and is packed with useful information including pretrip planning, emergency first aid, immunisation and disease information, and what to do if you get sick on the road. Other recommended references include *Traveller's Health*, by Dr Richard Dawood, and *Travelling Well*, by Dr Deborah Mills – check out the website (www.travellingwell.com.au).

HEALTH

IN TRANSIT

DEEP VEIN THROMBOSIS (DVT)

Deep vein thrombosis (DVT) occurs when blood clots form in the legs during plane flights, chiefly because of prolonged immobility. The longer the flight, the greater the risk. Though most blood clots are reabsorbed uneventfully, some may break off and travel through the blood vessels to the lungs, where they may cause life-threatening complications.

The chief symptom of DVT is swelling or pain of the foot, ankle or calf, usually but not always on just one side. When a blood clot travels to the lungs, it may cause chest pain and difficulty in breathing. Travellers with any of these symptoms should immediately seek medical attention.

To prevent the development of DVT on long flights you should walk about the cabin, perform isometric compressions of the leg muscles (ie contract the leg muscles while sitting), drink plenty of fluids, and avoid alcohol and tobacco.

JET LAG & MOTION SICKNESS

Jet lag is common when crossing more than five time zones; it results in insomnia, fatigue, malaise or nausea. To avoid jet lag try drinking plenty of fluids (nonalcoholic) and eating light meals. Upon arrival, seek exposure to natural sunlight and readjust your schedule (for meals, sleep etc) as soon as possible.

Antihistamines such as dimenhydrinate (Dramamine) and meclizine (Antivert or Bonine) are usually a traveller's first choice for treating motion sickness. The main side effect is drowsiness. A herbal alternative is ginger, which works like a charm for some people.

IN MYANMAR

AVAILABILITY OF HEALTH CARE & COSTS

Local medical care is dismal, and local hospitals should only be used out of desperation. Contact your embassy for advice, as staff will usually direct you to the best options. Be aware that getting Western-style health care may not come cheap.

Self-treatment may be appropriate if your problem is minor (eg traveller's diarrhoea), you are carrying the appropriate medication and you cannot attend a recommended clinic in Yangon or Mandalay. If you think you may have a serious disease, especially malaria, do not waste time – travel to the nearest quality facility to receive attention. It is always better to be assessed by a doctor than to rely on self-treatment.

Buying medication over the counter is not recommended in Myanmar, as fake medications and poorly stored or out-of-date drugs are common.

INFECTIOUS DISEASES

Cutaneous Larva Migrans

This disease is caused by dog hookworm. The rash starts as a small lump, then slowly spreads in a linear fashion. It is intensely itchy, especially at night. It is easily treated with medications and should not be cut out or frozen.

Dengue

This mosquito-borne disease is becoming increasingly problematic throughout Myanmar. As there is no vaccine available it can only be prevented by avoiding mosquito bites. The mosquito that carries dengue bites day and night, so use insect-avoidance measures at all times. Symptoms include high fever, severe headache and body ache (dengue was previously known as 'breakbone fever'). Some people develop a rash and experience diarrhoea. There is no specific treatment, just rest and paracetamol – do not take aspirin, as it increases the likelihood of haemorrhaging. See a doctor to be diagnosed and monitored.

Filariasis

A mosquito-borne disease that is very common in the local population, yet very rare in travellers. Mosquito-avoidance measures are the best way to prevent this disease.

Hepatitis A

This food- and water-borne virus infects the liver, causing jaundice (yellow skin and eyes), nausea and lethargy. There is no specific treatment for hepatitis A; you just need to allow time for the liver to heal. All travellers to Myanmar should be vaccinated against hepatitis A.

Hepatitis B

The only sexually transmitted disease that can be prevented by vaccination, hepatitis

B is spread by body fluids, including sexual contact. In some parts of this region up to 20% of the population are carriers of hepatitis B, and usually are unaware of this. The long-term consequences can include liver cancer and cirrhosis.

Hepatitis E

Hepatitis E is transmitted through contaminated food and water and has similar symptoms to hepatitis A, but is far less common. It is a severe problem in pregnant women and can result in the death of both mother and baby. There is currently no vaccine, and prevention is achieved by following safe eating and drinking guidelines.

HIV

Myanmar has one of the highest rate of HIV infection in Asia – and the problem is increasing. Heterosexual sex is now the main method of transmission.

Influenza

Present year-round in the tropics, influenza (flu) symptoms include high fever, muscle aches, runny nose, cough and sore throat. It can be very severe in people over the age of 65 or in those with underlying medical conditions such as heart disease or diabetes vaccination is recommended for these individuals. There is no specific treatment, just rest and paracetamol.

Japanese B Encephalitis

This viral disease transmitted by mosquitoes is a rare disease in travellers, but at least 50,000 locals are infected each year. Most cases occur in rural areas, and vaccination is recommended for travellers spending more than one month outside cities. There is no treatment, and a third of infected people will die, while another third will suffer permanent brain damage.

Malaria

For such a serious and potentially deadly disease, there is an enormous amount of misinformation concerning malaria and malaria medication. You must get expert advice as to whether the destinations you are going to will put you at risk. For most rural areas the risk of contracting the disease far outweighs the risk of any tablet side effects. Remember that malaria can be fatal. Before you travel, seek

medical advice on the right medication and dosage for you.

Malaria is caused by a parasite transmitted by the bite of an infected mosquito. The most important symptom of malaria is fever, but general symptoms such as headache, diarrhoea, cough or chills may also occur. Diagnosis can only be made by taking a blood sample.

Two strategies should be combined to prevent malaria – mosquito avoidance and antimalarial medications. Most people who catch malaria are taking inadequate or no antimalarial medication.

Travellers are advised to prevent mosquito bites by taking these steps.

- Use an insect repellent containing DEET on exposed skin. Wash this off at night, as long as you are sleeping under a mosquito net. Natural repellents such as citronella can be effective but must be applied more frequently than products containing DEET.
- Sleep under a mosquito net impregnated with Permethrin.
- Choose accommodation with screens and fans (if not air-con).
- Impregnate clothing with Permethrin in high-risk areas.
- Wear long sleeves and trousers in light colours.
- Use mosquito coils.
- Spray your room with insect repellent before going out for your evening meal.

Some available medications:
- **Artesunate** – derivatives of Artesunate are not suitable as a preventive medication. They are useful treatments under medical supervision.
- **Chloroquine and Paludrine** – the effectiveness of this combination is now limited in most of Southeast Asia. Common side effects include nausea (40% of people) and mouth ulcers. Generally not recommended.
- **Doxycycline** - this daily tablet is a broad-spectrum antibiotic that has the added benefit of helping to prevent a variety of tropical diseases, including leptospirosis, tick-borne disease, typhus and meliodosis. The potential side effects include photosensitivity (a tendency to sunburn), thrush in women, indigestion, heartburn, nausea and interference with the contraceptive pill. More serious side

HEALTH

effects include ulceration of the oesophagus – you can help prevent this by taking your tablet with a meal and a large glass of water and never lying down within half an hour of taking it. Must be taken for four weeks after leaving the risk area.

- **Lariam (Mefloquine)** – Lariam has received much bad press, some of it justified, some not. This weekly tablet suits many people. Serious side effects are rare but include depression, anxiety, psychosis and having fits. Anyone with a history of depression, anxiety, other psychological disorder or epilepsy should not take Lariam. It is considered safe in the second and third trimesters of pregnancy. It is around 90% effective in most parts of Southeast Asia. Tablets must be taken for four weeks after leaving the risk area.
- **Malarone** – this new drug is a combination of Atovaquone and Proguanil. Side effects are uncommon and mild, most commonly nausea and headache. It is the best tablet for scuba divers and those on short trips to high-risk areas. It must be taken for one week after leaving the risk area.

A final option is to take no preventive medication but to have a supply of emergency medication should you develop the symptoms of malaria. This is less than ideal, and you'll need to get to a good medical facility within 24 hours of developing a fever. If you choose this option the most effective and safest treatment is Malarone (four tablets once daily for three days). Other options include Mefloquine and quinine, but the side effects of these drugs at treatment doses make them less desirable. Fansidar is no longer recommended.

Measles

This highly contagious bacterial infection is spread by coughing and sneezing. Most people born before 1966 are immune, as they had the disease in childhood. Measles starts with a high fever and rash and can be complicated by pneumonia and brain disease. There is no specific treatment.

Rabies

This uniformly fatal disease is spread by the bite or lick of an infected animal – most commonly a dog or monkey. You should seek medical advice immediately after any animal bite and commence postexposure treatment. Having pretravel vaccination means the postbite treatment is greatly simplified. If an animal bites you, gently wash the wound with soap and water, and apply iodine-based antiseptic. If you are not prevaccinated you will need to receive rabies immunoglobulin as soon as possible.

STDs

Sexually transmitted diseases most common in Myanmar include herpes, warts, syphilis, gonorrhoea and chlamydia. People carrying these diseases often have no signs of infection. Condoms will prevent gonorrhoea and chlamydia but not warts or herpes. If after a sexual encounter you develop any rash, lumps, discharge or pain when passing urine, seek immediate medical attention. If sexually active during your travels, have an STD check on your return home.

Strongyloides

This parasite, also transmitted by skin contact with soil, is common but rarely affects travellers. It is characterised by an unusual skin rash called *larva currens* – a linear rash on the trunk that comes and goes. Most people don't have other symptoms until their immune system becomes severely suppressed, when the parasite can cause a massive infection. It can be treated with medications.

Tuberculosis

While rare in travellers, medical and aid workers and long-term travellers who have significant contact with the local population should take precautions. Vaccination is usually only given to children under the age of five, but pre- and post-travel TB testing is recommended for adults at risk. The main symptoms are fever, cough, weight loss, night sweats and tiredness.

Typhoid

This serious bacterial infection is spread via food and water. It gives a high and slowly progressive fever and a headache, and may be accompanied by a dry cough and stomach pain. It is diagnosed by blood tests and treated with antibiotics. Vaccination is recommended for all travellers spending more than a week in Myanmar and other parts of Southeast Asia. Be aware that vaccination is not 100% effective, so you must still be careful with what you eat and drink.

HEALTH

REQUIRED & RECOMMENDED VACCINATIONS

The only vaccine required by international regulations is yellow fever. Proof of vaccination will only be required if you have visited a country in the yellow-fever zone within the six days prior to entering Myanmar. If you are travelling to Myanmar from Africa or South America you should check to see if you require proof of vaccination.

The World Health Organization recommends the following vaccinations for all travellers to Myanmar:

Adult diphtheria and tetanus Single booster recommended if none in the previous 10 years. Side effects include sore arm and fever.

Hepatitis A Provides almost 100% protection for up to a year; a booster after 12 months provides at least another 20 years' protection. Mild side effects such as headache and sore arm occur in 5% to 10% of people.

Hepatitis B Now considered routine for most travellers. Given as three shots over six months. A rapid schedule is also available, as is a combined vaccination with Hepatitis A. Side effects are mild and uncommon, usually headache and sore arm. Lifetime protection occurs in 95% of people.

Measles, mumps and rubella Two doses of MMR required unless you have had the diseases. Occasionally a rash and flulike illness can develop a week after receiving the vaccine. Many young adults require a booster.

Polio No longer common in Southeast Asia. Only one booster required as an adult for lifetime protection. Inactivated polio vaccine is safe during pregnancy.

Typhoid Recommended unless your trip is less than a week and only to developed cities. The vaccine offers around 70% protection, lasts for two to three years and comes as a single shot. Tablets are also available; however, the injection is usually recommended as it has fewer side effects. Sore arm and fever may occur.

Varicella If you haven't had chickenpox, discuss this vaccination with your doctor.

These immunisations are recommended for long-term travellers (more than one month) or those at special risk, for example due to spending a lot of time in rural areas:

Japanese B Encephalitis Three injections in all. Booster recommended after two years. Sore arm and headache are the most common side effects. Rarely, an allergic reaction comprising hives and swelling can occur up to 10 days after any of the three doses.

Meningitis A single injection. There are two types of vaccination: the quadrivalent vaccine gives two to three years' protection; meningitis group C vaccine gives around 10 years' protection. Recommended for long-term backpackers aged under 25.

Rabies Three injections in all. A booster after one year will then provide 10 years' protection. Side effects are rare – occasionally headache and sore arm.

Tuberculosis A complex issue. Adult long-term travellers are usually recommended to have a TB skin test before and after travel, rather than vaccination. Only one vaccine given in a lifetime.

Typhus

Murine typhus is spread by the bite of a flea, whereas scrub typhus is spread via a mite. These diseases are rare in travellers. Symptoms include fever, muscle pains and a rash. You can avoid these diseases by following general insect-avoidance measures. Doxycycline will also prevent typhus.

TRAVELLER'S DIARRHOEA

Traveller's diarrhoea is the most common problem affecting travellers – between 30% and 50% of people will suffer from it within two weeks of starting their trip. In over 80% of cases, traveller's diarrhoea is caused by a bacterium (there are numerous potential culprits), and therefore responds promptly to treatment with antibiotics. Treatment with antibiotics will depend on your situation – how sick you are, how quickly you need to get better, where you are etc.

Diarrhoea is defined as the passage of more than three watery bowel movements within a 24-hour period, plus at least one other symptom such as nausea, vomiting, fever, cramps or feeling generally unwell.

Treatment consists of staying well hydrated; rehydration solutions such as Gastrolyte are the best for this. Antibiotics such as Norfloxacin, Ciprofloxacin or Azithromycin will kill the bacteria quickly.

Loperamide is just a 'stopper' and doesn't get to the cause of the problem. It can be helpful, for example, if you have to go on a long

HEALTH

bus ride. Don't take Loperamide if you have a fever or blood in your stools. Seek medical attention quickly if you do not respond to an appropriate antibiotic.

Amoebic Dysentery

Amoebic dysentery is very rare in travellers but is often misdiagnosed by poor-quality labs in Southeast Asia. Symptoms are similar to bacterial diarrhoea, ie fever, bloody diarrhoea and generally feeling unwell. You should always seek reliable medical care if you have blood in your diarrhoea. Treatment involves two drugs: Tinidazole or Metroniadzole to kill the parasite in your gut and then a second drug to kill the cysts. If left untreated complications such as liver or gut abscesses can occur.

Giardiasis

Giardia lamblia is a parasite that is relatively common in travellers. Symptoms include nausea, bloating, excess gas, fatigue and intermittent diarrhoea. 'Eggy' burps are often attributed solely to giardiasis, but work in Nepal has shown that they are not specific to this infection. The parasite will eventually go away if left untreated, but this can take months. The treatment of choice is Tinidazole, with Metronidazole being a second-line option.

ENVIRONMENTAL HAZARDS
Air Pollution

Air pollution, particularly vehicle pollution, is an increasing problem. If you have severe respiratory problems speak with your doctor before travelling to any heavily polluted urban centres. This pollution also causes minor respiratory problems such as sinusitis, dry throat and irritated eyes. If troubled by the pollution, leave the city for a few days and get some fresh air.

Diving

Divers and surfers should seek specialised advice before they travel to ensure their medical kit contains treatment for coral cuts and tropical ear infections, as well as the standard problems. Divers should ensure their insurance covers them for decompression illness – get specialised dive insurance through an organisation such as **Divers Alert Network** (DAN; www.danseap.org). Have a dive medical before you leave your home country – there are certain medical conditions that are incompatible with diving, and economic considerations may override health considerations for some dive operators that operate in Myanmar.

Food

Eating in restaurants is the biggest risk factor for contracting traveller's diarrhoea. Ways to avoid it include eating only freshly cooked food and avoiding shellfish and food that has been sitting around in buffets. Peel all fruit, cook vegetables and soak salads in iodine water for at least 20 minutes. Eat in busy restaurants with a high turnover of customers.

Heatstroke

Many parts of Myanmar are hot and humid throughout the year. For most people it takes at least two weeks to adapt to the hot climate. Swelling of the feet and ankles is common, as are muscle cramps caused by excessive sweating. Prevent these by avoiding dehydration and excessive activity in the heat. Take it easy when you first arrive. Don't eat salt tablets (they aggravate the gut), but drinking rehydration solution

---

DRINKING WATER

- Never drink tap water
- Bottled water is generally safe – check the seal is intact at purchase
- Avoid ice
- Avoid fresh juices – they may have been watered down
- Boiling is the most efficient method of purifying water
- The best chemical purifier is iodine but it should not be used by pregnant women or those with thyroid problems
- Water filters should also filter out viruses; ensure your filter has a chemical barrier such as iodine and a small pore size, eg less than four microns

or eating salty food helps. Treat cramps by stopping activity, resting, rehydrating with double-strength rehydration solution and gently stretching.

Dehydration is the main contributor to heat exhaustion. Symptoms can include feeling weak, headache, irritability, nausea or vomiting, sweaty skin, a fast, weak pulse and a normal or slightly elevated body temperature. Treatment involves getting the person out of the heat and/or sun, fanning them and applying cool, wet cloths to their skin, laying them flat with their legs raised, and rehydrating them with water containing a quarter of a teaspoon of salt per litre. Recovery is usually rapid, and it is common to feel weak for some days afterwards.

Heatstroke is a serious medical emergency. Symptoms come on suddenly and include weakness, nausea, a hot, dry body with a body temperature of over 41°C, dizziness, confusion, loss of coordination, fits and eventually collapse and loss of consciousness. Seek medical help and commence cooling by getting the person out of the heat, removing their clothes, fanning them and applying cool, wet cloths or ice to their body, especially to the groin and armpits.

Prickly heat is a common skin rash in the tropics, caused by sweat being trapped under the skin. The result is an itchy rash of tiny lumps. Treat by moving out of the heat and into an air-con area for a few hours and by having cool showers. Creams and ointments clog the skin, so they should be avoided. Locally bought prickly-heat powder can be helpful.

Tropical fatigue is common in long-term expats based in the tropics. It's rarely due to disease and is caused by the climate, inadequate mental rest, excessive alcohol intake and the demands of daily work in a different culture.

Insect Bites & Stings

Bedbugs don't carry disease but their bites are very itchy. They live in the cracks of furniture and walls and then migrate to the bed at night to feed on you. You can treat the itch with an antihistamine.

Lice inhabit various parts of your body but most commonly your head and pubic area. Transmission is via close contact with an infected person. Lice can be difficult to treat and you may need numerous applications of an an-

tilice shampoo such as Permethrin. Pubic lice are usually contracted from sexual contact.

Ticks are contracted after walking in rural areas. Ticks are commonly found behind the ears, on the belly and in the armpits. If you have had a tick bite and experience symptoms such as a rash at the site of the bite or elsewhere, or fever or muscle aches you should see a doctor. Doxycycline prevents tick-borne diseases.

Leeches are found in humid rainforest areas. They do not transmit any disease, but their bites are often intensely itchy for weeks afterwards and can easily become infected. Apply an iodine-based antiseptic to any leech bite to help prevent infection.

Bee and wasp stings mainly cause problems for people who are allergic to them. Anyone with a serious bee or wasp allergy should carry an injection of adrenaline (eg an Epipen) for emergency treatment. For others pain is the main problem – apply ice to the sting and take painkillers.

Most jellyfish in Southeast Asian waters are not dangerous, just irritating. First aid for jellyfish stings involves pouring vinegar onto the affected area to neutralise the poison. Do not rub sand or water onto the stings. Take painkillers, and anyone who feels ill in any way after being stung should seek medical advice. Take local advice if there are dangerous jellyfish around and keep out of the water.

Parasites

Numerous parasites are common in local populations; however, most of these are rare in travellers. The two rules to follow if you wish to avoid parasitic infections are to wear shoes and to avoid eating raw food, especially fish, pork and vegetables. A number of parasites are transmitted via the skin by walking barefoot; these include strongyloides, hookworm and cutaneous *Larva migrans*.

Skin Problems

Fungal rashes are common in humid climates. There are two common fungal rashes that affect travellers. The first occurs in moist areas that get less air such as the groin, the armpits and between the toes. It starts as a red patch that slowly spreads and is usually itchy. Treatment involves keeping the skin dry, avoiding chafing and using an antifungal cream such as Clotrimazole or

HEALTH

Lamisil. *Tinea versicolor* is also common – this fungus causes small, light-coloured patches, most commonly on the back, chest and shoulders. Consult a doctor.

Cuts and scratches easily become infected in humid climates. Take meticulous care of any cuts and scratches to prevent complications such as abscesses. Immediately wash all wounds in clean water and apply antiseptic. If you develop signs of infection (increasing pain and redness) see a doctor. Divers and surfers should be particularly careful with coral cuts as they easily become infected.

Snakes

Myanmar is home to many species of both poisonous and harmless snakes. Assume all snakes are poisonous and never try to catch one. Always wear boots and long pants if walking in an area that may have snakes. First aid in the event of a snakebite involves pressure immobilisation with an elastic bandage firmly wrapped around the affected limb, starting at the bite site and working up towards the chest. The bandage should not be so tight that the circulation is cut off, and the fingers or toes should be kept free so the circulation can be checked. Immobilise the limb with a splint and carry the victim to medical attention. Do not use tourniquets or try to suck the venom out. Antivenom is available for most species.

Sunburn

Even on a cloudy day sunburn can occur rapidly. Always use a strong sunscreen (at least factor 30), making sure to reapply after a swim, and always wear a wide-brimmed hat and sunglasses outdoors. Avoid lying in the sun during the hottest part of the day (10am to 2pm). If you become sunburnt stay out of the sun until you have recovered, apply cool compresses and take painkillers for the discomfort. A 1% hydrocortisone cream applied twice daily is also helpful.

TRAVELLING WITH CHILDREN

The main point to keep in mind is that children get dehydrated very quickly, so they will need to take liquids on a regular basis. This becomes more critical if they are suffering from diarrhoea.

WOMEN'S HEALTH

Pregnant women should receive specialised advice before travelling. The ideal time to travel is during the second trimester (between 16 and 28 weeks), when the risk of pregnancy-related problems is at its lowest and pregnant women generally feel their best. During the first trimester there is a risk of miscarriage and in the third trimester complications such as premature labour and high blood pressure are possible. It's wise to travel with a companion. Always carry a list of quality medical facilities available at your destination and ensure that you continue your standard antenatal care at these facilities. Avoid rural travel in areas with poor transportation and medical facilities. Most of all, ensure that your travel insurance covers all pregnancy-related possibilities, including premature labour.

Malaria is a high-risk disease in pregnancy. WHO recommends that pregnant women do *not* travel to areas with Chloroquine-resistant malaria. None of the more effective antimalarial drugs are completely safe in pregnancy.

Traveller's diarrhoea can quickly lead to dehydration and result in inadequate blood flow to the placenta. Many of the drugs used to treat various diarrhoea bugs are not recommended in pregnancy. Azithromycin is considered safe.

In Yangon and Mandalay, supplies of sanitary products are readily available. Birth-control options may be limited, so bring adequate supplies of your own form of contraception. Heat, humidity and antibiotics can all contribute to thrush. Treatment is with antifungal creams and pessaries such as Clotrimazole. A practical alternative is a single tablet of Fluconazole (Diflucan). Urinary tract infections can be precipitated by dehydration or long bus journeys without toilet stops; bring suitable antibiotics.

TRADITIONAL MEDICINE

Throughout Myanmar traditional medical systems are widely practised. There is a big difference between these traditional healing systems and 'folk' medicine. Folk remedies should be avoided, as they often involve rather dubious procedures with potential complications. In comparison, traditional healing systems such as traditional Chinese medicine are well respected, and aspects of them are being increasingly used by Western medical practitioners.

All traditional Asian medical systems identify a vital life force, and see blockage or imbalance as causing disease. Techniques such as herbal medicines, massage and acupuncture are utilised to bring this vital force back into balance or to maintain balance. These therapies are best used for treating chronic disease such as chronic fatigue, arthritis, irritable bowel syndrome and some chronic skin conditions. Traditional medicines should be avoided for treating serious acute infections such as malaria.

Be aware that 'natural' doesn't always mean 'safe', and there can be drug interactions between herbal medicines and Western medicines. If you are using both systems ensure that you inform both practitioners what the other has prescribed.

HEALTH

Language

CONTENTS

Myanmar's official language is Burmese, the language of the Bamar majority. Speakers of Burmese and related dialects comprise nearly 80% of the population. Making up another 10% of the population are speakers of Tai languages, which include the Shan, Khün, Tai Lü and even a little-known group of Lao living near Payathonzu – descendants of refugees from Lao–Siamese wars in the 19th century. Linguists estimate that there are 107 languages spoken within Myanmar.

Travellers will find basic English widely spoken in urban areas and around popular tourist sites such as Bagan, but venturing further afield will require at least some basic Burmese. Learning a few words of the language will make your travel in Bamar-majority areas much more enjoyable and rewarding. Travellers who have spent some time in northern Thailand or Laos and learned some of the respective languages will be pleasantly surprised to find that many of these words are understood in Shan State as well.

PRONUNCIATION

Mastering Burmese pronunciation is a dizzying proposition for the average traveller. While there are elements that don't exist in English, with a little practice it's not as daunting as it at first seems.

Vowels

Burmese has many vowel sounds, which occur in open, nasalised and stopped forms. Nasalisation is produced by pronouncing vowels so that the air is released through the nose, rather than the mouth; English speakers can approximate this by putting a weak 'n' at the end of such a syllable. In this guide the nasalisation is indicated by **n** after the vowel, eg *ein* (house).

Non-nasalised

i	as in 'police'
e	as in 'they'
eh	as the first 'e' in 'elephant'
a	as in 'father'
aw	as the British pronounce 'law'
o	as in 'go'
u	as in 'chute'

Nasalised / Stopped

Nasalised		Stopped	
in	as in 'sin'	**iq**	as in 'sit'
ein	as in 'vein'	**eiq**	as in 'late'
		eq	as in 'bet'
an	as in 'fun'	**aq**	as in 'mat'
oun	as in 'bone'	**ouq**	as in 'boat'
un	as in German *Bund*	**uq**	as in 'foot'
ain	as in German *mein*	**aiq**	as in the English 'might'
aun	as in 'brown'	**auq**	as in 'out'

Consonants

Consonants only occur at the beginning of a syllable; there are no consonants that occur after the vowel. The consonants **b**, **d**, **j**, **g**, **m**, **n**, **ng**, **s**, **sh**, **h**, **z**, **w**, **l** and **y** are pronounced as in English. The 'w' sound can occur on its own, or in combination with other consonants. Pronouncing the combination **ng** at the beginning of a syllable can be tricky for Westerners; try saying 'hang on', then leave off the 'ha-' to get an idea of the sound. The following consonants and combinations may cause confusion:

th – as in 'thin'
dh – as the 'th' in 'their'
ny – similar to the sound at the beginning of the British 'new'

hm, hn, hny, hng, hl – made with a puff of air
   just before the nasal or **l** sound
ng – as the 'ng' in 'hang'

Aspirated Consonants
The aspirated sounds are made with an audible puff of air after the consonant; in English, the letters 'p', 't' and 'k' are aspirated when they occur at the beginning of a word, eg 'pit', 'tab' and 'kit'. Unaspirated examples of these sounds occur in words such as 'spin', 'stir' and 'skin'.

The unaspirated **c** and aspirated **c'** are similar to the 'ch' in 'church'. Remember that **sh** as in 'ship', **s** as in 'sip' and the aspirated **s'** are three different sounds.

TONES
Burmese tones seem very tricky, but are essentially a matter of relative stress between adjoining syllables. There are three tones, plus two other possibilities.

Creaky High Tone Don't worry about the funny name! This is made with the voice tense, producing a high-pitched and relatively short, creaky sound. In the transliterations it's indicated by an acute accent above the vowel, eg *ká* (dance).

Plain High Tone The pitch of the voice starts quite high, then falls for a fairly long time, similar to the pronunciation of words such as 'squeal', 'car' and 'way'. It's indicated by a grave accent above the vowel, for example *kà* which, conveniently, is also the Burmese word for 'car'.

Low Tone The voice is relaxed and stays at a low pitch for a fairly long time, without rising or falling in pitch. If a vowel is unaccented, it indicates that it carries a low tone, eg *ka* (shield).

Stopped Syllable This is a very short and high-pitched syllable, cut off at the end by a sharp catch in the voice (a glottal stop); it's similar to the 'non-sound' in the middle of the exclamation, 'oh-oh', or the Cockney pronunciation of 't' in a word like 'bottle'. It's indicated by a 'q' after the vowel, eg *kaq* (join). Be aware that the 'q' isn't pronounced.

Reduced (Weak) Syllable This is a shortened syllable, usually the first of a two-syllable word, which is said without stress, like the 'a' in 'ago' in English. Only the vowel 'a' (sometimes preceded by a consonant) occurs in a reduced syllable; this is indicated by a small 'v'-like symbol above the vowel, eg *ǎlouq* (work). Any syllable except the last in a word can be reduced.

TRANSLITERATION
The system used in this language guide is just one of many ways that Burmese script can be rendered into the Roman alphabet, a process known as 'transliteration'. In Burmese writing, the sounds **c, c', j** are represented by the letters for **k, k', g** plus **y** or **r**, so anglicised forms of Burmese often represent them as **ky, gy** and so on. One example of this is the unit of currency, *caq*, which is usually written 'kyat' in the Roman alphabet. Aspirated consonants (**k', s', t'** and **p'**) may be transliterated with an 'h' either before or after the consonant. A creaky tone may be indicated by a final **t**, eg Hpakant (a town in Kachin State).

Various combinations of letters may be used to represent the same vowel sound: **e** and **eh** are both often transliterated as 'ay'; **ain** may be represented as 'aing', **auq** as 'auk' and so on.

There is no 'r' in Burmese but the sound appears in some foreign words such as *re·di·yo* (radio). Sometimes it's substituted with a **y**. Similarly there is no 'f' or 'v' in Burmese; loan words containing these consonants often use **p'** and **b** respectively.

In this guide, dots have been used to separate syllables (with the exception of the reduced syllable **ǎ**) to make it easier to determine the divisions between syllables. However, you'll notice that native speakers don't speak with such clear division between words or syllables.

ACCOMMODATION
Is there a ... near here?
... ဒီနားမှာရှိသလား။
... di·nà·hma shí·dhǎlà?
   hotel
   ဟော်တယ်   *ho·teh*
   guesthouse
   တည်းခိုခန်း   *tèh·k'o·gàn*

Can foreigners stay here?
နိုင်ငံခြားသား ဒီမှာတည်းလို့ရသလား။
nain·ngan·gyà·thà di·hma tèh·ló yá·dhǎlà?
May I see the room?
အခန်း ကြည့်ပါရစေ
ǎk'àn cí·bayá·ze?
Is breakfast included in the price?
အခန်းခထဲမှာ မနက်စာ ပါသလား။
ǎk'àn·k'á·dèh·hma mǎneq·sa pa·dhǎlà?
Can I pay in kyat?
ကျပ်နဲ့ပေးလို့ရလား။
caq·néh pè·ló yá·là?

LANGUAGE

I will stay for two nights.
နှစ်ရက်တည်းမယ်။
hnǎyeq tèh·meh

How much is ...?
... ဘယ်လောက်လဲ။
... beh·lauq·lèh?
   one night
   တစ်ရက်   *tǎyeq*
   two nights
   နှစ်ရက်   *hnǎyeq*
   a single room
   တစ်ယောက်ခန်း   *tǎyauq·k'an*
   a double room
   နှစ်ယောက်ခန်း   *hnǎyauq·k'an*

This room is good.
ဒီအခန်း ကောင်းတယ်။ *di ǎk'àn kaùn·deh*
clean
သန့်တယ်   *thán·deh*
dirty
ညစ်ပတ်တယ်   *nyiq·paq·deh*
fan (electric)
ပန်ကာ   *pan·ka*
noisy
ဆူညံတယ်   *s'u·nyan·deh*
pillow
ခေါင်းအုံး   *gaùn·oùn*

CONVERSATION & ESSENTIALS
Hello. (literally, 'It's a blessing')
မင်္ဂလာပါ။
min·gǎla·ba
How are you? (Are you well?)
ခင်ဗျား/ရှင် နေကောင်းရဲ့လား။
k'ǎmyà (m)/shin (f) ne·kaùn·yéh·là?
I'm well.
နေကောင်းပါတယ်။
ne·kaùn·ba·deh
Have you eaten?
ထမင်းစားပြီးပြီလား။
t'ǎmìn sà·pì·bi·là?
I've eaten.
စားပြီးပါပြီ။
sà·pì·ba·bi
Where are you going?
ဘယ်သွားမလိုလဲ။
beh thwà·mǎló·lèh?

To this, a general, non-specific reply is *di·nà·lè·bèh*, which means literally, 'just around here'. However, you could say:

I'm going back to my hotel.
ဟိုတယ်ကို ပြန်တော့မယ်။
ho·teh·go pyan·táw·meh
I'm leaving now. (Goodbye)
သွားပါအုံးမယ်။
thwà·ba·oùn·meh

A smile is often enough to express thanks in Myanmar, but it will still always be appreciated if you say 'thank you' in Burmese.

Thank you.
ကျေးဇူးပဲ။   *cè·zù·bèh*
Thank you very much.
ကျေးဇူးတင်ပါတယ်။   *cè·zù tin·ba·deh*
It's nothing. (You're welcome)
ကိစ္စ မရှိပါဘူး။   *keiq·sá mǎshí·ba·bù*
Yes.
ဟုတ်ကဲ့။   *houq·kéh*
No. (for questions containing nouns)
မဟုတ်ပါဘူး။   *mǎhouq·pa·bù*
What's your name?
ခင်ဗျား/ရှင် နာမည် ဘယ်လို ခေါ်သလဲ။
k'ǎmyá (m)/shín (f) na·meh beh·lo k'aw·dhǎlèh?
My name is ...
ကျွန်တော့်/ကျွန်မ ... လို့ ခေါ်ပါတယ်။
cǎnáw (m)/cǎmá (f) ... ló k'aw·ba·deh
I'm glad to meet you.
ခင်ဗျား/ရှင်နဲ့ တွေ့ရတာ ဝမ်းသာပါတယ်။
k'ǎmyà (m)/shin (f) néh twé·yá·da wùn·tha·ba·deh

DIRECTIONS
Is this the way to ...?
ဒီလမ်း ... သွားတဲ့လမ်းလား။
di·làn ... thwà·déh·làn·là?
How do I get to ...?
... ကို ဘယ်လိုသွားရသလဲ။
... ko beh·lo thwà·yá· dhǎlèh?
Can I walk there?
လမ်းလျှောက်ရင် ရမလား။
làn·shauq·yin yá·mǎlà?

Is it nearby?
ဒီနားမှာလား။   *di·nà·hma·là?*
Is it far?
ဝေးသလား။   *wè·dhǎlà?*

left

ဘယ်ဘက်   *beh·beq*

right

ညာဘက်   *nya·beq*

straight (ahead)

တည့်တည့်   *téh·déh*

very far away

သိပ်ဝေးတယ်॥   *theiq wè·deh*

not so far away

သိပ်မဝေးဘူး॥   *theiq măwè·bù*

north

မြောက်ဘက်   *myauq·p'eq*

south

တောင်ဘက်   *taun·beq*

east

အရှေ့ဘက်   *ăshé·beq*

west

အနောက်ဘက်   *ănauq·p'eq*

SIGNS

အဝင်	Entrance
အထွက်	Exit
ဝင်ခွင့်မရှိ	No Entry
ကလ်ဂလီဂုန်း	Telephone
ဆေးလိပ် မသောက်ရ	No Smoking
အမျိုးသမီးများ မဝင်ရ	Women Forbidden
ဓါတ်ပုံ မရိုက်ရ	No Photographs
တားမြစ်နယ်မြေ	Prohibited Area
အိမ်သာ/ရေအိမ်	Toilets
မ	Women
ကျား	Men

What ... is this?

ဒါ ဘာ ... လဲ॥

da ba ... lèh?

   town

   မြို့   *myó*

   street

   လမ်း   *làn*

   bus

   ဘတ်စကား   *baq·săkà*

In the Country

beach	ကမ်းခြေ	*kàn·gye*
countryside	တော	*tàw*

field (irrigated)	လယ်ကွင်း	*leh·gwìn*
hill	တောင်/ကုန်း	*taun/koùn*
island	ကျွန်း	*cùn*
lake	အိုင်	*ain*
lake (small, artificial)	ကန်	*kan*
map	မြေပုံ	*mye·boun*
river	မြစ်	*myiq*
sea	ပင်လယ်	*pin·leh*
track/trail	လမ်းကြောင်း	*làn·jaùn*
village	ရွာ	*ywa*
waterfall	ရေတံခွန်	*ye·dăgun*

EMERGENCIES

Help!

ကယ်ပါ॥   *keh·ba!*

I'm ill.

နေမကောင်းဘူး॥   *ne·măkàun·bù*

I'm lost.

လမ်းပျောက်နေတယ်॥   *làn pyauq·ne·deh*

I've been robbed.

အခိုးခံရတယ်॥   *ăk'ò·k'an·yá·deh*

Go away!

သွားစမ်း॥   *thwà·zàn!*

Call a doctor!

ဆရာဝန်ကို ခေါ်ပေးပါ॥   *s'ăya·wun·go k'aw·pè·ba!*

Call an ambulance!

လူနာတင်ကားခေါ်ပေးပါ॥   *lu·na·din·gà k'aw·pè·ba!*

HEALTH

Where is the ...?

... ဘယ်မှာလဲ॥

... beh·hma·lèh?

   chemist/pharmacy

   ဆေးဆိုင်   *s'è·zain*

   doctor

   ဆရာဝန်   *s'ăya·wun*

   hospital

   ဆေးရုံ   *s'è·youn*

Please call a doctor.

ဆရာဝန် ခေါ်ပေးပါ॥

s'ăya·wun kaw·pè·ba

I'm allergic to penicillin.

ကျွန်တော်/ကျွန်မ ပင်နီစလင်နဲ့ မတည်ဘူး။

cănaw (m)/cămá (f) pănăsălin·néh mătéh·bù

I'm pregnant.

ဗိုက်ကြီးနေတယ်/ကိုယ်ဝန်ရှိတယ်။

baiq cì·ne·deh/ko·wun shí·deh

It hurts here.

ဒီမှာ နာတယ်။

di·hma na·deh

I vomit often.

ခဏခဏ အန်တယ်။

k'ăná·k'ăná an·deh

I feel faint.

မူးလဲတယ်။

mù·lèh·deh

asthma

ပန်းနာရင်ကျပ်

(pàn·na·)yin·caq

have diarrhoea

ဝမ်းလျှောတယ်/

wùn·shàw·deh/

ဝမ်းသွားနေတယ်

wùn·thwà·ne·deh

have a fever

ဖျားတယ်

p'yà·deh

have a headache

ခေါင်းကိုက်နေတယ်

gàun kaiq·ne·deh

have a stomachache

ဗိုက်နာတယ်

baiq na·deh

aspirin

အက်စပရင်

eq·săpărin

bandage (for sprain)

ပတ်တီး

paq·tì

LANGUAGE DIFFICULTIES

Do you understand?

နားလည်သလား။

nà·leh·dhălà?

I understand.

နားလည်ပါတယ်။

nà·leh·ba·deh

I don't understand.

နားမလည်ပါဘူး။

nà·măleh·ba·bù

Please repeat that.

ပြန်ပြောပါဦး။

pyan·pyàw·ba·oùn

I can't speak Burmese.

ဗမာ စကား မပြောတတ်ဘူး။

băma·zăgà lo măpyàw·daq·bù

I speak English.

အင်္ဂလိပ်စကား ပြောတတ်တယ်။

ìn·găleiq·zăgà lo pyàw·daq·teh

Can you speak English?

ခင်ဗျား/ရှင် အင်္ဂလိပ်စကား ပြောတတ်သလား။

k'ămyà (m)/shin (f) ìn·găleiq·zăgà lo pyàw·daq·thălà?

What do you call this in Burmese?

ဒါ ဗမာလို ဘယ်လိုခေါ်သလ။

da băma·lo beh·lo k'aw·dhălèh?

NUMBERS

1	၁	*tiq/tă*
2	၂	*hniq/hnă*
3	၃	*thòun*
4	၄	*lè*
5	၅	*ngà*
6	၆	*c'auq*
7	၇	*k'ú·hniq/k'ú·hnă*
8	၈	*shiq*
9	၉	*kò*
10	၁၀	*(tă)s'eh*
11	၁၁	*s'éh·tiq*
12	၁၂	*s'éh·hniq*
20	၂၀	*hnăs'eh*
35	၃၅	*thòun·zéh·ngà*
100	၁၀၀	*tăya*
1000	၁၀၀၀	*(tă)t'aun*
10,000	၁၀၀၀၀	*(tă)thàun*
100,000	၁၀၀၀၀၀	*(tă)thèin*
1,000,000	၁၀၀၀၀၀၀	*(tă)thàn*

(One hundred thousand can often also be called one *lakh*.)

SHOPPING & SERVICES

Where is the ...?

... ဘယ်မှာလဲ။

... beh·hma·lèh?

bank

ဘဏ်တိုက်

ban·daiq

bookshop

စာအုပ်ဆိုင်

sa·ouq·s'ain

chemist/pharmacy

ဆေးဆိုင်

s'è·zain

market

ဈေး

zè

museum

ပြတိုက်

pyá·daiq

post office

စာတိုက်

sa·daiq

shop

ဆိုင်

s'ain

I'd like to make a call.
ဖုံးဆက်ချင်တယ်။ *p'oùn·s'eq·c'in·deh*
Can I send a fax?
ဖက်စ်ပို့လို့ ရသလား။ *fax pó·ló yá·dhălà?*

I want to change ...
... လဲချင်ပါတယ်။
... lèh·jin·ba·deh

dollars	
ဒေါ်လာ	*daw·la*
pounds	
ပေါင်	*paun*
foreign currency	
နိုင်ငံခြားငွေ	*nain·ngan·gyà ngwe*
money	
ပိုက်ဆံ	*paiq·s'an*
travellers cheques	
ခရီးချက်လက်မှတ်	*k'ăyì·c'eq·leq·hmaq*

How many kyat to a dollar?
တစ်ဒေါ်လာ ဘယ်နှစ်ကျပ်လဲ။
tădawla beh·hnăcaq·lèh?
Please give me smaller change.
အကြွေ လဲပေးပါ
ăkywe lèh·pè·ba

Where can I buy ...?
... ဘယ်မှာဝယ်ရမလဲ။
... beh·hma weh·yá·mălèh?
Do you have ...?
... ရှိလား။
... shí·là
How much is ...?
... ဘယ်လောက်လဲ။
... beh·lauq·lèh?

matches	
မီးခြစ်	*mì·jiq*
shampoo	
ခေါင်းလျှော်ရည်	*gaùn·shaw·ye*
soap	
ဆပ်ပြာ	*s'aq·pya*
toothbrush	
သွားပွတ်တံ	*dhăbuq·tan*
toothpaste	
သွားတိုက်ဆေး	*thwà·taiq·s'è*
toilet paper	
အိမ်သာသုံးစက္ကူ	*ein·dha·thoùn·seq·ku*

Do you have a cheaper one?
ဒါထက် ဈေးပိုပေါတာ ရှိသလား။
da·t'eq zè po·pàw·da shí·dhălà?
OK (literally, 'good')
ကောင်းပါပြီ။ *kàun·ba·bi*
expensive
ဈေးကြီးတယ် *zè·cì·deh*
cheap
ဈေးပေါတယ် *zè·pàw·deh*

TIME & DATES

What time is it?
ဘယ်အချိန်ရှိပြီလဲ။ *beh·ăc'ein shí·bi·lèh?*
At what time?
ဘယ်အချိန်မှာလဲ။ *beh ăc'ein·hma·lèh?*
7am
မနက် ခုနစ်နာရီ *măneq k'ú·hnăna·yi*
1pm
နေ့လည် တစ်နာရီ *né·leh tăna·yi*
4.30pm
ညနေ လေးနာရီခွဲ *nyá·ne lè·na·yi·qwèh*
10.15pm
ညဆယ်နာရီဆယ့်ငါး မိနစ် *nyá s'eh·na·yi s'éh·ngà·măniq*

hour	နာရီ	*na·yi*
minute	မိနစ်	*măniq*
morning (6am to noon)	မနက်	*măneq*
midday (noon to 3pm)	နေ့လည်	*né·leh*
afternoon/ evening (3pm to 7pm)	ညနေ	*nyá·ne*
night (7pm to 6am)	ည	*nyá*

today	ဒီနေ့	*di·né*
tomorrow	မနက်ဖြန်	*măneq·p'yan*
day after tomorrow	သဘက်ခါ	*dhăbeq·k'a*
next week	နောက် အပတ်	*nauq ăpaq*
yesterday	မနေ့က	*măné·gá*
Sunday	တနင်္ဂနွေနေ့	*tănìn·gănwe·né*
Monday	တနင်္လာနေ့	*tănìn·la·né*
Tuesday	အင်္ဂါနေ့	*in·ga·né*

LANGUAGE

Wednesday	ဗုဒ္ဓဟူးနေ့	*bouq·dăhù·né*
Thursday	ကြာသပတေးနေ့	*ca·dhăbădè·né*
Friday	သောကြာနေ့	*thauq·ca·né*
Saturday	စနေနေ့	*săne·né*

TRANSPORT

Where is the ...?
... ဘယ်မှာလဲ။
... *beh·hma·lèh?*

airport
လေဆိပ် — *le·zeiq*

railway carriage
မီးရထားတွဲ — *mì·yăt'à·dwèh*

train station
ဘူတာရုံ — *bu·da·youn*

bus station
ဘတ်စကားဂိတ် — *baq·săkà·geiq*

riverboat jetty
သင်္ဘောဆိပ် — *thìn·bàw·zeiq*

When will the ... leave?
... ဘယ်အချိန်ထွက်မလဲ။
... *beh·ăc'ein t'weq·mălèh?*

bus
ဘတ်စကား — *baq·săkà*

express train
အမြန်ရထား — *ămyan·yăt'à*

local train
လော်ကယ်ရထား — *law·keh·yăt'à*

plane
လေယာဉ်ပျံ — *le·yin·byan*

riverboat
သင်္ဘော — *thìn·bàw*

train
မီးရထား — *mì·yăt'à*

I'd like ...
ကျွန်တော်/ကျွန်မ ... လိုချင်ပါတယ်။
cănaw (m)/cămá (f) ... lo·jin·ba·deh

one ticket
လက်မှတ်တစ်စောင် — *leq·hmaq·dăzaun*

two tickets
လက်မှတ်နှစ်စောင် — *leq·hmaq hnăsaun*

Where does this bus go?
ဒီဘတ်စကား ဘယ်ကိုသွားသလဲ။
di baq·săkà beh·go thwà·dhălèh?

Where should I get off?
ဘယ်မှာဆင်းရမလဲ။
beh·hma s'ìn·yá·mălèh?

Can I get there by ...?
... နဲ့ သွားလို့ရမလား။
... *néh thwà·ló yá·mălà?*

Please go slowly.
ဖြည်းဖြည်းသွားပါ။
pyè·pyè thwà·ba

Please wait for me.
ကျွန်တော်/ကျွန်မကိုစောင့်နေပါ။
cănaw (m)/cămá (f) go saún·ne·ba

Stop here.
ဒီမှာ ရပ်ပါ။
di·hma yaq·pa

What time does the boat leave?
သင်္ဘော ဘယ်အချိန်ထွက်မလဲ။
thìn·bàw beh·ăc'ein t'weq·mălèh?

Can I get on board now?
အခု တက်လို့ရသလား။
ăk'ú teq·ló yá·dhălà?

bicycle
စက်ဘီး — *seq·bein*

4WD/'jeep'
ဂျစ်ကား — *jiq·kà*

motorcycle
မော်တော်ဆိုင်ကယ် — *mo·ta s'ain·keh*

taxi
အငှါးကား — *ăhngà·kà*

Also available from Lonely Planet:
Burmese Phrasebook

LANGUAGE

Glossary

See p78 for some useful words and phrases dealing with food and dining, and p380 for more comprehensive language information.

ABBREVIATIONS

AM – Air Mandalay
DIY – do it yourself
FEC – Foreign Exchange Certificate
IWT – Inland Water Transport
KIA – Kachin Independence Army
KNLA – Karen National Liberation Army
KNU – Karen National Union
MA – Myanma Airways
MTT – Myanmar Travels & Tours
NLD – National League for Democracy
NMSP – New Mon State Party
Slorc – State Law & Order Restoration Council
SPDC – State Peace & Development Council
SSA – Shan State Army
UWSA – United Wa State Army
YA – Yangon Airways

WORDS

acheiq longyi – *longyi* woven with intricate patterns and worn on ceremonial occasions
a-le – opium weights
a-nyeint pwe – traditional variety of *pwe*

Bamar – Burman ethnic group
betel – the nut of the areca palm, which is chewed as a mild intoxicant throughout Asia
Bodhi tree – the sacred banyan tree under which the Buddha gained enlightenment; also 'bo tree'
Brahman – pertaining to Brahma or to early Hindu religion (not to be confused with 'brahmin', a Hindu caste)

chaung – *(gyaung)* stream or canal; often only seasonal
cheroots – Myanmar cigars; ranging from slim to massive, but very mild as they contain only a small amount of tobacco mixed with other leaves, roots and herbs
chinlon – extremely popular Myanmar sport in which a circle of up to six players attempts to keep a rattan ball in the air with any part of the body except the arms and hands
chinthe – half-lion, half-dragon guardian deity

deva – Pali-Sanskrit word for celestial beings
dhamma – Pali word for the Buddhist teachings; called *dharma* in Sanskrit

eingyi – traditional long-sleeved shirt worn by Myanmar men

flat – covered pontoon used to carry cargo on the river; often up to 98ft long
furlong – obsolete British unit of distance still used in Myanmar; one-eighth of a mile

gaung baung – formal, turbanlike hat for men made of silk over a wicker framework
gu – cave temple

haw – Shan word for 'palace', a reference to the large mansions used by the hereditary Shan *sao pha*
hgnet – swallow-tailed boat
hintha – mythical, swanlike bird; *hamsa* in Pali-Sanskrit
hneh – a wind instrument like an oboe; part of the Myanmar orchestra
hpongyi – Buddhist monk
hpongyi-kyaung – monastery; see also *kyaung*
hsaing – traditional musical ensemble
hsaing waing – circle of drums used in a Myanmar orchestra
htan – *(tan)* sugar palm
hti – umbrellalike decorated pinnacle of a stupa
htwa – half a *taung*

in – lake; eg Inle means little lake

Jataka – stories of the Buddha's past lives, a common theme for temple paintings and reliefs

kalaga – embroidered tapestries
kamma – Pali word for the law of cause and effect; called *karma* in Sanskrit
kammahtan – meditation; a *kammahtan kyaung* is a meditation monastery
kammawa – lacquered scriptures
kan – *(gan)* beach; can also mean a tank or reservoir
karaweik – a mythical bird with a beautiful song; also the royal barge on Inle Lake; *karavika* in Pali
kutho – merit, what you acquire through doing good; from the Pali *kusala*
kyaik – Mon word for paya
kyauk – rock
kyaung – *(gyaung)* Myanmar Buddhist monastery; pronounced 'chown'
kye waing – circle of gongs used in a Myanmar orchestra
kyi – *(gyi)* big; eg Taunggyi means big mountain
kyun – *(gyun)* island

làn – road or street

lei-myet-hna – four-sided buddha sculpture

Lokanat – Avalokitesvara, a Mahayana Bodhisattva (buddha-to-be) and guardian spirit of the world

longyi – the Myanmar unisex sarong-style lower garment, sensible wear in a tropical climate; unlike men in most other Southeast Asian countries, few Myanmar men have taken to Western trousers

Mahayana – literally 'Great Vehicle'; the school of Buddhism that thrived in north Asian countries like Japan and China, and also enjoyed popularity for a time in ancient Southeast Asian countries; also called the Northern School of Buddhism

makara – mythical sea serpent

mi-gyaung – crocodile lute

mudra – hand position; used to describe the various hand positions used by buddha images, eg *abhaya mudra* (the gesture of fearlessness)

Myanma let-hwei – Myanmar kickboxing

myit – river

myo – town; hence Maymyo (after Colonel May), Allanmyo (Major Allan) or even Bernardmyo

myothit – 'new town', usually a planned new suburb built since the 1960s

naga – multiheaded dragon-serpent from mythology, often seen sheltering or protecting the Buddha; also the name of a collection of tribes in northwest Myanmar

nat – spirit being with the power to either protect or harm humans

nat-gadaw – spirit medium (literally 'spirit bride'), embraces a wide variety of *nat*

nat pwe – dance performance designed to entice a *nat* to possess a *nat-gadaw*

ngwe – silver

nibbana – nirvana or enlightenment, the cessation of suffering, the end of rebirth; the ultimate goal of Buddhist practice

oozie – elephant handler or *mahout*

pagoda – generic English term for *zedi* or stupa as well as temple; see also *paya*

pahto – Burmese word for temple, shrine or other religious structure with a hollow interior

Pali – language in which original Buddhist texts were recorded; the 'Latin' of Theravada Buddhism

pa-lwe – bamboo flute

paq-ma – Myanmar bass drum

parabaik – folding Buddhist palm-leaf manuscripts

parinibbana – literally, final *nibbana;* the Buddha's passing away

pattala – bamboo xylophone used in the Myanmar orchestra

paya – a generic Burmese term meaning holy one; applied to buddha figures, *zedi* and other religious monuments

pe-sa – palm-leaf manuscripts

pin – *(bin)* banyan tree

pi ze – traditional tattooing, believed to make the wearer invulnerable to sword or gun

pwe – generic Burmese word for festival, feast, celebration or ceremony; also refers to public performances of song and dance in Myanmar, often all-night (and all-day) affairs

pyatthat – wooden, multiroofed pavilion, usually turret-like on palace walls, as at Mandalay Palace

Sanskrit – ancient Indian language and source of many words in the Burmese vocabulary, particularly those having to do with religion, art and government

sao pha – 'sky lord', the hereditary chieftains of the Shan people

saung gauq – 13-stringed harp

sawbwa – Burmese corruption of the Shan word *sao pha*

saya – a teacher or shaman

sayadaw – 'master teacher', usually the chief abbot of a Buddhist monastery

shinpyu – ceremonies conducted when young boys from seven to 20 years old enter a monastery for a short period of time, required of every young Buddhist male; girls have their ears pierced in a similar ceremony

shwe – golden

sikhara – Indian-style, corncob-like temple finial, found on many temples in the Bagan area

sima – see *thein*

soon – alms food offered to monks

stupa – see *zedi*

t'ämìn zain – *(htamin zain)* rice shop

Tatmadaw – Myanmar's armed forces

taung – *(daung)* mountain, eg Taunggyi means 'big mountain'; it can also mean a half-yard (measurement)

taw – *(daw)* a common suffix, meaning sacred, holy or royal; it can also mean forest or plantation

tazaung – shrine building, usually found around *zedi*

thanakha – yellow sandalwood-like paste, worn by many Myanmar women on their faces as a combination of skin conditioner, sunblock and make-up

thein – ordination hall; called *sima* in Pali

Theravada – literally 'Word of the Elders'; the school of Buddhism that has thrived in Sri Lanka and Southeast Asian countries such as Myanmar and Thailand; also called Southern Buddhism and Hinayana

thilashin – nun

Thirty, the – the '30 comrades' of Bogyoke Aung San who joined the Japanese during WWII and eventually led Burma (Myanmar) to independence

thoun bein – motorised three-wheeled passenger vehicles

Tripitaka – the 'three baskets'; the classic Buddhist scriptures consisting of the Vinaya (monastic discipline), the Sutta (discourses of the Buddha) and Abhidhamma (Buddhist philosophy)

twin – *(dwin)* well, hole or mine

vihara – Pali-Sanskrit word for sanctuary or chapel for buddha images

viss – Myanmar unit of weight, equal to 3.5lb

votive tablet – inscribed offering tablet, usually with buddha images

wa – mouth or river or lake; Inwa means 'mouth of the lake'

wa leq-hkouq – bamboo clapper, part of the Myanmar orchestra

yagwin – small cymbals

Yama pwe – Myanmar classical dancing based on Indian epic the Ramayana

ye – water, liquid

yodaya zat – Ayuthaya theatre, the style of theatre brought into Myanmar with Thai captives after the fall of Ayuthaya in 1767

yoma – mountain range

youq-the pwe – Myanmar marionette theatre

ywa – village; a common suffix in place names such as Monywa

zat pwe – Myanmar classical dance-drama based on Jataka stories

zawgyi – an alchemist who has successfully achieved immortality through the ingestion of special compounds made from base metals

zayat – an open-sided shelter or resthouse associated with a *zedi*

zedi – stupa, a traditional Buddhist religious monument consisting of a solid hemispherical or gently tapering cylindrical cone and topped with a variety of metal and jewel finials; *zedi* are often said to contain Buddha relics

zei – *(zay* or *zè)* market

zeigyo – central market

The Authors

ROBERT REID
Coordinating Author

Raised in Oklahoma, Robert has worked for years for Lonely Planet, both in-house and out. No place he's been to for Lonely Planet (such as Chiapas, Petropavlovsk, Sliven, Transylvania, Nebraska) equals Myanmar – particularly for things like shirtless old men who chased him down to return a dropped K500 note or stopped him to talk family and football. He first visited the area when he moved to Vietnam in the mid '90s. This is his second time working on this guide, writing most front-matter and back-matter chapters, plus Bagan & Central Myanmar, Mandalay, Around Mandalay and Western Myanmar. He now lives in Brooklyn, New York.

JOE BINDLOSS
Eastern Myanmar & Northern Myanmar

Joe first visited Myanmar in the early '90s, and something clicked. He jumped at the chance to get deep into the north of the country for this guide. Joe was born in Cyprus and grew up in England, but he's since lived and worked in half a dozen countries, including the USA, Australia and the Philippines. When he isn't rumbling around Myanmar on rattletrap jeeps, Joe lives in London with his partner, Linda, and a growing collection of Buddhist curios and obscure musical instruments that he still hopes to one day learn how to play.

STUART BUTLER
Yangon, Around Yangon, Southeastern Myanmar & Environment

English-born Stuart Butler was first inspired to visit Myanmar after listening to a friend wax lyrical over the Shwedagon Paya. He went, he saw and he too was hooked. Since that first captivating trip he has contributed a number of Myanmar-based articles and photographs to magazines. In 2003 he became one of just a few lucky souls to have surfed the wild west coast of Myanmar. He now calls the beaches of southwest France home, though his travels have taken him across Southeast Asia and beyond, from the desert beaches of Pakistan to the coastal jungles of Colombia. He still waxes lyrical over the Shwedagon Paya.

LONELY PLANET AUTHORS

Why is our travel information the best in the world? It's simple: our authors are passionate, dedicated travellers. They don't take freebies in exchange for positive coverage so you can be sure the advice you're given is impartial. They travel widely to all the popular spots, and off the beaten track. They don't research using just the internet or phone. They discover new places not included in any other guidebook. They personally visit thousands of hotels, restaurants, palaces, trails, galleries, temples and more. They speak with dozens of locals every day to make sure you get the kind of insider knowledge only a local could tell you. They take pride in getting all the details right, and in telling it how it is. Think you can do it? Find out how at **lonelyplanet.com**.

Behind the Scenes

THIS BOOK

This 10th edition of *Myanmar (Burma)* was written by Robert Reid, who also coordinated it. He was assisted by Joe Bindloss and Stuart Butler, and Dr Trish Batchelor wrote the Health chapter. The first three editions of this book were penned by Tony Wheeler, and Joe Cummings took over the writing of the next three editions. Joe Cummings was assisted on the 7th edition by Michael Clark, while the 8th edition was updated by Steve Martin and Mic Looby. The 9th edition was written by Robert Reid and Michael Grosberg. This guidebook was commissioned in Lonely Planet's Melbourne office, and produced by the following:

Commissioning Editors Carolyn Boicos, Tashi Wheeler
Coordinating Editor Kirsten Rawlings
Coordinating Cartographer Sam Sayer
Coordinating Layout Designer Jim Hsu
Managing Editors Sasha Baskett, Melanie Dankel
Managing Cartographers David Connolly, Adrian Persoglia
Managing Layout Designer Sally Darmody
Assisting Editors Monique Choy, Janet Austin, Diana Saad, Ali Lemer
Cover Designer Pepi Bluck
Project Managers Chris Love, Glenn van der Knijff
Language Content Coordinator Quentin Frayne

Thanks to Mark Germanchis, Nicole Hansen

THANKS
ROBERT REID

I'd love to be able to name all the people in Myanmar who helped answer weird and panicked questions over the course of tracking down all the information in this guide. But I'll just go with a simple thanks to all. Also thanks to Carolyn Boicos at Lonely Planet, my fellow authors Stuart and Joe, many travellers met along the way (particularly Jan from Belgium), the readers who sent in so many informative letters, and Mai for calling on the road with progress reports of the football season back home.

JOE BINDLOSS

First up, I would like to thank my partner, Linda Nylind, for putting up with my peripatetic lifestyle for all these years. In Yangon, thanks to Piers and Nikki Benatar for finding an extra place at the Christmas dinner table, and to Stella, Beatrice, and Bart, for body-boarding tips and giving up bedrooms at various times so I had a place to sleep. In Kalaw, thanks to Harri Singh for a fascinating introduction to the customs and herbal lore of the hills. Thanks also to Adam McFarlane and Isabel for the inside track on crossing the border from Thailand to Myanmar. Lastly, a big cheers to everyone who wrote in with tips and warnings about travel in the northeast.

THE LONELY PLANET STORY

Fresh from an epic journey across Europe, Asia and Australia in 1972, Tony and Maureen Wheeler sat at their kitchen table stapling together notes. The first Lonely Planet guidebook, *Across Asia on the Cheap*, was born.

Travellers snapped up the guides. Inspired by their success, the Wheelers began publishing books to Southeast Asia, India and beyond. Demand was prodigious, and the Wheelers expanded the business rapidly to keep up. Over the years, Lonely Planet extended its coverage to every country and into the virtual world via lonelyplanet.com and the Thorn Tree message board.

As Lonely Planet became a globally loved brand, Tony and Maureen received several offers for the company. But it wasn't until 2007 that they found a partner whom they trusted to remain true to the company's principles of travelling widely, treading lightly and giving sustainably. In October of that year, BBC Worldwide acquired a 75% share in the company, pledging to uphold Lonely Planet's commitment to independent travel, trustworthy advice and editorial independence.

Today, Lonely Planet has offices in Melbourne, London and Oakland, with over 500 staff members and 300 authors. Tony and Maureen are still actively involved with Lonely Planet. They're travelling more often than ever, and they're devoting their spare time to charitable projects. And the company is still driven by the philosophy of *Across Asia on the Cheap*: 'All you've got to do is decide to go and the hardest part is over. So go!'

BEHIND THE SCENES

STUART BUTLER

A huge thanks to everyone who knowingly or unknowingly helped out. I'm sorry that, for obvious reasons, so many people in Myanmar cannot be named – without your help it would have been impossible. Also, thank you to M T Davis, Natalya Marquand, Hannah Matthews and Steve Thompson, Vicky Deresa, Sue and Tony Wright, Douglas Long and Bill Hobdell, all of whom shared meals, buses and tips with me. Finally, and as always, I would like to thank Heather for once again making this project a little easier and for being the best travel companion I could ever want.

OUR READERS

Many thanks to the travellers who used the last edition and wrote to us with helpful hints, useful advice and interesting anecdotes:

A Moksha Abels, Rika Altenburg, Raymond Ang, Sarah Ang, Aage Antila, Markus Arendt, Cortney Arnold **B** John Badgley, Josep Bagà, Joy Barnes, Justin Barron, Marton Bede, Angelique Berhault, David Berry, Klaus Bettenhausen, Amei Binns, Don Birch, Jørgen Borg, Anthony Bromley, Sabine & Clemens Bronner, Werner Bruyninx, Susanne Bulten, Timea Burjan, Stefan Burmeister **C** Ricardo Cabecos, Andrew Callister, Popelka Herzfeld Juan Carlos, Ruth Fredman Cernea, Kwan Cynthia Chan, Andrew Sheerman Chase, Ckaaij@Wanadoo, Karine Cormier, Jocelyn Corniche, Nicholas Cupaiuolo **D** Joan Daly, Jai Damle, Gillian Dank, Caroline Dearden, Jeroen Decuyper, Cathy Degaytan, Mark Degaytan, Florian Deising, Wendy De Vrede, Vera Donk, Richard Driessen, Heather Dunn **E** Martin Eichner, Omar Enciso **F** Winker Felix, Sandra Feyko, Susan Fleming, Jesse Foster **G** Bill Gasteyer, Rachel Godley, Rob Green, Kay Grimmesey, Maaike Groskamp **H** Andreas Hartung, Damien Hatcher, Volker Heiden, Ralph Heijstek, Claire Henault, Bernard Herman, Patsy Hetherington, Peter Hilbig, Chi Yuen Ho, David Hogarth, Kok Hon, Johnny Hopper, Lim Cheng How, Khin Maung Htay, Daniel Hürlimann, Aaron Hurvitz **I** Lior Itzkovitz **J** Tri Jaturanon, Nancy Jenkins, Craig Johnston, Guido Jung **K** Iris Kaidar, Elizabeth Kalnin, Carole Karp, Alex Kaufman, Shella Keilholz, Nicolas De Kerchove, Wesley King, Gregory Kleiman, K Kohncke, Chek Yong Kong **L** John Lancaster, T Joe Larive, Ema Lee, Jan-Pleun Lens, Roberta Leung, Olaf Liebegott, Jan Lignell, York Lin, Jennifer Lorenzi, Katharina Lupp **M** Tim M, Rios Garcia Manuela, Frank Marchetti, Yossi Margoninsky, Dilshad Marikar, Paul Martyn, Michael Mason, Sarah Massey, Heath Mcallister, Dan Mckechnie, James & Debbie Middleton, Olga Moereels, Rachel Morris, Silvia Muheim, Susan Mulholland, Kevin Murphy **N** Silke Neumann, Zoe Newman **O** Martin Oklyu, Jane Osbaldiston, Dieter Overhoff **P** Duncan Parker, Ryan Parker, Reggie Pawle, Ralph Perrella, Anders Petterson, Giampaolo Pilia, Sylvia Pollex, Simon Pons, Robert Poppelen **R** David Ragg, Anton Rijsdijk, Stephanie Rivera, Eva Robinshaw, Carla Rodrigues, Amrita Ronnachit, Beatrice Roth, Susanne Rothenbaecher-Gogniat, Renata Rover, Sonja Rücker-Böhm, Andreas Rynes **S** Jackie Sanders, Colin Schatz, Brigitte Schumann, Don Seekins, Thae Nu Nu Seinn, Malcolm Sell, Arthur Sellier, Belinda Shorland, Janet Smith, Thawta Soe, Richard Stilling, Claudia Stransky, Peter Stronach, Natalie Sykes **T** Hock Guan Tee, C A Teo, Kris Terauds, Malcolm Tetley, Hari Thorpe, Prendan Tom, Noemi Tracy, Julian Turner **U** Jamie Uhrig, Derek Uram **V** Fudil Valasr, Simon van Hemert, Ray Varnbuhler **W** Jane Ward, Tom Warden, Dr Weinberg, Paul Whittle, Gil Wiener, Peter Soe Wynn **Y** Qua Chern Yin **Z** Paul Zakus

ACKNOWLEDGMENTS

Many thanks to the following for the use of their content:

Globe on title page ©Mountain High Maps 1993 Digital Wisdom, Inc.

SEND US YOUR FEEDBACK

We love to hear from travellers – your comments keep us on our toes and help make our books better. Our well-travelled team reads every word on what you loved or loathed about this book. Although we cannot reply individually to postal submissions, we always guarantee that your feedback goes straight to the appropriate authors, in time for the next edition. Each person who sends us information is thanked in the next edition – and the most useful submissions are rewarded with a free book.

To send us your updates – and find out about Lonely Planet events, newsletters and travel news – visit our award-winning website: **lonelyplanet.com/contact**.

Note: we may edit, reproduce and incorporate your comments in Lonely Planet products such as guidebooks, websites and digital products, so let us know if you don't want your comments reproduced or your name acknowledged. For a copy of our privacy policy visit lonelyplanet.com/privacy.

Index

INDEX

INDEX

000 Map pages
000 Photograph pages

INDEX

INDEX

MAP LEGEND

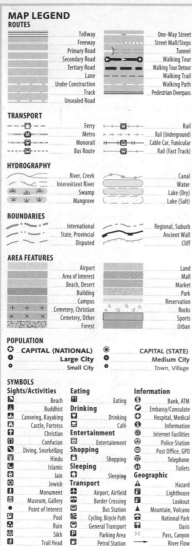

ROUTES

Tollway		One-Way Street	
Freeway		Street Mall/Steps	
Primary Road		Tunnel	
Secondary Road		Walking Tour	
Tertiary Road		Walking Tour Detour	
Lane		Walking Trail	
Under Construction		Walking Path	
Track		Pedestrian Overpass	
Unsealed Road			

TRANSPORT

Ferry		Rail
Metro		Rail (Underground)
Monorail		Cable Car, Funicular
Bus Route		Rail (Fast Track)

HYDROGRAPHY

River, Creek		Canal
Intermittent River		Water
Swamp		Lake (Dry)
Mangrove		Lake (Salt)

BOUNDARIES

International		Regional, Suburb
State, Provincial		Ancient Wall
Disputed		Cliff

AREA FEATURES

Airport		Land
Area of Interest		Mall
Beach, Desert		Market
Building		Park
Campus		Reservation
Cemetery, Christian		Rocks
Cemetery, Other		Sports
Forest		Urban

POPULATION

✪ **CAPITAL (NATIONAL)**	◉	**CAPITAL (STATE)**
● **Large City**	●	**Medium City**
◦ Small City	◦	Town, Village

SYMBOLS

Sights/Activities	Eating	Information
Beach	Eating	Bank, ATM
Buddhist	**Drinking**	Embassy/Consulate
Canoeing, Kayaking	Drinking	Hospital, Medical
Castle, Fortress	Café	Information
Christian	**Entertainment**	Internet Facilities
Confucian	Entertainment	Police Station
Diving, Snorkelling	**Shopping**	Post Office, GPO
Hindu	Shopping	Telephone
Islamic	**Sleeping**	Toilets
Jain	Sleeping	**Geographic**
Jewish	**Transport**	Hazard
Monument	Airport, Airfield	Lighthouse
Museum, Gallery	Border Crossing	Lookout
Point of Interest	Bus Station	Mountain, Volcano
Pool	Cycling, Bicycle Path	National Park
Ruin	General Transport	Oasis
Sikh	Parking Area	Pass, Canyon
Trail Head	Petrol Station	River Flow
Zoo, Bird Sanctuary	Taxi Rank	Waterfall

LONELY PLANET OFFICES

Australia
Head Office
Locked Bag 1, Footscray, Victoria 3011
☎ 03 8379 8000, fax 03 8379 8111
talk2us@lonelyplanet.com.au

USA
150 Linden St, Oakland, CA 94607
☎ 510 250 6400, toll free 800 275 8555
fax 510 893 8572
info@lonelyplanet.com

UK
2nd fl, 186 City Rd,
London EC1V 2NT
☎ 020 7106 2100, fax 020 7106 2101
go@lonelyplanet.co.uk

Published by Lonely Planet Publications Pty Ltd
ABN 36 005 607 983

© Lonely Planet Publications Pty Ltd 2009

© photographers as indicated 2009

Cover photograph: U Bein's Bridge, Amarapura, Myanmar, Bruno Morandi/Hoa-Qui/Eyedea/HeadPress. Many of the images in this guide are available for licensing from Lonely Planet Images: www.lonely planetimages.com.

All rights reserved. No part of this publication may be copied, stored in a retrieval system, or transmitted in any form by any means, electronic, mechanical, recording or otherwise, except brief extracts for the purpose of review, and no part of this publication may be sold or hired, without the written permission of the publisher.

Printed through Colorcraft Ltd, Hong Kong.
Printed in China.

Lonely Planet and the Lonely Planet logo are trademarks of Lonely Planet and are registered in the US Patent and Trademark Office and in other countries.

Lonely Planet does not allow its name or logo to be appropriated by commercial establishments, such as retailers, restaurants or hotels. Please let us know of any misuses: www.lonelyplanet.com/ip.

Mixed Sources
Product group from well-managed forests and other controlled sources
www.fsc.org Cert no. SGS-COC-005002
© 1996 Forest Stewardship Council

Although the authors and Lonely Planet have taken all reasonable care in preparing this book, we make no warranty about the accuracy or completeness of its content and, to the maximum extent permitted, disclaim all liability arising from its use.

BIBLIO RPL Ltée

G - AOUT 2009